Never Marry a Woman with Big Feet

Never Marry a Woman with Big Feet

Women in Proverbs from Around the World

MINEKE SCHIPPER

Yale University Press

New Haven and London

TO OUR FOREMOTHERS

Designed by Adam Freudenheim
Set by Alliance Interactive Technology in Van Dijck and Trajan MT
Printed in the United Kingdom at the University Press, Cambridge

Library of Congress Cataloging-in-Publication Data
Schipper, Mineke.
   Never marry a woman with big feet: women in proverbs from around the world / Mineke Schipper.
      p. cm.
Includes bibliographical references and index.
   ISBN 0–300–10249–6 (hardback : alk. paper)
   1. Proverbs. 2. Proverbs—History and criticism. 3.
   Women—Quotations, maxims, etc. I. Title.
   PN6405 .S35 2003
   398.9' 082—dc22   2003023095

A catalogue record for this book is available from the British Library
10 9 8 7 6 5 4 3 2 1

Contents

Acknowledgements

First of all, I must thank all those people, from every part of the world, who have shared proverbs with me, often along with enlightening explanations. It is impossible to acknowledge individually the names of all the friends, colleagues, students, and others who have contributed to my collection over the years—but I have provided oral and written sources of proverbs in the anthologies following each chapter.

Some friends and colleagues, however, I must thank personally. I am very grateful to Sanjukta Gupta, Sabine Cohn and Angélica Malinarich-Dorfman for their generous permission to draw from the materials they had contributed, respectively, to small Asian, Jewish, and Latin American collections of proverbs we co-authored in Dutch in the 1990s. I also want to thank Huang Mingfen from Xiamen for a long list of Chinese proverbs; Kwame Anthony Appiah for Twi proverbs his mother Peggy Appiah had collected in Ghana; Clémentine Faïk-Nzuji for Congolese proverbs; Dobrinka Parusheva for Bulgarian proverbs; Mavis Noordwijk for sending me Sranan proverbs from Surinam; Anne van de Zande for bringing me a Russian book of proverbs from Moscow, and Beer Schröder for a book of Asian proverbs he found for me in Singapore. My colleague Yang Enhong at the Institute of Minority Cultures of the Chinese Academy of Social Sciences introduced me to renowned proverb specialist Liu Xiaolu in Beijing.

The University of Leiden has always been extremely supportive of my research, and I am happy to acknowledge its indispensable support. For many years, the Arts Faculty, with its Research Schools covering the study of cultures in East and West, has been a dynamic and stimulating workplace, with ample space for interdisciplinary and intercultural contacts and exchange of ideas, thanks to its specialists on a large variety of cultures, as well as to a continuous stream of visitors from all over the world.

In 1999 and 2000 I received several grants which, together, made it possible to create a database, which has considerably facilitated working with the ever-growing collected material. I wish to express my sincere gratitude for this funding to the Netherlands Foundation for Scientific Research (NWO); the Arts Faculty and the Research School for African, Asian and Amerindian Studies at the University of Leiden; and the Leiden University Fund (Leids Universiteitsfonds) as well as the Gratama Foundation. Without those financial contributions it would not have been possible to do the preparatory research for this book.

I thank Gijs van Rij and Mieke van der Stel for their help with the numerous computer problems that had to be solved when the database was in the making. Thanks, as well, to Hedda Post, who worked indefatigably on introducing file card material into the database program and also provided insightful comment on the material. Further thanks go to Juanita Diemel who typed a number of filecards; to Andrea Lion who found many bibliographical references for me; and to Thera Giezen who has been a wonderful student assistant over the past two years. My Leiden colleagues linguists Uwe Blaesing (Comparative Linguistics) and Felix Ameka (African languages) gave helpful comments on the list of countries and languages.

I spent the year 2000-2001 at the Netherlands Institute for Advanced Study (NIAS) in Wassenaar. Without this invitation, the book would certainly not yet have been born. I sincerely thank the rector, the executive director, and the staff who made life perfect for this NIAS fellow. I especially mention Petry Kievit-Tyson and Anne Simpson who cheerfully checked my English, and Yves de Roo who thought up an ingenious computer program facilitating a comparative perspective on the material. At NIAS I was able to write a first rough draft of the bulk of most chapters. I wish to thank my co-fellows for comments on my work in progress. For their useful feedback on various chapters I thank Philip van der Eijk, Henk Maier, Christine Oppong and Agnes Verbiest. I feel particularly indebted to Mark Geller who read the various versions of the chapters as they developed and whose unwavering interest and enjoyable friendship have been extremely encouraging and stimulating.

In the summer of 2002 I spent six marvellous weeks at the estate of Les Treilles in Tourtour in the south of France. I am very grateful to the Fondation des Treilles and its Présidente, Mme Anne Postel-Vinay, for the generous invitation to work on my project in La petite maison with its idyllic surrounding landscape. The excellent care of the Foundation's staff members enabled me to concentrate completely on the last part of the book.

Special thanks go to my agent Laura Susijn, my editor Adam Freudenheim, and my copy editor, Christopher Fagg, for their great expertise and unflagging enthusiasm. And, last but not least, thank you, Jan, for being such an emancipated husband.

Prologue

THE MOTHER OF ALL SCIENCES

In my opinion, Sancho, there is no proverb that is not true, as they are all observations based on experience itself, the Mother of all Sciences. (M.Cervantes, *Don Quixote*)

Humanity consists of relatives who have hardly bothered to meet. As people belonging to different cultures, and as men and women in the world at large, we have to learn how to communicate.[1] How do we learn to think and speak and write and meet inclusively instead of exclusively? We need to gain information and knowledge not only about what we have been thinking and saying and writing about ourselves and about other people, but also to finally become familiar with what other people have been thinking, saying, and writing about themselves and about us.

Mutual knowledge is an important key to peaceful coexistence at all levels. Looking at what we share as humans is absolutely fruitful and today more urgent than ever before. It is a much better starting point than continuously insisting on 'us' versus 'them', on those who belong versus those who don't, in the worst case projecting dangerous axes of good and evil between 'us' and 'them'.

No need to say that those who look for differences will only find differences, but those who look for similarities will find out what people experience or have experienced jointly. What we have in common as humans is not only due to globalization, as some seem to believe, but also to old human universals, because we share not only the shape of our bodies but also some fundamental needs and experiences as human beings. Some observations written down on Sumerian clay tablets about 4000 years ago have ideas in common with later Greek or Latin, Sanskrit or Chinese reflections, or with African or Asian or South

American ideas orally transmitted until this very day—in spite of the local cultural differences, and the historical changes which, of course, also exist.

Proverbs about women also tend to reflect the old habit of setting 'us' against 'them', not in terms of culture but in terms of sexual embodiment. It is true that today for the first time in history men and women are being equally educated and doing the same jobs, but this truth holds only for the happy few, globally speaking. And we have to be aware of the numerous impediments invented and cherished over the centuries, and all over the world, to prevent this from happening. It is quite significant that many proverbs tend to sketch equal access to education and roles as a most unwelcome or even nightmarish scenario.

Over the years I have been comparing oral as well as written texts from different cultural origins. My research into proverbs has been a long, often breathtaking, but also very rewarding research into humanity's history. Over the last few years I have given talks about the results in many places, addressing academics (from New York to Paris to Beijing), as well as rural women, and widely diverse audiences in a synagogue in Leiden, a mosque in Nairobi, university students in many countries, the European Parliament in Brussels, etc.

A conversation about proverbs is a wonderful experience. It can be carried out at all levels of society in all cultures. Everywhere people love it, and are fascinated, because proverbs have to do with human existence. Proverbs about women are telling about men as well, and therefore this study has to do with all of us.

I found most revealing that people seem to understand without much difficulty proverbs from cultures they had not even heard of. Proverbial observations about the most preoccupying elements of life we share form an excellent starting point for a better mutual understanding without suspicion, hostility or polarization. Looking together, in brotherly and sisterly fashion, at our cultural legacies in a concrete way makes for an excellent beginning towards building bridges between cultures.

CREATION AND PROCREATION

The best means against dying is giving birth. (*Fulfulde, Cameroon/Guinea/Niger*)

Men and women have been moulded from the same clay, a Sumerian proverb stated long ago, and we all come to the world in the same way, a more recent Russian proverb added thousands of years later. We may agree with both, but why did the small physical differences men and women are born with have such enormous consequences?

If we look back at how it all began, we find that, worldwide, sex and gender issues have been expressed in oral traditions such as myths and origin stories, fairytales, animal fables, love poems or cradle songs—and proverbs. Such oral 'wisdom', transmitted from generation to generation, represents a fascinating cultural history. Proverbs, the world's smallest literary genre, are a most telling part of that serial narrative about humankind. They are our main topic here, but a brief look beforehand into how men and women came into being in creation myths is an illuminating point of entry.

The Sumerian wisdom that men and women have all been moulded from the same clay must have inspired the story about Adam's first wife, created by God from the same dust as Adam. Her name was not Eve, but Lilith. Their having been created on an equal footing had terrible consequences, because Lilith wanted to have sex on top, and she insisted on her right. According to some variants, Adam refused this, divorced her and sent her away, but in other versions she was the one who abandoned him. She pronounced the name of God, flew up out of Paradise into the air, and went off to the Red Sea. God sent angels to capture her and bring her back to Adam, threatening that if she didn't come along, she would lose a hundred of her demon children daily, but she preferred even that to returning to Adam. Ever since, she has taken her revenge on Eve (her rival) by strangling babies, and swallowing the sperm of men who sleep alone at night.[2]

Apparently, lying on top in sexual intercourse is an enviable position of power. In Tanzania I recently attended a discussion about who was entitled to have the couple's children after divorce, the husband or the wife. Most men insisted that it ought to be the husband, and one of their half-joking arguments was that 'it is the man who is physically on top when the children are being made.' The main conclusion of the Lilith story is that equality between men and women is not such a good idea.

Eve has inspired other origin stories, first in Jewish culture, but also in the Arab world, Africa and Europe. Some variants doubt Eve's originating from Adam's rib, because of an incident that preceded her creation. Here is a version of that story I heard from a Sudanese refugee in Congo a number of years ago:

> God sends the archangel Gabriel from heaven down to the earth to take the rib from sleeping Adam's body. Flying back to heaven, Gabriel meets the Devil on his way. The Devil says: 'Hi, Gabriel, how are you?' Gabriel answers politely and hurries on to heaven. The Devil has not failed to notice the curious object in Gabriel's hand: he gets closer and flies along with the archangel. 'What's that?' he asks curiously. 'None of your business,' replies Gabriel curtly. The Devil insists, but the archangel keeps quiet. Then, with a sudden move, the Devil snatches the rib from Gabriel who immediately goes after the Devil. The Devil escapes from Gabriel's grip and makes off as quickly as he can, but Gabriel does not want to return to God empty-handed, and resolutely holds onto his enemy. For a long time, they fly and wrestle, wrestle and fly, before the Devil succeeds in struggling free. On they fly, silently, one after the other. The Devil tries to give Gabriel the slip, but the archangel is determined not to let go. Finally, Gabriel catches up and succeeds in grabbing the Devil's tail. Of course the Devil tries his best to struggle free again, but Gabriel holds no less firmly on, until, all of a sudden, the Devil's tail breaks off. Since the archangel did not succeed in getting Adam's rib back, it is this part of the Devil's body he brought to God in heaven, and this is what the first woman has been made of ...

Women have always visibly (pro-)created with their bodies, whereas, in the remote past, men may not have been so sure whether they contributed at all to this miracle of pregnancy and birth. In creation myths, strange enough, women's role in procreation has sometimes conspicuously been ignored. The creation of Adam and Eve in the Bible is a case in point: Eve originates from Adam's body, not the other way round.

In many a myth women's involvement in birth-giving is denied, and a male god or first ancestor is the potter or sculptor or artisan fabricating human creatures. He shapes the human race with his own hands from mud or dust, or gives birth to them in one way or another. The Egyptian God Atum, for example, vomits twins, or, in another variant, produces them by masturbating. An oral narrative from the Congolese Kuba people tells of how, in the beginning, God has a sick stomach. He feels so ill that his whole body aches and he begins to throw up. He creates everything from his insides, by vomiting—all the plants, trees, animals, and human beings, one after the other onto the earth. In a Fang myth from Gabon, the mystery of human origin is explained by having the first woman come out of the first man's toe or by having her manually created from a piece of wood by the first man. We do not know why such self-sufficient creators have been thought up: was it a 'natural drive to compensate intellectually for what women produced physically?'[3]

More down to earth than myths, proverbs wholeheartedly acknowledge procreation as an indispensable female quality, and motherhood as a crucial domain of life: 'It is the woman who bears the man', a Twi proverb from Ghana observes. Being able to give birth is apparently considered so unique that numerous proverbs express not only respect but also fear *vis-à-vis* this awesome creativity.

Myths are a powerful genre, and the dogmas and statements they have given birth to are not supposed to be questioned by believers. Myths confirm and explain how 'man' created order out of chaos, and how, by means of culture, he succeeded in imposing his own will on nature. In oral traditions women have often been associated with the uncontrollability of nature. There are many myths about how, in the beginning, women were in charge, and men felt forced to rob them of their secrets, justifying the right to do so by arguing that the women were the ones who 'had everything'. Having 'everything' meant being able to giving birth, having a clitoris (interpreted as having a small penis) as well as a vagina.[4]

The story of Genesis and numerous other passages from the Bible have often been interpreted by Christian theology as a confirmation of the superiority of men over women. After Jesus' death, the equality of women to men was already questioned by the apostle Paul who insisted that 'man' is the head of 'woman', a view eagerly taken up later by Church Fathers. This wishful belief gradually became more influential than Jesus' own words, and has been echoed in many proverbs. The same holds for the interpretation of the Koran by later *ulamas* or Muslim interpreters,[5] and it seems to be no less true for orthodox views on Hindu women derived from old religious Sanskrit texts.[6] As for Buddhism, women's position was upgraded in Buddha's time, whereas after his death there has been a regression due to forces hostile to women.[7] The policy of creation stories and proverbs about women is one of trying to find a 'balance' between the domain of birth giving and the other domains of life—possibly the same 'balance' strived for in men's monopolizing of world religions.

Proverbs refer to stories, and stories to proverbs. Thus, womankind is rather reprovingly referred to as 'Eve' in Hebrew and European proverbs. The Genesis story from the Bible is regularly referred to in proverbs, for example in Russian: 'We should not expect anything good from our rib', or in Romanian: 'Even the best of women has still a Devil's rib in her.'[8] Even though, unlike Lilith, Eve was not created from the same clay, she still took undesirable initiatives instead of being humble and obedient. Here is a Russian proverbial example of her opinionatedness: ' "I go by myself", Eve said, and with her elbow she pushed away the one showing her out of heaven.' In some proverbs originating from Europe, the ideal wife is compared to the Virgin Mary in the Bible who is presented as modest and submissive. Proverbs stress that such an ideal dream wife is extremely rare: 'Not everyone has a wife like Maria, but him whom God gave.' Of course, Eve is presented as the antipode of Mary.

In other parts of the world there are also proverbial references to goddesses from myths and stories, such as the Sumerian grain goddess Ezinu-Kusu: '[As] a plant sweeter than a husband, a plant sweeter than a mother, may Ezinu-Kusu live with you in the house'; or the popular Chinese Goddess of Mercy, Kuan Yin: 'Young, she's a Kuan Yin; old, she's a monkey.'

The legacy of oral traditions is a moral one: it teaches people what to do or what to think in a given situation. They formulate some part of common sense, values and ways of doing.[9] Endowed with authority, proverbs, like other prestigious oral and written texts, present how things ought to be from certain perspectives. Such authoritative views have contributed to moulding people's roles and identities, and continue to have an impact in many ways. Although we hardly ever know whether originally a man or a woman created a certain proverb, we can look into the interests at stake. What these interests are and how they are given shape in particular cultures—rhetorically and thematically— are questions to be born in mind when looking into proverbs about women, which is what this book is about.

COLLECTING AND QUESTIONING

An old proverb will never break. (*Russian*)

Like most people in the contemporary western world, I had never paid much attention to the genre of the proverb—until I went to Africa. In oral cultures,[10] proverbs continue to be the 'palm oil with which words are eaten', as the Nigerian writer Chinua Achebe once put it. When I lived in Congo, I sometimes wrote down the proverbs I heard people saying, because their poetic power was fascinating. A few years later, back in Europe, a publisher invited me to be the editor of a book which was to be published under the title *Unheard Words: Women and Literature in Africa, The Arab World, Asia, the Caribbean and Latin America* (1985). For that book I wanted to preface each of the five sections about women writers with a small nominal selection of proverbs from the area concerned. That is how my interest in proverbs about women started.

Although my material at the time was limited, something unexpected occurred. In contrast to the assumption that cultures would mainly be marked by differences, I found fascinating resemblances in proverbs originating from across the world and throughout history. Could it be that, in spite of huge differences between cultures, the similarities in those about women were not pure coincidence? And if they were not, what could be the common ground? To answer such questions I started recording proverbs whenever I came across them, over the past fifteen years or so.

I have been able to collect my material, thanks to the enthusiastic contributions of a multitude of people from all over the world. Over the years I have been keenly looking for material, and that attitude was very rewarding. Everywhere people generously shared and discussed proverbs with me, from market women to taxi drivers, from shopkeepers to restaurant owners, from clerks or cleaners to bus, train or airplane passengers sitting next to me. I also enjoyed the help of many friends, colleagues, and students in many countries. As my collection grew to more than 15,000 from both oral and written sources, originating from more than 240 languages and all continents—dealing with all the aspects women's lives possibly have in common on the basis of physical characteristics, and real or imagined behavioural characteristics—I decided that the time had come to study this intriguing data collection thematically, as a corpus of comparable texts.

Proverbs and their variants about themes that I found in one culture, country, language or area often exist in other regions as well. How is this possible? Researchers are very outspoken when agreeing that standard patterns exist in the attribution of status and the division of labour, even though things are changing nowadays:

> In virtually all societies men fare better than women. Men exercise more power, have more status and enjoy more freedom. Men usually head the family, exercise considerably more force in legal, political, and religious matters, take alternative sexual partners, may often take more than one wife, have greater freedom in the choice of a spouse, usually reside near their own kin, and have easier access to alcoholic beverages and drugs. Women, on the other hand, are often segregated or avoided during menstruation, must often share their husbands with one or more co-wives, are blamed for childlessness, and are often forced to defer to men in public places. Child rearing is the only domain where women regularly exert more influence than men.[11]

Oral literature plays an important role in confirming 'traditional' ideas. In particular, proverbs provide us with a rich collection of reflections on the female body and an equally rich mosaic of the social consequences people's sexual differences have brought about. In this book, the starting point is that proverbs about women throw a fascinating light upon the worldwide existing gender division of roles in life. Questions to be answered are:

- What do proverbs say about women?
- Why do cultures believe that men and women are to be treated differently?
- Are the arguments presented in favour of different roles for men and women cross-culturally similar, and what kind of differences are to be found?

Answers to those three questions will be looked for in the next chapters. But first another question needs to be dealt with: How is it possible that we be able to understand proverbs originating from all sorts of 'foreign' cultures?

As human beings we share a number of things. We belong to the human species and, so far, we live on one and the same planet. We have in common with both our ancestors and our contemporary fellow humans the fact that basic drives and needs such as food, shelter, safety, and procreation determine our lives, at least in part. Our respective body shapes have yielded up male and female roles, called 'cultural traditions' in the communities where they apply, and large numbers of proverbs refer, directly as well as metaphorically, to the female body or parts of the female body, the roles of women and men, and the relations between the sexes. Thanks to common characteristics and experiences many proverbs can be understood without too much difficulty outside the culture that created them, even in translation.

It is quite revealing that people understand without much difficulty proverbs from cultures they have not even heard of. I have frequently experienced this immediate recognition among audiences from different ages, backgrounds, cultures, and continents. This amazing cross-cultural understanding must have to do with proverbs largely tapping into common body and gender experience. On the other hand, there are also proverbs which tap into specific local cultural contexts, and are therefore more difficult to understand without supplementary information.

Comparison requires comparable data. In order to keep data comparable, a practical rule is that 'the larger the geographical space one wants to study, the smaller should the unit of analysis be.'[12] A collection of proverbs, selected on the basis of the unifying theme of women as a 'kind', makes it particularly well suited for intercultural comparison. First, proverbs consist of concise statements; and second, the genre exists worldwide. Opting for intercultural comparison, we miss something—the extra meanings the local cultural context would add in the 'live' quoting context—but we also gain something. What we gain in our case is new insight into mankind's ideas about gender patterns.

In their terse and memorable fashion, proverbs reveal ways of seeing life. Musical, direct, frank, they reflect not only cultural uniqueness but also commonalities shared across the globe and throughout history, thanks to our all being equipped with either a male or a female body. People have been programmed as men and women mostly without their being aware of it. The proverbial messages are an excellent yardstick for finding out to what extent, individually and socially, we continue to swallow those stubborn ideas, or have come to look differently at the world than our ancestors did. Consciously or subconsciously, we have all been influenced by such messages, in spite of local and regional differences, and in spite of historical developments and changes.

Quite a few of the ideas presented in proverbs are no longer as self-evident as they must have looked in the past, which means that 'traditions' are changing, especially in industrialized societies. These changes mainly benefit privileged groups, and have much less affected the large majority without much educational opportunity, whose proverbial ideas about what is male and what is female are usually quite persistent. This does not mean, however, that such ideas are no longer present in the internalized subconscious legacy of socially privileged groups—as can be seen in the lives of contemporary 'career women' whose very success in their working lives often still causes them great difficulty in finding suitable partners, if at all.

Proverbs about women substantially help explaining how and why, worldwide, sexual differences have resulted in a growing gap, a gap that has estranged men and women from sharing both public roles in life and responsibilities at home. Teaching and preaching the preservation of such a gendered gap, on the basis of relatively insignificant body differences, proverbs have reinforced prevailing hierarchies and established rigid images of what it means not to be a man but a woman, thus legitimating accessory roles for life for both sexes. The inescapable other side of this prescriptive coin is that women and men who do not fit the prescribed behaviour are stigmatized—no less by other women than by men. Privileges are never given up easily. Those used to having others do unpleasant work for them want to keep things that way. As the French writer Madame de Sévigné observed in the seventeenth century: 'The humbling of inferiors is necessary to the maintenance of social order.' Or in the words of a German proverb: 'One makes the bed and the other lies down in it.'

The generous offer to share annoying tasks equally rarely occurs to those in a comfortably dominant position. 'A bad home sends you for water and firewood' is a Rwanda complaint; it means that a man becomes his wife's slave if he would accept to do such humiliating 'woman's work' in her place. If the wife does not conform to her social role, she will be the object of censure. In Europe such a woman used to be blamed for 'wearing the trousers', a frequently heard complaint in proverbs.

All those warnings for men, alongside compelling prescriptions and rules for women, reveal a great deal of uncertainty as well as fear for loss of the status quo. If women had been as subservient as they ought to be according to the endless series of prescriptions and proscriptions, the proverbs would have been completely superfluous, would they not?

It must be stressed right from the start that this book is not about 'reality': proverbs do not reflect 'reality'. The numerous tiny texts represent ideals—as well as regretted deviations from such ideals, as imagined by those whose interests they defend. Whose ideals are they talking about? As a public genre, the proverb is believed to serve and follow 'the tradition', without ever specifying whose tradition is actually being referred to. Instead of representing the 'reality' of what women were or are, the book presents an intriguing mirror of mainly male-inspired interests and fears and inherited ideas about 'ideal' and 'deviant' womanhood, and in doing so reveals at the same time inherited views of 'ideal' and 'deviant' norms of manhood. Thanks to the witty images and original comparisons the material is quite striking and often amusing. In some ways, though, this is also a disturbing book in that it demonstrates wide currency of misogynistic sentiment, especially in the proverbs about wives, transmitted from generation to generation in hundreds of different languages across the globe.

In the mirror of proverbs we'll meet them all—the prescribed and accepted, rejected and acclaimed, past and remaining gender roles. The mirror shows that times and images are changing, and at the same time reminds us that, because of those living legacies, even today, innumerable women still enjoy considerably less freedom than men.

PROVERBS AND THEIR IMPACT

Hold fast to the words of your ancestors.[13]

Who among us can quote proverbs off the cuff? In the Western world they are today much less current than advert slogans. Nevertheless, every now and then a proverb can be heard being quoted in conversation, on radio or television, or by politicians in speeches. Readers in the West may believe that proverbs are no longer alive in their society, but the *Penguin Dictionary of Proverbs* stresses their lasting impact: 'Though the proverb is abandoned, it is not falsified'.[14] Although their importance in twenty-first century writing cultures has been declining, proverbs may actually be more widely known than one might expect. When I quoted Chinese proverbs in China, people confirmed that they knew many of them. In Africa people are very familiar with proverbs, they have an 'ear' for them. In Europe too they seem to be alive. In a recent radio broadcast about this project, listeners were called upon to react if they still remembered any proverbs referring to women. The five telephones of the studio rang continuously during that hour-long program, and quite a number of letters containing proverbs about women were sent to me later. Indeed, the genre is not dead; on the contrary, the interest in the written proverb may even be increasing, if the number of important nineteenth-century collections reprinted in the last few decades is anything to go by. In the meantime, proverbs continue to be used in daily life in oral cultures all over the world.

LEGACIES

The bearded mouth does not lie. (Bemba)

The proverb came into being long before written history. Over the centuries this important living genre has mainly been passed on through oral traditions. My collection is based on oral as well as written sources from widely diverse cultural communities in all continents. The oldest written examples date back to ca. 2600–2550 BCE. Those early Sumerian proverbs were inscribed on clay tablets and only discovered in 1963 about 150 kms southeast of Baghdad, but their oral traditions must be much older. The only thing that is certain about them is their approximate date of inscription, but that does not tell us about the generations that have been quoting them orally long before that time. This holds true for proverbs in general: in most cases we know little or nothing about their creation, their age and their currency. Their being used or their being incorporated in written collections means that they have been preserved and transmitted, first orally and then in written form, first locally, and later nationally, and today more and more often also internationally.

Proverbs have been defined in many ways. A proverb tends to be seen as more generally than a saying applicable in a large variety of contexts. Proverbs close a discussion, make up for a misunderstanding, disguise ignorance, or put a good gloss on a bad cause. Although no satisfactory all-embracing definition exists, proverbs are quickly recognized as such by users and listeners. One might describe them as short, pithy sayings, ingeniously embodying an admitted truth or cherished belief. Definitions generally emphasize four main characteristics of the proverb: (1) its concise fixed artistic form; (2) its evaluative and conservative function in society; (3) its authoritative validity; and (4) its anonymous origin.

The original sources of proverbs and sayings can hardly ever be traced. Sometimes they seem to derive from holy books or valued scriptures, or well-known literary texts. Even then, however, the reverse is most likely to be the case: it is the writers who plunder oral traditions at will. This means that we hardly ever know who thought the proverbs up, nor do we usually know how old they really are, even approximately. This means that it is impossible to classify them historically. Some must be very old and are still being quoted today. Others are no longer quoted in their language of origin (because the language died out), but are still alive in other languages, as for example several Latin proverbs that live on in other languages all over Europe so many centuries later. In many cases it is not possible either to know how often one and the same proverb has been quoted or is still being quoted, even though a number of proverbs are known to be very popular, even today, as some of their sources kept stressing.

In different cultures proverbs warmly recommend themselves as a genre to be taken seriously. 'Proverbs are the horses of speech' means in Yoruba that if the dialogue gets lost, proverbs are there to retrieve it. Here are some examples:

> A hundred proverbs, a hundred truths. (*Spanish*)
> Proverbs are the daughters of everyday experience. (*Dutch/Krio*)
> Proverbs are the cream of language. (*Afar*)
> All proverbs walk upon stilts. (*Swedish*)

Such proverbs about proverbs have contributed to the prestige and the impact of the genre.

How do proverbs and sayings function in practice? Whether they come from traditional wisdom, the Talmud, the Bible, the Koran, the Veda Book of Hindu Scripture, from political or religious leaders, philosophers, or poets, they are used as quotes. In an oral culture, the experts are—mainly or exclusively—chiefs and elders, who refer to the ancestral tradition, and view themselves as its pre-eminent representatives.

The proverb is associated with established wisdom. Its powerful impact is further strengthened by forceful references such as: 'The tradition has taught us...' or: 'As our ancestors used to say...'. If the authority has said so, who are we to swim against the tide of so much traditional, religious or sound judgment? By referring to the wisdom's unquestionable validity, the speakers also command respect and authority for themselves, or in a concise Shona self-praise from Zimbabwe: 'The words of men do not fall down.' Thus, dominant values are confirmed, to the speaker's advantage, and, ultimately, this should all work out, as confirmed in another Shona proverb: 'The one who quotes proverbs gets what he wants.' The proverbs' authority thus has the function of legitimizing certain role patterns as well as preventing those patterns being possibly questioned.

In societies with rich oral traditions, people are impressed by those who have many proverbs at their disposal and who know how to use them at the right moment. Quoting is an art, and quotations can be used to convey something that, for whatever reason, one does not wish to say outright. The proverb creates a sense of detachment and generalization. It allows the speaker to stand back and broach sensitive matters in an indirect artful manner, to express what one has to say, but safely, since the speaker cannot be held responsible personally for a 'traditional' statement. The quote provides a safe way to criticize, mock or even insult.

Proverbs as part of people's cultural legacies, most sources keep telling us, confirm by their very nature *the* societal norms and values. The fact that the ruling values are the values of the rulers is usually not taken into consideration. The user of proverbs insists on the collective acceptance of the dominant norms and values to be taken for granted.[15] People tend to romanticize the past, and engage in a somewhat softened, cuddly style as soon as proverbial traditions are being discussed. It is obvious that great caution is needed here.[16]

MEDIA

Proverbs are like butterflies, some are caught, others fly away. (German)

Proverbs are not only communicated orally, they are to be found in print as well, in books and dictionaries, in magazines and newspapers, as well as in the work of writers. Cervantes' *Don Quixote* is a European case in point, Chinua Achebe's early novels are well-known African examples, while Luo Guanzhong is a famous sixteenth-century Chinese novelist making use of the popular genre. All over the world, proverbs and sayings have been and are still being transcribed and published in an ever-growing series of national and international book collections and dictionaries.

Proverbs can also be discovered on other objects than just pages: nicely drawn on wall plates, posters, jugs, mugs, pots, and other objects sold in tourist shops. A hairdresser in Dakha pasted the following Bengali proverb at the top of the mirror for her clients: 'A happy family life is because of a woman's virtue', and added on her own behalf: 'but only if she has a virtuous man by her side.'[17] Sayings of all kinds can be found in African public places, such as cafés, or on passenger vehicles. Such bus inscriptions are not always proverbs or sayings from the oral tradition, but when they are, they frequently refer to gender relations, for instance: 'Men suffer, women don't know'; 'No business, no wife'; 'A beautiful woman never stays with one man'; 'Fear woman and play with snake.'[18]

Although proverbs are mostly transmitted verbally—by word of mouth, or in the written or printed form—they also circulate by means of other media, for example, sculpted on pot-lids, engraved on calabashes, woven in or printed on textiles, and visualized in paintings. Especially in Africa, the proverb has been communicated through a larger variety of channels than in other parts of the world: via drumbeats, and by means of other signs and symbols.

In Africa messages are sometimes communicated through a type of skirt (also called *pagne, lappa, leza,* or wrapper) worn by women. The social function of the *pagnes* is illustrated by the example of how household quarrels between co-wives of the same husband are fought out through textiles. For instance, if the cloth has its knot tied at the back instead of the usual front side, it refers to the saying: 'A fool follows behind me' and applies to the co-wife the husband has decided to marry or has already married, against his first wife's wish.[19]

Husbands also receive messages from their wives by means of the specific cloth they wear. For instance, she can remind him of the old saying that 'A good husband is expensive' and this is also the name of expensive cloth material much wanted by women.[20] Some other visual channels, through which proverbs are transmitted among the Akan in Ghana, are designs in funeral cloths (*adinkra*), multi-coloured *kente* cloths referring to significant objects in that culture, and others.[21]

A highly original form of the non-verbal communication of proverbs is the pot-lid message, used exclusively (as far as I know), by Fiote women.[22] The Fiote live in Cabinda, an

Angolan enclave. Pot-lids are used to indicate truths women would not be permitted to express verbally to their husbands. The lids are round boards with a diameter of about 18 cm. On the top, images expressing a proverb or saying are sculpted in relief. Traditionally, wife and husband do not eat together; the clan's men eat together under the clan meeting-house roof. The wives put the food for their husbands in an earthen pot, cover it with a piece of banana leaf and call for a child to bring it to the men's place. This is what normally happens.

However, when a woman is not pleased with her husband's behaviour or when they have a quarrel, she chooses a meaningful proverb pot-lid from her collection or orders an artist to make a new one according to her instructions. This pot-lid then replaces the usual banana leaf and when the food with the sculpted cover arrives, the commotion is visible: What, a special pot-lid? Whose is it and what does it mean? The husband in question has to confess what the problem is and a palaver starts. It could be about his laziness, his impotence, his avarice, his wife's being sexually frustrated or her objecting to his taking a second wife. If he says he does not understand, a specialist will examine the pot-lid and, depending on his verdict, the husband will get advice from his companions. The sculpture may, for example, show a cooking-pot on three stones. The proverb depicted is: 'Three stones support the cooking-pot; three rights a woman has in marriage' (namely clothing, food, sex). The wife's message is that she has a complaint about one or more of these marital rights.

This very special means of communication has some unique advantages. For instance, she avoids her husband's initial outburst of rage, since she is not there when her message arrives. He, on the other hand, is likely to moderate his reaction in the presence of the other members of the clan. The pot-lid communication shows that, for reasons of tact, women would rather avoid direct confrontations and prefer instead to broach delicate subjects concerning their husbands in an indirect way, if at all. Many proverbs confirm that women are not called upon to speak. The artistically expressed Fiote pot-lid communication shares with other non-oral forms the fact that they use other proverb channels than the human voice, which gives to their messages an extra dimension of indirectness.

FEATURES

A proverb is the ornament of speech. (*Persian*)

Proverbs display a number of similarities in formulation as well as in terms of poetic devices, and are easily recognisable thanks to their compact form. Some of those formulations appear to be intriguingly similar in proverbs from different parts of the world.[23] Here are a few examples of the most frequently occurring patterns and, in the context of this book, these will, of course, be proverbs about women:

- A is (like) B:
    A house full of daughters is like a cellar full of sour beer. (*Dutch/German*)
    A beautiful woman is a feast for the eyes and loneliness for the soul.(*Filipino*)
    A wife is [like] a protecting wall for her husband. (*Hebrew*)

- A is not (like) B:
  Woman is not a corncob to be valued by stripping off its leaves. (*Baule*)
  A bad wife is not a good mother. (*Spanish*)
  Your wife is not a prayer shawl you replace when you don't like her anymore.
    (*Hebrew*)
- No A without B:
  No young woman without a mirror, no old one without advice. (*Spanish*)
  No bride without a veil, no woman without jealousy. (*Ladino*)
  No woman without charms, no poet without rum. (*Portuguese, Brazil*)
- Better A than B:
  Better a stupid wife than a ruinous house. (*Bassari*)
  Better to live with a dragon than with a bad woman. (*English, UK*)
  Better to starve than eat cats' dinner, better to freeze than wear old woman's
    clothes. (*Chinese*)
- If A, then B:
  If an old woman dances, she invites death in her yard. (*German*)
  If the father doesn't behave like a father, the daughter should still behave like a
    daughter. (*Chinese*)
  If a woman does not want to dance, she says her skirt is too short.
    (*English, Jamaica*)
- Said-sayings[24]:
  'Respected!' said the bride on learning she was pregnant. (*Oromo*)
  'More by hit than by wit,' said the man when, throwing a stone at his dog, he
    struck his mother-in-law. (*Danish*)
  'The truth is hard,' the man said, and he hit his wife on the head with the
    Bible. (*Frisian*).

The concise form, striking artistic devices, metrical and rhyme patterns, and other deviations from ordinary speech make proverbs easily recognisable as such. The poetic devices used are so numerous that only the most frequent ones can be discussed. The main forms of artistic language in proverbs are *metaphors*, *metonyms* and *similes*. They are so common and numerous in proverbs that they deserve our special attention separately in Chapter Five, 'Messages of Images'.

Quite a number of proverbs transmit exactly the same idea; they are *synonyms*, even though this idea is expressed in widely different images. Take for instance the widespread idea that the world is full of women:

Women are like shoes, they can always be replaced. (*Rajasthani, India*)
Women are like buses: if one leaves, another one will come. (*Spanish, Venezuela*)

The Minyanka proverb 'Even an old calabash is useful' is an example of *personification*. Not only animals, but also parts of the body and all sorts of lifeless objects are personified and thus enabled to reason or act. 'A mother's back sins when it is seated' (*Rundi*). 'A teapot can serve five teacups, but who has ever seen one teacup serving five teapots?' (*Chinese*).

Exaggeration is another amusing device, as illustrated in the following proverbs: 'A thousand wives, a thousand palavers' (*Ashanti*); 'Love turns pockmarks into dimples' (*Japanese*); 'Die from hunger small disaster, lose your chastity big disaster' (*Chinese*).

Proverbs usually consist of one sentence and seldom of more than two. Their characteristically concise fixed artistic form has been mentioned earlier. Some are even marked by *telegram style*: words—especially articles, verbs, pronouns—are often omitted, so that the shortened form turns into rather cryptic speech. The Bengali example from Bangladesh, 'A big cigar and a small wife' tersely expresses that both are part of the good life, provided that their size respects the ideally required dimensions. Because of its telegram style, a popular Wolof saying from Senegal, may sound somewhat mysterious at first sight: 'Family-name-woman-wife: Yes. Don't go, I stay; don't speak, I'm silent; don't do, I renounce', meaning: The family-name of the woman who becomes a wife is Yes; if you say: 'Don't go', she will reply: 'I stay'; if you say: 'Don't speak', she will say: 'I am silent'; if you say: 'Don't do', she will say: 'I renounce'.

Many proverbs use *parallelisms* (repetition with a difference). It means that formal parallels in verbs, nouns or adjectives effectively reinforce *similarities* as well as *contrasts* in meaning, as does the verb 'bear' in a Tigrinya proverb from Eritrea: 'To bear a girl is to bear a problem.' Two other examples are: 'Women's wisdom, monkeys' wisdom' (*Japanese*); 'The boat follows the rudder, the woman follows the man' (*Vietnam*). Devices, such as assonance, alliteration, rhyme, rhythm, repetition, and word play, to name just a few, may or may not completely survive translation, even though some philosophers hold that all languages are translatable and can be understood by non-native speakers.[25] Rhymes in proverbs get usually lost and such losses are regrettable, but even so many proverbs do stay vigorous and eloquent in spite of their being translated. And the fact remains that without translation they would not have been accessible at all to non-natives.[26]

A last proverbial feature is the frequent use proverbs make of persistent stereotypes. Proverbs about women make abundantly use of stereotype body characteristics, age, sex or stature, and the like, to highlight certain traits, while ignoring others. Such 'typical' traits presented in proverbs aim at people's suspending their own independent thought, so that they automatically agree. It is exactly the same use of cliché and rhetoric that is so effectively used in global advertising. In some stereotyping proverbs the gender of the speaker seems obvious. Would a woman ever say: 'Women and steaks, the more you beat them, the better they'll be' (*German*)? Or: 'A woman is like a goat: you tether her where the thistles grow' (*Rwanda*)? Or: 'Never trust a woman, even after she has given you seven sons' (*Japanese*)?

Is it highly unlikely that one would launch derogatory statements about one's own group. However, things are not so simple, because whose group are we talking about? It is all a question of belonging and taking sides, which is a matter of interest. The following Congolese Lingala example makes this point clear: 'To eat with a woman is to eat with a witch.' In Congo there are situations in which a woman, especially a mother, avidly quotes this popular proverb to her son, especially when his wedding day approaches. She uses the proverb to warn him against his future wife whose motives he should suspect. From her perspective as a mother, it is only 'natural' to take sides with her son against her daughter-in-law to be. Her interest lies foremost with her own blood relatives, and first of all with her own son. From that perspective the future daughter-in-law is just an unreliable outsider. In her case as in others, strategies and interests play a crucial role. So, indeed, she does not have in mind to pull her own group to pieces, and she does not do that at all. But she does not actually consider 'women' to be her first loyalty. Women's interests and loyalties are a very complex issue, and proverbs about women can certainly not be reduced to simple gender oppositions.

CHANGING CONTEXTS, CONSTANT CORES

A thing must happen to necessitate a proverb. (*Igbo*)

A few last points before we turn to 'The Female Body.' First of all, some proverb specialists have argued that a proverb acquires its concrete contextual meaning only at the very moment it is being used.[27] I agree that new shades of meaning are added each time a proverb is quoted, and those can be fruitfully studied. In the meantime, however, there is in each proverb a hard core that keeps its meaning in spite of all the changing contexts. Given the nature of our material—a large corpus of proverbs from widely different backgrounds—it is this comparative approach we opt for by concentrating on the intrinsic core meanings and messages of proverbs originating from all over the world.[28]

Another question: do proverbs contradict and thereby neutralize each other? This appears to be a question of little relevance for the use of proverbs in every day life and language. Take, for example, the issue of monogamy versus polygamy in the following two Congolese Luba proverbs: 'To have one wife is to be one-eyed' and 'If you marry two, you'll die all the younger'. They both put forward advantages and disadvantages of each option, so that, depending on one's own personal interests, one can opt for one or for the other. This is indeed a matter of strategy.

Finally, there is the point of literal and figurative meanings of proverbs and sayings. Two kinds of proverbs are said to exist: 1) originally direct statements, and 2) proverbs considered to be figurative right from the beginning. This also holds for proverbs about gender. There are first of all proverbs referring explicitly to women and men, daughters and sons, mothers and fathers, or in terms of parts of the body: breasts and beards, vaginas and penises. Proverbs take the body seriously, to the advantage of those who quote them, as for example in this Oromo proverb: 'A man holds and urinates with what he has', meaning that a man should use his anatomy to his profit, while stressing *en passant* the sexual differences between men and women. Such proverbs about the body or about various categories of men and women may or may not be used to make a point about gender. Secondly, there are proverbs not at all referring to male and female physical features directly, but 'traditionally' considered as most appropriate messages to refer to ideal or deviant gender roles and relations, such as: 'Get a cage before you get a bird', which means that a man should find a house before getting married (*Creole, Trinidad/Tobago*).

The two categories are difficult to separate. Literalness has always been a problematic concept: where does it end and where does the figurative sense begin? Sayings are either being seen as the vague umbrella under which all proverbs, maxims and precepts etc.

shelter, or defined as simple 'direct' non-metaphoric statements as against real (i.e. metaphoric) proverbs. Thus the Ashanti proverb (*Ghana*) 'The hen knows when it is morning, but she looks at the mouth of the cock' is no lesson in natural history but aims at metaphorically reminding a wife that her husband should do the speaking, while she should not. Being figurative it would be a 'real' proverb.

In this book, the so-called 'direct sayings' are not rejected as invalid specimens of the genre (as proverb specialists are sometimes inclined to do), but fully taken into account, in whatever way they refer to womankind. One could quote 'A whole night of labour and then only a daughter' as a literal statement or as a disappointed metaphorical (*Spanish*) proverb about any lack of success after much effort. In the latter case, however, the lack of appreciation for the birth of a daughter no less persists under the surface. Or take the following Baule example from Ivory Coast in which a poor man complains about his misery by quoting the following saying: 'Whether the widow has her period or not, it makes no difference.' Literally, it means in his society, that a widow has no right to have sexual intercourse, and neither does a woman who has her period. In this man's particular situation, it refers to his own poverty: whether it is a festive day or an ordinary day makes no difference to the poor, since their situation is always grim and monotonous. Thus, the 'commonsense' comment about gender, taken for granted, becomes metaphorical in being used to make a point about something else in the practice of its being quoted. Therefore a distinction between literal and figurative statements does not seem appropriate here. The example demonstrates that direct statements cannot be separated from so-called 'real' (that is metaphorical) proverbs, because they do take on unexpected metaphorical meanings. Nevertheless, their original direct meaning is not lost either. Even though the quoted Baule proverb on the widow engages in completely new and unexpected directions, the 'hard core' subsists, as the statement continues to remind a listener that in the Baule culture the widow's freedom is curtailed.

For the purpose of this book, then, proverbs literally referring to women as well as those that were metaphorically referring to the female sex right from the start have been collected and taken into account. Both categories yield information about women in different ways: directly, in observations, prescriptions, proscriptions and so forth, or indirectly, by means of messages using figurative language and images of all kinds. It is obvious that the second category may need more background knowledge to identify them as potentially being about gender. Wherever necessary, explanations have been added.

Proverbs exaggerate, idealize, simplify, stereotype, jest and joke, and in contextual usage their truth is less relevant than their potential for negotiable meaning. Thus, in local contexts, the weight of misogynistic sentiments so largely present in proverbs may well have been tempered through debate and irony. Their value in the context depends on what suits the speaker for the purpose of the argument.[29] Nonetheless, proverbs about gender usually represent a dominant view.

All the 15,735 examples that I found in written sources or came across in oral conversations have been taken into consideration, and proverbs in their widest sense have been examined as part of a rough and ready cross-cultural genre. However, the preponderance of proverbs representing male perspectives, promoting male superiority and defending male interests and privileges, is indeed striking. If proverbs present a 'truth', it is of course always a truth hiding underlying interests. 'Truths' as seen from women's perspectives are hard to come by, and not only in proverbs.

As much as they have been under-represented or excluded from the public arena and from public functions in most societies, women's views are significantly under-represented in the proverbs I collected from oral sources, as well as from written sources such as collections and dictionaries—even though I have especially looked for them and asked for them. It has always been difficult to study women's past inner thoughts and personal ideas in a systematic way, as relatively little written material is available. Proverbs, then, are no exception to the rule of human history in which women's views and voices, especially the controversial ones, are a relatively recent part of the public space. It is even likely that the silent majority of our foremothers have formally complied with the dominant social order, which the majority of proverbs refer to as the 'natural' order. Nonetheless, as we shall see, the enormous impact and power of women is strikingly present in proverbs, against all odds, in remarkably persistent ways.

1

The Female Body

When a girl is born, don't take care of her, she will grow like a cactus; when a boy is born, take good care of him, as you would with a rose-tree. (*Rajasthani, India*)

As the starting point of orientation in life the human body has been for people all over the world an inexhaustible source of proverbial images. Thanks to our body we move from one place to the other; thanks to our body we are able to handle objects, and to create, heal or destroy whatever we touch in the world around us. With our bodies we go through our successive phases of life between birth and death. Our bodies make us worry about illnesses, handicaps, or lack of physical attractiveness. The body is needed in making love, getting pregnant and having children. Thanks to our bodies we can touch and taste, talk and listen, gather and share knowledge, work and relax. Our bodies also reveal our characters and moods, whether we are bossy or submissive, fearful or courageous, tired or energetic, friendly or angry, frustrated, sad, or happy. The basic themes of proverbs are all derived from elementary human experience and activities. Through the body we express how we feel and who we are—or at least who we are allowed to be in the midst of the social pressure we all suffer to a larger or smaller extent—in the cultural context we live in. It is not amazing, then, that proverbs have taken the body seriously.

FROM HEAD TO FOOT

Whoever marries a woman for her body will lose the body and keep the wife.
(*Mandinka / Dutch / Papiamentu*)[30]

All over the world, male bodies are on average bigger than female bodies: the difference amounts to about 10 cm. At birth, male babies tend to be longer and also heavier than female babies, and the same holds true for adult males: they are on average about ten per cent heavier and seven per cent taller than females. According to statistics, however, female babies are less vulnerable to disease than male babies, while there are more still-born baby boys than baby girls.[31] 'A girl is an olive-tree, a boy a tadpole', the Ovambo in Namibia and Angola say, which means that a girl grows faster than a boy. In situations of poverty, a girl with many brothers may risk not to have enough to eat. 'Brought up among boys, a girl weakens', a Gikuyu proverb observes, which means that, the available food being scarce, usually the boys who are physically stronger will take possession of most of the available food.

Although adult males normally have more solid bones and greater muscular power than women, adult women seem to have more vitality and endurance than men, physically as well as psychologically, with a higher average life-expectancy and longevity, as worldwide statistics have indicated.

STATURE AND APPEARANCE

A woman who loves her man says: 'I look up to you.' (Twi)

The superior size and superior physical strength of men and the fact that women are the birth-givers have had far-reaching consequences for the gender history of mankind. In many ways the male sex has been able to make effective use of its physical size and power for its own gain and benefit.

Physical stature plays a role in power relations, probably because of the simple fact that smaller people have to 'look up to', and behaviour researchers have argued that taller people may impress simply because of their physical height. In fact, the same phenomenon can be noticed in social relationships. People of high rank underline their importance by sitting on 'higher' seats, and emperors, kings and queens not only sit on thrones but they also put crowns on their heads which make them even taller, and therewith more important. Tall males are often considered more attractive than short males, and people assume a 'natural' correspondence between male stature and social importance.[32] Women themselves may be inclined to prefer as their partners men taller than they are themselves.

Most women and all young children are physically smaller than adult men, and thus often literally looked down upon. In quite some proverbs women and children are equally considered to be 'minors'. Tall women, then, seem to breach the dominant norm of ideal gender stature by their sheer size. The idea that women ought to be physically smaller than their husbands is often explicitly expressed:

My misfortune is bearable, the man said, and married a small wife. (*Frisian*)
Of women, misfortunes and gherkins, the smallest are always the best.
   (*Hungarian*)
Women and sardines, the smaller the better. (*Spanish*)
Women and sardines: pick the small ones. (*Portuguese, Brazil/Spanish, Argentina*)
A wife and a plough handle are best when shorter than the man. (*Oromo*)
A housewife likes a small pot; a husband likes a small wife. (*Khiongtha*)

Smallness also seems to suggest youth (or childishness?): 'A small woman always looks just married' (*Italian*). Large or small body stature is used in the literal as well as in the figurative sense. Small females may seem easier to control physically than larger females, yet they still do not seem to guarantee an easy relationship, as a German proverb warns: 'Even a small woman surpasses the Devil in artifice', a proverb with variants in other European languages. Metaphorically the same message is presented in Latin America:

> The good essence comes in a small jar, but so does poison. (*Spanish, Chile / Cuba*)
> What they lack in size, they have extra in astuteness. (*Spanish, Bolivia*)

In proverbs, a woman who is physically taller than her partner is considered far from being ideal. An Ashanti proverb presents the problem as follows: 'When a tall woman carries palm nuts, birds eat them off her head.' A tall woman who proudly carries nuts in a bowl on her head is presented as one who is showing off, and she is warned that she will be punished for it. The explanation given is that such 'male' behaviour is condemned in a woman. The proverb is warningly quoted to girls who display what society considers to be male traits, and the palm nuts are a metaphor for 'the male world': as long as men are alive and around, a woman is not supposed to crack nuts.[33] The proverb reminds women to refrain from getting involved in designated male roles.

Of course, it does happen in real life that women are taller than the average man, and for those cases proverbs provide society with arguments to make sure that the problem is not getting too serious. Trying to conjure the eerie damage done to men by a female's imposing stature, a North American proverb whistles in the dark that 'A big wife and a big barn will never do a man any harm', whereas a Polish proverb argues that prevention is better than cure: 'Choose yourself a wife of the same weight if you don't want quarrels all the time.'

When a man is not the tall strong person he is supposed to be, there are plenty of comforting proverbs, especially in Africa, arguing that his smallness does not undo his superiority *vis-à-vis* women. He is in charge anyway:

> A man, even a man of small size, will be called great in comparison to women.
>   (*Arabic, Lebanon*)
> Even small, a man is old. (*Minyanka*)

Respect for old age, and especially the prestige of old men, as formulated in the above Minyanka proverb, is thus extended to the superiority of the male sex as such. Males always come first, even as young boys—goes the argument. For safety reasons it is sometimes argued that by their very nature men cannot be belittled in life. In the words of an Ashanti saying: 'There are no small men', because each man is 'higher' than any woman *ex officio*. A Gikuyu proverb from Kenya could not agree more: 'The man comes out of childhood, but the woman never comes out of womanhood', and a German proverb confirms a similar hierarchy with 'Boys will be men, girls will be brides.' The West African Mamprusi in Burkina Faso say quite simply: 'A woman can't become a man', which means that there is no way to ever change the gender status you receive at birth.

The Ngbaka who live in the Central African Republic have taken the small stature problem encountered by males so seriously that they have invented several reassuring proverbial metaphors:

A small string binds a big parcel.
A small squirrel can lift up a big nut.
The small hawk can carry off a big chick.

The small string refers to a small man, whereas the big parcel represents a tall woman. It argues and justifies that a small man can marry a tall woman without difficulty. As the reverse is no common situation, the couple's physical 'gender imbalance' has to be made up for by a convincing argument. The 'tallness' of the parcel also refers metaphorically to any superior qualities the woman might possibly own and the man possibly not. All three messages argue that a short husband can marry a huge woman without any risk, because he will stay in power, according to the established rule that the smallest of the strong (i.e. male) is always more powerful than the tallest of the weak.

This idea is also expressed in the Ikwere proverb: 'Whatever the size of the woman, it's the man who mounts her', with other variants saying 'climbs on her' or 'rides on her' meaning that lying on top while making love, there can be no doubt about who is the boss, as the mythical Lilith had well understood when she quarrelled with Adam about the issue. In proverbs about tall women in the figurative sense, many solutions are looked for to keep them 'small' in the sense of insignificant, as we shall see.

In fact, then, tall or small, why should a man bother at all about the size of the female body, as long as he is in control? What seems to be most unsettling about the female body is fertility rather than size, and about a thousand proverbs in my collection refer to this crucial issue. 'What a tall bride needs, a small one needs as well', as the Digor in the Russian Federation put it. And the Oromo argue that: 'A girl and a clay pipe are never too small.' In other words, young girls are big enough to be married, and, by extension, things may appear small but still serve their purpose. Smallness in the Oromo proverb refers to a girl's sex. Universally, proverbs express that it is posterity in the first place that men need women for—and women, men: a female's first and main utility is her fertility —in addition to her doing 'woman's work'. Still, the theme of stature and the impending threat of female imposing appearance have preoccupied proverbs extensively.

In the animal world, it is often the males of a species that display themselves to attract the females. Among birds, male peacocks court peahens with their seductive tails and colourful feathers, and with their beauty. This is also the case for some mammals, such as impressive lions who use their manes and male deer who use their antlers to scare away rivals.[34] In the human world, it has generally been taken for granted that beauty is a feminine trait. Alluring female trappings are being warned against in numerous proverbs that no less tend to think of women in terms of appearance than today's advertising business. The female physique has often been imagined to be so confusing that in some cultural or religious contexts it is required that the female body, head and face be hidden under concealing clothes and veils, in order to prevent male 'chaos'. Proverbs do not insist on men's face, hair, and beard to be hidden and covered in order to prevent female desire and sexual 'confusion'. If they do not want to lose their good name, women are not supposed to desire the male body at all, whereas a majority of proverbs referring to the female body reflect male desire as well as anguish.

In Europe in the past breasts were covered, and the first European décolleté seems to date from the Renaissance. If it is true that in the context of the western world the exposure of the body takes place where individual self-controls are high, women's ever more trustfully exposing her body might suggest a degree of (male) self-control that allows women to expose their body without being accused of 'immodesty', according to the idea that one can only expose oneself where there are guarantees against the risk of being exploited. Conversely, then, the female covering of (the head as well as) the body would mean a lack of trust and of 'sexual safety'.[35]

Nonetheless, the physical difference between female and male bodies has mainly come down to showing and looking respectively. True, in glossy magazines, films, videos etc., the number of scantily clad bulging males is growing. Overall, however, far more glamorous female nudes are commercialized to attract consumers in the advertising market. In Western Europe more than anywhere else in the world, female breasts, bellies, and buttocks are aggressively advertised on large billboards, which do not seem to disturb many people (at least few protests are heard). No less than in proverbs, it is evident who is the object and who is doing the goggling.

In the eternal competition for selective breeding this long term development has been explained as follows. In terms of evolution women wanted the best possible male candidate to father their children, and they tried to be as seductive as possible to achieve their goal, viz. to find a better candidate for procreation than their female rivals. In the course of human history, men instinctively internalized their ideal image of the female body and of what they considered to be female physical attractiveness. Thus women became 'the beautiful sex.' Women, however, gradually developed their ideal image of the male sex into a much less physical perspective: they came to appreciate in men qualities such as intelligence, spirit, and creativity. The fact that male physical strength and stature have gradually lost much of their selective value seems to have had a crucial effect on male behaviour: they were strongly stimulated to strive for the required accomplishments, and responded obediently and actively. However, the majority of men have never refrained from stressing their passionate interest in female physical beauty, and women have relentlessly strived for beauty and worked at beautifying.[36]

One may wonder whether Bertrand Russell was influenced by the above outline of human history—or by proverbs echoing the effects of such developments—when he said that women tend to love men for their character while men tend to love women for their appearance.

BODY AND SOUL

Husband and wife should not just become one body but one soul as well. (Hebrew)

Proverbs reflect an ongoing struggle about the possession of both the female soul and the female body. It is often argued that a wife is her husband's property, that he owns her. 'A devout wife is her husband's body' it is said in German, and the underlying idea is that he is the head (and the brains) of that body.

Ideally, man and wife are meant to be a couple, uniting not only their bodies, but also their minds and souls. The motto at the head of the section, an old Jewish proverb, has spread all over Europe. In practice, neither the bodies nor the souls of the spouses are harmoniously united all the time. There are quarrels and disagreements in wedlock, as expressed in a Korean proverb: '[When they] lie face to face, one body; [when they] turn around, strangers.' Especially in the Western part of the world, body and mind came to be seen as separate entities, with the mind being considered superior to the body, and guiding the body, if things would be as they should be. An Awar example from the Russian Federation explains what happens to those who follow their drives: 'Yield to the desires of your body, then endure the disasters that follow', and a Dutch one: 'Lascivious business breaks the body.' In Europe, this separation can be traced to the influence of ancient Greek culture on Christianity: Greek philosophers such as Plato emphasized the contrast between body and soul, and Christian Church Fathers came to associate women with the (despised) inferior body and its emotions, and men with the superior soul and mind.

In the Judeo-Christian cultures, many proverbs present mind and body as two forces involved in an ongoing competition. Mind equates control over body, whereas the body is considered a container of uncontrollable drives. It is as if men have tried to negate those uncontrollable drives of their bodies by projecting the blame for such 'sinfulness' on to the female body. In the Western world, Judeo-Christian ideas have incessantly alerted men to the dangers of womankind in general and to attractive female bodies in particular:

> Keep afar from the love of women, for their beauty is lewdness and their body a
>   graveyard of lust. (*Hebrew*)[37]
> A pretty woman has the Devil in her body. (*German*)

Not only the particularly beautiful ones but the whole of womankind is often presented as dangerous in European proverbs: women are simply associated with, and reduced to 'the female body.' Equated with their bodies, women are often presented as both attractive and unreliable.

Strong disapproval is expressed of women who offer their bodies for sex or for money. Women are advised not to accept gifts, because accepting some gift from a man's hands, she would have to offer her 'honour', meaning her body, in return. In the words of a Spanish proverb: 'A woman who takes, sells her body.'

According to many European proverbs, a woman's visible interest in some man qualifies her as unchaste, and women are strongly advised not to take such initiatives. Taking the lead in matters of love and sex would be interpreted as a woman's offering her body for consumption.

Human biology is an important key to understanding human behaviour, as proverbs referring to the female body illustrate. The female physique is the subject of numerous assumptions and projections in oral traditions, regarding what is good, bad, desirable, repugnant etc. From hair to toes, the female body and female beauty are commented upon.

HEAD AND NECK

A good woman goes without a head. (*Dutch*)

The head is usually the first thing people see when they meet. It is a sort of business card presenting a first impression of who the person is. One might think that it is very fortunate that women have a head, but some proverbs argue the opposite. In the above Dutch proverb the head is a metaphor for women's personal views, will, and opinions. The message is of course that the best female marriage partner is of the submissive type. Being blamed for having a head of her own, a woman is in fact blamed for having a will and ideas of her own. The Ovambo in Angola and Namibia refer more explicitly to the consequences for girls of this type: 'A girl with a will of her own will not get married.' When accepting that women do have a head, some proverbs hasten to add that it does not really serve any purpose, since there is nothing inside anyway, particularly when it is beautiful.

In daily life the head can be made use of in many ways; for example, one can put and carry things on top. Although women are sometimes considered the weaker sex, they have been used to transporting heavy loads on their heads, a case of beer or a plate of vegetables, a bundle of sticks or a pot filled with water. This is no longer the practice in most parts of the Western world, but still common in many cultures, particularly in rural areas, and proverbs illustrate this. Both examples below admonish women to work harder:

> The vegetables on her head have dried out long ago and still she does not stop talking.
> (*Arabic/Jewish, Yemen*)
> Words in the mouth are no loads on the head. (*English, Jamaica*)

It is often recommended that a woman's head be made less visible, by means of a hat, a shawl, a mantilla or a veil, as the custom prescribes in the cultures concerned. Serious reasons are given for keeping to the custom of covering a woman's head, arguing that it is for her good, virtue, submission, and respectability. Whether the cover is obligatory or not, in various cultures it is recommended that a woman bow her problematic head, because, apparently, her eyes sow confusion. An Arabic proverb puts it this way: 'A woman is like an onion, she must always have her head down.' A Tibetan proverb also tells girls to bow their heads instead of looking up and around, as a rule for everyday life, but still more to be respected on festive days when, dressed in their bright aprons and coloured boots, the girls look especially attractive to the men: 'Whether there is brilliance or not, look down; whether dancing or not, look at the feet.' In Argentina, brides to be are reminded of the ideal of submissiveness: 'Bend your head, bride, if you want to enter the church.'

Far more numerous and repetitious than the ones claiming that a woman should not *have* a head or show her head, are the proverbs claiming that she should not *be* a head. The idea that females cannot or should not exercise public power or even be head of the family is expressed in countries all over the world, in a large variety of direct as well as metaphorical observations. The proverb 'Man is the head of woman' originates, among other sources, from Paul's letters to the Corinthians (I, 11:3) in the Bible, and has thus turned into a widely used saying in Europe, but this hierarchical idea about gender relations can also be found elsewhere, as in the following Persian example: 'The God of women is man, therefore all women must obey man.'

Many references are being made to the inevitable crisis resulting from having two heads in one and the same house. Sometimes the idea that man be the one and only head and master in the house is expressed by explicitly rejecting the idea of two heads: 'You can't have two heads under one hood' (*Turkish*). One hood is not meant to cover two heads, but more often this very idea is presented in other metaphors, such as the hen leaving the floor to the cock, or the horse that needs its rider's tight reins and sharp spurs in order to be 'good'.

Proverbs thus try to construct a wished-for hierarchy. In practice the acceptance of this hierarchy is not as self-evident as proverbs suggest. In Europe and North America, for example, the negotiation for power between men and women is represented as a struggle between head and neck, in which, or so it seems, head is not given full credit by neck, in spite of its lower position on the body, and therefore 'naturally' doomed to submissiveness from the head's perspective. In most variants of this message, head, being the boss, is no less contradicted and manipulated by neck:

> Man is the head, but woman turns it. (*Dutch/English, USA*)
> The husband is the head, the wife is the neck; she can turn him whichever way she wants. (*Russian*)

'Neck' thus serves as a metaphor for women's influence on 'head'. Negotiations are going on below the surface of the ideal gender hierarchy sketched in proverbs.

Neck is not a part of the body that is frequently mentioned in proverbs. There are a few allusions to the neck as an essential element of female beauty, next to one other point being made quite violently: a girl's or a woman's—and more specifically a wife's—neck is recommended to be 'dealt with', twisted or wrung, just like a chicken's. Without such ostentatious exhibition of male power, she will not be a 'good girl':

> Wring a wife's and a hen's neck, if you want them good. (*Europe and both Americas*)
> Woman and candle, twist their necks if you want them at their best. (*Spanish*)
> Girls that whistle and hens that crow should have their necks twisted betimes. (*English, USA*)

Arguments alleged to explain why a woman should not whistle or 'crow' (i.e. manifest herself in public), and not govern or dominate are often directly based on body images: as there is space for only one head on the neck or on the body, there is space for only one head in the house. The 'logic' is that, on the basis of sexual differences, a man is presented as superior and a woman as inferior—or rather this is how things ought to be, if life were ideal. Thus, wherever the head is considered superior to the body, men are associated with the head and women with the body: two heads in one house inevitably clash: there should be no doubt about who is going to be the head. Still, it is also stressed, in German and Russian for example, that head and body cannot do without each other: 'Man without wife, head without body; woman without husband, body without head.' The idea of men being the head is complementary with the idea of women being the heart. Ideally, both complement each other:

The man may be the head, but the wife is the heart of the home. (*Gikuyu*)
Happy is the marriage where the man is the head and the woman the heart.
   (*Portuguese, Brazil*)

This idea is widely underscored by the argument that, all things being well, a man follows his head, while a woman follows her heart.

As for man, wisdom; as for woman, affection. (*Japanese*)
Men have a reason, women a heart. (*Dutch*)

The heart is sometimes believed to provide a woman with insights a man is supposed to be blind to. Associated with 'female' intuition, 'A woman's heart sees more than a man's eyes' (*Swedish*), or even, in a variant, 'more than ten men's eyes.' On the other hand, the heart is considered much less reliable, because it is hierarchically associated with (lower) emotions and naivety, while the head is considered to be the residence of supreme logic and reason:

The heart can be short-sighted, like the eyes. (*Russian*)
A heart that trusts is easily betrayed. (*German*)
When the heart gives orders, the body becomes its slave. (*Hausa*)

Accordingly, one is to perform certain tasks and to refrain from doing others: 'Woman may govern heart and pan, cup and head are for the man' (*German*). The main point being made is that the head is the top in all senses, superior to all the other parts of the body. In proverbs men have metaphorically colonized the head. However, more important are the brains inside: the contents are more important than the container.

BRAINS

Beauty you've got, my daughter, and intelligence I will buy for you. (*Ladino, Morocco*)

Recently I heard the following joke: A man needs a brain transplant. The surgeon says: 'I can offer you a man's brain or a woman's, what do you prefer? Men's brains are of course much more expensive, they cost $2000, women's brains are much less, only $200.' 'Why the difference?' the man asks. 'Well, you know, women's brains have been used.'

Proverbs tell a rather different story. Here, the point is not so much whether brains have been used or not but who has got them and who has not, in gender terms. Brains become a metaphor for intelligence. Men's heads are associated with brains, intelligence, wisdom and talents, while women in general, and wives in particular, are mainly associated with feelings, emotions, lack of logic, and irrationality. The phenomenon of one individual man without brains or a man being blamed for not using his brain effectively is sometimes referred to, although this is rather rare. Here is an example from Estonia which *en passant* also underlines woman's complete dependence on man: 'A man without brains and a woman without a man will never stand on their own legs.' Usually, however, proverbs referring to both sexes equate only men with brains and with using them well.

Innumerable reasons are invented for refusing women access to domains other than those considered 'essentially' female, and the other way round. The way in which the male and female domains are delineated is illuminating. For convenience's sake women's 'nature' is defined such as to deny them a sharp intelligence:

> A woman has the shape of an angel, the heart of a snake, and the brains of an ass. (*German*)
>
> Woman's intelligence is a child's intelligence. (*West Africa*)

In a number of cultures women are taught through proverbs that, by their very nature, they have no brains, i.e. no intellectual and artistic qualities. Whenever a girl appears to be so clever that she cannot be denied having brains, an explanation has to be offered for such a transgression of gender boundaries: 'Made for a boy, turned for a girl', as a Russian proverb puts it. Sometimes a solution is found by turning an extraordinary woman into an 'honorary male', so that the stereotype gender categories need not be questioned or affected: 'What a man Mother Aisha is!' is an Arabic example of this mechanism from Tunisia. The main strategy used, however, is to systematically discourage women gifted in other domains than those designated as female. They ought to suppress their talents, in order to become or at least look like a modest and well-behaved member of their species.

Various proverbs exclude women altogether from having brains or intelligence by their very physique. For example an Oromo proverb says: 'A woman, as her breasts hang down, so her brain hangs down.' In quoting this proverb the Oromo who live in Ethiopia and the north of Kenya mean that women are unable to make good decisions. Without any further argument, a Jewish proverb states: 'A bosom instead of brains', and an Arabic saying admits that actually a female brain does exist, but to be on the safe side it is kept limited: 'Women have only half a brain.' Having only half a brain should prevent her from ever trying to compete with the (supposedly whole) male brain.

In proverbs, brains and beauty are generally considered to be mutually exclusive. Women are mostly associated with beauty, and men with intelligence. This idea is 'naturally' used to reconfirm that women, especially when beautiful, have no brains. Some examples: 'More beauty than a peacock, but the intelligence of a block of wood' (*Mongolian*); 'A doll's head and an empty brain' (*Polish*).

As a sign of beauty, attractive hair has also been widely associated with an alleged lack of brains in women. Here are just a few examples picked at random:

> A head of hair and no brain inside. (*Mongolian*)
> Women have long hair and a short mind. (*Swedish*)
> Though a girl's hair be long, her brain is short. (*Kalmuk*)
> Long hair, little brain. (*Turkish*)

What do girls look for in a future husband, and what do men look for when they are in search of a bride? In proverbs intelligence is usually set against beauty, beauty being associated with women and intelligence with men. As a rule, men are inclined to look for beauty in their future partners, whereas women look for intelligence in theirs: 'The girl is looking for a clever husband; the boy, for a beautiful wife' (*Vietnamese*).

There are a few revealing reflections on what a daughter is expected to need for marriage: beauty and a well-to-do father who can pay her dowry in exchange for her future husband's intelligence, as expressed in the motto to this section. The importance of a scholarly husband for one's daughter is especially emphasized in Jewish culture, as the following proverb illustrates: 'A man should marry his daughter to a scholar, even if it means that he will have to sell everything' (*Hebrew*), in order to be able to pay her dowry. The study of the Talmud is absolutely crucial for men in orthodox Jewish circles. The question is clearly not in the first place as to whether the daughter herself has brains: it is her future husband who will provide for that. Modest household skills and sheer dedication will do for women, it is argued, as other talents risk distracting them from their female duties: 'A girl who reads, sings, and makes music, will rarely become a good wife' (*Polish*).

Women's heads and brains, then, are suspicious parts of the female body, and in need of severe control.

EYES

When her eyes are radiant, the grass withers. (*Russian*)

'The eye is the pupil of the body', the Yoruba in Benin and Nigeria say to express the essential importance of the eye, although they mainly quote this proverb to refer to its mirror function in matters of love. It is indeed the eyes that reflect (or rather betray) love's beginning and end. Through the eyes the world enters our body and mind, not only the physical world we live in, but also the people we meet. According to proverbs, what we see provokes immediate feelings, and it is through the eyes that vehement emotions such as desire and love are conjured up, since eyes are the gates of love, as it is said in German as well as in Russian. Significantly, seeing women is compared to seeing food, and women are 'eaten' with the eyes:

> Food and women enter first through the eyes. (*English, USA; Spanish, Mexico*)
> Watching feeds the eyes. (*Creole, Guadeloupe*)

The eyes are referred to as a mirror of feelings, but the mirror may turn out to be rather deceiving. In proverbs it is therefore often advised to see whether various body signs confirm one another's message: 'When a woman is speaking, listen to what her eyes say.' (*English, USA*) Alas, in a number of cases, body signs appear to be confusing. Apparently, the signs given by various body parts of one and the same person, such as eyes and heart, or eyes and mouth, do not match: 'Cries with the eyes, laughs with the heart' (*Russian*).

One part of the body may seem better equipped than another one to detect the truth about the beloved's feelings, although there is certainly no common opinion about which one is taken to be the most reliable. A special link is suggested to exist between the eyes and the heart when referring to feelings, and between the eyes and the ears when referring to the effect of reliable or unreliable words. The impact caused by the eyes on the mind or the heart is strongly emphasized. Their close links are also reflected in warnings against the chagrin that love may cause, and therefore not seeing may be preferable to seeing. This is expressed in proverbs from widely different areas:

That which does not enter through your eyes, does not get to your soul. (*Spanish*, *Chile*)
If the eyes don't see, the heart won't care. (*Creole, Haiti*)
What the eye has not seen will not touch the heart. (*Greek*)
The most effective defence against temptation is this: shut your eyes. (*Hebrew*)

Eyes enable us to see the world and its beauty. However, they never see objectively, as people project their own ideas onto what they see, and therefore usually see what they want to see:

Beauty is in the eyes of the beholder. (*English*)
Leila must be seen through Majnun's eyes.[38] (*Persian*)

Beauty is pleasant to the eyes, but eyes are also presented as a thing of beauty in themselves: 'A person's beauty is the face; the face's beauty are the eyes', a Turkish proverb argues, while the Hebrew proverb 'If a bride has beautiful eyes, do not study the rest of her body' is used in situations where, in spite of an obvious good point, someone continues to concentrate on negative aspects, while once more underlining the importance attached to eyes.

The powerful impact of the eyes may well be, at least partly, due to a woman's matching eyebrows, as a special finishing touch to the female eye. The ideal Chinese eyebrow, for example, ought to look like a willow leaf.

A house's beauty is in [the use of] water and a broom; a girl's, in her eyes and eyebrows.
(*Persian*)
A house without curtains is like a woman without eyebrows. (*Romanian*)
If eyes and eyebrows did not exist, there would be neither sin nor love for women.
(*Romanian*)

Proverbs pay some attention to the colour, size, beauty and shape of a woman's eyes. Proverbs referring to either black or blue eyes come from countries where both kinds exist, such as in Europe, the Americas, and also sometimes in North Africa. I found no proverbs about eye colour in Africa south of the Sahara, in Asia and Oceania, where people mostly share the same eye colour. There is usually not made much of a difference between women with blue or brown eyes:

If there are no black eyes, kiss the blue ones instead. (*Moldovan*)
Women's eyes cannot be trusted, neither the black nor the blue. (*German*)

In just one Arabic proverb from Morocco, women with blue eyes are explicitly warned against: 'Don't marry a blue-eyed woman, even though she has money in her box.' A blue-eyed person is reputed to have an evil eye, meaning that she has destructive powers. The negative connotations of beautiful eyes are often associated with the (evil?) power of the female gaze, and this power is in the first place associated with eyes of a 'deviant' colour, but not exclusively. Two examples:

Turquoise eyes, black heart. (*Russian*)
Beautiful eyes, villainous heart. (*Creole, Guadeloupe*)

A special power is ascribed to the evil eye, based on the idea that a person is able to harm someone by merely looking with envy or hatred, thus causing illness, and even death. One can take measures to prevent such harm by wearing amulets, or by making specific gestures, by spitting, or by uttering formulas to protect oneself. An Arabic saying from Morocco especially refers to this: 'If you meet a woman who has an evil eye, spit in her path and wish her the Qrîna.' The Qrîna is a female spirit causing the death of infants, a seriously destructive wish that makes clear how much the evil eye is feared.

Women's radiant eyes are considered so powerful that they make the grass wither, as the Russians say. Here are some more examples from various parts of the world:

> A woman's eye is like an arrow to men in the prime of life. (*Greek*)
> No better lye than a woman's eye. (*Frisian*)
> A woman asks, takes, despises, and kills with her eyes. (*Spanish*)
> Beautiful, big eyes sting sharper than lemons. (*Spanish, Cuba*)
> Hell can lie between the lashes of a beautiful woman's eye. (*Hebrew*)
> Too beautiful looks snatch the eyes [of those who look at them]. (*Japanese*)

There are hundreds of proverbs about eyes in general and women's eyes in particular. Which brings us to gender differences associated with the eyes: 'The woman is the left eye, the man the right', the Danish say. This can mean two things: on the one hand, two eyes need each other to co-ordinate seeing, and two people who live together need one another. On the other, there could be a different status referred to here: left and right are not equally appreciated as will be discussed later in the context of 'Hands'.

The Tanzanian Hehe proverb 'Long eyes' refers to a woman 'who runs with men.' It means that some women's eyes are considered so powerful that her look suffices to endanger a man. In spite of their different origins, the element of power and danger attributed to women's eyes is quite common. Is that why she is so often ordered to keep her head down or wear a veil? The talking about the impact of the female eyes in proverbs is mainly done from a male perspective, and the question of who is the subject and who is the object of the talking as well as the seeing is answered by the Romanian and Moldavian proverb: 'Man has eyes to see, woman to be seen.'

NOSE AND EARS

Every face, if only it has a nose, is beautiful. (Serbian / Croatian)

The nose is not much discussed. Some proverbs connect the way a woman's nose looks, its form or its length, with her character or qualities: 'A woman with a turned-up nose is the Devil's gift', says a Portuguese proverb. In Europe a turned-up nose is often associated with self-willed behaviour, and this goes against the unwritten rule of female submissiveness. This underlying idea may have led to associating such a nose, and the connected behaviour, with the Devil.

The length of a nose is considered too: 'An inch makes a world of difference when it's in a woman's nose' is an Irish proverb, declaring that an inch is not much but relative to a small object it may have considerable consequences. The nose seems secondary in the message, but it is no less associated with woman's looks, although one might argue that the same holds for a man's nose.

In some Japanese proverbs, however, the female nose has another familiar dimension, as it is used to indicate the severe limits of her intelligence and her lack of wisdom. The fact that men's noses are generally not much larger does not seem to be a point of consideration: 'Women's thoughts go as far as the tip of their noses' means to say that women are intellectual lightweights, while another version argues that 'A woman's wisdom extends to the end of her nose.' A Russian proverb once more presents beauty and intelligence as mutually exclusive: 'Lovely little nose but nothing in the little head.'

Whether large or small, whether or not used as a measure for one's intelligence, no one can deny that a nose is indispensable in making a face complete. What then to do with the hidden urge of a revengeful husband *vis-à-vis* what he considers to be an unbearably demanding wife? 'The wife asks for a nose-ring whereas the husband wants to cut her nose off' is a Telegu example from India reflecting a complete lack of marital communication.

Finally, the nose can be used in other, sometimes unexpected, ways. How many people, for example, have tried the Burmese practice of kissing with the nose: 'Even if you have no love, be brave and kiss; if you cannot, substitute an intake of breath.' A warm recommendation is added: 'You may think it rather chilling, but to sniff a lover's cheek, like sucking lips, can be quite thrilling!'

On the whole, the ear harvest of proverbs is very limited. In some proverbs, there is an emphasis on gender difference in communication, again with reference to the effect of woman's verbal talents: 'Talking to a man goes into one ear and out from the other; to a woman, it goes into both ears and out from the mouth' is a proverb from Slovenia.

Male and female love is sometimes associated with different parts of the body: 'A man loves with eyes, a woman with ears' (*Polish*) suggests that men are more easily attracted by a woman's looks than by her words. This would justify the following warning: 'Choose a wife rather by your ear than by your eye' (*Hebrew/English, USA*). In comparison to the male emphasis on female beauty, not much attention is paid to women's appreciation of the male appearance. If women are attracted more by a man's promising words than by his appearance, as some proverbs suggest, this could be partly due to women's economic dependence on men's material achievements.

I found one Chilean proverb about the ear from an outspoken female perspective: 'A husband at home is like a flea in your ears', meaning that a housewife does not like the irritating presence of her spouse in the house: as long as he is away, she is her own boss and freely decides what to do in the house and how to do it. Exactly the same idea is expressed in a Kurdish proverb of Jewish origin: 'A husband who is at home is like a toothache to his wife'—which brings us to the next parts of the body.

LIPS, MOUTH, TEETH, TONGUE

'You are right,' said the husband to his wife, 'but all the same, keep your mouth shut.' (*Frisian*)

Women's lips are considered sweet and attractive: 'Women's lips have cured many', as the French put it. A nubile girl whose lips have never been touched by any man is highly recommended in Arabic: 'No-one ever smelled her lips except her mother', means that her honour is guaranteed, but how can one be sure? A torturing question! Proverbs are never short of warnings against the everlasting dangers projected on to men's association with women:

> Women have honeyed lips, but their heart is full of poison. (*Bengali*)
> The mouth is a rose, and the tongue a thorn. (*Hungarian*)
> Free of her lips, free of her hips. (*English*)
> If it is not beauty of her lips, it is beauty of her sex. (*Bisa*)

How to be sure that a woman is really in love with you? The Mongolians provide a simple proof to be taken: 'The lips of a woman who does not love, are cold.'

Proverbs associate women's lips and mouth not only with love but also with talking and eating. There are many proverbs specifically addressing the female mouth. If, according to an earlier-mentioned Dutch proverb, a good woman does not have a head, a Beti proverb from Cameroon states that 'Woman has no mouth', meaning that women are not allowed to speak publicly.

In several countries and cultures, it is explicitly emphasized that a woman's mouth is only meant for taking food: 'A woman should not open her mouth but to eat' (*German and Albanian*). In the Arab culture, a taciturn girl deserves high praise, for belonging to 'the good and quiet type.' It is of her that people say: 'She has a mouth which eats but does not speak' (*Lebanon*)—a warm recommendation. However, to be sure, you need to put her to the test. Another piece of Arabic advice, this time from Syria, is therefore: 'Break a woman's spinning thread and you'll see what language will come from her mouth.' If her mouth remains silent even under those trying circumstances then, yes, she deserves the First Prize for total tolerance and submissive self-control. Sometimes the occasions for women's right to use their tongues for speaking are specified:

> No hen is allowed to sing in the cock's presence. (*Rwanda*)
> Where men are speaking, women should keep their mouths shut. (*Dutch*)

As the Frisian motto to this section jokingly argues, it is not so much a question of a woman's being right or wrong. The main message dictated in such proverbs about the mouth is that it would be against the rules for women to use their mouths in the discussion, nor should they comment or talk back on an equal footing with men. In order to prevent this from happening, women are told to be silent, or, as a Rwandese proverb states: 'No woman is called upon to speak', arguing that a female opinion has no weight. Women sometimes also quote such proverbs for strategic reasons, when they prefer not to give their opinion on certain matters.

All sorts of beliefs surround women's teeth. A Jamaican proverb warns, for example, that 'A woman has teeth and her bite is dangerous', whereas a French proverb reassuringly states, that 'The woman who dresses herself up, loses her teeth', meaning that she is no longer 'dangerous' when she wants to please. The Quecha in Ecuador believe that a woman who has given birth should fast, the poor thing: 'A woman who does not fast will be nursing rotten teeth.' Fasting after childbirth is common amongst Quechua people, and prescribed by traditional doctors, and bad teeth are believed to be due to the transgression of this unwritten rule. Finally, the Romanian proverb, 'A woman cuts her wisdom teeth when she is dead' argues once more that a woman will never come to her senses during her life and will therefore have to be excluded from 'serious' business.

The Kweli in Cameroon see an analogy between wedlock and the extraction of teeth in the sense that both spoil beauty. However, a man can also lose his teeth in a fight with his lover. To indicate that a man has power over his wife and not over his lover, the Oromo in Ethiopia use the following said-saying or wellerism: '"Break some firewood", the man said to his wife and she did so; "Kiss me", he said to his lover and she broke his teeth.' Teeth also serve as a metaphor for the unity in marriage, for example in Ossetian: 'Husband and wife have the same teeth.' Every society has its rules for relationships, and in most societies it is just not allowed for a man to touch another man's wife. The Yaka in Congo express this as follows: 'Other man's wife, teeth pleasure'—meaning that, if you feel attracted to her, there is nothing much that can be done about it. As my Yaka commentator explained: 'One can just smile or laugh, and that's all…'

In proverbs, a woman's tongue is often warned against as a powerful and dangerous part of her body. The dimensions and dangers of a woman's tongue and talking are sometimes expressed in exaggerated terms, as in the following Creole example from Saint Lucia: 'A woman's tongue is more than seven meters long.' A woman's tongue is indeed a factor to be reckoned with, at least as far as proverbs are concerned. A Moldavian proverb sighs that 'If a woman's tongue were shorter, the life of her husband would be longer.' Another example from the Maghreb—'Who can have the last word with his wife since her tongue goes around her neck?'—is in fact an Arabic acknowledgement of male verbal submission or defeat. In the context of the earlier discussed metaphor of wringing necks, the female tongue can be interpreted as literally serving to prevent her neck from being twisted. In other words, her tongue protects her neck, which, figuratively, stands for her body, a vulnerable body that badly needs such preventive measures. However, the other side of the medal is shown in an Estonian proverb: 'A tongue of flesh cuts through a bony neck', expressing that the strong necks of the verbally less gifted feel threatened by the sharp and wounding words uttered by the strong tongues of the physically weak in society.

SHOULDERS AND ARMS

A husband should use his wife's shoulder to cry on. (Irish)

The rare proverbs regarding the shoulders all point to different things. That 'The shoulders carry the head' is a Kundu proverb meaning that a leader or high official needs other people to support him—or that a man needs two wives. The shoulder is considered a reliable part of the body: 'If a modest woman's livelihood is gone, her shoulders are not gone.' This Arabic proverb is quoted to encourage her to carry on. We already met the shoulder in the Kweli proverb used to metaphorically confirm that a wife should submit to her husband. Hierarchy or not, man and wife are linked to each other like shoulder and arm, for better and for worse, in a Congolese Yaka proverb: 'The shoulder does not run away from the arm because it is sick.' A Russian proverb, on the contrary, associates shoulders and arms with the freedom of love and the shackles of marriage respectively: 'Love has wings on its shoulders; matrimony has crutches under its arms.'

Descending from her shoulders to her arms, proverbs reflect that a woman's arms are a comfortable place to be. Inevitably there are proverbs about the mother's arms as related to child care and mother love, but there are also other women's arms and wives' arms. 'While during the day he is a monk, at night he is in our arms', is an ancient Sumerian example from Mesopotamia, from a female perspective. It is not always easy to say whether the perspective in a proverb is gender bound. The following North American proverb might be quoted by men (as a warning) as well as by women (tenderly or even complacently): 'Strong men-of-arms become like putty in the arms of women.'

There is often an undertone of fear in proverbs about women, fear of losing control. How can you be sure about the other's feelings, and what will happen next? These are torturing questions that both sexes, of course, ponder. From a male perspective, a Rwandan proverb relates a man's suspicions: 'An unworthy woman betrays you while offering her arm as a pillow.'

Anguish and disappointment are expressed in many ways, e.g. in the following Jewish proverb from Morocco: 'Before a girl gets married she has seven arms and one mouth; after she is married she has seven mouths and only one arm.' How to prevent this from happening? A man's fears of the consequences of falling in love and throwing himself into a woman's arms must have inspired the following North American proverb: 'A woman would be more charming if one could fall into her arms without falling into her hands.' Falling into someone's hands without being able to get away holds equally for both sexes. The question is: who falls into whose hands?

HANDS AND FINGERS

The wife is a wife because of [her] hands. (Zulu)

Usually people have a left hand as well as a right hand, but in most, if not all, cultures the right hand seems to be more positively viewed than the left hand:

> What resemblance, more perfect than that between our two hands! And yet what a striking inequality there is! To the right hand go honours, flattering designations, prerogatives: it acts, orders, and takes. The left hand, on the contrary, is despised and reduced to the role of a humble auxiliary: by itself it can do nothing; it helps, it supports, it holds.[39]

This quotation reads as a metaphorical reflection on gender relations. How is the relation between the two hands expressed in proverbs? 'The left hand should not know what the right hand does' is originally a saying from the Bible referring to the giving of alms that should be done modestly and without any fuss. In a Creole proverb from Martinique it has got a different interpretation: a wife should not meddle in her husband's affairs. The husband is associated with the preferable right hand, and the wife with the left.

In other proverbs, the wife is sometimes referred to as the right hand: 'A woman is her husband's right hand' (*Mordvin*). The hierarchy is kept intact nonetheless. When she is referred to as the right hand, it is as a submissive part of the head, or of the whole body representing the husband; yet when they are both referred to as hands, he becomes the right hand and she the left, so that the hierarchy is reassuringly confirmed.

There are also 'neutral' cases in which no gender is attached to either hand, such as the above quotation from the Bible or the following Igbo example: 'The right hand washes the left hand, the left hand washes the right hand.' This proverb from Nigeria means not only that in marriage one needs to help each other, but also, more generally, reminds people to repay kindness to those who are kind to you.

'You can't clap with one hand' as the Burmese say to express that you need a partner in life, while a Malay proverb compares the misery of a one-sided love with 'trying to clap with one hand', meaning that instead of useless pining, one does better to look for another partner, as it 'takes two to make a quarrel or a love affair', and who would deny that?

Hands can be warm or cold, although only in proverbs originating from cold climates it is emphasized that the warm hand of a woman can make a man happy. The warmth of the hand refers to the warmth of the whole woman. Thus, for example, the hand of an average warm woman in combination with a good pint makes an Irishman feel as if he is a relative of royalty—which apparently means much: 'A beer, a warm woman's hand, and the queen is my aunt.' Paradoxically, in several European countries it is also stressed that cold hands express a burning passion: 'Cold hands, hot love' (*German/ French/Italian*).

Things are always enjoyed more when we love those who present them to us: 'Whatever a mother gives from her hand, tastes sweet', as the Adyg proverb goes. That a mother's hand also means power and influence is made clear by the well-known but rather overstated English proverb that 'The hand that rocks the cradle rules the world.' However, the hand of a beauty has more impact than what the mother can achieve: 'Tea tastes even more delicious when given to you by the beautiful hand of a lady', is an Arabic example of this truth, although a complementary warning is launched in the same culture: 'Drink from the hand of the woman you love, but do not let her drink from yours.' Too much intimacy threatens a man's emotional independence.

Asking for a woman's hand is a widely used expression underlining that the hand is a crucial part of the body. All over the world, a girl is 'asked for her hand' as the expression goes, and inexperienced young men who have to do the asking are strongly advised to be careful in their choice. How can a man be sure that he asks for the right one? Beauty is no guarantee; perhaps, on the contrary 'A white glove conceals a dirty hand', as the English say to emphasize that one has to look further than a girl's outer appearance only. Proverbs emphasize that young men should be choosy, even before a girl's hand is officially asked for:

When you go to dance, take heed whom you take by the hand. (*Danish*)
To ask for a woman's hand is like buying a horse: groom, open your eyes. (*German*)

In order to remain on the safe side, the advice is not to look for a girl from afar, for a man must know what he is doing, as it is argued in this example from Estonia: 'Take a wife from a neighbouring farm, you know her hands and legs.' You know her background as well as her working capacities, and a farm's future depends on a profitable wife with solid hands and solid legs.

There are a thousand-and-one stories that must have inspired proverbs about asking a girl's' hand in marriage. Strikingly, I found most of them in Arabic. When reading such a series of proverbs about the asking for and giving of a girl's hand, one sees them arriving, as in a film, the young men who want to marry, advised by friends or fathers to first walk by the house where the girl in question lives. The proverb 'See his house and ask for the hand of his daughter' has many Arabic and also Jewish (*Ladino*) variants from the Maghreb.

If a suitor decides that the house looks acceptable, he presents himself to her father. If the girl hesitates or dares to say no, she is warned of others who did the same and were sorry afterwards. Sayings originating from all over the Arab world or from specific countries emphasize that some girls are so obstinate as to refuse all suitors that present themselves and are explicitly marked as 'bad' girls and seriously criticized for such un-cooperative be-haviour:

> They came to your house to ask for your hand, but you were not there.
>   She replies: They could come now!
> They asked for her hand in marriage, she coquettishly refused; they left her alone, she
>   broke down and began to supplicate.
> Now that a man has come to ask for her hand, she says that he is one-eyed. (*Lebanon*)
> A bad woman refuses every man who asks for her hand. (*Iraq*)

The main message is that she will regret her own behaviour, when it is too late. In spite of her longing for a suitor, a girl may look for reasons to decline the proposal of the wrong suitor who arrives first to ask for her hand. Dilemma. Should she say no now, hoping and waiting for the longed for beloved to present himself? And what if the loved one never turns up? In the Maghreb, the story may then continue either as: 'After she got married, many men asked for her hand' or as: 'The first one asked for her hand, the second one mar-ried her.' Usually in life things happen in the wrong order.

In cultures where a bride price has to be paid to the bride's family, asking for a girl's hand is a costly business for a groom to be, and sometimes 'The hand is more expensive than the dish', as a Russian proverb puts it, in which the girl has metaphorically become a dish of food to be eaten by the groom. On the other hand, in cultures where a dowry accompanies the bride, there are suitors who are more interested in the money than in the girl, as in an Irish proverb: 'He asks for the girl's hand, but marries the money.'

The female hand alludes suggestively to its profitable working force. A Sotho proverb puts it this way: 'A woman is a monkey: her hands are eatable.' Indeed, for those who eat monkey meat, the hands are the most important and the most tasty part—and this also holds for women: not a woman's beauty but her obedient hardworking hands are the most crucial aspect to be looked for. The South African Zulu motto to this section also stresses that a wife should be handy and skilful in practical work, and from the northern part of Africa the same message is echoed in an Oromo proverb from Ethiopia, arguing that both a woman and a dog are useful to the household, each in their own way: 'A woman is a hand; a dog is a voice.' The female hands have to keep a good home, and the dog has to guard the house by barking. In the Ladino proverb 'The hands of a notable housewife are the grease in the dish'— 'grease', being a delicacy, stands for a most profitable housekeeper.

In proverbs related to hands one finds messages similar to those associated with earlier discussed parts of the body. First, existing hierarchies have to be respected and a strong woman should remember that 'Even though her hand might hold the reigning sceptre, she remains a woman'—as an Arabic Jewish proverb from Yemen insists. Second, 'A man shouldn't wash his wife's hands', as a Kenyan Nandi proverb puts it, meaning that he should never ever spoil her.

Ideally, instead of being difficult, a woman 'asked for her hand' offers this hand willingly to the man who wants to marry her, whereas men are warned not 'to fall into the hands of women', because 'He who has fallen into a woman's hands, has fallen on burning coals', as a Ladino proverb from Morocco states. A man, then, must keep all control in his own male hands.

In many cultures, a girl's finger is given a ring as a symbol of betrothal or the promise of marriage, and a number of proverbs refer to this. Here are three examples from widely different parts of the world:

> The handsome finger gets the ring. [lit. A ring around it]. (*Swahili*)
> When the finger is ringed, the girl is occupied. (*Danish*)
> The promises of marriage are wind, the only thing that counts is the ring on the finger.
> (*Creole, Guadeloupe*)

Other proverbs associate a woman's working capacities with her finger or fingers:

> When a woman wets her finger, fleas had better flee. (*English, USA*)
> To her every finger is a man. (*Hebrew*)

This last proverb expresses the highest praise for a housewife, because she works for ten, and to have such a wife is of course most profitable to her husband. In an Arabic proverb with many variants the importance for a woman to be on good terms with her husband is expressed in the metaphor of the finger:

> She who has her husband's agreement can rule the universe with her little finger.
> She who has her husband with her shall turn the moon with her finger. (*Syria*)

This proverb is obviously very popular, as I found it in many versions, sources and countries all over the Arab world. Evidently, such a good relationship blesses a woman with both power and possibilities, although they all seem to depend exclusively on this partnership.

SEX CHARACTERISTICS

God protect us from hairy women and beardless men. (Arabic)

The number of proverbs devoted to female sexual characteristics varies in different parts of the world.[40] Depending on the culture and the context, breasts are either taken for granted, seen as a pedestrian, functional body part for nurturing, or considered as objects of erotic arousal. In China no special attention seems to be paid to the female breast as an erotic object. The Chinese phrase for breasts, *ru fang*, means 'house of milk', referring to nursing and motherhood. In Chinese classic poetry, unlike the Psalms and the Song of Solomon, the praise of its beauty seems to be lacking, even the Book of Odes[41] contains no mention of breasts. Why should this be? Perhaps it is due to the fact that in the rural areas (especially in rich families) Chinese boys (not girls) are breastfed for a relatively long time, often until their sixth year. It may well be that, rightly or wrongly, Chinese men consider breasts as something of importance for children only.[42]

Could this be the reason why I found no Chinese proverbs about breasts? In fact there were conspicuously few proverbs on breasts, wombs, and vaginas from Asia in general, particularly in comparison with Africa. Is this a matter of decency to be respected in the written sources, as in the United States? In my collection of North American proverbs I found hardly any references to breasts either, and none to wombs or vaginas. In this case, it does not necessarily mean that breasts are not considered to be exciting nor that such statements did not exist but that they have been kept out of collections for reasons of puritanism, austerity, decency, or as a form of political correctness *avant la lettre*.[43] In fact, the North American proverbs on women are the most 'decent and respectable' (and therewith on average also somewhat 'sterile'): it is possible that the original oral traditions were censored and 'cleansed' before being published in official collections, although this cannot be proved. In Europe, a number of proverbs on breasts and wombs have survived in spite of Victorian prudery.

Where does discretion end and prudery begin, as far as the exhibition of female nudes, and breasts in particular, are concerned? Breasts are sexualized as aesthetic objects, at least in the contemporary Western world, and only occasionally looked at from the functional perspective of breastfeeding. In Africa, south of the Sahara, a striking abundance of proverbs are related to breasts—in the two senses: on the one hand they deal with breastfeeding and motherhood, on the other hand, with beauty and sex appeal. Those two aspects are also found in the other continents (with North America as the exception), although to a lesser extent than in Africa.

Proverbs present the male beard as a sign of time-honoured respectability in many cultures: 'Under a white beard lives an honest woman', according to a Mexican proverb meaning that she will be well protected by the social esteem he enjoys due to his respectable age. It is significant that she is situated 'under' his beard.

Incidentally, young women themselves do not necessarily feel attracted by the wealthy old 'man with the white beard.' An Arabic proverb looks at the matter from a young woman's point of view: 'A woman flees from a white beard like a sheep flees from the jackal.' Apart from that, the respected whiteness of the beard may well be caused less by the man's wisdom than by his worries: 'If the wife is bad, the husband's beard will soon turn white', as a Tati saying from Iran observes. However that may be, having a beard is having power, and sharing that power with one's wife is strongly advised against in the following Spanish proverb: 'To a married woman don't give a piece of the beard.' Or, in Persian: 'Rather pull the beard off than give it to your wife.' A beard makes a man worthy of respect—but not a woman. On the contrary, a beard on a woman's face is considered unbearable, figuratively no less than literally. It is a sign of 'maleness' and female 'maleness' risks overthrowing the existing order.

A woman who grows a beard or moustache 'naturally' is obviously very disturbing. Proverbs see it as a sign that something is very wrong:

> A woman with a beard is of a wicked kind. (*Dutch*)
> When a family is going to ruin, a beard grows on the face of the eldest daughter-in-law. [a bad presage] (*Korean*)
> A bearded woman, God help us! (*Portuguese, Brazil*)
> May God spare me from a bearded, old woman. (*Spanish, Argentina*)

A proverb even blames a woman who accommodates to the requirements by taking the trouble to shave her face. No way! 'From a shaved woman you should turn away your face' (*Spanish*). Finally, a proverb about the moustache has obviously travelled from the Iberian peninsula to South America: 'A woman with a moustache: greet her at a distance' has variants in Spain and Portugal as well as in Colombia and Brazil. It is a warning to men who do not want to run the risk of being kissed by such a woman. Apparently a female with hair on the face is the absolute in repulsiveness for Iberian men and their South American descendants.

'If my aunt grows a moustache, she will be my uncle', the Tamil in India say, to express that changing roles in life is unlikely, especially in the field of gender. This idea is confirmed by proverbs from other areas, for example, the following Dutch one: 'Beard, breeches and billfold, these are a man's three b's that a woman should avoid.' A Danish proverb jokingly explains women's smooth skin by referring to another presumed stereotype female quality: 'Women don't have beards because they cannot keep their mouths shut while shaving.' If having a beard means having power, could the derision about a woman's facial hair be seen as an encroachment of the male privileged domain?

In some cultures men do not shave, e.g. Orthodox Jews or fundamentalist Muslims. An Eastern European proverb pretends that: 'It is easier to bear a child once a year than to shave every day.' Whether such claims are being made by men or by women, or indifferently by both, is difficult to know.

In spite of cultural differences, there seems to be a rather general agreement that a woman needs to have an abundance of hair on her head, but that most, and in some cultures all, of the other parts of her body should ideally be hairless, and depilated if they are not 'naturally' smooth. Depending on the culture, she may therefore have to smoothen her arms and legs, and to shave her armpits and even her pubic hair. So much time-consuming work!

There are indeed some proverbs about such undesirable hair on body parts other than the head: 'Only on horseback did she realize she had forgotten to shave herself' originates from Morocco. It refers literally to a bride who is on her way to her new home; in the Berber culture it is unworthy for a bride not to depilate her armpits and pubic hair. The proverb is figuratively used to express that people usually think of doing something when it is already too late.

So far we have seen that breasts are female attributes, and a man is not supposed to have them, just as a woman is not supposed to have a beard or a moustache. There should be no confusion about the order of things: 'Sky is adorned with stars, man with his beard, woman with her hair', insists a Tatar proverb from the Russian Federation. A man may have, and in some cultures is highly recommended to have, a fully-grown beard. As for the rest, his hair is allowed to sprout at will, which is not at all acceptable in a woman's case. In North America, this is expressed as follows: 'A hairy man's rich, a hairy wife's a bitch', while in an Arabic proverb the difference is marked in slightly more elegant terms: 'God blesses the hairy man and the smooth woman.'

Women are really caught by those various unwritten norms and rules regarding female face and body hair. The main line of argument is that the differences between men and women need to be made unambiguously clear. Echoes of the above prescriptions make the slightest trace of female hair on the wrong part of the body, undesirable. Therefore, even a faint moustache on a woman's face begins to look like a serious disaster, as two Portuguese proverbs from Brazil state:

Not even the Devil can handle a woman with a moustache.
Not even the Devil can put up with a woman with hair in her nostrils.

Again, for a man this is a completely different matter. In Japan, even a man's nostril hairs are obviously interesting: a geisha who is allowed to count the hairs in the nostrils of her favoured patron feels very flattered, because this privilege is considered as a sign of respect and trust. It grants her power as well: 'A woman can do what she pleases with the man who lets her count the hairs in his nostrils.'

If a woman is 'disqualified' for developing male sex characteristics, it is no less considered bad for a man to develop female sex characteristics, such as breasts. This may be due to hormonal changes, or, as some proverbs suggest, be the result of eating certain plants or food. The Quecha Indians in Ecuador warn men against eating and even touching a plant whose seeds contain a milky liquid: 'If you touch a *chuchu muyu* seed, you will develop breasts.'

Although in the eyes of many men breasts are considered intriguing and attractive, they prefer not to develop them on their own body. On the other hand, some proverbs insist that breasts (like beards) are not very special as such:

A woman is more than her breasts; goats also have two. (*Rwanda*)
Breasts are like a beard: even a barren woman has them. (*Ganda*)

There are also women who do not develop real breasts. Wrongly, it has sometimes been believed that a woman without breasts is sterile and men would not lightly take the risk to marry such a woman. If a teenage girl does not develop breasts, some proverbs conclude that such a woman will grow old without having any children: 'The proof of a girl's lack of breasts is her white hair' (*Rwanda*) means that she will grow old without being married. The Kundu in Cameroon refer to this link of breast and womb as well, by saying that 'A girl has the other thing because of her breasts', in which 'the other thing' refers to a womb and fertility, although breasts or breast size do not really guarantee motherhood, and have nothing to do with female reproductive capacity.

NURSING BREASTS AND BREASTS AS OBJECTS OF DESIRE

You can always soothe a child with the breast, but how to handle a husband? (*Estonian*)

For millions of years the first provider of food in people's life has been the mother. She starts suckling and nurturing right from the child's first day of life. She is willing to do this, but the child also has to remind her of his needs. This familiar image of a baby who cries to remind his mother of his need to be breastfed is widely used in proverbs:

> An infant must cry to get its mother's milk. (*Sinhalese, Sri Lanka*)
> Until the baby cries, the mother doesn't suckle him. (*Romanian*)
> If the child doesn't cry, the mother won't find out. (*Russian*)
> The mother gives the child no milk until it cries for it. (*Persian*)
> A mother does not suckle a child until it cries. (*Tibetan*)
> A crying baby gets a suck; but a babbler only gains dislike. (*Khiongtha*)

Being indispensable to the young baby's survival, breastfeeding has served as a metaphor for a mother's taking care in general as the basis for one's later life 'Everyone acts according to the amount of his mother's milk he has drunk' (*Kurdish, Turkey*). The majority of proverbs on breastfeeding argue that a female breast is meant to suckle children. Proverbs on this subject, however, do not only associate the mother's breast with its actual bodily function but, as usual, bring along other messages. Thus the Oromo observation that 'Breasts are two but the milk is the same' metaphorically reminds listeners of the old wisdom that different means may yield the same result or, as a European saying from a totally different domain puts it: 'More than one road leads to Rome.'

Several proverbs aptly combine the issue with familiar messages declaring that 'naturally' a female is supposed to act like a female. The act of breastfeeding serves as a pretext to justify the separation of roles along the lines of the sexes:

> Let a female develop her breast, eventually she must give it to her child. (*Igbo*)
> Little girl, you suck your mother's breast, and yours will be sucked. (*Lega*)
> A man's breast does not give milk. (*Hehe*)
> Breast-ache is not a man's ache. (*Minyanka*)

Thus the female breast serves to exclude the sexes from each other's culturally established domains in life: men cannot suckle children and women should not be intellectually too talented—exactly the mechanism we came across in the discussion about brains.

The metaphor of breastfeeding is used to underscore the truth that right from the beginning a baby learns from those who surround him or her, in particular the mother:

> Whatever the mother has eaten, the child will take in at the breast. (*Sranan*)
> That which you sucked from the tit will be spilled over your grave. (*Spanish, Bolivia*)

However, the opposite is not impossible. This idea is also reflected in proverbs about the breast, for example in the following one from Botswana: 'All women's breasts can feed wise children', arguing that even foolish mothers can give birth to and feed a child that is very different. Conversely, even wise mothers have no guarantee that their children will turn out to be reasonable creatures: 'The mother puts a breast in the child's mouth but not sense in its head', several versions of a widespread European proverb make clear. The same unpredictability regarding posterity is expressed in numerous proverbs about wombs, as we shall see.

One's children are never too much of a burden to care for, and female breasts are metaphors *par excellence* for a mother's love and care for her children, and also, more generally, for the responsibilities one has to take on in life, as the following Creole proverb from Haiti expresses: 'The breasts are never too heavy to be carried', or in a variant 'too heavy for the owner to run with'.

Everywhere people seem to agree about the wonderful experience of being breastfed by one's mother:

> A mother's love, a breast-clinging child. (*Maori*)
> A mother's breast is better than rays of sunlight. (*Adyg*)
> A mother's breast is paradise for a child. (*Kabardino-Balkar*)
> My home is my mother's breast. (*Spanish*)

Breasts are associated with nourishment, meaning that mothers look for and find ways to feed their children. Some proverbs stress that, luckily, there still is life after having been breast-fed. Mothers continue to be generous, and if need be, one has to improvise in life and look for an alternative source of survival:

> A mother's breast may dry but her hand does not. (*Oromo*)
> A child does not die because its mother's breasts are dry. (*Nigeria*)

The breast as an image of being attached to one's mother survives during a man's whole life: 'A mother always has breasts, a healer always has medicine' is a Yaka proverb which means that a man who is leaving his mother's house does not cut bonds with her. Some African proverbs about breasts remind people to take care of their old mothers who took such good care of them and breastfed them in their childhood years:

> The breast of your mother is not to be forgotten. (*Tonga*)
> A mother's breast cannot be abandoned because of a wound. (*Mboshi*).

Such messages teach the younger generation to take care of those who cared for them in the past—one's old mother in the first place, but also, by extension, one's older relatives in general. In cultures and countries where social security is non-existent, people depend on their children as a form of insurance for their old age, no less than children on their mother's breast. In this sense breastfeeding is an early investment in children that hopefully yields output in times of sagging and withering.

In addition to proverbs about the nourishing function of breasts, there are others expressing fascination with their sex appeal: 'The sweetness of the breasts lasts until the grave', according to an Arabic proverb.

Although paradise could be dreamt of in different terms, from a male perspective the female breast as a metaphor for paradise extends long after breast-feeding is over.

The breasts of a woman are in general more developed than a young girl's, and some proverbs pay special attention to the irresistible and therefore problematic attractiveness of big breasts, as expressed in a Spanish proverb: 'A woman with big breasts you should marry, bury, or put into a nunnery.' The observer here seems completely obsessed with those confusing objects. All three suggested options in the proverb are meant to solve the man's problem with his own drives and desires, whereas, ironically, his solutions consist of far-reaching measures taken against the innocent woman whose only fault is to have breasts!

Obviously, female breasts have a special appeal to men, and proverbs warn the male sex against the dangers they provoke and the confusion they sow: 'Do not desire the breasts of somebody else's wife', the Yaka in Congo say, for example. Young girls seem unaware of the power of their breasts but they can also be coquettish:

> A girl flutters her breasts without knowing the consequences. (*Rwanda*)
> The girl that goes out dancing does not hide her breasts. (*Oromo*)

Quite a number of sayings suggest that the attractiveness of the female body has power over male reason. Women's breasts seem to fascinate, and there are many proverbs about the irresistible appeal of the female bosom:

> There is nothing that is not the breast of a woman. (*Zulu*)
> Two tits pull more than a hundred wagons. (*Spanish, Panama*)

Numerous variants exist in many places, in which sometimes 'hair' replaces 'tits'. One of men's main worries expressed in proverbs is the capital question of their wives' and daughters' chastity. It is as if 'breasts' as a seductive part of the body, and 'chastity' are thought of as being mutually exclusive:

> The hair of a tiger, the gem of a snake, the breast of a chaste woman, the tusk of an elephant, the sword of a brave man, the riches of a Brahman, one gets them only after their death. (*Hindi*)

In other proverbs, however, the problem is rather that women (especially the chaste ones) reject men who wish to grab at their breasts. Therefore men are advised to flatter women extensively. It is also stressed, though, that timidity will prevent a man from reaching the goal of his desire:

> Sweet mouths suck two breasts. (*Greek*)
> A timid heart will not see a white breast. (*Kurdish*)

To comfort those who have been rejected by a woman, an African proverb recommends just a bit of patience: 'If a girl says no to marriage, just wait for her breasts to sag' (*Rundi*), whereas those who complain about the consequences of their own choice, are reminded that they should blame themselves instead: 'He that takes an old wife should not complain about sagging breasts' (*German/Romanian*). Indeed, breasts grow old with their owners and their attractiveness is likely to diminish with suckling and age: 'Breastfeeding makes old, the childbed makes young', as it is said all over Europe.

Both the nurturing and the aesthetic side of the female breasts have inspired the making of proverbs praising either their motherly warmth and nourishing qualities or their lovable sweetness and powerful attractiveness.

WOMB

In woman's womb lies the destiny of the home. (German)

The womb is the fundamental organ to distinguish women from men: 'A womb makes a woman', a Latin proverb states, and an Italian proverb goes so far as to say that 'Women reason with the womb.' Here, once more, we find the familiar argument excluding women from the male domain of rationality on the basis of the female body shape or a specific body part—this time the womb.

Most proverbs about wombs are concerned with what the womb is actually meant for: procreation—the wonders and worries of bearing a child. Both men and women seem to attach crucial importance to having children. Wombs are receptacles for posterity, several proverbs argue:

> Love for a girl lies below the navel. (*Rwanda*)
> The woman with a storehouse under her navel will not die of hunger or cold.
> (*Ladino/Hebrew*)

The storehouse under the navel is considered a good investment by an older generation. Therefore girls need to be fertile and fertility is signalled by menstruation—yet I found only a few proverbs dealing with the matter. The Zulu sound the drum for a girl's first menstruation to celebrate and announce that she is now nubile, but 'Unhappy the girl for whom the drum does not sound.' In an Arabic proverb, there are obviously mixed feelings about the event: 'When a girl begins to menstruate, either give her in marriage or bury her.' The proverb reflects the same need for drastic control as expressed in the Spanish proverb we came across earlier, and the same options of either marrying or burying her.

According to Islam, menstruation is considered as 'uncleanness' and during her period a woman is exempted from the usual duties of prayer and fasting. A menstruating woman, even if she is not allowed to pray, can still go to the mosque. Of course, nobody would be able to check whether she has her period, and therefore the fact is simply ignored. A Persian proverb refers to this by saying that: 'They don't close the mosque for one menstruating woman.'[44]

In a number of cultures, traditionally, menstruating women were or are not allowed to prepare food for others. I only found one Baule proverb from Ivory Coast referring to the idea of food thus being 'polluted': 'Better to sleep hungry than wait for food prepared by a woman having her period.' Among the Baule (but also among a number of other peoples), there is another rule about menses: menstruating women are not allowed to have sex, and the same holds for widows. Hence the proverb 'Whether the widow has her period or not, it makes no difference': she cannot have sexual intercourse anyway.[45] Finally, having one's period means not being pregnant. A Congolese Mboshi proverb expresses the worries of the married woman who desperately wants to conceive. Each month she hopes that her period will not appear, and then feels disappointed again: 'The chance of motherhood fades with regular menstruation.'

The fact that women carry their children in the womb for nine months before giving birth establishes strong links between them. The mother's love for their children is considered endless, she has loved them even before she gave birth. For her the child is 'The one whom the heart has seen before the eye could see him' (*Arabic, Lebanon*). It is sometimes suggested that a child can only be completely happy as long as it is in the mother's womb, which the Yaka metaphorically refer to as 'the big forest', when they ask rhetorically: 'A child, will he weep in the big forest?' Before the womb can carry anything, action has to be taken, as recommended from a female or from a male perspective:

> He loves me well that makes my belly swell. (*English, UK*)
> It is not enough for a woman to put her hands on her belly to get a son.
>   (*Arabic, Syria/Lebanon*).

Sometimes, however, women seem to love their husband more than their child. In such a case 'The belly precedes the child' and this preference is socially disapproved of among the Rundi where this proverb comes from, but not only there. In all cultures, children are considered to be the hope of the future, and therewith the most important contribution women make to society.

When my first son was born in Congo, all the people from the neighbourhood came, one after the other, knocking at the door, to say 'thank you' to me for having given birth to a child. It meant that by giving life to a newborn I had contributed new strength to society. This idea is not acknowledged so movingly and explicitly everywhere, but the underlying truth is a universally acknowledged. In the words of a Gikuyu proverb: 'The foetus in the womb carries the future.' In Arabic, a mother of attractive children is praised as follows: 'The womb is a mine of precious stones' (*Lebanon*), meaning that she has been a successful birth-giver.

Proverbs seem to observe mainly two different things about the content of the womb. First, children look like their mother and also resemble each other, an idea concisely expressed in English: 'The child follows the womb.' Secondly, and more frequently, it is argued that one cannot tell what the womb will bring, as it produces all sorts of children:

> A mother's womb does unexpected things. (*Digor*)
> A womb is an indiscriminate container: it bears a thief and a witch. (*Shona*)
> The womb is like the *muwogo* [cassava root]: it brings forth both beautiful and ugly.
>   (*Ganda*)
> A mother's womb is like a slave ship, bringing both good and bad. (*Sranan*)

Such widely different container metaphors as the cassava plant, and the slave ship refer to ideas about the womb as developed in various continents. One Russian proverb suggests that it all depends on the man and his sperm: 'A woman is like a bag, whatever you put into it, she will carry.'

Having children makes people worry about them, right from conception and forever after. 'The child hurts inside and outside', as the Tonga in Zambia put it, meaning that mothers always suffer because of their children. 'Wombs see trouble', as the Ganda aptly summarize this world of sorrow.

VAGINA

Even if your wife's sex is small, dawn will find you there. (*Minyanka*)

The vagina, this narrow path leading to the womb, is looked upon with mixed feelings by men and presented with mixed feelings by women. Metaphorically a Thai proverb warns men to handle the small vagina of a young woman with care: 'Thread the small-eyed needle slowly.' On the other hand, a Creole saying from Guadeloupe observes that 'A vagina is like a pig's snout', meaning that it is so solid that it is never worn out, thus recommending that it should be well used throughout life. Apparently this is not so self-evident. A Sumerian proverb preserved in cuneiform writing on a clay tablet from thousands of years ago contains a complaint on the matter: 'My vagina is fine, [yet] according to my people [its use] for me is ended.' This complaint is attributed to an old prostitute defending her ability to continue her profession in spite of her aging. Had she known the Creole proverb, it might have served her as an argument!

Other proverbs emphasize that a woman should not be too eager or too willing to accept men's proposals. All over the world metaphorical warnings are provided to remind females of the serious consequences of such willingness. The following examples—all from Africa south of the Sahara—illustrate this by literally referring to the part of the body concerned:

Let-me-please, let-me-please! grazes the vagina. (*Rwanda*)
If a woman offers her sex to everyone, pestles are used on it. (*Minyanka*)
The kind woman has a hairless vagina. (*Mamprusi*)

Sexual indulgence can be detrimental, goes the warning. The Mamprusi image refers to the belief that abundant hair on a woman's private parts is a sign of health, and the proverb indicates more generally that the presence of one thing is a sign of something else that is hidden for the time being. All three proverbs literally refer to sex, but they express metaphorically that profiteers take advantage of the notorious goodness of people who sacrifice themselves to other people's pleasure. The violent Minyanka image of the pestle stresses that such behaviour is abused as well as despised.

Sometimes the vagina stands for a woman's nakedness: 'He who sees a vulva in the morning should go on to the market at once'(*Arabic, Algeria*), as it is considered good luck for a man to see a naked woman. It means misfortune, though, if it incidentally happens the other way round. Again, a woman is the object who brings good luck to the man, whereas seeing a 'penis', i.e. a naked man, is just bad luck, but for whom?

Although many proverbs speak about the dangers and powers of women's sexual attractiveness, I found only one proverb directly referring to the frightening archetype of the *vagina dentata*, originating from the Mapuche in Chile: 'A woman of striking appearance has a biting vagina.' In some cases the vagina is referred to without being mentioned explicitly, as in the following Rwanda proverb: 'A happy girl thinks that hers must be better.' It is quoted when people attribute their luck to their own merits.

As we have seen, most examples in this section are from Africa, and only a few are from Asia and South America. Indeed, in daily life the vagina is not a part of the body that is openly talked about.[46] Nevertheless, having or not having a vagina is a decisive question, and the answer makes a no less decisive difference in life.

BUTTOCKS

She who offers a half-cooked meal is better than she who offers her buttocks. (Rwanda)

Proverbs about female buttocks almost always refer to their sexual appeal. Buttocks are like breasts, in some respects: the same round forms, the same attractiveness. A woman who goes without pretty buttocks is disadvantaged: 'Neither a beautiful face, nor a supple behind' says an Arabic proverb disapprovingly, referring to anybody or anything in the world with nothing to recommend.

In Africa, the Caribbean, and South America, there seems to be more emphasis on this part of the body than in Europe or Asia. The ideal behind should be a large one, so that it can be shown off:

> No one shows her buttocks unless they are big. (*Rwanda*).
> A woman is like the merino sheep—she is judged by her backside.
> (*Sotho, Lesotho/South Africa*)

Although buttocks are important in the overall male appreciation of a female's attraction, men are warned that they are not free of charge. In Cuba it is jokingly said that: 'A woman with a big behind consumes a lot of gasoline', meaning that being an attractive lady, she will cost a man a lot of money. Some women aptly exploit this part of their body to enlarge their impact or profit, as observed in an Armenian proverb: 'A smart bride shows her husband only half of her behind.'

In order to arm oneself against such vulnerability, men are reminded not to follow their desire in the first place, as argued in the Rwanda motto to this section: a less attractive but hard-working woman who produces good food is always better than the lazy one who has nothing else to offer than just a beautiful pair of buttocks.

Another point insisted upon is that, although attractive to the male eye, like breasts, a bottom is not necessarily available:

> A big behind is not a drum. (*Creole, Marie Galante*)
> Although a man may fondly love buttocks, he is only allowed what a woman allows.
> (*Dutch*)

Other aspects concern the temperature of female buttocks and the problem of breaking wind. Are women's buttocks cold or warm? Cold, says a Japanese proverb: 'Cold things are a cat's nose and a woman's buttocks.' Hot, states a Frisian saying from the Netherlands: 'Hot on hot, said the blacksmith, and he put his wife with her bare buttock on the stove.'[47]

Breaking wind is a natural function for both genders, so why it should be especially associated with women is a mystery. When it happens at the wrong moment, in the presence of other people, such an uncontrolled body sound causes female embarrassment: 'After the fart she squeezed her buttocks', says an Arabic proverb about the irrelevance of taking measures only after an unfortunate event—but why the 'she'?

The twofoldedness of the behind is used to explain that misunderstandings and quarrels are unavoidable for those who live closely together as partners: 'Two buttocks cannot
avoid brushing against each other' goes a Tonga proverb from Zambia. It also exists in
a number of other Bantu languages in the following form: 'Buttocks rubbing together
do not lack sweat.' A European proverb from Armenia has a comparable variant about
breasts: 'Even breasts rub against each other' in which, once more, the metaphor of buttocks and breasts serve the same purpose.

LEGS, KNEES, FEET

Heaven is at the feet of mothers. (*Arabic*)

Legs, knees and feet are noticed for their beauty but also for their ugliness. Let me begin
with the ugliness. Down on the scale are women who have no legs at all: 'Even a legless
[woman] begets what has legs', the Hehe people in Tanzania say to express that insignificant and powerless people sometimes succeed in achieving miracles. Proverbs about ugly
legs are quite rare. In fact I found only one, from Ireland, a mild jest about legs so badly
shaped that their owners need dispensation from the Vatican for such a terrible sin.

Young women's legs are considered highly attractive and therefore happily shown at
the dance: 'When the dance is in full swing, the girl's upper legs can be seen.' This Baule
proverb encourages people to put all their energy into their work so that the result will be
admired. Beautiful thighs can be dangerously powerful to the point of bewitching their
charmed victims: 'A devout witch hides her leg but shows her thigh', a Catalan proverb
warns. Another joking reference to the obsessive appeal of legs comes from Denmark:
'Reverends and girls' legs promise something better in higher spheres.'

Sometimes a woman's legs decide about the married status of their owner—but who *is*
the owner here? 'He rejected her and looked at her legs again' is an Arabic proverb. A
woman's legs thus have an impact on her fate and future, that is her marriage's fate and
future. In practice its meaning extends to someone's rethinking the situation he placed
himself in, and then revising an earlier decision.

A Maori recommendation advises a mother as follows: 'Massage the legs of your daughter, that she may have a good appearance when standing before the fire on the beach.'
Young Maori women, it is explained, used to dive to catch lobsters and afterwards they
dried themselves in front of the fire before getting dressed—a good opportunity for them
to proudly show their beautifully shaped legs before interested suitors.

As with shoulders and arms, there are very few proverbs about knees, and again they
seem to have little in common. A Dutch said-saying deals jokingly with two perspectives
on a woman's pair of knees:

> 'Cover them, cover them,' said the man to his wife. 'Why should I, I did not steal them,'
> said she, and sat with her skirt above her knees.

The husband jealously wants to protect his wife's knees from the eager gaze of other
men, while the wife claims that she has nothing to hide. If the appearances are against
you, a popular Yoruba proverb advises, it may take more time and energy to prove your

innocence than to accept the blame: 'A woman who admits guilt will not spend time on her knees.'

One proverb about knees is quoted in the context of work: 'Resting does not graze the knees.' A hardworking woman thus criticizes a lazy one: in the Berber culture, women work mostly on their knees when they are busy with laundering, cleaning, and even kneading dough.

Finally, feet are associated with old or young, beautiful or ugly women. To express that no conclusion is justified before one has finished, or to exhort those who lack persever-ance, some African proverbs use the image of old women's feet to comment critically on those who are full of enthusiasm in the beginning, but whose activities soon fizzle out. The Rundi say, for example: 'Old women's footsteps start firmly but don't last.' A woman who behaves as if her age does not count but who is unable to really manage is made fun of in a Frisian joke: '"Skating makes thirsty," said the old woman, and she stood with one foot on the ice.'

There are some strange beliefs about feet, such as the idea that a broom sweeping a woman's feet brings bad luck: 'She who has her feet swept, will marry an old man' is a Cuban belief, whereas the Quecha Indians in Ecuador advise against foot-binding for women who want to be pregnant: 'Do not tie up your feet; you will not [be able to] give birth.' One may wonder whether those who do tie their feet up could practice this as a method of anti-conception. And how would such a relation between tied feet and sterility have been found out about? Why would Quecha women have tied up their feet anyway? Was it for beauty's sake, as in China? Such questions need to be answered by Quecha specialists.

A small woman has usually small feet; both small women and small feet seem to be con-sidered more attractive than large size. In ancient China, many women's feet were bound from toe to heel, to make them more seductive. Larger female feet are not only literally regarded as a sexual turn-off but, when referred to in proverbs, they usually stand for something else. Metaphorically women's small feet indicate 'the right measure' in mari-tal relationships. In general, women that look vulnerable seem to have more sex appeal to men than strong-looking females, as female vulnerability confirms the established gender hierarchy. The 'right measure' presented in proverbs equates with a relationship on an unequal footing. The Sena who live in Malawi and Mozambique warn against the danger of big female feet, in a proverb with several variants:

Never marry a woman with bigger feet than your own.
Don't marry the one with the big feet, because she is your fellow-male.
Look for someone who has short feet, because one who has long feet is your fellow-male.

No doubt such a relationship would complicate a husband's life and should therefore be prevented from happening. The Sena explanation furnished as 'Bantu Wisdom' is that 'man is superior to woman'; therefore, when looking for a wife, he must choose one over whom he can exercise his authority.[48] Recently, I quoted the Sena proverb that inspired the title of this book in Beijing in a discussion with two proverb researchers of the Chi-nese Academy of Social Sciences. One colleague smiled and said that in Chinese a similar proverb exists: 'The woman with the long feet ends up alone in a room.' Ending up alone in a room is considered to be the fate of a talented woman, as she will not succeed in finding a husband. In Chinese culture long feet in females are not only pejorative figuratively; in the past the feet have also physically been shortened for reasons of beautifying.

There are many other references associating the size of feet (and shoes) with competence, e.g. in India there is a Telegu saying in which older women warn young ones not to develop their feet spectacularly: 'If a girl develops long feet, she will be in trouble after marriage.'[49] And the Hebrew saying 'I do not desire a shoe that is larger than my feet' means: I do not desire to marry a wife who is from a higher class than my own. Bigger feet do not only metaphorically refer to her belonging to a higher social class, but also to other matters threatening the status quo. The apparent male aversion to women with bigger feet reflects a deep-seated fear of losing control. Given the fact that, usually, women have shorter feet than men, proverbs have gratefully taken the image on as a convincing metaphor of how things ought to be arranged in gender relationships. That women have an impact in spite of all the messages trying to prevent this from happening, is also expressed in a European proverb: 'Without touching with her feet, woman leaves footmarks' (*e.g. Portuguese or German*).

A woman's feet, and especially her heels, are a standard for her beauty in some cultures, among the Ethiopian Oromo, for example, 'A girl's beauty can be recognized by her heels', referring to a woman's perfect heels as an indication of beauty. It is linked to the tradition of veiling the face. In that context, looking at a woman's naked feet is the only way to find out whether she is old or young. As my Kenyan friend Zera, born in Mombasa on the Islamized Swahili coast, told me: before she was married, her mother wanted her to veil herself, because that was what a virtuous woman ought to do. However, covering herself and wearing the veil did not protect her from men pinching her behind. 'But how', I asked her, 'did they know that you were not an old woman? Or did they just take that risk?' Her answer was that men guess your age by your feet, so that they always first look at your feet before deciding whether a pinch is worthwhile.

This comment may help to explain the meaning of some proverbs from North Africa where the covering of the face and the beauty of the feet are related: 'A woman with beautiful feet does not need to cover her face' is an example from the Maghreb, reasoning that if they find her feet beautiful, men immediately know that her face will be beautiful as well. This is indeed a matter of consideration in another proverb, applying to a woman who, in order to look more attractive, has beautified her feet with henna in the Arab tradition. However, the harsh critique is that this effort is totally useless: 'Cover your feet, you silly woman—there is no beauty other than the one you were born with.'

The climate may play a role in proverbs about naked feet: I found references to uncovered feet only in the Maghreb and in Ethiopia, where women's feet may be the only part of the body that is not hidden. In such a context a woman's naked feet, at the utmost shod in slippers or sandals, evidently attract more male attention than in colder places where such parts of the body are usually hidden in stockings and shoes.[50]

The next part of my friend Zera's story is illuminating as well. After she had become a nurse and went to work in a hospital, she had to wear a uniform without a veil, to the despair of her mother who was afraid that her daughter's 'honour' would be at stake now.

According to Zera however, it turned out to be very different: 'As soon as I started wearing my uniform, I have never ever been pinched against my own will!' In different times and cultural contexts, modesty has been attached to a variety of parts of the female body, from hair to breasts, from buttocks to feet. Shifting erogenous zones has been associated with shifting norms of modesty, considering now this, then that part of the body as more (or less) provocative than other parts. Thus in proverbs from (at least some parts of) orthodox Islamic culture, men do not seem to have a problem with nude female feet, but with nude female faces, whereas, for example, in ancient China and in Western Victorian times it was immodest for women to exhibit their feet. Most of the underlying standards for such practices have been projected on to the female body as measures of control.

The proverb about losing the body and keeping the wife with which we began this head-to-foot survey of women advises men to look for a wife with more solid qualities than just appearance. Nonetheless, female beauty appears to be an inexhaustible source of proverbial inspiration in all parts of the world.

BEAUTY AND BEAUTIFYING

A woman's beauty makes fish sink and wild geese fall from the sky. (Chinese)

People are judged by the way they look. Attractive people are believed to be more socially and intellectually competent and are better liked.[51] Some proverbs argue in the same sense: 'Beauty of the face is the reflection of a beautiful character' (*Arabic, Lebanon*) or 'A good-looking person also has a beautiful heart' (*Japanese*). Beautiful and attractive people are often more successful than ugly or less attractive ones, and make friends more easily. According to a Russian proverb, 'The beautiful one is well liked by everyone', or using metaphors in Indonesian and Korean respectively: 'There where the sugar is, ants are to be found', and: 'Butterflies come to pretty flowers.'

Stereotype thinking fuses inner qualities with outer beauty, thus giving beautiful people an advantage in life. Although some proverbs attest to the good fortune of the beautiful, many others hasten to set outward appearance against inner beauty and goodness, warning not only against confusing physical beauty with inner positive qualities, but also against the grave dangers beauty provokes. The female body and its aesthetic dimensions are submitted to endless (mainly) male comment.

RADIANCE

The beautiful one laughs and lets the ugly one cry. (Papiamentu)

Female looks and women's beautifying practices are mentioned in all their varieties and detail in proverbs: women are commented upon virtually from head to toe, from hairdo to ointment, from glittering earrings to colourful clothes. In order to define female beauty, proverbs inevitably also deal with its opposite—ugliness—and with the advantages and disadvantages of both. There are very few critical comments from the female perspective on the male obsession with female beauty. Here is one significant Chinese example: 'Don't pick withered blossoms on your way when you have a plum-flower back at home.' It is presented as a wife's lonely prayer. In order to have any impact on her husband's behaviour, she would need to 'pray' aloud in front of her husband, but would she really do so?

In spite of cultural differences, proverbs are of one mind with the Turkish statement that 'A beauty is a joy to everyone.' Wherever, women's beauty is praised. Most poetical terms express what a great source of visual pleasure women represent to the male beholder:

> Beautiful the girl who looks like a peony when she sits, like a columbine when she
>   stands, and like a lily when she walks. (*Japanese*)
> A beautiful woman is like newly forged gold. (*Indonesian*)
> When three women join together, the stars come out in broad daylight. (*Telegu*)
> A radiant beauty says to the moon: 'Don't bother to rise; I will.' (*Persian*)

Especially in Asian proverbs such as above, a rich variety of poetic praises is devoted to female beauty, though such praises do not lack in other parts of the world. Some proverbs stress that men would love to caress and serve such a woman.

> A beautiful woman stands on the palm of the hand. (*English*, *Hawaii*)
> Woman's beauty radiates in the brightness of her presence; a girl's beauty is in the
>   freshness of her innocence. (*Arabic*, *Morocco*)
> Nature meant woman to be her masterpiece. (*English*, *USA*)

A remarkable beauty, even a silent one, cannot easily be ignored, a Japanese proverb argues: 'Even silent, a beautiful woman cannot go unnoticed.' Beauties are absolutely striking when they are found amidst ordinary people who then become their backdrop. The Japanese expression 'Mountain trees around flowers' means that nothing is fair when seen at the side of beauty. Beauty itself loves to show off: 'A many-coloured hen does not stay in a corner of the house', it is said in a Cameroonian Kundu proverb, meaning that attractive women love to be admired. On the other hand, it would be regrettable for such beauty to be located in lonely landscapes or faraway corners, like cherry blossoms hidden in the mountains, inaccessible for human enjoyment and admiration:

> What is the use of the peacock strutting in the jungle? (*Malay*)
> Moonlight in the jungle. [no one around to admire her beauty.] (*Telegu*)

What is considered beautiful varies according to cultural and individual taste. It may be associated, for example, with the pure freshness of youth: 'A pretty girl is like freshly made cheese' (*Nenets*); or with a woman's beautiful hair: 'Beauty of the mountains is in the stones; beauty of the head is in the hair' (*Turkish*); the shape of the head: 'Spacious forehead, beautiful woman' (*Spanish*, *El Salvador*); or any of the graceful curves of the female body: 'A woman's beauty is in her slender waist' (*Tamil*, *India*). In some cases a description is provided of what the ideal beauty ought to be like: 'A pretty girl should have an eyebrow like a willow-leaf, an eye like the kernel of an apricot, a mouth like a cherry, a face the shape of a melon-seed, and a waist as thin as a poplar' (*Chinese*). Here are some proverbs about attractive eye-catching qualities:

Three traits of a woman; a broad bosom, a slender waist and a short back. (*Irish*)
Women and greyhounds should have thin waists. (*Spanish*)
A skinny woman is like a racehorse: fast and fun, but no good for work. (*English*, *USA*)
Fatness is part of beauty. (*Spanish*, *Chile*)
Beauty comes through the mouth. [Women should be fat.] (*Spanish*, *Colombia/Panama*)
A fat woman is a quilt for the winter. (*Multani*, *India*)

Unlike today's Western advertised thinness ideal, corpulence has been (and still is in many parts of the world) highly appreciated in women, as a sign of healthy beauty. Thin women are even ridiculed: 'Being slim is the property of the gazelle, being corpulent, the property of the big horse'—thus goes the apologetic response of a slim Arabic woman when she is being made fun of by more prestigiously weighty women (*Syria/Lebanon*). 'Plumpness redeems the seven deadly sins' is a very popular Arabic proverb. Being plump is a sign of beauty, wealth and health, especially in societies where people are used to the painful experience of famine and poverty:

A plump wife is a warm blanket in wintertime. (*Nandi*)
Harvest makes girls and orphans plump. (*Ovambo*)
Should a husband blame his wife for growing fatter? (*Mossi*)

Although the ideas about shape may vary, too much or too little of something, depending on the established norms in a given community, is always problematic:

A slim woman smells of fish. [slim women are little appreciated] (*Creole*, *Martinique*)
Big bread does not find customers. [meaning that very corpulent women will not find a
    husband] (*Portuguese*, *Brazil*)

THE IMPACT OF FEMALE ATTRACTION

Young and beautiful, access to everything. (*Kirghiz*)

Although beauty is a temporary good, it does not prevent young women from thoroughly enjoying this short-lived good fortune: 'No girl holds herself in contempt' as the Swahili say. A young and beautiful face and body benefit the self-esteem of the owner. It is a source of actual profit in dowry cultures, because a beautiful girl will be able to marry without the obligatory dowry to be paid by her father: 'With a beautiful face no wealth is needed' (*Ladino*). On the basis of nothing but appearance, beautiful girls are presented in proverbs as not only self-confident but also highly influential:

A pretty face is the key to locked doors. (*Tajik*)
To every beautiful girl beckons a golden future. (*Russian*)
Beauty is a good letter of introduction. (*Portuguese/German*)
A beautiful woman cannot be scared away like birds that eat the harvest.
    (*Swahili*, *East Africa*)
Advice from the mouth of a beautiful girl is listened to with benevolence.
    (*Spanish*, *Puerto Rico*)

Beauty is thus presented as a source of female power and influence believed to subdue not only ordinary humans, but also extraordinary men and supernatural beings:

Even God loves beauties. (*Pashto*)
Even an angel cannot resist a beautiful girl. (*Hebrew*)
However much he tries, even a hero is overcome by a woman's beauty. (*Chinese, Taiwan*)

And even animals—as we have seen, fish cease to swim and wild geese cease to fly when mesmerized by female beauty. A few more examples:

When she looks out of her window, the horse starts walking and moves into the garden, and the dogs bark for three days. (*Russian*)
When one has a beautiful wife, one has no fine pigs—because the pigs, instead of eating, spend all their time staring at her. (*French*)

The effect of beauty is considered more impressive than physical strength: 'A pleasing appearance is stronger than power' (*English, Jamaica*). Its impact does not yield to the power of money: 'The world is ruled by money and beautiful women' (*Portuguese, Brazil*). The profitability of beauty to girls is emphatically emphasized:

All beautiful girls sew with gold. (*Russian*)
A beautiful wife is a golden plough to the household. (*Romanian*)

From the perspective of proverbs, then, there is no doubt about the advantages of beauty for women—but most women do not receive it as a gift from nature.

BELLES

Nature provides woman with only three-tenths of her beauty. (Chinese)

Aware as they are that the male gaze is easily distracted, women work hard on their appearance, in order to keep abreast with aging, and not to lose the impact of their youth on the man of their choice. Large numbers of proverbs suggest that there is no guarantee that the female body he is pleased with today will still appeal to him tomorrow. A hungry husband has to be nourished not only on good meals, but also on daily doses of seductive beauty, in order to be satisfied. No wonder that all the required services to her needy husband are in themselves sometimes equated with a wife's being beautiful: 'The beauty of a woman is her devotion to her husband' (*Lokaniti*), or defined as the best beautifying practice, as argued in Sanskrit: 'To serve her husband is the best adornment of a wife.' Ideally, from a female perspective, a Ganda proverb says, 'In a good marriage you bring his food without having to dress up for it.' However, from their own experience, women know that just devotion is not enough—far from that, and therefore, one takes a certainty for an uncertainty:

A woman beautifies herself for the man who pleases her. (*Chinese, Taiwan*)
A wife who takes care of her appearance, keeps her husband away from other doors.
     (*Spanish, Argentina / Mexico / Puerto Rico*)

The beautifying inventiveness of women has no limits, or so it seems in proverbs. To begin with: there are two opposed views, often held in the same cultures. One holds that not much can be done about ugliness or aging, and that 'giving a hand to nature' is useless. Beautifying, or trying to, does not help at all; it can make things even worse, whereas an attractive woman needs no make-up, she can be poorly dressed, and still be attractive:

> Beauty unadorned, adorns the most. (*Hebrew*)
> True beauty needs no decoration. (*Hindi*)
> The ugliest woman is she who dresses herself up most. (*Portuguese*)
> And she powders, and puts on a blush, and still they won't look. (*Russian*)
> A pretty girl is also pretty in an old dress. (*Chechen*)

On the other hand, it is confidently, or rather hopefully, argued that beautifying makes up for the flaws of nature:

> A white complexion hides many defects. [a white skin was admired] (*Japanese*)
> A little bit of powder and a little bit of paint makes an ugly woman look like what she
>   ain't. (*English, USA*)
> The woman who arrays herself well is never ugly.
>   (*Portuguese, Brazil//Spanish, El Salvador/Venezuela*)

One proverb even completely dismisses a woman without make-up: she ought to be disposed of. One of the most repeated arguments holds that women should beautify themselves exclusively for their own husband: 'The woman who dresses in silk stays at home' (*English, USA*). The true intentions—decent or otherwise—of the blind man's dressed-up wife do not escape comment:

> The blind man's wife—for whom does she put on make-up?
>   (*Portuguese, Brazil; Spanish, Argentina*)
> The blind man's wife needs no make-up. (*English, USA*)
> For whom does the blind man's wife paint herself? (*Hebrew*)
> Blind man's wife for whom are you dressing up? (*Greek/Portuguese*)

She has to justify her behaviour in the gossipy community. And so has the shepherd's wife, whose husband spends the day out in the field. For her the rules are to be adapted: 'The shepherd's wife dresses fancily in the evening' (*Tatar*). Why should she beautify herself during the day? A widow, of course, has no reason at all to beautify herself.

Proverbs stress that, contrary to men, women enjoy appreciative looks: 'A man leaves the home to attend to business, a woman to show herself' (*Finnish*). This seems more acceptable for girls who need to find a husband, than for married women, although, for both categories virtue is presented as the first priority. After marriage, especially from a husband's perspective, beautifying exposes his wife to the risky desires of other men, and, willingly or unwillingly, she could seduce or be seduced by other men and lose her chastity. Therefore, in an Arabic proverb, men are warned to watch their 'property' carefully: 'Do not spread out your merchandise, it will diminish its value' (*Lebanon*). For their own good a Spanish proverb from Argentina advises men to ignore the strong sex appeal of beautified ladies they might find on their way: 'From a woman wearing make-up, one turns his face away', whereas in Hebrew the advice is to simply shut one's eyes. An Arabic recommendation from Algeria goes thus: 'Veil your women and repair your ramparts', two activities considered indispensable to protect men against imminent temptation.

As for women, and particularly wives, if they need to leave the house (though it is often argued that it were preferable to keep them at home all the time), only the most modest and inconspicuous ones are 'safe' outside:

> An unornamented calabash may safely be left outside. (*Maori*)
> A woman and a cherry are painted for their own harm. (*English, USA*)
> The little house that is whitened up wants to be rented. (*Spanish, Argentina*)

Thus, beautifying is considered a precarious activity, even though female beauty is presented as being immensely enjoyable. In proverbs a husband always feels like protecting his wife from the imagined consequences of the desiring and designing looks of other men. In some cultures the protection of men against seductive women as well as the protection of their wives against the beauty-hungry looks of other men was meant to be facilitated by women's wearing a veil. Still, the practice seems to be far from simple. Proverbs suggest that in spite of their veil women find ways to be charming: 'Though she covers her face with her veil, she still manages to be coquettish' (*Bengali*). Moreover, a veil leaves much to male guesswork and fantasy: 'Covered with a veil everyone is handsome' (*Azeri*), so that, without a veil, a woman may even come to be seen as less attractive: 'A woman without a veil is like food without salt', as a Pashto proverb stresses. In the meantime, for an ugly woman, the veil is presented, literally, as a blessing in disguise: 'An ugly woman will swap a silk belt for a woollen veil' (*Russian*), but such a solid veil makes a Turkish proverb jump to unjustified conclusions: 'The thicker the veil, the less worth the lifting.'

As for the beautifying practices themselves, all over the world proverbs reflect how ingeniously women put themselves out to meet what they imagine to be the male expectations of female beauty. The material is so vast that a severe selection has to be made, with only a few examples for illustration.

First of all, it is the skin, the face and the hair to which women pay endless attention. There are proverbs about the ways they anoint all three with oil or cream, the face is rouged or whitened, and the hair curled or coloured according to fashion or personal aesthetics. As usual, proverbs referring to beautifying practices include other messages, such as the Lega proverb, indicating that one should be critical in selecting one's advisers: 'Before you ask the varan [a large lizard] for a skin cream, look at its skin.' An Oromo proverb about hair explains the dilemma of making choices in life: 'Because she enjoyed the sweetness of the fresh milk, she left her hair dry', the custom being to use the cream of the milk to oil people's hair. Ovambo women use butter as a skin cream, if it is available for that luxury purpose: 'A woman who uses butter for her face will not lack any', reminding us that one needs to be rich in cattle to do so.

Especially in the Arab world, but also more widely in Islamic cultures, women's hair, hands and feet are beautified with henna: 'If you want to look more radiant, use henna and ointments' (*Morocco*); or 'She says to her husband: I would like to put henna on my nails; and he answers: I could not ask for anything better' (*Syria/Lebanon*), a proverb quoted when someone proposes something wonderful. Though it is argued that 'A black eye does not need make-up' (*Ladino*), a popular device is the darkening of the eyes and the dyeing of the eyebrows is highly popular:

> Kohl beautifies a woman, the parade beautifies the tribe, the saddle[-cloth] beautifies the horse. (*Arabic*)
> I got married in order to dye my eyebrows, not to sew patches on worn clothes. (*Persian*)

Hair is a beauty issue *par excellence*, it is called 'a woman's pride', in a Spanish Cuban proverb, and 'her crowning glory' in an English proverb from the United States. Ideas about the preferable colour differ:

> Better a charming brunette than a sad blonde. (*Portuguese, Brazil*)
> Where red hair and thorns grow, there is no good land. [A red-haired woman is usually considered a termagant and would not make a good wife] (*Pennsylvanian German*)
> A blonde head does not last long. (*Spanish, Colombia*)

In cultures where a woman's hair needs to be decently covered, the following proverb is a compliment to elegant women who work so hard in their home that their beautiful hair gets uncovered: 'Elegance and looks, the scarf fell down' (*Berber, Morocco*). On purpose or not?—one may wonder. The many ins and outs of women's hair are dealt with extensively: is it tangled or well combed, dyed or 'natural', straight or curled? Apparently, so many hairs, so many minds:

> Good is a horse with flowing tail and mane, bad the woman with dishevelled hair. (*Finnish*)
> Falseness often lurks beneath fair hair. (*Danish*)
> A curly-haired woman is amorous. [Before the Second World War, Japanese women loved to have straight hair; nowadays, many urban women prefer to have curly hair] (*Japanese*)
> Those with a curly fringe are from the wild cattle. [bulls and women] (*Spanish, Mexico*)
> Curled hair, curled wits. (*Dutch*)

In proverbs, small feet are not only seen as a sign of beauty, but they also wishfully refer to a smaller female body size and lesser intellectual capacities of the mind than her partner. An extreme case of small feet is the result of the Chinese tradition of foot binding, which dates back to the 10th century CE and remained fashionable for the next thousand years. It meant that a girl's feet were bound from toe to heel, to mark them out as objects of beauty. The description of the painful procedure and the sexual benefits meant to men reveals what extremes people went to in sacrificing parts of the body to imagined beauty:

> Having tiny feet was considered a sign of beauty, and men would not take wives with normal feet. The smaller the foot, the more erotic the woman, it was thought. Bound feet were on a par with sex organs—women would reveal them to their husbands only.... For admirers, a tiny foot was an erotic plaything, being viewed as a special sexual organ and possibly the most forbidden zone. The foot-binding procedure created a deep cleft in the sole where the instep had been—a deformity men considered highly stimulating ... in a foot you could find a heightened form of female beauty: the properly bound foot was rounded like a breast, small like a mouth made

more mysterious than other private parts of the body. Some fetishists delighted in the musty odour that came from a bound foot, and there were even gentlemen's handbooks devoted to the most erective ways of arousing a bound-foot consort. One technique was called 'Eating the Golden Lotus', which required the suitor to put the woman's unbound foot in his mouth. It was considered the pinnacle of erotic pleasure.[52]

For Chinese women this feudal practice caused extreme suffering. They were forced to have unnaturally small feet. It meant in fact lifelong torture because they could not walk properly with such deformed feet. It was economically necessary, as otherwise no well-to-do man would be interested in marrying them, as girls were told by their mothers: no family would be interested in taking a big-footed girl as a daughter-in-law: 'If you have large feet, how will the servants be able to tell if you are a bride or a newly purchased slave', as the argument went.[53] In spite of all the presumed advantages, the suffering is realistically reflected in the following proverb: 'Every bound foot conceals a jar of tears.' It was also an effective way to restrict women—they could not walk very far on such small bound feet.

Western women's wearing pointed high-heeled shoes as a beautifying practice has sometimes been compared to Chinese foot binding, as both are responsible for deformation, and both are restrictive and unnatural:

> Although a pale shadow of the Chinese footwear, [it] is nevertheless a gross distortion of what nature intended. Like the Chinese shoes, the Western high-heeled shoes incapacitate the wearers. They are far less extreme, of course, but they still make the wearer look more delicate, more vulnerable and therefore more likely to arouse the protective instincts of the human male ... it is only a matter of degree. The principle is just the same.[54]

Many other female beauty devices also require physical suffering, and a Dutch saying jokingly refers to the phenomenon: 'Who wants to be handsome has to suffer pain, said the maid, as she pinned the bonnet to her ears.'

All sorts of ornaments mentioned as beautifying extras for the female body, from earrings and necklaces to bracelets, rings, and nose-plugs, are commented upon positively or negatively:

> A woman without earrings is like a house without furniture. (*Spanish, Cuba*)
> A woman with many bracelets is capricious. (*French/Catalan*)
> With or without a nose-plug, women are always beautiful. (*Makua*)

However, it is also argued that inner jewels are more suitable to decent women than outer appearance. Next to the female ornament of silence, so much appreciated all over Europe, submissiveness is mentioned as an attractive necklace for girls (*Russian*); and there is of course decency, specified as an adornment for Greek women, or modesty, warmly recommended in German as an excellent dress.

In spite of such moving wisdom, a Russian proverb argues that 'Beautiful feathers make beautiful birds.' Clothes are indeed often presented as most important, and a wealth of proverbs comment on material, colours, and the effect dresses have on women as well as on the admiring men around them. First of all, it is stressed that if a man marries, he has to pay for a woman's clothes, which is a costly business: 'A wife is clothes, a banana plant is weeding', as the Swahili say. Secondly, daring colours are commented upon in different ways in some North and South American proverbs, yellow as brightly striking, black as the colour of mourning, and green as associated with youth on the one hand and with the grave (covered by grass) on the other:

> The woman who dresses in yellow trusts her beauty. (*English, USA*)
> She who dresses in green trusts her beauty. (*Spanish, Colombia*)
> She who dresses in black must rely on her beauty. (*Spanish, Mexico*)

The luxurious finery of silk, satin, lace, and velvet are appreciated, but their lack of practical use is immediately pointed out, e.g. in Romanian: 'A girl in lace and silk is suitable for dance and banquet, but not for lady of the house' or in Hebrew: 'Silks and satins put out the kitchen fire.' Attention is paid to different garments, from skirts to kimonos, from stockings to shoes and underwear. The comments related to the various kinds of wear associated with a woman's clothes are as detailed as they look familiar: the loss of love in marriage, the vanity of finery, the fatal attraction of beauty, the undesirability of a wife's power over her husband, the profitability of a daughter's beauty, and the boundaries of gender roles that should not be overstepped. The petticoat effectively illustrates the various issues:

> Love flies with the red petticoat. [Only unmarried girls wear this garment.] (*Japanese*)
> A woman's petticoat is the Devil's binder. (*Romanian*)
> Many an Irish property was increased by the lace of a daughter's petticoat. (*Irish*)
> The ribbons of a petticoat pull more than a team of oxen. (*Spanish, Mexico*)
> A foolish woman is known by her petticoats, showing her wealth by the number she possesses. (*English, UK*)
> If your petticoat fits you well, do not try to put on your husband's pants.
> (*Creole, Martinique*)

Although some proverbs argue that clothes do not make much difference, and that 'A beauty in ugly clothes is still a beauty' (*Uzbek*), there is a much stronger opinion stressing, on the contrary, that clothes are decisive for one's appearance. That a woman is made beautiful by her clothes, is confirmed metaphorically in a Tsonga proverb: 'A house is made beautiful by its thatch.' An Arabic Lebanese proverb rejects the idea that beauty comes naturally as follows: 'Neither my father nor my mother made me beautiful, but my clothes [did].' Even the most unattractive beings can become acceptable and even appealing thanks to outfit and adornment. Women who are jealous of the excellent finery of other women quote such proverbs:

> Dress the corncob and it will look like a bride. (*Arabic*)
> Nicely dressed, even a stick becomes beautiful. (*Ladino*)
> Even a log is beautiful if beautifully dressed. (*Hungarian*)
> Put jewels on a stump, then even the stump is beautiful. (*Estonian*)

The advantages of dressing versus undressing remain an open question, as I found only two (contradictory) proverbs on the issue:

> A woman without clothes is as unattractive as food without salt. (*Pashto*)
> If this is how she looks in beautiful garments, how will she look without them?
>   (*Turkish/Azeri*)

Thanks to the worldwide efforts, a multitude of beautiful women populate the earth. Abundance inevitably leads to inflation. If charming women are so abundant, why worry when one specimen decides to leave you? Men are advised not to feel sad about the loss of just one beauty:

> Beautiful women are like fresh banana leaves: they never come to an end in the
>   plantation. (*Ganda*)
> If you think Miss-this-year is pretty, Miss-next-year will be more so. (*Hausa*)
> It is easy to find a beautiful woman; it is difficult to find a good craftsman. (*Thai*)

A final point frequently made is that all women's beautifying efforts are nullified during the night. Defects disappear in the dark, and the observation that all differences between beauty and ugliness are reduced to nothing by darkness is made in different cultures and continents.

> Every woman is beautiful in the dark, from a distance and under an umbrella. (*Japanese*)
> In the dark all women are moons. (*Arabic, Tunisia*)
> In the dark every woman is [as beautiful as] the moon. (*Ladino*)
> The ugly woman has to switch off the light to say that she is pretty. (*Spanish, Cuba*)
> In the dark all cats and girls are beautiful. (*Hungarian*)

BEAUTY VERSUS INTELLIGENCE

A woman wants to be pretty rather than intelligent and shrewd, because men, in general, see better than they think. (*Hebrew*)

Many proverbs suggest that appearance is *the* important thing for women, and brains for men, while confirming the widespread idea is that beauty and brains cannot be found in one and the same person: 'God did not join brains with beauty' is a Polish example. Attractive hair has also widely been equated with an alleged lack of brains in women. Variants of the popular proverb 'Long hair, short brain' exist in languages and cultures, in Asia, Europe, the Americas and the Caribbean, as argued in the section on brains. All a woman seems to need in life is beauty:

> A daughter should be pretty and a son skilled. (*Nepalese*)
> The man by his hands, the woman by her beauty. (*Russian*)
> The brains of a woman are in her curls. (*Neo-Aramaic, Iraq*)
> Man has beauty in his excellence and woman excellence in her beauty. (*Spanish*)
> Man's brains are his jewels: woman's jewels are her brains. (*Yiddish*)
> Women are wacky, women are vain; they'd rather be pretty than have a good brain.
>   (*English, USA*)

Proverbs about body and beauty have set men against women as two separate categories to be appreciated differently, associating women with shallowness—transient prettiness, jewels, curls—and men with depth: solid skills, brains, excellence. Such messages have distanced men from their appearance while identifying women 'naturally' with theirs.[55]

TRANSIENCE

Woman's beauty, the echo in the forest, and a rainbow fade quickly. (*German*)

Beauty is transitory, it is perishable and fades quickly, or in the words of a Fang proverb from Cameroon and Gabon, 'Woman's beauty is a cloud's beauty' or, in the terms of a proverb with many variants in Europe, the Caribbean, and the Maghreb, 'Charms vanish, money goes, ugliness stays in the bed.' Proverbs are unanimous in stating that the beauty of the female body is transitory: 'A handsome shape sags out quickly' (*Russian*) or metaphorically speaking: 'No shoe is so beautiful, that it will not become a slipper' (*French*). In Japanese, it is put even stronger: 'Yesterday's lovely flower is but a dream today.'

Female beauty is destroyed by bearing, breastfeeding and aging. One Arabic proverb from Lebanon gives a pregnant wife the benefit of the doubt: 'A woman's physical beauty is proved only after pregnancy and nursing.' However, it is mostly agreed that pregnancy and breastfeeding ravage the body's fragile beauty, though some make a difference between nursing and childbed: 'Breastfeeding makes one wither, childbed makes beautiful' (*Catalan/French/German*):

> A dress is beautiful until it is washed for the first time, a woman, until she has her first child. (*Tamil, India*)
> Pregnancy spoils the waist. (*German*)
> The hen will only stay beautiful as long as she does not lay eggs. (*Serbian*)
> The pretty Creole does not die with her pretty bottom. (*Creole, Guadeloupe*)

Female aging tends to reduce male ardour. There are large numbers of proverbs on fleeting beauty. One Indonesian example: 'When the sweet taste has gone, the chewing [gum] is thrown away.' Nonetheless, a few voices argue in favour of the opposite, as in the following comforting messages from Europe: 'Wrinkled perhaps, but loved anyway' (*Russian*) and 'The heart has no wrinkles' (*French*).

OUTER BEAUTY AND INNER QUALITIES

A woman's beauty is not in her face. (*Swahili*)

Looks are often considered to compete with radiance or gracefulness. In such competition, beauty stands for a combination of qualities that please the aesthetic senses, and especially the sight, whereas grace means attractiveness in manner or movement. Contrary to transient, physical beauty, graceful behaviour is lasting. Grace is 'all over the body', as a Burmese proverb puts it, and inexplicably radiating from inside, as part of a charming personality. Beauty without grace is regarded as incomplete, and several proverbs even suggest that an ugly woman might well have more grace than a beautiful one:

Beauty without grace is a violet without smell. (*Hebrew*)
It is better to be graceful than to be pretty. (*Spanish, Bolivia*)
Beauty is in the face, grace in the body and you cannot exhaust it. (*Burmese*)
Beauty is a mirror, the silvering [the secret] of which is within. (*Turkish*)
Beauty without grace is a hook without a bait. (*French*)

Grace and gracefulness seem to win from beauty. Outward appearance is set against 'inner beauty', a quality equated with purity, goodness, honour, decency, docility, and virtue, whereas 'just good looks' are presented as superficial, problematic, or even as being mutually exclusive with goodness or chastity, the very qualities so desperately wanted for in wives:

A wife you love for her being, not for her beauty. (*Swahili*)
What is good is not necessarily beautiful. (*Japanese*)
Most good women are without beauty. (*Chinese*)
Beauty is null and void, when honour is lost. (*English, UK*)
Beauty without decency is wine without taste. (*Italian*)
Modesty and beauty do not come together. (*Hebrew*)

Ideally the two are combined, as suggested in Slovak: 'Virtue and beauty are a blessed association', as well as in Arabic: 'Chastity combined with beauty makes a woman perfect' (*Lebanon*), but such perfection is only of short duration, given the problem of aging. Therefore, many proverbs recommend men not to pursue their obsession with beauty in to marriage:

Do not take a wife because of her beauty but rather because of her virtues.
    (*Arabic, Lebanon*)
Beauty fades, but not goodness. (*Filipino*)
Do not follow after desire; do not love for beauty only. (*Khionghta*)
With character, ugliness is beauty, without character beauty is ugliness. (*Hausa*)

So, if female beauty perishes with age, then why not explore the advantages its much reviled antipole might hold in store?

UGLINESS

Beautiful roads won't take you far. (*Chinese*)

In a world of males obsessed by female beauty, ugliness tends to become a serious preoccupation for women: 'If ugliness suffered pains, it would cry out' (*Ladino*). An Arabic proverb from Tunisia portrays the ugly girl as such a desperate case that even the pig, an animal considered despicable and unclean in the culture concerned, would feel like refusing to take her for a wife: 'Offer her to the pig, he will say: "I'm in no hurry".' At first sight, therefore, a woman's destiny, prestige, and her accounts in matters of love and marriage seem to be settled mainly on her beauty, especially when she is young. However, there is more to it than just that.

Female ugliness has a wealth of advantages, and therefore seems preferable to ephemeral beauty. No proverb ever defines what exactly ugliness is. It is just taken for granted what ugliness means. There are only a few hints here and there. 'Beauty and ugliness are in the face', says a Tamil proverb from India, and an English proverb has this to offer: 'The three ugliest things of their own kind—a thin red-haired woman, a thin yellow horse, a thin white cow', but that does not bring us much further. Ugliness is defined by its practical usefulness, for example in a German proverb: 'An ugly wife is a good hedge around the garden' or, in Chinese: 'One's house is best protected by a wasted garden outside and an ugly wife inside.' In the United States it is argued that 'Ugliness is the guardian of the woman', of her chastity that means, and—another great advantage—'The ugliest girl makes the best housewife.'

Beauty and ugliness appear to be quite relative matters, as love changes the whole picture:

Nobody's sweetheart's ugly. (*Scottish*)
He who loves the ugly finds it beautiful. (*Spanish, Mexico / Chile*)

Another argument against attractive looks is that beauties can be extremely tedious: 'Rather an entertaining ugly one than a boring beauty' (*Arabic, Morocco*); or frigid like snow (*Ossetian*). Moreover, ugly women are far from lacking passion, as emphasized in two Japanese proverbs:

Ugly women are the more passionate ones.
When an ugly woman has a great passion—who should say thank you?

Many arguments are presented in favour of marrying an ugly woman. Not only is beauty dangerous and even deadly, it is also transitory, and the brideprice for an ugly one costs much less. Finally, and importantly, a man's emotional life will certainly be more peaceful with an ugly wife: 'A hedgehog and peace is better than a gazelle and grief' and, in another variant, 'A scarab giving me peace is preferable to a gazelle that kills me' are two Arabic warnings to a man planning to marry a beauty, in which the gazelle is a metaphor for the beautiful woman. Ugliness has hardly any disadvantages other than a lack of visual pleasure for the onlookers. This lack is balanced, though, by the comforting gift of peacefulness and harmony enjoyed by the souls of those who 'own' such an ugly woman. She will not easily tempt or be tempted by other men who, rather foolishly, feel attracted to the shallowness of beauty.

For men good looks simply do not seem to matter. Proverbs broaching the issue do not see male ugliness as a serious inconvenience: 'An ugly man takes a beautiful woman to be his wife' (*Chinese*), whereas, according to a Vietnamese proverb, 'Even a man as ugly as the Devil can chase girls.' 'Man is like a bear, the uglier, the more beautiful', is the message of a Spanish Colombian proverb. The argument that the more ugly a man is, the more attractive he becomes, significantly confirms the idea of beauty as against brains.

Only one proverb, from Tibet, observes that 'A woman is happy with an ugly husband', precisely because his ugliness might make other women reluctant to take him away from her, exactly the same argument frequently used from a male perspective about feeling safe and quiet with an ugly wife. Would women really not mind a man's being ugly? The point is that the available proverbs are so completely absorbed by male feelings, desires, and interests that they reveal very little about women's perspectives on male attractiveness.

Rationally 'An ugly person comforts him/herself by saying that prettiness is vanity' as an Igbo proverb from Nigeria states, but in practice female beauty preoccupies both the female and the male sex in extremis. There are so many aspects to the topic that only the three most widely mentioned are discussed here.

The first is that beauty makes it difficult for girls to keep out of trouble: 'The eye of the beautiful cannot see well', is an Acholi proverb from Uganda. The embarrassment of the many men jostling each other around her make a beauty marry the wrong man, whereas ugly women with fewer choices seem to be more privileged by destiny. This irony of destiny is reflected by the following widely popular South American proverb: 'The beautiful woman wishes for the happiness of the ugly one.' Many others agree that prettiness is often unfortunate and that beautiful girls tend to be born unlucky:

A fox's fur is its own enemy. (*Adyg/Kabardino-Cherkess*)
A pretty face is a punishment. (*Estonian*)
A fair woman is unfortunate. (*Japanese*)
A rosy-cheeked woman always has a difficult destiny. (*Chinese, Taiwan*)
The destiny of the ugly one is what the beautiful one longs for. (*Ladino*)
The woman who has a pretty face is usually unhappy. (*Spanish, Puerto Rico*)

The second frequent topic is that a woman's beauty does not yield material benefit to her man, whereas ugly women are profitable in many respects. In fact, beauty and work exclude one another, but marriage means business and therefore a man is advised not to take a wife for her outward appearance, because she will surely be a disappointing homemaker. The main question is: what does she bring in?

You can't fill your belly with beauty. (*Arabic*)
Beauty will not feed you a salad. (*Creole, Guadeloupe*)
You don't eat beauty with a spoon. (*French*)
The surface of the water is beautiful, but you can't sleep on it. (*Ga*)
A fair face will not keep the pot boiling. (*Hebrew*)
No bread grows on a pretty face, nor apples grow on the shoulders. (*Dargin*)

And so forth! Female beauty and the making of soup, for example, are absolutely irreconcilable in a variety of languages:

A woman who follows the fashion will never make a good soup. (*English, Jamaica*)
You can't put beauty in the *sjtsji* [cabbage soup]. (*Finnish*)
Beauty will not season your soup. (*Polish*)
Soon one will have enough of beauty, but not of cabbage soup. (*Russian*)
Nobody can make soup out of beauty. (*Estonian*)
Prettiness makes no pottage. (*Hebrew*)

Metaphorically the same idea is expressed in a Korean proverb: 'Cotton is the best flower.' Cotton, it means, is not very pretty, but is more useful than many prettier flowers, for it bears cotton wool. Beauties, however, seem to be so interested in their own appearance that they spend lots of time in front of the mirror—precious time lost to other activities:

> The wife who loves the looking glass, hates the saucepan. (*English, USA*)
> It is a sad house where the husband cries and the wife is standing before the mirror. (*Danish*)
> A woman that looks at herself in the looking-glass does not spend much time on housekeeping. (*Letzeburgish*)
> The more women look in their mirror, the less they look to their house. (*Hebrew*)

The ugly one just works, as she knows in advance that it would be a waste of time and a complete disappointment for her to even cast a glance in the mirror:

> A homely girl hates mirrors. (*Hebrew*)
> An ugly woman dreads the mirror. (*English, USA*)

Rarely proverbs go against this general trend of opposing beauty to ugliness. One Irish proverb critically questions the presumed guarantee of an ugly wife's profitability: 'A woman's beauty never boiled a pot but ugliness never filled it either.' And another European proverb acknowledges that beauty stimulates passion, though immediately adding that passionate lovemaking is detrimental to a woman's working hard in the house.

It is not only the working capacity of beautiful women that is believed to be unprofitable, but, more seriously, their fertility tends to be questioned. Men are warned that the outside may be beautiful, but inside there may be no profit at all:

> Beauty is an empty calabash. (*Kundu*)
> Charming girl, empty gourd. (*Spanish*)
> Splendid without but empty within. (*Thai*)
> The beauty of the bride can be seen at the cradle. (*Armenian*)

There may be several reasons underlying this association of beauty with an empty uterus. The first is the suggestion that a woman's seductive beauty must have led to her having intercourse with several men, and the venereal diseases resulting from such promiscuity easily lead to sterility. The Bassar in Togo say: 'Beautiful woman brings diseases.' Thus beauty is easily associated with prostitution, and its risks for men.

A Bengali proverb presents a husband as exceptionally lucky because his exemplary wife is not only very beautiful but has also given birth to a boy-child. The proverb refers to a radiant destiny, and a blameless perfection, thanks to both ravishing looks and successful procreation, i.e. producing a son instead of a daughter.

The third and last topic is that having a beautiful wife is a tricky business from a male perspective. As long as she is beautiful, she makes a man's life very problematic: 'Pity the man who marries a beautiful woman; until she grows old, fear will not leave him' (*Spanish, Colombia*). Thus, although female beauty is experienced as a pleasure to the male senses, and as a source of pride and prestige for him to show off, a pretty woman is presented as an endless source of worry and trouble. A beautiful wife means 'a man's death', according to a Sranan proverb, whereas a Brazilian proverb advises to stay on the safe side: 'He who marries an ugly woman is not afraid of another man.'

An American proverb argues that 'A true wife is her husband's flower of beauty' (*English*), but how to be sure of her devotedness? 'One's chattels are one's own, but a beautiful wife is common property' (*Khiongbta*). It is indeed in terms of 'possessions' and desirable goods that men speak about beautiful wives in proverbs. The rule is not to draw people's attention to desirable things one owns, as it might provoke other men's desire to snatch them from under your very eyes, or, as an Irish proverb warns: 'Three things which a man ought not to boast of—the size of his purse, the beauty of his wife, the sweetness of his beer.' The irony is, of course, that men are measuring women's cloth by their own yard, so to speak, as it is not possible to control a wife for a lifetime. As a Hebrew proverb reasonably observes, 'If your wife is chaste, why should you watch her? If she is not, you will watch her in vain.'

FATAL ALLUREMENTS

A beautiful woman is an axe that cuts off life. (Japanese)

A beautiful woman is presented as an object of immense desire, and men go to great lengths to possess her: 'Beauty is much desired, even if it lies at the bottom of the abyss' (*Arabic, Maghreb*). Even though a beauty's 'face shines like the moon', it fatally provokes chaos, and therefore proverbs urge men to fight their desires.

Multiple arguments have been woven into the discussion. The main point is that, although instinctively inclined to run after a beautiful woman, men must not follow their emotions, but remember that God himself rather loves the ugly one!

Female beauty is pleasurable and profitable, a number of proverbs stress. Pleasurable to whom, and of benefit to whom? Beauty is pleasant for others to see, but it is an advantage to women themselves in the first place: beautiful women receive more often a friendly ear than ugly ones, although proverbs predict them bad luck in love matters. Easily upset by female beauty, men appear to be vulnerable beings. Older members of society, sadder and wiser from their own experience, warn naïve young men against female beauty's traps and chaos:

> A beautiful wife is an enemy. (*Sanskrit, India*)
> Beautiful women are dangerous. You cannot keep them long. (*Spanish, Mexico*)

Women's beauty being considered so dangerous that it can kill a man is thus inevitably associated with women's power and men's weakness. Proverbs do not shy away from the strongest possible metaphors, such as crashing wild geese, or even a killing axe. In Europe and the Arab world beautiful women are often associated with the Devil. The metaphor of the single female hair equated with strong and sturdy animals, is widely used: 'A hair of a girl's head draws harder than ten oxen' (*Yiddish*), or: 'One hair on a pretty woman's head is enough to tether a big elephant' (*Japanese*)—just two examples among many variants of the same message found in different parts of the world. Proverbs do not stop cautioning against what is presented as the destructive forces of female beauty: misery, bad luck, diseases, witchcraft, war, devilry and death, thus positioning women 'in a space of danger and desire, and unconscious fears.'[56] They express those admonitions in almost the same terms in widely different areas:

Beautiful woman, beautiful trouble. (*English, Jamaica*)

Marry beauty, marry trouble. (*Krio/Mende/Kru/Jaba/Hebrew/English, USA*)

In proverbs men blame female beauty for their own getting involved in tricky business, even though, as observed in Chinese: 'Beauty does not lure people in to a trap; they enter it themselves.'

Summing up the pros and cons, then, beauty brings happiness, and beauty brings unhappiness; beauty is good and beauty is bad; beauty has advantages, and ugliness has advantages. Even though proverbs argue in favour of different things, they do not really contradict each other; rather do they show various negotiable aspects that prevail in social life. Female appearance is presented as a confusing threat, but, significantly, hardly any proverb turns the perspective around. In proverbs, women, especially beautiful women, are almost exclusively seen as objects of male desire. Women who desire an attractive man must hide such feelings; if not, their behaviour is quickly designated 'shameless', as if they ought to be prevented from becoming adults in their own right.

Proverbs pay a great deal of attention to the female body, and connect physical characteristics with mental qualities, character and behaviour. The body and its various parts inspire messages justifying and preserving specific norms and interests. That nature herself would have denied women superior talents and qualities by endowing them with a womb and breasts is an idea that has not only been transmitted by men. Many generations of women have willingly or unwillingly internalized such negative ideas regarding their own sex, and they have also been very good in passing such messages on to their own sons and daughters.

The Female Body Anthology

FROM HEAD TO FOOT

When a girl is born, don't take care of her, she will grow like a cactus; when a boy is born,
    take good care of him, as you would with a rose-tree. (*Rajasthani, India*): *o.s.*★ *Emmy de Goede*
The body ages, but the heart does not. (*Turkish*): *Geyvandov 29*
Whoever marries a woman for her body will lose the body and keep the wife.
    (*Dutch; Papiamentu, Netherlands Antilles; Mandinka, Mali*): *Mesters 103; Maduro 137; o.s.*
    Massa Makan Diabaté
A girl is an olive-tree, a boy a tadpole. [Girls grow faster than boys.]
    (*Ovambo, Namibia/Angola*): *Geyvandov 148*
Brought up among boys, a girl weakens. (*Gikuyu, Kenya*): *Ngumbu Njururu 76*

STATURE AND APPEARANCE
A woman who loves her man says: 'I look up to you.' (*Twi, Ghana*): *o.s. Peggy Appiah*
My misfortune is bearable, the man said, and married a small wife.
    (*Frisian, Netherlands*): *o.s. Jan Calsbeek*
Of women, misfortunes and gherkins, the smallest are always the best. (*Hungarian*): *Rauch 179*
Women and sardines, the smaller the better. (*Spanish*): *Geyvandov 246*
Women and sardines, the bigger they are, the bigger the damage. (*Portuguese*): *Suard II 29*
Women and sardines: pick the small ones.
    (*Portuguese, Brazil/Spanish, Argentina*): *Mota 44; Moya 489*

★ *o.s.* means 'oral source'; source names not preceded by *o.s.* are written sources.

A wife and a plough handle are best when shorter than the man. (*Oromo, Ethiopia*): *Cotter 56*
A housewife likes a small [also: new] pot; a husband likes a small wife.

(*Khiongtha, Bangladesh*): *Lewin 6*

A small woman always looks just married. (*Italian*): *Geyvandov 246*

Even a small woman surpasses the Devil in artifices. (*German*): *Wander I 1139*
The good essence comes in a small jar, but so does poison.

(*Spanish, Chili / Cuba*): *Sabiduría Guajira 31; o.s. Patricio Frano*

What they lack in size, they have extra in astuteness. (*Spanish, Bolivia*): *Paredes-Candia 142*
When a tall woman carries palm nuts, birds eat them off her head. (*Twi, Ghana*): *Oduyoye 7*
What a tall woman has hung up, a short man cannot undo. (*Sukuma, Tanzania*): *Ibekwe 53*
A big wife and a big barn will never do a man any harm. (*English, USA*): *Brown 970: 17*
Choose yourself a wife of the same weight if you don't want quarrels all the time.

(*Polish*): *Reinsberg-Düringsfeld 116*

A man, even a man of small size, will be called great in comparison to women.

(*Arabic, Lebanon*): *Abela 287*

Even small, a man is old. (*Minyanka, Mali*): *Cauvin 1980: 525*
There are no small men. [lit.: no men to be called small.] (*Twi, Ghana*): *Geyvandov 246*
The man comes out of childhood, but the woman never comes out of womanhood.

(*Gikuyu, Kenya*): *Barra 109*

Boys will be men, girls will be brides. (*German*): *Meier-Pfaller 38*
The small hawk can carry off a big chick. (*Ngbaka, Central African Republic*): *Thomas 748*
Whatever the size of the woman, it's the man who mounts her. (*Ikwere, Nigeria*): *o.s. Sylvester Osu*
What a tall bride needs, a small one needs as well. (*Digor, RF[57]*): *Geyvandov 246*
A girl and a clay pipe are never too small. (*Oromo, Ethiopia*): *Cotter 3*

BODY AND SOUL

Husband and wife should not just become one body but one soul as well.

(*Hebrew, widespread in Europe*): *Hazan-Rokem 136*

A devout wife is her husband's body. (*German*): *Haller 462*
Woman is man's body and life. (*Dutch*): *Harrebomée II 30*
[When they] lie face to face, one body; [when they] turn around, strangers.

(*Korean*): *Geyvandov 147*

Yield to the desires of your body, then endure the disasters that follow.

(*Awar, RF*): *Geyvandov 192*

Lascivious business breaks the body. (*Dutch*): *Mesters 103*
Keep afar from the love of women, for their beauty is lewdness and their body a graveyard of
lust. (*Hebrew, Israel*): *Alcalay 547*
A pretty woman has the Devil in her body. (*German*): *Meier-Pfaller 661*
A woman who takes, sells her body. (*Spanish*): *Bergua 342; Bohn 1875 : 13*

HEAD AND NECK

A good woman goes without a head. (*Dutch*): *Ter Laan 353*
In leap-years women declare themselves to men. (*Spanish, Cuba*): *Feijóo 17*

A copper-headed man is better than a gold-headed woman. (*Kazakh, RF*): *Geyvandov 270*

The vegetables on her head have dried out long ago and still she does not stop talking.
(*Jewish/Arabic, Yemen*): *Stahl 237*

Words in the mouth are no loads on the head. (*English, Jamaica*): *Llewellyn Watson 277*

Women do not carry men on their *torches* [a rolled piece of cloth placed on the head when carrying a load: they cannot control their men]. (*Creole, Guadeloupe*): *ACCT 62; Ludwig 426*

If your wife returns with a pot of water on her head, and asks you to help her put it down, you will do well to help her. (*Ashanti, Ghana*): *Oduyoye 9*

A woman is like an onion, she must have her head down.
(*Arabic, Maghreb/West Sahara*): *Duvollet 43*

Whether there is brilliance or not, look down; whether dancing or not, look at the feet.
(*Tibetan*): *Duncan 184*

Bend your head, bride, if you want to enter the church. (*Spanish, Argentina*): *Moya 342*

Man is the head of woman. (*All over Europe, e.g. Swedish; Russian*): *Holm 189; o.s. Anna Ravve*

You can't have two heads under one hood. (*Turkish*): *Haig 53*

Two pots cannot be put on one head. (*Mossi, Burkina Faso*): *o.s. A. Sawadogo*

Two cocks do not crow on the same roof. (*Mongo, Congo*): *Hulstaert 511*

A horse with the rein, a woman with the spurs. (*Spanish, Mexico*): *Glazer 38; Casasola 99*

Man is the head, but woman turns it. (*English, USA*): *Kin 282*

Man is the head and woman the neck on which it turns. (*Dutch*): *o.s. Van der Zee*

Wring a wife's and a hen's neck, if you want them good.
(*Spanish, and all over Europe and both Americas*): *Champion 310; Chaves 880*

Woman and candle, twist their necks if you want them at their best. (*Spanish*): *Bergua 343*

Girls that whistle and hens that crow should have their necks twisted betimes.
(*English, USA*): *Hoffman 198*

Man without wife, head without body; woman without husband, body without head.
(*Russian; German*): *Graf 169; Geyvandov 84*

The good wife is the crown on her husband's head.
(*Russian, probably from Jewish origin; Hebrew, Israel*): *Geyvandov 120*

A [nasty] woman is to her husband like a heavy burden to an old person; a soft and good woman, on the other hand, is a crown of gold for her husband; whenever he looks at her, it is a feast for his heart and his eyes. (*Arabic*): *Wijnaendts-Francken 92*

Happy is the marriage where the man is the head and the woman the heart.
(*Portuguese, Brazil*): *Souto Maior 92*

As for man wisdom, as for woman affection. (*Japanese*): *o.s. Anonymous*

Men have a reason, women a heart. (*Dutch*): *o.s. Hermans*

A woman's heart sees more than a man's eyes [or: more than ten men's eyes].
(*Swedish*): *Ström 164*

The heart can be short-sighted, like the eyes. (*Russian*): *Geyvandov 50*

A heart that trusts is easily betrayed. (*German*): *Geyvandov 58*

When the heart gives orders, the body becomes its slave.
(*Hausa, Nigeria/Niger*): *Geyvandov 40*

Woman may govern heart and pan, cup and head are for the man. (*German*): *Wander V 1270*

BRAINS

Beauty you've got, my daughter, and intelligence I will buy for you.
  (*Ladino, Marocco*): *Dahan 1318*

A man without brains and a woman without a man will never stand on their own legs. (*Estonian*): *Geyvandov 240*

A woman has the shape of an angel, the heart of a snake, and the brains of an ass.
  (*German*): *Haller 466*

Woman's intelligence is a child's intelligence. (*West Africa*): *o.s. Soulé Issiaka Adissa*

Women's understanding is about as deep as the two finger lengths of water they use to cook
  rice. (*Sinhalese, Sri Lanka*): *o.s. Gunasekare*

Made for a boy, turned for a girl. (*Russian*): *Geyvandov 269*

What a man Mother Aisha is! (*Arabic, Tunisia*): *Tetiv 5*

A woman, as her breasts hang down, so her brain hangs down.
  (*Oromo, Ethiopia/ Kenya*): *o.s. Jolanda Alkemade*

A bosom instead of brains. (*Hebrew, Israel*): *Alcalay 545*

Women have only half a brain. (*Arabic, Lebanon*): *Frayha II 651*

A head of hair and no brain inside. (*Mongolian*): *Geyvandov 72*

Women have long hair and a short mind. (*Swedish*): *Ström 159*

Though a girl's hair be long, her brain is short. (*Kalmuk, RF*): *Champion 488*

Long hair, little brain. (*Turkish*): *Champion 480*

The girl is looking for a clever husband; the boy for a beautiful wife. (*Vietnamese*): *Geyvandov 270*

A man should marry his daughter to a scholar, even if it means he will have to sell everything.
  (*Hebrew, Israel*): *Rosten 1977: 316, 401; Alcalay 94, 310; Rosen 416*

A girl who reads, sings, and makes music, will rarely become a good wife.
  (*Polish*): *Reinsberg-Düringsfeld 126*

EYES

When her eyes are radiant, the grass withers. (*Russian*): *Graf 208*

The eye is the pupil of the body. (*Yoruba, Benin/Nigeria*): *Geyvandov 26*

Food and woman enter first through the eyes.
  (*English, USA; Spanish, Mexico*): *West 42; Rubio 273*

Watching feeds the eyes. (*Creole, Guadeloupe*): *Ludwig 430*

The eye is the witness of the heart. (*German*): *o.s. Anonymous*

When a woman is speaking, listen to what her eyes say.
  (*English, USA*): *Mieder 1992: 668*

Cries with the eyes, laughs with the heart. (*Russian*): *Geyvandov 198*

That which does not enter through your eyes, does not get to your soul.
  (*Spanish, Chile*): *Laval 68*

If the eyes don't see, the heart won't care. (*Creole, Haiti*): *Hall 200*

What the eye has not seen will not touch the heart. (*Greek*): *Geyvandov 276*

The most effective defence against temptation is this: shut your eyes.
  (*Hebrew, Israel*): *Rosten 1977: 451*

Beauty is in the eye of the beholder. (*English, UK*): *Geyvandov 74*

Leila must be seen through Majnun's eyes. [Majnun and Leila are the Persian equivalents of
    Romeo and Juliet.] (*Persian*): *Elwell-Sutton 68*

A person's beauty is the face; the face's beauty is the eyes. (*Turkish*): *Geyvandov 69*

If a bride has beautiful eyes, do not study the rest of her body.
    (*Hebrew, Israel/Iraq*): *Stahl 418, Rosten 1977: 111*

[Beauty is] The neck of a swan, the trot of a peacock, the eyes of a falcon and brows like
    sabres. (*Russian*): *Geyvandov 70*

A house's beauty is in [the use of] water and a broom; a girl's in her eyes and eyebrows.
    (*Persian*): *Geyvandov 69*

A house without curtains is like a woman without eyebrows. (*Romanian*): *Günther 46–47*

If eyes and eyebrows did not exist, there would be neither sin nor love for women.
    (*Romanian*): *Gruber 16*

If there are no black eyes, kiss the blue ones instead.
    (*Moldovan; Romanian*): *Geyvandov 38; Günther 206–7*

Women's eyes cannot be trusted, neither the black nor the blue. (*German*): *o.s. Anonymous*

Don't marry a blue-eyed woman, even though she has money in her box.
    (*Arabic, Morocco*): *Westermarck 73*

Turquoise eyes, black heart. (*Russian*): *Geyvandov 76*

Beautiful eyes, villainous heart. (*Creole, Guadeloupe*): *Zagaya 235; Barbotin 118*

If you meet a woman with an evil eye, spit in her path and wish her the Qrîna [female spirit
    causing the death of infants]. (*Arabic, Morocco*): *Westermarck 65*

A woman's eye is like an arrow to men in the prime of life. (*Greek*): *Politès 3*

No better lye than a woman's eye. (*Frisian, Netherlands*): *Beintema 83*

A woman asks, takes, despises, and kills with her eyes. (*Spanish*): *Geyvandov 186*

Beautiful, big eyes sting sharper than lemons. (*Spanish, Cuba*): *Sánchez-Boudy 17*

Hell can lie between the lashes of a beautiful woman's eye. (*Hebrew, Israel*): *Rosten 1977: 494*

Too beautiful looks snatch the eyes [of those who look at them]. (*Japanese*): *Buchanan 29*

The woman is the left eye, the man the right. (*Danish*): *Geyvandov 113*

[A woman who runs with men has] Long eyes [She is dangerous].
    (*Hehe, Tanzania*): *Madumulla 82*

Man has eyes to see, woman to be seen. (*Romanian; Moldovan*): *Günther 34–35; Geyvandov 186*

Before you get married, keep two eyes open; afterwards, shut one.
    (*Creole, Jamaica*): *Anderson 85; Champion 629*

In marriage, the husband should have two eyes, and the wife but one.
    (*English, UK*): *Williams I 407*

If they [the children] were a thousand, they would be dearer than my eyes.
    (*Arabic, Egypt*): *Singer 58*

Your mother is like your eyes. (*Adyg, RF*): *Geyvandov 163*

Where the hen's eggs are, there are her eyes.
    (*Spanish, Argentina; Portuguese, Brazil*): *Moya 404; Lamenza 180; Magalhães Júnior 137; Mota
    149*

A good mother-hen sees a seed with one eye and a hawk with the other. (*Russian*): *Geyvandov 92*

Better a mother with one eye, than a father with two. (*Latvian*): *Geyvandov 166*

NOSE AND EARS

Every face, if only it has a nose, is beautiful. (*Serbian/Croatian*): *Karadžić 338*

A woman with a turned-up nose is the Devil's gift. (*Portuguese*): *Chavez 871*

An inch makes a world of difference when it's in a woman's nose. (*Irish*): *O'Farrell 87*

Women's thoughts go as far as the tip of their noses. (*Japanese*): *Huzii 65*

A woman's wisdom extends to the end of her nose. (*Japanese*): *Buchanan 266*

Lovely little nose but nothing in the little head. (*Russian*): *Graf 131*

The wife asks for a nose-ring while the husband wants to cut her nose off.
(*Telegu, India*): *o.s. S.W.A. Shah*

Even if you have no love, be brave and kiss; if you cannot, substitute an intake of breath.
(*Burmese*): *Myint Thein 63*

A husband at home is like a flea in your ear. (*Spanish, Chile*): *Cannobio 75*

Discreet women have neither eyes nor ears.
(*English, UK*): *Bohn 1855: 6; Kloeke 31; Politès 5; Chavez 908*

An honest woman does not have ears or eyes. (*Portuguese, Brazil*): *Souto Maior 47*

The smart woman has eyes but no ears. (*English, Jamaica*): *Llewellyn Watson 259*

The mother-in-law should have one blind eye and one deaf ear. (*Armenian*): *Geyvandov 151, 276*

Talking to a man goes in one ear and out the other; to a woman, it goes into both ears and out
from the mouth. (*Slovenian*): *Geyvandov 234*

A man loves with eyes, a woman with ears. (*Polish*): *Geyvandov 244; Mieder 1986: 286*

Choose a wife rather by your ear than by your eye.
(*Hebrew, Israel; English, USA*): *Cohen 1961: 511; Loomis 1955: 197*

The ears deceive, the eyes not. (*Mongolian*): *Krueger 77*

One eye informs better than two ears. (*German*): *Geyvandov 244*

LIPS, MOUTH, TEETH, TONGUE

A husband who is at home is like a toothache to his wife. (*Hebrew, Israel*): *Stahl 248*

You are right, said the husband to his wife, but all the same, keep your mouth shut.
(*Frisian, Netherlands*): *Beintema 50*

Women's lips have cured many. (*French*): *Geyvandov 47*

No-one ever smelled her lips except her mother. (*Arabic, Lebanon*): *Frayha II 601*

Women have honeyed lips, but their heart is full of poison. (*Bengali, India*): *o.s. Shobha Gupta*

The mouth is a rose, and the tongue a thorn. (*Hungarian*): *Geyvandov 234*

Free of her lips, free of her hips. (*English, UK*): *Bohn 1855: 46; Rayner 118*

If it is not beauty of her lips, it is beauty of her sex. (*Bisa, Burkina Faso*): *o.s. Honorine Mare*

Sweet melon lips, bitter melon heart. (*Chinese*): *Lunde & Wintle 120*

The lips of a woman who does not love are cold. (*Mongolian*): *Geyvandov 137*

While a woman's lips cry 'enough', her eyes call for more. (*Chinese*): *Wintle 120*

If a woman says no, she means yes. (*Europe*): *Cibotto 18; Ström 161; Molbech 171*

The eyes speak as much as the mouth does. (*Japanese*): *Huzii 94*

Woman has no mouth. (*Beti, Cameroon*): *Vincent 75; o.s. Peter Geschiere*

A woman should not open her mouth but to eat. (*German; Albanian*): *Meier-Pfaller 59; Rauch 19*

She has a mouth which eats but does not speak. (*Arabic, Lebanon*): *Frayha I 72*

In a closed mouth no fly enters, in an open mouth it nestles. (*Arabic, Algeria*): *Belamri 50*

Break a woman's spinning thread and you'll see what language will come from her mouth.

> (*Arabic, Syria*): *Feghali 233*

No hen is allowed to sing in the cock's presence. (*Rwanda*): *Crépeau 244, 345*

Where men are speaking, women should keep their mouth shut. (*Dutch*): *o.s. anonymous*

No woman is called upon to speak. (*Rwanda*): *Crépeau 339*

It's a good wife whose mouth is your mirror. (*Irish*): *O'Farrell 42*

Women and mules: if you want to make something good out of them, stop up their mouths.

> (*Spanish, Argentina*): *Villafuerte 22*

A man with a big [literally: wide] mouth is elegant; a woman with a big mouth is bad for the

> neighbours. (*Vietnamese*): *Nguyen 102*

A woman has teeth and her bite is dangerous. (*English, Jamaica*): *Geyvandov 88*

The woman who dresses herself up, loses her teeth. (*French*): *Ségalen 53*

A woman who does not fast will be nursing rotten teeth.

> (*Quecha, Ecuador*): *Santos Ortiz de Villalba 280*

A woman cuts her wisdom teeth when she is dead. (*Romanian*): *Mieder 1986: 539*

Extraction of teeth and wedlock spoil beauty. (*Kweli, Cameroon*): *Geyvandov 81*

'Break some firewood', the man said to his wife and she did so; 'Kiss me', he said to his lover

> and she broke his teeth [with a punch]. (*Oromo, Ethiopia*): *Cotter 86*

Husband and wife have the same teeth. (*Ossetian, RF*): *Geyvandov 113*

Other man's wife, teeth pleasure. (*Yaka, Congo DR*): *Beken 1993: 210*

A woman's tongue is more than seven metres long. (*Creole, Saint Lucia*): *ACCT 83*

If a woman's tongue were shorter, the life of her husband would be longer.

> (*Moldovan*): *Geyvandov 235*

Who can have the last word with his wife since her tongue goes around her neck?

> (*Arabic, Maghreb*): *Duvollet 40*

A tongue of flesh cuts through a bony neck. (*Estonian*): *Reinsberg-Düringsfeld 13*

SHOULDERS AND ARMS

A husband should use his wife's shoulder to cry on. (*Irish*): *O'Farrell 45*

Even if a modest woman's livelihood is gone, her shoulders are not.

> (*Arabic, widespread*): *Khalil Safadi 97*

The shoulder is lower than the head. (*Kweli, Cameroon*): *Geyvandov 129*

The shoulder does not run away from the arm because it is sick.

> (*Yaka, Congo DR*): *Beken 1993: 219*

Love has wings on its shoulders; matrimony has crutches under its arms.

> (*Russian*): *Mieder 1986: 286*

The woman has one child to her breast, the husband at her side, the second child in her arms

> and the third she carries on her neck. (*Estonian*): *Geyvandov 265*

First you hold the child in your arms; then, on your lap; finally, on your back.

> (*Japanese*): *Geyvandov 172*

If a child dies in its mother's arms, she cannot be blamed. (*Creole, Haiti*): *ACCT 33*

No man ever wore a scarf as warm as his daughter's arm around his neck. (*Irish*): *O'Farrell 51*

While during the day he is a monk, at night he is in our arms.

(*Sumerian, Mesopotamia*): *Geyvandov 200*

Strong men-of-arms become like putty in the arms of women. (*English, USA*): *Kin 14*

An unworthy woman betrays you while offering her arm as a pillow. (*Rwanda*): *Crépeau 474*

Before a girl gets married she has seven arms and one mouth; after she is married she has
seven mouths and only one arm. (*Hebrew, Israel; Ladino, Morocco*): *Moscona 25–6*

A woman would be more charming if one could fall into her arms without falling into her
hands. (*English, USA*): *Brown 1970: 114*

When a dancer retires [gives up dancing], her shoulders continue to sway.

(*Arabic, widespread*): *Lunde & Wintle 126*

It is sufficient for a woman to look over her shoulder to find a reason. (*Irish*): *Geyvandov 246*

HANDS AND FINGERS

The wife is a wife because of [her] hands. (*Zulu, South Africa*): *o.s. Veli Mnyandu*

The left hand should not know what the right hand does. (*Creole, Martinique*): *David 96*

A woman is her husband's right hand. (*Mordvin, RF*): *Geyvandov 191*

The right hand washes the left hand, the left hand washes the right hand.

(*Igbo, Nigeria*): *Penfield 116*

You can't clap with one hand. (*Burmese*): *Myint Thein 122*

Is not one-sided love a misery? It is like trying to clap with one hand. (*Malay*): *MBRAS 8*

A beer, a warm woman's hand, and the queen is my aunt. (*Irish*): *Geyvandov 254*

Cold hands, hot love. (*German; French; Italian*): *Herg 54–55*

Whatever a mother gives from her hand tastes sweet. (*Adyg, RF*): *Geyvandov 164*

The hand that rocks the cradle rules the world. (*English, USA*): *Kin 59*

Tea tastes even more delicious, when given to you by the beautiful hand of a lady.

(*Arabic*): *Geyvandov 253*

Drink from the hand of the woman you love, but do not let her drink from yours.

(*Arabic*): *Champion 343*

A white glove conceals a dirty hand. (*English, UK*): *Bohn 1855: 303*

When you go to dance, take heed whom you take by the hand. (*Danish*): *Bohn 1857: 376*

To ask for a woman's hand is like buying a horse: groom, open your eyes.

(*German*): *Geyvandov 100*

Take a wife from a neighbouring farm, you know her hands and legs. (*Estonian*): *Paczolay 194*

See his house and ask for the hand of his daughter.

(*Arabic/Ladino/Hebrew, Maghreb; many variants*): *Yetiv 130; Dahan 216*

They came to your house to ask for your hand, but you were not there. She replies: 'They
could come now!' [Regrets come always too late.] (*Arabic, Syria/Lebanon*): *Feghali 318–19*

They asked for her hand in marriage, she coquettishly refused; they left her alone, she broke
down and began to supplicate. [Bad behaviour.] (*Arabic, Lebanon*): *Frayha I 290*

Now that a man has come to ask for her hand, she says that he is one-eyed.

(*Arabic, Lebanon*): *Frayha II 388*

A bad woman refuses every man who asks for her hand. (*Arabic, Iraq*): *o.s. Muzan*

After she got married, many men asked for her hand. (*Arabic, Maghreb*): *Yetiv 13*

The first one asked for her hand, the second one married her.

(*Arabic, Maghreb*): *Cheneb III 22*

The hand is more expensive than the dish. (*Russian*): *Geyvandov 111*

He asks for the girl's hand, but marries the money. (*Irish*): *Geyvandov 98*

A woman is a monkey: her hands are eatable. (*Sotho, Lesotho*): *Geyvandov 74*

A woman is a hand; a dog is a voice. (*Oromo, Ethiopia*): *Cotter 102*

The hands of a notable housewife are [like] the grease in the dish.

(*Ladino, Morocco*): *Dahan 300*

Even though her hand might hold the reigning sceptre, she remains a woman.

(*Arabic / Hebrew, Yemen*): *Stahl 234*

A man shouldn't wash his wife's hands. (*Nandi, Kenya*): *Geyvandov 129*

He who has fallen into a woman's hands, has fallen on burning coals.

(*Ladino, Morocco*): *Dahan 191*

The handsome finger gets the ring [lit.: a ring around it]. (*Swahili, East Africa*): *Scheven 485*

When the finger is ringed, the girl is occupied. (*Danish*): *Molbech 172*

The promises of marriage are wind, the only thing that counts is the ring on the finger.

(*Creole, Guadeloupe*): *Ludwig 452*

When a woman wets her finger, fleas had better flee. (*English, USA*): *Taylor & Whiting 133*

To her every finger is a man. [She works for ten.] (*Hebrew, Israel*): *Stahl 419*

She who has her husband's agreement can rule the universe with her little finger.

(*Arabic, Lebanon*): *Abela 326*

She who has her husband with her shall turn the moon with her finger.

(*Arabic, Syria; many variants*): *Champion 336; Khalil Safadi 82*

SEX CHARACTERISTICS

God protect us from hairy women and beardless men.

(*Arabic; Lebanon*): *Feghali 115–16; Frayha I 71*

Under a white beard lives an honest woman. (*Spanish, Mexico*): *Casascola 109*

A woman flees from a white beard like a sheep flees from the jackal.

(*Arabic, widespread*): *Wijnaendts-Francken 64*

If the wife is bad, the husband's beard will soon turn white. (*Tati, Iran*): *Geyvandov 124*

Don't give a piece of the beard to a wife. (*Spanish*): *Bergua 110*

Rather pull the beard off than give it to your wife. (*Persian*): *Geyvandov 130*

A woman with a beard is of a wicked kind. (*Dutch*): *Cock 161*

When a family is going to ruin, a beard grows on the face of the eldest daughter-in-law.

(*Korean*): *o.s. B. Walraven*

A bearded woman, God help us! (*Portuguese, Brazil*): *Mota 124*

May God spare me from a bearded old woman. (*Spanish, Argentina*): *Moya 195*

From a shaved woman you should turn away your face. (*Spanish*): *Bergua 133*

A woman with a moustache: greet her from afar.

(*Spanish, Spain / Colombia; Portuguese, Portugal / Brazil; many variants*): *Bergua 133; Chaves 841;*
Meier-Pfaller 63; Acuña 89; Díaz Rivera 133; Moya 305; Fernández Valledor 154; Mota 106

If my aunt grows a moustache, she will be my uncle. (*Tamil, India*): *Geyvandov 253*

Beard, breeches and billfold, these are a man's three b's that a woman should avoid.

(*Dutch*): *Mesters 28*

Women don't have beards because they cannot keep their mouths shut while shaving.

(*Danish*): *Kjaer Holbek 195*

It is easier to bear a child once a year than to shave every day.

(*Russian; Czech*): *Mieder 1986: 70; Ley 86*

Only on horseback she realized she had forgotten to shave herself.

(*Berber, Morocco*): *Bentolila 76*

Sky is adorned with stars, man with his beard, and woman with her hair.

(*Tatar, RF*): *Geyvandov 69*

A hairy face denotes a hairy vagina. (*Mapuche, Chile*): *Guevara 53*

A hairy man's rich, a hairy wife's a bitch. (*English, USA*): *Whiting 1952: 345*

God blesses the hairy man and the smooth woman. (*Arabic, Tunisia*): *Lunde & Wintle 114*

Not even the Devil can handle a woman with a moustache.

(*Portuguese, Brazil*): *Mota 125; Souto Maior 45*

Not even the Devil can put up with a woman with hair in her nostrils.

(*Portuguese, Brazil*): *Mota 125*

A woman can do what she pleases with the man who lets her count the hairs in his nostrils.

(*Japanese*): *Lunde & Wintle 87*

If you touch a *chuchu muyu* seed, you will develop breasts. [The seeds of the *chuchu muyu*
   contain a milky liquid.] (*Quecha, Ecuador*): *Santos Ortiz de Villalba 288*

A woman is more than her breasts; goats also have two. (*Rwanda*): *Crépeau 476*

Breasts are like a beard: even a barren woman has them. (*Ganda, Uganda*): *Walser 36*

The proof of a girl's lack of breasts is her white hair. (*Rwanda*): *Crépeau 213*

A girl has the other thing because of her breasts. (*Kundu, Cameroon*): *Ittmann 117*

NURSING BREASTS AND BREASTS AS OBJECTS OF DESIRE

You can always soothe a child with the breast, but how to handle a husband?

(*Estonian*): *Geyvandov 121*

An infant must cry to get its mother's milk. (*Sinhalese, Sri Lanka*): *o.s. Gunasekare*

Until the baby cries, the mother doesn't suckle him. (*Romanian*): *Mieder 1986: 17*

If the child doesn't cry, the mother won't find out. (*Russian*): *Krylov 54*

The mother gives the child no milk until it cries for it. (*Persian*): *Roebuck 128*

A mother does not suckle a child until it cries. (*Tibetan*): *Gergan 120*

A crying baby gets a suck; but a babbler only gains dislike.

(*Khionghta, Bangladesh*): *Lewin 18*

Everyone acts according to the amount of his mother's milk that he has drunk.

(*Kurdish, Turkey*): *Geyvandov 163*

Breasts are two, but the milk is the same. (*Oromo, Ethiopia*): *Cotter 161*

Let a female develop her breast, eventually she must give it to her child.

(*Igbo, Nigeria*): *Penfield 112*

Little girl, you suck your mother's breast, and yours will be sucked.

(*Lega, Congo DR*): *o.s. Malasi*

A man's breast does not give milk. (*Hehe, Tanzania*): *Madumulla 80*

Breast-ache is not a man's ache. (*Minyanka, Mali*): *Cauvin 1980: 60*

A woman, as her breasts hang down, so even her brain hangs down. [Women don't make good decisions.] (*Oromo, Kenya*): *o.s. Jolanda Alkemade*

The breast that contains milk cannot contain intelligence. (*Somali*): *o.s. Wilma Fels*

Whatever the mother has eaten, the child will take in at the breast.
(*Sranan, Surinam*): *o.s. Mavis Noordwijk*

That which you sucked from the tit will be spilled over your grave.
(*Spanish, Bolivia*): *Paredes-Candia 143; Glazer 170*

All women's breasts can feed wise children. (*Tswana, Botswana*): *Ibekwe 145*

The mother puts a breast in the child's mouth but not sense in its head.
(*various European versions, e.g. Finnish*): *Kuusi 46*

The breasts are never too heavy to be carried.
(*Creole, Haiti*): *David 11; Barbotin 212; Ludwig 464; Zagaya 135*

Breasts are never too heavy for the owner to run with. (*Creole, Haiti*): *Préval 28*

The tusks are never too heavy for its owner. [One's children can never be too much of a burden to care for.] (*Chewa, Malawi*): *Milimo 14*

A mother's love, a breast-clinging child.
(*Maori, New Zealand*): *Brougham & Reed 72; Champion 640*

A mother's breast is better than rays of sunlight. (*Adyg, RF*): *Geyvandov 163*

A mother's breast is paradise for a child. (*Karachay-Balkar, RF*): *Geyvandov 163*

My home is my mother's breast. (*Spanish*): *Geyvandov 127*

A mother's breast may dry but her hand does not. [Mothers always find ways to feed their children.] (*Oromo, Ethiopia*): *Cotter 5*

A child does not die because its mother's breasts are dry. [Need for improvisation and for an alternative source of survival if need be.] (*Nigeria*): *Akporobaro & Emovon 92*

A mother always has breasts; a healer always has medicine. [A man who is leaving his mother's house does not cut the bonds that exist between mother and child.]
(*Yaka, Congo DR*): *Beken 1993: 132*

The breast of your mother is not to be forgotten. (*Tonga, Zambia*): *Milimo 11*

A mother's breast cannot be abandoned because of a wound. (*Mboshi, Congo*): *Obenga 290*

The sweetness of the breasts lasts until the grave. (*Arabic, Sudan*): *Singer 58*

Paradise on earth can be found on horseback, in reading books or between women's breasts.
(*Arabic, Maghreb*): *Cheneb III 135*

A woman with big breasts you should marry, bury, or put into a nunnery.
(*Spanish*): *Geyvandov 190*

Do not desire the breasts of somebody else's wife. (*Yaka, Congo DR*): *Beken 1993: 139*

The running woman holds her breasts for beauty's sake, not because she thinks she'll lose them. (*Twi, Ghana*): *o.s. Cameron Duodu*

The running woman holds her breasts for beauty's sake, not because she fears they might fall off. (*Mamprusi, Burkina Faso*): *Plissart 80*

When women run they hold their breasts, but when they panic they drop everything and lose control. (*Creole, Guadeloupe*): *Ludwig 464*

A girl flutters her breasts without knowing the consequences. (*Rwanda*): *Crépeau 488*

The girl that goes out dancing does not hide her breasts. (*Oromo, Ethiopia*): *Cotter 93*

There is nothing that is not the breast of a woman. [Women always find admirers.]

    (*Zulu, South Africa/Swaziland*): *Nyembezi 214*

Two tits pull [court] more than a hundred wagons. (*Spanish, Panama*): *Rubio 267*

One tit pulls more than a cart. (*Spanish, Argentina*): *Magalhães Júnior 519*

Tits pull more than oxen and carts.

    (*Spanish, Bolivia/Mexico; many variants*): *Lehman-Nitche 128; Fernández Naranjo 194*

The hair of a tiger, the gem of a snake, the breast of a chaste woman, the tusk of an
    elephant, the sword of a brave man, the riches of a Brahman, one gets them only after
    their death. (*Hindi, India*): *Champion 399*

Sweet mouths suck two breasts. (*Greek*): *Geyvandov 230*

A timid heart will not see a white breast. (*Kurdish, Turkey*): *Geyvandov 35*

If a girl says no to marriage, just wait for her breasts to sag. (*Rundi, Burundi*): *Rodegem 90*

He that takes an old wife should not complain about sagging breasts.

    (*Romanian; German*): *Wander V 1806.*

WOMB

In woman's womb lies the destiny of the home. (*German*): *Wander V 1272*

A womb makes a woman. (*Latin*): *De Mauri 165*

Women reason with the womb. (*Italian*): *Menarini 6*

Love for a girl lies below the navel. (*Rwanda*): *Crépeau 546*

The woman with a storehouse under her navel will not die of hunger or cold.

    (*Ladino/Hebrew, Israel*): *Moscona 118*

Unhappy the girl for whom the drum does not sound. [The drum sounds for a girl's first
    menstruation.] (*Zulu, South Africa*): *Nyembezi 118*

When a girl begins to menstruate, either give her in marriage or bury her.

    (*Arabic, Lebanon*): *Frayha I 198*

They don't close the mosque for one menstruating woman. [She is not allowed to pray.]

    (*Persian*): *Elwell-Sutton 46*

Better to sleep hungry than wait for food prepared by a woman having her period.

    (*Baule, Ivory Coast*): *Arbelbide 111*

Whether the widow has her period or not, it makes no difference. [She has no right to sexual
    intercourse, neither has the woman who has her period.]

    (*Baule, Ivory Coast PR*): *Arbelbide 56*

The chance of motherhood fades with regular menstruation. (*Mboshi, Congo*): *Obenga 299*

The one whom the heart has seen before the eye could see him.

    (*Arabic, Lebanon*): *Abela 231*

A child, will he weep in the big forest [the womb]? (*Taka, Congo DR*): *Ibekwe 14*

He loves me well that makes my belly swell.

    (*English, UK*): *Gluski 234; Reinsberg-Düringsfeld 66–67*

It is not enough for a woman to put her hands on her belly to get a son.

    (*Arabic, Syria/Lebanon*): *Feghali 177–178*

She ate fresh flour and so her keeper of love [the womb] swelled up.

  (*Mapuche, Chile*): *Guevara 57*

The belly precedes the child. (*Rundi, Burundi*): *Rodegem 121*

The foetus in the womb carries the future. (*Gikuyu, Kenya*): *Barra 95*

The womb is a mine of precious stones. (*Arabic, Lebanon*): *Abela 224*

The child follows the womb. (*English, UK*): *Williams IV 143*

A child in the mother's womb takes after her. (*Ganda, Uganda*): *Ibekwe 34*

A mother's womb does unexpected things. (*Digor, RF*): *Geyvandov 169*

A womb is an indiscriminate container, it bears a thief and a witch.

  (*Shona, Zimbabwe*): *Ibekwe 196*

The womb is like the *muwogo* [cassava root]: it brings forth both beautiful and ugly.

  (*Ganda, Uganda*): *Walser 143*

A mother's womb is like a slave ship, bringing both good and bad.

  (*Sranan, Surinam*): *o.s. Mavis Noordwijk*

The same womb gives birth to the thief and the wizard. [also: to a thief and a poisoner]

  (*Gikuyu, Kenya*): *Ngumbu Njururu 88; Barra 79*

From one womb, but not the same children. (*Russian*): *Geyvandov 169*

A mother's womb is like a patchwork quilt. (*Sranan, Surinam*): *o.s. Mavis Noordwijk*

A woman is like a bag, whatever you put into it, she will carry. (*Russian*): *o.s. Anna Ravve*

The child hurts inside and outside. (*Tonga, Zambia*): *Geyvandov 172*

Wombs see trouble. (*Ganda, Uganda*): *Walser 143*

Relations are like part of your body: if anything touches it, however small, you feel it.

  (*Hausa, West Africa*): *Akporobaron & Emovon 163*

VAGINA

Even if your wife's sex is small, dawn will find you there. (*Minyanka, Mali*): *Cauvin 1980: 519*

Thread the small-eyed needle slowly. (*Thai*): *Wintle 66*

A vagina is like a pig's snout. [Very solid, never worn out.] (*Creole, Guadeloupe*): *Ludwig 435*

My vagina is fine, [yet] according to my people [its use] for me is ended.

  (*Sumerian/Akkadian, Mesopotamia*): *Lambert 248*

Let-me-please, let-me-please! grazes the vagina. (*Rwanda*): *Crépeau 329*

If a woman offers her sex to everyone, pestles are used on it. (*Minyanka, Mali*): *Cauvin 1980: 342*

The kind woman has a hairless vagina. (*Mamprusi, Burkina Faso*): *Plissart 70*

He who sees a vulva in the morning should go on to the market at once.

  (*Arabic, Algeria*): *Westermarck 284*

A woman of striking appearance has a biting vagina. (*Mapuche, Chile*): *Guevara 53*

A happy girl thinks that hers must be better. (*Rwanda*): *Crépeau 488*

BUTTOCKS

She who offers a half-cooked meal is better than she who offers her buttocks.

  (*Rwanda*): *Crépeau 382*

Neither a beautiful face, nor a supple behind. (*Arabic, Syria/Lebanon*): *Feghali 124*

No one shows her buttocks unless they are big. (*Rwanda*): *Crépeau 355*

A woman is like the merino sheep—she is judged by her backside.

(*Sotho, Lesotho/South Africa*)

A woman with a big behind consumes a lot of gasoline. (*Spanish, Cuba*): *Sánchez-Boudy 16*

A small woman with a big behind: if she is not a whore, she is a thief.

(*Spanish, Colombia*): *Sierra García 117*

A wiggling behind throws you off the roof. (*Spanish, Cuba*): *Sánchez-Boudy 16*

A little arse, well administered, will give more profit than a farm in the valley.

(*Spanish, Bolivia*): *Paredes-Candia 226*

A smart bride shows her husband only half of her behind. (*Armenian*): *Sakayan 241*

A big behind is not a drum. (*Creole, Marie Galante/Caribbean*): *Barbotin 48*

Although a man may fondly love buttocks, he is only allowed what a woman allows.

(*Dutch*): *Mesters 106*

Cold things are a cat's nose and a woman's buttocks. (*Japanese*): *Buchanan 34*

Hot on hot, said the blacksmith, and he put his wife with her bare buttocks on the stove.

(*Frisian, Netherlands*): *Beintema 61*

After the fart she squeezed her buttocks. (*Arabic, Algeria*): *Belamri 124*

Two buttocks cannot avoid brushing against each other. (*Tonga, Zambia*): *Milimo 23*

Buttocks rubbing together do not lack sweat.

(*several Bantu languages, not specified*): *Finnegan: 406*

Even breasts rub against each other. (*Armenian*): *Sakayan 18*

LEGS, KNEES, FEET

Heaven is at the feet of mothers. (*Arabic, o.s. Myriem Fasla; English, USA*): *Kin 117*

Even a legless [woman] begets what has legs. (*Hehe, Tanzania*): *Madumulla 83*

Irishwomen have a dispensation from the Pope to wear the thick ends of their legs down-

wards. (*Irish*): *Gaffney & Cashman 92*

When the dance is in full swing, the girl's upper legs can be seen.

(*Baule, Ivory Coast*): *Arbelbide 34*

A devout witch hides her leg but shows her thigh. (*Catalan, Spain; French*): *Guiter 33*

Reverends and girls' legs promise something better in higher spheres.

(*Danish*): *Kjaer Holbek 181*

He rejected her and looked at her legs again. (*Arabic, Syria/Lebanon*): *Feghali 171–72*

Massage the legs of your daughter, that she may have a good appearance when standing

before the fire on the beach. (*Maori, New Zealand*): *Brougham & Reed 106*

'Cover them, cover them', said the man to his wife. 'Why should I, I did not steal them', said

she and sat with her skirt above her knees. (*Dutch*): *Mesters 123*

The virtuous woman and the broken leg must stay at home.

(*Portuguese; Spanish*): *Chavez 906; Champion 305*

A virtuous woman and a broken leg should stay at home and be kept on a chair.

(*German*): *Harrebomée I 39*

A woman who admits guilt will not spend time on her knees. [i.e. under interrogation]

(*Yoruba, Nigeria*): *o.s. Felix Mnthali*

Resting does not graze the knees. (*Berber, Maghreb*): *Bentolila 124*

Old women's footsteps start firmly but don't last. (*Rundi, Burundi*): *Rodegem 305*
'Skating makes thirsty', said the old woman, and she stood with one foot on the ice.
   (*Frisian, Netherlands*): *Beintema 114*
She who has her feet swept, will marry an old man. (*Spanish, Cuba*): *Sabiduría Guajira 43*
Do not tie up your feet; you will not [be able to] give birth.
   (*Quecha, Ecuador*): *Santos Ortiz de Villalba 293*
Never marry a woman with bigger feet than your own. (*Sena, Malawi/Mozambique*): *Milimo 24*
Don't marry the one with the big feet, because she is your fellow-male.
   (*Sena, Malawi/Mozambique*): *Milimo 116*
Look for someone who has short feet, because one who has long feet is your fellow-male.
   (*Sena, Malawi/Mozambique*): *Milimo 16*
The woman with long feet ends up alone in a room. (*Chinese*): *o.s. Tao Yang and Liu Xiaolu*
If a girl develops long feet, she will be in trouble after marriage. (*Telegu, India*)
I do not desire a shoe that is larger than my feet. (*Hebrew, Israel*): *Cohen 1912: 33*
Without touching with her feet, woman leaves footmarks. (*Portuguese; German*): *Chaves 955*
Paradise lies under the feet of the mother. (*Turkish*): *o.s. A.P. Kwak*
Paradise lies under the heel of the mother. (*Arabic, Algeria*): *o.s. Myriem Fasla*
The mother declares she is lying down, but her feet are outside.
   (*Baule, Ivory Coast*): *Arbelbide 82*
While the mother sleeps, her toes are awake. (*Creole, Guadeloupe/French Antilles*): *Ludwig 466*
A girl's beauty can be recognized by the heels of her feet. (*Oromo, Ethiopia*): *Cotter 8*
A woman with beautiful feet does not need to cover her face.
   (*Arabic, Maghreb*): *Dahan 1254*
Cover your feet, you silly woman—there is no beauty other then the one you were born
   with. (*Arabic, Morocco*): *Dahan 1277*

BEAUTY AND BEAUTIFYING

A woman's beauty makes fish sink and wild geese fall from the sky. (*Chinese*): *Shengzi 812*
Beauty of the face is the reflection of a beautiful character. (*Arabic, Lebanon*): *Frayha I 243*
A good-looking person also has a beautiful heart. (*Japanese*): *Buchanan 121*
A beautiful human is popular with everyone. (*Russian*): *Reinsberg-Düringsfeld 51*
There where the sugar is, ants are to be found. (*Indonesian*): *o.s. P. de Haas*
Butterflies come to pretty flowers. (*Korean*): *Ha 65; o.s. B. Walraven*

RADIANCE

The beautiful one laughs and lets the ugly one cry.
   (*Papiamentu, Netherlands Antilles*): *Brenneker 16*
Don't pick withered blossoms on your way when you have a plum-flower back at home.
   (*Chinese*): *Chen 135*
A beauty is a joy to everyone. (*Turkish*): *Geyvandov 78*
The saddle[-cloth] is the embroidery of the horse; woman the embroidery of life.
   (*Mongolian*): *Geyvandov 120*

Beautiful the girl who looks like a peony when she sits, like a columbine when she stands, and
    like a lily when she walks. (*Japanese*): *Wintle 62*

A beautiful woman is like newly forged gold. (*Indonesian*): *o.s. Maya Sutedja-Liem*

When three women join together, the stars come out in broad daylight.
    (*Telegu, India*): *Champion 438*

A radiant beauty says to the moon: 'Don't bother to rise; I will.' (*Persian*): *Geyvandov 68*

Beauty is like a morning star. (*Maori, New Zealand*): *Geyvandov 68*

A beautiful woman stands on the palm of the hand. [Man desires to caress and serve her.]
    (*English, Hawaii*): *o.s. Pukui 202*

Woman's beauty radiates in the brightness of her presence; a girl's beauty is in the freshness
    of her innocence. (*Arabic, Morocco*): *Messaoudi 88*

Nature meant woman to be her masterpiece. (*English, USA*): *Kin 281*

Even silent, a beautiful woman cannot go unnoticed. (*Japanese*): *Buchanan 264*

Mountain trees around flowers. (*Japanese*): *Huzii 56*

A many-coloured hen does not stay in a corner of the house. (*Kundu, Cameroon*): *Ittmann 77*

What is the use of the peacock strutting in the jungle? (*Malay*): *MBRAS 17*

Moonlight in the jungle. [No one around to admire her beauty.] (*Telegu, India*): *Geyvandov 102*

Cherry blossoms in a deep mountain. (*Japanese*): *Huzii 56*

A pretty girl is like freshly made cheese. (*Nenets, RF*): *Geyvandov 69*

Beauty of the mountains is in the stones; beauty of the head is in the hair.
    (*Turkish*): *Geyvandov 69*

Spacious forehead, beautiful woman. (*Spanish, El Salvador*): *Sánchez Duarte 109*

A woman's beauty is in her slender waist. (*Tamil, India*): *Geyvandov 70*

A pretty girl should have an eyebrow like a willow-leaf, an eye like the kernel of an apricot, a
    mouth like a cherry, a face the shape of a melon-seed, and a waist as thin as a poplar.
    (*Chinese*): *Lunde & Wintle 61*

Three traits of a woman; a broad bosom, a slender waist and a short back.
    (*Irish*): *Gaffney & Cashman 104*

Women and greyhounds should have thin waists. (*Spanish*): *Geyvandov 70*

A skinny woman is like a racehorse: fast and fun, but no good for work.
    (*English, USA*): *Mieder 1992: 665*

Fatness is part of beauty. (*Spanish, Chile*): *Aguilera 55*

Beauty comes through the mouth. [Women should be fat.]
    (*Spanish, Colombia/Panama*): *Acuña 49; Aguilera 55*

A fat woman is a quilt for the winter. (*Multani, India*): *Champion 425*

Being slim is the property of the gazelle, being corpulent the property of the big horse.
    (*Arabic, Syria/Lebanon*): *Feghali 684*

Plumpness redeems the seven deadly sins. (*Arabic, widespread*): *Lunde & Wintle 106*

A plump wife is a warm blanket in wintertime. (*Punjabi*): *Geyvandov 219*

Harvest makes girls and orphans plump. (*Ovambo, Angola/Namibia*): *Geyvandov 253*

Should a husband blame his wife for growing fatter? [It is a sign of health to be fat.]
    (*Mossi, Burkina Faso*): *o.s. A. Sawadogo*

A slim woman smells of fish. [Slim women are little appreciated.] (*Creole, Martinique*): *David 51*

Big bread does not find customers. [Very corpulent women will not find a husband.]
   (*Portuguese, Brazil*): *Mota 161*

Gaining weight, grown more beautiful, Madam has forgotten how she was before.
   (*Ladino, Morocco*): *Dahan 1300*

THE IMPACT OF FEMALE ATTRACTION

Young and beautiful, access to everything. (*Kirghiz*): *Geyvandov 78*

No girl holds herself in contempt. (*Swahili, East Africa*): *Scheven 485*

With a beautiful face no wealth is needed. (*Ladino, Morocco*): *Dahan 272*

A pretty face is the key to locked doors. (*Tajik*): *Geyvandov 78*

To every beautiful girl beckons a golden future. (*Russian*): *Graf 168*

Beauty is a good letter of introduction. (*Portuguese; German*): *Marwick 444*

A beautiful woman cannot be scared away like birds that eat the harvest.
   (*Swahili, East Africa*): *Scheven 485*

Advice from the mouth of a beautiful girl is listened to with benevolence.
   (*Spanish, Puerto Rico*): *Fernández Valledor 68*

It is tastier to eat a beautiful biscuit. (*Korean*): *Geyvandov 78*

The more beautiful the fruit, the tastier it seems to be. (*Pashto, Afghanistan*): *Geyvandov 78*

Even God loves beauties. (*Pashto, Afghanistan*): *Geyvandov 78*

Even an angel cannot resist a beautiful girl. (*Hebrew, Israel*): *Stahl 223*

However much he tries, even a hero is overcome by a woman's beauty.
   (*Chinese, Taiwan*): *o.s. H.V. Tseng*

When she looks out of her window, the horse starts walking and moves into the garden, and
   the dogs bark for three days. (*Russian*): *Geyvandov 80*

When one has a beautiful wife, one has no fine pigs—because the pigs, instead of eating,
   spend all their time staring at her. (*French*): *Marwick 444*

A pleasing appearance is stronger than power. (*English, Jamaica*): *Geyvandov 78*

The world is ruled by money and beautiful women. (*Portuguese, Brazil*): *Mota 83*

All beautiful girls sew with gold. (*Russian*): *Reinsberg-Düringsfeld 52*

A beautiful wife is a golden plough to the household. (*Romanian*): *Geyvandov 123*

BELLES

Nature provides woman with only three-tenths of her beauty. (*Chinese*): *o.s. Huang Mingfen*

The beauty of a woman is her devotion to her husband. (*Lokaniti, Myanmar*): *Gray 22*

To serve her husband is the best adornment of a wife. (*Sanskrit, India*): *Jha 167*

In a good marriage you bring his food without having to dress up for it.
   (*Ganda, Uganda*): *Walser 114*

A woman beautifies herself for the man who pleases her. (*Chinese, Taiwan*): *o.s. H.V. Tseng*

A wife who takes care of her appearance keeps her husband away from other doors.
   (*Spanish, Argentina/Mexico/Puerto Rico*): *Moya 488; Velasco Valdés 85; Díaz Rivera 129*

Beauty unadorned, adorns the most. (*Hebrew, Israel*): *Cohen 1961: 44*

True beauty needs no decoration. (*Hindi, India*): *Geyvandov 72*

The ugliest woman is she who dresses herself up most. (*Portuguese*): *Chaves 869*

And she powders, and puts on a blush, and still they won't look. (*Russian*): *Geyvandov* 97

A pretty girl is also pretty in an old dress. (*Chechen, RF*): *Geyvandov 72*

A white complexion hides many defects. [A white skin was admired.]

(*Japanese*): *Buchanan 265*

A little bit of powder and a little bit of paint make an ugly woman look like what she ain't.

(*English, USA*): *Mieder 1992: 478*

The woman who arrays herself well is never ugly.

(*Portuguese, Brazil; Spanish, El Salvador/Venezuela*): *Magalhães Júnior 196; Sánchez Duarte 39; Febres Cordero 43*

A woman who does not put on make-up will be thrown away.

(*Portuguese, Brazil*): *Magalhães Júnior 196*

The woman who dresses in silk stays at home. (*English, USA*): *West 42*

The blind man's wife—for whom does she put on make-up?

(*Portuguese, Brazil; Spanish, Argentina*): *Mota 125; Moya 488*

The blind man's wife needs no make-up. (*English, USA*): *Kin 155*

For whom does the blind man's wife paint herself? (*Hebrew, Israel*): *Cohen 1961: 60*

Blind man's wife, for whom are you dressing up? (*Greek; Portuguese*): *Politès 11; Chaves 803*

The shepherd's wife dresses fancily in the evening. (*Tatar, RF*): *Geyvandov 287*

A man leaves the home to attend to business, a woman to show herself.

(*Finnish*): *Geyvandov 269*

Do not spread out your merchandise, it will diminish its value. (*Arabic, Lebanon*): *Abela 32*

From a woman wearing make-up, one turns his face away. (*Spanish, Argentina*): *Moya 322*

Veil your women and repair your ramparts. (*Arabic, Algeria*): *Lunde & Wintle 71*

An unornamented calabash may safely be left outside.

(*Maori, New Zealand*): *Brougham & Reed 132*

A woman and a cherry are painted for their own harm. (*English, USA*): *Mieder 1992: 665*

The little house that is whitened up wants to be rented. (*Spanish, Argentina*): *Moya 356*

The woman who has put on make-up leaves her husband through the other door.

(*Spanish, Puerto Rico*): *Fernández Valledor 155*

Though she covers her face with her veil, she still manages to be coquettish.

(*Bengali, India*): *Long I 39*

Covered with a veil everyone is handsome. (*Azeri, Azerbaijan*): *Geyvandov 74*

A woman without a veil is like food without salt. (*Pashto, Afghanistan*): *Champion 463*

An ugly woman will swap a silk belt for a woollen [i.e. thick] veil.

(*Russian*): *Reinsberg-Düringsfeld 56*

The thicker the veil, the less worth the lifting. (*Turkish*): *Lunde & Wintle 156*

Before you ask the varan [monitor lizard] for a skin cream, look at its skin.

(*Lega, Congo DR*): *o.s. Malasi*

Because she enjoyed the sweetness of the fresh milk, she left her hair dry.

(*Oromo, Ethiopia*): *Cotter 41*

A woman who uses butter for her face will not lack any.

(*Ovambo, Angola/Namibia*): *Geyvandov 204*

If you want to look more radiant, use henna and ointments. (*Arabic, Morocco*): *Messaoudi 118*

She says to her husband: 'I would like to put henna on my nails'; and he answers: 'I could not ask for anything better.' (*Arabic, Syria/Lebanon*): *Feghali 173*

A black eye does not need make-up. (*Ladino, Morocco*): *Dahan 1287*

Kohl beautifies a woman, the parade beautifies the tribe, the saddle[-cloth] beautifies the horse. (*Arabic*): *Cheneb III 238*

I got married in order to dye my eyebrows, not to sew patches on worn clothes. (*Persian*): *Geyvandov 133*

Hair is a woman's pride. (*Spanish, Cuba*): *Cabrera n.p.*

A woman's hair is her crowning glory. (*English, USA*): *Mieder 1992: 666*

Better a charming brunette than a sad blonde. (*Portuguese, Brazil*): *Souto Maior 35*

Where red hair and thorns grow, there is no good land. [A red-haired woman is usually considered a termagant and would not make a good wife.] (*Pennsylvanian German, USA*): *Champion 635*

A blonde head does not last long. (*Spanish, Colombia*): *Acuña 63*

Elegance and looks, the scarf fell down. (*Berber, Morocco*): *Bentolila 19*

Good is a horse with flowing tail and mane, bad the woman with dishevelled hair. (*Finnish*): *Kuusi 66*

Falseness often lurks beneath fair hair. (*Danish*): *Bohn 1855: 357*

A curly-haired woman is amorous. [Before the Second World War, Japanese women loved to have straight hair; nowadays, many urban women prefer to have curly hair.] (*Japanese*): *Buchanan 232*

Those with a curly fringe are from the wild cattle [bulls and women]. (*Spanish, Mexico*): *Casasola 53*

Curled hair, curled wits. (*Dutch*): *o.s. Meyer*

Every bound foot conceals a jar of tears. (*Chinese*): *Wintle 156*

Who wants to be handsome has to suffer pain, said the maid, as she pinned the bonnet to her ears. (*Dutch*): *Beintema 108*

A woman without earrings is like a house without furniture. (*Spanish, Cuba*): *Cabrera n.p.*

A woman with many bracelets is capricious. (*French; Catalan, Spain*): *Guiter 33*

With or without a nose-plug, women are always beautiful. (*Makua, Mozambique*): *o.s. J. Wembah-Rashid*

Submissiveness is a girl's necklace. (*Russian*): *Geyvandov 71*

Woman's adornment is her decency. (*Greek*): *Haller 461*

Women's true adornment is modesty and not her dress. (*German*): *Haller 465*

Beautiful feathers make beautiful birds. (*Russian*): *Graf 243*

A wife is clothes, a banana plant is weeding. (*Swahili, Tanzania/Zanzibar*): *o.s. M. van Twillert*

The woman who dresses in yellow trusts her beauty. (*English, USA*): *West 42*

She who dresses in green trusts her beauty. (*Spanish, Colombia*): *Acuña 47*

She who dresses in black must rely on her beauty. (*Spanish, Mexico*): *Ballesteros 29*

A girl in lace and silk is suitable for dance and banquet, but not for the lady of the house. (*Romanian*): *Günther 26–7*

Silks and satins put out the kitchen fire. (*Hebrew, Israel*): *Cohen 1961: 281*

Love flies with the red petticoat. [Only unmarried girls wear this garment.]
    (*Japanese*): *Champion 442*

A woman's petticoat is the Devil's binder. (*Romanian*): *Mieder 1986: 372*

Many an Irish property was increased by the lace of a daughter's petticoat.
    (*Irish*): *O'Farrell 73*

A foolish woman is known by her petticoats, showing her wealth by the number she
    possesses. (*English, UK*): *Williams I 476*

The ribbons of a petticoat pull more than a team of oxen. (*Spanish, Mexico*): *Rubio 267*

If your petticoat fits you well, do not try to put on your husband's pants.
    (*Creole, Martinique*): *Hearn 34*

When ladies wear the breeches their petticoats ought to be long enough to hide 'em.
    (*English, USA*): *Mieder 1992: 359*

A beauty in ugly clothes is still a beauty. (*Uzbek*): *Geyvandov 72*

A house is made beautiful by its thatch. [A woman is made beautiful by her clothes.]
    (*Tsonga, Mozambique*): *Champion 593*

Neither my father nor my mother made me beautiful, but my clothes [did].
    (*Arabic, Lebanon*): *Geyvandov 72*

Dress the corncob and it will look like a bride. (*Arabic*): *Safadi 14*

Nicely dressed, even a stick becomes beautiful. (*Ladino, Morocco*): *Dahan 1309*

Even a log is beautiful if beautifully dressed. (*Hungarian*): *Paczolay 204*

Put jewels on a stump, then even the stump is beautiful. (*Estonian*): *Paczolay 204*

A woman without clothes is as unattractive as food without salt.
    (*Pashto, Afghanistan*): *Geyvandov 75*

If this is how she looks in beautiful garments, how will she look without them?
    (*Turkish; Azeri, Azerbaijan*): *Geyvandov 72*

Beautiful women are like fresh banana leaves: they never come to an end in the plantation.
    (*Ganda, Uganda*): *Walser 4*

If you think Miss-this-year is pretty, Miss-next-year will be more so.
    (*Hausa, Niger/Nigeria*): *Whitting 94*

It is easy to find a beautiful woman; it is difficult to find a good craftsman.
    (*Thai*): *Peltier 29*

Every woman is beautiful in the dark, from a distance and under an umbrella.
    (*Japanese*): *Geyvandov 75*

In the dark all women are moons. [Moon is a metaphor for beauty.] (*Arabic, Tunisia*): *Yetiv 63*

In the dark every woman is the moon [i.e. as beautiful as the moon].
    (*Ladino, Morocco*): *Dahan 277*

The ugly woman has to switch off the light to say that she is pretty.
    (*Spanish, Cuba*): *Cabrera n.p.*

In the dark all cats and girls are beautiful. (*Hungarian*): *Ley 50*

BEAUTY VERSUS INTELLIGENCE

A woman wants to be pretty rather than intelligent and shrewd, because men, in general, see
    better than they think. (*Hebrew, Israel*): *Alcalay 551*

God did not join brains with beauty. (*Polish*): *Mieder 1986: 197*

Beauty and mind are seldom of one kind. (*Russian*): *Graf 208*

A doll's head and an empty brain. (*Polish*): *Reinsberg-Düringsfeld 53*

More beauty than a peacock, but the intelligence of a block of wood. (*Mongolian*): *Geyvandov 71*

The intelligence [also: wisdom] of women is in their beauty, the beauty of men is in their intelligence [also: wisdom].

    (*Ladino / Arabic, Morocco; variants in Israel, Europe and Asia*): *Stahl 223; Dahan 242*

A daughter should be pretty and a son skilled. (*Nepalese*): *Pokhrel 13*

The man [achieves] by his hands, the woman by her beauty. (*Russian*): *Bläsing 68*

The brains of a woman are in her curls. (*Neo-Aramaic, Iraq*): *Geyvandov 71*

Man has beauty in his excellence, woman excellence in her beauty. (*Spanish*): *Meier-Pfaller 63*

Man's brains are his jewels; woman's jewels are her brains. (*Yiddish*): *Rosten 1970: 321*

Women are wacky, women are vain; they'd rather be pretty than have a good brain.

    (*English, USA*): *Mieder 1992: 669*

TRANSIENCE

Woman's beauty, the echo in the forest, and a rainbow fade quickly.

    (*German*): *Graf 252; Bohn 1857: 176*

Woman's beauty is a cloud's beauty. (*Fang / Bulu, Cameroon / Gabon*): *o.s. S. Eno-Belinga*

Charms vanish, money goes, ugliness stays in the bed.

    (*many variants in Europe, the Caribbean, and the Maghreb*): *Dahan 276*

The gold and the millions are gone, but the misfortune stays in the bed.

    (*Ladino, Morocco*): *Stahl 215*

A handsome shape sags out quickly. (*Russian*): *Geyvandov 82*

No shoe is so beautiful that it will not become a slipper. (*French*): *Ségalen: 80*

Yesterday's lovely flower is but a dream today. (*Japanese*): *Buchanan 168*

Where has the beautiful wife gone? (*Maori, New Zealand*): *Geyvandov 82*

A woman's physical beauty is proved only after pregnancy and nursing.

    (*Arabic, Lebanon*): *Frayha II 584*

Breastfeeding makes old, the childbed makes young. (*Catalan, Spain; French, German*): *Guiter 37*

A dress is beautiful until it is washed for the first time; a woman until she has her first child.

    (*Tamil, India*): *Geyvandov 82*

Pregnancy spoils the waist. (*German*): *Wander IV 418*

The hen will only stay beautiful while she does not lay eggs. (*Serbian*): *Karadžić 301*

The pretty Creole does not die with her pretty bottom.

    (*Creole, Guadeloupe*): *Ludwig 443; ACCT 71*

When the sweet taste has gone, the chewing [gum] is thrown away. (*Indonesian*): *o.s. P. de Haas*

Wrinkled perhaps, but loved anyway. (*Russian*): *Geyvandov 74*

The heart has no wrinkles. (*French*): *Geyvandov 29*

OUTER BEAUTY AND INNER QUALITIES

A woman's beauty is not in her face. (*Swahili, East Africa*): *o.s. J. Wembah-Rashid*

No woman as beautiful as the docile one. (*Rwanda*): *Crépeau 368, 476*

Kind words and few are a woman's ornament. (*Danish*): *Cordry 288*

There is no more shining dress for a woman than silence.
  (*Hebrew, Israel; Russian*): *Cohen 1961: 456; Graf 144*

Grace is all over the body. (*Burmese*): *Myint Thein 7*

Beauty without grace is a violet without smell. (*Hebrew, Israel*): *Cohen 1961: 43*

It is better to be graceful than to be pretty. (*Spanish, Bolivia*): *Paredes-Candia 157*

Beauty is in the face, grace in the body and you cannot exhaust it. (*Burmese*): *Hla Pe 24*

Beauty is a mirror, the silvering [the secret] of which is within. (*Turkish*): *Haig 105*

Beauty without grace is a hook without a bait. (*French*): *Geyvandov 70*

The ugly girl is a thousand times more gracious than the beautiful one.
  (*Spanish, Argentina*): *Villafuerte 158*

A wife you love for her being, not for her beauty. (*Swahili, Kenya*): *o.s. Ahmed Sheikh N.*

What is good is not necessarily beautiful. (*Japanese*): *Buchanan 123*

Most good women are without beauty. (*Chinese*): *Chen 193*

Beauty is null and void, when honour is lost. (*English, UK*): *Geyvandov 77*

Beauty without decency is wine without taste. (*Italian*): *Geyvandov 77*

Modesty and beauty do not come together. (*Hebrew, Israel*): *Stahl 211*

A woman's beauty is like a spring flower, but her purity is like a star in the sky.
  (*English, UK; USA*): *Geyvandov 71; Loomis 1955: 197*

Virtue and beauty are a blessed association. (*Slovak*): *Mieder 1986: 509*

Chastity combined with beauty makes a woman perfect. (*Arabic, Lebanon*): *Wortabet 69*

Do not take a wife because of her beauty but rather because of her virtues.
  (*Arabic, Lebanon*): *Wortabet 69*

Beauty fades, but not goodness. (*Filipino*): *Chua & Nazareno 24*

Do not follow after desire; do not love for beauty only. (*Khionghta, Bangladesh*): *Lewin 22*

With character, ugliness is beauty; without character, beauty is ugliness.
  (*Hausa, Nigeria*): *Akporobaro & Emovon 162; Champion 533*

Beauty without discipline, a rose without scent. (*Danish*): *Cordry 22*

UGLINESS

Beautiful roads won't take you far. (*Chinese*): *Geyvandov 77*

If ugliness suffered pains, it would cry out. (*Ladino, Morocco*): *Benazeraf 137*

Offer her to the pig, he will say: 'I'm in no hurry.' (*Arabic, Tunisia*): *Tetiv 35*

Beauty and ugliness are in the face. (*Tamil, India*): *Geyvandov 69*

The three ugliest things of their own kind—a thin red-haired woman, a thin yellow horse, a
  thin white cow. (*English, UK*): *O'Rahilly 77*

God loves the ugly one. (*Creole, Bahamas*): *Armbrister 274*

An ugly wife is a hedge around the garden. (*German*): *Meier-Pfaller 59*

One's house is best protected by a wasted garden outside and an ugly wife inside.
  (*Chinese*): *Lunde & Wintle 28*

Ugliness is the guardian of the woman. (*English, USA*): *Kin 263*

The ugliest girl makes the best housewife. (*English, USA*): *Kin 123*

Nobody's sweetheart is ugly. (*Scottish, UK*): *Champion 77*

He who loves the ugly finds it beautiful. (*Spanish, Mexico/Chile*): *Glazer 101; Cannobio 53*

Rather an entertaining ugly one than a boring beauty. (*Arabic, Morocco*): *Messaoudi 112*

Ugly women are the more passionate ones. (*Japanese*): *o.s. Kosunose*

When an ugly woman has a great passion—who should say thank you?
(*Japanese*): *Lunde & Wintle 120*

A hedgehog and peace is better than a gazelle and grief. (*Arabic, Morocco*): *Lunde & Wintle 25*

A scarab giving me peace is preferable to a gazelle that kills me.
(*Arabic*): *Wijnaendts-Francken 80*

An ugly man takes a beautiful woman to be his wife. (*Chinese*): *Geyvandov 81*

Even a man as ugly as the Devil can chase girls. (*Vietnamese*): *Geyvandov 83*

A man is like a bear: the uglier, the more beautiful. (*Spanish, Colombia*): *Acuña 47*

A woman is happy with an ugly husband. (*Tibetan*): *Duncan 235*

An ugly person comforts him/herself by saying that prettiness is vanity.
(*Igbo, Nigeria*): *Ibekwe 178*

The eye of the beautiful cannot see well. (*Acholi, Uganda*): *p'Bitek 30*

The beautiful woman wishes for the happiness of the ugly one.
(*Spanish, Costa Rica/Bolivia/Colombia/Dominican Republic*): *Hernández 144; Barneville Vásquez 50; Acuña 47; Rodríguez D. 171*

A fox's fur is its own enemy. (*Adyg, RF; Kabardino-Cherkess, RF*): *Geyvandov 77*

A pretty face is a punishment. (*Estonian*): *Geyvandov 77*

A fair woman is unfortunate. (*Japanese*): *Buchanan 265*

A rosy-cheeked woman always has a difficult destiny. (*Chinese, Taiwan*): *o.s. Tseng*

The destiny of the ugly one is what the beautiful one longs for.
(*Ladino/Hebrew*): *Benazeraf 95*

The woman who has a pretty face is usually unhappy.
(*Spanish, Puerto Rico*): *Fernández Valledor 154; Díaz Rivera 48*

Beautiful girls tend to be born unlucky. (*Chinese*): *o.s. Huang Mingfen*

Prettiness is often unfortunate. (*Papiamentu, Curaçao, Netherlands Antilles*): *Brenneker 44*

You can't fill your belly with beauty. (*Arabic, widespread*): *Lunde & Wintle 155*

Beauty will not feed you a salad. (*Creole, Guadeloupe*): *Ludwig 418*

You don't eat beauty with a spoon. (*French*): *Ségalen: 51*

The surface of the water is beautiful, but you can't sleep on it. (*Ga, Ghana*): *Geyvandov 73*

Ugly wives and stupid maids are invaluable. (*Chinese*): *Champion 383; Scarborough 213*

A fair face will not keep the pot boiling. (*Hebrew, Israel*): *Cohen 1961: 43, 174; Boecklen 89*

No bread grows on a pretty face, nor do apples grow on the shoulders.
(*Dargin, RF*): *Geyvandov 74*

A woman who follows the fashion will never make a good soup.
(*English, Jamaica*): *Llewellyn Watson 267*

You can't put beauty in the *sjtsji* [cabbage soup]. (*Finnish*): *Geyvandov 73*

Beauty will not season your soup. (*Polish*): *Mieder 1986: 24*

Soon one will have enough of beauty, but not of cabbage soup. (*Russian*): *Graf 123*

Nobody can make soup out of beauty. (*Estonian*): *Mieder 1986: 448; Reinsberg-Düringsfeld 111*

Prettiness makes no pottage. (*Hebrew, Israel*): *Cohen 1961: 409*

Cotton is the best flower. (*Korean*): *Ha 65*

The wife who loves the looking glass, hates the saucepan. (*English, USA*): *Kin 151*

It is a sad house where the husband cries and the wife is standing before the mirror.
(*Danish*): *Kjaer Holbek 111*

A woman that looks at herself in the looking-glass does not spend much time on
housekeeping. (*Letzeburgish*): *o.s. Laure Wolter*

A homely girl hates mirrors. (*Hebrew, Israel*): *Cohen 1961: 215*

An ugly woman dreads the mirror. (*English, USA*): *Kin 263*

A woman's beauty never boiled a pot but ugliness never filled it either.
(*Irish*): *O'Farrell 16, 87; O'Rahilly 6; Geyvandov 74*

Who takes a woman because of her beauty, has good nights, but bad days.
(*Danish; German*): *Wander I 1135*

Beauty is an empty calabash. (*Kundu, Cameroon*): *Ittmann 34*

Charming girl, empty gourd. (*Spanish*): *Bergua 329*

Splendid without, but empty within. (*Thai*): *o.s. Baas Terwiel*

The beauty of the bride can be seen at the cradle. (*Armenian*): *Geyvandov 82*

By looking at the monkey's face, one cannot tell what kind of milk she will give.
(*Spanish, Argentina*): *Moya 650*

Beautiful woman brings diseases. (*Bassar, Togo*): *Szwark 59*

Not all little seats are good to occupy. [refers to the risk of venereal diseases]
(*Mandinka, West Africa*): *Meyer 128*

Oh you who are whitened outwardly, how do you fare inwardly?
(*Arabic, Morocco*): *Westermarck 85*

No one is warmed by the beauty of snow. (*Ossetian, RF/Georgia*): *Geyvandov 218*

Not only is she fair but she also has a boy-child. (*Bengali, India*): *o.s. Shobha Gupta*

Pity the man who marries a beautiful woman; until she grows old the fear will not leave him.
(*Spanish, Colombia*): *Ramírez S. 38*

He who has a beautiful wife, has death; he who has an ugly wife, has life.
(*Sranan, Surinam*): *o.s. Mavis Noordwijk*

He who marries an ugly woman is not afraid of another man. (*Portuguese, Brazil*): *Mota 179*

Who has a fair wife, needs more than two eyes. (*English, UK*): *Bohn 1855: 7*

You need a thousand eyes to watch her. (*Tamil, India*): *Geyvandov 68*

A true wife is her husband's flower of beauty. (*English, USA*): *Mieder 1992: 653*

One's chattels are one's own, but a beautiful wife is common property.
(*Khionghta, Bangladesh*): *Lewin 16*

Three things which a man ought not to boast of—the size of his purse, the beauty of his
wife, the sweetness of his beer. (*Irish*): *O'Rahilly 77*

With a white horse and a beautiful wife, a man is always in trouble.
(*Danish; Italian*): *Bohn 1857: 376; Haller 514; Cibotto 1976: 11*

A white mare washing; a pretty wife watching. (*Latvian*): *Mieder 1986: 311*

A man's peace is an ugly wife and a castrated horse. (*Portuguese, Brazil*): *Mota 214*

If your wife is chaste, why should you watch her? If she is not, you will watch her in vain.
(*Hebrew, Israel*): *Alcalay 528*

FATAL ALLUREMENTS

A beautiful woman is an axe that cuts off life. (*Japanese*): *Buchanan 264*

Beauty is much desired, even if it lies at the bottom of the abyss. (*Arabic, Maghreb*): *Stahl 227*

Her face shines like the moon, but her soul is the poison of a snake.

   (*Tamil, India*): *Geyvandov 198*

A beautiful wife is an enemy. (*Sanskrit, India*): *Jha 214*

Beautiful women are dangerous. You cannot keep them long. (*Spanish, Mexico*): *Glazer 201*

A hair of a girl's head draws harder than ten oxen.

   (*Yiddish; and all over the world*): *Landmann 191*

One hair on a pretty woman's head is enough to tether a big elephant. (*Japanese*): *Wintle 86*

Beautiful woman, beautiful trouble. (*English, Jamaica*): *Ibekwe 11; Champion 634*

Marry beauty, marry trouble. (*Krio/Mende, Sierra Leone*): *o.s. Eldred Jones*

If you marry a beautiful woman, you marry trouble. (*Kru/Jaba, Liberia*): *Ibekwe 122*

Marry a beautiful woman, marry trouble. (*Jaba, Nigeria*): *Geyvandov 123*

If you marry a beautiful woman, you marry trouble. (*Hebrew, Israel; English, USA*): *Kin 157*

Beauty does not lure people in to a trap; they enter it themselves. (*Chinese*): *Geyvandov 40*

2

Phases of Life

GIRLS, DAUGHTERS, BRIDES

Every girl has her own luck. (Uzbek)

Children are the greatest treasure on earth, says a Japanese proverb, and I never found a proverb contradicting this firm belief. Everywhere it is stated that children are the support of their parents and ornaments to the house. However, as the Tibetans say, 'If you say there is a difference, there is a difference, as there is a difference between a son and a daughter.' In many proverbs the difference between the sexes is not only stressed, but it takes on amazing dimensions. In most cultures, as soon as they are born, children of the two sexes are placed in opposed categories, as if they had nothing else in common than their having come into the world in the same way.

Both sexes are equally needed for humanity to flourish and prosper, but most societies favour one sex over the other, and the birth of a boy and that of a girl are far from being greeted with the same enthusiasm. This can be seen in the ways people have organized their social groups and the access to resources: mainly only one sex decides where the couple is going to have residence after marriage and that only one sex inherits, either the male or the female, but most societies traditionally favour the male sex.[58]

A BOY OR A GIRL?

Who leaves a son behind is not really dead. (Danish)

In most societies girls are married off and end up in another household or village, where they will spend the greater part of their lives among 'strangers', i.e. their in-laws.

Therefore, young girls are reminded that they are just in 'transit' in their own home, as in the following Chinese proverb: 'The parents' home is owned country for boys and a restaurant for girls', or in Korean: 'The girl who gets married is no relative anymore.' Daughters are doomed to depart, and in many cases her children will belong to her husband's clan.[59] When a girl marries into the family of her husband, she is usually not considered to belong to that family either: 'A woman is nobody's relative,' says a Mongo proverb. It all depends on the cultural system, of course. Proverbs look at the matter mainly from the perspective of extended family interests. The fact that, in so many cultures, a girl had (or still has) to move and live under the supervision of her husband and his family must have (had) an impact on her identity. The contradictory loyalties she has to develop in such a situation towards her own family and her husband's make her uncertain and vulnerable. Such a permanent feeling of alienation in girls only becomes manageable by unconditionally adopting the ruling principles and internalizing the resulting messages.

Around the world numerous proverbs express that giving birth to girls is less appreciated than giving birth to boys. Proverbs from China, for example, are uncompromisingly clear about this preference:

Eighteen goddess-like daughters are not equal to one son with a hump.
Ten fine girls are not equal to one cripple boy.
One lame son is more valuable than eighteen golden daughters.
A stupid son is better than a crafty daughter.
It is a blessing to bear a son, a calamity to bear a daughter.
A girl is worth one-tenth of a boy.

However, posterity being considered important, daughters may be welcomed if there is no other choice. Metaphorically this situation is expressed in the following proverbs, also from China: 'In a pond without fish, shrimps are highly prized', meaning that in a home without sons, daughters are spoken of favourably. Or: 'If you cannot get any mercury, red earth becomes valuable.' In other words, girls are better than nothing.

A preference for boy children over girls can be found in other cultures in Asia as well: 'A son counts as one; ten daughters do not count at all' (*Vietnamese*). A Telegu proverb from India sees the birth of girls as a punishment for bad behaviour: 'Those who spread lies will give birth to daughters.'[60] A Jewish proverb associates the arrival of a daughter with other disagreeable experiences, even if male children 'neutralize' the birth of a female child: 'Three things a man prefers not to have: weeds in his garden, a girl among his sons and vinegar in his wine,' while an Arabic proverb states that 'Every daughter is a handful of trouble.' Other Arabic examples:

When a daughter is born, the threshold weeps for forty days. (*Widespread*)
A girl is always a source of trouble, even when she is a queen on a throne.

In Africa the same preference is expressed: 'To bear a girl is to bear a problem' is a Tigrinya example from Eritrea. Nevertheless, proverbs from Africa also refer to the various advantages of daughters, their work in the household, their loyalty to their family and their ability to procreate[61]:

A woman without a daughter should bury herself alive. (*Ladino*)

No one knows when the man without daughters dies. [It is the daughters who wail, expressing grief when a father dies.] (*Arabic*)

A clan with female posterity cannot perish. (*Woyo/Kongo*)

In African cultures south of the Sahara, the profitable bride-wealth a future husband has to pay for the girl of his choice to her family makes people appreciate having both sons and daughters: bride-wealth offered to the family for the daughter provides for the son's future bride.

In Europe, too, there are plenty of proverbs containing depreciative comments on the birth of daughters (as against sons):

A whole night of labour, and then only a daughter. (*Spanish*)

Many sons, many blessings of God; many daughters, many calamities. (*German*)

When a girl is born, even the roofs cry. (*Bulgarian*)

When a wife gives birth to a boy even the walls of the house rejoice. (*Armenian*)

Better nine sons than one daughter. (*Estonian*)

Woe the mother who has only a daughter [and no son]. (*Serbian/Croatian*)

Many proverbs do not only express a preference for boy children; they also forward reasons why boys are considered preferable. The main idea behind the negative statements is indeed based on the traditional organization of society. In a majority of cultures a daughter who marries is destined to leave the family. Her commitment and her children are then considered to be economically 'lost' to her own family, as she will belong to her husband's family. In contrast, a son keeps the family name alive. This can even mean that a daughter-in-law may be considered more important than one's own daughter. The list of proverbs on this issue is endless: a daughter is presented as another man's child (*Korean and Vietnamese*); she has wings (*Ladino*); she is a lost child (*Bengali*); spilt water (*Chinese*), cigarette's ashes (*Arabic*) or she becomes a fig tree, because the one who plants does not get the profit (*Ganda*), as fig trees take a long time before they bear fruit. The above considerations explain how little a girl's family seems to have expected from her after marriage. Her fate is to 'face out' as a Chinese proverb puts it, whereas boys are 'facing in', meaning that a boy will remain in the house he's born in, while a girl will have to leave.[62]

Next to numerous explicitly negative proverbs about the birth of daughters, some mitigating circumstances are produced. The acceptance of a daughter is made easier by the hope for a son in the future, politely expressed to parents when the news of a little girl's birth is received. The mother is greeted by encouraging statements such as: 'First a girl, then a boy' (*Japanese*), in other words, keep hoping for better! Such words meant to cheer up the baby girl's parents also stress that the girl will soon be able to help her mother in the house, and to take care of the ones to be born next. In a Korean proverb, this practical advantage is expressed very clearly: 'A first daughter is worth a capital in the household' and a Vietnamese proverb agrees: 'The eldest daughter is a babysitter for her younger siblings.' Thus, the patterns for gendered division of labour are impeccably passed on to the next generation at birth.

Such ambiguous wishes exist in other cultures as well: 'Blessed the house where the daughter arrives before the son' is a consolation uttered after the birth of a girl in the Jewish tradition. A similar saying exists in the Muslim tradition: 'He whose first child is one with a vulva was gladdened by God.' An Arabic reference to the Prophet Mohammed argues for resignation and modesty: 'The ideal of the Prophet is having a daughter and a son.' This means that humans should accept what Allah has in stock for them, although it no less reflect that girls are not valued as highly as boys, when it is quoted to the mother who has just given birth to a daughter. If she had given birth to a boy, the enthusiasm would have been much warmer.

The issue is also discussed in a proverb from the United States: 'First a daughter then a son and the family's well begun.' Or, as the Ganda say comfortingly: 'She who brings forth a daughter, also gets a son', meaning that a son-in-law will join the family, when she marries. Another form of consolation is: 'Rather than begetting a bad son, better to beget a good daughter and depend on a son-in-law.' This Oromo proverb is quoted in situations where a less important thing becomes the more important thing: the daughter's importance will depend on the man who will marry her. This female dependence on the added value of having found a husband is also expressed in Bengali: 'One good daughter is worth ten sons if she can find a good bridegroom.'

Often, a woman's prestige is presented as depending on her giving birth to male children. Some African proverbs reflect the lower position of mothers without sons, as in this Rwanda example: 'A mother of only daughters does not laugh before the others laugh.' The Oromo in Ethiopia and Kenya also refer to a woman who gives birth to a daughter: 'The mother of a girl child does not laugh at the things of girls.' If the norm in a society is to look down on girls, mothers of sons may feel inclined to join in the negative chorus, but how could mothers of daughters do this?

For all those who give birth to daughters while hoping for sons, the main question is of course: what will happen next time? In proverbs, optimism prevails, even after four girls, at least according to an old Chinese argument: 'Four girls make up the four feet of a bed: a steady basis for a boy who is the fifth'—to be born in that comfortable bed! In Rwanda a father keeps up his courage as follows: 'None is abused for having a daughter as long as he still can bring forth.' To have a one and only daughter after a number of boys, however, usually makes parents happy. She is carefully referred to in the singular:

> Who only has one daughter, will make her a wonder. (*Spanish*)
> A family without a daughter is like an oven without heat. (*Korean*)

The more daughters, however, the more their burdening effect is emphasized, especially in families without a single son. I found only one proverb complaining about sons as a financial problem: 'Who has daughters, has bread, who has sons, goes begging.' In this Catalan proverb daughters are praised for their working capacity in the family business, especially in farming. The profit brought to the house by hardworking daughters is also expressed in a North American proverb: 'Farmer's luck: bull calves and girl babies.' In such a case, the marriage and departure of a girl are the more regrettable, because, as a South African Zulu proverb observes: 'Marriage decreases their support', to the girls' own relatives that means. This is not much of an issue in proverbs from Muslim communities, where

traditionally (at least in the middle and higher classes) women were preferably not working outside the house.

BRIDE-WEALTH AND DOWRY

The candle of a father of daughters burns all night. (*Ladino*)

Both bride-wealth and dowry are connected with marriage, and both are part of the social
and economic system of property exchange. Bride-wealth (or bride-price) is an official
payment (in money or cattle or in the form of other gifts such as metal objects), made by
the groom's family to that of the bride, and is meant to establish their marriage relations
in an official way. However, this wealth does not go to the bride herself.[63] In this exchange,
the groom's family offers bride-wealth goods to the family of the bride and is offered certain rights regarding the bride by her family. The role of this deal is to make sure that the
children of the marriage will be affiliated to the father's kin, and to prevent the family of
the bride from having too much control over the bride, so that there is less risk of divorce,
and more compensation in case of adultery.

In contrast, a dowry goes with the bride to the groom's family.[64] This explains the
worrying father of daughters' sleepless nights in the Ladino motto to this section. The
raising of dowry means that the family members—that is the father or brothers—have to
make sacrifices in order to secure a decent marriage for the daughters of the family. Thus,
daughters are a costly business and this is one of the reasons why the birth of more than
one daughter in a family is presented as a tragic and worrisome event in cultures with a
dowry system:

> Better two scorpions [in the house] than two daughters.
> (*Arabic, Maghreb / Western Sahara*)
> One girl is a girl, two girls are half a girl and three girls are no girl at all. (*English, USA*)
> One daughter, a good girl; two daughters, enough girls; three daughters, too many girls,
>   four daughters and a wife, five devils against one father.
> (*Catalan; also Spanish, Argentina*)[65]
> The world cannot exist without males and females, yet happy the father of sons and un-
>   happy the father who has only daughters. (*Hebrew*)

Especially for families with many daughters it requires much effort to marry girls off in an
acceptable way without completely ruining the family. Some of the girls, especially the
less attractive ones, may end up with a husband they don't like. An Arabic proverb
stresses this very strongly, using the metaphor of the dog, an animal considered unclean:
'A father of lots of girls runs the risk of getting a dog for a son-in-law.' Preferring sons to
daughters results from the financial consequences such a system involves. The family's
worries are apparently so insuperable that the untimely death of a daughter is even presented as a welcome relief, expressed in an Arabic proverb from Lebanon: 'The death of a
girl is fortunate though she may be ready to get married.' The dowry is clearly a huge
problem for a poor family. In some cultures parents try for cross-cousin marriage arrangements, so that the property does not get lost to 'foreigners':

> The daughter of a maternal uncle is not obtained for money. (*Arabic, Tunisia*)
> Cousin, let us get married and keep the dowry in the family. (*English, Jamaica*)
> Marry your cousin—if trouble comes it will not involve another family. (*Maori*)

Cousin marriages have other advantages too: a man knows what sort of woman his cousin is. On the other hand, Arabic proverbs from the Maghreb stress that such an arrangement can also provoke family quarrels.

What the girls think themselves is hardly ever brought to the fore in proverbs. Others decide what will make them happy: 'You can marry whoever you like, as long as it is cousin Manuel', a Portuguese proverb from Brazil jokingly observes. 'A girl with a nice disposition is always happy, and so is a girl with potential husbands through relationship agreements', in the words of an Afar proverb recommending cross-cousin marriages.

Bride-wealth exists mainly in Africa, and dowry mainly in Europe and Asia, although the dowry has been introduced in Africa in places where Islamic or Christian influence has been established. The bride-wealth received for giving the daughters in marriage enables her brothers to take a wife. Summarizing the two systems in a somewhat simplistic way, one could say that in the case of bride-wealth the girl is paid for, and in the case of dowry, the girl is paid off.[66] Depending on the society, then, the exchange of a girl brings money or costs money.

Only a few proverbs refer to mother-centred societies where girls have the advantage of staying in their own family after marriage. A Twi proverb from Ghana explicitly states that 'The child resembles the father but belongs to the clan [of the mother].' Examples of the father being belittled as 'a little dust on a tree trunk', as it happens in a Minangkabau proverb, are however extremely rare in proverbs.

The financially disastrous effects of the dowry system are strongly reflected in numerous precarious proverbs on daughters from the Arab world, Europe, Asia, and Latin America:

> A house of girls is a house of ruin. (*Arabic*)
> Daughters in the cradle, dowry in the chest. (*Russian*)
> A lot of girls and a large garden ruin the best farm. (*German*)
> A family of elegant daughters is the worst thief of all. (*Chinese*)
> Even a king begetting more than five [daughters] becomes a pauper. (*Tamil*)
> To have three daughters is to run through one's fortune. (*Japanese*)
> He who marries off his daughter, will stay behind broke. (*Portuguese, Brazil*)
> The poor do not marry off their daughters. (*Spanish, Venezuela*)

Great is the despair echoing in many such proverbs: the birth of just one daughter is like 'seven thieves in your safe' (*Polish*), more than one daughter means poverty (*Romanian*); and a house full of them is 'a cellar full of sour beer' which makes you poor (*Dutch*); their dresses 'devour the harvest' (*Catalan*), and so forth. According to a Korean proverb, 'He who has three daughters may sleep with his door open': the father need not be afraid of thieves in the night because their marriages cost so much that there is nothing of value left in the house. Finally, an Indian Bhojpuri example argues that, like digging a well, a girl's marriage is equally necessary and expensive.

The worst and most feared scenario is the one in which a married daughter is sent back to her parents by her husband. Not much can be done to prevent this from happening, except perhaps generous marriage gifts: 'Because of the presents, the bride is not sent back' (*Bulgarian*); 'A money-bag makes the marriage of the ugly one possible' (*Swedish*). Although money helps, there is no guarantee. Even after a number of years, a daughter can turn up again, to her father's deep despair: 'I married my daughter off in order that I might relieve myself of worry, but there she comes back to me with four little ones behind her' (*Arabic, Lebanon*). Worries about his daughters mark the father: 'He who has a daughter will age quickly' (*Turkish*). Therefore a Spanish proverb advises 'When a good offer comes for your daughter, don't wait until her father returns from the market.' Female beauty smoothens the negotiations. If a suitor appreciates the girl's appearance, it may occur that the father gets rid of her with a modest dowry or even without: 'If you like beauty, you should not discuss the amount of the dowry' (*Arabic, Tunisia*). This is also a rather general idea in Europe:

> The beauty of the girl is half the dowry. (*Russian*)
> Fair maidens need no purses. (*German*)
> Born handsome is born married. (*Italian*)
> Beauty wears the dowry in the face. (*English, UK*)

The ugly one needs extra money, but, ugly or beautiful, marrying too rich a bride is dangerous. In cases where the bride brings along important property, the nature of the marriage relationship will change, as a wealthy bride will have more say in the relationship: 'A great dowry is a bed full of brambles', goes an English warning. A Belorussian admonition holds the other way round, when the proposed groom is rich but unsympathetic: 'Don't pay attention to the silver, if life is not nice.' In Hebrew the warning is expressed both ways: 'A marriage for money is made by the Devil.' As for the girl, she is supposed to be the passive object exchanged between men of two families: 'Unmarried, a woman obeys her father; married, her husband', as the Chinese say, or, in Korean: 'Girls and water go wherever they are sent.'

VIRGINITY AND VIRTUE

Comb your daughter's hair until she is twelve, safeguard her until she is sixteen, after sixteen say thank you to whomsoever will wed her. (Czech)

A Hebrew poetic definition of a virgin is: 'A rose that still has to unfold its petals.' In many cultures, a girl was (and often still is) considered nubile early, at the age of about fifteen or sometimes as early as ten: 'As soon as she can bring a pot to her mouth, she can carry what her mother carries' (*Arabic, Maghreb*). A comment adds that desert girls are precocious. Among the Tamil, where a girl used to be old enough to get married even under the age of ten, usually with a much older man, a proverb refers to the phenomenon of child brides: 'When the bride starts growing up, the husband dies.' From Ancient Mesopotamia, there are references to very early girl child marriages, in which a girl child before puberty is compared to 'bread that has not had time to mature.'[67] In Russia the difference in age is commented upon somewhat ironically: 'The bride has been born, the groom mounts a horse.' A Portuguese proverb from Brazil stresses the difference between physical maturity and psychical immaturity: 'A young girl is like a pineapple: on top she is green, but below she is capable.'

Proverbs insist on the importance of a girl's being 'intact' until marriage. The fear that a girl might lose her virginity before marriage is omnipresent, because 'The herbalist has no herbs for lost innocence,' as a Sorbian proverb puts it. Lost innocence would spoil her good name and diminish her chances for finding a decent husband: 'A girl's chastity is her dowry', says a Tamil proverb from India, but, more important, her having lost this precious treasure would stain the honour of the whole family, and especially the father's respectability.

From a father's perspective, a Berber proverb from Morocco states that girls are a humiliation anyway. A Portuguese Brazilian proverb puts the disaster thus: 'A disgraced maiden dishonours her whole family.' Decent daughters of good families ought to stay inside the house. Anxious fathers worry about their daughter's honour as their own good name depends on her being intact:

> If your daughter is out in the streets, check your honour to see if it is still there.
>   (*Arabic, Tunisia*)
> The flower is picked, the stalk is trampled. [The stalk refers to her parents] (*Malay*)
> Money, like girls, should not sleep in the yard. (*Creole, Haiti*)
> A daughter is a treasure and a cause of sleepless nights. (*Ladino*)

Fathers have a dilemma: to marry their daughters off either too early or not at all. If the first suitor is mediocre, how to be sure that another one will come? There are two risks here: one is that the girl loses her chastity (or, even worse, becomes pregnant), and therewith her 'value'; the other is that she will stay virgin forever, a spinster who is looked down upon, even ridiculed. This is likely to happen if the father declines all offers either because he continues to hope for a better candidate, or because he loves his daughter so much that he demands the impossible: 'He who does not want to give his daughter in marriage, raises her price' (*Arabic, Lebanon*). In various parts of the world, but especially in Europe, many proverbs warn against this dangerous scenario:

> Only three things warrant haste: the marriage of a daughter, the burial of the dead, and the feeding of a guest. (*Persian*)
> The deceased and the daughter should leave the house quickly. (*Dutch*)
> Daughters and dead fish are no keeping wares. (*English, UK*)
> Girls and eggs cannot be kept for a long time. (*German/Letzeburgish*)
> Girls are like horses, if you don't give them away when they are young, they lose their luck. (*Italian*)
> Sweet pears and young women can't last long. (*Frisian*)

Men can always find a wife, even when they are older, but for girls it is soon 'too late': 'Marry your son when you will, your daughter when you can' is a popular proverb in Europe, both Americas, the Caribbean, and the Arab world. Daughters—just like eggs or cucumbers, or fruits, or even the dead—are not 'keeping wares', and their parents must remove them from the house in due time: 'Apples at Easter and girls of thirty have lost their flavour' (*French/German/Letzeburgish*). A girl's getting married is so crucial that a Hebrew proverb recommends: 'If your daughter is getting on in years, free your slave and let them get married.' A Tamil proverb presses parents into a similar direction: 'A girl older than ten has to get married, if need be, to a pariah.'

The longer the marriage is postponed, the greater the danger of her being exposed to temptations. The girl's chastity is as sacrosanct as it is vulnerable. In a wide variety of cultures metaphors such as glass and crystal are used to express the fragility of virginity.

> Girls and glasses are always in danger. (*German*)
> A girl is thin glass. (*Ossetian, RF*)
> Daughters are brittle ware. (*English, USA*)
> A girl is like crystal: if shattered, it cannot be restored. (*Armenian*)
> The bottle [is good] with its sealingwax, the girl with her hymen. (*Arabic, Maghreb*)
> Glass and maidens are easily broken. (*Korean*)

The last proverb is followed by this comment: 'The old etiquette kept the sexes apart to protect girls in order to retain their rosebud freshness until marriage.' How to prevent this freshness from being spoilt? The dangers are uncountable. How to be sure that she stays untouched? 'Hair and virgins, many are fake', the Spanish proverb goes, and it is suggested that a girl's virginity is even more unlikely when she is attractive:

> A virginal womb and a warm sun at Christmas are rarities. (*Danish*)
> A girl's honesty is like snow; when it melts the whiteness is no longer seen.(*Romanian*)
> How rare a thing it is to match virginity with beauty. (*Hebrew*)
> Chaste is [only] she whom no one has asked. (*English, USA/Dutch*)

Proverbs insist that girls must fight against the continuous temptation of losing their virginity. If people say about a girl that she is 'No longer clean' (*Indonesian*), it means that she 'has lost it', and she is despised for that. Proverbs in many languages repeat that a girl should keep herself 'intact'; it is her responsibility, and she is the one to blame if she fails. Risks surround her, even though, as a Dutch proverb observes, 'A young virgin does not want to be injured by fire.' She is in danger even inside the house, goes the Punjabi warning: 'A virgin girl in her parents' house is like a lump of dough; if kept outside crows peck at it, if kept inside rats nibble at it.' There is a variety of advice to prevent such 'pecking' and 'nibbling' and to encourage her to behave decently and modestly. Proverbs do not seem to make much of a problem about the loss of virginity for boys, though. The fact that it needs two people to make love is hardly taken into account in the context of virginity and virtue, and there is no emphasis on shared responsibilities.

> An embrace breaks a bracelet. (*Pashto*)
> A girl worth kissing is not easily kissed. (*English, USA*)
> Take the road that keeps innocence [virginity] intact. (*Nepalese*)
> A girl gets pregnant only once. (*Rwanda*)
> Stay in your nest, until he comes, the one who will make you fly away.
> (*Arabic, Maghreb*)

Proverbs considering virginity unimportant are almost nonexistent. Here is one rare exception: 'If you really are in love, you don't need care if she's a virgin or not' (*Creole, Haiti*). Most proverbs, however, consider it a scandal if a girl 'misbehaves' before marriage, especially when a pregnancy results from such 'unchasteness.'

The disapproval is general. An Estonian proverb contemptuously describes the horror: 'The affair is finished, the slut is in the corner, the child sits on the lap, milk is in the nipples.' In Christian Europe no less than in Islamic cultures such girls used to be called 'sinners': 'One who has secretly sinned will give birth in public' (*Dargin/Tatar*). The extent of the scandal is stressed in all cultures, telling girls that one moment of thoughtlessness has far-reaching consequences:

> Whoever puts out a net in the water, wants to catch fish. (*Creole, Martinique*)
> Five minutes of pleasure, nine months of torment. (*Portuguese, Brazil*)
> We praised the bride, and she was found pregnant. (*Arabic, Tunisia*)
> The impatient virgin becomes a mother without being a bride. (*English, USA*)
> The girl who is praised for dancing will be gossiped about when pregnant out of
>   marriage. (*Oromo*)

In a Nama proverb from Namibia, a girl who has allowed herself to become pregnant has forfeited the chance of ever finding an excellent candidate: 'A pregnant girl is not married for the first kitchen'—she will never become a chief's first wife. The warnings are numerous and widespread:

> She never used to go to the washing place [a place known to be dangerous for girls]—
>   and yet. (*Mapuche, Argentina/Chile*)
> Once there was a time ... now only pregnancy is left. (*Russian*)
> It is too late to scratch your backside after the child has been made. (*Danish*)
> Frequent kisses end in a baby. (*Hungarian*)
> Better a bad dowry than a bad gift [i.e. illegitimate pregnancy]. (*Fulfulde*)

The spiteful rumours of the community cannot be avoided, in spite of a wide coat and a man who accepts to marry the pregnant girl:

> A beautiful dress cannot conceal the shame. (*Serbian*)
> The coat of the girl makes the neighbours gossip. (*Catalan/French*)

Such comments mainly address the girl. In only one proverb a man's annoyance with an unintended pregnancy is mentioned: 'The man who made a virgin pregnant hates each new moon' (*Oromo*). Without safe birth control, strictly disciplined behaviour is needed to prevent a pregnancy before the wedding day, and serious agreements have to be made beforehand: 'Without earrings no kisses' (*Catalan/French*). Like rings, earrings are an engagement present, even though fiancés do not always keep their promises, as girls are reminded in an Arabic proverb: 'You promised me earrings and I pierced my ears; you did not give me earrings and made me suffer for nothing.' An official wedding ceremony has to solemnize the union, or in the words of a Dutch proverb: 'To marry in the hay is wonderful, but in church it is true forever.'

The choice of a partner looks like a lottery: 'Marriage and hanging are determined by destiny.' (*English, UK*). Marriages are made in heaven, it is suggested in Judeo-Christian cultures. God, destiny or higher powers are believed to bring two people together, as an Indonesian proverb metaphorically observes: 'Fishes in the sea, *asam* tree on the mountain, they meet each other in the stew pot.' Parents can only wait and see what destiny has in stock for their daughters: 'As for marriage, I have married you off; but as for luck, where could I get it for you?'(*Arabic*).

SPINSTERS

Better a spinster than being with a husband you don't love. (*Russian*)

Those who do not conform to the social expectation become the object of gossip and derision. Women who live alone—spinsters, widows, prostitutes—are 'deviant' and therefore suspect. Spinsters are despised as left on the shelf. Their fate is sketched in a Ghanaian Adangme proverb: 'If she cannot be married, she will be a fig tree.' This means that everybody will try to profit from her 'available' body, just like people pick figs from a 'free' tree at the gate or along the roadside. An unmarried girl, it is emphasized, risks to miss the train or the boat, and a spinster is associated with 'a moonless night' (*Bengali*); 'a sack of rice on which duty has not yet been paid' (*Chinese*); 'a palm tree without dates' (*Arabic*); 'a horse without reins' (*Turkish*), and so forth. Nothing can be done but accepting; society tolerates no alternative, as a Ladino example stresses: 'Were it not because of mockery and shame, no single [woman] would have come under the canopy', in which the canopy refers to the Jewish wedding ceremony. In Hebrew a spinster is compared to wasteland, and in Hungarian she becomes 'an undelivered letter.' The land has to be tilled and the letter to be delivered, because 'The spinster is difficult to govern.' (*Spanish, Argentina*). According to a Bulgarian proverb, 'Spinsterhood is far worse than a life in bad wedlock', and girls usually submit to the pressure: 'We married in order not to be called spinster, we gave birth to sons in order not to be called sterile.' (*Ladino Morocco*)

Old unmarried girls, however, did not conform to the norm of marriage as a must. In most societies, living alone as a woman meant (and often still means) that something must be wrong with you as a woman: with your appearance, behaviour, health or whatever. Otherwise, some man would have been interested in 'taking' you for a wife. An Arabic proverb compares the spinster to an object dropped on the road, ignored if she has no luck, and found if she has: 'Everything that falls is picked up by someone, and even spinsters may sometimes get lucky.'

In all of the above examples, it is obvious, who is the subject and who the object, who is choosing and who is to be chosen, rejecting or being rejected, picking up or being ignored. The old girl is presented as the one who has to wait and see whether she will be leftover forever or not. It is argued that not all hope is lost for older single women:

> Happiness looks at an old spinster. (*Digor*)
> An old spinster will become a young wife. (*Hungarian*)

In spite of all the compelling promotion of marriage, a few proverbs argue that remaining a spinster does have certain advantages. First of all, if you have no husband, you cannot lose him either; second, love tends to disappear after the wedding; third, it is tough to slave for a husband who benefits from his wife's efforts without being interested in her as a person:

> Unmarried girls do not risk widowhood. (*Ladino*)
> The married chicken pecks, the unmarried chicken pecks. Better unmarried then: she'll peck for herself. (*Fulfulde*)
> Better a good spinster's life than badly married. (*Spanish, Mexico*)
> Better be an honest old spinster, than a bored husband's wife. (*Estonian*)

In the majority of messages, though, negativity prevails: spinsters are looked down upon and spoken about in disapproving terms. A Minyanka proverb illustrates the point to which the woman who never married is despised: 'Who has no work to do can dig the spinster's grave.'

WEDDING DAY

Girl, rejoice not over your wedding dress; there is much trouble behind it. (Arabic)

The wedding celebration is presented as the most important day in a girl's life. The irrevocableness makes it a day full of emotions, in the first place for the bride herself: 'At the wedding feast, the one to eat the least is the bride' (*Spanish, Puerto Rico*), but also for her mother: 'All brides are child brides in their mother's eyes' (*English, USA*). The bride's lack of appetite has to do with her being at the centre of everybody's attention. She suddenly becomes a public figure, an exceptional situation for girls, and very limited at that. It ends with the wedding day: 'The bride is respected for one day' (*Chinese*).

A Russian proverb states without reserve that 'Any bride is born for the sake of her groom.' It is a decisive day for the bride, because, in most cultures, on her wedding day a girl leaves her parents' house for good. In the words of an Indian proverb: 'A girl leaves her father's house in a bridal carriage and returns only in a coffin.' At the wedding all people comment on her appearance, or gossip behind her back:

> The bride is a frog, but the wedding a cyclone. [The bride is insignificant, but the wedding a great, ostentatious show] (*Arabic*)
> An ugly bride spends much money on the veil. (*Dutch*)
> Our bride is flawless, except for her blindness, her pimples and fits.
>   (*Persian; also: Hebrew/Ladino*)
> If the bride is ugly, what good is the beauty of her mother? (*Pashto*)
> The pearls the bride wears at her wedding, are the tears she will cry afterwards.
>   (*Spanish*)

Tears flowing from a bride's eyes are not believed to be a bad omen; on the contrary, from China to Russia or the United States, wedding tears foretell a happy marriage:

> Weeping bride, laughing wife; laughing bride, weeping wife. (*Russian*)
> The girl will have little fortune if she doesn't cry on her wedding ceremony. (*Chinese*)
> A sad bride makes a glad wife. (*English, USA*)

The weather on the wedding day also seems to predict the future, particularly in European proverbs. Sunshine is seen as a happy presage, but sometimes rain is also positive:

Happy the bride the sun shines on, and happy the corpse the rain rains on.
(*English, UK/USA*)
Rain during the wedding is a good omen. (*Russian*)
If rain falls on the lap of the bride, she will soon be pregnant. (*Dutch*)
If bride and groom get wet feet, they will be three within a year. (*French*)

How reliable is the groom, even on the wedding day? 'Only one woman needs to dress up and the girl loses her bridegroom' (*Vietnamese*). There are many other worries, especially if there is no man in the house: 'A daughter without a father, her marriage will be discussed outside the house' (*Oromo*). Such a girl is likely to be kidnapped, as custom allows in the culture concerned: people always take advantage of an unprotected person. Apparently, a girl has to be prepared to whatever happens to her before, during and after the wedding. 'Even during the process of getting dressed for her wedding, a bride does not always know who shall marry her', says an Arabic proverb. This means that, on her wedding day, in spite of official agreements between her own family and the bridegroom's family, a bride may run the risk of being kidnapped—though not always against her will.

'A cousin has the right to take the bride off the mare's back' is another Arabic example on this matter: he can kidnap her on the wedding day, and thus claim the right to marry her. The risk of being kidnapped is not limited, alas, to action taken by a relative; the bride can also be kidnapped by a complete outsider. To make her immune to such events, a Bengali proverb recommends that she be taught not to be easily hurt: 'Do not pamper your daughter; what would she do if abducted by a Turk?' This refers to such a wedding ceremony where a bridegroom's rival kidnaps the bride. The custom of bride snatching seems to exist or have existed in widely diverse cultures, from the Chilean Mapuche via Scotland to New Guinea.[68]

Another understandable worry is the bride's fear for the in-laws with whom she will have to live, as is the norm in many cultural traditions. In Arabic, sadder and wiser older wives temper a girl's innocent joy over her wedding day. They have seen the trouble behind the wedding dress and the wedding presents. In the words of a Japanese proverb: 'A caught fish is no longer fed.' Many proverbs forcefully express the shining prospect waiting for her: 'The husband's house is filled with seven barrels full of bile', as is said to the bride in Iran, before she follows the bridegroom to her in-laws' house.

In proverbs, marriages between young girls and old men are frequently mentioned and often recommended, whereas the reverse is advised against. The difference in age is expressed in all kinds of ways. In Greek as well as in other European languages it is recommended that: 'A young girl should be laid on an old man', and in a Dutch proverb the result promises numerous posterity: 'A young girl and an old lecher fill the cradle for years to come.' A large number of proverbs on the topic stress that old men do not stop being keenly and passionately interested in young girls: 'The eyes are young forever' (*Spanish, Argentina/Uruguay*).

Even though 'A young woman married to an old man must behave like an old woman'

(*English, USA*), several proverbs see not only disadvantages for girls in such a deal: 'A rich man is never old for a girl', as a French proverb puts it, and 'The youthfulness of an old man is in his wallet' is the way to express a girl's profit in Puerto Rico. On the other hand, the old man is not always at ease: how to satisfy the young lady, and how to be sure of her fidelity, in case she is unsatisfied?

> An old man marrying a young girl is like buying a book for someone else to read.
> (*English, USA*)
> An old man who marries a young woman buys a newspaper for others to read.
> (*Portuguese, Brazil*)
> An old man who marries a young girl should not leave the house. [He needs to control her behaviour] (*Spanish, Costa Rica*).
> An old man with a young woman, either a cuckold or the grave. (*Portuguese, Brazil*)
> An old man is a bed full of bones. (*English, UK*)
> Young women are the horses on which old men ride to hell. (*Dutch/Polish*)
> A young woman is an old man's coffin. (*Frisian*)

Although by far most of the proverbs recommending relations between young girls and old men come from South America, they also occur in other continents. A Jewish and Russian proverb observes rather cynically: 'When an old man takes a young wife, death laughs.'

All over the world, girls dream of husbands and love. The Rwanda proverb: 'Better "little wife" than "little girl"' suggests that a girl's fate is worse than a wife's, because motherhood will crown her with prestige. When the wedding dress has been laid aside, real life begins.

WEDLOCK

Husbands are the only resort for wives both in this life and in the hereafter. (*Sanskrit*)

Perfect marriage is romantically associated with blossoming flowers and full moon. Such idyllic views of enduring heavenly harmony hide the other side of the coin. Right from the wedding day men and women are mutually confined, as aptly expressed in the English word *wedlock*. This point is dealt with in proverbs in which the non-married are struggling with the heavy pressure towards getting married, while the married are struggling with the inexorable consequences of their having been 'caught': 'To marry is a disaster, not to marry is a disaster.' (*Lithuanian*). Proverbs try to balance the pros and cons with mixed feelings:

> The bachelor feels bored, and the husband feels shackled. (*Ladino*)
> Marriage is like a cage: the birds without despair to get in and those within despair to get out. (*Hebrew*)
> Marriage is not a journey: by marrying you have put your head through the hangman's rope. (*Creole, Martinique*)
> Wedlock is like a chicken run, one wants to get in, another wants to get out. (*Russian*)
> Marriage is like an eel-trap: those within want to get out; those without want to get in.
> (*Danish/German*)

Shackles, hangman's rope, chicken run, and eel-trap are only a few of the nightmarish metaphors used. Some proverbs express doubts or social pressure from a female perspective:

> The girl that thinks no man is good enough for her is right, but she is left. (*English, USA*)
> The hen would have been happy not to take part in the wedding, but they pulled her
>   there by her wings. (*Russian*)
> The cow does not want to marry, but she is taken along on a leash. (*Ukrainian*)

Although proverbs pressure all young people into marriage, for girls wedlock is often presented as their profession, their only acceptable career, whereas married young men go on with their 'real' profession after the wedding day. Or, in the words of a Khiongtha proverb from Bangladesh: 'Man's life is ambition; woman's life is man.'

Looking back from an older women's perspective proverbs remind girls that wedlock will not be the paradise they have dreamt of: 'Mother, what is marriage? To spin, give birth and then to cry', goes the dialogue between daughter and mother in Europe and the Americas, or in a Russian variant: 'to knead dough, weave, have children and cry.'

> Girls do not know the worries of wives. (*Minyanka*)
> If young girls only knew what old wives know, they would never marry.
>   (*English, Jamaica*)
> She cried for marriage and when married she cried again. (*Oromo*)
> Marriage is the supreme blunder that all women make. (*English, USA*)

Why opt so massively for wedlock in spite of the above warnings? 'A girl marries to please her parents', according to a Chinese proverb. In addition to the parents, society at large wants them to get married. For a decent woman, then, a husband is as indispensable as a centre-post for a house, and wedlock, the only 'career' for a girl advertised in proverbs.

> A woman is a wife only through her husband. (*Rundi*)
> A girl's marriage is a protection for her. (*Arabic, Lebanon*)
> A woman's delight is her husband. (*Sinhalese, Sri Lanka*)

Even a fake husband will do: 'It is better to get a bridegroom made of wood than to remain single' (*Arabic, Lebanon*). Becoming somebody's wife, then, means being (economically and socially) protected as well as being controlled by a husband. Such dependence does not mean that the husband has all the advantages. Men are constantly reminded of their serious material responsibilities and heavy duties in marriage *vis-à-vis* their wife to be. This is not only a matter of paying a bride price. Many proverbs insist that men are obliged to support their wife or wives materially, an issue referred to not only in literal terms, but also in metaphors:

> He who has money can marry the sultan's daughter. (*Arabic*)
> Your duty to your wife does not end with [paying her] a cloth. (*Baule*)
> Lay good food and betel nuts before the guests; lay presents before a woman. (*Khionghta*)
> To feed a cow you need a store of grass. (*Tibetan*)
> Prepare a nest for a hen and she will lay eggs for you. (*Portuguese*)

Look for a house, before you look for a wife. (*Italian; French*)
It is cheaper to find a wife than to feed a wife. (*English, USA*)
Get a cage before you get a bird. [a house before you get married]
    (*Creole, Trinidad/Tobago*)

Apparently there is some space for negotiation on both sides. What to conclude? For various reasons, the position of girls, daughters, and brides in proverbs is related to defined roles. Daughters are often less appreciated than sons, especially in societies where dowry has to be paid and usually also in those cultures where the bride is obliged to leave her family to go and live with her husband and his kin. In the traditions of most cultures, the girl's future has been (and quite often still is) associated almost exclusively with marriage, while the boy's future is seen in a completely different light.

WIVES, CO-WIVES, WIDOWS

WIVES

A wife is like a blanket: cover yourself, it irritates you; cast it aside, you feel cold. (Ashanti)

'All those who were once virgins are married now', sighs a Russian proverb. Indeed, girls turn into wives. Most proverbs being presented from a male perspective, the main 'wife' issues dealt with vary from: how to find a good wife, to: how not to end up in the arms of a bad wife. When the wedding and the honeymoon are over, life seems to have some nasty disappointments in store for husbands (and no less for wives). Young girls' faults, perhaps overlooked at first, and still be given the benefit of the doubt for a while, because they were inexperienced and attractive, are looked upon differently as soon as men are married a bit longer. At least this is what is being suggested. Many proverbs complain about the radical change that takes place in girls once they have become wives. Often a rhetorical question is posed about this matter:

Girls are beautiful, sweet and tender; where do all those wicked wives come from?
    (*Russian*)
All are good girls, but where do the bad wives come from? (*English, USA*)
A girl's heart is put to the test by the wife's cloth. [All girls are perfect; where do the
    nasty wives come from?] (*Rwanda*)
When they marry they warp, and when their husbands die they are needy.
    (*Arabic, Maghreb*)
As long as she is with her mother, kind as a lamb; as soon as she has got a husband, she
    pulls out a long-drawn tongue. (*Serbian/Croatian*)

Such messages—there are many more of them—do they reflect that women are disappointed so soon after the wedding, and is that why they no longer look up to their men as they were taught to do? Are the young wives rebellious, or are they exploring the boundaries of their freedom? And what about the men: have they been so spoiled by their mothers, that any wife must be a disappointment? In proverbs, the main criticism is that wives work less and talk more than husbands appreciate. It is suggested that women turn 'bad' right after marriage, but what is good and what is bad? The most frequent terms associated with the 'bad' wife are 'evil', 'anger', and 'wickedness'. In contrast, words such as 'goodness', 'submissiveness', 'angelic nature', and 'heavenliness' are used to describe the ideal and idealized 'good' wife.

GOOD OR BAD?

Darkness covers everything except a bad wife. (Hebrew)

A wife is often presented as a decisive factor in marriage: she seems to be able to make it or to break it. A wife either has a good influence on her husband or she destroys his life; she either makes him young or she makes him old; she makes a man out of him or turns him into dust; she is either a treasure or a pestilence, and so forth. A Hebrew proverb refers to the strong impact of women: 'After they were divorced, the man married a bad woman and she made him bad; the woman married a bad man and she made him good.' The positive influence of the good wife is also stressed in a Persian proverb: 'A good wife makes a good husband.' It is as if a wife is a miraculous mirror that enchants her husband. The same idea is also expressed in Europe, and other parts of the world. In proverbs, the good wife is praised endlessly and the 'bad' wife blamed endlessly:

> There is no end to the goodness of a good wife nor to the wickedness of a bad one.
> (*Hebrew*)
> If you have a good wife, do not go to weddings; you have one everyday in your house. If
> you have a bad wife, do not go to funerals; you have one every day in your house.
> (*Armenian*)
> He that has a good wife has an angel at his side; he that has a bad wife has a devil at his
> elbow. (*English, USA*)
> There is nothing better for a man than a good wife, nothing worse than a bad one.
> (*Greek*)

Still, we have no definition of 'good' and 'bad'. One Romanian proverb states pessimistic-ally that a good husband is nonexistent: 'There is no such thing as a good husband or a sweet onion.' It is not easy to find out what an ideal husband is, because proverbs on the issue are rare. If we do not assume that men are quite naturally good husbands, their ab-sence means that women's perspectives on this matter are hardly represented:

> A good husband will not squeeze juice out of his wife. (*Komi*)
> A good dog does not kill the chickens; a good husband does not beat his wife. (*Chinese*)
> A good husband is better than a friend and a brother. (*Tajik*)
> One good husband is worth two good wives; for the scarcer things are the more they're
> valued. (*English, USA*)

The last proverb suggests that good husbands are rare, the other three examples above are mainly defined in negative terms: a good husband would not exploit his wife or beat her, whereas an Indian Telegu proverb observes that it is up to the wife to 'earn' a good hus-band by her own deeds: 'Good deeds bring good husband; charity brings good children.'

There are remarkably few proverbs about a husband's badness. The two examples I found are both from the Russian Federation: 'A bad man's wife is always stupid' (*Russian*) and: 'A bad man always suspects his wife of being unfaithful' (*Digor*). In proverbs where the 'badness' of both partners is discussed and compared, female wickedness is usually believed to be worse than male wickedness. And not only that, even a woman's 'goodness' is worse than a man's 'badness' in this line of thinking: 'Better a man's wickedness than a woman's virtue' (*Hebrew*).

It looks as if proverbs tend to protect a husband's reputation and to smear the wife's character. As for the bad husbands, it looks like an issue that did not really interest the inventors, audiences, and collectors of proverbs. Exceptionally, a Chinese proverb compares a bad husband to a 'luckless tomb' for his wife, and a Russian one states that: 'It is better to suffer cold than to live with a wicked husband.' A widespread Arabic proverb points jokingly to the profit to be gained by men from being a 'good' husband: 'Be good to your own wife and you can have your neighbour's.'

THE 'GOOD' WIFE

She is gracious and chaste, and moreover has a golden heart. (Arabic)

A good wife is absolutely crucial, the proverbs argue, but she is considered a rare species: 'The [ideal] wife is [like] the *mvuumbu* mushroom: one must be lucky to find her' (*Taka*). Her worth is expressed in poetic praises of all kinds. She is 'the pride of men' (*Uzbek*), more important to the home than kitchenware (*Japanese*) and the 'best piece of furniture' in the house (*Dutch/Frisian/German/Danish*); she is 'happiness' (*Hebrew*) or at least 'halfway happiness' (*Kirghiz*), more than 'heaven' (*Bulgarian*), or at least brings you 'halfway to heaven' (*Swedish*); a 'cornerstone' (*Uyghur*), the 'pillar of the house' (*Minangkabau, Indonesia*), or even better than 'a golden pillar' (*Czech*); the 'crown on her husband's head' (*Russian/Hebrew*); the 'crown of the home' (*Hungarian*), the 'honour of the home' (*Estonian*), the 'heart of the home' (*Gikuyu*); a 'great treasure' (*Icelandic*), a 'golden key' (*Latvian*), and so forth, and so on. In short: 'For a good wife there is no price' (*Czech*).

From the ensemble of qualities mentioned in a wide variety of cultures, the portrait of the ideal wife comes out clearly. She is chaste, constantly takes care of her husband and all his needs, is an excellent housekeeper, cleaner, and cook without ever moaning or grumbling; she is dedicated and full of zeal in all female domains; she attends to her man's health, his food, his clothes, his sex life, his children, his problems:

> You can tell the husband of a good wife by his clothes. (*Turkish/Bulgarian*)
> He that hath a good wife shows it in his dress. (*English, USA*)
> Glorify your husband; glorify him with a cassava root. [Love is expressed in good food and other good deeds] (*Taka*)
> A woman who does not take care of her husband, cannot be a good wife. (*Kru*)
> A good wife will reduce sorrows to half their size and increase fortune to double the amount. (*Georgian/Hebrew*)

The good wife prevents her husband from being embarrassed by anything that she would do or that he himself would do, or even other people would do. She is submissive, admires, adapts, and accepts her lower position *vis-à-vis* her husband. She does not draw public attention to her own person. She does not interfere with her husband's business or engage in any male role or activity whatsoever. She looks up to him and adapts to him:

> As water takes on the colour of the earth, so a wife takes on the manners of her husband. [She adapts to his influence] (*Oromo*)
> A girl is 'parwe'.[69] (*Yiddish/Dutch*)
> A corset is made to fit the size of the breasts. [A woman should know how to adapt] (*Creole, Guadeloupe*)

A good wife is a chaste wife; she keeps herself away from the public space; like the cat she stays at home; her name is Yes, and she never grumbles. She supports and protects her man, she sees but keeps silent, and she definitely does not talk about his weaknesses to anybody:

> A good wife guards her husband from bad ways. (*Chinese*)
> A good wife mends what the husband spoils. (*Spanish, Chile*)
> A wife is a cloth for her husband. [i.e. a good wife hides the failings of her husband from the public]. (*Oromo*)

A Russian ideal wife is described thus: 'Meek as a sacrificial lamb, busy as a bee, beautiful as a bird of paradise, faithful as a turtle-dove.' Some proverbs refer to motherhood as an essential aspect of the ideal wife's role. 'A wife should be like one's mother,' says a Swahili proverb from Tanzania; a Spanish example from Costa Rica almost literally repeats this message: 'A good wife is like a mother', whereas a Georgian proverb states that 'The wife that looks after your every need is your mother.' In fact, the mother seems to be irreplaceable in a man's life.

And, of course, 'A good wife is content with one man' (*Latin*). Considering the various observations on the matter, one wonders whether there are any suitable couples at all. It is regularly noted that a man's life would be much less complicated without women, and wives in particular, although, admittedly, life with a good wife is not a bad option: 'There's only one thing in the world better than a good wife ... no wife' (*English, UK/USA*).

Not without irony an English proverb says that 'There is but one good wife in the world and every man thinks he has her', but there is a reverse variant in Hebrew: 'There is only one bad wife in the world and every man thinks he has got her' and an equally cynical German variant: 'There have only been three good women: the first walked out the world, the second drowned in the Rhine, the third they are still looking for.' Rather gloomily a Chinese proverb concludes that: 'Good wives have bad husbands and good husbands have bad wives'—there is no justice in this world.

'WICKEDNESS'

Is one veil sufficient to cover a woman's wickedness? (Tamil, India)

Women are accused of all kinds of 'badness': morally wicked, offensive, naughty or bad behaviour. The meanings of 'bad' and 'wicked' merge. In proverbs a rich variety of options of what 'bad' or wicked women are, what they do, and what it means to live with a wicked wife is made available: she 'ruins the family' (*Chinese/English USA*); she is 'sixty years bad harvest in a row' (*Japanese*); she is 'leprosy to her husband' (*Hebrew*); she 'sells her husband' (*Khiongtha*). She is blamed for 'quarrelling endlessly' (*Nogay*), for 'scorching and choking' the poor man (*Hebrew*), for not forgiving him his 'drunken fit' (*Danish*). She behaves like 'an enemy in the house' (*Karachay-Balkar*), she grills him 'on the stove' (*Russian*), and she does not seem inclined to swallow her husband's advice (*English, UK; Somali*). She even frightens a man in his sleep (*Hebrew*). Proverbs consider a 'bad' or 'wicked' wife a disruptive element in marriage:

> A wicked wife is a daily fever. (*Italian*)
> A man who has a wicked wife grows old sadly. (*Oromo*)
> A bad wife is like a dreary, rainy day. (*Hebrew*)
> A desert is more desirable than a wicked wife. (*Yiddish*)

Wives *have* to be ruled, proverbs have no doubt about that. A sign of wickedness is non-submissive behaviour *vis-à-vis* a husband. Women do not seem to be automatically impressed by their husband's authority. A Chinese proverb compares an unruly wife to an unruly horse: 'It is difficult to rule a bad wife as it is a hard thing to climb a fierce horse.' Such proverbs reveal male apprehension of female power, even to the extent that sometimes womankind as a whole is assigned inherent negative forces:

> From a garment flutters a moth and from a woman her wickedness; better the
>   wickedness of a man than a woman's virtue. (*Hebrew*)
> Woman is more wicked than the Devil. (*Bulgarian*)

All complaints about female wickedness put men in the role of innocent and vulnerable victims who do not know how to face female adversity, let alone be in charge: 'The husband commands and the wife does what she likes', a Catalan proverb concludes pessimistically. Ultimately a wife may not even like to see her man at home. Two examples of ultimate male misery:

> A bad wife wishes her husband's heel turn homewards and not his toe. (*Danish*)
> A bad wife likes to see her husband's heels turned to the door. (*English, USA*)

The scenario can still be worse: 'May God protect you from rising hunger and a bad wife who wants a divorce', goes a Ladino prayer. Why keep such a bad creature in the house anyway? The answer is not difficult to imagine: she is needed to run the household, and to produce posterity, and, as long as the gains are greater than the losses, the married status quo is by far preferable:

> The thing [penis] that has paid the bride-wealth for a wicked one spends the night with
>   her. (*Rwanda*)
> One keeps a wicked woman because of the children. [Not all is bad in a given situation]
>   (*Minyanka*)

Reluctantly, proverbs admit that however 'wicked' a wife's behaviour, a man depends on her presence in so many respects:

Better a bad wife than an empty house. (*Baule*)
Better to have a bad wife than to sleep alone. (*Twi*)
It's bad with the bad [woman], but worse without the bad. (*Hungarian*)
Bad with your wife, but even worse without her. (*Russian*)
Women are like bees: in spite of their wickedness you'll always draw some honey.
    (*Bamum*)

In proverbs, then, the much referred to 'wickedness' of wives equates the husbands' fear of their wives' threatening the ideal marriage balance as the men see it. Of course, not only a husband profits from his wife, but also vice-versa. Despite (or due to?) this interdependence, only very few proverbs refer to friendship between spouses:

Wife is husband's best friend. (*Bulgarian*)
At home, the best friend is one's wife. (*Sanskrit*)
Your husband, cherish him as your best friend, but distrust him as your worst
    enemy.(*Ladino*)

CO-WIVES

A teapot can serve five teacups, but who has ever seen one teacup serving five teapots? (*Chinese*)

Polygamy can be traced in the histories of many peoples, but nowhere is it the exclusive form of marriage, as even in those cultures that permit it, the large majority of people practice monogamy. In the past polygyny, as the system in which a man is married to several women at the same time, has existed in widely different cultures and continents, in today's world the custom subsists on a less extensive scale, but it has by no means disappeared.

In China and Japan, concubinages were sometimes considered as lawful relationships, hardly to be distinguished from the position of officially married wives. In Japan concubinage was only abolished in 1880. In China Mao's puritan revolution started a tenacious struggle against concubinage and bigamy in 1949. Many African peoples have a strong tradition of polygamy. Among the ancient Egyptians polygamy was permitted but was unusual, whereas Babylonian marriages were mostly monogamous. Among the Israelites there was theoretically no limit to the number of wives a man could take, and there was no difference in their legal status, but monogamy became the norm. In Arabia, Mohammed ordained that, legally, a man could have no more than four wives.

Polygamy has also been permitted among many of the Indo-European peoples—Slavs and Teutons, for example, or ancient Irish, and Vedic Indians—although the practice was mostly confined to kings and noblemen. None of the Hindu law books seems to have restricted the number of wives a man can marry; yet there is a preference given to monogamy. In Greece, monogamy was the only recognized form of marriage, although concubinage existed as well. Roman marriage was also monogamous, in spite of married men's liaisons and mistresses. In Christian Europe, many kings continued to practice polygamy in those countries where it had been considered acceptable before the arrival of Christianity. Charlemagne, for example, had two wives and many concubines.[70]

Most proverbs about co-wives come from Africa and Asia, but some do exist in the Americas and Europe as well. There are also references to consecutive wives of the same husband, concubines, mistresses, and extramarital one-night stands. It is sometimes argued that an official marriage protects the rights of women better than unofficial relationships. In many ways proverbs comment upon the ins and outs of institutional polygamy, as the system under which a man is officially married to more than one woman at the same time.[71]

Polyandry—having more than one husband—is not considered an option for a woman by most societies. Reason: the husband's wish to be sure that he really fathers the children his wives give birth to, a reason reflected in proverbs by reminding women directly or metaphorically that their only option is to have one partner only:

> Two male hippopotamuses cannot live in one pool. (*Mandinka*)
> There can only be one tiger in each cave. (*Spanish, El Salvador*)
> Two male bears do not winter in one hole. (*Yakut*)
> She who is wife to one man cannot eat the rice of two men. (*Chinese/English, USA*)[72]

Pool, cave and hole refer to the womb, of course. The message that women should refrain from having two (let alone multiple) partners is stressed in metaphors explicitly referring to female as well as male anatomy. I have chosen three examples from different parts of the world to illustrate this. A metaphor from the Arab world is 'The needle does not hold two threads', in which the (eye of the) needle refers to the vagina, and the two threads to two competitive penises, whereas the Ovambo also use the container image of the kettle (again referring to the womb) and its contents: 'You don't cook two big bones in the same kettle.' The gender hierarchy for polygamy is made most visible in the Chinese metaphor of the actively pouring teapot and the passively receiving teacups in the motto quoted above.[73]

Throughout the world, polyandry is in fact extremely rare.[74] In some examples, children may recognize different men as having the status of true father; often such fathers are full brothers. In other cases, women bear legitimate children to several men in succession; or even a single legitimate husband allows other men sexual access to his wife. This last rare type includes wife lending, as a sign of hospitality. Generally proverbs refer extremely negatively to this practice:

> One should never lend either one's wife or one's razor. (*Maltese*)
> A knife and a wife are not to be lent. (*Spanish, Argentina*)
> A wife and a pen are not to be lent, because both will get spoiled. (*Venezuela*)
> A wife and a wristwatch should not be lent. (*Portuguese, Brazil*)
> He who lends his wife to dance, or his horse to the bullfight, has no complaint to make.
>   (*English, USA*)
> If you lend your girl, your watch or your knife you get them back spoilt. (*Dutch*)
> One can show a wife and a gun, but not lend them. (*Serbian/Croatian*)
> Do not lend three things: power, a wife, a gun. [You'll have difficulty in getting them
>   back, and they will be abused]. (*Fulfulde, Senegal*)

In such proverbs, wives are jokingly associated with other precious objects owned by men, and, last but not least, power. I found only one example in the same vein from a woman's perspective: 'One could lend rice or a dress, but no-one would lend her husband' (*Vietnamese*). This proverb differs from the others quoted above, first, in the choice of objects here belonging to the female domain, and second: because for once the wife is presented as the subject and the husband as the object of the lending, and because except for the husband the two other objects *are* being lent in this proverb! That a woman's lending is so amazingly rare in proverbs is probably due to the fact that in reality, certainly in the past, women usually did not own, but were owned. Therefore they were generally unable to lend things of some importance, let alone husbands:

> A married woman has nothing of her own but her wedding ring and her hair lace.
> (*English, UK*)
> A girl possesses nothing but a veil and a tomb. (*Arabic, Saudi Arabia*)

WHY AN EXTRA WIFE?

When a man has two pairs of trousers, he thinks of a new wife. (Persian)

The above Persian statement is presented as 'a women's saying.' What motivates a husband's need to take more than one wife? In proverbs the following arguments come to the fore. A man who feels attracted to the freshness and beauty of a woman younger than his own wife wants to marry her. Some proverbs simply argue that a man should take two, if he can afford to keep two: 'Don't take one wife, if you can maintain two' is a Swiss example, and 'A supplementary dish of rice can always be added', is Malaysian. The proverb refers to a Malay feast where attendants serve rice to the guests, but a large dish of rice is additionally set before the guests, from which they can take as much as they feel like. The proverb pleads for a man to have not only the (according to Islamic law) allowed legal number of four wives, but also the right to have concubines (which is not acceptable in Islamic law).

Posterity is a second important argument: a man desires more children than he is able to have with only one wife. Having several wives solves problems arising in societies where it is the custom for a husband to abstain from sex with his wife during the latter stage of her pregnancy, after childbirth and during lactation, a period of several years. In Mesopotamia having more than one wife was recommended as 'human' if a man's wife was ill, or if she remained childless: 'Marrying several wives is human; getting many children is divine' (*Sumerian*). Another invented justification for a man's polygamous inclinations has been that it is in line with 'nature':

> Even a wolf is allowed to marry two. (*Awar*)
> Two flowers, one insect. (*Turkish*)

And a man's motive might be prestige: he wants to show the community that he is a wealthy man capable of paying bride-wealth for several wives. 'A man with one wife is chief among the unmarried', says a Ganda proverb. Profit is another point abundantly made: having more children means more security for one's old age but also a greater investment, whereas having more wives means more 'woman power' in the home and on the land. With more than one wife, a man always has somebody to work for him. The comment emphasizes that if one's only wife would be absent or ill, the husband will need another one to cook, go for firewood and fetch water for him, if he does not want to do 'women's work' himself. From a man's point of view, it would be ideal to have two wives, one rich and one beautiful, to satisfy his different needs in life, as a Galla proverb stresses: 'One wife warms the heart, the other one warms the kettle.'

Another aspect of this argument is that the disaster of a wife dying is much less tragic for a husband if he still has another wife (or more) to take care of him. In both northern and southern Africa it is referred to through the metaphor of the eye: 'One wife, one eye' (*Ovambo, Angola*), made even more explicit in the Oromo proverb using the same image: 'The person of one eye and the man of one wife die equally.' Both proverbs suggest that as a widower a man cannot survive. This risk of loss is also expressed in metaphors referring to fragile objects: 'Only one wife, only one jar in one's basket' (*Yaka*).

A further aspect is punishment. In order to discipline the uncontrollable wife or wives he has got already, a man may 'punish' them by taking a new one, as an effective means to 'bring a wife back to reason': 'Flog the bad wife with a new wife' (*Nubian*).

Do the co-wives themselves see any advantage at all in sharing a husband? Although most proverbs undeniably represent a world in which men decide, comment and command, the arrival of a co-wife is emphatically greeted with bitterness and despair from the perspective of the senior wife or wives:

> Even if she were a date, the taste of the co-wife is bitter. (*Arabic, Algeria*)
> A co-wife, even when made of unbaked flour, is undesirable. (*Rajasthani*)
> The very voice of a co-wife is intolerable. (*Persian*)
> A wife will not respect her co-wife. (*Mamprusi*)

HIERARCHIES AMONG WIVES

The feet of the first wife do not walk in the dew wet morning grass. (*Fang*)

The first wife has certain privileges. 'The first one drinks no muddy water' (*Ovambo*). She drinks from the well before the others, she is allowed to sleep a little longer, and speaks before the others in case of quarrels or complaints: 'You, first wife, speak; you, second, be silent' (*Yaka*). It goes without saying that such proverbs are used in other hierarchical contexts as well.

Proverbs tend to stress that the first wife is the best. As a Tonga proverb from Zambia says: 'The first fish is real', meaning that a man should be happy with his first wife and that the second one is mere illusion. 'The first [wife] possesses the marriage; the one who comes later is like the shoots of the banana tree', according to a Yaka proverb. The first wife is considered more reliable than the other wives, and, in case of problems, proverbs recommend that the husband should turn or return to her. Such proverbs warn men not to despise their first wife. She is the one who knows her husband best. She will look after him and support him in times of trouble. As the Gikuyu say: 'If your young wife dies, return to your old one.'

When a new wife arrives, the older wife wonders how to survive materially. She tries to make herself indispensable, by working hard or by pleasing her husband in other ways. A Haya woman swallows her feelings of pain and disappointment by reminding herself of the following proverb which reflects the first wife's fear of being driven off: 'I've got to make them happy, the first wife says, and eats with them.'

In Africa south of the Sahara, the rule is that a decent polygamous husband does not reject his first wife when he gets a second one, and proverbs remind men of this obligation:

> If you have a new earthen pot, don't throw away the old one. (*Swahili*)
> If you take a new wife, don't forget the old one. (*Ngwana*)
> Don't chase your old wife when you take a new one. (*Mamprusi*)

The first wife is compared to the mother in an Acholi proverb from Uganda: 'Your first wife is your mother.' This is not a mere compliment though, although it refers to the vital part first wives play in running homes. A husband quotes this proverb to flatter his first wife, and to comfort her when he informs her of his intention to take a second wife. The Swahili in East Africa have an almost identical proverb: 'Your first wife is like a mother.' Most proverbs on first and other wives I found originate from Africa, although they do exist in other parts of the world as well.

In India a Bengali proverb says: 'When she was the only wife, she was treated like a goddess; now that she has a co-wife, she is cast out on the garbage heap.' It is humiliating for her to see how much her husband prefers his new wife. The proverb 'My first wife my sandal, my second wife my turban' (*Turkish*) means that in a man's eyes the second wife by far excels the first, at least for the time being, in spite of his first wife's hierarchical position.

Even though the first wife is unlikely to succeed in preventing her husband's second marriage from taking place, she stays a formidable factor to be reckoned with, particularly in non-Islamic societies in Africa south of the Sahara. 'The first wife is like magic: you never get rid of her', the Mongo say, but they also try to diminish the hierarchy: 'A woman's value is not her being the first wife', which means that a wife's value has to be earned by her dedication to her husband. A Yaka proverb expresses that the authority of the husband is incontestable: 'The young wife, place her at the end, it's up to you, place her next to the fire, it's up to you.' In other words, he has the sole right to decide about the place of his new wife in the hierarchy.

Other proverbs state that there is (or rather should be) no difference between wives of the same husband, when it comes to discipline, as expressed in a Krio proverb: 'The stick that has beaten the senior wife will beat the junior wife' with a slightly different Yoruba variant: 'The rod that is used to beat the senior wife is waiting in the roof for the junior'— as a cold comfort to the first wife.

For a husband it appears to be difficult to be 'neutral' and to hide his preferences: 'The butter is for Emm Zbeid and the thrashing is for Emm Obeid' states ironically how one wife is favoured over the other (*Arabic*). Most men try to be more tactful: 'The polygamous man will hesitate long time before deciding whom he will give the piece of cloth to' (*Yaka*). As he has only one piece to give to one of his wives, he can be sure that the others will be jealous.

The newly arrived wife may feel superior, but she must show respect to her senior. It would be unwise for her to mock the first wife. 'The new cooking-pot never scorns the old one', as the Minyanka say. Newly married, she may underestimate her husband's attachment to his older wife: 'The new wife does not know that the first one is loved' (*Baatomun*).

Wives of the same husband hate favouritism—unless they are themselves the cherished favourite. Still, this is not only a pleasure, as the favourite wife lives under constant stress, due to tough competition: 'The favoured wife does not grow fat', according to a Kundu proverb. Her position unavoidably creates the enmity of the other wives and their constant jealousy.

Many proverbs express how difficult it is for a wife to live with a co-wife. Being kind to her does not help: 'You measure some flour for your co-wife and this flour makes your husband spend the night with her' (*Rundi*). Saying bad things about her does not make things any better: 'You scorn the small vulva of your co-wife, but it takes away your husband' (*Rwanda*). A complete lack of solidarity makes a woman maliciously delight in her co-wife's misery: 'When the favourite wife commits a fault, you, the despised one, rejoice' (*Ganda*), and envy her successes in life: 'When your co-wife gives birth, you do not wear your festive ornaments' (*Rwanda*). Jealousy prevails and may even go so far that widowhood seems preferable to sharing your man with another wife: 'It is better to let one's husband die than to give him to a co-wife' (*Bengali*).

Thus, loyalty and sympathy between co-wives are not in the line of things. On the contrary, a wife seems mostly interested in hurting her co-wife: 'Even when their rival co-wife is not guilty, the other co-wives call: "It's her!" ' (*Sotho*). A wife is always on her guard against the bad tricks she may expect from her co-wife: 'If you dance with your co-wife, don't close your eyelid' (*Rundi*): she would inevitably try to trip you up. However, a wife can only harm a co-wife without being punished for it, when she is sure of her husband's favouritism: 'If a wife has kicked her co-wife, it is on the husband's shoulder she has found support' (*Fulfulde*). Such a proverb is also quoted in the context of other power politics.

A wife can be obsessed by hatred to the point of explicitly wishing for her co-wife's death: 'Oh weasel! Eat this fish and spare my husband but eat my co-wife' (*Bengali*). After a co-wife's incidental death, this obsessive preoccupation melts away quickly: 'When a woman's rival dies, she is no longer interested in her' (*Wolof, Gambia*). It is even likely that when the husband dies, the enmity between co-wives disappears, as a Bengali proverb observes: 'Fortunately the husband died. Now the two co-wives are friendly to each other.' A sad story, or rather, millions of sad stories starring women who are not happy about their husbands' polygamy: 'It is better to die young than to be a co-wife', is a Vietnamese conclusion.

PROBLEMS AND DISILLUSIONS

Two wives, two pots of poison. (*Gikuyu*)

Obviously, women are not happy about their husbands' polygamy. How do men manage with more than one wife? Many a proverb argues against the idea. It is as inadvisable as binding two horses to one tree (*Turkish*); an impossible job, as impossible as climbing two oil palms at the same time (*Kundu*); running after two gazelles (*Ndebele*); rowing two boats at the same time (*Ovambo*); carrying two watermelons under one arm (*Hebrew*), and so forth.

Other messages reflect the fate of those who have not followed the above good advice. A polygamous man is a sick man, a victim, a worrier, a martyr:

> A day's disease: drink brandy. A life's disease: take two wives. (*Russian*)
> Two wives is two problems, three wives is like walking around without trousers.
>   (*Ossetian/Arabic, Lebanon*)
> One woman, what a glory; two women, what a worry. (*Turkish*)
> A house with two mistresses will be deep in dust. (*Persian*)
> Farming in two villages and having two wives are equally bad. (*Telegu*)
> Buying two ploughs makes a family flourish; marrying two wives makes a family grow
>   poor. (*Chinese*)

Financially too, it is difficult to support an extra wife: 'A poor man does not take a second wife' (*Tamil, India*). In times of adversity, a man may even be obliged to abandon one of them, for reasons of survival: 'We cannot suffer a burning sun together', is an Ovambo proverb meaning that a husband of two wives will leave one of them when there is famine in a year of drought. Will she starve in solitude? More wives also means more children, and more expenses: 'Many children, many debts; many wives, many fires to keep', a Vietnamese proverb points out.

Polygamous men feel trapped and torn by the endless tensions and quarrels with their wives and between their wives: 'To have two wives is being [ground] between two millstones' (*Karachay-Balkar*). A similar proverb exists in the Maghreb: 'A husband of two wives has no peace: he is crushed between the stones of the hand-mill' (*Ladino*).[75] Polygamous relationships are frequently expressed in such terms of dispute, rivalry and conflict. The following Awar proverb is another example: 'Two wives, two enemies.' In proverbs polygamy equates disharmony in the family:

> With two camels you have peace, with two wives you have war. (*Mongolian*)
> If you tether two goats at the same post, you can be sure that the ropes get entangled.
>   (*Fiote, Angola/Cabinda*)

The idea that a monogamous relation is more harmonious than a polygamous marriage seeps through in many proverbs, sometimes in surprisingly similar terms in totally different parts of the world, as two examples, from China and Nigeria, demonstrate. Both remind men that monogamy is much less tempestuous:

> A single bracelet does not jingle. [There is peace with one wife] (*Fulfulde*)
> A single key doesn't rattle. (*Chinese*)

In a Berber proverb from Morocco, the husband's instability in taking decisions is compared to the cock's feathers in the wind. Tossed to and fro between his two wives who constantly oppose each other, a man feels unsure: 'The polygamous husband is like the cock's tail.' Or, to use a Kurdish image: 'A man with two wives has two faces.' A polygamous man is unlikely to find peace in his own home. There are many references to the misfortune of a man married to two quarrelsome wives:

> Quarrel sleeps in the house of the man with two wives. (*Swahili*)
> The husband of two parrots [is like] a neck between two sticks [that strike it].
> (*Arabic, Egypt*)
> A thousand wives, a thousand palavers. (*Ashanti*)

The dream of being lovingly surrounded, cherished and pampered by co-wives is shattered in Asian as well as in African proverbs. Deception seems to be the order of the day for the polygamous man, as expressed in a Mongo proverb: 'The foolish wife imagines her co-wife has taken care.' Take for example a simple request for a bath: 'He has twenty wives but has not been able to take just one bath' is a Kru proverb from Ivory Coast and Liberia. A husband asks one wife after the other to fetch water for him, and they all tell him that the next one will do the job. Disappointments only:

> A bamboo pressed between two trees is apt to crack; a man with two wives frequently suffers hunger. (*Khiongtha*)
> A man with one wife gets his food served in time; with two wives, he waits a long time for his food to come. (*Bengali*)
> A sick man with many wives dies of hunger. (*Twi*)
> A husband of two wives [and he] has to sleep outside. (*Ladino, Morocco*)
> Owner of mill, owner of garden, owner of co-wives—none of them ever has a quiet night. (*Arabic, Maghreb*)
> When the head of a large household [with many wives] wants clean premises, he has to sweep them. [This is a woman's task, but the women are of no use] (*Kundu*)

If we draw up the balance-sheet, then, nothing is left but a gloomy scenario which ultimately leads to the husband's miserable and premature death:

> If you marry two, you'll die all the younger. (*Luba*)
> He who has a piece of land in two villages will go bankrupt; he who has two women will die. (*Tamil, India*)

In spite of the negative prognoses in proverbs, polygamy continues to be practised officially in a number of countries in Africa as well as Asia (except in the former communist areas).[76]

WIDOWS

Cold rice is still rice; a widow is still a woman. (Khmer)

The tragedy of losing one's partner in life echoes in proverbs all over the world. As a shared experience the death of one's husband creates mutual understanding, as expressed in Chinese: 'Only a widow knows the widow's grief'. However, in Korean, 'A widow's suffering is not understood by a widower.' The ideal solution would be for them to marry each other, and 'To arrange the marriage of a widower with a widow, is to please two persons,' as the French say, but, according to a Polish proverb, 'Widower and widow seldom join.'

A Japanese husband who loves his wife and wishes that they grow old together, may prefer to die before she does: 'May you live up to one hundred years and I up to ninety-nine.' He wants his wife to live longest, because she has to mourn and pray for and to his departed spirit.[77] The Arabic proverb 'The woman that God gives his blessings will accompany her husband on his funeral' wishes for the couple's common death, but for a completely different reason: she would be best off to die when her husband dies because no one will be interested in her anymore nor take good care of her after his death. Implicitly it also means that she is incapable of managing her own life.

DEATH OF WIFE, DEATH OF HUSBAND

The lucky woman dies before her husband's death, the unlucky woman dies after it. (Chinese)

A preference for the consecutive order of a wife's and a husband's death from a woman's point of view is expressed in a proverb from China: 'If she dies before her husband, that will ensure the wife of a bunch of flowers at the tomb; if she dies after him, she will have a heart like a bunch of rags.' It means that, as a widow, she cannot expect much from life; that is why it is preferable for her to die before her husband.

A difference in mourning over the loss of a wife and a husband respectively is also stressed in several proverbs from China: 'When the husband dies, the wife will be in deep mourning for three years; when the wife dies, she won't be remembered for more than a hundred days.' Comparing this observation about the death of a wife to those represented in Western proverbs, this proverb still reflects some respect. Many other proverbs about the loss of a wife, especially from Europe and the Americas, are surprisingly sanguine. From the number of proverbs on the issue, it seems that Western men did not hesitate to express, openly and without any restraint, great relief and even happiness about the death of a wife, presenting her as nothing but an easily replaceable commodity, and her death as a profitable event. Proverbs can be aptly used to make the most cynical statements, because the quoter cannot be personally held responsible for the quoted phrase:

> Grief for a dead wife lasts to the door. (*Catalan; also French and Italian*)
> The death of the wife is the renewal of the wedding. [Allusion to the custom of taking a new wife immediately after the death of a former]. (*Arabic, Egypt*)
> A wife brings but two good days: her wedding day and the day of her death. (*English, UK*)
> A dead wife is the best goods in a man's house. (*Catalan*)
> A dead goose gives life, a dead woman gives heaven. (*Spanish*)
> Women are a four-days' fever and only death frees from them. (*German*)
> A man regrets his wife's death no more than he does a broken whip. (*Chuwash*)
> The wife's death, a replacement in bed. (*Chechen*)
> Happy the door through which a dead woman leaves. (*Portuguese, Brazil*)
> The pain caused by the wife's death lasts unto the door. (*Spanish, Argentina*)
> Grief for a dead wife, and a troublesome guest, continues to the threshold, and there is at rest. (*English, USA*)

Where do such ideas come from? In the Christian tradition divorce was practically prohibited (except for some very special grounds such as insanity or impotence). The only way to dissolve marriage was death. Man and wife were sentenced to living with each other for life, whether they liked it or not. Money matters often played a considerable role in the making of marriages.[78] A wife's death could be quite profitable, especially when the new bride brought a new dowry:

> Death of the wife and health of the cattle help the poor man forward. (*Italian*)
> The death of wives and the life of sheep make men rich. (*French/English, UK*)
> New wife, new silver. (*French*)

It is unfortunate that in most proverbs only the husbands' perspectives on the death of wives are represented, and hardly ever the other way round. Still, there are a few rural proverbs in the 'said-saying' form, a genre well represented in the Nordic countries of Western Europe, in which the death of a spouse is jokingly referred to, either from the point of view of the husband, or from that of the wife:

> 'Every little bit lightens,' said the skipper, and he threw his wife overboard. (*Frisian*)
> 'Never make a toil of pleasure,' as the man said when he dug his wife's grave only three feet deep. (*Irish*)
> 'Every man for himself and God for us all,' said the farmer who saw his wife drown, without lifting a finger. (*Dutch*)
> 'A feast with no breakages is rubbish,' said the woman, when her husband broke his neck. (*Danish*)
> 'That clears a space,' said Grietje, when her husband died. (*Dutch*)

Although the above said-sayings are meant as jokes, they are no more positive about wedlock as the cornerstone of society than the earlier proverbs about the death of one's wife.

As many marriages were made for economic reasons, spouses were often eagerly interested in holding on to what they had contributed to the conjunction (and preferably, also, to possess what the spouse had brought in). As a consequence, premeditated murder (by husbands as well as by wives) for reasons of economic profit and inheritance seems to have occurred in Europe.[79] Stories about such murders may have contributed to superstitious beliefs and stereotypical ideas about widows in proverbs.

However, such beliefs are certainly not limited to Europe. When a husband dies, his surviving wife is made suspect in proverbs from five continents:

> Never marry a widow unless her husband was hanged. (*English, UK/USA*)
> A woman who buries a husband does not mind burying another one. (*French*)
> The man who marries a widow should expect to suffer a few deaths in the family. (*Spanish, Mexico*)
> Every time a woman who was born in the water-snake year opens her mouth, a husband is swallowed. [Husbands of women born in the year of the water snake were believed to die prematurely]. (*Tibetan*)
> Avoid the woman who has it within her fate to destroy eight lives. [When she marries her husband will die]. (*Chinese*)
> You flirted with the widow, but do you know what killed her husband? [Warning not to marry a widow too quickly]. (*Bassar, Togo*)

A man who wants to marry a widow has to find out first whether she has been involved in her husband's death. A widow is associated with the power of death, simply because death has visited her house and seized her husband. The proverbs just quoted all refer to such beliefs, in one way or another.[80]

In proverbs, no such observations about widowers exist, in spite of well-known cruel stories such as that of Bluebeard, and hardly any concerning a widow's cheerfulness after the death of a husband.

LOSS AND SORROW

Whether a woman is clever or not will become clear once she is a widow; whether a man is clever or not, will become clear once he starts talking. (Tangut, China)

In fairytales, couples live happily ever after they have found each other. This ideal is expressed in good wishes on the wedding day. One such wish is for the couple's longevity. It is expressed in the following Assam proverb from India: 'Never let the spot of *kinowari* disappear from your forehead.' That symbol of marital bliss indicates that the woman who wears it is married. The proverb expresses the wish for a woman not to become a widow.

In most cultures, even today, the position of adult women is strongly determined by their marriage. A widow finds herself in a difficult position: with her husband she has lost her anchor in life. When he dies, she is 'reduced', so to speak: 'Widows are the leftovers from dead men', in the words of a Portuguese proverb from Brazil.

Proverbs reflect the issues that make life most difficult for widows. The first problem is that the loss of a husband means loss of status for the wife. This is very well expressed through the Minyanka metaphor of the fallen tree: 'The baobab has fallen; now the goats start climbing on it' (*Mali*). It means that a woman was respected in the community as long as she was a wife, but this esteem is lost once she becomes a widow. Therefore, women who (still) have husbands feel sorry for those who lack this prestige: 'Widows and young girls have the pity of married women' (*Arabic, Lebanon*), and those who have become widows ardently pray for a way to find their lost status back: 'Please, God, let us not stay a widow' (*Russian*). There is not much comfort to be offered. The Igbo just say: 'One can tell a widow only this: have patience.' Perhaps another man will come, but for the time being a widow's situation is not very bright. A woman who was respected when her husband was alive does not really interest people after her status provider's death. Why?

No less than the spinster, a widow constitutes an 'irregularity', a problem to be solved in society. She disturbs the existing gender structures and thus she risks destabilizing the social order: 'A widow is a boat without a rudder' expresses the idea. This proverb does not only exist in Asia in China, with variants in Vietnamese, but also in both Americas. Women are supposed to obey men, but, if the husband passes away, whom will she obey? In order to prevent the problem from getting out of hand, a Spanish proverb suggests the following three solutions for 'the problem' of a widow, especially if she looks attractive: 'A buxom widow must be married, buried, or shut up in a convent.'[81] The metaphor of the horse without a rider reflects the lost control:

A mare without a rider finds the meadow. (*Spanish*)
A widow feels as happy as a horse that has thrown off its rider. (*Malayalam*)
Widows are as frolicsome as a horse that has thrown off its rider. (*Malay*)
It's dangerous marrying a widow, because she hath cast off her rider. (*English, UK*)

Many proverbs stress that a woman needs a man's protection during her whole life: a father before marriage, a husband in later life. It is therefore frequently suggested that a widowed wife is completely dependent on the care of others: 'The widow and the capon: all they eat is the food they're given'[82] (*Portuguese, Brazil*). The loss of a husband is sometimes presented as the ultimate tragedy in a woman's life: 'Loss of goods is one spoiled day, loss of a husband is a ruined life' (*Burmese*).

After her husband's death she needs a deputy, so to speak, a 'looking-glass husband', or 'shield husband'. Those two Malay expressions refer to an arrangement created for widows on their re-marriage, which is a substitute marriage for purposes of protection or convenience. Another regular safety haven for widows is to take shelter in a son's protective presence. In some cultures the disaster is complete if she has no male child, or when her son dies. That makes her spineless:

The childless one [widow] is like an overgrown field. (*Amharic*)
What will support the spineless one? (*Chinese*)

Still another solution has been the tradition of the levirate, a marriage whereby the widowed woman is 'inherited' by the deceased man's brother who has the duty to marry her and to breed her children in his name.[83] This is considered a matter of group responsibility. It is a practice referred to in the Bible, in both the Old and the New Testament, and one finds it in proverbs as well: 'The widow is not free for all' (*Kweli/Kundu*), i.e. she must be inherited by the brother of the dead man, as custom dictates that a widow has to stay in the clan of the deceased. Or, a Pashto example: 'While looking at her dead husband's brother, she let another husband go.' She had to. Again, the 'irregular situation' of the widow is 'repaired' for her, or rather behind her back, under the show of her not being able to handle her own life.[84] In the face of so many proverbs suggesting that she would be incapable of solving her own problems, there is the refreshing Chinese motto to this section, which at least gives a widow the benefit of the doubt. The idea that she might be able to survive by herself is rather exceptional.

One of a widow's believed incapacities is that she would be unable to bring up her children on her own:

A child brought up by a widow is like a bullock without a nose-rope. (*Telegu*)
A widow's son is either badly brought up, or is a vicious character. (*Spanish*)

This and other incapacities are tersely expressed in Arabic proverbs: 'A widow's dog does not bark; her ox does not plough', or in a more elaborate version: 'When a widow raises a child, she does not make a man out of him; when she teaches a dog, it does not bark; when she places a bull in front of the plough, it does not work; whatever she undertakes will fail.' This is either meant to discourage her before she has even tried—or just wishful thinking which, as usual, easily results in a self-fulfilling prophecy.

WIDOWS' TEARS

A widow's dress shows the past, her tears weep for the present, and her heart seeks the future. (German)

Oceans of tears are shed daily by widows worldwide for all sorts of reasons. A first reason is the pain of the loss: 'A black shirt and veil do not release a soul from pain' (*Spanish*). A second reason has to do with all the consequences that such a loss has in store for her. And thus the widow weeps and weeps. Proverbs refer to her tears in various ways.

Attending a wedding she thinks of her lost husband: 'The widow weeps and the others laugh at the wedding' (*French*). She may weep but she also reflects on the future: 'The widow weeps for the dead and thinks of the living' (*Italian*). The more tears, the sooner she will remarry, a North American proverb says: 'There is nothing like wet weather for transplanting.' Lack of tears should not amaze the community either. Crying is a luxury in harsh circumstances. 'A widow who cries for two years has somebody to help her', according to a Yaka proverb—otherwise she will have to work on the land, or find food some other way.

Tears or lack of tears, a widow's real feelings *vis-à-vis* her dead husband are considered a mystery in many proverbs. Did she love him and does she miss him? How soon will she have forgotten about him? Especially the young ones may want to remarry: 'The hearts of young widows and stone bowls grow cold very quickly', an Estonian proverb reasons. And what do her tears and sighs mean? 'A widow who sighs, wants to get married' is a Spanish explanation from Argentina.

Although nobody knows for sure, proverbs are quick to accuse a widow of hypocrisy: 'Onions can make even heirs and widows weep' (*English, USA*), and in Latin America there are cynical expressions such as 'cry like a widow' or 'have the memory of a widow.' The malevolent suggestion is that a widow's tears, meaning widows—or even women's tears and women in general—are unreliable: 'Good and honest is a buried widow' (*Portuguese, Brazil*). Sometimes a woman's fate is symbolized by a constant flow of tears. Still, when tears are shed continually they have so little impact that they become meaningless:

> A widow weeps because she is a widow, and perhaps a woman with a husband living [has also cause to weep]; but in their company a spinster also weeps! (*Bihari, India*)
> Widows cry, what does it matter, girls cry no less. (*Bulgarian*)

No matter how a widow's tears are interpreted, her position rouses little envy among her fellow humans.

SLANDER

At the widow's gate many a scandal will occur. (Chinese)

A widow may easily damage her delicate position. Her uncontrollability is inversely proportional to people's malicious inclination to endless gossip and slander about her behaviour. She has constantly to face the inquisitive eyes of the people who surround her:

> The widow is like an open field: every wind touches her. (*Karelian*)
> Slander clusters around the widow's door. (*Hebrew, Israel; also Chinese*)

After Jacques has died, we will watch Thérésine's conduct. (*Creole, Guadeloupe*)
Looking here and looking there, makes a widow forget her husband. (*Mamprusi*)

In a number of cultures a woman has to show through her dress and hairstyle that she is a widow. Her outfit is a metaphor for the risks she runs by her very status. If she deviates, even slightly, she knows that she will be condemned without mercy:

One tells a widow by her hair. [A widow is not allowed to do her hair nicely and has to wear a white headband]. (*Senufo/Minyanka*)
When you see a cloud speckled like the wing of a partridge and a widow applying scented oil to her hair, the former will rain and the latter will elope. (*Bihari*)
The widow's dress is long and everyone steps on it. (*Dutch*)
Even her skirts are the widow's enemy. [A widow is always under scrutiny for her morality.] (*Bulgarian*)
Even the train of her dress will be an enemy to the widow. (*Turkish*)
After the husband is buried, the widow beautifies herself. (*Italian*)
There is no Saturday without sun, nor a widow without rouge. (*Spanish, Puerto Rico*)

If her hair, clothes and make up reflect the slightest frivolity, she is rebuked for indecency. A widow should not draw attention to herself, because it might be interpreted as showing off as a candidate for remarriage. By doing so she would ridicule herself. An old Sumerian proverb already mocked a widow's begging for attention by comparing her (in a pun) to a donkey breaking wind: 'A widowed donkey makes a show of farting.'

A rich widow rejoices in the constant attention of the community she belongs to. Many proverbs comment on her. She is much better off than the poor widow, as she does not depend on other people's charity. The more her husband has left behind for her, it is suggested, the more quickly she is inclined to forget him: 'The favourite wife does not mourn her husband', a Kundu proverb observes. The world tends to be ungrateful. In Europe and both Americas, the rich widow is presented as a person who is certainly not as desperate as others might wish her to be:

The rich widow's tears soon dry. (*Danish*)
A rich widow, with one eye she cries and with the other she bells the clock [for a new wedding]. (*Spanish*)
The rich widow cries with one eye and blinks with the other. (*Spanish/Portuguese, also Brazil*)
The rich widow weeps with one eye and laughs with the other. (*English, USA*)

Being well-to-do she will quickly find a new husband, and therefore her mourning is ambivalent. As much as the rich widow is considered lucky (mostly because men tend to be interested in her), the poor widow has to calculate and to drudge for her survival:

There are no plump mice in the house of a widow. (*Japanese*)
Widows do not eat fat meat. (*Kundu, Cameroon*)
Being a poor man's friend is the helplessness of a widow. (*Sumerian*)

Widows who cannot (or are not allowed to) earn a living, eat up their savings: they 'sell their silver to eat', as the Koreans say.

REMARRYING

The widow in a hurry passes by the handsome man. (*Bassar*)

In addition to the argument that she might well have killed her husband, there are other reasons to dissuade someone from marrying a widow.[85] One is that she costs money: for example, if she has children and is not in easy circumstances, particularly if she has got daughters in cultures where dowries have to be paid:

> To marry a widow with a daughter is to ruin your home in a year's time.
> (*Arabic, Lebanon*)
> A man who married a widow with two daughters has got three back doors.
> (*Scottish/English, USA*)
> He that marries a widow with three daughters marries four thieves.
> (*Danish/English,UK/USA*)

The above examples are familiar variants of proverbs earlier discussed in the section on daughters. The only difference is that the 'real' fathers had no choice, while the potential husband of a widow with daughters does have a choice.

Another argument presented against marrying a widow is that such a wife has already been trained and 'modelled' by her earlier husband: 'A mule tamed by someone else will always keep some remnants' (*Spanish, Antigua*). What kind of 'remnants' is the proverb referring to? There is, in the first place, the possibility that the vivid memory of her deceased husband will condition the new marriage:

> He that marries a widow will often have a dead man's head thrown into his dish.
> (*English, USA*)
> Whoever marries a widow has to put up with the 'stiff' [i.e. the dead husband].
> (*Spanish, Mexico*)
> Who gets the widow into bed, gets the dead man in his house. (*Danish*)
> A widow dreams a double dream on her lonely lot. [First of her dead husband and again
> of her new love]. (*Pashto*)
> When the tiger looks into a mirror, there are two tiger heads. [Refers to a woman who
> has taken a second husband]. (*Chinese*)
> Never marry a widow, even when her cheeks are a bunch of flowers: you will love her but
> she will say: God blesses the blessed one [i.e. her dead husband]. Arabic/ Ladino)
> A widow never fails to praise her dead husband. (*Ganda*)
> Never marry a widow: each time you'd quarrel she'd remind you of her dead husband.
> (*Bamum*)

In China a virtuous widow is strongly advised not to marry again, as good horses do not 'turn back to eat grass' nor do they 'bear two saddles.' Both are metaphors for having sex. A widow would be able to compare the sexual performances of her earlier husband with those of the new one, and some European proverbs suggest, without much reserve, an involuntary sexual competition with the dead man:

> Taking a widow is like buying trousers at the flea market; who knows who wore
> them before. (*Polish*)

A widow is like a liver pie: one never knows what has been put into it. (*Dutch*)
The widow certainly has the ready-made bread, but it's sour. (*Polish/Russian*)

Ambivalent feelings *vis-à-vis* the widow's former husband's sexual achievements is still more openly expressed in another Polish proverb: 'It is dangerous to get a horse after a brave horseman, and a widow after a strong man.'[86] Such feelings of reluctance, or rather fear, to marry a widow are supported by strong pressure *vis-à-vis* widows to refrain from remarrying—as a matter of loyalty to her deceased husband:

The widow who marries again loses esteem. (*French*)
The widow does not need soap. [i.e. she should not remarry. The soap refers to her
    washing herself after having slept with a man]. (*Bulgarian*)
A faithful wife doesn't marry twice. (*Japanese*)

In several African cultures there is a taboo on a widow's having sex, and proverbs refer to it:

'Mine is useless,' said the widow [referring to her sex]. (*Oromo*)
One who eats when the cock is dead, breaks a taboo. [Refers to a man who has—
    forbidden—sex with a widow]. (*Zulu*)

A last strong point against marrying a widow is her presumed power and independence. She is known for taking initiatives, which goes against the usual rules of female decency and virtue. It is the man's role to be in control, but a widow develops a will of her own:

You cannot marry a widow for the widow marries you. (*English, USA*)
A maid marries according to the will of her parents; a widow decides her marriage by
    herself. (*Chinese*)
I shall not tie the donkey at the place of the horse. (*Arabic, Morocco*)

This last Arabic proverb means that if a man of lower birth wants to marry the widow of a man of higher birth, she turns him down by means of the quotation. An English hint is to strike the iron while it is hot, so to speak: 'Marry a widow before she leaves mourning', that is while she is still intimidated by the events. Obviously, a man cannot deal with a widow as he can with a young and inexperienced girl. A widow knows things about love-making a virgin would not yet be aware and could even be afraid of. This 'knowledge' is commented upon positively:

Young widows are like green wood: it burns at one end, while water is trickling down at
    the other end. (*Danish*)
The pan of a widow: small and patched up. (*Spanish*)
A widow's pot: small but well stirred. (*Portuguese, Brazil*)
[Nothing is] Hotter than a grass widow's kiss. (*English, USA*)
A widow is good to love, for a calf won't go into the yoke of its own accord. (*Pashto*)
Rather marry a young widow than an old virgin. (*Hebrew*)

As well as negatively:

Widows carry the Devil. (*Italian*)
The widow, if she does not scare you she will weaken you. (*Spanish, Bolivia*)

The ambivalence of a widow's position and the prohibition in so many societies to take her own life into her hands, then, make a wife vulnerable to the greed of relatives and profiteers after her husband's death.[87]

MOTHERS AND MOTHERS-IN-LAW

MOTHERS

Every river runs to its mamma. (English, Jamaica)

After all those rather hostile comments on wives, what a relief to broach the subject of the mother! Mothers are put on a pedestal, and choruses of sweetly glorifying voices start singing in proverbs about mothers. The mother is set apart as the most valuable representative of womankind, and even of humankind, in endless songs of praise. She is adored as a divinity, she *is* the presence of God, or at least as a superhuman being, and a source of endless love and impeccable selflessness. 'God could not be everywhere, therefore he decided to make mothers,' an English proverb sweetly observes. A few more examples, picked at random from different cultures and continents:

> Mother is God number two. (*Chewa*)
> Hearing the approaching step of his mother, Rab Joseph would say: 'I must stand up, for the Shekhinah [the 'Divine Presence'] enters.' (*Hebrew*)
> Life is a mother. [Everything in life depends on one's mother]. (*Arabic, Lebanon*)
> Whoever has a mother should not cry. (*Spanish, Argentina*)
> No temple is more beautiful than one's mother. (*Tamil, India*)
> Mother's milk is holy. (*Mongolian*)

UNIQUENESS

Mothers are incomparable. (Kongo)

Why are mothers so unique? Right from birth children experience her loving presence as something special. Her generosity knows no limits: 'The mother says not "will you" but gives at once' (*Maltese*). She radiates warmth, care, and protection: 'It is warm in the sun, and nice with a mother' (*Russian*). Her smell is wonderful: 'Of all perfumes, the mother has the best scent' (*Greek*). She is full of understanding and patience; and she never tires with all the efforts, as expressed in a variety of metaphors:

> The climbing plant's fruits are not a burden to it. (*Sinhalese, Sri Lanka*)
> The elephant never tires from carrying her own tusks. (*Chewa/Haya/Shona/Vai*)
> Breasts are never too heavy for the owner to run with. (*Creole, Haiti*)
> No hen is burdened by her feathers. (*Spanish, Dominican Republic*)

A mother's love is referred to as unfailing and exemplary: 'The origin of love for fellow humans lies in the mother' a Kongo proverb observes, and in Greek the message is no less flattering: 'The only generous love is the love of a mother': it knows no limits (*Russian*), is lifelong (*Filipino*), and omnipresent, and it 'even dashes up from the sea' (*English, USA*). It has the 'soothing freshness of a shadowy fig tree' (*Bengali*). A mother is always ready to take care, to comfort, and to cure. She knows how to handle the problems of her children—at least in proverbs:

> A mother understands the language of her mute child. (*Letzeburgish*)
> A mother understands the child's babbling. (*Armenian*)
> A mother has a cure for every injury. (*Italian*)
> When the boy's foot is broken, he finds his mother's yard. (*English, Jamaica*)
> It's the mother who knows how to carry her one-legged child. (*Mandinka*)
> The mother of the dumb one speaks his language. (*Arabic, Lebanon*)

Whenever there is an emergency, a mother goes to great length to help her children survive: 'For her children a mother will swim across the sea', according to a Lak proverb, while a well-known southern African proverb observes that 'The child's mother catches the knife at the sharp end' (*Sotho/Tswana*). The bond between mothers and children reaches beyond the grave: 'A mother hears the cries of her child from the grave' (*Ossetian*). She even has and gives access to eternity: 'Paradise will be opened at the command of a mother' (*Arabic, Lebanon*). For sure, 'Who has a mother has a friend' (*Catalan*). A Tamil proverb from India asks the question and gives the answer: 'Who are related to each other? The mother and her child.' A mother is to be confided:

> Cry, tree, to the one who bore you. [Tell your mother your problems]. (*Ovambo*)
> Give your love to your wife but tell your secrets to your mother.
> (*Irish/Spanish, Guatemala*)

She repairs her children's damage and covers their wrongs and failures:

> The child gets dirty and tears his clothes, the mother sews and cleans. (*Czech*)
> Both a mother and an apron cover many a gap. (*Hebrew*)
> A mother is like a coverlet: she won't cover a corpse, but she will cover your disgrace.
> (*Sranan*)
> A mother is like a good cooking pot with a lid. [She hides her children's weaknesses].
> (*Creole, Martinique*)

Children feel cherished and treasured by their mother so much so that they tend to deny that no other woman can compete with her:

> Better your own mother's rod than your stepmother's bread and butter.
> (*German/Finnish*)
> Rather in your mother's hands than in the nurse's. (*Papiamentu*)
> There are thousands of women but only one mother. (*Spanish, Bolivia*)
> Your mother is your mother, your wife is just a woman. (*Sranan*)
> One hundred aunts are not equal to one mother. (*Krio*)
> Not even a thousand aunts can replace your own mother. (*Azeri*)
> Wife for counsel, mother-in-law for a greeting, but nothing sweeter than your own
> mother. (*Russian*)

What about fathers? In quite a few proverbs, fathers and mothers are both highly appreciated and praised on an equal footing: they are a divinity and a treasure respectively

(*Telegu*); the only ones in the world who are no strangers (*Arabic*); their hands are soft (*Lithuanian*); you cannot buy them (*Tamil*), and so forth:

> The feelings of a father are higher than the mountains, the feelings of a mother deeper than the ocean. (*Japanese*)
> Pleasant is the shade of a tree; pleasanter that of a parent, a father or a mother. (*Burmese*)
> The mother is a garden of blessings, the father a rock. (*Arabic-Jewish, Yemen*)
> There is no greater love than that of a mother or a father. (*Spanish, Mexico*)

In other proverbs, however, the father is not given the same credit as the mother. On the contrary, a hierarchy is ostentatiously established between the two:

> One mother is worth more than ten fathers. (*Korean*)
> Mother is gold, father is a mirror. [A mirror easily breaks]. (*Yoruba*)
> There are many fathers, but only one mother. (*Papiamentu*)
> There are a few like your father, nobody like your mother. (*Danish*)
> The father is the shoulder, the mother the soul. (*Tatar*)

More than the father, it is suggested, the mother feels the pain when her child suffers. According to a German proverb: 'Whatever hurts the children the father feels in his little finger and the mother in her whole body', while in Russian it is argued that 'What touches the mother's heart, touches but the father's knee.' I could find no proverb in which the father's loving care was more highly praised than that of the mother.

Usually people have good memories of those who nurtured them when they were young, dependent and vulnerable. In most cases, such memories include a mother's loving care. In proverbs a role of selflessness is associated with the mother, who does not seem to ask much in return.

IDEAL CHILDREN AND WORRYING MOTHERS

If you don't have children, the longing for them will kill you; and if you do, the worrying for them will kill you. (Igbo)

Mothers tend to idealize their children, and proverbs reflect this: 'There is only one pretty child in the world and every mother has it' (*e.g. Hebrew/English, USA*). For a child this is very fortunate. This loving care and admiration is expressed in animal metaphors in which, for example, a little monkey becomes a gazelle in its mother's eyes (*Arabic/Hebrew*), and an owlet, a beauty (*Russian*). The same holds for the baby bug, duck, goose, hedgehog, raven, etc., all presented as their mother's most extraordinary progeny in a wide range of countries and cultures. Here are some more examples:

> The beetle saw its child on the wall and said: 'a pearl on a thread.' (*Arabic, Lebanon*)
> The porcupine caressed her children and said: 'May God take care of your silken skin.' (*Kurdish*)
> To the female weasel her baby is very precious. (*Sinhalese*)
> Cockroaches call their children suns. (*Spanish, Cuba*)
> When asked to bring the most beautiful thing, the crow brought its chick. (*Chechen*)

Next to such good-natured and humorous statements about the animal world, direct statements also mildly mock the mothers' adoration of whatever children they give birth to:

> She who bore the child will like his slobbering. (*Portuguese, Brazil*)
> Every mother thinks it is on her own child the sun rises. (*Irish*)
> The mother said to her blind son, 'Morning star of mine'; and to her lame son, 'Straight river of mine.' (*Oromo*)
> A blind son is considered sighted by the mother. (*Cherkess*)

And thus 'Ugly children have no mother', as it is said in Latin America. Even criminals have a loving mother, as argued in a Sinhalese proverb about Devadatta, a son so wicked as to try to murder the Buddha: 'Devadatta is pleasing to his mother.'

For those who want to please a mother, the best trick is to be nice to her children: 'If you take the child by the hand, you take the mother by the heart' (*English, USA*) or, again, by means of an animal metaphor: 'The tigress does not bite when you tell her that her young are beautiful' (*Korean*). As the mother is so uncritical, her judgment has to be taken with a pinch of salt:

> Mother's eyes are enchanted and see it wrong. (*Italian*)
> What the mother praised, leave and run; what the neighbour praised, take and run. (*Armenian*)
> The truth is not as mothers tell it, but as the neighbours tell it. (*Hindi*)

That a mother is so fond of her children has still other consequences: 'You can't weigh worries but many a mother has a heavy heart', says an Irish proverb. From a mother's perspective her children's survival depends completely on her taking care, her being there. She is courageous and enterprising whenever her children and their wellbeing are at stake. She foresees their problems, and is alert all the time. This is very realistically expressed in a Krio proverb from Sierra Leone as well as in a Creole proverb from the Caribbean:

> A mother lying down sees farther than a child on a tree. (*Krio*)
> While the mother sleeps, her toes are awake. (*Creole, Guadeloupe*)

A mother worries helplessly when she no longer feels in control over the events or situations her children are or might become involved in. Growing children no longer depend on their mother all the time, and gradually the maternal influence on their lives begins to diminish. This does not prevent her from continuing to care and to worry. In her mind she plays out the worst scenarios, as the following Greek proverb illustrates: 'Dear God, don't send the child what his mother is afraid will happen to him.' Indeed, 'A child is a sure care and an uncertain joy' as observed in Swedish, or, in Chinese: 'The child knows not what trouble it has given its mother.'

The helplessness of parents, and especially mothers, *vis-à-vis* the adult problems of their grown-up children, is reflected in the widespread saying that having small children means small problems and grown-up children, big problems, with variants in many languages:

Small children give you headache, big children heartache. (*German*)
The little child sucks the breast, the big one the heart. (*Russian*)
Small children eat porridge; big ones eat their parents' hearts. (*Czech*)
As long as the child is growing up, it is heavy for the hands; when it has grown up, it is
    heavy for the heart. (*Tajik*)
A small child brings joy; once grown up, sadness. (*Uyghur*)
First you hold the child in your arms; then, on your lap; finally, on your back. (*Japanese*)

The mother's deepest fear is that of losing a child forever, particularly an only one: 'One child: eternal anxieties for a mother' (*Bengali, Bangladesh*). The likelihood of sons dying is greater than for daughters. Male children are more likely to take risky initiatives when they leave the house: 'A mother worries about her son when he is travelling far away' (*Chinese*); but, in spite of that, boys will often stray. 'A man does not die where his mother is' (*Mongo*), meaning that it is natural for a son to leave his home and travel or, worse, go to war. It is the sons who have often been called to fight in wars in far-off places. Thus, 'The woman who does not give birth to a son has no worries' (*Spanish, Colombia*). In proverbs, mothers are referred to as especially fearful of having a hero for a son, who is likely to perish in some hazardous enterprise:

The mother of a hero is the first to weep. (*Serbian/Croatian*)
The mother of the brave wept, the mother of the timid laughed. (*Giryama*)
The mother of a timid son never weeps. (*Turkish*)
A child [who is] a coward saves his mother worries. (*Ladino, Morocco*)

Throughout history, there has been 'No grief greater than a mother's' (*Maltese*) over the continuing waste of the lives of children they gave birth to. 'Mother means martyr', as the Italians say.

MOTHERS AND CHILDREN, MOTHERS AND SONS

A good oven bakes good bread. (*Romanian*)

Inescapably, mother and child not only look alike but also behave alike. In proverbs certain plants and animals express this idea metaphorically. For example, 'A *girauman* [a vegetable] does not bear calabashes' (*Creole, Haiti*), and 'A guinea hen cannot bring forth a ram' (*Creole, Trinidad/Tobago*), simply because they are not meant to do so in 'nature'. Here are first some examples without moral judgment about the result:

Every tree has its root. (*Sranan*)
A slanted branch has a slanted shadow. (*Japanese*)
The child of a piebald cow will always come out stained. (*Spanish, Colombia*)
What is born of a cat will catch mice. (*Czech/Serbian/Croatian/Romanian/Spanish, Chile*)
A goat does not generate a lamb. (*Romanian*)
If you planted a pear tree, do not expect peaches. (*Chinese*)
The pear falls under the pear tree. (*Albanian*)
How could the apple be but as the apple tree? (*Irish*)
The horse-dung does not fall far from the horse. (*Dutch*)

The observation that a good mother may have a bad child does not lack in figurative proverbs either: 'A beautiful branch can bear ugly fruit' (*Burmese*) whereas the opposite seems hardly likely: 'There will never be a good plant from a bad shrub' (*Spanish, Dominican Republic*). Mothers are prepared to do anything for their children, but they seem to have an especially weak spot for their sons, as expressed, among other examples, in Fulfulde: 'The son goes to heaven thanks to his mother.' Mothers and sons are believed to feel particularly attached to each other, and some of the ways in which proverbs refer to their strong bonds would not have surprised Sigmund Freud. For example: 'The mother of an impotent male neither rejoices nor grieves.' (*Arabic*)

A Hausa proverb even states that if it were possible to marry one's mother, she would be preferable to any other wife: 'Lack of a mother one takes a wife', arguing that a mother is more useful and less trouble. Two proverbs go so far as to look into sexual relationships with the mother, be it in a disapproving sense: 'If a man has sexual intercourse with his mother, it is as if he did it in the *ka'bah*', which would be as scandalous as having sex with somebody in a public place (*Arabic, Morocco*). In a Catalan example the idea serves as a crude example of *force majeure* in life: 'One sleeps with one's mother out of sheer necessity' (*Catalan*). Most other proverbs restrict themselves to stressing the strong bond of close friendship between mother and son:

> The embrace of his mother is a cradle for a son. (*Pashto*)
> There is no finer sweetheart than one's mother. (*Turkish*)
> A boy's best friend is his mother and there's no spancel[88] stronger than her apron string. (*Irish*)
> In sunshine it is warm, with his mother a son feels comfortable. (*Russian*)
> Every man carries his mother in his heart. (*Spanish, Cuba*)

Actually a mother would love to keep her darling son safe and near to her all her life: 'The eldest son should not leave the family home; the youngest does not leave his mother's room' (*Chinese*). She has more difficulty in letting her son go than her daughter: 'The back of a mother got bent when her son got married, but is erect again when her daughter marries' (*Chechen*).

A mother's fate is to step back as soon as her son falls in love: 'The boy's best friend is his mother, until he becomes himself his sweetheart's best friend' (*Irish*). Nevertheless, a son's mother fixation may last until her death, so that it is only after her death that a man will bind himself to his wife, according to a Hebrew proverb. Even after her death, an Adyg proverb insists, the mother's impact is not gone, as in moments of distress, a man may instinctively shout her name: 'When the river took him, the old man screamed: "Mama".'

'Your mother's love and your wife's support' is the Italian male ideal: both should accompany a freshly married man. In reality, though, it may be more likely that a silent (or even not so silent) competition will be set in motion between mother and wife.[89] Who will be better at pampering and understanding him? The resulting tensions are expressed in the following Telegu proverb: 'The mother will look at his belly, the wife at his back', meaning that the noble mother will be interested in how her son fares, and his wife in what he brings home. Some proverbs suggest a tense triangular relationship in which a man needs to make difficult choices and decisions:

> When the mother receives much, the wife receives little. (*Chuwash*)
> The son who loves his wife more than his mother is unfilial; the mother who joins the son in hating his wife is not good. (*Chinese*)
> Mother loves her son, but the son loves his wife. (*Khionghta*)
> Mother's heart is tender but her son's heart is like a stone. (*Tibetan*)
> The mother loves excessively while the son has a heart of stone. (*Pashto, Pakistan*)
> Sacrifice your mother, another woman will give you offspring. [Used when choices are to be made]. (*Haya*)

Apparently, it is not easy for a son to severe the bond with the mother. He wallows in her warm and caring presence and she is not keen on letting him go. However, being mollycoddled prevents him from becoming the 'real man' society expects him to be:

> Mothers' darlings make but milk-porridge heroes. (*English, USA*)
> A child who remains in his mother's house believes her soup the best. (*Efik/Ga*)
> A son who never leaves home always thinks his mother's is the loudest fart. (*Gikuyu*)

His mother gets in the way if she keeps too close to him: 'If a boy is raised by a woman, he'll not become a man', a Somali proverb argues. If he continues to identify with her, as he 'naturally' did in his early childhood, he will never be able to fulfil his role as he should: 'A man does not look like his mother' (*Ovambo, Angola*) means that a grown-up male child must behave like a real man. This message of 'manliness' is widespread, even though the idea of what a 'real man' is may differ according to the cultural context concerned. In their own specific way, then, proverbs put pressure on sons reminding them that they have to prepare for roles men are to play in life, roles incompatible with a strong mother-son bond.

MOTHERS AND DAUGHTERS

The daughter of a good mother will be the mother of a good daughter. (*English, USA*)

Proverbs on mothers and daughters have usally only the message that they inevitably resemble each other. The direct statement 'Like mother, like daughter' can be found in many languages in the Western world and the Middle East, e.g. in Danish, Italian, Hungarian, Estonian, Bulgarian, Dutch, English (*UK and USA*), Hebrew and Arabic. Other variants include:

> Look at the mother rather than [at] her daughter. (*Japanese*)
> See the mother, comprehend the daughter. (*Pashto, Afghanistan*)
> Know the mother and pick up the daughter. (*Arabic*)
> The habits of the mother go to the daughter. (*Finnish*)
> Have a [good] look at the mother before you take the daughter. (*Widespread in Europe*)

The supposed similarity of mothers and daughters is also expressed by means of meta-phors and comparisons:

The worth of the bread depends on the flour. (*Telegu*)

The daughter's merits come from her mother; the goodness of butter depends on the
    quality of the cow. (*Bengali, Bangladesh*)

Look at the mother before you take a daughter; see how much milk the buffalo gives be-
    fore you buy her. (*Telegu, India*)

Observe the edge and take the linen; observe the mother and take the daughter.
    (*Turkish*)

The filly is judged after the mare, the daughter is known after the mother.
    (*Estonian*)

Whether a daughter will be a 'good' wife or a 'bad' wife seems to depend exclusively on the mother: she is the one to be praised when the girl turns out well, she is the one to be blamed when the girl does not stick to the norm of a well-behaved daughter:

Lascivious mothers, strumpet daughters. (*Dutch*)

Bravo for the mother of the girl. (*Bulgarian*)

Lenient housewife, lazy daughters. (*Estonian*)

A bustling mother makes a slothful daughter. (*French*)

A tender mother breeds a scabby daughter. (*German*)

It is the mother who needs to be good; in the proverbs just quoted, the father is not even mentioned. In a rare English proverb referring to a bad father, it is even explicitly argued that his presence has no influence whatsoever on his daughter: 'Choose a good mother's daughter, though her father were the Devil' (*English, UK*). I found only one (*Portuguese*) example about a father's negative influence on a daughter: 'An impertinent father gets a disobedient daughter.'

The point that daughters look like and behave the way their mothers do is mainly made from the perspective of a man who wants to marry. His perspective and his interest are at stake in proverbs discussing whether the daughter of a 'good' mother is to be a good wife.

There are astonishingly few proverbs about the relationship between mothers and daughters as women. A Spanish example refers to a daughter's understanding of her mother: 'Even when the daughter is mute, she understands her mother', and a Ladino one refers to their closeness: 'Mother and daughter are like nail and flesh.' In another Jewish proverb the mother is mentioned as a confidante to her daughter: 'A daughter tells her secrets only to her mother.' That is about all. Mutual understanding between the mother and daughter is significantly less elaborated upon than the mother-son relationship. It is, apparently, not much of an issue from a male perspective.

WHO IS TAKING CARE OF THE MOTHER?

The son was asked: 'How will you repay your mother?' 'I'll raise a son.' (Georgian)

What an impossible task to return such endless motherly generosity and selflessness: 'Even if the son fries her an egg on his hand, he can't repay his mother' (*Dargin*). A grandson is suggested as the best remuneration. A few proverbs, mostly from Africa, reflect some measure of gratitude and appreciation:

An old hare gets suckled by her young. (*Ganda*)

The hide that served the mother to carry the child will serve the child to carry the mother. (*Mboshi*).

Chick, find food for your mother; she used to search for it for you. (*Ovambo, Namibia*)

Other proverbs, however, point out that children easily forget what their mother (or both parents) did for them, and that solidarity often is one way only: 'When the mother feeds her children, she gives as much as heaven and sea; when the children feed their mother, they count every day' (*Vietnamese*). In Sranan this difference in attitude is graphically expressed in the metaphor of boiling and eating: 'Boil the mother and her child will eat; boil the child and its mother won't' or, in a variant: 'A mother has no pot big enough for her to boil her child in.' In other words, the mother will not take advantage of her children, while this is quite likely the other way round. A Tibetan proverb puts it quite cynically: 'The young magpie plucking its mother's feathers thinks that it is showing gratitude to her.' This deceptive lack of mutual solidarity is visibly criticized all over, in almost literally the same wording:

A mother can feed ten children; ten children cannot feed their mother. (*Vietnamese*)

A mother can take care of ten children, but sometimes ten children can't take care of one mother. (*English, USA*)

A mother can provide in the needs of twelve children, but not the other way round. (*Letzeburgish*)

A poor mother is able to feed seven children in the same way as seven children one mother. (*Czech*)

One mother for a hundred children, and not a hundred children for one mother. (*Spanish, Chile*)

The same complaint is to be found expressed in a number of other ways revealing no less bitter disappointment about children's egoism and lack of concern:

The kind-hearted mother dies unhappy. (*Arabic*)

Love can be passed downwards; love that goes upwards does not exist. [Parents love children, children do not love parents]. (*Korean*)

Parents for their children, children for themselves. (*Abkhaz*)

A Japanese proverb reminds people that it is better to show kindness to the parents during their life than to express filial piety by means of impressive tombstones: 'Don't try to cover the stone with a quilt.' The main message is that even beloved mothers live in an ungrateful world.

MOTHERLESS

You do not know how to cry until your mother dies. (Ovambo)

As long as they are needed mothers toil for their children. Taking care is presented as the heart of a mother's life. Sometimes it is suggested that a mother's life loses its meaning, as soon as the children leave her. Metaphorically, a Papiamentu proverb expresses this as follows: 'Once the little scorpions leave the mother's back, she dies.' A mother's death is presented as a catastrophe for children at all ages. Again, the loss of the mother seems to be a worse disaster than the father's, especially when the child is still young:

> Without a mother, the children are lost like bees. (*Russian*)
> A child that has lost his mother, his help is behind. (*English, UK*)
> A fatherless child is half an orphan, a motherless one a whole orphan.
> (*Finnish/Bulgarian/Estonian*)
> Orphaned of his mother, the child has the doorstep as his pillow, orphaned of his father,
> he still has his mother's lap. (*Arabic, Tunisia*)
> If the mother dies, the father becomes an uncle. (*Tamil, India*)

The father 'becomes an uncle', when he remarries, and his new wife will become the child's stepmother, who will be much more interested in her new husband and her own children than in his earlier children[90]: 'One can only truly value the love of a mother once the stepmother has arrived' (*Ladino*).

In regions with imminent famine, the consequence of a mother's death means an immediate struggle for survival:

> With your mother at home you are fed with good olive oil; with your mother at the
> cemetery, you are fed with remnants [waste]. (*Arabic, Maghreb*)
> A child does not get enough food, when the [real] mother is not there. (*Ganda*)
> When your mother dies, you'll eat yam peels. (*Ngbaka*)

However, it is not only young children who miss their mother terribly. A Mongo proverb serves as a conjuration against her ever passing away: 'A mother cannot die.' It is a wish uttered by a man who does not want to lose his mother—she simply should not die. Proverbs refer to the event with deep sadness and despair:

> Whoever has lost his mother has lost his life. (*Jewish/Arabic, Yemen*)
> The one who has lost his mother, where is the house where he will be harboured?
> (*Arabic, Algeria*)
> One does not cry on the day of his mother's death. [The pain gets worse over time].
> (*Creole, Guadeloupe*)

Some proverbs comfort those who have lost their mother by suggesting that, even dead, a mother will always be there: 'A good mother warms beyond the grave' (*Letzeburgish*) and, because her children keep on praising her, she will live on: 'A mother does not die' (*Ganda*). Memories of parents who passed away provoke emotions in their children of all ages. As a Twi proverb from Ghana puts it: 'At someone's funeral we weep for our own mothers and fathers.' Still, the mother seems to be much more painfully missed than the father:

> Better the father seven times dead, than the mother once. (*Lak*)
> When my father died I hardly noticed, when my mother died I broke down the house.
> (*Arabic/Jewish, Iraq*)

The large majority of proverbs about mothers are overwhelmingly positive. I found only three referring to her being a burden to her children. One is an elaboration of a more general praise saying in Spanish: 'A mother you have only one.' In Venezuela it has been extended as follows: 'A mother you have only one—thank God!' The second is a Kundu proverb, 'The mother has died: now for the good times.' It refers to people's hope that they will fare better when they are finally independent. The third is Tibetan: 'After its mother died, the colt's coat became glossy.' Such messages refer to the suffocating effects of too much loving care and overprotection.

> The monkey smothers its young by hugging them too much. (*Creole, Martinique*)
> Too much mothering can be harmful. (*Hebrew*)

As we have seen, proverbs pay a great deal of attention to the bond of love between mothers and sons and much less to the solidarity between mothers and daughters. They also suggest that mothers have different relationships with sons than with daughters.[91] Mothers are blamed for being too indulgent with their male children—especially in social and cultural contexts where the 'male' domains of society are not only considered more prestigious but also most inaccessible to girls.

It is nothing new that mothers tend to be more tolerant and accepting towards their sons than towards their daughters. Such attitudes exist already in an ancient Sumerian proverb: 'A chattering girl is silenced by her mother; a chattering boy is not silenced by his mother.' In many cultures fathers as well as mothers ascribe to the traditional idea that raising small children is exclusively the mother's domain, a message clearly reflected in proverbs. Every child, an Arabic proverb argues, 'depends for its upbringing on the mother.' According to the following proverb in different languages: 'Your son shall be the way you raise him to be, your husband shall be the way he was raised to be' (*Adyg/ Arabic/Ladino*) This observation, stressing the enormous impact the mother's upbringing has on the mentality of sons, is echoed in the following Bulgarian proverb: 'A mother gets ruined by daughters, but she herself ruins for them her son [by spoiling him].' Both proverbs create awareness of the generational gender chain of being—and in this respect both can be seen as warnings of great wisdom.

In most social and cultural contexts fathers do not 'mother' as much as (or rather much less than) mothers do. Therefore the mother has a much greater impact on the children's future behaviour than the father, particularly in the crucial early years of childhood. There is a hidden likelihood that a mother will confirm existing gender patterns and hierarchies, even without being aware of doing so. The more the mother's praise is to be sung, the more the 'motherhood ideology' is upheld, including the view that a mother needs to be constantly and exclusively available to her children. This very view scares fathers away from taking up duties and responsibilities in the children's crucial early years. The mothers themselves can go so far as to exclude fathers altogether from such important tasks. In a system of strictly separate gender roles, the idea that only mothers intuitively know what is good for the child leads to the myth of the 'essential' mother, who has to restrict herself to being a biological and social mother and who is morally forced to sacrifice herself to death for her children, like the scorpion. 'Women are mothers and men are men' according to an old Dutch saying, re-emphasizing anew the old idea that women ought to opt for motherhood and abandon all other ambitions in life.

MOTHERS-IN-LAW VERSUS DAUGHTERS-IN-LAW

To find a wife is easy, to find suitable parents-in-law is difficult. (Malagasy)

As much as mothers are adored and praised, mothers-in-law are detested in proverbs, and they do not like their daughters-in-law either. 'If our child catches a snake, what can be done with it?' asks an Indonesian proverb in despair. The son's choice of wife, no matter how ungracious or wicked she is, is to be respected by his parents.

The situation is mainly presented from a mother-in-law or daughter-in-law perspective. From the parents' point of view, there is an intruder who joins the family and comes to live with your child, often even in your own house, under your very eyes. Inevitably this creates tensions. Perhaps it is to do with primitive urges and uncontrollable instincts: the safe and familiar nest smell is suddenly disturbed by unknown aromas emanating from a foreign element, and the instinctive reaction of blood relatives is to stick together and drive the intruder out.

Generally, blood relations have priority over in-law relations in proverbs. This is expressed, for example, in Yaka: 'Birth comes first, marriage follows.' As opposed to blood relatives, all in-laws are usually valued negatively. 'The stranger is not one of us', says a Bulgarian proverb marking the outsiders once and for all.

Everywhere, mothers-in-law are at the proverbial centre of negative in-law qualifications. It is suggested that she hates her in-law children: 'A mother-in-law is not a relative but a punishment' (*Portuguese, Brazil*). She sees her daughter-in-law as *the* alien, she gives orders and is constantly meddling: 'A mother-in-law is like a pig's snout digging here and digging there' (*Yaka*). She is unreliable, and her friendliness is suspect:

> Who counts on his mother-in-law's soup, will go to sleep without dinner.
>   (*Creole, Dominican Republic*)
> Never rely on the glory of a morning or on the smiles of your mother-in-law. (*Japanese*)
> The friendship of a mother-in-law is like dry weather in the wet season. (*Papiamentu*)
> Friendship between mothers-in-law and daughters-in-law only goes as deep as the teeth
>   [of the smile]. (*Portuguese, Brazil*)

Proverbs argue that there can be no sweetness in a mother-in-law: 'even one made out of sugar is no good' (*Catalan/Greek/Spanish/Spanish, Bolivia*). Wherever she goes she leaves a taste of bitterness behind, like the *mangosa* tree (*Telegu*) or bitter carrots (*Italian*); or she tastes like sour grapes (*Romanian*). A mother-in-law is not only considered devoid of goodness, but also explicitly called malicious and evil:

> No evil is as bad as a mother-in-law. (*Greek*)
> The evil words of a mother-in-law are worse than a donkey's kicks. (*Creole, Saint Lucia*)
> The tail of a pike is always black; nowhere in the world will you find a good mother-in-
>   law. (*Bengali, Bangladesh*)
> The best mother-in-law ate her son-in-law. (*Spanish, Chile*)

The cannibalistic desire to exterminate the son- or daughter-in-law may have a very different outcome than the mother-in-law had in mind: 'A tooth, sharpened for the daughter-in-law, will bite the son' (*Chechen*) or: 'While gnawing the daughter-in-law, the son is consumed' (*Awar*). The destructive mood of the mother-in-law may thus accidentally hurt her own child and ultimately cause the couple's misfortune, as well as her own besides: 'The tongue of a bad mother-in-law brings divorce' (*Yiddish/Hebrew*) or, in an Arabic example: 'Is thy mother-in-law quarrelsome? Divorce her daughter' (*Egypt*). The final outcome could be that the husband drives both the mother-in-law and her daughter out of the house, and the proverb is quoted as a general practical advice to cut evil by the root.

Children-in-law are no less equipped with hatred. They may feel like cursing their mother-in-law, as happens in the following saying: 'Stones, run in the river; shrimps, under the bridge; cockroaches and rats, run over my mother-in-law's legs' (*Spanish, Panama*). Just like mothers-in-law, they are warned that the curse might unexpectedly bounce back in an unwished-for direction, as in a Haitian proverb: 'The curse that you meant for your mother-in-law will come down on your mother' (*Creole*).

A mother-in-law's wickedness is associated with the Devil and Hell in proverbs originating from Europe:

> The husband's mother is the wife's Devil. (*German*)
> The wife's mother is the husband's Devil. (*German*)
> Forty leagues down from hell there is a special hell for mothers-in-law.
> (*Spanish, Colombia*)

Such persistent prejudices prevent people from being kind: 'Not even if she were made of clay would a mother-in-law be welcome' (*Hebrew/Spanish, Mexico*). It is recommended to stay away from one's mother-in-law as far 'as the swallows are from the stars' (*Spanish, Peru*). This, alas, is an impossible wish for those who are forced to live with their in-laws in the same house.

RIVALS

Mother-in-law and daughter-in-law: you can cook them together, but it will never be sweet. (French)

In proverbs, mothers-in-law and daughters-in-law quarrel at the slightest provocation. Making them live together 'is like introducing a pestilence in the house', as a Thai proverb puts it. Impossible mother- and daughter-in-law relationships are compared to other impossible situations:

> The daughter-in-law has taken the oath to love her mother-in-law on the day when charcoal turns white. (*Arabic, Morocco*)
> When will there be peace between daughter-in-law and mother-in-law? When a donkey climbs a ladder. (*Hebrew*)
> Where a hundred soldiers fit, a mother-in-law with her daughter-in-law doesn't. (*Estonian*)

Their bad relations are also represented by means of a large variety of animals that are notorious for being on bad terms with each other:

Brides and mothers-in-law are like dogs and monkeys. (*Japanese*)

Mother-in-law, daughter-in-law, dog and cat never eat from the same plate.
(*Italian/Spanish, Chile*)

A daughter-in-law can no more live under the same roof with her mother-in-law than a
goat can live in the same barn with a tiger. (*Hebrew*)

In proverbs the message is that they will never come to love each other. A popular Arabic
proverb from Lebanon expresses this bad relationship as fatal: 'Inscribed on the gates of
Paradise: No daughter-in-law ever loved her mother-in-law.' According to an Iraqi proverb 'If a daughter-in-law would have loved her mother-in-law, all women would have gone
to heaven' (*Arabic/Jewish*). There are two prejudices here. One is that all mothers-in-law
and daughters-in-law hate each other; the other is that women don't have an easy access
to heaven because of their 'wickedness'. If they hate each other so deeply, could it be that
in point of fact they resemble each other? Quite a few proverbs refer to the mutually negative feelings and reactions both categories cherish *vis-à-vis* each other.

Mother-in-law and daughter-in-law are made of the same crooked rib. (*Chechen*)

In the daughter-in-law there's a piece of the mother-in-law. (*Yiddish, Eastern Europe*)

Mother-in-law and daughter-in-law are a tempest and hailstorm. (*English, UK/USA*)

The spots on the antelope are those on her mother-in-law. (*Cameroon*)

More examples would not add much to the argument. The emphasis on their resemblance
implies that you should not blame others—and especially in-laws—for qualities you have
yourself as well.

NEWLY ARRIVED

Once, long ago, there was one good mother-in-law, but a wolf ate her. (French)

As long as the future daughter-in-law does not live in the mother-in-law's house the two
may get along without serious problems. Under the surface, however, the proverbial rule
is that 'Every mother-in-law dislikes the young wife' (*Serbian/Croatian*), and a Spanish
proverb warns that: 'Daughter-in-law and mother-in-law, they mess already at the door.'
Many proverbs refer to the tensions that erupt after the wedding, especially when in-laws
are forced to live in the same house: 'Before the wedding, embraces and kisses, later violence and strangling' (*Ladino*).

In the beginning, the new daughter-in-law seems willing to make the best of the situation. A Chinese proverb refers to her zeal: 'A new daughter-in-law is very diligent on her
first arrival.' However, for the mother-in-law, the new woman's arrival is experienced as
an announcement of her own death, in the words of another Chinese proverb: 'When a
new daughter-in-law enters the house, to the mother-in-law it is like entering her coffin
on her burial.' Mothers-in-law are presented as revengeful *vis-à-vis* the 'intruding' daughter-in-law. An Estonian proverb reminds the girl how to survive: 'A daughter-in-law has a
horse's patience and a dog's obedience.'

Proverbs from different parts of the world reflect the harrowing difficulties experienced
by the young daughter-in-law.[92] Her tireless efforts are not really appreciated: 'Rarely is a

servant praised, a daughter-in-law never', as a Finnish proverb states. It is echoed in Korean: 'Good deeds of a daughter-in-law or a cat go unnoticed.' A Persian proverb asks rhetorically: 'In the presence of the mother-in-law what rank is the bride!' If the daughter-in-law has any rank at all, she seems to be her mother-in-law's unpaid handmaid.

In proverbs, the poor young woman is denied the best food: 'To give eggplant to a daughter-in-law is too great a kindness' (*Japanese*). Eggplants are expensive, and the despised daughter-in-law does not deserve such a delicacy. On the contrary: 'A dry piece of bread, salted with a tear, is the fate of a young daughter-in-law', is the way a Komi proverb from the Russian Federation depicts her situation. Indeed, instead of being served food as a daughter, she is given the most odious tasks that nobody else wants to do, as in the following African Rundi proverb: 'Your mother-in-law does not serve you cooked corn but she engages you to grind.'

The mother-in-law may see it as her duty to take over her daughter-in-law's life: 'Raise your child from early years, raise your daughter-in-law from the first days' (*Nogay*). The son's young wife's behaviour is commented upon. Sometimes this is done more or less subtly, as in the following widespread proverbs:

> My mother-in-law scolds her daughter in order to teach me. (*Bengali*)
> I speak to you neighbour, that my daughter-in-law might hear. (*Arabic*)
> Hear me daughter, so that the daughter-in-law will understand.
> (*Spanish, Mexico/English, USA*)

More often the young wife is submitted to all sorts of ordeals, while she has to obey the whimsical orders of the mother-in-law, who makes unpleasant scenes. Two proverbs from India illustrate this:

> If a mother-in-law breaks a huge vessel, it is nothing; if the daughter-in-law breaks a
>   tiny bowl, the household is ruined. (*Tamil*)
> It is very distressing for a daughter-in-law to be controlled by a wicked mother-in-law.
>   (*Bengali*)

In proverbs, a mother-in-law comments negatively on whatever displeases her and her critical eyes constantly follow her daughter-in-law. She does not fail to notice the slightest mistake the young woman makes: 'Better the glares of a foreigner than those of a mother-in-law.' This Rundi proverb from Burundi argues that you may suffer more from your relatives' hatred than from that of foreigners. The critical eyes as well as the ears of a bad mother-in-law are also referred to in two Russian proverbs:

> The wicked mother-in-law has eyes at the back.
> The evil mother-in-law has also ears at the back.

It would be wise for the daughter-in-law to follow the popular advice to 'Always sweep where your mother-in-law looks' (*English, USA; Spanish, Dominican Republic; Hebrew, Israel*). Extreme submissiveness leads to looking ridiculous, as a whole series of Bulgarian proverbs mockingly points out. Here is just one example: 'Eat until the evening, father-in-law, then I will delouse you.'

In many different cultures, the daughter-in-law is defined as stupid and good for nothing from the mother-in-law's malicious perspective, in nasty proverbs such as the following, Bengali and Arabic respectively: 'My daughter-in-law is very good at doing useless things like chopping a gourd', and: 'When foolishness was distributed, my daughter-in-law received a generous share of it.'

REVENGE

Daughters-in-law become mothers-in-law. (*English, USA*)

The disgusted daughter-in-law has to cope with all the pressure, and does not at all feel at ease in the house of the in-laws. Her instant impulse is to run away as soon as she can: 'The daughter-in-law's shawl always hangs closest to the door' (*Finnish*). Three common reactions are presented. The first is that she flees the house of her in-laws in terror: 'A daughter-in-law will run to her parental house on bare feet' (*Armenian*). The second is anger. Having, at first, heroically and patiently accepted all humiliations, her anger cannot but get the better of her, as a Sumerian proverb states: 'The pleasure of a daughter-in-law is anger.' As long as she does not dare confront her mother-in-law openly, she looks for other outlets for her rage: 'Angry with her mother-in-law, the daughter-in-law kicks her [mother-in-law's] dog' (*Korean*). If the son-in-law finds the actual enemy too powerful, he also seeks a surrogate as an outlet for his anger, and finds one comfortably close by, as expressed in an Arabic proverb from Egypt: 'He was no match for his mother-in-law, he then rose against his wife', or in a Lebanese variant: 'Unable to prevail against his mother-in-law he takes vengeance on his wife.' An Amharic proverb also mentions a husband taking out on his wife the accumulated irritation against his mother-in-law: 'A mother-in-law that meddles with everything, should get a third of the strokes of the stick the wife gets.' Ultimately, the daughter-in-law cannot help but burst out in uncontrollable rage, confronting her in-laws with her pent-up wrath: 'For nine years she kept silence, and in the tenth year when she started speaking again, she ruined nine villages' (*Bulgarian*). The son-in-law's hateful reactions are presented as no less violent. A series of mainly Arabic proverbs refers to such fantasies about radical revenge:

> [A man] who takes the trouble to beat his mother-in-law should cleave her skull.
> (*Arabic, Maghreb*)
> Who comes to strike his mother-in-law must be sure to give her a well-deserved beating.
> [To make her pay in advance for all her faults to come]. (*Arabic, Algeria*)
> If you have pulled down your mother-in-law, press hard! God knows when you will have
> another chance. (*Fulfulde*)
> 'More by hit than by wit,' said the man, when he threw a stone at his dog and struck his
> mother-in-law. (*Danish*)

The third reaction that seems to keep a daughter-in-law going is the prospect that one day she herself will be a mother-in-law: 'The patience of a daughter-in-law results from her desire to become mother-in-law in the future' (*Chinese*). This generational succession is extensively referred to in proverbs from Japan to Europe and the Americas. Bad mothers-in-law produce bad daughters-in-law, so that a vicious circle of negative power seems doomed to dominate mother- and daughter-in-law relationships from one generation to the next:

> There comes a time that the daughter-in-law becomes a mother-in-law, and she will be even worse than her own mother-in-law. (*Korean*)
> As a daughter-in-law she could do nothing right in the eyes of her mother-in-law; when she became a mother-in-law herself, she hated her daughter-in-law. (*Basque*)

It is often suggested that mothers-in-law have a bad, or certainly a rather selective memory. Proverbs emphasize that over the years they have completely forgotten their own earlier in-law experiences:

> Mother-in-law, have you not been a daughter-in-law? Yes, I have forgotten all about it. (*Arabic, Lebanon*)
> The mother-in-law remembers not that she was a daughter-in-law. (*English, UK/ USA*)
> There is no mother-in-law who remembers she has also been a daughter-in-law. (*Spanish, Venezuela*)

DEATH AND THE MOTHER-IN-LAW

Adam was the first happy person, for he had no mother-in-law. (Hebrew)

In proverbs an instinctive mutual death wish preoccupies in-laws; they simply want to get rid of each other. The 'intruder' should disappear—the earlier, the better:

> Death stepped on the threshold and everybody looked at the daughter-in-law. (*Greek*)
> When grief is predestined to a house, may the daughter-in-law die, and if she is not at home, the son-in-law. (*Chechen*)

This death wish is, of course, not restricted to the in-law children only, but also strikes the parents-in-law, and especially the mother-in-law:

> Fathers-in-law, mothers-in-law, maize and beans do best in the earth. (*Portuguese, Brazil*)
> The mother-in-law is good but better when buried in the earth. (*Catalan*)
> A mother-in-law is like a *yuca* [a cassava root], good enough to be buried. (*Spanish, Antigua*)
> The best mother-in-law is in the goose-field [buried]. (*German*)
> The mother-in-law's final breath is better than the nightingale's song. (*Persian*)

In proverbs, the death of the mother-in-law is experienced, and sometimes even applauded, as the ultimate relief. According to the Fulfulde proverb 'As long as you have not buried your mother-in-law, your wife does not belong to you', it is only after her death that a man really 'owns' his wife, because from then on her mother will no longer influence her. Two Indian proverbs exult at the very thought of the mother-in-law passing away. In Bengali it is said: 'I shall be the mistress of the homestead and go to the bathing-place with my keys hanging on my sari', which means that after the death of the mother-in-law, the wife claims authority, symbolized by the bunch of keys. In Rajasthani there is also a triumphant sigh of relief following the mother-in-law's passing away: 'The mother-in-law died, the shackle is broken and she [daughter-in-law] climbs onto a pedestal.' Lucky the daughter-in-law who has no mother-in-law:

> The bride is happy, there is neither a mother-in-law nor a sister-in-law. (*Persian*)
> The woman who is happily married has neither a mother-in-law nor sisters-in-law.
>   (*Spanish, Chile*)

The height of hypocrisy, it is argued, is a daughter-in-law who sheds tears at the death of her parents-in-law, as referred to in two Asian proverbs:

> A daughter-in-law crying for her father-in-law's death. (*Telegu*)
> A daughter-in-law's mourning for her mother-in-law is false and feigned. (*Chinese*)

However, a mother-in-law is remembered after she is gone, when her contribution to the household chores is painfully missed: 'Even a dead mother-in-law is brought to mind when pounding rice' (*Korean*)—a daughter-in-law could do with some help, even from her mother-in-law.

Amongst proverbs about in-laws, a sympathetic mother-in-law is considered so rare that in a dry country she would be valued as more precious than a piece of land containing a water source, in the words of a Jewish proverb in Arabic. Very few proverbs believe that something can be done about bad in-law relationships. A Bulgarian proverb suggests that 'Gifts reconcile even the wicked mother-in-law', whereas a Spanish proverb matches the old Dutch saying, 'Who does good, gets good', with an in-law variant: 'Good mother-in-law, good daughter-in-law.' Both possibilities are imagined in rates of one in a thousand, or even two thousand, in a last Arabic proverb from Lebanon: 'Among a thousand daughters-in-law, one may love her mother-in-law; among two thousand mothers-in-law, one may cherish her daughter-in-law.'

OLD AGE

It is wonderful to be married to an archaeologist. The older you get, the more interested he gets.
(*Agatha Christie*)

In all parts of the world women outlive men, and the largest proportion of the aged population consists of women.[93] Life expectancy, and the cultural and social contexts of aging vary considerably. The perspective on age is somewhat arbitrary, and people have different ideas about age and lifetime, individually, as age groups, within cultures as well as across cultures. It is therefore difficult to indicate where old age is actually supposed to start. Although quite a few proverbs indirectly answer questions of age, and thus give an indication of people's views of female aging, hardly any consistent reference is given:

> At fifteen, a scent of milk; at twenty, blooming; at thirty, smelly; at forty, faugh!
>   (*Spanish, Chile*)
> The longest five years in a woman's life is between twenty-nine and thirty. (*English, USA*)

At the age of thirty, a man is still as attractive as a flower, while a woman looks old.
   (*Chinese*)
A man at forty is youthful as a flower, but a woman at forty resembles an old potsherd in
   the sweepings. (*Chinese*)
Forty years is grandma's age. (*Russian*)
When she becomes forty, a woman withers. (*Ukrainian*)
Forty-five-years old and the woman is a berry again. (*Russian*)
A woman is an angel at ten, a saint at fifteen, a devil at forty and a witch at fourscore.
   (*English, UK*)

Thus, women's aging seems to be set between thirty and forty. A Bengali proverb from
India takes sex as the main criterion: 'A woman who is not sexually active is counted as
old', and an Uyghur proverb from China observes that 'While the child is growing up, the
mother becomes an old woman.'

In most respects, grandmothers are served with the same sauce as the rest of old
womankind. 'Grandmother' and 'old woman' appear to be interchangeable terms in many
proverbs. In some cultures younger people address elderly women as 'grandmother', or
even as 'great-grandmother', even though there is no family connection. The meanings of
the terms simply overlap, as illustrated in the following African proverbs:

Everyone knows the old woman's name, yet everyone calls her [great-]grandmother.
   (*Mamprusi/Mossi*)
The old woman who boils water for porridge does not lack grandchildren. (*Rwanda*)
The well-to-do old woman discovers she has a crowd of grandchildren. (*Rundi*)

GRANDMOTHERS AND OLD WOMEN

Respect your grandmother, because without her your mother would not have existed.
(Umbundu)

Grandmothers are special and children are taught to look up to them with respect, as the
above Umbundu proverb underlines. Grandmothers as well as grandfathers adore their
grandchildren: 'There is nothing sweeter than a grandchild', as a German proverb puts
it. Grandmothers are represented as those who cannot refuse their grandchildren anything:

In granny's basket there is always *waranawa* fish. (*Papiamentu*)
A grandmother always thinks that she cannot do enough to show her love for her
   grandchildren. (*Chinese*)
Pleasantly lives he who lets his grandmother look after him. (*Russian*)
Whoever does not know about grandmothers, does not know what is good.
   (*Spanish, Chile*)

Grandmothers are no less blamed for the consequences of spoiling their grandchildren
than mothers for spoiling their children: 'A mother is responsible for a bad son, a grandmother for a bad grandson', as the Vietnamese say. Proverbs explicitly warn against the
consequences of such grave behaviour:

The baby nursed by its grandmother can never be corrected. (*Gikuyu*)

Those who have been reared by grandmothers are cheaper by three hundred
[coins].(*Japanese*)

Grandparents' love makes grandchildren naughty. (*Catalan*)

The grandmother's correction makes no impression. (*English, UK*)

Jokingly a Russian proverb underlines grandmother's spoiling her grandson as follows:
"'Grandma, what will you refuse me?' 'I don't know, maybe admission to church.'"

In spite of their age, grandmothers are considered useful to their kin in many ways.
Their working capacity is highly valued in the family, and some proverbs refer to their
work and life experience sometimes as superior to that of mothers: 'Your grandmother
has taught you this and you want to ask your mother?' This rhetorical Baule question reveals a generational hierarchy: a grandmother knows better, as her daughter, the mother
of the child, has learnt from her all she knows.

A grandmother fulfils the roles and activities she has been used to carrying out in her
earlier life as a mother, simply moving from loving childcare to loving grandchild care.
This is significantly expressed in a Fulfulde proverb on breastfeeding: 'Lacking-his-
mother sucks his grandmother' (*West Africa*). The grandmother stands in and takes the
place of the mother wherever needed, it is argued in several Caribbean and Latin American proverbs:

If the child does not have a mother, let the grandmother raise it. (*Creole, Haiti/Jamaica*)

He who does not have a mother will have to make do with a grandmother.
(*Spanish, Panama/Argentina*)

If you do not see your mother, go and find your grandmother. (*English, Jamaica*)

Just as a Chewa proverb called a mother 'God number two', so an Ovambo proverb associates God with a grandmother: 'God is not only one person's grandmother' (*Namibia*),
meaning that s/he takes care of all, whereas a Dutch proverb argues that: 'God cannot be
everywhere, that's why he created grandmothers.'

GOOD OLD AGE

A good grape turns into a good raisin. (Spanish, Argentina/Bolivia)

As long as their minds do not get lost in senility, grandmothers and old women are
appreciated as very useful people. Their skills and wisdom—the fruits of a lifelong
experience—gain them respect, while they are also praised for the assistance they provide to kin and social surroundings. The highest praise is her being a *mater familias*, 'a large
tree on which all things hang, or are entwined: if she falls, all perish', as an Efik proverb
from Nigeria states. An Arabic description of a strong, prudent, and respected old woman
goes as follows: 'She dies free and noble; she keeps the moneybag; she chases the enemy
out.' It is fair to add immediately that this is a rather exceptional statement, as most other
Arabic proverbs on this subject are extremely negative.

Most cultures express appreciation for the contributions of older people to the well-
being of the relatives they live with. 'If you have luck you have an old person at home'

(*Turkish*), and in Dutch this is expressed in 'White hair, wise hair', both meaning that it is good to have someone of experience to consult with. Old women are considered more profitable than old men. This is especially stressed in several Jewish proverbs:

> An old woman in the house makes it a joyful place. (*Hebrew*)
> An old man in the house is a burden; an old woman in the house is a treasure. (*Hebrew*)
> An old man and an old woman [wife] in the home: he is a burden [to bear with], she is
>   bearing the burden [also: she herself is the yoke]. (*Ladino*)

Other proverbs support this idea. Old women make the home more comfortable: they have household expertise, and participate in all sorts of activities, as they have done all their life. Proverbs from African origin also refer to their being profitable, either directly or metaphorically:

> Even an old calabash is useful. (*Minyanka*)
> An old pot is not thrown away: it can still be useful. (*Yaka*)
> Even old women run on God's errands. (*Oromo*)
> An old woman is not old in a song she dances well. [i.e. she has expertise]. (*Nigeria*)
> The old woman—if she does not serve for a pot, she'll serve for a cover. (*Spanish*)

Proverbs refer to the specific activities grandmothers and old women continue to practice in their declining years, and to the special knowledge or utensils they have at their disposal. In many cultures, older women are experienced midwives, herbalists and healers. In an outcry against misbehaviour, one Bulgarian proverb reflects that a child's grandmother has been a midwife at his birth: 'Why did grandmother, who cut your belly-button, not cut your head as well?' Further, thanks to her experience as a birthgiver, it is argued, that nobody can teach her a lesson on that matter: 'Do not instruct *baba* [grandmother], how to give birth to children', and, also in Bulgarian, 'The grandmother does not need science.'

Proverbs also refer to old women's kitchen activities, crafts, or agriculture:

> In the luggage of the old woman one finds mortar and pestle. (*Lega*)
> Even if she is crooked she still kneads the bread. (*Lithuanian*)
> Little by little the old woman spins the flock. [A flock is a tuft of wool, a flock is also the
>   sheep: she works her way through all the wool produced by the flock]
>   (*Spanish, El Salvador / Argentina*)
> A kiss doesn't spoil a girl, a knitting needle doesn't spoil an old woman. (*Bulgarian*)
> Old baskets are used again in the peanut harvest. [Serving others' needs when required.]
>   (*Yaka*)

In a number of proverbs the old woman is presented as an absolute treasure, from the perspective of an old husband, and even by far preferable to a young one whose beautiful looks he appreciates:

> If there is an old woman by the fireside, a ram will not hang himself. (*English, Jamaica*)
> There are three faithful friends: an old wife, an old dog and ready money. (*English, USA*)
> If you have an old wife at home, your mind can rest easy. (*Ladino, Morocco*)
> A young woman gets a man's glances, an old woman his heart. (*Irish*)

By the time the couple is growing older, both husband and wife are likely to have adapted to each other's funny habits and have come to appreciate each other's familiar presence. From a man's perspective it is argued—mainly in Asian proverbs—that wives are easier to get along with after you have had them for a longer time:

> Wives and pots and kettles are better when old. (*Japanese*)
> Wives and shoes are better when old. (*Japanese*)
> One can curl up like a dog if one cannot stretch out like a dog; there is yet more if one
>   has relations with an older woman. [Put up with what there is and be happy]
>   (*Tibetan*)

Older people don't necessarily think of themselves as old people: 'Every woman keeps a corner in her heart where she is always twenty-one' (*English, USA*). According to a Turkish proverb, the body may age, but the heart does not, and the French agree: 'The heart does not grow old.' The husband's view of the beloved wife as a young girl is expressed in an Oromo proverb: 'An old wife is a child to her old husband', and in Kabardino-Cherkess it is recommended not to leave one's old wife: 'Don't forget the well-trodden roads.' However, Asian proverbs describe the full depth and enjoyment of a matured love relationship:

> Pearls are found in old shells. (*Vietnamese*)
> In love, a mature [older] woman is best. (*Japanese*)

Not all men and women, alas, succeed in realizing the ideal of a mature love partnership that develops continuously and blooms no less in old age than in the earlier phases of life. 'An old he-monkey will choose an old she-monkey,' is the advice given in an African Twi proverb, whereas in Vietnam women are wisely advised to adapt to the realities of life: 'As long as you are beautiful, choose young men; when beauty fades, you get married to an old man.' Only a few rare proverbs emphasize the advantages for a young man's union with an older woman:

> As an old woman likes her young husband, so the master loves his best scholar.
>   (*Khiongbta*)
> The old woman gives pleasure to the one who marries her. (*Ila*)
> Always marry an older woman; you won't starve and you'll benefit from her experience.
>   (*Indonesian*)

Usually, though, a love relationship between an older woman and a young man is not at all considered the 'natural' way of doing things. It is commented upon and gossiped about, and people wonder about the underlying interests: 'If a nubile girl is exchanged for an old woman, there must be a reason' (*Minyanka*). Perhaps a matter of material advantage, as suggested in some European proverbs:

> Rather have an old woman with money as the better half than a young lover with golden
>   hair. (*German/Dutch*)
> He who takes an old woman loves her money better than he loves her. (*French*)

Only the wise who look further than outward appearance or filthy lucre will enjoy the comfortableness of old shoes and savour the pleasures of surprising pearls hidden in old shells.

BAD OLD AGE

To have a long life is to lose beauty. (*Turkish*)

In most cultures, it is a scandal for an older woman to be in love with a younger man and equally for a young man to love an older woman, as for example expressed in a Rundi proverb: 'The young man's eye disdains the old woman' and, even stronger, in an English proverb from Britain: 'A young man and an old woman [are] of the Devil's making.' The most outspoken comments against such a union are numerous Arabic proverbs from the Maghreb:

> Don't marry an old woman, even though you will eat with her young pigeons and lamb's
> meat [the most delicious food]. (*Morocco*)
> He who has an old woman [for a wife] has a plague. (*Morocco*)
> Three things darken the face: carrying heavy loads on your neck, walking barefoot,
> marrying an old woman. (*Maghreb*)
> If you want your sorrow to be complete, marry a woman of your mother's age.
> (*Maghreb; Lebanon; Egypt*)

In other words, 'Young woman good luck, old woman bad luck'—a wish addressed to a man in search of a wife (*Arabic, Maghreb*). A Berber proverb from the same area looks at the age problem from a female perspective: 'O *iskni*, it is the barley that made you attractive, but what use are you after the harvest?' An *iskni* is a harvest basket, serving here as a metaphor for a wife loved by her husband when she was young and beautiful, and abandoned when she has grown old. Some proverbs express outright contempt, as for example in the following Arabic Jewish proverb from Yemen: 'An old man should be welcomed by a young girl; an old woman should be thrown out like garbage.' In Europe too, a relationship with an old woman is seriously dissuaded:

> Drink wine, not *braga* [home brewed beer], love a girl, and not an old woman. (*Russian*)
> One should not pay much for old women's love, young people's intellect and tiny horses.
> (*German*)
> A pointless business is to grind straw, a pointless job to marry an old woman. (*Karelian*)
> Who doesn't have any better, sleeps with his old wife. (*Dutch*)

A variant of the last message also exists in a Baule proverb from Ivory Coast: 'If you are ashamed of an old wife, you'll sleep alone.' Although the general idea here is that you have to accept your fate, the proverb also suggests that an older man prefers to forsake his aging wife, as if he were not aging himself.

The majority of proverbs about relationships with older women reflect older men's restless eagerness to conquer girls at least half their age: 'A bee does not sit on faded flowers' (*Spanish, El Salvador*). However, the young flowers have to adapt to the older bees:

> A young woman married to an old man must behave like an old woman. (*English, UK*)
> A young woman who marries an old man, will be treated as an old woman.
> (*Portuguese, Brazil*)
> An old man thinks his wife is old [though she may be young]. (*Oromo*)

The explanation for older men's keen interest in young women is possibly a manoeuvre to prove that they are still young, whereas an older wife, like a mirror, confronts her husband with the frightening fact of his own aging. This 'fact' holds no less true the other way round, but women's views and feelings are scarce in proverbs. Although one Russian proverb observes that: 'An old cow loves the bull too', proverbs mainly and keenly present male perspectives on men's 'natural' passion for young girls, and an older wife as second-best:

> An old wife who coughs is preferable to an empty hut. (*Mossi, Burkina Faso*)
> To mount a donkey is better than to go by foot. (*Arabic, Maghreb*)

There are different views of old women's appearance. On the one hand they are worthy of being adored and adorned: 'Prop up an old house, cherish an old wife' (*Khiongbta*) or 'Buttressing an old house is adorning an old woman with flowers' (*Burmese*); more often, however, brightening up an older woman is considered either indecent or embarrassing: 'Beautiful flowers are ashamed when they are stuck in an old woman's hair' (*Chinese*), because beautiful clothes and adornments cannot bring back juvenile beauty. An older woman's dressing up creates a dangerous illusion of youth: 'When an old woman pretends to be young there could be somebody whose eye falls on her', is a German way of warning young men against falling in love with older women. Even though they may look younger, the result is likely to be a childless relationship: 'An old hen does not lay eggs anymore' (*Italian*), or, at least: 'The older, the slower the childbirth' (*Dutch*).

With age people gradually lose some of their faculties. According to proverbs, aging women are less in demand with men than in earlier phases of life, unless they dispose of other forms of profitability or prestige than their physical attractiveness. The overall hard truth of female aging is expressed in a Baule proverb from Ivory Coast: 'Old women make space for girls.' Stepping back with old age holds of course for both sexes. However, for those women whose lives depend, economically and otherwise, mainly on men, the loss of female beauty means the loss of male attention, with all the risks implied, socially, materially and sexually.

OLD AGE BEHAVIOUR

Did any mountain flower ever intend to wither? (*Korean*)

Courageously, women fight a tragic battle against the aging of body and face, a battle without hope of victory: 'As long as your beauty has not been buried with you, don't say "I saved my body"', as a Kundu proverb from Cameroon imperturbably states. Ultimately none will survive. All over the world, physical aging is presented in words and images expressing how helpless women, especially, feel about this irreversible process:

> Old age eats youth [i.e. of women]. (*Gikuyu*)
> Old age ruins *akeyo*. [In full bloom a very beautiful plant that soon withers]. (*Acholi*)
> Age is a garland of nettles; youth, a garland of roses. (*Hebrew*)
> Holding on to beauty, by using make-up, cannot be compared to the flower of
>   youth. (*Chinese*)

However noisy a crow may be, he will not become a goose: however hard an old woman
    tries, she will not become young. (*Kirghiz/Karakalpak*)
You can hide much, but where can you hide your wrinkles? (*Assam*)

Enough examples of how much women's aging makes them worry. Ironically, worrying does
not solve the problem, on the contrary: 'Worries make you age before old age' (*Ladino*).
Some proverbs try to cheer older women up by stating that old age does not necessarily
mean the loss of all former beauty: 'What remains of wealth is still wealth and what remains
of beauty is still beauty' (*Arabic, Tunisia*). Poor comfort, as there is no way back to youth.

There is no way back to youth for men either, but they have invented proverbs to explain
their own aging problem away: 'If man gets old, he becomes a ram, if woman gets old, she
becomes naught [nothing]' which means that a man is a man at any age (*Turkish*). Many
such proverbs make explicitly clear who is the subject and who the object of looking, feeling, and deciding who is young or old—thus jokingly suggesting that aging is not at the
same level of disquietude for men as it is for women. All examples below are from the West:

A man feels only as old as the woman he feels. (*Irish*)
A man is as old as he feels: a woman as old as she looks. (*Widespread in Europe*)
A woman is as old as she looks. A man is old when he quits looking. (*English, USA*)

Old age brings losses and regrets, in proverbs depicted as lost youth and former beauty:
'Those that would have seen me before, their hearts would have opened; those that would
see me now, would be running back [and] back', says a Turkish proverb, referring to the
pleasures of youth and the aversion to old age, whereas a Tamil proverb from India reflects
impatience *vis-à-vis* women's old age: 'A young woman is joy; an old one, irritation.'

The loss or impotence of a partner is painfully felt. Especially older women, either
widowed or abandoned by their husbands for younger ones, are affected in this way: 'Yesterday is not today, as the old woman said when she thought of her [lonely] nights at
home' (*Hausa*). A Hebrew proverb refers to a husband's impotence as a form of widowhood for his wife: 'A young woman married to an old man is a lady by day and a widow by
night', and the same image is used in Arabic: 'The child of an old man is like an orphan,
[and] the woman of an old man is like a widow.'

It is of course more likely for a younger woman to have such a nightly 'widowhood'
problem with an older husband, than the other way round. Strangely enough, proverbs
prefer to ignore this possibility and instead plead strongly in favour of giving the old man
a young girl to replace his aging wife. A point that could well be related to men's fear of
impotence is that older women are presented as sexually eager and skilful. This sexual experience is commented upon in different ways. It is considered either as an advantage or
as an indecency. The most widespread metaphor in proverbs referring to sex with an older
woman is the old pot or hen that produces 'good soup', with variants in Central and Western Europe as well as in the Caribbean and South America:

Even old goats like to lick salt. (*Estonian/Hungarian*)
Up there: white hair; down there: desire. (*Spanish, Bolivia*)
An old hen makes a good soup. (*Creole/Papiamentu/Spanish*)

In fact such proverbs express that sexual needs do not change with aging, and even that experience makes older women more desirable sexual partners. Another frequently used metaphor on this matter is fire and burning:

> Wood: the drier it is, the faster it burns. (*Spanish, El Salvador*)
> Old hay burns more fiercely. [Referring to women of a riper age.] (*Kurdish, Turkey*)
> When an old barn [old maid] begins to burn, there is no extinguishing it.
>   (*Dutch/German*)
> It's easier to heat an old oven than a new one. (*French*)

Musical instruments are often used as metaphors to make the point, that older instruments are easier to tune and handle than new ones, as in the following English proverb: 'There's many a good tune played on an old fiddle.'[94] And a Creole proverb example from Belize stresses: 'The older the violin, the sweeter the music.' Thus, it is suggested in a variety of ways that older women are certainly not less but rather more capable of making love than younger ones. Old women's sexual desire is nonetheless often referred to in rather disapproving terms. An old lady's eagerness seems to be felt either as a lack of decency or as a threatening form of negative power, and often associated with witchcraft. It is believed to have eerie consequences, as expressed in an Arabic proverb from Morocco: 'Sexual intercourse with an old woman gives one lice and long hair on the head.'

In old age no less than in earlier phases of life, female behaviour is submitted to restrictions, in spite of incidental freedoms to be gained after menopause. No less than younger ones, old women are classified as 'good' and 'bad', depending on their subscribing to the norms set for what an older woman should do or refrain from. Older women are held to behave moderately, whereas they are commented upon, criticized or even mocked when paying attention to their looks, or wearing colourful clothes.

> For a young woman, liveliness; for an old witch, prudishness. (*Nepalese*)
> Being old and grey-haired, should I wear a red gown? (*Arabic, Lebanon*)
> A hundred years old, a green dress. [i.e. still coquettish, or dead: wearing a green dress
>   also refers to being buried under the grass]. (*Catalan/French*)

Thus, it is not done for an older woman to fall in love or to long for a partner: 'Love is a virtue in the young, a vice in the aged' is Italian, and 'An old nag shouldn't be brisk, a grey broad shouldn't kiss', Ukrainian. A Frisian proverb holds that 'Old in love is foolish in love' whereas in Greek an old woman is ridiculed for wanting a partner: 'Seeing the crowd, the old woman said: "Give me a man".' In the Estonian proverb: 'An old woman and a bronze kettle are always virtuous', *are* simply means 'ought to be.' A mortal blow is given to old women's sex by English proverbs from Britain associating old wives with gunpowder:

> What should be done with an old wife but make gunpowder of her?
> An old woman is better than saltpetre for making gunpowder.

Gunpowder was made from saltpetre, a product used to reduce man's libido and given as a sedative to men in prison.

Two Chinese prescriptions refer to old women who are (supposed to be) serene and devoid of passion: 'Old wells do not bubble' and: 'At an advanced age a good woman has no need of a man.' A Malagasy proverb states that: 'A [woman's] last husband is a brother' (*Madagascar*) which suggests that old couples (ought to) live without having sex. If an old woman should preferably not fall in love nor feel like having sex anymore, what about her being interested in marriage or remarriage? Two German proverbs comment: 'A late wedding is a letter to the grave-digger', especially when the old woman has grandchildren: '"Our mother is the bride", is possible, "our grandmother is the bride" sounds awful.' An older woman should not be pregnant either: 'An old woman who bears a child does not know where to leave it' (*Kazakh*).

Youthful activities, such as whistling, running, or dancing, openly expressing cheerfulness and other forms of 'exuberance' are considered unsuitable for women in old age.[95] Multiple proverbs warn aged ladies against visible or audible indecencies: 'Old women's laugh ends up in coughing', as it is said in both Danish and German, and 'laugh' here refers to unbecoming behaviour of any kind, or, in Spanish and Greek: 'An applauding old woman throws up a cloud of dust.' In Latin it is even stressed, that old women should not indulge in having fun: 'When an old hag has fun, death chuckles.' A similar proverb also exists in German: 'Old women's joy is death's rejoicing.'

Women's old-age 'exuberances' are acceptable only in exceptional circumstances, or in case of emergencies:

> Old women do not whistle without reason.[96] (*Rundi*)
> Even an old woman may run when a goat carries her snuffbox. (*Nigeria*)
> Need makes the old woman trot.
> (*Danish/Dutch/English/German/French/Irish; Pidgin, Jamaica*)
> No matter the age of a woman, when she catches fire she jumps. (*Danish/Spanish*)

Next to beautifying, dancing is widely considered unsuitable for old women: they are no longer able to perform the dances of the young, and they should not even try to do so:

> To dance with an old woman is like riding a donkey. (*Spanish, Mexico*)
> To dance like young girls is not becoming for a grandmother.
> (*Russian/Romanian*)
> The she-cat is on the roof and the old woman with blackened eyes is dancing [wanting to prove that she is as agile as a cat]. (*Arabic, Algeria*)
> As long as her dance is not finished, don't say: 'Grandma, your foot is nimble.'
> (*Mandinka*)
> The morning rain is like an old woman's dance, soon over. (*English, USA*)

Such behaviour provokes death's intervention punishing the breaker of the norm: 'An old woman's dance brings death to her yard', a German proverb warns. It is difficult to decide to what extent such proverbs function as observations, admonitions, or prescriptions as to how things ought to be. But one thing comes across clearly: old women must behave discreetly; having passed the age of attractiveness, they should by no means draw any attention to themselves in the public space.

DECREPITUDE AND DEATH

To encourage each other, old ladies say: 'O young lady!' (Oromo)

In the Oromo proverb 'One old woman will call another old woman Grandmother', the message is that, under the pretence of being respectful, one of the two old ladies addresses the other as 'really old', in the meanwhile pretending that she herself is still 'younger'. The proverb means that people usually prefer to talk about the bad situation of others, unwilling to recognize that their own situation is not that glorious either. Another African proverb from Rwanda is of the same tenor: 'The old woman who outstrips another one says: "Spare me those hollow eyes".'

Old women manage quite well until they reach a great age, and 'There's a tough sinew in an old wife's heel', as the English proverb puts it. Sometimes it is suggested that their power takes on almost supernatural dimensions: 'A solid old woman, even the mill could not grind her' (*Lithuanian*), but even without such extraordinary forces, there are many ways of overcoming the limitations of old age, as it is nicely expressed in a Mamprusi proverb: 'The toothless old woman still chews cola nut.'

Nevertheless, old age generates inconveniences and, next to diminishing beauty, deterioration of health is mentioned as one of the negative consequences of advanced old age:

Ten old women, eleven diseases. (*German*)
'In former days the cocks used to crow, now they yawn,' said the old woman when she
    had become deaf. (*Frisian*)
There is no Saturday without sun, nor an old woman without pain, nor a maiden with-
    out love. (*Spanish, Bolivia/Argentina*)
Old houses and old ladies always need repairing. (*English, USA*)

The loss of energy ultimately leads to the inability to take care: 'An old woman cannot control the pestle anymore' (*Hehe*). In other words, old age involves defects undreamed of in earlier life. This is either reflected in terms of the way she dresses: 'Grandmother's wrinkled skirt never used to be wrinkled' (*Sranan*), or, metaphorically: 'The old cow gets stuck in every mud puddle' (*Spanish, Colombia*). There are hardly any proverbs referring to the mental deterioration of elderly women, and it is not even sure that the following three examples fall into that category:

Grandma only knows her old-hag's talk. (*Bulgarian*)
The seagull, the older, the crazier. (*Spanish, Argentina*)
The old, blind, deaf, mute and cripple [woman] spins the cotton, reports the news from
    anywhere and frisks about the rocks; she prays her chaplet [rosary], gossips and
    breaks the dog's teeth if he interferes by barking. (*Arabic, Maghreb/West Sahara*)

Old people are bound to die and to leave some legacies. Proverbs reveal people's greedy thoughts *vis-à-vis* their older relatives: 'Old grandmothers have old savings' (*German*) and 'If an old woman falls down twice, the things in her basket will be counted' (*Igbo*). Openly expressed curses and death wishes regarding old women are not lacking, although none of those come from Asia:

Kill the old woman for her locust bean cakes. (*Hausa*)
Old maids and young dogs should be drowned. (*Romanian*)
An old woman and a new plough are nowhere better than in the earth. (*German*)

The encouragement to stand up for one's rights is expressed in Ganda: 'The polite and shy old lady let people bury her alive.' Does the proverb, indirectly, refer to death-hastening, a practice in which elderly people are killed or abandoned or exposed to the natural elements?[97] There is only one direct reference to this custom, in Spanish: 'Take the old woman who cannot walk to the sandy plain.' A Lega proverb argues against the option: 'Don't kill my grandmother, a frying pan that will break soon,' i.e. of its own accord.

In a Persian proverb, impatience is expressed *vis-à-vis* an old woman who delays dying: 'The winter is past and the old woman is not dead' (*Iran*). It refers to improvident people who make no preparation for the future. To express that things occur at inconvenient times, another Persian proverb—'The old woman did not die until a rainy day'—reflects irritation, not about the death of an old woman as such, an event causing no regret, but because of the burial taking place in the rain. No one chooses his or her own time of dying, as death harvests indiscriminately: 'Both an old woman and a young girl will go to the grave' (*Spanish, El Salvador*). A proverb from Rwanda observes that death is inclined to take away the wrong people on purpose: 'When an old woman sees Death and asks him to come back and pass the night, he will return and kill all her children.'

A final issue frequently mentioned is that those who despise or ridicule older people, forget that old age is no less their own future:

Girl, never laugh at an old woman, because soon you will be dried up like the moon yourself. (*Bulgarian*)
Superb tree, don't ridicule dead wood: you'll die too. (*Lega*)

STATUS AND AUTHORITY

A woman with withered breasts drinks beer like a man. (Ganda)

It has been suggested that in a wide variety of societies aging following menopause gains women more status and authority.[98] The Ganda motto to this section was the only proverb I found explicitly confirming some post-menopausal right. Several proverbs reflect that older women after menopause acquire a little more respect than they enjoyed before, because of their life experience, and because they are no longer attractive enough to create 'chaos' and confusion among men once they have lost their youthful and powerful sex appeal. For this same reason, as we have seen, old women are despised in contexts where youth and beauty are overvalued. Old women (not old men) are advised to make themselves invisible, even more than younger women or wives, and to behave as if they are asexual beings. Proverbs, then, do not give much reason to celebrate a supposed 'freedom' of women after menopause.

Even though the hierarchies in proverbs discussed here are mainly associated with gender matters, some internal female hierarchies can be discerned in the context of women's phases of life. A Lao proverb refers to both: 'To have a husband is to live like a servant; to have a child is to be master of your own kingdom.' Broadly outlined, then, girls are low-est on the female ladder, they still have to prove what they're worth, and first need to get married and produce posterity in order for the community to take them a little more seriously. Spinsters are 'lower' than wives, and sterile wives are the lowest category of wives.

Undeniably, mothers are the most respected category of women at large, but then, there are mothers and mothers, and the various kinds are differently judged, from mothers of one or more daughters to, higher up, mothers of one son, and, at the top of the hierarchy, the mother of many sons (including possibly one daughter). Grandmothers and old women are sometimes appreciated for their wisdom and practical knowledge, and of course respected for having grandchildren. The fear of women's (especially old women's) awesome powers is reflected in proverbs about secret knowledge and destruc-tive forces such as witchcraft and devilry—to be dealt with later. As a fitting end to this long chapter on women's phases of life, let me quote just one example of the mysterious powers ascribed to women: 'A woman can turn a man into whatever she wants, even into an old woman' (*Frisian*).

Phases of Life Anthology

GIRLS, DAUGHTERS, BRIDES

Every girl has her own luck. (*Uzbek*): *Geyvandov 95*

The greatest treasure on earth is children. (*Japanese*): *Geyvandov 160*

If you say there is a difference, there is a difference, as there is a difference between a son and
a daughter. (*Tibetan*): *Duncan 172*

A BOY OR A GIRL?

Who leaves a son behind is not really dead. (*Danish*): *Ley 111*

The parents' home is owned country for boys and a restaurant for girls.
(*Chinese*): *o.s. Huang Mingfen*

The girl who gets married is no relative anymore. (*Korean*): *o.s. P. Touw*

A woman is nobody's relative. (*Mongo, Cong DR*): *Hulstaert 132*

Eighteen goddess-like daughters are not equal to one son with a hump.
(*Chinese*): *Champion 335*

Ten fine girls are not equal to one cripple boy. (*Chinese*): *Plopper 99*

One lame son is more valuable than eighteen golden daughters. (*Chinese*): *Lunde & Wintle 151*

A stupid son is better than a crafty daughter. (*Chinese*): *Scarborough 201*

It is a blessing to bear a son, a calamity to bear a daughter. (*Chinese*): *Scarborough 196*

A girl is worth one-tenth of a boy. (*Chinese*): *Champion 361*

In a pond without fish, shrimps are highly prized. (*Chinese*): *Fabre 10*

If you cannot get any mercury, red earth becomes valuable. (*Chinese*): *Champion 369*

A [one] son counts as one; ten daughters do not count at all. (*Vietnamese*): *Dình Khuê Duong 25*

Those who spread lies will give birth to daughters. (*Telegu, India*): *Murty 226*

Three things a man prefers not to have: weeds in his garden, a girl among his sons and vinegar in his wine. (*Hebrew, Israel*): *Alcalay 93*

Every daughter is a handful of trouble. (*Arabic, widespread*): *Lunde & Wintle 121*

When a daughter is born, the threshold weeps for forty days.
   (*Arabic, widespread*): *Lunde & Wintle 121; Champion 334*

A girl is always a source of trouble, even when she is a queen on a throne.
   (*Arabic, Syria/Lebanon*): *Feghali 189*

To bear a girl is to bear a problem. (*Tigrinya, Eritrea*): *o.s. Ghirmai Negash*

A woman without a daughter should bury herself alive. (*Ladino/Hebrew, Morocco*): *Stahl 214*

No one knows when the man without daughters dies. [It is the daughters who wail, expressing grief when a father dies.] (*Arabic, Morocco*): *Lunde & Wintle 43*

A clan with female posterity cannot perish. [A clan prospers as long as there are nubile girls.]
   (*Kongo, Congo DR*): *Clémentine Faik-Nzuji 12*

A whole night of labour and then only a daughter. (*Spanish*): *Collins 202*

Many sons, many blessings of God; many daughters, many calamities.
   (*German*): *Meier-Pfaller 75*

When a girl is born, even the roofs cry. (*Bulgarian*): *Arnaudov 53*

When a wife gives birth to a boy, even the walls of the house rejoice. (*Armenian*): *Sakayan 240*

Better nine sons than one daughter. (*Estonian*): *Geyvandov 148*

Woe the mother who has only a daughter [and no son].
   (*Serbian/Croatian*): *Karadžić 287*

A daughter is a child of other people; only a daughter-in-law is really our child.
   (*Vietnamese*): *Dình Khuê Duong 135*

A daughter is another man's child. (*Korean*): *Geyvandov 177; Dình Khuê Duong 135*

Daughters have wings. (*Ladino, Morocco*): *Dahan 42*

A female child is worthless, if it dies it is lost; if given into marriage it is lost.
   (*Bengali, India*): *o.s. Shobha Gupta*

Married daughter, spilt water. (*Chinese*): *o.s. Huang Mingfen*

A girl is [no more important than a] cigarette's ashes.
   (*Arabic, Maghreb/West Sahara*): *Duvollet 40*

A girl-child is like a *mutuma* [fig tree]: the one who did not plant gets the profit.
   (*Ganda, Uganda*): *Walser 269*

A boy is born facing in; a girl is born facing out. (*Chinese*): *Plopper 99*

First a girl, then a boy. (*Japanese*): *Huzii 89*

A first daughter is worth a capital in the household. (*Korean*): *Geyvandov 177*

The eldest daughter is a baby sit for her younger siblings. (*Vietnamese*): *Geyvandov 173*

Blessed the house where the daughter arrives before the son.
   (*Ladino/Hebrew, Morocco*): *Benazeraf 90*

He whose first child is one with a vulva was gladdened by God. (*Arabic*): *Westermarck 89*

The ideal of the Prophet is having a daughter and a son. (*Arabic, Syria/Lebanon*): *Feghali 192*

First a daughter then a son and the family's well begun. (*English, USA*): *Mieder 1992: 135*

She who brings forth a daughter, also gets a son [i.e. a son-in-law, when she marries].
(*Ganda, Uganda*): *Walser 68*

Rather than begetting a bad son, better to beget a good daughter and depend on a son-in-law. (*Oromo, Ethiopia*): *Cotter 7*

One good daughter is worth ten sons if she can find a good bridegroom.
(*Bengali, India*): *Geyvandov 177*

A mother of only daughters does not laugh before the others laugh. (*Rwanda*): *Crépeau 380*

The mother of a girl child does not laugh at the things of girls. (*Oromo, Ethiopia*): *Cotter 4*

Four girls make up the four feet of a bed: a steady basis for a boy who is the fifth.
(*Chinese*): *Fabre 70*

None is abused for having a daughter as long as he still can bring forth. (*Rwanda*): *Crépeau 350*

Who only has one daughter, will make her a wonder. (*Spanish*): *Meier-Pfaller 83*

A family without a daughter is like an oven without heat. (*Korean*): *Geyvandov 177*

Who has daughters, has bread; who has sons, goes begging. (*Catalan, Spain*): *Guiter 123*

Farmer's luck: bull calves and girl babies. (*English, USA*): *Person 181*

Marriage decreases their support [i.e. married daughters are no longer available to support their own relatives]. (*Zulu, South Africa*): *Geyvandov 177*

A father of lots of girls runs the risk of getting a dog for a son-in-law.
(*Arabic, Syria/Lebanon*): *Feghali 185*

BRIDE-WEALTH AND DOWRY

The candle of a father of daughters burns all night. [He passes sleepless nights because of worries.] (*Ladino, Morocco*): *Dahan 38*

Better two scorpions [in the house] than two daughters.
(*Arabic, Maghreb/West Sahara*): *Duvollet 40*

One girl is a girl, two girls are half a girl and three girls are no girl at all.
(*English, USA*): *Mieder 1992: 251*

One daughter, a good girl; two daughters, enough girls; three daughters, too many girls; four daughters and a wife, five devils against one father.
(*Catalan, Spain; Spanish, Spain/Argentina*): *Guiter 137; Collins 373; Bergua 495; Champion 298, 614*

One son, no son; second son, half son; third [one is] a son. (*Estonian*): *Paczolay 78*

The world cannot exist without males and females, yet happy the father of sons and unhappy the father who has only daughters. (*Hebrew, Israel*): *Malka 23*

A son born after three daughters is destined to become a beggar; a daughter born after three sons will rule a kingdom. (*Bhojpuri, India*): *Champion 396*

The death of a girl is fortunate though she may be ready to get married.
(*Arabic, Lebanon*): *Frayha II 691*

The daughter of a maternal uncle is not obtained for money. [Priority for the full cousin.]
(*Arabic, Tunisia*): *Duvollet 38*

Cousin, let us get married and keep the dowry in the family. (*English, Jamaica*): *Geyvandov 96*

Marry your cousin, so that if evil comes it will be kept to yourself.
(*Maori, New Zealand*): *Brougham & Reed 37–8*

You can marry whoever you like, as long as it is cousin Manuel.
  (*Portuguese, Brazil*): *Magalhães Júnior 65*
A girl with a nice disposition is always happy, and so is a girl with potential husbands
  through relationship agreements. (*Afar, Eritrea/Ethiopia*): *Parker 286*
The child resembles the father but belongs to the clan [of the mother].
  (*Twi, Ghana*): *Geyvandov 166*
A house of girls is a house of ruin. (*Arabic, Lebanon*): *Abela 171*
Daughters in the cradle, dowry in the chest. (*Russian*): *Geyvandov 96*
A lot of girls and a large garden ruin the best farm. (*German*): *Meier-Pfaller 75*
A family of elegant daughters is the worst thief of all. (*Chinese*): *Lunde & Wintle 60*
Even a king begetting more than five [daughters] becomes a pauper.
  (*Tamil, India*): *Subramanian 111*
To have three daughters is to run through one's fortune. (*Japanese*): *Huzii 95*
He who marries off his daughter, will stay behind broke. (*Portuguese, Brazil*): *Lamenza 211*
The poor do not marry off their daughters. (*Spanish, Venezuela*): *Febres Cordero 60*
The birth of a daughter is like seven thieves in your safe. (*Polish*): *Geyvandov 147*
Many daughters at home, much poverty. (*Romanian*): *Günther 22–3*
A house full of daughters is a cellar full of sour beer [i.e. makes you poor].
  (*Dutch*): *Mesters 74; Meier-Pfaller 78*
The dresses of the daughters devour the harvest. (*Catalan, Spain*): *Guiter 137*
He who has three daughters may sleep with his door open. [Their marriages cost so much
  that there is no longer anything of value in the house, and therefore the father needs not
  be afraid of thieves in the night.] (*Korean*): *o.s. B. Walraven*
Marrying off a daughter is like digging a well [i.e. equally essential and expensive].
  (*Bhojpuri, India*): *Champion 396*
Because of the presents, the bride is not sent back. (*Bulgarian*): *Arnaudov 103*
A money-bag makes the marriage of an ugly one possible. (*Swedish*): *Geyvandov 98*
I married my daughter off in order that I might relieve myself of worry, but there she comes
  back to me with four little ones behind her. (*Arabic, Lebanon*): *Frayha I 248, 342*
He who has a daughter will age quickly. (*Turkish*): *Geyvandov 178*
When a good offer comes for your daughter, don't wait until her father returns from the
  market. (*Spanish*): *Champion 298*
If you like beauty, you should not discuss the amount of the dowry.
  (*Arabic, Tunisia*): *Yetiv 35*
In the upper classes people provide their daughters with a lot of money when they get
  married; in the middle classes people simply marry off their daughters, and in the lower
  classes people try to enrich themselves by the marriage of their daughters.
  (*Chinese*): *Geyvandov 97*
The beauty of the girl is half the dowry. (*Russian*): *Graf 174*
Fair maidens need no purses. (*German*): *Reinsberg-Düringsfeld 41*
Born handsome is born married. (*Italian*): *Bohn 100; Menarini 7; Speroni 191*
Beauty wears the dowry in the face. (*English, UK*): *Geyvandov 96*
A great dowry is a bed full of brambles. (*English, UK*): *Bohn 1855: 289*

Don't pay attention to the silver, if life is not nice [i.e. when the proposed groom is rich but unsympathetic]. (*Belorussian*): *Geyvandov 99*

A marriage for money is made by the Devil. (*Hebrew, Israel*): *Cohen 1961: 325*

Unmarried, a woman obeys her father; married, her husband. (*Chinese*): *Scarborough 14*

Girls and water go wherever they are sent. (*Korean*): *Geyvandov 203*

VIRGINITY AND VIRTUE

Comb your daughter's hair until she is twelve, safeguard her until she is sixteen, after sixteen say thank you to whomsoever will wed her. (*Czech*): *Champion 98*

A virgin is a rose that still has to unfold its petals. (*Hebrew, Israel*): *Alcalay 510*

As soon as she can bring a pot to her mouth, she can carry what her mother carries.
(*Arabic, Maghreb*): *Cheneb II 280*

When the bride starts growing up, the husband dies. (*Tamil, India*): *Geyvandov 137*

A thing which has not occurred since time immemorial: a young girl broke wind in her husband's lap. [Even child brides must be of suitable age.]
(*Sumerian, Mesopotamia*): *Lambert 260*

The bride has been born, the groom mounts a horse. (*Russian*): *Geyvandov 101*

A young girl is like a pineapple: she may be green on top, but the fruit below is ready.
(*Portuguese, Brazil*): *Mota 122*

The herbalist has no herbs for lost innocence. (*Sorbian*): *Herrmann 59*

A girl's chastity is her dowry. (*Tamil, India*): *Geyvandov 104*

Girls are a humiliation. (*Berber, Morocco*): *Bentolila 87*

A disgraced maiden dishonours her whole family. (*Portuguese, Brazil*): *Vascondellos 67*

If your daughter is out in the streets, check your honour to see if it is still there.
(*Arabic, Tunisia*): *Tetiv 69*

The flower is picked, the stalk is trampled. [The flower is the daughter, the stalk refers to her parents.] (*Malay*): *Lunde & Wintle 140*

Money, like girls, should not sleep in the yard. (*Creole, Haiti*): *ACCT 47*

A daughter is a treasure and a cause of sleepless nights.
(*Hebrew/Ladino, Morocco*): *Rosten 1977: 153*

He who does not want to give his daughter in marriage, raises her price.
(*Arabic, Lebanon*): *Abela 24; Frayha I 533*

Marry off your daughter and eat fresh fish betimes. (*English, USA*): *Franklin 1736*

Only three things warrant haste: the marriage of a daughter, the burial of the dead, and the feeding of a guest. (*Persian*): *Lunde & Wintle 59*

The deceased and the daughter should leave the house quickly. (*Dutch*): *Ter Laan 63*

Daughters and dead fish are no keeping wares. (*English, UK*): *Bohn 1855: 233; Bohn 1857: 342*

Girls and eggs cannot be kept for a long time.
(*German; Letzeburgish*): *Reinsberg-Düringsfeld 40; Meier-Pfaller 41*

Girls are like horses, if you don't give them away when they are young, they lose their luck.
(*Italian*): *Reinsberg-Düringsfeld 40*

Sweet pears and young women can't last long. (*Frisian, Netherlands*): *Beintema 107*

A woman is not a cow to be kept forever. (*Kru, Liberia*): *Geyvandov 111*

Marry your son when you will, your daughter when you can.

   (*Turkey, Europe, the Americas, the Caribbean, the Arab world*): *Champion 91, 629; Franklin 1734;*
   Geyvandov 93; Yetiv 141; Champion 91, 629; Geyvandov 93; Moya 355; Vasconcellos 97; Mota 65;
   Llewellyn Watson 115; o.s. A.P. Kwak

Apples at Easter and girls of thirty have lost their flavour.

   (*French; German; Letzeburgish*): *o.s. Laure Wolter*

If your daughter is getting on in years, free your slave and let them get married.

   (*Hebrew, Israel*): *Alcalay 93*

A girl older than ten has to get married, if need be, to a pariah. (*Tamil, India*): *Geyvandov 93*

Girls and glasses are always in danger. (*German*): *Meier-Pfaller 53; Pineaux 94*

A girl is thin glass. (*Ossetian, RF*): *Geyvandov 283*

Daughters are brittle ware. (*English, USA*): *Kin 64*

A girl is like crystal: if shattered, it cannot be restored. (*Armenian*): *Sakayan 244*

The bottle [is only good] with its sealing-wax, the girl with her hymen.

   (*Arabic, Maghreb*): *Cheneb III 230*

Glass and maidens are easily broken. (*Korean*): *Ha 211*

Hair and virgins, many are fake. (*Spanish*): *Bergua 161*

A virginal womb and a warm sun at Christmas are rarities. (*Danish*): *Molbech 158*

A girl's honesty is like snow; when it melts the whiteness is no longer seen.

   (*Romanian*): *Champion 254; Mieder 1986: 231; Geyvandov 200*

How rare a thing it is to match virginity with beauty. (*Hebrew, Israel*): *Cohen 1961: 535*

Chaste is [only] she whom no one has asked. (*English, USA; Dutch*): *Kin 45; Mesters 104*

The girl [who has lost her virginity] is no longer clean. (*Indonesian*): *o.s. P. de Haas*

[A girl who has lost her virginity:] Touched by man. (*English, Hawaii*): *Pukui 311*

A young virgin does not want to be injured by fire. (*Dutch*): *Cock 109–10*

A virgin girl in her parents' house is like a lump of dough: if kept outside crows peck at it, if
   kept inside rats nibble at it. (*Punjabi, India*): *Bedi 170*

An embrace can break a bracelet. (*Pashto, Afghanistan*): *Geyvandov 91*

A jug only breaks once. (*Uzbek*): *Geyvandov 92*

It costs so much to preserve your honour, said the good virgin. (*Dutch*): *Mesters 104*

A girl worth kissing is not easily kissed. (*English, USA*): *Mieder 1992: 250*

Take the road that keeps innocence [virginity] intact. (*Nepalese*): *Geyvandov 104*

A girl gets pregnant only once. (*Rwanda*): *Crépeau 177*

Stay in your nest, until he comes, the one who will make you fly away.

   (*Arabic, Maghreb*): *Cheneb I 53*

If you really are in love, you don't need care if she's a virgin or not. (*Creole, Haiti*): *Ibekwe 118*

As long as the belly keeps silence, all whores are virgins. (*German*): *Wander I 249*

The affair is finished, the slut is in the corner [has given birth], the child sits on the lap, milk
   is in the nipples. (*Estonian*): *Geyvandov 264*

One who has secretly sinned will give birth in public. (*Dargin/Tatar, RF*): *Geyvandov 272*

Whoever puts out a net in the water, wants to catch fish. (*Creole, Martinique*): *David 45*

Five minutes of pleasure, nine months of torment. (*Portuguese, Brazil*): *Vasconcellos 117*

We praised the bride, and she was found pregnant. (*Arabic, Tunisia*): *Yetiv 101*

The impatient virgin becomes a mother without being a bride. (*English, USA*): *Kin 128*

The girl who is praised for dancing will be gossiped about when pregnant out of marriage.
(*Oromo, Ethiopia*): *Cotter 55*

A pregnant girl is not married for the first kitchen. (*Nama, Namibia*): *Knappert: 196*

She never used to go to the washing place [a place known to be dangerous for girls]— and yet
… (*Mapuche, Argentina / Chile*): *Koessler-Ilg 117*

Once there was a time … now only pregnancy is left. (*Russian*): *Geyvandov 286*

It is too late to scratch your backside after the child has been made. (*Danish*): *Kjaer Holbek 168*

Frequent kisses end in a baby. (*Hungarian*): *Mieder 1986: 260*

Better a bad dowry than a bad gift [i.e. illegitimate pregnancy]. (*Fulfulde, Senegal*): *Gaden 27*

A beautiful dress cannot conceal the shame. (*Serbian*): *Karadžić 183*

The coat of the girl makes the neighbours gossip. (*Catalan, Spain; French*): *Guiter 101*

A wide coat and a husband often conceal a big shame. (*Danish*): *Kjaer Holbek 100*

The man who made a virgin pregnant hates each new moon. (*Oromo, Ethiopia*): *Cotter 87*

Without earrings no kisses. (*Catalan, Spain; French*): *Guiter 103; Ségalen 33*

You promised me earrings and I pierced my ears; you did not give me earrings and made me
suffer for nothing. (*Arabic, Syria / Lebanon*): *Feghali 30*

To marry in the hay is wonderful, but in church it is true forever. (*Dutch*): *Mesters 82*

Marriage and hanging are determined by destiny. (*English, UK*): *Geyvandov 106*

Fishes in the sea, *asam* tree on the mountain, they meet each other in the stewpot. [Even
when two people live far apart, if they are meant for each other, nothing can prevent their
marriage.] (*Indonesian*): *o.s. Sylvia Schipper*

As for marriage, I have married you off; but as for luck, where could I get it for you?
(*Arabic, Lebanon*): *Frayha I 236*

SPINSTERS

Better a spinster than being with a husband you don't love. (*Russian*): *Geyvandov 102*

If she cannot be married, she will be a fig tree. (*Adangme, Ghana*): *Geyvandov 200*

Spinsters miss the train. (*Spanish, Chile*): *o.s. Lucero*

A young girl without a husband is like a night without the moon.
(*Bengali, India*): *o.s. Sanjukta Gupta*

An unmarried daughter is like a sack of rice on which duty has not yet been paid.
(*Chinese*): *Lunde & Wintle 61*

A woman without a husband is a palm tree without dates.
(*Arabic, Maghreb / West Sahara*): *Duvollet 41*

A woman without a husband is like a horse without reins. (*Turkish*): *o.s. A.P. Kwak*

Were it not because of mockery and shame, no single [woman] would have come under the
canopy. (*Ladino, Maghreb*): *Dahan 208*

Untilled land is like a widow or a lonely spinster. (*Hebrew, Israel*): *Alcalay 270*

[An old spinster] is no more appreciated than an undelivered letter.
(*Hungarian*): *Geyvandov 104*

The spinster is difficult to govern. (*Spanish, Argentina*): *Magalhães Júnior 488*

The old spinster takes care of the home. (*Rwanda*): *Crépeau 250*

Spinsterhood is far worse than a life in bad wedlock. (*Bulgarian*): *Champion 92*

We married in order not to be called spinster, we gave birth to sons in order not to be called
    sterile. (*Ladino, Morocco*): *Dahan 169*

The married one has a lot of sorrows, but the unmarried one has one more.
    (*Finnish*): *Ley 168; Geyvandov 89*

The spinster wishes to be like the married woman even though she is sterile.
    (*Oromo, Ethiopia*): *Cotter 74–5*

Everything that falls is picked up by someone, and even spinsters may sometimes get lucky.
    (*Arabic, Oman*): *Lunde & Wintle 137*

Happiness looks at an old spinster. (*Digor, RF*): *Geyvandov 105*

An old spinster will become a young wife. (*Hungarian*): *Geyvandov 105*

Unmarried girls do not risk widowhood. (*Ladino / Hebrew*): *Dahan 200*

The married chicken pecks, the unmarried chicken pecks. Better unmarried then: she'll peck
    for herself. (*Fulfulde, Senegal*): *Gaden 33*

Better a good spinster's life than badly married.
    (*Spanish, Mexico*): *Casasola 177; Rodríguez D. 183*

Better be an honest old spinster than a bored husband's wife. (*Estonian*): *Geyvandov 105*

Who has no work to do can dig the spinster's grave. (*Minyanka, Mali*): *Cauvin 1980: 204*

WEDDING DAY

Girl, rejoice not over your wedding dress; there is much trouble behind it.
    (*Arabic, widespread*): *Khalil Safadi 79*

Girls do not know the worries of wives. (*Minyanka, Mali*): *Cauvin 1980: 687*

If young girls only knew what old wives know, they would never marry.
    (*English, Jamaica*): *Llewellyn Watson 119*

The bride is respected for one day. (*Chinese*): *o.s. Huang Mingfen*

Any bride is born for the sake of her groom. (*Russian*): *Geyvandov 106*

A girl leaves her father's house in a bridal carriage and returns only in a coffin.
    (*India*): *zaza.com / awomansplace / description.html*

At the wedding feast, the one to eat the least is the bride.
    (*English, USA; Spanish, Puerto Rico*): *Brown 1970:18; Fernánez Valledor 46*

All brides are child brides in their mother's eyes. (*English, USA*): *Mieder 1992: 70*

The bride is a frog, but the wedding a cyclone. [The bride is insignificant, but the wedding a
    great, ostentatious show.] (*Arabic, Lebanon*): *Frayha II 428*

An ugly bride spends much money on the veil. (*Dutch*): *Harrebomée I 99*

Our bride is flawless, except for her blindness, her pimples and fits.
    (*Persian; Hebrew / Ladino*): *Geyvandov 253*

If the bride is ugly, what good is the beauty of her mother?
    (*Pashto, Afghanistan*): *Geyvandov 248*

The pearls the bride wears at her wedding, are the tears she will cry afterwards.
    (*Spanish*): *Geyvandov 114*

Weeping bride, laughing wife; laughing bride, weeping wife.
    (*Russian*): *Mieder 1986: 47; Rauch 132*

The girl will have little fortune if she doesn't cry on her wedding ceremony.
   (*Chinese*): *o.s. Huang Mingfen*

A sad bride makes a glad wife. (*English, USA*): *Kim 520*

Happy the bride the sun shines on, and happy the corpse the rain rains on.
   (*English UK/ USA*): *Bohn 1855: 44; Hines 118*

Rain during the wedding is a good omen. (*Russian*): *Graf 1960*

If rain falls on the lap of the bride, she will soon be pregnant. (*Dutch*): *Harrebomée I 99*

If bride and groom get wet feet, they will be three within a year. (*French*): *Ségalen 35*

Only one woman needs to dress up and the girl loses her bridegroom. (*Vietnamese*): *Geyvandov 97*

A daughter without a father: her marriage will be discussed outside the house.
   (*Oromo, Ethiopia*): *Cotter 19n*

Even during the process of getting dressed for her wedding, a bride does not always know
   who shall marry her. (*Arabic, Lebanon*): *Frayha II 428–9; Geyvandov 286*

A cousin has the right to take the bride off the mare's back. (*Arabic, Lebanon*): *Frayha I 10*

Do not pamper your daughter; what would she do if she is abducted by a Turk?
   (*Bengali, India*): *Long I 43*

A caught fish is no longer fed. (*Japanese*): *o.s. Keiko Kosunose*

The husband's house is filled with seven barrels full of bile. (*Persian*): *Geyvandov 153*

A young girl should be laid on an old man. (*Greek*): *Politès 1*

A young girl and an old lecher fill the cradle for years to come.
   (*Dutch*): *Mesters 104; Ter Laan 248*

The eyes are young forever. (*Spanish, Argentina/Uruguay*): *Guarnieri 27*

A rich man is never old for a girl. (*French*): *Roux de Lincy 235*

The youthfulness of an old man is in his wallet. (*Spanish, Puerto Rico*): *Díaz Rivera 33*

An old man marrying a young girl is like buying a book for someone else to read.
   (*English, USA*): *Thompson 484*

An old man who marries a young woman buys a newspaper for others to read.
   (*Portuguese, Brazil*): *Souto Maior 60*

An old man who marries a young girl should not leave the house. [He needs to control her
   behaviour.] (*Spanish, Costa Rica*): *Hernández 261*

An old man with a young woman: either a cuckold or the grave.
   (*Portuguese, Brazil*): *Magalhães Júnior 146*

An old man is a bed full of bones. (*English, UK*): *Browning 356*

Young women are the horses on which men ride to hell. (*Dutch*): *Mesters 67*

A young woman is an old man's coffin. (*Frisian, Netherlands*): *o.s. J. Calsbeek*

When an old man takes a young wife, death laughs.
   (*Hebrew, Israel; Russian*): *Cohen 1961: 550; Graf 42*

Better 'little wife' than 'little girl'. (*Rwanda*): *Crépeau 373*

WEDLOCK

Husbands are the only resort for wives both in this life and in the hereafter.
   (*Sanskrit, India*): *Jha 41*

To marry is a disaster, not to marry is a disaster. (*Lithuanian*): *Geyvandov 89*

Marriages are made in heaven. (*Hebrew, Israel*): *Alcalay 310*

Marry or don't marry, whichever you do, you will repent it. (*Hebrew, Israel*): *Cohen 1961: 326*

The bachelor feels bored, and the husband feels shackled. (*Ladino, Morocco*): *Dahan 218*

Marriage is like a cage: the birds without despair to get in and those within despair to get
out. (*Hebrew, Israel*): *Cohen 1961: 325*

Marriage is not a journey: by marrying you have put your head through the hangman's rope.
(*Creole, Martinique*): *David 42*

Wedlock is like a chicken run, one wants to get in, another wants to get out.
(*Russian*): *Graf 69*

Marriage is like an eel-trap: those within want to get out; those without want to get in.
(*Danish; German*): *Storm Petersen 20; Brix 121; Meier-Pfaller 67*

The girl that thinks no man is good enough for her is right, but she is left.
(*English, USA*): *Mieder 1992: 251*

The middle of the day has come and breakfast has not been eaten. (*Tibetan*): *Duncan 235*

The hen would be happy if she did not have to take part in the wedding, but they pulled her
there by her wings. (*Russian*): *Rauch 139; Geyvandov 280*

The cow does not want to marry, but she is taken along on a leash. (*Ukrainian*): *Geyvandov 280*

She cried for marriage and when married she cried again. (*Oromo, Ethiopia*): *Cotter 18*

Marriage is the supreme blunder that all women make. (*English, USA*): *Brown 1970:114*

A girl marries to please her parents, a widow to please herself.
(*Chinese*): *Scarborough 13; Geyvandov 155*

The woman is beautiful with the man, without a man she is no woman.
(*Russian*): *o.s. Anna Ravve*

Man's life is ambition; woman's life is man. (*Khionghta, Bangladesh*): *Lewin 26*

A maiden not yet given is under her own power; once given she is in the power of the man.
(*Tibetan*): *Duncan 235*

A girl's dignity exists only when she is with her father. [She has to be accompanied.]
(*Arabic, Maghreb*): *Cheneb III 210*

A girl who has no brother stays at home. (*Armenian*): *Sakayan 245*

Not she who's with her father, but she who's with her husband, is happy.
(*Russian*): *Geyvandov 65*

If you have no husband, you are naked [i.e. vulnerable to all kinds of trouble, with no one to
protect you]. (*Ovambo, Angola/Namibia*): *Geyvandov 126*

A woman is a wife only through her husband. (*Rundi, Burundi*): *Rodegem 192*

A girl's marriage is a protection for her. (*Arabic, Lebanon*): *Frayha I 348*

A woman's delight is her husband. (*Sinhalese, Sri Lanka*): *o.s. Gunasekare*

It is better to get a bridegroom made of wood than to remain single.
(*Arabic, Lebanon*): *Frayha II 429*

He who has money can marry the sultan's daughter. (*Arabic, widespread*): *Kalil Safadi 80*

Your duty to your wife does not end with [paying her] a cloth. (*Baule, Ivory Coast*): *Arbelbide 30*

Marriage is more than paying a dowry. (*Kundu, Cameroon*): *Ittmann 35*

Lay good food and betel nuts before the guests; lay presents before a woman.
(*Khionghta, Bangladesh*): *Lewin 5*

To feed a cow you need a store of grass. (*Tibetan*): *Gergan 65*

Prepare a nest for a hen and she will lay eggs for you. (*Portuguese*): *Champion 251*

Look for a house before you look for a wife. (*Italian; French*): *Geyvandov 96; Pineaux 87*

It is cheaper to find a wife than to feed a wife. (*English, USA*): *Kin 279*

Get a cage before you get a bird [i.e. a house before you get married].
  (*Creole, Trinidad/Tobago*): *Ottley 89*

Only with plenty of water does the water lily bloom. [A woman's conditions depend on her
  husband.] (*Burmese*): *Geyvandov 126*

All those who were once virgins are married now. (*Russian*): *Geyvandov 264*

No cocksure girl has beaten the skin skirt. [Marriage will tame a girl; the skin skirt or *isid-
  waba* is a dress women start wearing after marriage.] (*Ndebele, Zimbabwe*): *Finnegan 406*

The union must be solemnized in heaven. (*English, UK*): *Geyvandov 106*

WIVES, CO-WIVES, WIDOWS

WIVES

A wife is like a blanket: cover yourself, it irritates you; cast it aside, you feel cold.
  (*Ashanti, Ghana*): *Rattray 139*

Girls are beautiful, sweet and tender; where do all those wicked wives come from?
  (*Russian*): *Graf 251; Geyvandov 112; Rauch 149; Reinsberg-Düringsfeld 163*

All are good girls, but where do the bad wives come from? (*English, USA*): *Mieder 1992: 251*

A girl's heart is put to the test by the wife's cloth. [All girls are perfect; where do the nasty
  wives come from?] (*Rwanda*): *Crépeau 513*

When they marry they warp and when their husbands die they are needy.
  (*Arabic, Maghreb*): *Cheneb III 78*

As long as she is with her mother, kind as a lamb; as soon as she has got a husband, she pulls
  out a long tongue. (*Serbian/Croatian*): *Reinsberg-Düringsfeld 144*

A diamond daughter turns to glass as a wife. (*English, USA*): *Mieder 1992: 135*

A neat maiden often makes a dirty wife. (*English, USA*): *Mieder 1992: 395*

GOOD OR BAD?

Darkness covers everything except a bad wife. (*Hebrew, Israel*): *Alcalay 525*

After they were divorced, the man married a bad woman and she made him bad; the woman
  married a bad man and she made him good. (*Hebrew, Israel*): *Rosten 1970: 439*

A good wife makes a good husband.
  (*Persian*): *Shaki 516; Italian; English, USA: Geyvandov 120; Brown 1970: 109*

There is no end to the goodness of a good wife and none to the wickedness of a bad one.
  (*Hebrew, Israel*): *Alcalay 524*

If you have a good wife, do not go to weddings; you have one every day in your house. If you
  have a bad wife, do not go to funerals; you have one every day in your house.
  (*Armenian*): *Sakayan 231*

He that has a good wife has an angel at his side; he that has a bad wife has a devil at his elbow.
  (*English, USA*): *Mieder 1992: 653*

There is nothing better for a man than a good wife, nothing worse than a bad one.

(*Greek*): *Van Dijk-Hemmes 3*

A real man has a wife like a lioness, a bad man has a wife like a slave. (*Turkish*): *Geyvandov 125*

There is no such thing as a good husband or a sweet onion. (*Romanian*): *Mieder 1986: 245*

A good husband will not squeeze juice out of his wife. (*Komi, RF*): *Geyvandov 124*

A good dog does not kill the chickens; a good husband does not beat his wife.

(*Chinese*): *Fabre 41*

A good husband is better than a friend and a brother. (*Tajik*): *Geyvandov 126*

One good husband is worth two good wives, for the scarcer things are, the more they're
valued. (*English, USA*): *Kin 124*

Good deeds bring good husband; charity brings good children. (*Telegu, India*): *o.s. Naidu*

A bad man's wife is always stupid. (*Russian*): *Geyvandov 127*

A bad man always suspects his wife of being unfaithful. (*Digor, RF*): *Geyvandov*

Better a man's wickedness than a woman's virtue. (*Hebrew, Israel*): *Alcalay 544*

For a woman to be married to a bad man is like being buried in a luckless tomb.

(*Chinese*): *Scarborough 207*

It is better to suffer cold than to live with a wicked husband. (*Russian*): *Geyvandov 127*

Be good to your own wife and you can have your neighbour's.

(*Arabic, widespread*): *Lunde & Wintle 87*

THE 'GOOD' WIFE

She is gracious and chaste, and moreover has a golden heart. (*Arabic, Maghreb*): *Cheneb III 76*

The [ideal] wife is [like] the *mvuumbu* mushroom: one must be lucky to find her.

(*Yaka, Congo DR*): *Beken 1993: 201*

If you have a good name, it is the world's honour; if you have a good wife, it is the pride of
men. (*Uzbek*): *Geyvandov 120*

Take a good wife even if you have to sell your pots and kettle. (*Japanese*): *Buchanan 91*

A good wife is the best piece of furniture.

(*Dutch; Frisian, Netherlands; German; Danish*): *Beintema 141; Wander I 1116; Harrebomée II 419*

Happy is he who has found a good wife. (*Hebrew, Israel*): *Geyvandov 119*

A good wife is halfway happiness. (*Kirghiz*): *Geyvandov 119*

With a good wife, who needs heaven? (*Bulgarian*): *Geyvandov 184*

He who has a good wife is halfway to heaven. (*Swedish*): *Ström 164*

If your wife is a good wife, do not call her a wife, but rather call her a cornerstone.

(*Uyghur, RF*): *Geyvandov 120*

The woman is the pillar of the house. (*Minangkabau, Indonesia*): *o.s. J. van Reenen*

A good wife is better than a golden pillar. (*Czech*): *Reinsberg-Düringsfeld 161*

A good wife is the crown of the home. (*Hungarian*): *Paczolay 28*

A good wife is the honour of the home. (*Estonian*): *Paczolay 28*

The man may be the head, the wife is the heart of the home. (*Gikuyu, Kenya*): *o.s. M.G. Mugo*

Is there a greater treasure than a good wife? (*Icelandic*): *Geyvandov 122*

For a man a good wife is a golden key. (*Latvian*): *Geyvandov 122*

For a good wife there is no price. (*Czech*): *Reinsberg-Düringsfeld 161*

You can tell the husband of a good wife by his clothes. (*Turkish; Bulgarian*): *Arnaudov 74*

He that hath a good wife shows it in his dress. [She washes and mends his clothes.]
(*English, USA*): *Loomis 1955: 198*

A good wife is a good housekeeper. (*Japanese*): *Champion 447*

Glorify your husband; glorify him with a cassava root. [Love is expressed in good food and
other good deeds.] (*Taka, Congo DR*): *Beken 1993: 219*

A woman who does not take care of her husband, cannot be a good wife.
(*Kru, Ivory Coast/Liberia*): *Geyvandov 121*

A good wife will reduce sorrows to half their size and increase fortune to double the amount.
(*Georgian/Hebrew, Israel*): *Hazan-Rokem 129*

As water takes on the colour of the earth, so a wife takes on the manners of her husband.
[She adapts to his influence; surroundings influence people.] (*Oromo, Ethiopia*): *Cotter 16*

A girl is *parwe*. [A girl adapts to her groom.] (*Yiddish, Netherlands; Dutch*): *Beem 153*

A corset is made to fit the size of the breasts. [A woman should know how to adapt.]
(*Creole, Guadeloupe*): *Ludwig 459*

The name of the woman-wife is Yes: Don't go; I stay; Don't speak; I am silent; Don't do; I
renounce. (*Wolof, Senegal*): *o.s. P.G. N'Diaye*

It is a good horse that never stumbles, and a good wife that never grumbles.
(*English, USA*): *Kin 245*

A good wife has her empire behind the front door.
(*Ladino, Maghreb; Hebrew, Israel*): *Moscona 120*

A good wife and a good cat are best at home. (*English, UK*): *Williams I 433*

A good wife keeps herself away from public and thus keeps her good name.
(*Sanskrit, India*): *Jha 3*

A chaste wife's tears never fall on the ground. [As she is a good wife, she has no reason to cry.]
(*Sanskrit, India*): *Jha 167*

A good wife guards her husband from bad ways. (*Chinese*): *Geyvandov 120*

A good wife mends what the husband spoils. (*Spanish, Chile*): *Cannobio 79*

A wife is a cloth for her husband. [A good wife hides the failings of her husband from the
public.] (*Oromo, Ethiopia*): *Cotter 8–9*

Meek as a sacrificial lamb, busy as a bee, beautiful as a bird of paradise, faithful as a turtle-
dove. (*Russian*): *Geyvandov 68*

A wife should be like one's mother. (*Swahili, Tanzania*): *o.s. J. Wembah-Rashid*

A good wife is like a mother. (*Spanish, Costa Rica*): *Hernández 256*

The wife that looks after your every need is your mother. (*Georgian*): *Geyvandov 121*

A good wife is content with one man. (*Latin*): *Haller 596; Plautus*

A good man will not find a good wife. (*Creole, Martinique*): *David 52*

There's only one thing in the world better than a good wife … no wife.
(*English, UK/USA*): *Gaffney & Cashman 67; Bohn 1855: 459; Loomis 1955: 197*

There is but one good wife in the world [also: in the country] and every man thinks he has her.
(*English, UK/USA*): *Bohn 1855: 43; Williams IV 148; Loomis 1955: 197*

There is only one bad wife in the world and every man thinks it is his.
(*Hebrew, Israel*): *Stahl 246*

There is only one wicked wife and every man supposes he has got her. (*Dutch*): *Mesters 175*

There have only been three good women: the first walked out of the world, the second
   drowned in the Rhine, the third they are still looking for. (*German*): *Meier-Pfaller 59*

Good wives have bad husbands and good husbands have bad wives. (*Chinese*): *Wintle 157*

'WICKEDNESS'

Is one veil sufficient to cover a woman's wickedness? (*Tamil, India*): *Champion 435*

What the good husband brings home in his hands, some wives throw out with a spoon.
   (*Papiamentu, Netherlands Antilles*): *Brenneker 46*

Man makes the money, woman builds the home. (*Arabic, widespread*): *Lunde & Wintle 62*

The man is a river, the wife a dam against it. [The husband's earnings have to be guarded by
   the wife.] (*Armenian*): *Sakayan 232*

A bad wife can carry away more in her apron than a man can bring in with seven horses.
   (*Estonian*): *Paczolay 76*

A wife who squanders money is the ruin of the house. (*Spanish, Argentina*): *Moya 531*

A bad wife ruins a family. (*English/Chinese, USA*): *Mieder 1989: 54*

A bad wife is sixty years' bad harvests in a row. (*Japanese*): *Champion 447; Geyvandov 124*

A wicked wife is like leprosy to her husband. (*Hebrew, Israel*): *Alcalay 525*

A wicked woman sells her husband. (*Khiongtha, Bangladesh*): *Lewin 11*

A bad dog digs into the ground, a bad wife quarrels every day. (*Nogay, RF*): *Geyvandov 142*

A bad wife scorches you worse than a fire and chokes you worse than a rope or water.
   (*Hebrew, Israel*): *Alcalay 525*

It is a bad wife that does not forgive her husband his drunken fit. (*Danish*): *Brix 35*

He who has taken a bad wife, has an enemy in his house. (*Karachay-Balkar, RF*): *Geyvandov 142*

The husband of a bad wife lies on the stove. [Burning with suffering.]
   (*Russian*): *o.s. Anna Ravve*

There is some remedy for a fool who will listen, but no medicine for a bad wife who refuses
   good advice. (*English, UK; Somali*): *Gaffney & Cashman 67; Andrzejewski 102*

The man who sees a wicked woman in his dreams should dread lest it portends some
   calamity. (*Hebrew, Israel*): *Alcalay 548*

A wicked wife is a daily fever. (*Italian*): *Haller 467*

A man who has a wicked wife grows old sadly. (*Oromo, Ethopia*): *Cotter 87*

A bad wife is like a dreary, rainy day. (*Hebrew, Israel*): *Rosten 1977: 488*

A desert is more desirable than a wicked wife. (*Yiddish, RF*): *Geyvandov 219*

It is difficult to rule a bad wife as it is a hard thing to climb a fierce horse. (*Chinese*): *Fabre 59*

From a garment flutters a moth and from a woman her wickedness; better the wickedness of
   a man than a woman's virtue. (*Hebrew, Israel*): *Alcalay 544*

Woman is more wicked than the Devil. (*Bulgarian*): *Arnaudov 50*

The husband commands and the wife does what she likes. (*Catalan, Spain; French*): *Guiter 35*

A bad wife wishes her husband's heel turn homewards and not his toe. (*Danish*): *Bohn 1855: 394*

A bad wife likes to see her husband's heels turned to the door. (*English, USA*): *Hines 285*

May God protect you from rising hunger and a bad wife who wants a divorce.
   (*Ladino, Morocco*): *Dahan 350*

The thing [i.e. the penis] that has paid the bride-wealth for a wicked one spends the night
   with her. (*Rwanda*): *Crépeau 448*

One keeps a wicked woman because of the children. [Not all is bad in a given situation.]
   (*Minyanka, Mali*): *Cauvin 1980: 258*

Better a bad wife than an empty house. (*Baule, Ivory Coast*): *Arbelbide 62*

Better to have a bad wife than to sleep alone. (*Twi, Ghana*): *Oduyoye 7*

It's bad with the bad [woman], but worse without the bad. (*Hungarian*): *Paczolay 173*

Bad with your wife, but even worse without her. (*Russian*): *Geyvandov 219*

Women are like bees: in spite of their wickedness you'll always draw some honey.
   (*Bamum, Cameroon*): *o.s. Chimoun*

Wife is husband's best friend. (*Bulgarian*): *Geyvandov 220*

At home, the best friend is one's wife. (*Sanskrit, India*): *Jha 214*

Your husband: cherish him as your best friend, but distrust him as your worst
   enemy.(*Ladino, Maghreb*): *Benazeraf 32*

CO-WIVES

A teapot can serve five teacups, but who has ever seen one teacup serving five teapots?
   (*Chinese*): *Lunde & Wintle 86*

Two male hippopotamuses cannot live in one pool. (*Mandinka*): *o.s. Habib Koite*

There can only be one tiger in each cave. (*Spanish, El Salvador*): *Sánchez Duarte 217*

Two male-bears do not winter in one hole. [A woman should only have one husband.]
   (*Yakut, RF*): *Geyvandov 38*

Who is the wife of one cannot eat the rice of two. (*English, USA*): *Mieder 1992: 654*

A girl can't drink tea from two families. (*Chinese*): *o.s. Huang Mingfen*

The needle does not hold two threads. (*Arabic, Egypt*): *Singer 22*

You don't cook two big bones in the same kettle. (*Ovambo, Nambia/Angola*): *Geyvandov 118*

Two thunderclaps cannot live in one cloud. (*Rwanda*): *Geyvandov 38*

A girl is respected to have fulfilled her obligations when she gets married and sticks to a
   husband. (*Haya, Tanzania*): *Nestor 56*

If it is to their advantage, two men will share one wife. (*Arabic, Syria/Lebanon*): *Feghali 595*

If there is any profit in partnership, two will share a woman. (*Arabic, Tunisia*): *Yetiv 94*

One should never lend either one's wife or one's razor. (*Maltese*): *Lunde & Wintle 107*

A knife and a wife are not to be lent. (*Spanish, Argentina*): *Moya 457*

A wife and a pen are not to be lent, because both will get spoiled.
   (*Spanish, Venezuela*): *Febres Cordero 43*

A wife and a wristwatch should not be lent. (*Portuguese, Brazil*): *Mota 126*

Wife, gun and horse: do not even think of lending them.
   (*Portuguese, Brazil*): *Mota 124; Glazer 39*

He who lends his wife to dance, or his horse to the bullfight, has no complaint to make.
   (*English, USA*): *West 43*

If you lend your girl, your watch or your knife you get them back spoilt. (*Dutch*): *Mesters 105*

One can show a wife and a gun, but not lend them.
   (*Serbian/Croatian*): *Reinsberg-Düringsfeld 140*

Do not lend three things: power, a wife, a gun. [You'll have difficulty in getting them back, and they will be abused.] (*Fulfulde, Senegal*): *Gaden 22, 63*

One could lend rice or a dress, but no-one would lend her husband.

(*Vietnamese*): *Geyvandov 206*

One's wife and one's sandals cannot be shared. (*Ladino, Morocco*): *Dahan 217*

A married woman has nothing of her own but her wedding ring and her hair lace.

(*English, UK*): *Williams I 466*

A girl possesses nothing but a veil and a tomb. (*Arabic, Saudi Arabia*): *Lunde & Wintle 52*

WHY AN EXTRA WIFE?

When a man has two pairs of trousers, he thinks of a new wife. [A women's saying.]

(*Persian*): *Geyvandov 132*

Don't take one wife, if you can maintain two. (*Switzerland*): *Geyvandov 116*

A supplementary dish of rice can always be added. (*Malay*): *MBRAS 43*

Marrying several wives is human; getting many children is divine.

(*Sumerian, Mesopotamia*): *Gordon 126*

Even a wolf is allowed to marry two. (*Awar, RF*): *Geyvandov 116*

Two flowers, one insect. (*Turkish*): *Haig 117*

A man with one wife is chief among the unmarried. (*Ganda, Uganda*): *Walser 420*

One wife warms the heart, the other one warms the kettle.

(*Galla, Ethiopia; Nigeria*): *Geyvandov 116; Akporobaro & Emovon 185*

One wife, one eye. (*Ovambo, Angola*): *Geyvandov 116*

The person of one eye and the man of one wife die equally. (*Oromo, Ethiopia*): *Cotter 165*

Only one wife, only one jar in one's basket. (*Taka, Congo DR*): *Beken 1978: 69*

Flog the bad wife with a new wife. (*Nubian, Sudan*): *Werner 327*

Without the strong ones the weak wives would already be dead. (*Berber, Morocco*): *Bentolila 37*

Even if she were a date, the taste of the co-wife is bitter. (*Arabic, Algeria*): *Belamri 28*

A co-wife, even when made of unbaked flour, is undesirable. (*Rajasthani, India*): *Bhatnagar 71*

The very voice of a co-wife is intolerable. (*Persian*): *Roebuck 319*

A wife will not respect her co-wife. (*Mamprusi, Burkina Faso*): *Geyvandov 62*

HIERARCHIES AMONG WIVES

The feet of the first wife do not walk in the dew-wet morning grass.

(*Fang, Cameroon / Gabon*): *o.s. S. Eno-Belinga*

The first one drinks no muddy water. (*Ovambo, Namibia*): *Geyvandov 117*

You, first wife, speak; you, second, be silent. (*Taka, Congo DR*): *Beken 1978: 66*

The first fish is real. (*Tonga, Zambia*): *Geyvandov 117*

The first [wife] possesses the marriage; the one who comes later is like the shoots of the banana tree. (*Taka, Congo DR*): *Beken 1993: 204*

It is the first [wife] that makes the home. (*Tonga, Zambia*): *Milimo 16*

If your young wife dies, return to your old one. (*Gikuyu, Kenya*): *Geyvandov 39*

'I've got to make them happy', the first wife says and eats with them.

(*Haya, Uganda*): *Geyvandov 117*

If you have a new earthen pot, don't throw away the old one.
    (*Swahili, East Africa*): *o.s. Clémentine Faïk-Nzuji*
If you take a new wife, don't forget the old one. (*Ngwana, Congo DR*): *o.s. Clémentine Faïk-Nzuji*
Don't chase your old wife when you take a new one. (*Mamprusi, Burkina Faso*): *Geyvandov 214*
Your first wife is your mother. (*Acholi, Uganda*): *o.s. Molara Ogundipe*
Your first wife is like a mother. (*Swahili, East Africa*): *Scheven 486*
When she was the only wife, she was treated like a goddess; now that she has a co-wife she is
    cast out on the garbage heap. (*Bengali, India*): *Maity 297*
My first wife my sandal, my second wife my turban. (*Turkish*): *Haig 119*
The first wife is like magic: you never get rid of her. (*Mongo, Congo DR*): *Hulstaert 647*
A woman's value is not her being the first wife. (*Mongo, Congo DR*): *Hulstaert 643*
The young wife, place her at the end, it's up to you, place her next to the fire, it's up to you.
    (*Taka, Congo DR*): *Beken 1993: 205*
The stick that has beaten the senior wife will beat the junior wife.
    (*Krio, Sierra Leone; Mamprusi, Burkina Faso*): *Plissart 344; o.s. Eldred Jones*
The rod that is used to beat the senior wife is waiting in the roof for the junior.
    (*Yoruba, Nigeria*): *o.s. Biodun Jeyifo*
The butter is for Emm Zbeid and the thrashing is for Emm Obeid. [No equal treatment for
    co-wives.] (*Arabic, Syria/Lebanon*): *Feghali 172*
The polygamous man will hesitate a long time before deciding whom he will give the piece of
    cloth to. (*Taka, Congo DR*): *Beken 1993: 206*
The man of many wives will mow only one field. (*Tonga, Zambia*): *Anonymous*
The new cooking-pot never scorns the old one. (*Minyanka, Mali*): *Cauvin 1981: 95*
The new wife does not know that the first one is loved. (*Baatomun, Benin*): *Cauvin 1981: 95*
The favored wife does not grow fat. (*Kundu, Cameroon*): *Ittmann 139*
You measure some flour for your co-wife and this flour makes your husband spend the night
    with her. (*Rundi, Burundi*): *Rodegem 255*
You scorn the small vulva of your co-wife, but it takes away your husband.
    (*Rwanda*): *Crépeau 427*
When the favorite wife commits a fault, you, the despised one, rejoice.
    (*Ganda, Uganda*): *Walser 255*
When your co-wife gives birth, you do not wear your festive ornaments. (*Rwanda*): *Crépeau 319*
It is better to let one's husband die than to give him to a co-wife.
    (*Bengali, India*): *o.s. Shobha Gupta*
Even when their rival co-wife is not guilty, the other co-wives call: 'It's her!'
    (*Sotho, Lesotho*): *Geyvandov 195*
If you dance with your co-wife, don't close your eyelid. (*Rundi, Burundi*): *Rodegem 366*
If a wife has kicked her co-wife, it is on the husband's shoulder she has found support.
    (*Fulfulde, Senegal*): *Gaden 70*
Oh weasel! Eat this fish and spare my husband but eat my co-wife.
    (*Bengali, India*): *o.s. Sanjukta Gupta*
When a woman's rival dies, she is no longer interested in her.
    (*Wolof, Gambia*): *Geyvandov 37*

Fortunately the husband died. Now the two co-wives become friendly to each other.
(*Bengali, India*): *Maity 300*

It is better to die young than to be a co-wife. (*Vietnamese*): *Geyvandov 117*

PROBLEMS AND DISILLUSIONS

Two wives means two pots of poison. (*Gikuyu, Kenya*): *o.s. Gacheche Waruingi*

One does not bind two horses to one tree. (*Turkish*): *Geyvandov 136*

One cannot climb two oil palms at the same time. (*Kundu, Cameroon*): *Geyvandov 246*

One cannot run after two gazelles. (*Ndebele, South Africa*): *Geyvandov 246*

A man cannot row two boats at the same time. (*Ovambo, Angola / Namibia*): *Geyvandov 246*

Two watermelons cannot be carried under one arm. (*Hebrew, Israel*): *Cohen 1961: 26*

A day's illness: drink brandy. A life's illness: take two wives. (*Russian*): *Rauch 143*

Having two wives is having two problems, having three wives is like walking around without
trousers. (*Ossetian, RF / Georgia; Arabic, Lebanon*): *Geyvandov 118; Lunde & Wintle 62*

Every man with two wives is a porter. (*Arabic, widespread*): *Lunde & Wintle 87*

One woman, what a glory; two women, what a worry. [A man will never be happy with two
wives.] (*Turkish*): *Haig 128*

A house with two mistresses will be deep in dust. (*Persian*): *Elwell-Sutton 65*

Farming in two villages and having two wives—equally bad. (*Telegu, India*): *Murty 229*

Buying two ploughs makes a family flourish; marrying two wives makes a family grow poor.
(*Chinese*): *o.s. Huang Mingfen*

A poor man does not take a second wife. (*Tamil, India*): *Geyvandov 132*

We cannot suffer a burning sun together. (*Ovambo, Angola / Namibia*): *Geyvandov 37*

Many children—many debts, many wives—many fires to keep.
(*Vietnamese*): *o.s. Būi Văn Hâu 163*

To have two wives is being [ground] between two millstones.
(*Karachay-Balkar, RF*): *Geyvandov 118*

A husband of two wives has no peace: he is crushed between the stones of the handmill.
(*Ladino, Morocco*): *Dahan 285*

Two wives, two enemies. (*Avar, RF*): *Geyvandov 118*

With two camels you have peace, with two wives you have war. (*Mongolian*): *o.s. Shoupu*

If you tether two goats at the same post, you can be sure that the ropes get entangled.
(*Fiote, Angola / Cabinda*): *Vissers 39*

A single bracelet does not jingle. [There is peace with one wife.]
(*Fulfulde, Nigeria*): *Akporobaro & Emovon 117*

A single key doesn't rattle. [There is peace with one wife.] (*Chinese*): *Champion 336*

The polygamous husband is like the cock's tail. (*Berber, Morocco*): *Bentolila 81*

A man with two wives has two faces. (*Kurdish, Turkey*): *Geyvandov 118*

Quarrel sleeps in the house of the man with two wives. (*Swahili, Kenya / Congo DR*): *Geyvandov 118*

The husband of two parrots [is like] a neck between two sticks [that strike it]. [Refers to the
misfortune of a man married to two quarrelsome wives.] (*Arabic, Egypt*): *Burckhardt 99*

A thousand wives, a thousand palavers. (*Ashanti, Ghana*): *Rattray 139; Oduyoye 8*

The foolish wife imagines her co-wife has taken care. (*Mongo, Congo*): *Hulstaert 369*

He has twenty wives but has not been able to take just one bath.

(*Kru, Ivory Coast/Liberia*): *Geyvandov 121*

A bamboo pressed between two trees is apt to crack; a man with two wives frequently suffers hunger. (*Khiongtha, Bangladesh*): *Lewin 79*

A man with one wife gets his food served on time; with two wives, he waits a long time for his food. (*Bengali, India*): *De 49*

Two rats on a tree trunk. [Two wives are pregnant at the same time: neither of them prepares you dinner.] (*Taka, Congo DR*): *Beken 1993: 205*

A sick man with many wives dies of hunger. (*Twi, Ghana*): *Geyvandov 245*

A husband of two wives [and he] has to sleep outside. (*Ladino, Morocco*): *Stahl 419*

Owner of mill, owner of garden, owner of co-wives—none of them ever has a quiet night.(*Arabic, Maghreb*): *Duvollet 4*

When the head of a large household [with many wives] wants clean premises, he has to sweep them. [This is a woman's task, but the women are of no use.]

(*Kundu, Cameroon*): *Geyvandov 245*

If you marry two, you'll die all the younger. (*Luba, Congo DR*): *o.s. Clémentine Faïk-Nzuji*

He who has a piece of land in two villages will go bankrupt; he who has two women will die.

(*Tamil, India*): *Geyvandov 246*

WIDOWS

Cold rice is still rice; a widow is still a woman. (*Khmer, Cambodia*): *Geyvandov 155*

Only a widow knows the widow's grief. (*Chinese*): *o.s. Huang Mingfen*

A widow's suffering is not understood by a widower. (*Korean*): *Geyvandov 260*

The sorrow of a widow is known to her widow friend. (*Korean*): *o.s. B. Walraven*

To arrange the marriage of a widower with a widow, is to please two persons. (*French*): *Ségalen 42*

Widower and widow seldom join. (*Polish*): *Reinsberg-Düringsfeld 121*

A widow or a widower is a house without a roof. (*Finnish*): *Ley 168*

A woman without a husband is a house without a roof. (*Vietnamese*): *Nguyen 127*

Your wife's death is your roof collapsed. (*Chechen, RF*): *Geyvandov 153*

Only after her death does a husband respect his wife. (*Hebrew, Turkey*): *Stahl 249; Alcalay 529*

Being a widow you begin to love your husband. (*Russian*): *o.s. Ravve*

The death of a woman is felt by no-one so much as by her husband.

(*Hebrew, Israel*): *Rosten 1977: 156, 492*

A good wife lost is God's gift lost. (*English, USA*): *Franklin 1733*

Widows [and widowers] are very brave; they look to right, they look to left [i.e. flirt], and are not afraid to try again. (*Palaung, Myanmar*): *Champion 348*

May you live up to one hundred years and I up to ninety-nine. (*Japanese*): *Buchanan 90*

The woman to whom God gives his blessings will accompany her husband at his funeral.

(*Arabic, Syria/Lebanon*): *Feghali 165*

DEATH OF WIFE, DEATH OF HUSBAND

If she dies before her husband, the wife will have a bunch of flowers at her tomb; if she dies after him, she will have a heart like a bunch of rags. (*Chinese*): *Fabre 63*

The lucky woman dies before her husband's death, the unlucky woman dies after it.

(*Chinese*): o.s. *Huang Mingfen*

When the husband dies, the wife will be in deep mourning for three years; when the wife
   dies, she won't be remembered for more than a hundred days.

(*Chinese*): *Scarborough 317; Fabre 578*

Grief for a dead wife lasts to the door.

(*Catalan, Spain; French; Italian*): *Roux de Lincy 222; Guiter 415; Bohn 1857: 93; Cibotto 8*

The death of the wife is the renewal of the wedding. [Allusion to the custom of taking a new
   wife immediately after the death of a former.] (*Arabic, Egypt*): *Lunde & Wintle 87*

A wife brings but two good days: her wedding day and the day of her death.

(*English, UK*): *Williams I 405, III 407*

A dead wife is the best goods in a man's house.

(*Catalan, Spain; French; English, UK*): *Guiter 115; Williams III 382; Bohn 1855: 43*

A dead goose gives life, a dead woman gives heaven. (*Spanish*): *Haller 80*

Women are a four-days' fever and only death frees from them. (*German*): *Haller 466*

A man regrets his wife's death no more than he does a broken whip. (*Chuwash, RF*): o.s. *Bläsing*

The wife's death, a replacement in bed. (*Chechen, RF*): *Geyvandov 153*

Happy the door through which a dead woman leaves. (*Portuguese, Brazil*): *Mota 99*

The pain caused by the wife's death lasts unto the door.

(*Spanish, Argentina*): *Moya 131; Mota 86; o.s. Castellanos*

Grief for a dead wife, and a troublesome guest, continues to the threshold, and there is at
   rest. (*English, USA*): *Franklin 1734*

Death of the wife and health of the cattle help the poor man forward. (*Italian*): *Geyvandov 153*

The death of wives and the life of sheep make men rich.

(*French; English, UK*): *Reinsberg-Düringsfeld 249; Rayner 241*

New wife, new silver. (*French*): *Roux de Lincy 228*

'Every little lightens', said the skipper, and threw his wife overboard.

(*Frisian, Netherlands*): *Beintema 83; Mesters 140*

'Never make a toil of pleasure', as the man said when he dug his wife's grave only three feet
   deep. (*Irish*): *Gaffney & Cashman 67*

'Every man for himself and God for us all', said the farmer who saw his wife drown, without
   lifting a finger. (*Dutch*): *Mesters 56*

'A feast with no breakages is rubbish', said the woman, when her husband broke his neck.

(*Danish*): *Brix 36*

'That clears a space', said Grietje, when her husband died. (*Dutch*): *Mesters 59*

Never marry a widow unless her husband was hanged. (*English, UK/USA*): *Williams I 466*

A woman who buries a husband does not mind burying another one.

(*French*): *Roux de Lincy 232*

The man who marries a widow should expect to suffer a few deaths in the family.

(*Spanish, Mexico*): *Ballesteros 49*

Every time a woman who was born in the water-snake year opens her mouth, a husband is
   swallowed. [The belief was that men married to women born in the year of the
   water-snake died prematurely.] (*Tibetan*): *Duncan 237*

Avoid the woman who has it within her fate to destroy eight lives. [When she marries her
    husband will die.] (*Chinese*): *Plopper 126*

You flirted with the widow, but do you know what killed her husband? [Warning not to
    marry a widow too quickly.] (*Bassar, Togo*): *Szwark 68*

LOSS AND SORROW

Whether a woman is clever or not will become clear once she is a widow; whether a man is
    clever or not, will become clear once he starts talking. (*Tangut, China*): *Geyvandov 237*

Never let the spot of *kinowari* disappear from your forehead. (*Assam, India*): *Geyvandov 115*

Widows are the leftovers from dead men. (*Portuguese, Brazil*): *Mota 229*

The baobab has fallen; now the goats start climbing on it. (*Minyanka, Mali*): *Cauvin 1980: 577*

Widows and young girls have the pity of married women. (*Arabic, Lebanon*): *Abela 146*

Please, God, let us not stay as a widow in mourning. (*Russian*): *Geyvandov 153*

One can tell a widow only this: have patience. (*Igbo, Nigeria*): *Njoku 69*

A widow is a boat without a rudder.
    (*Chinese; variants in Vietnamese; Portuguese, Brazil; English, USA*): *Lunde & Wintle 28; Dình*
    Khuê Duong 13; Geyvandov 126; Kin 29; Lamenza 266

A buxom widow must be married, buried, or shut up in a convent.
    (*Spanish*): *Champion 310; Meier-Pfaller 55; Bergua 514*

A mare without a rider finds the meadow. (*Spanish*): *Collins 388*

A widow feels as happy as a horse that has thrown off its rider.
    (*Malayalam, India*): *Geyvandov 155*

Widows are as frolicsome as a horse that has thrown off its rider.
    (*Malay*): *Lunde & Wintle 163*

It's dangerous marrying a widow, because she hath cast off her rider.
    (*English, UK*): *Bohn 1855: 43*

The widow and the capon: all they eat is the food they're given.
    (*Portuguese, Brazil*): *Lamenza 250*

Loss of goods is one spoiled day, loss of a husband is a ruined life. (*Burmese*): *Hla Pe 50*

A 'looking-glass husband', or a 'shield husband'. [Expression commonly used by widows on
    their re-marriage, a marriage for purposes of protection or convenience.]
    (*Malay*): *Champion 453*

The childless one [widow] is like an overgrown field. (*Amharic, Ethiopia*): *Geyvandov 158*

What will support the spineless one? What will support the widow whose son has died?
    (*Chinese*): *Fabre 63*

The widow is not free for all. (*Kweli/Kundu, Cameroon*): *Ittmann 96*

While looking at her dead husband's brother, she let another husband go.
    (*Pashto, Pakistan*): *o.s. S.W.A. Shah*

A child brought up by a widow is like a bullock without a nose-rope.
    (*Telegu, India*): *Champion 435*

A widow's son is either badly brought up, or is a vicious character. (*Spanish*): *Collins 173*

A widow's dog does not bark; her ox does not plough.
    (*Arabic, widespread*): *Safadi 26*

When a widow raises a child, she does not make a man out of him; when she teaches a dog, it does not bark; when she places a bull in front of the plough, it does not work; whatever she undertakes will fail. (*Arabic, Syria/Lebanon*): *Feghali 229*

WIDOWS' TEARS

A widow's dress shows the past, her tears weep for the present, and her heart seeks the future. (*German*): *Champion 184; Giusti 89*

A black shirt and veil do not release a soul from pain. (*Spanish*): *Collins 77*

The widow weeps and the others laugh at the wedding. (*French*): *Guiter 105*

The widow weeps for the dead and thinks of the living. (*Italian*): *Alaimo 70*

Widows who cry easily are the first to marry again. [There is nothing like wet weather for transplanting]. (*English, USA*): *Hendricks 92*

A widow who cries for two years has somebody to help her. (*Yaka, Congo DR*): *Beken 1993: 118*

The hearts of young widows and stone bowls grow cold very quickly.
(*Estonian*): *Geyvandov 154*

A widow who sighs, wants to get married. (*Spanish, Argentina*): *Moya 652*

Onions can make even heirs and widows weep. (*English, USA*): *Franklin 1734*

Good and honest is a buried widow. (*Portuguese, Brazil*): *Souto Maior 43*

A widow weeps because she is a widow, and perhaps a woman with a husband living [has also cause to weep]; but in their company a spinster also weeps!
(*Bihari, India*): *Champion 397*

Widows cry, what does it matter, girls cry no less. (*Bulgarian*): *Arnaudov 118*

SLANDER

The widow is like an open field: every wind touches her. (*Karelian, RF*): *Geyvandov 154*

Slander clusters around the widow's door.
(*Hebrew, Israel; Chinese*): *Cohen 1961: 550; Lunde & Wintle 26; o.s. Huang Mingfen*

At the widow's gate many a scandal will occur. (*Chinese*): *Geyvandov 155*

After Jacques has died, we will watch Thérésine's conduct.
(*Créole, Guadeloupe*): *Zagaya 249; Barbotin 30*

Looking here and looking there, makes a widow forget her husband. [Accepting temptation leads to infidelity.] (*Mamprusi, Burkina Faso*): *Plissart 276*

One tells a widow by her hair. [A widow is not allowed to do her hair nicely and has to wear a white headband.] (*Senufo, Ivory Coast; Minyanka, Mali*): *Cauvin 1980: 221*

When you see a cloud speckled like the wing of a partridge and a widow applying scented oil to her hair, the former will rain and the latter will elope. (*Bihari, India*): *Champion 397*

The widow's dress is long and everyone steps on it. (*Dutch*): *Mesters 87*

Even her skirts are the widow's enemy. [A widow is always under scrutiny for her morality.]
(*Bulgarian*): *Arnaudov 74, 118*

Even the train of her dress will be an enemy to the widow. (*Turkish*): *Geyvandov 154*

After the husband is buried, the widow beautifies herself. (*Italian*): *Menarini 15*

There is no Saturday without sun, nor a widow without rouge.
(*Spanish, Puerto Rico*): *Fernández Valledor 209*

A widowed donkey makes a show of farting. (*Sumerian, Mesopotamia*): *Alster I 61*

The favourite wife does not mourn her husband. (*Kundu, Cameroon*): *Geyvandov 227*

The rich widow's tears soon dry. (*Danish*): *Cordry 280*

A rich widow, with one eye she cries and with the other she watches the clock [for a new
   wedding before too much time has elapsed]. (*Spanish*): *Bergua 515*

The rich widow cries with one eye and blinks with the other.
   (*Spanish; Portuguese, Brazil*): *Bohn 1857: 268; Bergua 515; Guiter 45; Magalhães Júnior 315;*
   Fernández Valledor 35; Díaz Rivera 88; Moya 497

The rich widow weeps with one eye and laughs with the other.
   (*English, USA*): *Mieder 1986: 524*

There are no plump mice in the house of a widow. (*Japanese*): *Lunde & Wintle 180*

Widows do not eat fat meat. (*Kundu, Cameroon*): *Ittmann 96; Geyvandov 154*

The widow sells her silver to eat. (*Korean*): *Fabre 58*

REMARRYING

The widow in a hurry passes by the handsome man. (*Bassar, Togo*): *Szwark 68*

To marry a widow with a daughter is to ruin your home in a year's time.
   (*Arabic, Lebanon*): *Frayha I 37*

A man who married a widow with two daughters has got three back doors.
   (*Scottish, UK; English, USA*): *Geyvandov 134; Whiting 1952: 345*

He that marries a widow with two daughters marries four thieves.
   (*English, UK/USA; Danish*): *Champion 34; Bohn 1855: 45; Cordry 170; Brown 1970:113; Mieder*
   1992: 653

Whoever marries a widow becomes responsible for her children.
   (*Arabic, Lebanon*): *Frayha I 87*

He who takes the widow, takes the children. [Think of the consequences of something
   before you act.] (*Arabic, Syria/Lebanon*): *Feghali 164, 181*

Never marry a widow, because a mule tamed by somebody else always turns out to have a bad
   temper. (*Spanish, Colombia*): *Acuña 44; Sierra García I 88*

A mule tamed by someone else will always keep some remnants [old habits].
   (*Spanish, Antigua/Barbuda*): *Sierra García I 76*

He that marries a widow will often have a dead man's head thrown into his dish.
   (*English, USA*): *Loomis 1956: 175*

Whoever marries a widow has to put up with the 'stiff' [i.e. the dead husband].
   (*Spanish, Mexico*): *Rubio 200*

Who gets the widow into bed, gets the dead man in his house. (*Danish*): *Brix 26*

A widow dreams a double dream on her lonely lot. [First of her dead husband and again of
   her new love.] (*Pashto, Afghanistan*): *Champion 463*

When the tiger looks into a mirror, there are two tiger heads. [Refers to a woman who has
   taken a second husband.] (*Chinese*): *Plopper 106*

Never marry a widow, even when her cheeks are a bunch of flowers: you will love her but she
   will say: God blesses the blessed one [i.e. her dead husband].
   (*Ladino/Hebrew, Morocco*): *Dahan 307; Stahl 222; Duvollet 43; Westermarck 74*

A widow never fails to praise her dead husband. [A widow will not fail to praise the
generosity of her deceased husband in the presence of the new husband, to remind him
that he should live up to his predecessor's example.] (*Ganda, Uganda*): *Walser 256*

Never marry a widow: each time you'd quarrel she'd remind you of her dead husband.
(*Bamum, Cameroon*): *o.s. Chimoun*

Though you may become the wife of a divorced man, don't become the wife of a widower.
(*Japanese*): *Buchanan 92*

Good horses do not turn back to eat grass; good wives do not remarry.
(*Chinese*): *Lunde & Wintle 161*

A good horse will not bear two saddles; a virtuous wife will not remarry.
(*Chinese*): *o.s. Huang Mingfen*

She who is the wife of one man cannot eat the rice of two. (*Chinese*): *Scarborough 213*

Taking a widow is like buying trousers at the flea market; who knows who wore them before.
(*Polish*): *Reinsberg-Düringsfeld 120*

A widow is like a liver pie: one never knows what has been put into it. (*Dutch*): *o.s. Anonymous*

The widow certainly has the ready-made bread, but it's sour.
(*Russian; Polish*): *Reinsberg-Düringsfeld 119*

It is dangerous to get a horse after a brave horseman, and a widow after a strong man.
(*Polish*): *Reinsberg-Düringsfeld 119*

The widow who marries again loses esteem. (*French*): *Ségalen: 42*

The widow does not need soap. [i.e. she should not remarry. The soap refers to her washing
herself after having slept with a man.] (*Bulgarian*): *Arnaudov 118*

A faithful wife doesn't marry twice. (*Japanese*): *o.s. Keiko Kosunose*

'Mine is useless,' said the widow [referring to her sex]. (*Oromo, Ethiopia*): *Cotter 57*

One who eats when the cock is dead, breaks a taboo. [It refers to a man who has—
forbidden—sex with a widow.] (*Zulu, South Africa*): *Geyvandov 219*

Do but dally not [that's the widow's phrase]. (*English, UK*): *Williams I 473*

You cannot marry a widow, for the widow marries you. (*English, USA*): *Thompson 484*

A maid marries according to the will of her parents; a widow decides her marriage by herself.
(*Chinese*): *Lunde & Wintle 63; o.s. Huang Mingfen*

I shall not tie the donkey at the place of the horse. (*Arabic, Morocco*): *Westermarck 71*

Marry a widow before she leaves mourning. (*English, UK*): *Champion 44*

A mourning widow or a snivelling girl are best to make love with. (*Dutch*): *Mesters 104*

Young widows are like green wood: burning at one end, water [i.e. widow's tears] at the
other to avoid indelicate. (*Danish*): *Storm Petersen 27*

The pan of a widow: small and patched up. (*Spanish*): *Bergua 386*

A widow's pot: small but well stirred. (*Portuguese, Brazil*): *Souto Maior 50*

[Nothing is] Hotter than a grass widow's kiss. (*English, USA*): *Taylor 50*

A widow is good to love, for a calf won't go into the yoke of its own accord.
(*Pashto, Afghanistan*): *Champion 463*

Rather marry a young widow than an old virgin. (*Hebrew, Israel*): *Stahl 222*

Widows carry the Devil. (*Italian*): *Santoro 64*

The widow will either scare you or weaken you. (*Spanish, Bolivia*): *Barneville Vásquez 51*

MOTHERS AND MOTHERS-IN-LAW

MOTHERS

God could not be everywhere; therefore he made mothers. (*English, USA*): *Kim 169*

All over the world mothers are the same. (*Italian*): *Cibotto 13*

Mother is God number two. (*Chewa, Malawi*): *o.s. Mathieu Schoffeleers*

Hearing the approaching step of his mother, Rab Joseph would say: 'I must stand up, for the
    Shekhinah enters.' [Shekhinah is the 'Divine Presence'.] (*Hebrew, Israel*): *Rosten 1977: 333*

The mother is the mother, the rest is just air. (*Ladino, Morocco*): *Benazeraf 91*

Life is a mother. [Everything in life depends on one's mother.]
    (*Arabic, Lebanon*): *Lunde & Wintle 157; Abela 340*

Whoever has a mother should not cry. (*Spanish, Argentina*): *Moya 608*

There is nothing like your own mother. (*Spanish, Colombia*): *Acuña 58*

No temple is more beautiful than one's mother. (*Tamil, India*): *Champion 433*

Mother's milk is holy. (*Mongolian*): *Geyvandov 163*

UNIQUENESS

Mothers are incomparable. (*Kongo, Congo DR*): *Geyvandov 165*

The mother says not 'will you' but gives at once. (*Maltese*): *Busuttil 8, 49*

It is warm in the sun, and nice with a mother. (*Russian*): *Geyvandov 164*

Of all perfumes, the mother has the best scent. (*Greek*): *Politès 12*

The climbing plant's fruits are not a burden to it. (*Sinhalese, Sri Lanka*): *o.s. Gunasekare*

The elephant never tires from carrying her own tusks.
    (*Shona, Zimbabwe; Chewa, Malawi; Vai, Liberia; Haya, Tanzania*): *Milimo 14; Jablow 126; o.s.
    Mutembei*

No hen is burdened by her feathers. (*Spanish, Dominican Republic*): *Cruz Brache 16*

The origin of love for fellow humans lies in the mother. (*Kongo, Congo DR*): *Geyvandov 163*

The only generous love is the love of a mother. (*Greek*): *Geyvandov 164*

The tenderness of a mother knows no limits. (*Russian*): *Günther 27; Rauch 150*

A mother's love for her child will never fade away. (*Filipino*): *Chua & Nazareno 22*

Your mother's love even dashes up from the sea. (*English, USA*): *Kin 169*

The shade of a fig tree is the best; the love of a mother is the best.
    (*Bengali, India*): *o.s. Sanjukta Gupta*

A mother's love is a blessing. (*Irish*): *O'Farrell 19*

A mother understands the language of her mute child. (*Letzeburgish*): *o.s. Laure Wolter*

A mother has a cure for every injury. (*Italian*): *Geyvandov 164*

A mother understands the child's babbling. (*Armenian*): *Geyvandov 165*

When the boy's foot is broken, he finds his mother's yard.
    (*English, Jamaica*): *Llewellyn Watson 113*

It's the mother who knows how to carry her one-legged child.
    (*Mandinka, West Africa*): *Meyer 162*

The mother of the dumb child speaks his language. (*Arabic, Lebanon*): *Abela 457*

For her children a mother will swim across the sea. (*Lak, RF*): *Geyvandov 164*

The child's mother catches the knife at the sharp end.

    (*Sotho/Tswana, South Africa*): *Kuzwayo 1998: 25; Ibekwe 130; o.s. V. Mnyandu*

A mother hears the cries of her child from the grave. (*Ossetian, RF*): *Geyvandov 164*

Paradise will be opened at the command of a mother. (*Arabic, Lebanon*): *Wortabet 72*

Who has a mother, has a friend. (*Catalan, Spain*): *Guiter 141*

Who are related to each other? The mother and her child. (*Tamil, India*): *Champion 433*

Cry, tree, to the one who bore you. [Tell your mother your problems.]

    (*Ovambo, Angola*): *Geyvandov 163*

Give your love to your wife but tell your secrets to your mother.

    (*Irish; Spanish, Guatemala*): *o.s. Rosa*

The child gets dirty and tears his clothes, the mother sews and cleans.

    (*Czech*): *Reinsberg-Düringsfeld 190*

Both a mother and an apron cover many a gap. (*Hebrew, Israel*): *Moscona 205*

A mother is like a coverlet: she won't cover a corpse, but she will cover your disgrace.

    (*Sranan, Surinam*): *Hoen 48; o.s. Mavis Noordwijk*

A mother is like a good cooking pot with a lid. [She hides her children's weaknesses.]

    (*Creole, Martinique*): *David 46; Ludwig 447*

Better your own mother's rod than your stepmother's bread and butter.

    (*German; Finnish*): *Kuusi 58*

Rather in your mother's hands than in the nurse's.

    (*Papiamentu, Netherlands Antilles*): *Brenneker 58; Hoefnagels 84, 87; o.s. Willems*

There are thousands of women but only one mother.

    (*Spanish, Bolivia*): *Paredes-Candia 151; David 48*

Your mother is your mother, your wife is just a woman. (*Sranan, Surinam*): *o.s. Mavis Noordwijk*

One hundred aunts are not equal to one mother. (*Krio, Sierra Leone*): *o.s. Eldred-Jones*

Not even a thousand aunts can replace your own mother. (*Azeri, Azerbaijan*): *Geyvandov 165*

Wife for counsel, mother-in-law for a greeting, but nothing is sweeter than your own mother.

    (*Russian*): *Geyvandov 165*

A mother is a divinity, a father a treasure. (*Telegu, India*): *Champion 437*

After my father and my mother all are strangers. (*Arabic, Egypt*): *Singer 56*

The hands of fathers and mothers are soft. (*Lithuanian*): *Schleicher 183*

One may buy everything except a mother and a father. (*Tamil, India*): *Champion 433*

The feelings of a father are higher than the mountains, the feelings of a mother deeper than

    the ocean. (*Japanese*): *Geyvandov 166*

Pleasant is the shade of a tree; pleasanter that of a parent, a father or a mother.

    (*Burmese*): *Gray 12*

The mother is a garden of blessings, the father a rock. (*Hebrew/Arabic, Yemen*): *Stahl 201*

There is no greater love than that of a mother or a father. (*Spanish, Mexico*): *Glazer 13*

One mother is worth more than ten fathers. (*Korean*): *Geyvandov 166*

Mother is gold, father is a mirror. [The mother is much more valuable to the child than the

    father is expected to be: a mirror easily breaks.] (*Yoruba, Nigeria*): *Lindfors & Owomoyela 28*

There are many fathers, but only one mother.

    (*Papiamentu, Netherlands Antilles*): *Brenneker 84; Fernández Valledor 141*

There are a few like your father, nobody like your mother. (*Danish*): *Brix 50*

The father is the shoulder, the mother the soul. (*Tatar, RF*): *Geyvandov 166*

Whatever hurts the children the father feels in his little finger and the mother in her whole
body. (*German*): *Wander II 1309*

What touches the mother's heart, touches but the father's knee. (*Russian*): *Graf 60*

IDEAL CHILDREN AND WORRYING MOTHERS

If you don't have children, the longing for them will kill you; and if you do, the worrying for
them will kill you. (*Igbo, Nigeria*): *o.s. M. Ogundipe*

As many times as a woman gives birth, so many clever men there are on earth.
(*Arabic*): *Safadi 46*

There is only one pretty child in the world and every mother has it.
(*e.g. Hebrew, Israel; English, USA*): *Cohen 1961: 349; Whiting 1952: 383*

The little monkey is a gazelle [a symbol for beauty] in its mother's eyes.
(*Arabic, widespread; Hebrew, Israel*): *Safadi 12; Cohen 1961: 22*

An owlet is a beauty in his mother's eyes. (*Russian*): *Mieder 1986: 357*

The beetle saw its child on the wall and said: 'a pearl on a thread.'
(*Arabic, Lebanon*): *Frayha I 293*

The porcupine caressed her children and said: 'May God take care of your silken skin.'
(*Kurdish, Turkey*): *Geyvandov 161*

To the female weasel her baby is very precious. (*Sinhalese, Sri Lanka*): *o.s. Gunasekare*

Cockroaches call their children suns. (*Spanish, Cuba*): *Sabiduría Guajira 20*

When asked to bring the most beautiful thing, the crow brought its chick.
(*Chechen, RF*): *Geyvandov 161*

She who bore the child will like his slobbering. (*Portuguese, Brazil*): *Magalhães Júnior 239*

Every mother thinks it is on her own child the sun rises. (*Irish*): *Gaffney & Cashman 26*

The mother said to her blind son, 'Morning star of mine'; and to her lame son, 'Straight
river of mine.' (*Oromo, Ethiopia*): *Cotter 4*

A blind son is considered sighted by the mother. (*Cherkess, RF*): *Geyvandov 107*

Ugly children have no mother [also: no parents].
(*Spanish, Argentina; Chile*): *Guarnieri 27; Moya 574; o.s. Aurora Lazcano*

Devadatta is pleasing to his mother. [Even though he was a wicked man who tried to murder
the Buddha.] (*Sinhalese, Sri Lanka*): *o.s. Alex Gunasekare*

If you take the child by the hand, you take the mother by the heart. (*English, USA*): *Kin 169*

The tigress does not bite when you tell her that her young are beautiful. (*Korean*): *Geyvandov 230*

Mother's eyes are enchanted and see it wrong. (*Italian*): *Speroni 209*

What the mother praised, leave and run; what the neighbour praised, take and run.
(*Armenian*): *Sakayan 243*

The truth is not as mother tells it, but as the neighbours tell it. (*Hindi, India*): *Champion 403*

You can't weigh worries but many a mother has a heavy heart. (*Irish*): *O'Farrell 36*

A mother lying down sees farther than a child on a tree. (*Krio, Sierra Leone*): *o.s. Eldred Jones*

Dear God, don't send the child what his mother is afraid will happen to him.
(*Greek*): *Suard II 171*

A child is a sure care and an uncertain joy. (*Swedish*): *Ley 448*

The child knows not what trouble it has given its mother. (*Chinese*): *Scarborough 196*

Small children give you headache, big children heartache. (*German; Russian*): *Meier-Pfaller 80; Mesters 70; Mieder 1986: 72*

The little child sucks the breast, the big one the heart. (*Russian*): *Geyvandov 172*

Small children eat porridge; big ones eat their parents' hearts. (*Czech*): *Mieder 1986: 72*

Small child, small trouble; big child, big trouble.

(*Hungarian; Estonian; Romanian*): *Paczolay 79; Günther 36–7*

As long as the child is growing up, it is heavy for the hands; when it has grown up, it is heavy for the heart. (*Tajik*): *Geyvandov 172*

A small child brings joy; once grown up—sadness. (*Uyghur, China*): *Geyvandov 162*

One child: eternal anxieties for a mother. (*Bengali, Bangladesh*): *Geyvandov 102*

A mother is worried about her son when he is travelling far away. (*Chinese*): *o.s. Huang Mingfen*

A man does not die where his mother is. (*Mongo, Congo DR*): *Hulstaert 354*

The woman who does not give birth to a son has no worries.

(*Spanish, Colombia*): *o.s. Anonymous*

The mother of a hero is the first to weep. (*Serbian/Croatian*): *Mieder 1986: 336*

The mother of the brave wept, the mother of the timid laughed. (*Giryama, Kenya*): *Ibekwe 199*

The mother of a timid son never weeps. (*Turkish*): *Champion 481*

The coward belongs to his mother. [The fearful person who won't fight or hunt stays in safety.] (*Oromo, Ethiopia*): *Cotter 10*

A child [who is] a coward saves his mother worries. (*Ladino, Morocco*): *Dahan 66*

No grief greater than a mother's. (*Maltese*): *Lunde & Wintle 93*

Mother means martyr. (*Italian*): *Giusti 117*

MOTHERS AND CHILDREN, MOTHERS AND SONS

A good oven bakes good bread. (*Romanian*): *Günther 40–1*

All raindrops that fall on the roof, end up in the gutter. [Children usually follow the example of their parents.] (*Indonesian*): *Geyvandov 167*

A *girauman* [a vegetable] does not bear calabashes. (*Creole, Haiti*): *Hall 193*

A guinea hen cannot bring forth a ram. (*Creole, Trinidad/Tobago*): *Ottley 89*

Every tree has its root. (*Sranan, Surinam*): *Hoen 22*

A slanted branch has a slanted shadow. (*Japanese*): *Geyvandov 168*

The child of a piebald cow will always come out stained. (*Spanish, Colombia*): *Acuña 57*

What is born of a cat will catch mice.

(*Czech; Serbian/Croatian; Romanian; Spanish, Chile*): *Mieder 1986: 62; Karadžić 315; Cannobio 59*

A goat does not generate a lamb. (*Romanian*): *Günther 40–1*

If you planted a pear tree, do not expect peaches. (*Chinese*): *Geyvandov 167*

The pear falls under the pear tree. (*Albanian*): *Reinsberg-Düringsfeld 108*

How could the apple be but as the apple tree? (*Irish*): *O'Rahilly 4*

The horse-dung does not fall far from the horse. (*Dutch*): *o.s. Elly Westerhof*

The mother is round but the children are square. (*Vietnamese*): *Geyvandov 169*

A beautiful branch can bear ugly fruit. (*Burmese*): *Geyvandov 169*

There will never be a good plant from a bad shrub.

(*Spanish, Dominican Republic*): *Rodríguez D. 210*

The son goes to heaven thanks to his mother, the daughter thanks to her husband.

(*Fulfulde, West Africa*): *Geyvandov 178*

The mother of an impotent male neither rejoices nor grieves.

(*Arabic, widespread*): *Lunde & Wintle 123*

If a man has sexual intercourse with his mother, it is as if he did it in the *ka'bah* [as if he had sex with somebody in a public place]. (*Arabic, Morocco*): *Westermarck 86*

One sleeps with one's mother out of sheer necessity. (*Catalan, Spain*): *Guiter 141*

The embrace of his mother is a cradle for a son. (*Pashto, Afghanistan*): *Geyvandov 163*

There is no finer sweetheart than one's mother. (*Turkish*): *o.s. A.P. Kwak*

A boy's best friend is his mother and there's no spancel [a rope tie used to hobble cattle during milking] stronger than her apron string. (*Irish*): *O'Farrell 44*

In sunshine it is warm, with his mother a son feels comfortable. (*Russian*): *Rauch 145*

Every man carries his mother in his heart. (*Spanish, Cuba*): *Cabrera n.p.*

The eldest son should not leave the family home; the youngest does not leave his mother's room. (*Chinese*): *Lunde & Wintle 28*

The back of a mother gets bent when her son is married, but gets straight again when her daughter marries. (*Chechen, RF*): *Geyvandov 176*

The boy's best friend is his mother, until he becomes himself his sweetheart's best friend.

(*Irish*): *Geyvandov 149; O'Farrell 57*

Usually a man is bound to his mother and only after she has died does he bind himself to his wife. (*Hebrew, Israel*): *Rosen 410*

When the river took him, the old man screamed: 'Mama'. (*Adyg, RF*): *Geyvandov 164*

Your mother's love and your wife's support. (*Italian*): *Attanasio 33*

The mother will look at his belly, the wife at his back. (*Telegu, India*): *Champion 437*

When the mother receives much, the wife receives little. (*Chuwash, RF*): *Geyvandov 149*

The son who loves his wife more than his mother is unfilial; the mother who joins the son in hating his wife is not good. (*Chinese*): *Scarborough 197; Lunde & Wintle 185*

Mother loves her son, but the son loves his wife. (*Khionghta, Bangladesh*): *Lewin 28*

Mother's heart is tender but her son's heart is like a stone. (*Tibetan*): *Gergan & Asboe 73*

The mother loves excessively while the son has a heart of stone.

(*Pashto, Pakistan*): *o.s. S.W.A. Shah*

Sacrifice your mother, another woman will give you offspring. [Used when choices are to be made.] (*Haya, Tanzania/Uganda*): *Geyvandov 175*

Mother's darlings make but milk-porridge heroes. (*English, USA*): *Loomis 1956: 175*

A child who remains in his mother's house believes her soup the best.

(*Efik, Nigeria; Ga, Ghana*): *Jablow 38; Ibekwe 95*

A son who never leaves home always thinks his mother's is the loudest fart.

(*Gikuyu, Kenya*): *o.s. Gacheche Waruingi*

If a boy is raised by a woman, he'll not become a man. (*Somali, Somalia/Kenya*): *Geyvandov 149*

A man does not look like his mother. (*Ovambo, Angola*): *Geyvandov 179*

MOTHERS AND DAUGHTERS

The daughter of a good mother will be the mother of a good daughter. (*English, USA*): *Kin 244*

Like mother, like daughter.

> (*In many languages in the Western world and the Middle East, e.g. in Danish; Italian; Hungarian; Estonian; Bulgarian; Dutch; English, USA; Hebrew; Arabic*): *Kuusi 90; Ter Laan 220; Pineaux 90; Spezzano 68; Krylov 22; Arnaudov 78; Alcalay 93; Safadi 22; Mieder 1992: 419*

Look at the mother rather than [at] her daughter. (*Japanese*): *Buchanan 64*

See the mother, comprehend the daughter. (*Pashto, Afghanistan*): *Champion 462*

Know the mother and pick up the daughter. (*Arabic, widespread*): *Safadi 22*

The habits of the mother go to the daughter. (*Finnish*): *Geyvandov 250*

Have a [good] look at the mother before you take the daughter.

> (*Hungarian; Bulgarian; widespread in Eastern Europe*): *Krylov 22; Arnaudov 78*

The worth of the bread depends on the flour. (*Telegu, India*): *o.s. Hema Naidu*

The daughter's merits come from her mother; the goodness of butter depends on the quality of the cow. (*Bengali, Bangladesh*): *Jalil 24*

Look at the mother before you take a daughter; see how much milk the buffaloe gives before you buy her. (*Telegu, India*): *Champion 437*

Observe the edge and take the linen; observe the mother and take the daughter.

> (*Turkish*): *Haig 27; Champion 478*

The filly is judged after the mare, the daughter is known after the mother.

> (*Estonian*): *Paczolay 23*

Lascivious mothers, strumpet daughters. (*Dutch*): *Harrebomée II 92*

Bravo for the mother of the girl. (*Bulgarian*): *Arnaudov 79*

Lenient housewife, lazy daughters. (*Estonian*): *Krylov 22*

A bustling mother makes a slothful daughter.

> (*French*): *Roux de Lincy 232; Bohn 1857: 280; Champion 252; Harrebomée II 92*

A tender mother breeds a scabby daughter.

> (*German*): *Meier-Pfaller 84; Bohn 1857: 47, 106; Roux de Lincy 232; Pineaux 91*

Choose a good mother's daughter, though her father were the Devil.

> (*English, UK*): *Champion 71*

An impertinent father gets a disobedient daughter. (*Portuguese*): *Geyvandov 168*

Even when the daughter is mute, she understands her mother. (*Spanish*): *Meier-Pfaller 82*

Mother and daughter are like nail and flesh. (*Ladino, Israel*): *Stahl 201*

A daughter tells her secrets only to her mother. (*Hebrew, Israel*): *Alcalay 93*

WHO IS TAKING CARE OF THE MOTHER?

The son was asked: 'How will you repay your mother?' 'I'll raise a son.'

> (*Georgian*): *Geyvandov 174*

Even if the son fries her an egg on his hand, he can't repay his mother.

> (*Dargin, RF*): *Geyvandov 173*

An old hare gets suckled by her young. (*Ganda, Uganda*): *Walser 357*

The hide that served the mother to carry the child will serve the child to carry the mother.

> (*Mboshi, Congo*): *Obenga 284*

Chick, find food for your mother; she used to search for it for you. (*Ovambo, Namibia*): *Ibekwe 24*

When the mother feeds her children, she gives as much as heaven and sea; when the children feed their mother, they count every day. (*Vietnamese*): *Geyvandov 164*

Boil the mother and her child will eat; boil the child and its mother won't.
(*Sranan, Surinam*): *David 6; Ottley 89; Llewellyn Watson 257; o.s. Mavis Noordwijk*

A mother has no pot that is big enough for her to boil her child in.
(*Sranan, Surinam*): *o.s. Mavis Noordwijk*

The young magpie plucking its mother's feathers thinks that it is showing gratitude to her.
(*Tibetan*): *Duncan 188*

A mother can feed ten children; ten children cannot feed their mother.
(*Vietnamese*): *Geyvandov 174*

A mother never complains, even [when] she has given birth to ten children, but her children are reluctant to bear the responsibility of taking care of her. (*Chinese*): *o.s. Huang Mingfen*

A mother can take care of ten children, but sometimes ten children can't take care of one mother. (*English, USA*): *Titelman 239*

A mother can provide for the needs of twelve children, but not the other way round.
(*Letzeburgish*): *o.s. Laure Wolter*

A poor mother is able to feed seven children in the same way as seven children one mother.
(*Czech*): *Reinsberg-Düringsfeld 189*

One mother for a hundred children, and not a hundred children for one mother.
(*Spanish, Chile*): *Cannobio 71; Hernández 256; Moya 643; Sánchez Duarte 232*

She gave birth and brought up [children], but has to sleep outside.
(*Ladino, Morocco*): *Dahan 129*

The kind-hearted mother dies unhappy. (*Arabic, widespread*): *Lunde & Wintle 94*

Love can be passed downwards; love that goes upwards does not exist. [Parents love children, children do not love parents.] (*Korean*): *Geyvandov 173*

The mother is sweet to the child, the child cruel to the parents. (*Estonian*): *Geyvandov 174*

Parents for their children, children for themselves. (*Abkhaz, Georgia*): *Geyvandov 174*

Don't try to cover the stone with a quilt. (*Japanese*): *Buchanan 96*

MOTHERLESS

You do not know how to cry until your mother dies. (*Ovambo, Namibia*): *Ibekwe 119*

Once the little scorpions leave the mother's back, she dies.
(*Papiamentu, Netherlands Antilles*): *Brenneker 81*

Without a mother, the children are lost like bees. (*Russian*): *Reinsberg-Düringsfeld 190*

A child that has lost his mother, his help is behind. (*English, UK*): *Whiting 1968: 82*

A fatherless child is half an orphan, a motherless one a whole orphan.
(*Finnish; Bulgarian; Estonian*): *Cordry 181; Arnaudov 76; Mieder 1986: 69*

Orphaned of his mother, the child has the [threshold] doorstep as his pillow, orphaned of his father, he still has his mother's lap. (*Arabic, Tunisia*): *Lunde & Wintle 101*

If the mother dies, the father becomes an uncle. (*Tamil, India*): *Champion 431*

One can only truly value the love of a mother once the stepmother has arrived.
(*Ladino / Hebrew, Morocco*): *Stahl 204*

With your mother at home you are fed with good olive oil; with your mother at the cemetery,
  you are fed with remnants [waste]. (*Arabic, Maghreb*): *Duvollet 31*
A child does not get enough food when the [real] mother is not there.
  (*Ganda, Uganda*): *Walser 397*
When your mother dies, you'll eat yam peels.
  (*Ngbaka, Central African Republic*): *Thomas 743*
A mother cannot die. (*Mongo, Congo DR*): *Hulstaert 434*
Whoever has lost his mother has lost his life. (*Hebrew, Yemen*): *Stahl 416*
The one who has lost his mother, where is the house where he will be harboured?
  (*Arabic, Algeria*): *Belamri 38*
One does not cry on the day of his mother's death. [The pain gets worse over time].
  (*Creole, Guadeloupe*): *Ludwig 433*
A good mother warms beyond the grave. (*Letzeburgish*): *o.s. Laure Wolter*
A mother does not die. [i.e. her children keep on praising her]. (*Ganda, Uganda*): *Walser 393*
At someone's funeral we weep for our own mothers and fathers. (*Twi, Ghana*): *Ibekwe 40*
Better the father seven times dead, than the mother once. (*Lak, RF*): *Geyvandov 166*
When my father died I hardly noticed, when my mother died I broke down the house.
  (*Hebrew / Arabic, Iraq*): *Stahl 416*
A mother you have only one.
  (*Spanish*): *Paredes-Candia 151; David 48; Brenneker 84; Fernández Valledor 141*
A mother you have only one—thank God! (*Spanish, Venezuela*): *o.s. Rafael Sánchez*
The mother has died: now for the good times. (*Kundu, Cameroon*): *Ittman 71*
After its mother died, the colt's coat became glossy. (*Tibetan*): *Gergan & Asboe 118*
The monkey smothers its young by hugging them too much. (*Creole, Martinique*): *Hearn 7*
Too much mothering can be harmful. (*Hebrew, Israel*): *Cohen 1961: 349*
A chattering girl is silenced by her mother; a chattering boy is not [silenced by his mother].
  (*Sumerian, Mesopotamia*): *Alster I 37*
The child depends for its upbringing on the mother. (*Arabic, Maghreb*): *Cheneb III 194*
Your son shall be the way you raise him to be, your husband shall be the way he was raised to
  be. (*Arabic, Maghreb; Ladino, Israel; Adyg, RF*): *Lunde & Wintle 124; Duvollet 28*
A mother gets ruined by daughters, but she herself ruins for them her son [by spoiling him].
  (*Bulgarian*): *Arnaudov 284*
Women are mothers and men are men. (*Dutch*): *o.s. anonymous*

MOTHERS-IN-LAW VERSUS DAUGHTERS-IN-LAW

To find a wife is easy, to find suitable parents-in-law is difficult.
  (*Malagasy, Madagascar*): *Geyvandov 147*
If our child catches a snake, what can be done with it? (*Indonesian*): *o.s. Sylvia Schipper*
Birth comes first, marriage follows. (*Taka, Congo DR*): *Beken 1993: 75*
The stranger is not one of us. (*Bulgarian*): *Arnaudov 72*
A mother-in-law is not a relative but a punishment. (*Portuguese, Brazil*): *Vasconcellos 62*
A mother-in-law is like a pig's snout digging here and digging there.
  (*Taka, Congo DR*): *Beken 1993: 216*

Who counts on his mother-in-law's soup, will go to sleep without dinner.
(*Creole, Dominican Republic*): *ACCT 101; Zagaya 253; David 49*

Never rely on the glory of a morning or on the smiles of your mother-in-law.
(*Japanese*): *Lunde & Wintle 443*

The friendship of a mother-in-law is like dry weather in the wet season.
(*Papiamentu, Netherlands Antilles*): *Brenneker 6*

Friendship between mothers-in-law and daughters-in-law only goes as deep as the teeth [of
the smile]. (*Portuguese, Brazil*): *Mota 43*

A mother-in-law, even one made out of sugar, is no good.
(*Spanish, Spain/Bolivia; Greek; Catalan, Spain*): *Bergua 480; Glazer 282; Sánchez Duarte 210;
Cannobio 108; Ballesteros 52; Politès 13; Guiter 147; o.s. José Paz*

There is no goodness in a mother-in-law or sweetness in a Mangosa tree [a very bitter plant].
(*Telegu, India*): *Murty 227*

Mothers-in-law are like carrots, they are all bitter, more or less. (*Italian*): *Raimondi 56*

A mother-in-law tastes like sour grapes. (*Romanian*): *Geyvandov 147*

No evil is as bad as a mother-in-law. (*Latin; Greek*): *Otto 246*

The evil words of a mother-in-law are worse than a donkey's kicks.
(*Creole, Saint Lucia*): *ACCT 83*

The tail of a pike is always black; nowhere in the world will you find a good mother-in-law.
(*Bengali, Bangladesh*): *Jalil 25*

The best mother-in-law ate her son-in-law. (*Spanish, Chile*): *Laval 74*

A tooth, sharpened for the daughter-in-law, will bite the son. (*Chechen, RF*): *Geyvandov 149*

While gnawing the daughter-in-law, the son is consumed. (*Awar, RF*): *Geyvandov 149*

The tongue of a bad mother-in-law brings divorce.
(*Yiddish, RF; Hebrew, Israel*): *Geyvandov 147, 236*

Is thy mother-in-law quarrelsome? Divorce her daughter. (*Arabic, Egypt*): *Burckhardt 63*

Stones, run in the river; shrimps, under the bridge; cockroaches and rats, run over my
mother-in-law's legs. (*Spanish, Panama*): *Aguilera 124*

The curse that you meant for your mother-in-law will come down on your mother.
(*Creole, Haiti*): *ACCT 34*

The husband's mother is the wife's devil. (*German*): *Champion 169*

The wife's mother is the husband's devil. (*German*): *Meier-Pfaller 67*

Forty leagues down from hell there is a special hell for mothers-in-law.
(*Spanish, Colombia*): *Ramírez S. 173*

Not even if she were made of clay would a mother-in-law be welcome.
(*Hebrew, Israel; Spanish, Mexico*): *Alcalay 335; Casasola 67; Mota 213*

Anyone who owns just three ounces of flour should never have to depend on his wife's family.
(*Japanese*): *Wintle 17*

I want to be as far from my mother-in-law as the swallows are from the stars.
(*Spanish, Peru*): *Arora 121*

My youth, come back to me, for my poor daughter-in-law to see what I was capable of then,
for my dear husband to be proud of me. (*Arabic, Morocco*): *Messaoudi 108*

You, daughter-in-law, will get older and see what I have seen. (*Arabic, Tunisia*): *Yetiv 132*

RIVALS

Mother-in-law and daughter-in-law: you can cook them together, but it will never be sweet.
(*French*): *Ségalen: 38*

To make a daughter-in-law and a mother-in-law live together is like introducing a pestilence in the house. (*Thai*): *Peltier 11*

Brides and mothers-in-law are like dogs and monkeys. (*Japanese*): *Buchanan 93*

Mother-in-law, daughter-in-law: dog and cat never eat from the same plate.
(*Spanish, Chile; Italian*): *Cannobio 108; Menarini 20*

When cat and mouse will make peace, mother-in-law and daughter-in-law will forgive each other. (*Ladino, Morocco*): *Dahan 356*

A daughter-in-law can no more live under the same roof with her mother-in-law than a goat can live in the same barn with a tiger. (*Hebrew, Israel*): *Rosten 1977: 153*

Inscribed on the gates of Paradise: No daughter-in-law ever loved her mother-in-law.
(*Arabic, Lebanon*): *Lunde & Wintle 123; Frayha II 665*

If a daughter-in-law would have loved her mother-in-law, all women would have gone to heaven. (*Arabic/Jewish, Iraq*): *Stahl 418*

The daughter-in-law has taken the oath to love her mother-in-law on the day when charcoal turns white. (*Arabic, Morocco*): *Messaoudi 106*

When will there be peace between daughter-in-law and mother-in-law? When a donkey climbs a ladder. (*Hebrew, Israel*): *Moscona 48*

Where a hundred soldiers fit, a mother-in-law with her daughter-in-law can't.
(*Estonian*): *Geyvandov 151*

Mother-in-law and daughter-in-law are made of the same crooked rib.
(*Chechen, RF*): *Geyvandov 151*

In the daughter-in-law there's a piece of the mother-in-law.
(*Yiddish, Eastern Europe*): *Geyvandov 151*

Mother-in-law and daughter-in-law are a tempest and hailstorm.
(*English, UK/USA*): *Bohn 1857: 455; Wander IV 475; Whiting 1977: 298*

The spots on the antelope are those on her mother-in-law. (*Cameroon*): *o.s. N. Zwaal*

NEWLY ARRIVED

Once, long ago, there was one good mother-in-law, but a wolf ate her. (*French*): *Ségalen 39*

Every mother-in-law dislikes the young wife. (*Serbian/Croatian*): *Reinsberg-Düringsfeld 195*

Daughter-in-law and mother-in-law, they mess up already at the door. (*Spanish*): *Bergua 380*

Before the wedding, embraces and kisses, later violence and strangling.
(*Ladino, Morocco*): *Dahan 357*

A new daughter-in-law is very diligent on her first arrival. (*Chinese*): *Scarborough 201*

When a new daughter-in-law enters the house, to the mother-in-law it is like entering her coffin on her burial. (*Chinese*): *Fabre 35*

A daughter-in-law has a horse's patience and a dog's obedience. (*Estonian*): *Geyvandov 150*

Mothers-in-law are always talkative, thus daughters-in-law need to be hard of hearing.
(*Chinese*): *o.s. Huang Mingfen*

The sister-in-law is a stinging nettle. (*Russian*): *Geyvandov 150*

The sister-in-law is a birchen splinter. (*Russian*): *Geyvandov 150*

The mother-in-law is a fever and the sister-in-law is a poisonous scorpion.
(*Arabic, Lebanon*): *Abela 353*

The elder sister of one's husband is as authoritative as one's mother-in-law, and the younger
sister is as terrible as the King of Hell. (*Chinese*): *o.s. Huang Mingfen*

Two sisters-in-law hit each other, the mother-in-law paid the penalty for it.
(*Bulgarian*): *Arnaudov 85*

Rarely is a servant praised, a daughter-in-law never. (*Finnish*): *Kuusi 58*

Good deeds of a daughter-in-law or a cat go unnoticed. (*Korean*): *Geyvandov 150*

In the presence of the mother-in-law what rank is the bride! (*Persian*): *Roebuck 312*

To give eggplant to a daughter-in-law is too great a kindness. (*Japanese*): *Lunde & Wintle 170*

A dry piece of bread, salted with a tear, is the fate of a young daughter-in-law .
(*Komi, RF*): *Geyvandov 150*

Your mother-in-law does not serve you cooked corn but she engages you to grind.
(*Rundi, Burundi*): *Rodegem 224*

Raise your child from early years, raise your daughter-in-law from the first days.
(*Nogay, RF*): *Geyvandov 168*

My mother-in-law scolds her daughter in order to teach me. (*Bengali, India*): *o.s. Shobha Gupta*

I speak to you, neighbour, that my daughter-in-law might hear.
(*Arabic, Lebanon*): *Singer 66; Frayha I 162*

Hear me, daughter, so that the daughter-in-law will understand.
(*Spanish, Mexico; English, USA*): *Glazer 156; Yoffie 149*

If a mother-in-law breaks a huge vessel, it is nothing; if the daughter-in-law breaks a tiny
bowl, the household is ruined. (*Tamil, India*): *Subramanian 113*

It is very distressing for a daughter-in-law to be controlled by a wicked mother-in-law.
(*Bengali, India*): *o.s. Shobha Gupta*

Better the glares of a foreigner than those of a mother-in-law. (*Rundi, Burundi*): *Rodegem 78*

The wicked mother-in-law has eyes at the back [of her head]. (*Russian*): *Graf 211*

The evil mother-in-law has also ears at the back [of her head]. (*Russian*): *Rauch 145*

Always sweep where your mother-in-law looks.
(*English, USA; Spanish, Dominican Republic; Hebrew, Israel*): *Mieder 1989: 88; Henríquez Ureña
109; Rodríguez D. 65*

Eat until the evening, father-in-law, then I will delouse you. (*Bulgarian*): *Arnaudov 71*

My daughter-in-law is very good at doing useless things like chopping a gourd.
(*Bengali, India*): *o.s. Sanjukta Gupta*

When foolishness was distributed my daughter-in-law received a generous share of it.
(*Arabic, Morocco*): *Messaoudi 108*

REVENGE

Daughters-in-law become mothers-in-law. (*English, USA*): *Mieder 1992: 135*

The daughter-in-law's shawl always hangs closest to the door. (*Finnish*): *Geyvandov 150*

A daughter-in-law will run to her parental house on bare feet. (*Armenian*): *Geyvandov 153*

The pleasure of a daughter-in-law is anger. (*Sumerian, Mesopotamia*): *Alster I 89*

Angry with her mother-in-law, the daughter-in-law kicks her [mother-in-law's] dog.
  (*Korean*): *o.s. B. Walraven*

He was no match for his mother-in-law, he then rose against his wife.
  (*Arabic, Egypt*): *Burckhardt 221*

Unable to prevail against his mother-in-law, he takes vengeance on his wife.
  (*Arabic, Lebanon/Egypt*): *Frayha I 115, 240*

A mother-in-law that meddles with everything should get a third of the strokes of the stick
  the wife gets. (*Amharic, Ethiopia*): *o.s. Anonymous*

For nine years she [daughter-in-law] kept silence, and in the tenth year when she started
  speaking again, she ruined nine villages. (*Bulgarian*): *Arnaudov 215*

He who bothers to hit his mother-in-law may as well break open her head [i.e. do it prop-
  erly]. (*Arabic, Algeria*): *Lunde & Wintle 123*

[A man] who takes the trouble to beat his mother-in-law should cleave her skull.
  (*Arabic, Maghreb*): *Lunde & Wintle 123; Cheneb I 111; Belamri 46*

Who comes to strike his mother-in-law must be sure to give her a well-deserved beating. [To
  make her pay in advance for all her faults to come.] (*Arabic, Algeria*): *Belamri 46*

If you have pulled down your mother-in-law, press hard! God knows when you will have another chance. [If you can harm her, don't have mercy.] (*Fulfulde, Senegal*): *Gaden 36*

'More by hit than by wit', said the man, when he threw a stone at his dog and struck his
  mother-in-law. (*Danish*): *Kjaer Holbek 256*

The patience of a daughter-in-law results from her desire to become a mother-in-law in the
  future. (*Chinese*): *o.s. Huang Mingfen*

Yesterday's bride is today's mother-in-law. [According to Japanese customs, a bride severely
  treated by her mother-in-law will soon become one herself and treat her daughter-in-law
  equally badly] (*Japanese*): *Buchanan 92*

There comes a time that the daughter-in-law becomes a mother-in-law, and she will be even
  worse than her own mother-in-law. (*Korean*): *Ha 100; Geyvandov 151*

As a daughter-in-law she could do nothing right in the eyes of her mother-in-law; when she
  became a mother-in-law herself, she hated her daughter-in-law.
  (*Basque, Spain*): *Geyvandov 219*

The mother-in-law does not remember that she was a daughter-in-law.
  (*Hebrew, Israel*): *Cohen 1961: 350; Stahl 418*

Mother-in-law, have you not been a daughter-in-law? Yes, I have forgotten all about it.
  (*Arabic, Lebanon*): *Abela 575*

The mother-in-law remembers not that she was a daughter-in-law.
  (*English, UK/USA*): *Rayner 149; Wander IV 475; Guiter 147; Bergua 378*

No mother-in-law can remember she has also been a daughter-in-law.
  (*Spanish, Venezuela*): *Mota 132; o.s. Claudia Tones*

DEATH AND THE MOTHER-IN-LAW

Adam was the first happy person, for he had no mother-in-law. (*Hebrew, Israel*): *Geyvandov 147*

Death stepped on the threshold and everybody looked at the daughter-in-law.
  (*Greek*): *Geyvandov 150*

When grief is predestined to a house, may the daughter-in-law die, and if she is not at home,
   the son-in-law. (*Chechen, RF*): *Geyvandov 150*

Fathers-in-law, mothers-in-law, maize and beans do best in the earth.
   (*Portuguese, Brazil*): *Vasconcellos 62; Lamenza 250; Mota 213*

The mother-in-law is good but better when buried in the earth. (*Catalan, Spain*): *Guiter 147*

A mother-in-law is like a *yuca* [cassava plant], good enough to be buried. [A yuca is a plant.]
   (*Spanish, Antigua*): *Sierra García I 99*

The best mother-in-law is in the goose-field [buried]. (*German*): *Wander IV 475*

The mother-in-law's final breath is sweeter than the nightingale's song. (*Persian*): *Geyvandov 148*

Until you have buried your mother-in-law, your wife does not belong to you.
   (*Fulfulde, West Africa*): *o.s. Pinto-Bull*

I shall be the mistress of the homestead and go to the bathing-place with my keys hanging on
   my sari. (*Bengali, India*): *De 49*

The mother-in-law died, the shackle is broken and she [daughter-in-law] climbs onto a
   pedestal. (*Rajasthani, India*): *Bhatnagar 72*

The bride is happy, there is neither a mother-in-law nor a sister-in-law. (*Persian*): *Roebuck 312*

The woman who is happily married has neither a mother-in-law nor sisters-in-law.
   (*Spanish, Chile*): *Mota 124; Vasconcellos 62; Acuña 43; Moya 328; o.s. R. Sanchez*

A daughter-in-law crying for her father-in-law's death [i.e. likely to be feigned].
   (*Telegu, India*): *Geyvandov 198*

A daughter-in-law's mourning for her mother-in-law is false and feigned.
   (*Chinese*): *Scarborough 317*

Even a dead mother-in-law is brought to mind when pounding rice. (*Korean*): *o.s. B. Walraven*

Rather a good mother-in-law than an inheritance with a well. (*Arabic/Jewish, Yemen*): *Stahl 232*

Gifts reconcile even the wicked mother-in-law. (*Bulgarian*): *Arnaudov 85*

Good mother-in-law, good daughter-in-law. (*Spanish*): *Wander IV 475*

Among a thousand daughters-in-law, one may love her mother-in-law; among two thousand
   mothers-in-law, one may cherish her daughter-in-law.
   (*Arabic, Lebanon*): *Lunde & Wintle 123*

OLD AGE

At fifteen, a scent of milk; at twenty, blooming; at thirty, smelly; at forty, faugh!
   (*Spanish, Chile*): *Laval 66*

The longest five years in a woman's life is between twenty-nine and thirty.
   (*English, USA*): *Mieder 1992: 667–8*

At the age of thirty, a man is still as attractive as a flower, while a woman looks old.
   (*Chinese*): *o.s. Huang Mingfen*

A man at forty is youthful as a flower, but a woman at forty resembles stale tea leaves.
   (*Chinese*): *Chen 194*

A man at forty is youthful as a flower; but a woman at forty resembles an old potsherd in the
   sweepings. (*Chinese*): *Fabre 17*

Forty years is grandma's age. (*Russian*): *Geyvandov 81*

When she becomes forty, a woman withers. (*Ukrainian*): *Geyvandov 81*

Forty-five-years old and the woman is a berry again. (*Russian*): *o.s. Ravve*

A woman is an angel at ten, a saint at fifteen, a devil at forty and a witch at fourscore.

    (*English, UK*): *Champion 45*

A woman who is not sexually active is counted as old. (*Bengali, India*): *o.s. Shobha Gupta*

While the child is growing up, the mother becomes an old woman.

    (*Uyghur, China*): *Geyvandov 165*

Everyone knows the old woman's name, yet everyone calls her [great-]grandmother.

    (*Mamprusi/Mossi, Burkina Faso*): *o.s. A. Sawadogo*

The old woman who boils water for porridge does not lack grandchildren. (*Rwanda*): *Crépeau 43*

The well-to-do old woman discovers she has a crowd of grandchildren.

    (*Rundi, Burundi*): *Rodegem 30*

GRANDMOTHERS AND OLD WOMEN

Respect your grandmother, because without her your mother would not have existed.

    (*Umbundu, Angola*): *Geyvandov 181*

There is nothing sweeter than a grandchild. (*German*): *Meier-Pfaller 74*

In granny's basket there is always *waranawa* fish. (*Papiamentu, Netherlands Antilles*): *Brenneker 56*

A grandmother always thinks that she cannot do enough to show her love for her

    grandchildren. (*Chinese*): *o.s. Huang Mingfen*

Pleasantly lives he who lets his grandmother look after him. (*Russian*): *Rauch 137*

Whoever does not know about grandmothers, does not know what is good.

    (*Spanish, Chile*): *Cannobio 20*

A mother is responsible for a bad son, a grandmother for a bad grandson.

    (*Vietnamese*): *Geyvandov 181*

The baby nursed by its grandmother can never be corrected. (*Gikuyu, Kenya*): *Barra 29*

Those who have been reared by grandmothers are cheaper by three hundred [coins]. [They

    are so thoroughly spoiled that they are not of much value.] (*Japanese*): *Buchanan 102*

Grandparents' love makes grandchildren naughty. (*Catalan, Spain*): *Guiter 123*

The grandmother's correction makes no impression. (*English, UK*): *Bohn 1855: 506*

'Grandma, what will you refuse me?' 'I don't know, maybe admission to church.'

    (*Russian*): *Geyvandov 209*

Your grandmother has taught you this and you want to ask your mother?

    (*Baule, Ivory Coast*): *Arbelbide 157*

Lacking-his-mother sucks his grandmother. (*Fulfulde, West Africa*): *Issa 46; Gaden 117*

If the child does not have a mother, let the grandmother raise it.

    (*Creole, Haiti/Jamaica*): *Préval 76; Anderson 79*

He who does not have a mother will have to make do with a grandmother.

    (*Spanish, Panama/Argentina*): *Maduro 69; Villafuerte 134*

If you do not see your mother, go and find your grandmother.

    (*English, Jamaica*): *Llewellyn Watson 255*

God is not only one person's grandmother. (*Ovambo, Namibia*): *Geyvandov 118*

God cannot be everywhere, that's why he created grandmothers. (*Dutch*): *o.s. A. Wagenmakers*

GOOD OLD AGE

A good grape turns into a good raisin.
  (*Spanish, Argentina/Bolivia*): *Moya 600; Paredes-Candia 42*

She is a large tree on which all things hang, or are entwined: if she falls, all perish.
  (*Efik, Nigeria*): *Ibekwe 97*

She dies free and noble; she keeps the moneybag; she chases the enemy out.
  (*Arabic, Lebanon*): *Frayha I 162*

Even an old woman can make mistakes. (*Russian*): *Krylov 169*

If you have luck you have an old person at home. (*Turkish*): *Haig 42*

White hair, wise hair. (*Dutch*): *Anonymous*

An old woman in the house makes it a joyful place. (*Hebrew, Israel*): *Moscona 208*

An old man in the house is a burden; an old woman in the house is a treasure.
  (*Hebrew, Israel*): *Rosten 1977: 338; Malka 67; Cohen 1912: 24*

An old man and an old woman [wife] in the home: he is a burden [to bear with], she is bearing
  the burden [also: she herself is the yoke]. (*Ladino, Morocco*): *Dahan 1237*

Even an old calabash is useful. (*Minyanka, Mali*): *Cauvin 1981: 80*

An old pot is not thrown away: it can still be useful. (*Yaka, Congo DR*): *Beken 1993: 129*

Even old women run on God's errands. (*Oromo, Ethiopia*): *Cotter 25*

An old woman is not old in a song she dances well [i.e. she has expertise]. (*Nigeria*): *Ibekwe 59*

The old woman [i.e. grandmother]—if she does not serve for a pot, she'll serve for a cover.
  (*Spanish*): *Bohn 1855: 227*

Why did grandmother, who cut your belly-button, not cut your head as well?
  (*Bulgarian*): *Arnaudov 116*

Do not instruct *baba* [grandmother], how to give birth to children. (*Bulgarian*): *Arnaudov 115*

Why teach your grandmother to grope ducks? (*English, UK*): *Bohn 1855: 494*

Don't teach your grandmother how to pick [pluck?] ducks, or to suck eggs.
  (*English, USA*): *Atkinson 79*

Do you intend to teach your grandmother to suck eggs?
  (*Maltese; English, UK*): *Busuttil 29; Bohn 1855: 494*

You do not teach your grandmother how to suck eggs. [Respect experience]
  (*Ronga, Zimbabwe*): *p'Bitek 6*

The grandmother does not need science. (*Bulgarian*): *Arnaudov 89*

If you show a medicine to an old woman, you'll have to pluck the leaves.
  (*Baule, Ivory Coast*): *Arbelbide 36*

In the luggage of the old woman one finds mortar and pestle. (*Lega, Congo DR*): *o.s. Malasi*

Even if she is crooked she still kneads the bread. (*Lithuanian*): *Schleicher 154*

Little by little the old woman spins the flock. [A flock is a tuft of wool, a flock is also the
  sheep: she works her way through all the wool produced by the flock.]
  (*Spanish, El Salvador/Argentina*): *Sánchez Duarte 191; Moya 583*

A kiss doesn't spoil a girl, a knitting needle doesn't spoil an old woman.
  (*Bulgarian*): *o.s. Dobrinka Parusheva*

Old baskets are used again in the peanut harvest. [Only serving others' needs when
  required.] (*Yaka, Congo DR*): *Beken 1993: 207*

If there is an old woman by the fireside, a ram will not hang himself.
   (*English, Jamaica*): *Llewellyn Watson 277*
There are three faithful friends: an old wife, an old dog and ready money.
   (*English, USA*): *Franklin 1738*
If you have an old wife at home, your mind can rest easy. (*Ladino, Morocco*): *Dahan 1236*
A young woman gets a man's glances, an old woman his heart. (*Irish*): *O'Farrell 10*
Wives and pots and kettles are better when old. (*Japanese*): *Buchanan 91*
Wives and shoes are better when old. (*Japanese*): *Buchanan 91*
One can curl up like a dog if one cannot stretch out like a dog; there is yet more if one has re-
   lations with an older woman. [One can put up with what there is and be happy.]
   (*Tibetan*): *Duncan 219*
Every woman keeps a corner in her heart where she is always twenty-one.
   (*English, USA*): *Mieder 1992: 667*
The heart does not grow old. (*French*): *Meier-Pfaller 43*
An old wife is a child to her old husband. (*Oromo, Ethiopia*): *Cotter 20*
Don't forget the well-trodden roads, don't discard your old wife.
   (*Kabardino-Cherkess, RF*): *Geyvandov 122*
Pearls are found in old shells. (*Vietnamese*): *Geyvandov 29*
In love, a mature [older] woman is best. (*Japanese*): *Geyvandov 28*
Old maids make good lovers. (*English, USA*): *West 43*
Old love cannot be compared to new love. (*Korean*): *Geyvandov 27*
A fully opened flower becomes the freshest of buds. [An old man or woman in love affect the
   playful ways of extreme youth.] (*Malay*): *MBRAS 47*
An old he-monkey will choose an old she-monkey. (*Twi, Ghana*): *Geyvandov 62*
As long as you are beautiful, choose young men; when beauty fades, get married to an old
   man. (*Vietnamese*): *Geyvandov 104*
As an old woman likes her young husband, so the master loves his best scholar.
   (*Khionghta, Bangladesh*): *Lewin 18*
The old woman gives pleasure to the one who marries her. (*Ila, Zambia*): *Geyvandov 251*
If a nubile girl is exchanged for an old woman, there must be a reason.
   (*Minyanka, Mali*): *Cauvin 1980: 481*
He who has many troubles should take a wife as [old as] his mother.
   (*Arabic, Morocco*): *Westermarck 115*
Rather have an old woman with money as the better half than a young lover with golden
   hair. (*German Dutch, Germany/Netherlands*): *Wander I 56*
He who takes an old woman loves her money better than the lady. (*French*): *Roux de Lincy 220*

BAD OLD AGE

To have a long life is to lose beauty. (*Turkish*): *Anonymous*
The young man's eye disdains the old woman. (*Rundi, Burundi*): *Rodegem 96*
A young man and an old woman [are] of the Devil's making. (*English, UK*): *Williams III 410*
Don't marry an old woman, even though you will eat with her young pigeons and lamb's
   meat [the most delicious food]. (*Arabic, Morocco*): *Westermarck 73*

He who has an old woman [for a wife], has a plague. (*Arabic, Morocco*): *Westermarck 73*

Three things darken the face: carrying heavy loads on your neck, walking barefoot, marrying
an old woman. (*Arabic, Maghreb*): *Cheneb III 130*

If you want your sorrow to be complete, marry a woman of your mother's age.
(*Arabic, Maghreb; Lebanon; Egypt*): *Cheneb III 101; Frayha II 685; Burckhardt 79*

Young woman good luck, old woman bad luck. [A wish addressed to a man who is in search of
a wife.] (*Arabic, Maghreb*): *Cheneb II 25*

O *iskni* [harvest basket], it is the barley that made you attractive, but what use are you after
the harvest? (*Berber, Maghreb*): *Bentolila 123*

An old man should be welcomed by a young girl; an old woman should be thrown out like
garbage. (*Arabic/Jewish, Yemen*): *Stahl 226*

Drink wine, not *braga* [home-brewed beer], love a girl, and not an old woman.
(*Russian*): *Geyvandov 104*

One should not pay much for old women's love, young people's intellect and tiny horses.
(*German*): *Wander V 2*

A pointless business is to grind straw, a pointless job to marry an old woman.
(*Karelian, RF*): *Geyvandov 138*

Who doesn't have any better, sleeps with his old wife. (*Dutch*): *Mesters 21*

If you are ashamed of an old wife, you'll sleep alone. (*Baule, Ivory Coast*): *Arbelbide 101*

A bee does not sit on faded flowers. (*Spanish, El Salvador*): *Sánchez Duarte 141*

A young woman married to an old man must behave like an old woman.
(*English, UK*): *Bohn 1855: 305*

A young woman who marries an old man will be treated as an old woman.
(*Portuguese, Brazil*): *Mota 122*

An old man thinks his wife is old [though she may be young]. (*Oromo, Ethiopia*): *Cotter 9*

An old cow loves the bull too. (*Russian*): *Geyvandov 65*

An old wife who coughs is preferable to an empty hut. (*Mossi, Burkina Faso*): *o.s. A. Sawadogo*

To mount a donkey is better than to go by foot. [Marrying old women is better than to stay a
bachelor.] (*Arabic, Maghreb*): *Cheneb III 169*

Prop up an old house, cherish an old wife. (*Khionghta, Bangladesh*): *Lewin 7*

Buttressing an old house is adorning an old woman with flowers. (*Burmese*): *Hla Pe 24*

Beautiful flowers are ashamed when they are stuck in an old woman's hair.
(*Chinese*): *Geyvandov 73*

When an old woman pretends to be young there could be somebody whose eye falls on her.
(*German*): *Raub 34*

An old hen does not lay eggs anymore. (*Italian*): *Santoro 26*

Old women make space for girls. (*Baule, Ivory Coast*): *Arbelbide 50*

The white hair lies, the wrinkles do not lie. (*Arabic, Morocco*): *Westermarck 73*

OLD AGE BEHAVIOUR

Did any mountain flower ever intend to wither? (*Korean*): *Geyvandov 280*

As long as your beauty has not been buried with you, don't say 'I saved my body.'
(*Kundu, Cameroon*): *Ittman 34*

Old age eats youth [i.e. of women]. (*Gikuyu, Kenya*): *Barra 111*

Old age ruins *akeyo*. [In full bloom this plant is very beautiful, but it soon withers.]
    (*Acholi, Uganda*): *p'Bitek 37*

Age is a garland of nettles—youth a garland of roses. (*Hebrew, Israel*): *Geyvandov 278*

Holding on to beauty, by using make-up, cannot be compared to the flower of youth.
    (*Chinese*): *Geyvandov 81*

However noisy a crow may be, he will not become a goose: however hard an old woman tries,
    she will not become young. (*Kirghiz; Karakalpak, RF*): *Geyvandov 277*

You can hide much, but where can you hide your wrinkles? (*Assam, India*): *Geyvandov 239*

Worries make you age before old age. (*Ladino/Hebrew*): *Dahan 1260*

What remains of wealth is still wealth and what remains of beauty is still beauty.
    (*Arabic, Tunisia*): *Yetiv 8*

If man gets old, [he] becomes [a] ram, if woman gets old, [she] becomes naught [nothing].
    (*Turkish*): *Haig 89*

A man feels only as old as the woman he feels. (*Irish*): *O'Farrell 9*

A man is as old as he feels: a woman as old as she looks.
    (*Throughout Europe; English, UK/USA; Italian; Frisian, Netherlands*): *Beintema 93; Browning
    353; Williams I 474; Geyvandov 278*

A man is as old as he feels, a woman as old as she feels like admitting.
    (*English, USA*): *Titelman 227*

A woman is as old as she looks. A man is old when he quits looking. (*English, USA*): *Bradley 98*

A man is young when a girl can make him happy or unhappy; he enters middle age when a
    woman can make him happy but not unhappy; he becomes old when a woman can make
    him neither happy nor unhappy. (*Hebrew, Israel*): *Rosten 1970: 321*

Those that would have seen me before, their hearts would have opened; those that would see
    me now, would be running back [and] back. (*Turkish*): *Haig 93*

A young woman is joy; an old one, irritation. (*Tamil, India*): *Geyvandov 279*

Yesterday is not today, as the old woman said when she thought of her [lonely] nights at
    home. (*Hausa, West Africa*): *Whitting 96*

A young woman married to an old man is a lady by day and a widow by night.
    (*Hebrew, Israel*): *Cohen 1961: 326*

The child of an old man is like an orphan, [and] the woman of an old man is like a widow.
    (*Arabic*): *Geyvandov 138*

Even old goats like to lick salt. (*Estonian; Hungarian*): *Paczolay 110*

Up there: white hair; down there: desire. (*Spanish, Bolivia*): *Paredes-Candia 189*

You eat the best soup from an old pot. (*French*): *Ségalen 55*

Wood: the drier, the more it burns. (*Spanish, El Salvador*): *Sánchez Duarte 132*

Old hay burns more fiercely. [Referring to women of a riper age.]
    (*Kurdish, Turkey*): *Geyvandov 29*

When an old barn [old maid] begins to burn, there is no extinguishing it.
    (*Dutch; German*): *Mesters 164; Geyvandov 29*

It's easier to heat an old oven than a new one. (*French*): *Geyvandov 27*

There's many a good tune played on an old fiddle. (*English, UK*): *o.s. Anonymous*

Sexual intercourse with an old woman gives one lice and long hair on the head.
    (*Arabic, Morocco*): *Westermarck 73*

For a young woman, liveliness; for an old witch, prudishness. (*Nepalese*): *Geyvandov 280*

Being old and grey-haired, should I wear a red gown? (*Arabic, Lebanon*): *Frayha I 185–186*

A hundred years old, a green dress. [i.e. still coquettish, or dead: wearing a green dress also
    refers to being buried under the grass.] (*Catalan, Spain; French*): *Guiter 37*

Love is a virtue in the young, a vice in the aged. (*Italian*): *o.s. Joseph Ricapito*

An old nag shouldn't be brisk, a grey-haired woman shouldn't kiss. (*Ukrainian*): *Geyvandov 29*

Old in love is foolish in love. (*Frisian, Netherlands*): *Beintema 54*

Seeing the crowd, the old woman said: 'Give me a man.' (*Greek*): *Geyvandov 190; Politès 15*

An old woman and a bronze kettle are always virtuous. (*Estonian*): *Geyvandov 29*

What should be done with an old wife but make gunpowder of her? (*English, UK*): *Rayner 242*

An old woman is better than saltpetre for making gunpowder. (*English, UK*): *Williams III 420*

Old wells do not bubble. (*Chinese*): *Shengzi 815*

At an advanced age a good woman has no need of a man. (*Chinese*): *Shengzi 821*

A [woman's] last husband is a brother. (*Malagasy, Madagascar*): *Geyvandov 118*

A late wedding is a letter to the grave-digger. (*German*): *Wander I 56*

'Our mother is the bride' is possible, 'our grandmother is the bride' sounds awful.
    (*German*): *Wander III 812*

An old woman who bears a child does not know where to leave it. (*Kazakh*): *Geyvandov 165*

Old women's laugh ends up in coughing. (*Danish; German*): *Wander V 1*

An applauding old woman throws up a cloud of dust.
    (*Spanish; Greek*): *Leutsch & Schneidewin 154; Politès 15*

When an old hag has fun, death chuckles. (*Latin*): *Geyvandov 62*

Old women's joy is death's rejoicing. (*German*): *Wander V 100*

Old women do not whistle without reason. (*Rundi, Burundi*): *Rodegem 346*

Even an old woman may run when a goat carries off her snuffbox.
    (*Nigeria*): *Akporobaro & Emovon 133*

Need makes the old woman trot.
    (*Dutch; Danish; German; French; Irish; English, USA; Pidgin, Jamaica*): *Gluski 102; Mesters 79;*
    Bohn 1855: 227; O'Rahilly 30; Gaffney & Cashman 92; Llewellyn Watson 221

No matter the age of a woman, when she catches fire she jumps.
    (*Danish; Spanish*): *Bohn 1857: 346; Geyvandov 30*

The head of an old woman is not shown for nothing. [Old women normally wear a kerchief
    and do not display their heads without it. Quoted when a request is answered with
    another request.] (*Minyanka, Mali*): *Cauvin 1980: 239*

An old woman who dances raises a lot of dust. (*Spanish, Argentina*): *Villafuerte 327*

To dance with an old woman is like riding a donkey. (*Spanish, Mexico*): *Casasola 14*

What then wishes grandma while dancing? (*Bulgarian*): *Arnaudov 93*

To dance like young girls is not becoming for a grandmother. (*Russian*): *Rauch 137*

Girls' dances are improper to a grandmother. (*Romanian*): *Günther 47*

The old woman bought herself a place in the dance; and afterwards paid double to be
    released. (*Serbian/Croatian*): *Karadžić 341*

The she-cat is on the roof and the old woman with blackened eyes is dancing [wanting to
  prove that she is as agile as a cat]. (*Arabic, Algeria*): *Westermarck 198*
As long as her dance is not finished, don't say: 'Grandma, your foot is nimble.'
  (*Mandinka, West Africa*): *Meyer 148*
The morning rain is like an old woman's dance, soon over. (*English, USA*): *Boatwright 219*
An old woman's dance brings death to her yard. (*German*): *Wander V 134; Meier-Pfaller 53*

DECREPITUDE AND DEATH

To encourage each other, old ladies say: 'O young lady!' (*Oromo, Ethiopia*): *Cotter 111*
One old woman will call another old woman 'Grandmother'. (*Oromo, Ethiopia*): *Cotter 9*
The old woman who outstrips another one [in health, energy etc.] says: 'Spare me those hol-
  low eyes.' (*Rwanda*): *Crépeau 43*
There's a tough sinew in an old wife's heel. (*English, UK*): *Williams I 464*
A solid old woman, even the mill could not grind her.
  (*Lithuanian*): *Schleicher 185; Reinsberg-Düringsfeld 200*
The toothless old woman still chews cola nut. (*Mamprusi, Burkina Faso*): *Plissart 121*
Ten old women, eleven diseases. (*German*): *Meier-Pfaller 662*
In former days, the cocks used to crow, now they yawn, said the old woman when she had be-
  come deaf. (*Frisian, Netherlands*): *Beintema 61*
There is no Saturday without sun, nor an old woman without pain, nor a maiden without
  love.
  (*Spanish, Bolivia/Argentina*): *Barneville Vásquez 63; Moya 550; Villafuerte 250; o.s. Ollantay*
Old houses and old ladies always need repairing. (*English, USA*): *Kin 214*
An old woman cannot control the pestle anymore. (*Wahehe, Tanzania*): *Madumulla 165*
Grandmother's wrinkled skirt never used to be wrinkled.
  (*Sranan, Surinam*): *o.s. Mavis Noordwijk*
The old cow gets stuck in every mud puddle. (*Spanish, Colombia*):*Ramírez S. 162*
Grandma only knows her old-hag's talk. (*Bulgarian*): *Arnaudov 88*
The seagull—the older, the crazier. (*Spanish, Argentina*): *Lehmann-Nitche 128; Moya 509*
The old, blind, deaf, mute, cripple [woman] spins the cotton, reports the news from any-
  where and frisks about the rocks; she prays her chaplet [rosary], gossips and breaks the
  dog's teeth if he interrupts by barking. (*Arabic, Maghreb/West Sahara*): *Duvollet 41*
Old grandmothers have old savings. (*German*): *Wander II 1621*
If an old woman falls down twice, the things in her basket will be counted.
  (*Igbo, Nigeria*): *Penfield 61*
May God curse the woman in her sixties, even on the day she dies: she counts her beads,
  makes the dog bark, and pulls out his teeth while he is barking. [Old women are seen as
  nasty, nagging, treacherous, real Delilas] (*Arabic, Maghreb*): *Cheneb II 7*
Kill the old woman for her locust-bean cakes. (*Hausa, Nigeria*): *o.s. Erna Berg*
Old maids and young dogs should be drowned. (*Romanian*): *Champion 254*
An old woman and a new plough are nowhere better than in the earth.
  (*German*): *Champion 175; Meier-Pfaller 59; Wander I 56*
The polite and shy old lady let people bury her alive. (*Ganda, Uganda*): *Ibekwe 23*

Take the old woman who cannot walk to the sandy plain. (*Spanish*): *Bergua 114*

Don't kill my grandmother, a frying pan that will break soon. (*Lega, Congo DR*): *o.s. Malasi*

The winter is past and the old woman is not dead. (*Persian*): *Roebuck 259*

The old woman did not die until a rainy day. (*Persian*): *Roebuck 154*

Both an old woman and a young girl will go to the grave.
   (*Spanish, El Salvador*): *Sánchez Duarte 23*

Old people have to die; children may die. (*Papiamentu, Netherlands Antilles*): *Brenneker 13*

When an old woman sees Death and asks him to come back and pass the night, he will return
   and kill all her children. (*Rwanda*): *Crépeau 487*

Girl, never laugh at an old woman, because soon you will be dried up like the moon yourself.
   (*Bulgarian*): *Geyvandov 232*

You mock the old: soon you will be among them. (*Yoruba, Nigeria*): *Knappert 90*

Superb tree, don't ridicule dead wood: you'll die too. (*Lega, Congo DR*): *o.s. Malasi*

STATUS AND AUTHORITY

A woman with withered breasts drinks beer like a man. (*Ganda, Uganda*): *Walser 372*

To have a husband is to live like a servant; to have a child is to be master of your own kingdom. (*Lao, Laos*): *Geyvandov 121*

A woman can turn a man into whatever she wants, even into an old woman.
   (*Frisian, Netherlands*): *Beintema 45*

3

Basics of Life

LOVE

Love is a ring and a ring has no end. (Russian)

'All you need is love' was one of the most popular song that The Beatles sang in the second half of the twentieth century. Humans love and want to be loved. Love embellishes life in many ways—'Where love is sown, joy comes up', in the words of a German proverb—but what *is* love? The number of answers to that question is endless. There are many thousands of proverbs about love, its sweetness, blindness, miracles, misery, jealousy, irrationality, unreliability, its happy beginnings and lamentable endings. It is impossible to address in a few pages the enormous variety of wise observations and sad reflections on the crucial emotion that a love relationship represents in people's lives. Love is sometimes referred to in dream images. A Persian proverb uses the image of thirst: 'A thirsty person dreams of water.' For lovers to sit together on one lotus flower in paradise is a Japanese dream: 'One open lotus, grasp life.' The proverb refers to the tragic double suicide of frustrated lovers who wish to fulfil that dream. There are more such lovers' dreams of longing for their beloved. Dreams express desire and fulfilment of love. Optimistically, a Hungarian proverb believes that 'In dreams and love nothing is impossible', but this is a rather rare statement, the worries and fears and deceptions being much more numerous than the joys, at least in proverbs.

Here the most central issues will be addressed. To start with, love is considered to be a very confusing emotion and one's first love in particular, to leave ineffaceable traces:

The first love is the only true love. (*Arabic*)
First love and first fruit taste best. (*Portuguese*)

There is no love like the first. (*Spanish, Mexico*)
A young girl never quite gets over her first man. (*English, USA*)
First love is like a snake; if it doesn't destroy you, it will paralyze you. (*Polish*)

A first love can be so impressive that it is never forgotten. All sorts of metaphors have been invented to express the experience, e.g. a sawn willow that grows again, salt consumed long ago that makes you thirsty again, old ice that easily freezes again, old fires that flare up again, and so forth. However, a well-developed stable and mature love brings more harmony, and is compared to precious materials. In some Asian proverbs mature love is ranked highly above intense short-lived loves and passions:

The longer you wash mother-of-pearl, the more beautiful it is. (*Mongolian*)
The love of young people is like a pair of silver buds but the love of mature people is
    like golden flowers. (*Japanese*)

FALLING IN LOVE

There are a thousand miseries in one love. (*Punjabi*)

'Falling in love' is the English expression for the amazing sensations of attraction that start bubbling up in unexplainable ways. It expresses adequately that love's victims are no longer able to control their own steps and decisions in life. It is such a puzzling experience that proverbs have been looking for the right words to deal with what is happening. A Kurdish proverb sees it as what happens after the first lightning has struck the heart of its victim: 'The usual occupation of the love-struck is silence.' One feels helpless. That is why proverbs from Africa and of African descent advise people not to act in a hurry when such confusion gets hold of you:

Who falls in love quickly, will separate quickly. (*Amharic*)
Quick loving a woman means quick not loving a woman. (*Yoruba*)
To fall in love quickly is to fall out of love quickly. (*Papiamentu, Aruba*)

Better, then, to think twice. The multiple objections are expressed either through images or directly. The main points being made are that such a stormy passion or sudden love affair is like a tree trunk without roots easily blown down by the wind, or a river that never reaches the sea. Short loves, in other words, only cause long sighs and enduring pain.

Such warnings sound very reasonable, but the problem is that falling in love is *not* reasonable. Falling in love just happens, even at first sight, without people being prepared for it. When the beloved one rejects the lover or a love relationship is ended against the wish of one of the lovers, torture and suffering unavoidably follow. The fate of the unhappy lover is deplorable, as all those who have had the experience know. Probably nobody has loved without suffering one way or another: 'You can suffer without love, but you can't love without suffering', as the Germans say. Love can be a rebellious obsession difficult to get rid of in spite of all strong logic arguing against it: 'Heartache cannot be discarded like a nutshell' (*Udmurt*). Its unbearable pain is already referred to in humanity's oldest-known legacy of proverbs, as a wish or prayer addressed to the goddess of love: 'May Inanna pour oil on my heart that aches.' (*Sumerian*)

Unhappy love is frequently associated with physical pain, hurt, diseases, burns etc. 'If pangs of love were a disease of the legs, many people would limp', a Wolof proverb from Senegal observes, and, indeed, if this were the case, it would be easier to find out about what is in reality mostly a silent and hidden form of suffering:

> Love breeds offences [being hurt]. (*Korean*)
> Frost hurts the ears, love the heart. (*Basque*)
> No worse disease than love. (*Romanian*)

There are also hints at a happy solution according to the simple law that love itself heals lovesickness: 'Diseases of the heart are healed with a heart-potion', a Chinese proverb says comfortingly. Both pain and cure of a lovesick person proceed from the beloved, a Persian proverb acknowledges, and a Maltese proverb addresses the beloved directly and concisely: 'Break my heart and bring me a plaster.'

In various parts of the world proverbs reflect both sides of the coin of love, using similar metaphors opposing the sweetness of flowers and honey to the pain caused by thorns or an insect's sting:

> He who wants a rose must respect the thorn. (*Persian*)
> Without thorns no love. (*Romanian/Slovene*)
> The roses fall and the thorns remain. (*Italian*)
> The one who wants honey has to endure the stings of the bees. (*Arabic*)
> First she kisses, then she stings. (*Indonesian*)
> If you tease a bee, she will sting. (*Vietnamese*)
> A woman is like a bee, she either gives you honey or a sting. (*Portuguese, Brazil*)

Obviously, the beauty of roses and the stings of thorns, the sweetness of honey and the stings, or 'the hell of bees' in the words of a Turkish proverb, originate from women, at least from a male perspective, and it is men that are warned against this female threat.

After the sting, love's suffering begins with painful longing. 'The more longings, the more disappointments,' the Bengali say. In order to limit love's uncontrollable pain and damage, a Pashto proverb from Afghanistan bravely states: 'I really do love you, but I will not drown myself for you.' The point is, alas, that the painful passion of unilateral love silently grips and consumes its victim. 'Unlike the singing cicadas, the silent fireflies burn themselves,' says a Japanese proverb referring to a woman deeply in love; she is silent, or rather has to be silent, while the cruel flames of desire consume her. Speaking out is considered a man's initiative, and by doing so herself, a woman would disastrously reverse the order of things, like a mortar seeking the pestle, as a Malay metaphor puts it. Such going against the order of things is disapproved of in all corners of the world:

> If a man runs after a woman, he falls into marriage; if a woman runs after a man, she falls
>   into ruin. (*Khionghta*)
> A hen shall not crow. (*Ovambo*)
> The horse cannot sell itself. (*Tiv*)

Other mocking images are a pond in search of a field (*Indonesian*), hay following a horse (*Dutch*), a horse in desperate need of a rider (*Spanish*), someone going around with the bit in one hand and the saddle in the other (*Spanish, Uruguay*), and so on.

It is the eyes that play a crucial role in this falling in love: 'Love is born through the eyes', as a Mexican proverb observes. As soon as two people's eyes meet, their hearts might fall in love, as an Uzbek proverb puts it, or, in an Assam example from India: 'Love at first sight is a bond between four eyes.' Eyes are a dangerous part of the body, and people are advised against giving those painful pangs of love a chance. They should simply stop carelessly looking around because the price to be paid, a broken heart, is too high. A Creole wisdom states: 'That which the eye has not seen, cannot cause a heartache.'

The eyes not only see, they also betray the profound and passionate feelings of people in love: 'Eyes give away lovers' and 'Love sparkles in the eyes', as it is said in Norwegian and Digor, respectively. Not just the eyes, though, but the whole body language easily betrays people's being in love. In many languages and in many ways, proverbs express the idea that those who fall in love do not succeed in hiding their emotions. Silent lovers are like other things that cannot stay hidden, such as a mosquito (*Pashto*), a hunchback (*Ladino*), a cough (*Portuguese*), poverty (*Danish*), going up a mountain or riding a camel (*Arabic*). Lovers are just bad keepers of secrets (*Russian*).

Love, then, cannot be 'locked away', as it is said in Kirghiz, a sorry matter not only for all those whose love affairs go against the rules of society, but also for those who cherish this secrecy as a very special experience:

> The extreme form of passionate love is secret love. (*Japanese*)
> A secret love is always a true love. (*Slovak*)

Passionate love is both idealized and warned against in many ways. 'What you love passionately is like henna on your hand palm' (*Arabic, Maghreb*): it is as transient as it is beautiful. A Japanese proverb sees the outcome of passion as unpredictable: 'Passionate love is the origin of a hundred fruits'—sometimes good and sometimes evil. To 'divide your passionately burning love over all the days of your life' is a Ladino recommendation, and a Danish message also advocates controllable passion: 'A small fire that warms is better than a large one that burns'—as if love were a 'reasonable' emotion.

THE LOGIC OF LOVE

Ardent love and cold reason seldom go together. (Frisian)

Who falls in love with whom? The popular idea of passionate love as a 'logical' basis for marriage as it usually exists today in the West and its spheres of influence, has not always been so self-evident, even there. In the past, passion was not considered a motive for founding a family, and feelings were an unreliable guide for courting a girl to be married. In many societies passionate love is or was not necessarily the first motive for marriage at all. Falling in love means losing one's rationality: 'When the heart bends, the mind falls,' according to a Portuguese proverb. Lovers tend to suffer serious disorientation of the senses:

> Five senses we have, five senses we lose when we fall in love. (*Spanish, Mexico*)
> Love is no prison, but it does make people's senses disappear. (*Russian*)
> When love enters through the door, the mind jumps out through the window.
>   (*German*)

The first sense that gives up is sight. That love is blind is literally acknowledged and repeated all over the world. Love is presented as a friend of blindness (*Arabic*), and a twin sister of blindness (*Russian*). Those in love are blind with open eyes (*English*). Here are some more examples illustrating the seriousness of the matter:

> An owl is blind in daytime, a crow is blind at night; but lovers are blind in daytime and
>   at night. (*Hindi*)
> Love is blind: it descends with as much ease on cow manure as it does on a nice girl.
>   (*Switzerland*)
> Love is blind and thinks others don't see either. (*Danish*)
> Love is blind, but the neighbours are not. (*Spanish, Mexico/Puerto Rico*)

A Surinamese proverb reminds blind lovers that ultimately insight is bound to occur: 'Love blinds the eyes and only regret will open them.' In the meantime, biased perspectives make lovers see the beloved in a different light, so that, for example, from Africa to Asia no beloved one has a skin problem. The beloved one is the most extraordinary human being ever, no matter how he or she looks or behaves. Under the spell of their feelings lovers unconditionally idealize the beloved and adore anything associated with him or her. Love even includes outright banalities:

> Love is blind to blemishes and faults. (*Irish*)
> The foot of a sweetheart makes a trodden track green. (*Italian*)
> When you are in love, even a monkey is beautiful; when you are not, even a lotus flower
>   is ugly. (*Chinese*)
> A wolf is handsome in the eyes of a lovesick girl. (*English, USA*)
> Love does not notice patches on the trousers. (*Creole, Guadeloupe*)
> Love extends even to the crow on the roof. (*Japanese*)

Other senses are switched off as well. For example, lovers do not seem to feel the cold or the rain as long as they are together:

> Hot lovers don't feel the cold. (*Dutch*)
> Lovers do not notice the rain. (*Malagasy*)
> Two wet swallows under one umbrella. (*Japanese*)

Love brings about a change of character or at least of behaviour, and thus 'Love turns the sensible stupid, and the shy wild' (*Russian*). Distance and other impediments become insignificant to lovers who challenge any difficulty. For lovers no roads are too long and no barriers too high:

> Love is following your beloved, even when that means walking through twelve thousand
>   mountain passes. (*Korean*)
> For the one who is in love, Baghdad is not far. (*Turkish*).
> The road of love does not know distance. (*Sranan*)

To a lover going to and fro, a thousand *ri*[99] is but one. (*Japanese*)
Between lovers, there are no barriers. (*Kurdish*)

This idea applies even to the social barriers between higher and lower classes or ranks. Feelings are stubborn and don't care about norms and rules. Women, especially, are presented as ingenious in eliminating all obstacles that might prevent them from uniting with their lover:

Not even God is smart enough to catch a woman in love. (*Yoruba*)
Women know how to find their lover even when they are locked up in a chest. (*German*)
When a woman cooks up a trick she can outwit a hundred men. (*Abkhaz*)
When the she-hedgehog loves a he-hedgehog, she gives herself to him in spite of the quills. (*Arabic, Maghreb*)

Love, then, has a logic of its own that lies below the border of reason, as a Japanese proverb puts it. A lover's argument is like a shower in spring, according to an Arabic observation: it is as fleeting as it was unforeseen. Proverbs from various origins warn that people in love are inconsistent. They say one thing and do the opposite. They are in love but keep denying it. According to a Mexican proverb, a woman who appears to be indifferent to a man is only pretending. She is compared to a saw bird, a bird with a beak like a saw: 'The saw refuses the corn but ventures to nibble.' People seem to feel too vulnerable to admit their real feelings openly, and conceal their vulnerability by bizarre or contradictory reactions:

To say 'I hate you' is to say 'I love you.' (*Japanese*)
With one hand she hits you, with the other she hugs you. (*Tamil, India*)
When a woman says no, she often means yes. (*Swedish*)
The 'no' of a girl is the 'yes' of a boy. (*Danish*)
A woman's Nay is a double yea, they say. (*English, UK*)

The more you feel attracted, proverbs argue, the more your beloved feels like flying away. In cultures from Africa to Europe and America, one finds the following proverb: 'Woman is like a shadow, follow her and she flees from you, flee from her and she follows you.' The suggested tactics seems to be that, for a while, one should simply ignore the beloved. In proverbs this holds especially for girls. An American proverb preaches this logic: 'The more a girl runs, the harder a boy chases.' And here is the Ladino advice to a wondering lover: 'Dislike a woman and she will love you, love her and she will dislike you.' All such pretending and denying makes courting quite complicated.

And, of course, there is jealousy. In all continents proverbs observe that love and jealousy go hand in hand. Jealousy is sometimes considered the soul of love. In Japan women in love who are not jealous are even compared to a ball that does not bounce. How serious is a non-jealous love? 'Love without jealousy is no love', says a Hebrew proverb. On the other hand, jealousy causes pain and despair, and, moreover, risks to ruin love:

The smile in love is like honey; the smile in jealousy is like a thorn in the heart. (*Filipino*)
Jealousy bites deeper than fleas. (*Icelandic*)
Jealousy will destroy love. (*Spanish, Mexico*)

'Doubt is the beginning of the disease that kills love', in the words of a Burmese proverb. Real jealousy, many proverbs agree, gradually deteriorates the health of the jealous:
sleepless nights are their lot and ultimately they suffocate all feelings of love.

LOVE IN MARRIAGE

The gloves you put on, you shall wear. The wife you choose, you shall live with. (Latvian)

After the wedding, marriage lasts until death, 'like the feathers of a bird: they don't leave
her till the end of her days' in a poetic Malagasy image. The ideal of a harmonious union
and mutual understanding is expressed in proverbial images:

> Husband and wife are like tongue and teeth. (*Burmese*)
> Husband and wife are like chopsticks: always together. (*Vietnamese*)
> Husband and wife are tied together like an axe and the handle of the axe. (*Ossetian*)
> Husband and wife are each other's spade and pickaxe. [They support each other]
>   (*Kurdish*)
> What the yam feels, the knife understands. [The knife is the closest to the yam; the hus-
>   band, the closest to his wife] (*Yoruba*)

Ideally, love and marriage coincide and ideally partners fully understand each other, a
wonderful situation presented in a Chinese proverb: 'Loving spouses say a thousand
things to each other, without saying a word.' They develop 'such harmony that not even
water can come between them' (*Lithuanian*). As if marriage were not an institution full of
contradiction, misunderstanding, confusion, irritation, and even feelings of disgust or
hate, as reflected in large numbers of other proverbs. Usually marriage is not seen in terms
of love. It is much more social compatibility and custom that keep two people together
than romantic love, as expressed in a Tamil proverb from India: 'If the bullock and the
cart keep together, what does it matter how many ups and downs there are?'

In paradoxical terms a proverb in Catalan as well as in French recommends women:
'Love your husband like a friend, fear him like an enemy.' In spite of such mixed marital
feelings, outsiders are seriously advised not to interfere in the life of a married couple:

> Do not try to come between the tree and its bark. (*Arabic*)
> Do not even put a pin between a husband and a wife. (*Spanish, Panama*)
> Do not put a spoon between a husband and a wife. (*Portuguese, Brazil*).

Such warnings address those who want to interfere in a marital relationship, though they
also indirectly confirm that: 'Where there is much love, there are few freedoms.' It is unclear whether this Spanish proverb refers to love within marriage or without, but, it is
true, love and freedom are frequently opposed to each other in proverbs. It is repeatedly
suggested that lovers are much freer and happier in their relationship than spouses who
are officially forced to live together and who sacrifice individual freedom to keep their
marriage intact. 'Obligation suffocates love', as an Uzbek proverb argues, and therefore
proverbs from widely different origins oppose love to marriage as if the two were contradictory terms, and marriage the beginning of the end of love:

Love is a magnificent garden, but the field of marriage is covered with stinging nettles.
   (*Finnish*)
Desire of two young lovers, and regret of husband and wife. (*Urdu*)

An Akan proverb suggests that 'Happiness is like palm-wine: if you mix it with too much water, it loses its taste.' If marriage is just a diluted form of happiness, how much added water is then bearable for a marriage to last and for spouses not to lose their love (not even to mention passion)? There are opposite opinions, depending on cultural or religious traditions, social norms, infatuation of the (ex-)lovers concerned, and so forth. People may feel disappointed about their married status but resign themselves to drink the diluted palm-wine, in spite of their disappointment. Some proverbs cynically warn against marrying for love, and in a Russian proverb marriage is even called 'the tomb of love'. In many areas and cultures, proverbs accept the difference between love and marriage: 'Love leads you to a wonder, money to a marriage.' This French example openly doubts that love has much to do with marriage. Marriage was (and often still is) arranged between two families who are less interested in the couple's love than in the material consequences of the alliance. The married couple has to understand what this means in terms of emotion. According to a Kirghiz proverb: 'You do not long for the one they married you off to, but for the one you love.' Many proverbs explicitly emphasize that love and marriage are mutually exclusive:

The bride in her silliness and inexperience calls marriage 'love'. (*Ganda*)
Wedlock is not 'love me'. [Many see their mistake soon] (*Kundu*)
Whoever marries for love, must live in sorrow. (*Spanish, Chile*)
Love provides wings, but wings of wax melt with the torch of marriage. (*Russian*)
He that marries for love has good nights but sorry days. (*English/French/Italian/Spanish*)

An Arabic proverb exhorts girls to show a happy face on their wedding day even when they get married against their will and feel unhappy: 'They call you the newly wed one, do not be sad.' Just play the game! Nevertheless, a few proverbs advise against acting 'as if it were raining when the sun shines,' as the Cubans say:

A marriage without love is like a garden without flowers, a shirt without sleeves or a
   bull without a blanket. (*Kurdish*)
Who marries without love, lives in distress. (*Portuguese*)
Marriage without love is a vexation. (*Estonian*)
Sauce makes the couscous, love makes the marriage. (*Berber*)

A few proverbs optimistically predict that love will come after marriage, whereas others fear that love will end soon after it has been solemnized or even on the very wedding day:

Love ends at the altar. (*Estonian*)
Before the wedding, you say, 'my love', and afterwards you sigh, 'If I had known.'
   (*Creole*)
The first night of the marriage is sometimes the last of love. (*Dutch*)

Women are warned not to obey their own feelings, and to marry a man who loves them instead of the man they love:

The woman who marries the man who loves her will do better than the woman who
    marries the man she loves. (*Arabic*)
A wise woman will marry the man who loves her, rather than the one she loves.
    (*Slovene/Serbian/Croatian*)
When you love, you are a slave; when you are loved, you are the boss. (*Polish*)

'Better to be waited-for than to wait', as a Japanese proverb reflects the fate of a lovelorn
woman who passes weary hours waiting and suffering for the man of her dreams. As a rule,
the one who is most in love is also the most dependent and dominated in a relationship.
The combination of love and marriage looks rather unlikely in proverbs, but a miracle is
never excluded: 'To marry for love is risky, but God smiles at it', a German proverb states
hopefully. Indeed, God is often actively involved in uniting partners in proverbial love:
'God brings to all wheat its measurer' (*Arabic, Morocco*). Still, partners themselves must
look for equality, as expressed in metaphors of pairs of wooden shoes or boots (*Russian*) or
a birch-bark sandal looking for another birch-bark sandal (*Estonian*). From Puerto Rico to
Serbia and Iraq, love between unequal people is considered suspect, even though proverbs
mainly run to the rescue of equality whenever a 'superior' wife comes into the picture.

    Being completely 'equal' in the physical sense does not occur in the proverbial order of
things. Lesbian love is rarely mentioned, and 'two women kissing each other'—as it is
defined in the English context—is simply rejected and disapproved of:

Butter with butter is no sauce. (*Scottish*)
Bread and cheese is very well, but cheese and cheese is no sense. (*English, UK*)
Fine looking and a lesbian, like an itchy bitch in a straw hut. (*Arabic, Morocco*)[100]

One Oromo proverb refers to a woman's impossible love for a homosexual man, in which
she is jokingly presented as a man's rival for another man's affections: '"Oh my troublesome fellow!" said the woman who mourned for a homosexual.' It is a proverb quoted in
cul-de-sac situations. That there are so few proverbs about love relationships between
women reflects the extent to which lesbianism was—and still is—tabooed.

LOVE AND OTHER MEN'S WIVES

Don't place your spoon where your bowl is not. (Abkhaz)

Many proverbs sympathize with a man's falling in love with another woman than his own
wife, and, as we have seen, in a number of cultures he can simply marry one, two or more
co-wives. This does not hold for women, as insistently observed, or rather prescribed, for
example in Vietnamese: 'A man is allowed to have more than one woman, a good wife has
only one man', or in Yaka: 'Woman is a gazelle skin on which only one man can sit'. The
gazelle being a small animal, there is no space for two husbands to sit on its hide at the
same time.

    However, having a love affair with someone else's wife is another cup of tea. Men all over
the world are advised not to fall in love with other men's dishes of food, fruits, animals,
shoes, as they are the other man's 'property', not to be touched, tasted, eaten, looked at,
sit upon, etc.:

Married women are like elephant tusks: don't touch them. (*Swahili*)
Another man's wife is like the mongoose skin: only one person can sit on it. (*Luba*)
One doesn't taste another man's wife. (*Bassar*)
Do not lure another man's hen. (*Songye*)
One should close one's mouth to someone else's apple. (*Karakalpak*)
In someone else's millet, don't put your horns. (*Russian*)
Don't place your foot in someone else's shoe. (*Karachay-Balkar*)
Do not look at someone else's dish. (*Spanish, El Salvador*)
Do not hibernate on an open spot; do not love another man's wife. (*Mongolian*)
Better catch a serpent and suck its poison than to have dealings with another man's wife.
   (*Urdu, India*)

Alas, reasonable advice does not work when love seizes its victim like a bolt from the blue. 'Owned' wives look the more irresistible as they are untouchable. In a Spanish proverb from Mexico the 'tastiest dish' necessarily comes from somebody else's home. Things belonging to others seem more valuable than one's own belongings. Whether the 'belongings' agree or not is no point of concern:

Another man's hen is a goose; another man's wife, a beauty. (*Turkish*)
Another man's wife is always the prettiest. (*Hebrew*)

Once a man 'possesses' a wife, his love shortly turns into boredom, as argued in a Persian proverb: 'To kiss your own wife is like chewing cotton wool.' Ironically, wives are unlike other products men cherish:

Men love their own compositions and other men's wives. (*Chinese*)
A horse is fun if it's your own, a wife if she's someone else's. (*Awar/Chechen*)
One favours somebody else's wife, but one's own son. (*Russian*)

Even though one Creole proverb from Martinique optimistically sees adultery as a knife cutting through water without leaving a trace, it is frequently suggested that a man takes high risks in secretly beginning a love affair with a married woman. Proverbs refer to the lover's fear and the 'owner's' legitimate revenge should he find out. Ever since ancient times the intrepid lover has been warned that he pays dearly for such a dangerous passion:

He who makes love to a married woman is killed on her doorstep. (*Ancient Egyptian*)
He who loves somebody else's wife always looks pale, not because of the love he feels but from fear of the husband. (*Spanish, Mexico*)
He who loves prickly pears must not fear thorns, and he who loves a married woman must not fear death. (*Maltese*)

From the perspective of the cuckolded man, though, the idea that his wife be unfaithful is presented as utterly unbearable. Numerous expressions depict a wife's having an affair as an absolutely humiliating situation for her husband, especially in Latin America. A multitude of metaphors describe him as the one who 'preheats the oven for somebody else to bake his bread'; or who 'dresses up the altar for others to celebrate mass'; he 'hangs a swing for somebody else to swing on' or 'heats up the water and somebody else drinks the *mate*',[101] and so forth. Next to revenge, compensation is seen as a solution to the infringement of the norm. A Hebrew proverb on the matter is formulated as a rhetorical question: 'Can anyone walk on glowing coals without burning his feet?' One way or the other, a man who falls in love with another man's wife, has to pay for it—to the owner, her lawful husband. Let us end on a more positive Hungarian note: 'True love does not fear infidelity.'

BITTER WORRIES AND SWEET WORDS

The tongue is the translator of the heart. (Arabic)

Even though love is opposed to fear, it often leads to fearful worries. 'One who loves intensely, has intense fears,' in the words of a Spanish proverb, so much so that it risks to drive love off completely. Fear in matters of love has inspired frightening images of drowning, disappearing and getting lost, for example. The intimidating emotions involved are reflected in all minor keys:

> Love is a sea: who cannot swim, drowns. (*Turkish*)
> Love is bottomless. (*Udmurt*)
> Love is a dark pit. (*Hungarian*)
> Love is like a nettle that stings badly. (*Russian*)
> Violent love, violent anger. (*Burmese*)

All sorts of images are used to express doubt about love's absurd beginnings, its inscrutable paths and its usually disappointing endings, for example in Spanish: 'Love is like soup, the first mouthful is very hot, and the ones that follow become gradually colder.' On both the eastern and the western sides of the African continent, seaweed has become a familiar metaphor for love's inescapability:

> Love is like seaweed: pushing it away will not prevent it from coming back. (*Fulfulde*)
> Love is like seaweed, you go to her, she leaves you, you leave her, she follows you.
> (*Malagasy*)

Love is also given the benefit of the doubt, or even a chance for happiness in messages encouraging lovers not let themselves be scared away by fear, worries and insecurity. Instead they should explore the treasures love holds in store for them. Again, love is kneaded into all sorts of metaphors: a farm that has to start anew every day (*Dutch*), oatmeal porridge to be prepared every day (*Irish*), or a baby to be treated tenderly (*Afrikaans*). Here are a few more:

> Love is like silk: it can be wrapped around the dead and clothe the living. (*Malagasy*)
> Love is like the sun to flowers: to the strong she gives strength, the weak she dries up.
> (*Irish*)
> Faithful love will not burn in fire nor drown in water. (*Russian*)

Women's love is associated with transience, for example in Russian: 'Women's love is like morning dew, the wind blows, and it's gone.' Or with capriciousness, as in the following Thai proverb: 'A female heart is as unstable as water rolling on a lotus leaf.'

Although lovesickness is sometimes referred to as incurable, there are many more proverbs stating that new loves will make one forget former loves.

> A new love will let you forget the old ones. (*Spanish, Mexico*)
> New loves make us forget old ones. (*Spanish*)
> New saints make us forget the old ones. (*Danish*)
> New dishes give satisfaction, old dishes are given to the fire. (*Latin/German*)
> Love and eggs should be fresh to be enjoyed. (*Russian*)
> A change of saddle yields pleasure. (*Arabic*)

Disappointed lovers are comfortingly told that the world is full of women: 'Not a hand
full but a land full', as it is said in Dutch to those whose relationship goes to pieces. Men
are told to set their eyes on other women instead of fixing forever their love and desire on
the unattainable lost one (and even, without having lost one): 'Kiss a mouth and you'll
forget the other mouth' (*Ladino/Hebrew, Morocco*). This message is enveloped in images
associating women with widely available objects:

> Women are like buses, if one leaves, another one will come along.
>   (*Spanish, Venezuela*)
> Women are like the bullets of a revolver, one comes out the barrel and another one is
>   ready in the cylinder. (*Portuguese, Brazil*)
> Women are like frogs, for every one diving into the water four others turn up to the sur-
>   face. (*Spanish, Peru*)

Are such statements really effective in the eyes of those who are helplessly in love with an
unreachable ideal? They may feel closer to the sentiment expressed in a poetic Malay
proverb: 'Many are the flowers which bloom in the garden, but one flower alone maddens
my heart with love.'

In a large variety of cultures, another point is the importance lovers ought to attach to
material wellbeing. In proverbs about love and poverty two opposite ideas are widely
present. The first is based upon romantic idealism: love simply makes up for all lack.
Lovers live in a palace when they share a shack, and their piece of dry bread tastes like a
wonderful dinner. The only thing they need is each other's loving presence:

> To lovers, even water tastes sweet. (*Chinese*)
> When two loving hearts are united, they take a hayloft for a feather bed. (*Turkish*)
> With you: bread and onions. (*Spanish, Bolivia*)
> With a sweetheart you can have paradise in a hut. (*Russian*)
> Harmony makes space and love widens the blanket. (*Scandinavian*)
> Better a piece of bread in happiness than a gold bar in sorrow. (*Finnish*)

In many languages and variants, though, more practically oriented proverbs strongly
oppose this view, arguing that love without a solid material basis will soon vanish. An
overall repeated European message is, for example: 'When poverty enters through the
door, love jumps out through the window.' The importance of food and shelter, even in
the life of lovers, is emphasized in many ways:

Of mere love a chimney does not smoke. (*German*)
Love is a fire: without food it will extinguish. (*Russian*)
Eating is preferable to amorousness. (*Japanese*)
Love cannot exist without bread and salt. (*Polish*)

It is even strongly argued that money can be used to seduce women into marriage, and that women chase after wealthy men. Women are blamed for being after their lover's money:

Love can do much, money everything. (*French*)
If you supply food, fancy presents and love, women remain tame. (*Hindi*)
Deposit the money and the wife will arrive. (*Arabic, Maghreb*)
In both war and love, gold is the winner. (*Spanish, Venezuela*)

Last but not least, the role of language. Many proverbs emphasize that in love words have a crucial impact: 'Poetry softens the relationship between men and women', a Japanese proverb observes. Verbal intercourse normally precedes sexual intercourse, and the importance of verbal courtship is explicitly stressed in several proverbs:

With sweet words you can break stones. (*Russian*)
With sweet words you can milk a mountain goat. (*Georgian*)
All girls lap up sweet words. (*Yiddish*)
Pleasant words are the hunters of men's hearts. (*Persian*)

A Pashto proverb from Afghanistan observes that from the union of heart and tongue love is born. In Asian proverbs, in particular, love is praised in romantic terms, as people imagine it to happen in their most beautiful dreams and fantasies:

Two hearts united will break down a mountain. (*Persian*)
Two hearts can put one mountain on top of another. (*Kurdish*)
The united couple can make gold out of earth. (*Chinese*)
Befriended spouses can pump all the water from the Pacific Ocean. (*Vietnamese*)

There is also the role that music plays. An American proverb even calls it 'the key to the female heart.' Nature, flowers, and gardens also play their part in the poetic ambiance of romantic love.

A heart without love is a garden without flowers. (*Japanese*)
The merit of the rose is known to the nightingale. (*Turkish*)
The gratification of my beloved is dear to me, and the leaf of the rose, very delicate.
    (*Persian*)
Without you, the flowers won't flower, the oaks won't grow in the oak garden. (*Russian*)

Exemplary love covers up all errors and weaknesses, taking thoughtful and patient care of the beloved. A Malagasy saying compares such love to the process of spinning and weaving cotton: 'Love me the way cotton is made: give the thin parts a little extra and connect the broken threads.'

As soon as love is found to be so strong that it 'lifts the coat and the shirt', in the words of a Danish proverb, time has come to move on to sex, ideally love's closest counterpart: 'It's heaven on earth to make love while in love,' as the Dutch say.

SEX

The pan said: 'My bottom is [made] of gold', and the dipper answered: 'I've just been there.' (Akkadian)

There is more to sex than the innocent manifestation of love's natural desire. Next to lust, pleasure, jokes and enjoyment, the one and a half thousand proverbs or so on sex at my disposal reflect considerable fear, insecurity, helplessness, awkwardness, selfishness and cheating. Sex refers not only to the organic and functional differences between men and women but also to copulation, and to love in its physical aspect with all emotions and cravings involved. The English verb 'to make love' and the French 'faire l'amour' express the multiple ways in which people sexually reveal their love and feelings of mutual attraction by means of their bodies. In addition to the many metaphorical references to sex, a limited number of proverbs, mainly from Africa openly name the relevant parts of the body.[102] Still, whether in metaphorical form or not, proverbs give us a wide perspective on humanity's sexual weal and woe.

PRIVATE PARTS

The penis does not know what the vagina thinks. (Igbo)

Proverbs stress that showing for the first time one's most intimate parts of the body to one's partner in love is as inevitable as it creates uneasiness. Such uneasiness is no surprise. Even in circles where sex is apparently talked about freely and easily, there continues to be a lot of embarrassment in sexual matters, if we take into account today's growing market of sexual surgery, and not only in the Western world. Such an operation can only be afforded by the happy or unhappy few who are courageous enough and wealthy enough to let surgeons work on their private parts. Around the world, however, there must be countless men and women who feel that they do not live up to what they imagine to be the ideal size and shape of sexual organs. They have to live and bear with what they've got, which is their own business, until someone else starts looking at those intimate parts of the body: what will he or she think and how will you feel without the safety of your clothes? Will your private parts fall short of the other's expectations? Will his or her nakedness live up to your own expectations? Eerie and perhaps familiar questions broached by proverbs carrying the message that people must overcome their embarrassment and pluck up courage. What ever one has, bodily speaking, is to be shown and used for its purpose:

> It is the woman's private parts that are shown to the husband. (*Igbo*)
> Even when the bird's sex is small, he will show it to his wife. (*Mossi*)

As in the above Mossi example, some proverbs refer to the size and particularities of both penises and vaginas, and to the advantages or disadvantages this size represents to the respective owners of the crucial parts concerned: 'Better a short penis than sleeping alone' is a Baule proverb, while in a Minyanka proverb from Mali the short penis is varnished, so to speak, as an effective apparatus in spite of its modest size: 'Even if the penis is short, it can cover a woman's sex as well as a Fulfulde hat', a large hat that can cover a man's head. Still, both proverbs give us to understand indirectly that a bigger penis might have been more desirable, although nothing much can be done about it. The message of both is that people ought to be content with whatever life has in store for them.

On the other hand, in a Ganda proverb, size extra large is used as a bogey to warn young women. They should be aware of the consequences of their acts and behaviour: 'She who has undressed should not fear a long penis.' Having sex is indispensable for having children, and for that very reason the Swahili recommend that both men and women have to do their job, whether they like it or not, whereas a Rwanda proverb reminds sexually unwilling women that it is their duty not to bar access to their uterus: 'Sitting on her heel, a woman closes the entrance to numerous offspring.' Men, too, are encouraged to do their utmost:

> A woman is like a flower: it sprouts only if you water it. (*Guaraní*).
> He who is too shy to live in matrimony with his wife will not get children.
> (*Arabic, Syria/Lebanon*)

Such considerations address beginners. An experienced woman is much less easily intimidated than a young girl, as the wisdom in proverbs from Southern and West Africa reflects:

> The pregnant woman is not afraid of her husband's penis. (*Ovambo*)
> The mother of twins does not fear a huge penis. (*Baule*)

There are not only proverbs about the size of the penis, but also about the size of the vagina: 'Even if your wife's sex is small, dawn will find you there,' as a Minyanka proverb observes, meaning that one uses and appreciates the few things in life one is entitled to. In a Tibetan proverb, the pros and cons of sizes are compared: 'A large penis is like an inheritance for a girl; a large vagina is like beating wheat in a famine', the former being considered pleasing to a woman and the latter hard to satisfy for a man. In a Creole proverb, male fear of the power of the vagina is expressed in a rather frightening image: 'A woman with the genitals of a large octopus is stronger than God and even stronger than the devil.'

In sexual relationships the mutual involvement of both partners can be effective as much as it can be problematic: 'What affects the penis affects the vagina', the Igbo wisely say. Proverbs repeatedly stress that experience is needed to teach people what sex is all about. Here are a few indirect comments on women's 'penis experience':

> You only know if something is long or short after you have tried it on. (*Korean*)
> A man is like pepper; only when you have tasted, do you know how hot it is. (*Hausa*)
> Even a bent sugar spoon will taste sweet. (*Telegu*)

In some proverbs a warning about the world being ungrateful is expressed by means of sexual metaphors:

> If you cure someone of his impotence, it's your wife that he'll rape. (*Mossi*)
> You cured his testicles and he used them on your wife. (*Ganda*)
> Whenever you cure your enemy's penis, he'll use it to impregnate your wife. (*Mamprusi*)

In Egypt this is expressed more indirectly but it comes to the same thing: 'He gets his passage for nothing, and winks at the wife of the captain.'

Proverbs comment upon either a woman's readiness or her reserve to offer her vagina for sex. In anecdotes and jokes as well as in proverbs penis and vagina are sometimes presented as independent personalities leading a life of their own. In some proverbs, vaginas are personified as if they were thinking, feeling, and acting independently. The Igbo motto to this section, for example, presents both as conscious personages, whereas a Rwanda proverb admonishes against excessive female lust by means of the vagina as an independent character: 'The desiring vagina dies by making a bed for herself on the road.' In ancient Mesopotamia, both were already introduced as leading personalities in a proverb: 'Has an unfaithful penis ever done damage to an unfaithful vulva?' If both consent, what is the harm? The answer to such a question will depend on the sexual identity and the norms of their owners. In proverbs, men usually consider themselves to be the legal owners not only of their own, but also their wives' private parts.

DESIRE

Desire calls, modesty halts. (Telegu)

'Who knows the limits of desire?' asks a concise Sanskrit proverb. 'Desire has no limit', is a concise Chinese answer. According to a Hausa definition 'Desire is the door that leads to problems', but many proverbs suggest that not only men but also women are interested in opening the door that gives access to sex, thus taking all the surrounding problems for granted. Numerous proverbs ostentatiously sympathize with, or even justify, the male urge as being 'in man's nature.' All sorts of arguments seem to hold. What can a man do to subdue his drive when life is chaotic, women are physically so pleasurable, and so forth:

> Woman and money tempt even Brahma the creator. (*Telegu*)
> In stormy weather, every hole seems like a harbour. (*Spanish*)
> Woman and soup taste good the whole year. (*Catalan/French*)
> The red fruit of the palm by day and the pleasure of women by night. (*Maori*)

'Man's nature' is even justified by male anatomy. The Creole proverb from Guadeloupe 'A penis does not have shoulders', compares the glans to the head of the human body. Unlike the 'real' head, anatomically hampered by the shoulders and possibly also by human reason, there appears to be nothing to hamper this little part of the male body. So, the simplistic reasoning goes, why should the penis not go ahead?

Proverbs about sex centre round desire, and fear. First, desire. There is ongoing understanding and approval regarding male desire and disapproval regarding female desire: 'The woman too eager to make the bed will not notice that she does not please' (*Rwanda*). In proverbs, male adultery frequently meets with sympathy and understanding whereas female infidelity is discarded as disastrous, or as the Komi say: 'When the husband has a lover, one stake in the barn burns. When the wife has an affair, all the buildings burn.' From China via Europe to the US this view is shared by means of one and the same image and argument:

If a man is unfaithful to his wife, it is like spitting from a house into the street, but if a
woman is unfaithful to her husband, it is like spitting from the street into the house.
(*Chinese; English, USA*)
If a man sins it is like spitting out of the window, if a woman sins it is like spitting in
through the window. (*Estonian*)

This talk of 'spitting' is a metaphor for male sperm leaving the home or brought into
the home. A man can permit himself to spit into the street (even though he may have to
pay some compensation), a wife cannot. A Russian proverb also refers to the difference between a man's 'trespass' and a woman's: 'The husband's sin is left before the threshold, his
wife brings everything into the house.' The house is of course a metaphor for the womb,
and 'everything' refers to the possible consequences. A man does not feel responsible for
the results of his behaviour outside his own home. He does not seem to mind 'fertilizing
another man's field' so to speak, but he does mind his own house or field being affected by
an outsider's seed. Women are simply not allowed to play the same game in sex matters as
men. Those double gender standards go without much questioning. An Oromo proverb
admonishes an unhappy wife to just accept her fate: 'It is better to be content with a bad
husband than to wish for the good husband of someone else.' Women who desire another
man than their husband were—and, in spite of modern contraception, often still are —
stigmatized, heavily punished and in some cultures even stoned to death when caught in
the act. The outright advice is to reject or divorce such a wife:

If the wife is unfaithful, even though she has a child, divorce her, don't love her.
(*Arabic, Morocco*)
A wife who loves two: may the Devil take her away. (*Spanish, Colombia*)
Books, wife, wealth when taken by others are lost. (*Sanskrit*)

One of the main issues in proverbs is this male concern about how to prevent one's 'own'
wife being led into temptation. As soon as she goes out, she is exposed to outsiders' eyes
and desire: 'When the nanny-goat is in the garden, the billy-goat will look over the fence'
(*Russian*). A Creole proverb from the small Caribbean island of Marie-Galante expresses
this same idea by comparing women to cows who take their liberty as soon as they get the
chance: 'There where the fence is low, the cow will climb over.' A Berber proverb from Morocco mocks a woman who in spite of all her usual precautions is seen by strangers: 'She
covers herself like eggs in a basket.' The ideal woman is the chaste and decent one who, in
some Muslim countries and communities, covers and veils herself, and thus safely avoids
being seen by men, but even then a Tamil proverb cynically wonders whether 'one veil is
sufficient to cover a woman's wickedness.' There is no end to this male obsessive fear: the
less female freedom, the more control seems to be needed to set the scared husband's mind
at rest. One Arabic proverb explains this irrational weakness as measuring other people's
cloth by your own yard: 'The fickle husband mistrusts his wife's faithfulness, the thief
fears to have his house robbed.'
    Unfathomable male fear sees a wife's desire fatally flaring up and uncontrollable sexual
affairs glaring around each and every corner, like evil spirits. In this projection of desire,
the fruits are blamed for the uncontrolled hunger of those who want to swallow them, so

to speak, to the effect that men become less, and women more guilty in matters of seduction. Streams of proverbs blame women for unfaithfulness while completely glossing over men's behaviour. The earlier-quoted Digor proverb 'A bad man always suspects his wife of being unfaithful' is a rare exception to the ruling message that womankind, and especially wives, are suspected or accused:

> If the cow were honest, the bull wouldn't have horns. (*Spanish*, *Argentina/Bolivia*)
> When the husband is away, the wife will play. (*English*, *USA*)
> Palm-wine is not kept in a transparent bottle. [A wife is unreliable] (*Krio*)
> A horse, a wife and a sword, these three are unfaithful. (*Kashmiri*)
> Who ever saw a horse, a woman, or a sword faithful? (*Persian*)
> Never trust a horse or a woman. (*Turkish*)

A woman is even to be blamed for 'suspect' thoughts projected onto her: 'There is no worse adultery than that of the woman who, while making love to her husband, thinks of another man' (*Hebrew*). The proverbs' understanding of male desire, on the contrary, goes sometimes so far as to encourage men to seize any opportunity offered, an understanding to be found especially in Caribbean and South American proverbs: 'Any piece of rug with an opening for your head, can serve as a poncho', is a metaphorical Spanish example from Mexico, to argue that any woman's body can serve a man's sexual purposes, especially when she is considered not to be 'virtuous':

> The thief is not to be blamed if he finds the gate open. (*Spanish*, *Colombia*)
> The man, who sees a saddled horse, will often decide he needs to take a ride.
>   (*Spanish*, *Mexico*)
> No one will ever miss a slice on a loaf that has already been cut. (*English*, *Jamaica*)
> Once the ears have been pierced, any earring can go in. (*Creole*, *Guadeloupe*)
> A girl and sugarcane should not be passed by. (*Oromo*)

The idea that any woman will do is further strengthened by the widespread argument that all women are the same in the dark:

> All women look the same after the sun goes down. (*English*, *USA*)
> Put the light out, all women are alike. (*Arabic*, *Tunisia*)
> Switch the light off, and all women are equal. (*German*)
> At night all women are equal. (*Italian*)
> Under the sheets the black one is as good as the white one. (*Spanish*)
> After the light has been turned off, we are all the same colour.
>   (*Spanish*, *Dominican Republic*)
> In the dark, the queen is worth as much as the black cook. (*Portuguese*, *Brazil*)

I did not find even one example of this idea in its reverse form. Are women believed to be choosier? That proverbs tend to present facile solutions to meet with men's physical needs and fantasies does not mean that there are no proverbs reminding men that sex relationships are to be taken seriously. Quite a few do so, using the strikingly identical formula 'a woman/wife is not (like)', followed by all sorts of associative terms, referring to desirable goods. Thus, women are associated with food, musical instruments, garments, and so forth. The messages resemble each other in content and form, in spite of widely different origins:

> A wife is not like a bedcover. (*Creole, Haiti*)
> A wife is not a shirt you can change according to your needs. (*Ladino*)
> A woman is not cassava to be valued by roasting and tasting. (*Baule*)
> A woman is not a boot; you cannot kick her off. (*Russian*)
> A woman is not a *goesli* (fiddle, or other stringed instrument); having played you cannot hang it on the wall. (*German / Finnish / Russian*)

The extreme advice to refrain completely from sexual relations is almost non-existent. The Tamil example arguing, without gender nuances, that 'Abstinence is the best medicine', is the only one in my collection. A few other proverbs explicitly warn men against messing around. Two examples of which the first one is Mongolian: 'A man always desiring women destroys his body; a man always desiring possessions destroys his life.' Interestingly, the proverb expresses only concern about the effect on *his* body, not about what his behaviour could mean to the bodies of the women he desires. The second one is Arabic: 'Piety lies between earrings and cheeks, not on top of the mountains,' which means that a man should not only piously pray and look up to heaven, but also control himself in the presence of women.

In general, such references to restriction, control and, indeed, self-control, do not address men but women. Significantly, the bulk of proverbial lessons regarding chastity and decency, are commandments directed to women and not men, starting from ancient Egypt: 'The great praise of a wise woman is self-control in her manner of life.' Those prescriptions and proscriptions cover a wide field of behaviour, though, indirectly, there is always some link with sex.

Desire being so strong and sex being so crucial, proverbs highly recommend couples not to keep quarrelling after sunset—and to make it up before the night falls—unless they want to sleep alone. From China to Costa Rica and from the Russian Federation to Indonesia, proverbs insist that at bedtime all brawls should be over. The bed proves to be a powerful means of keeping people together, as jokingly expressed in this Arabic saying from Iraq: 'I told her: "I divorce you!" She said: "Come to bed!"'

> Quarrels between spouses and wind from the west stop when the night falls. (*Japanese*)
> Unless you want to sleep alone do not curse your wife after sundown. (*Chinese*)
> During daytime they fight, but at night they sleep together. (*Indonesian*)
> Husband and wife call one another names but they lie under one fur coat. (*Russian*)
> Two who hate each other in daytime love each other at night. (*Estonian*)
> Better the blows of a sledgehammer than a wife's complaints in bed. (*Arabic, Lebanon*)
> During the day she is my dustbin, during the night she is my beauty.
> (*Arabic, Algeria*)

If marriage looks rather like a battlefield than a field of roses, as a Hebrew proverb observes, a Kurdish view is more optimistic about bed life, believing that 'the blankets will make peace' between man and wife. Happy or unhappy, the two inevitably find each other

in bed and have to sleep together, in spite of all the blames and beatings possibly exchanged during the day.

Nevertheless, promises are made in bed that women are advised not to believe, because,
made of butter, they 'melt away when the first sunrays appear', as it is said in Arabic,
meant to stress that the only purpose of such promises is to satisfy male desire at short
notice.

PLEASURE

Woman and horse want a worthy rider. (Greek)

The travel guide to pleasure has shorter and longer roads in store which vary from playing, pinching, touching, kissing, smelling, sniffing, to gradually more intense caressing
and undressing. In most cultures a long distance needs to be covered before desire is allowed (if at all) to end in fulfilled pleasure. It is all part of the game, although in proverbs
the rules for what is allowed and forbidden where, when and to whom, vary. Even though
'a kiss does not come under your shirt', as a Russian proverb argues, proverbs are inclined
to estimate that a boy and a girl should not be left alone together, as in this Spanish
proverb from Panama: 'The more they play, the more the dogs get entangled.'

Suggestions can be picked at random about how to proceed when exploring the map of
physical pleasure and tenderness. In an Estonian proverb the body is poetically compared
to a tree of which 'Love pushes the branches from each other' and 'joy lifts the clothes.'
That a careful prelude is an important part of the game of pleasure is stressed in different
ways. The proverbs' basic rule seems that this is a male responsibility. Men are the ones
who ought to bring women into the mood for making love, not the other way round. This
principle is expressed in a variety of direct as well as indirect statements:

If a woman is cold, it's her husband's fault. (*Russian*)
Stroke a cow before you milk her. (*Hausa*)
A woman is like the legs of a hide; if you don't rub them, they won't become soft. (*Ganda*)
A woman is like a bottle of medicine: shake before use. (*Portuguese, Brazil*)
With a hammock as with women: sideways and patiently. (*Spanish, Colombia*)
A woman and a guitar are tuned before using them. (*Spanish*)
Fire and women burn when you put them into motion. (*Korean*)
You mustn't rush a lady. (*English, USA*)
The eggplant is eaten slowly. (*Arabic, Morocco*)

Musical instruments are favourite images for lovemaking throughout different cultures.
In this metaphorical play, men are always the ones who actively play whereas women's role
is to be the passive instruments tuned and played upon:

If you carve a harp-lute, you must know how to play it. (*Ngbaka*)
A woman is like a guitar, as soon as you play her, she sounds. (*Spanish, Mexico*)
One should know how to tune a woman and a guitar. (*Spanish*)

It is all a matter of initiation, as a Turkish proverb observes: 'At first she acts coyly, later
enjoys.' A Japanese proverb also confirms the advantages of experience by presenting a

girl's initial (feigned?) shyness as evolving into the boldness of 'a running hare'. Some metaphors associate pleasure with experience, as illustrated by the following examples:

Old ovens are soon heated. (*English, UK*)
A new sleeping mat is no pleasure to sleep on. (*Swahili*)

Earlier we came across proverbs stressing the reverse idea, i.e. that older men are keenly interested in sex with young girls. This eagerness for youth is also expressed in the following Filipino proverb: 'Fresh young coconut tastes better than the ripe one', an idea that seems to contradict the plea in favour of female sexual maturity and experience. In reality such ideas are not really contradictory to each other, they rather represent various angles of incidence. From a male perspective, those who have the luxury of choice ought to compare the pros and cons of the physical attractiveness of a young but inexperienced girl against the perhaps more satisfying enjoyment to be had with a mature and experienced woman.

Another point concerns clothes. To be dressed or undressed seems to be a puzzling question for those who are struck by desire. Some proverbs contain warnings against undressing, others are hesitant, and others still recommend courage. A Romanian proverb advises both parties to refrain, at least for the time being (until marriage?): 'Don't undress, it's still a long way to go to the river.' This message is addressed to women only in an Adyg proverb: 'Do not lift your skirts before you need to wade', and to men only in a Frisian proverb: 'Keep God before you and the trousers closed'—a well-known message of fathers to sons who went a-courting. There are proverbs in favour of both options, depending on the situation, but ultimately the outcome is clear, as reflected in a Creole proverb from Martinique: 'If you do not lift the bride's dress, you will not know what is underneath.'

The courage needed to undress yourself, to undress someone else, to let someone undress you and, finally, to be with someone undressed, concerns men and women, and proverbs reflect the discomfiture of both sexes when it comes to it. Visibly, it concerns men in the following Japanese observation: 'More to be feared than a tiger is the scarlet silk-crêpe'. In Japan, scarlet silk-crêpe is used for young women's undergarments. Hence, to be with a woman clothed in just underwear, or even less, is a fearful thing for a man not used to the situation. In a Chinese proverb, it is women who are encouraged to see undressing for their husband as 'normal': 'Dress to meet your in-laws; undress to meet your husband.'

'If you feel her thigh, don't fear her sex' is a West African Mandinka proverb exhorting young men not to be afraid in sexual matters, but it applies of course no less to other contexts where courage is needed. The same holds for other proverbs about dressing and undressing, or sex matters in general. A Zambian Bemba proverb reminds people of the wisdom that one's own experience is the best guarantee for a good judgment by means of the metaphor of a dressed girl that cannot be condemned right away: 'Do not despise a woman you have not undressed.' A Creole proverb from Guadeloupe assents to this commonsense: 'One has to undress the sweetcorn to judge its quality.' The other side of the coin is presented in a Baule proverb—another example of the series 'a woman is not'—resolutely advising against such undressing without further commitment: 'A woman is not a corncob to be valued by stripping off its leaves.'

Again, most proverbs about desire are presented exclusively from a male perspective, as the following Papiamentu proverb from Aruba once more illustrates: 'Nobody un-dresses a girl in order to sit beside her and look into her eyes.' Undressing is not an end in itself, it is rather a plea in favour of going all the way—at least from a male perspective. Hardly any information is given about how girls or women feel about undressing or being undressed. In fact who is undressing whom? And who has paid for the dress? Those two questions get answered in a Frisian proverb: 'The one who dresses a woman is allowed to undress her.' This statement reflects, freely and easily, the self-evidence of women's eco-nomic dependence in marriage and consequently their obligation to grant their husband sexual services in return. The one who has spent money on a woman's clothes seems to consider himself the 'owner' of both the dress and the body it envelops.

Proverbs from a female perspective in which a desiring woman is the subject are almost completely lacking. Here is one rare example, from Estonia: 'The head thinks of the man, the eyes think of the he-goat.' The rarity of such messages is probably due to the taboo on openly expressed female desire, as it goes against the prescription for female modesty.

Proverbs about sex tend to present a hierarchy in action and power. This is frequently expressed by means of the well-known sexual metaphor of the horse and its rider, as in the following popular South American proverb: 'The one who mounts, commands.' Here are a few more examples:

> A husband is like a rider on his horse. (*Ladino*)
> The horse depends on the rider, the woman depends on the man. (*Arabic, Maghreb*)
> Whatever the size of the woman, it's the man who mounts her. (*Ikwere*)
> A horse rears according to its rider. (*Turkish*)

THE FIRST TIME AND NEXT

The penis comes erect as if it intends to kill, but the vagina swallows and tames it. (*Igbo*)

Wedding-night secrets are given only scant comment, but some proverbs pass on a few indirect observations. Grooms need to know that girls can be fearful or reluctant to 'give themselves' to their husband. Inexperienced men are warned not to force things, in Turk-ish for example: 'A rose untimely opened, will soon fade', meaning that abrupt attempts are sure to deter the girl. Some proverbs also advise men not to appear too pleased after the first time, because such eulogy might spoil the bride right from the beginning:

> Do not praise the bride after the first night and do not praise the shepherd after his first year. (*Hebrew*)
> Do not praise the girl before the morning, do not praise the day before the evening. (*Lithuanian*)

It is the newly wed husband's role to take the initiative—that is at least the role he gets ascribed in proverbs—whereas the young wife's role is to be just passive in his hands, as she is (imagined to be) without any experience. In that respect, she is different from a woman who marries for the second time: 'With a girl the way you want, with a widow, the way she wants' (*Polish*). Still, girls are not always as willing as they should be, and even wives' eagerness cannot be fully guaranteed:

It is hard to teach unwilling brides how to dance. (*Dutch*)
There's no end to a virgin's resistance or to a wife's resentment. (*Chinese*)

Mothers and other experienced married women see it as their task to prepare girls for the wedding night, and to teach them how to behave, to be patient and to accept whatever is going to happen. This is especially necessary when the young bride feels scared and disgusted *vis-à-vis* her prospective (and perhaps much older) groom, whom she may not like at all, but with whom she will have to share her life wherever this has been decided for her. She is advised to grow up and accept:

A grown-up girl is not afraid of her groom. (*Basque*)
Endure, young bride, it's a man. (*Bulgarian*)
Be quiet and lie down at his side. (*Oromo*)

A young girl who has just been married to an old man must accept the inevitable without complaint, however frightening it seems to her. After the wedding night women keep quiet about what happened, about the groom's behaviour as well as the pains they may have suffered in losing their virginity: 'The mortar is under the bride and still she keeps quiet.' This Berber proverb refers to people who suffer in silence, like a bride who does not dare complain about her experience. From a girl's perspective, a Bengali proverb expresses the young woman's mixed feelings in the wedding night: 'The bride is ashamed to eat, but nonetheless swallows the banana whole.'

Men have their own fears: 'He who would eat the kernel, must crack the shell' (*English / Polish*). They are expected to take action, but what if they fail to perform? A Berber proverb pities and commiserates with the groom instead of the bride: 'May God have mercy on the husband; as for the wife she knows what awaits her.' This proverb mockingly refers to the husband's duty of deflowering his virgin bride during the wedding night: he must be able to pierce the hymen, in spite of his inexperience or his advanced age.

Men need boldness and self-confidence to convince women of their performance capacities. There is a variety of proverbs in which male fear rather than joy sets the tone—fear of scary vaginas and presumed female insatiability, and insecurity about sexual potency as well as men's limits in satisfying women:

Before the time, great courage; when at the point, great fear. (*English / Spanish*)
The rat will die, and the hole will not be satisfied. (*Arabic, Tunisia*)
Women, land and belly are insatiable. (*/Arabic-Jewish, Yemen*)
Water, fire and women will never say 'enough'. (*Polish*)
The man as long as he can, the woman as long as she wants to. (*Spanish, Bolivia*)
Women's appetite is twice that of a man, their intelligence four times, and their desire eight times. (*Burmese*)

Just like the above Igbo motto to this section about the vagina 'swallowing' and 'taming' the erect penis, a Chilean Mapuche proverb sexualizes female power: 'Women are violent, they can overthrow even a man's penis.' The fear of female sexual appetite is sometimes associated with the dangers of fire. A woman is 'fire bearing fire' according to a Hebrew proverb and therefore men are advised to be careful. A Fulfulde proverb contains a similar warning and recommends male self-control to prevent excessive burnings: 'Woman is fire; if you have to, take a little.'

Age is certainly an issue in proverbs about sex. It is undeniably true, as Bette Midler once said in a TV show, that it is easier for a man of twenty with a woman of eighty than the other way round. In some proverbs, mature women are presented as sexually eager and skilful. This makes them now praised now feared. The age difference between girls and old men is no less ambiguously commented upon. No doubt that girls have sexual power, no doubt that young as well as older men desire them, and no doubt that fear and awe are part of the sexual game. The main fear for an old man is not being able to satisfy a young woman sexually, so that in the worst scenario his lack of potency would make her seek for a better sex partner. Proverbs look at the problem from both male and female perspectives:

> Woman is like a corncob: you have no teeth, you hardly eat. (*Fang*)
> When an old man takes a young wife, he lives in an oasis and she lives in a desert.
>   (*Hebrew*)
> An old man who marries a younger woman will end up finding her with a younger man.
>   (*Ladino*)
> An old man is a cold bedfellow. (*English, UK*)
> Woman is to an old man like a book to an illiterate. (*Russian*)
> To a woman an old man is like a hedgehog to a dog. (*Polish*)

'Neither lovemaking nor baking always succeed', as a German proverb rightly stresses, seemingly in agreement with the sombre judgments above. Baking could be interpreted here as being successful in having a child. However, the proverb's meaning can also be explained positively—that, be it surprisingly, both sex and baking may not always fail either, not even in marriage, as expressed in a Russian proverb: 'The husband mated and surprised his wife', a surprise not necessarily limited to one occasion only. The main and most comforting rule of the game is that everyone makes love in his own way:

> All women kiss their men in their own way. (*Sranan*)
> Every man kisses a woman in his own way. (*Papiamentu*)

However true and simple this rule may be, men feel obsessed by the idea of competition in matters of sex, if we have to believe what proverbs say. In Jewish culture, the Talmud warns men not to marry a divorced woman, because 'All fingers are different', a statement in which finger stands for penis. Knowing different fingers enables women to compare: a frightening idea. 'Do not cook in your neighbour's saucepan' is a warning possibly motivated in part by the same fear as the warning against marrying a widow or a divorced woman, as they have had 'the' experience. If a man desires a woman who has lost her virginity, the fundamental underlying worrisome question in proverbs seems to be whether he is the better sexual performer. Would this be one of the very reasons why in most cultures a girl's virginity is (or was) considered so crucial? If she is still ignorant, there is no competition problem. The opposite question, as to whether a woman might worry about being (or not being) a better performer than other women her man has (had) experience with is simply not put to the fore.

Ideally, then, a woman 'knows' only one man in her entire life, physically speaking, so

that a husband can always be sure to be the exclusive and the only one who ever made love
to his wife. This proverbial principle makes the borderline between good and bad women
completely neat:

> Don't eat a bitten pea, don't take a deflowered woman as a wife. (*Bulgarian*)
> A woman without character flees one penis for another one. (*Lega*)
> [A bad woman is she who] left the lyre in the willow and went on to play the lute. (*Arabic*)
> Lost is the girl who plays with men before her marriage. (*Oromo*)

Very few proverbs comment on changing partners from a female perspective; in fact, I
found only two. A Yoruba proverb holds that 'A woman who has not been married several
times cannot know what perfect marriage is' and, according to an Arabic proverb from the
Maghreb: 'Who has never changed turban has never seen sweetness' with variants in
which 'sweetness' is replaced by happiness. Women who have had several husbands quote
this proverb literally, but, as usual, it is also quoted in a figurative sense. It should be
quickly added that these two examples reflect the exception to the overall rule, aptly expressed in two significant variants of a very popular Latin American proverb:

> For the chaste woman, God suffices. (*Spanish, El Salvador / Argentina*)
> For the chaste woman, her husband suffices. (*Spanish, Colombia*)

Being devoted to God or to one's husband practically amounts to the same thing. Notice-
ably, this message originates from the continent from which also originate the majority of
macho proverbs in Spanish as well as in Portuguese of the type: 'He who does not have
anything better, sleeps with his wife.' Variants of this saying exist in Puerto Rico, Cuba,
Brazil, Chile, etc. but I found some similar messages also in Europe and elsewhere.

Double standards in matters of sex and lovemaking are the cradle from which the confusion originates between natural female desire and the social norm that forbids women to
give way to their sexual feelings. In Chinese this embarrassment is expressed thus: 'When
a woman's lips say "It is enough," she looks at you and her eyes say "Again".' An American proverb not only reflects women's desire, confusion, and vacillation, but also society's
imminent condemnation of female 'indecency' and 'immodesty'—here euphemistically
referred to as 'unladylike' behaviour: 'When a lady says no, she means perhaps; when she
says perhaps, she means yes; when she says yes, she is no lady.' The overall taboo on female
sexual desire further explains the earlier referred to yes-and-no logic of love. Women are
pressed into ambivalence and irresolution in sexual matters, due to the strict reserve imposed upon them in societies all over the world.

HEAVENLY DELIGHT

Let nothing on earth make you sad as long as you can make love. (*Hungarian*)

Ideal sex is referred to in just a few proverbs. Once more, a male perspective prevails, as
the following examples illustrate:

> Nothing is so pleasant to one's physical well-being as having a wife. (*Sanskrit*)
> Bed, wine and woman comfort the body. (*German*)

Described as a wonderful bodily satisfaction, it is hard to guess what those who bring this perfect condition of male well-being about are feeling themselves.

Some proverbs subtly refer to the night's pleasure while leaving the question open as to whose pleasure it was, the man's or the wife's, or whether both enjoyed it equally:

> The blushes on a woman's cheeks are caused by her husband. (*Kurdish*)
> Where the heart was in the night the legs wake up in the morning. (*Haya*)

In cultures where several co-wives share one and the same man, each of the wives has sex with the husband in turn. Apparently the difference between the lucky one and the other wives is noticeable from the secret code of their understanding, as observed in a Minyanka proverb: 'The wife who has spent the night with her husband shows it in the way they greet.' A sign of closeness and intimacy—or is she showing off to make her co-wives jealous?

A man needs change, proverbs about sex insist, although, once in a while, the idea is put forward that a man could resort to his own legal wife. Getting out of the old routine, it is argued, creates the illusion of change: 'Even your own wife is better in another barn', is a piece of Finnish advice. Some proverbs argue in favour of a sexual variant of home sweet home: 'It's most convenient to make love under one's own roof,' according to a Dutch example.

Undoubtedly there have always been innumerable people who miraculously combine mutual love with mutual lovemaking, but such heavenly delight is disappointingly rare in proverbs. Exceptionally, sexual pleasure equally enjoyed by two people is made explicit in a charming Dutch proverb: 'When husband and wife give pleasure to each other, the little angels in heaven laugh.' Most proverbs, though, do not seem to care what love and sex mean to women, at least it is not much of an issue. For a girl, getting married is equated with being 'consumed'. Young women without sexual experience are often given a higher value than those who have slept with a man. Some Asian proverbs put such consumption on a par with devaluation:

> A married girl is like water that has been spat out: no one will drink it again. (*Chinese*)
> The fox was beautiful before it got killed; the bride was beautiful before she got
>   married. (*Mongolian*)

The idea that sex equates 'lost purity' and reduced value holds for women in other parts of the world as well. In the West the perfect ideal of the Virgin Mary, who stayed a virgin in spite of having given birth to Jesus, may in the past have created a guilt problem for 'ordinary' wives and mothers: for them such a perfect model of having a child without having sex would be forever unrealisable. Sexuality thus became associated with fear and shame. The more the idealization of virginity came to be held in esteem in the Catholic Church, the more defloration came to be considered a real loss of value for women in Western society, in spite of the miracle (and demographic necessity) of women's unique quality as birth-givers. The ideal motherhood of the Virgin Mary meant her being untainted by the desires of the female flesh. In Islam, too, young men have contempt for an unmarried girl who is no longer a virgin. Many believe that such a woman will be punished for such a terrible sin by giving birth to handicapped children.[103]

In proverbs originating from a majority of cultures a girl is taught 'asexual virtue' as against men's 'overt sexual needs.'[104] The girls must refuse sex before marriage, and remain virgin whereas men are usually allowed to find sexual fulfilment elsewhere, by going to 'bad' women. In a recent interview in a Dutch women's magazine, a Turkish girl living in the Netherlands confessed that she had agreed to her Turkish boyfriend making love to a Dutch girl—for the time being. Both she and her fiancé found Western girls 'shameless' anyway. This 'solution', she argued, would satisfy his hunger for sex and save her purity so that she would be able to marry him as a virgin bride.

If a wife has too strongly internalized virginal resistance as obligatory decent behaviour, she may never get rid of it after the wedding. The risk here is that love and sex may remain separate matters for husband and wife alike, and who knows how many wives never enjoyed (or never allowed themselves to enjoy) the pleasures of sex during a lifetime of marriage?

What should our conclusion be? Proverbs stress that in most societies men and men's desires, feelings and expectations (have to) predominate in sex matters. Men are the ones who ought to take sexual initiatives while women are supposed not to; and men are the ones having premarital and extramarital freedom, whereas women are not. In a majority of proverbs on the topic, having sex means for men satisfying their needs and for women being used sexually. In this context, there seems little or nothing to be gained for women in having the experience (except for those who earn their living that way and whom 'decent' people hold in contempt anyway). In proverbs sex as a source of pleasure for women is hardly ever referred to in a positive way. Adult love and sex relations between men and women are mainly presented as problematic, and the rare delight of making love while being in love looks like an ideal reserved for just the happy few.

FERTILITY, PREGNANCY, CHILDBIRTH

She who leaves a child behind lives eternally. (Chagga)

A truth confirmed in proverbs all over the world is that posterity is absolutely crucial. In the words of a Sinhalese proverb from Sri Lanka: 'The gem of the house is the child.' This idealization of the miracle of pregnancy and childbirth stands firm in spite of the fact that pregnancy and having children are frequently mentioned as the cause of deep pain and serious problems; the pain of childlessness is however considered to be much worse, and the fate of women without children, lamentable.

In order to make life less unbearable, a sterile woman is urged to adopt children from relatives who are unable to feed them:

Take thy luck from thy sister's lap. (*Arabic, Egypt*)
The womb that is not carrying, raises another woman's child. (*Oromo*)

Such proverbs comfort a desperate childless wife. It is mainly women who are quite unambiguously stigmatized, if a couple remains childless. Proverbs emphatically stress women's indispensability as birth-givers, and sterility as one of the worst possible disasters. In societies where women are valued mainly or only for achieving motherhood, they will go to any lengths to have a child. Even in societies where they are no longer appreciated only for giving birth, women are often ready to spare no pains for the purpose of having a child.

STERILITY

Do not accuse the bed of infertility. (Chinese)

A childless woman is not necessarily sterile, however. In the Minayanka culture, for example, friends and relatives will comfort a woman who has a miscarriage by saying that 'Miscarriage is not sterility.' Within the proverbial female procreation hierarchy, there are, at the very bottom, the sterile ones, followed by women who have had a miscarriage, a little higher up are the mothers of stillborn children, and those who have lost their child or children. They are somewhat 'higher up', as they have at least shown to be able to conceive, and, moreover, for them not all hope is lost. For the sterile woman there is no such comfort. When a woman is childless because her child has died, some African proverbs stress that such women are 'better off' than barren women, as they can always cherish hope for new pregnancies. A sterile woman, on the contrary, has no such hope. She cannot glory in having given birth, and she does not even have the consolation of crying at the graves of her children:

> The woman whose sons have died is richer than a barren woman. (*Gikuyu*)
> The one whose children are buried in her womb will not see their graves. (*Rundi*)
> Rather condolences for dead sons than no hope of giving birth to them. (*Ladino*)

Even in cultures where twins are believed to bring bad luck, giving birth to twins is preferable to barrenness: 'Better to bear twins than to be sterile' (*Frafra, Ghana*) means that although having twins is a tricky business, the birth-giver has at least proved to be a 'worthy' woman. In proverbs a sterile woman is conspicuously disapproved of. Her painful lack stays no less hidden than hunger, in the words of a Haya proverb. She has to be on her guard all the time against insults and contemptuous remarks such as the following:

> A woman without children doesn't know what love is. (*English/Italian*)
> The house without children is a cemetery. (*Sanskrit*)
> What can a sterile woman know about the happiness of having children? (*Telegu*)
> A barren sow is never kind to piglets. (*Danish*)

A sterile woman is advised not to make fun of those who have given birth and are therefore more prestigious and experienced, and the same holds for young girls—as a Creole proverb from Jamaica reminds them: 'You done no breed, so no laugh after your grannie.' And the mother of only one child should not mock a childless woman, according to a Ghanaian Mamprusi advice, as the risk of losing one's only treasure is always high.

In proverbs, infertility is mainly equated with female infertility. If, incidentally, male impotence is referred to, it is rather in the context of a man's not being able to have sex, and this may involve two threatening scenarios: a wife's 'punishment' consisting either of her refusal to take good care of a man who does not fulfil his 'duty' or of her being unfaithful in order to have a child:

> The impotent man does not eat seasoned food. (*Lunda, Zambia*)
> If the pestle were broken, the mortar will be lost. (*Malay*)

The broken pestle in the Malay proverb is of course a metaphor for the malfunctioning male organ, while the 'lost' mortar stands for the wife's womb getting out of control.

The gossipy question becomes: who made the wife of the sterile man pregnant? This question lies, for example, behind the following Yaka proverb: 'The adulterous man peoples the village, the sterile man doesn't.' The suspicion hinted at is that the wife of an impotent husband will try to have a child by some other man. This possibility is even more openly suggested in an Arabic proverb presented from a female perspective: 'If I had relied on you, husband, we would never have had children' (*Morocco*). A woman going so far as to take the high risk of being caught in the act of adultery must feel really desperate to have a child.

Fertility and sterility mark women for life. In proverbs the various disadvantages surrounding female barrenness are considered in detail. Families want to secure heirs. Therefore, in many cultures men are allowed to divorce a 'sterile' wife, that is a wife who has not given birth within a few years after marriage, as if this could only be a woman's fault:

> A marriage without children does not last long for men. (*Arabic, Maghreb*)
> A bride who bears no child after three years of marriage should be divorced. (*Japanese*)

The messages are harsh and destructive, whether expressed in metaphorical terms or not: 'Rather mud than an infertile wife', is an Andrah proverb from India. And what to do with a sterile tree? It is best chopped down and thrown into the fire according to variants of the same message in Hebrew or Romanian. Only one proverb gives women the benefit of the doubt for a longer period of time: 'Seven years is not too long for a pumpkin vine to start bearing fruit' (*English, Jamaica*). And miracles are never to be excluded, as a Ladino proverb from Morocco reminds people: 'When the sterile one begins to give birth, prepare many cradles!' Indeed, one can run from one extreme to another in life.

A Ganda proverb summarizes the very reasons men need women for—work and children: 'A useless person is like a woman who is both lazy and barren.' Fearing the threat of divorce, women without children try to spoil their husbands with more and better food than a co-wife with children would think of doing, so that the husband concerned might see some advantages in keeping her in spite of 'her problem'. Apparently such efforts are sometimes rewarded. Next to quite a few proverbs arguing that a sterile wife has to be sent back to her parents or to be divorced right away, a Yaka saying sets her as an example to the fertile co-wife: 'If you do not prepare food, should I hate the [sterile] one who prepares well?' Stigmatized by the community, they are forced to be exaggeratedly obliging towards other people, and thus they 'give birth to visitors', as the Ganda put it ironically. They feel defenceless against those who exploit them materially and sexually:

The one who visits the barren one chooses among the dough balls. (*Rwanda*)
A childless donkey will be eaten by the wolves. (*Uzbek*)

Female infertility is associated with all sorts of things: a tent without tent pegs (*Ladino*); an extinguished hearth (*Finnish*); blind windows (*Lithuanian*); a day without sun (*Czech/Serbian*); a cow without a bell (*German*); a lonely flower on a mountain top (*Vietnamese*); a birdless tree (*Thai*); a fruitless tree (*German/Tadjik*); a leafless tree (*Tibetan*), and so forth. Beautiful looks are often put on a par with sterility, whereas 'real' female beauty is associated with motherhood.

Inevitably, people try to discover the cause of such extremely bad luck, and many natural and supernatural causes and cures have been found or invented, although proverbs do not say much about them. According to the Mapuche in Chile it is believed that the scrapings of a mule's nail transmit infertility. It can also be caused by witchcraft. The idea that you can be rejected (and so lose your livelihood) if you do not get pregnant soon enough is apparently alarming. Of course, women pray, and visit priests or doctors if they do not conceive quickly. They practise customary rituals, and try to cure themselves by means of herbs, potions and magic in order to solve the problem, and it seems to work in a Telegu proverb: 'She had but just passed the holy tree and already felt signs of pregnancy.'

Especially in Africa and to a lesser extent also South Asia, sterility and childlessness are a more frequent issue in proverbs than in Europe and North America, although negative proverbs about female sterility are certainly not lacking in the West. In many societies the fate of a woman who cannot have children is far from enviable.

FERTILITY

Two can make ten. (*Mongolian*)

Although in many cultures girls and women seem to be less appreciated than boys or men, proverbs do acknowledge that the future of society depends on females. A Kamba metaphor compares humans to trees in the desert: 'In the desert there are two kinds of trees: dry ones and green ones.' The desiccated ones are associated with males and the green ones with females, meaning that males cannot give birth. Men are advised to carefully choose their wives with a view to their conceiving capacity. The problem is that the proof of the pudding is in the eating, so to speak. A risk has to be taken, especially in cultures where virginity must be respected until the wedding night. People can be lucky or not, a wife can conceive quickly or not, or even wait in vain for the faintest sign of pregnancy. If a bride can be bought, a child cannot, as the Bulgarians say. A Fulfulde proverb tells men who are in a hurry for posterity: 'If you are impatient to have a child, you marry a pregnant woman.'

Several Latin American proverbs compare the purchase of a wife for breeding to another serious matter of concern, the purchase of dogs or cattle for the same purpose:

Rooster, horse and wife should be chosen for their breed. (*Spanish, Mexico*)
Women and goats: choose them for their breed. (*Spanish, Puerto Rico*)
Women, horses and hunting-dogs: choose them for their breed. (*Portuguese, Brazil*)

A clan prospers as long as there are nubile girls who will bring forth a new generation. This point is especially emphasized in proverbs from African societies where infant mortality is experienced as an imminent threat:

> A girl is a peanut seed: she enlarges the clan. (*Woyo*)
> The wealth of a girl is in her frontside. (*Rwanda*)
> Girl, bring forth, that we may see [what you're worth]. (*Bembe*)
> The girl grows up in order to raise a family. (*Rundi*)
> May your daughter fill the house [with boys] and bear fruit, thanks to God. [A marriage wish] (*Arabic, Maghreb/West Sahara*)

Children are not only a precious treasure of family happiness, but also a source of practical profit. Thus, from a maternal perspective, even the very young ones will lighten their mother's daily burdens:

> Where the mother sends [her children], the childless goes herself. (*Ganda*)
> Who will draw water for the childless old woman? (*Gikuyu*)
> Those who have children arrive first at the water; the childless one fetches muddy water. (*Taka*)
> Mothers cuddle and play with children, but women without children stay glum. (*Sinhalese*)

Moreover, after a fight with her husband, a sterile woman cannot work off her emotions on her children, as an African Nyanja proverb argues: 'A childless woman has no one to scold.' Sterility is to fertility, then, as poverty is to wealth. This not only holds for mothers, but also for fathers. Having children is a long-term investment in the material sense, in societies where children are the only possible insurance in old age: 'Those who fear children's crying will cry in their old age', as the Swahili saying goes. From this perspective, the more numerous your offspring, the more chances you have that some will survive and take care of you in your last phase of life. Sons, especially, are considered a good investment:

> Children are the riches of the poor. (*Japanese*)
> If you have sons what would you need money for? (*Chinese*)
> A house full of sons is like a house full of pearls. (*Kurdish*)

Therefore men are advised to take the necessary measures in due time, instead of complaining when it is too late: 'If an elder grows slim, it is his fault,' a Yaka proverb stresses. He should have married several wives who would have given him many children in his younger years.

There are two sides to immense female fertility. Positively, 'getting many children is divine', according to a Sumerian proverb, as we have seen. Having children is often presented in terms of sheer happiness and profit, as in the following Oromo proverb: 'When the year is a good year, the women of the house have many children' (*Ethiopia*). Many proverbs express the good luck and prestige of having numerous offspring:

> And the tree keeps on giving. (*Spanish, Mexico*)
> The more children the more luck. (*German*)
> Many children are the riches of Romanians. (*Romanian*)

Just as the fireplace for cooking never has enough firewood, a woman never has enough
  children. (*Punjabi*)

This seems all very well from the perspective of those who don't have to bear with the
pregnancies and the actual birthing, and who don't have to think of how to feed so many
hungry mouths. Other proverbs, however, tone down the praise of such overwhelming
female wealth, or even blame women for conceiving too easily (or warn against women
who do):

Some women will conceive if you but shake a pair of breeches at them. (*English, UK*)
It happens that by leaping over a hedge you become pregnant. (*Estonian*)
A woman who gives birth to many children will get pregnant from the slightest wind.
  (*Hebrew*)
Every year a child, in nine years twelve. (*Bulgarian*)
Ill-starred women have two babies a year. (*Pashto*)

As a parody on the popular hunting proverb 'Where he puts the eye, he puts the bullet', a
Spanish Bolivian proverb refers with frank disapproval to such exuberant fertility:
'Where she puts her eye, she gets a baby.'
  Other proverbs look into the trouble and worries that a large family brings along. A
Korean proverb stresses that 'A tree with many branches has not a day without wind', in
which wind is a metaphor for adversity. The same idea can be found in more direct state-
ments:

To bear many children is to shed many tears. (*Shona*)
Many children, many debts; many wives, much malicious gossip. (*Vietnamese*)
May God save us from many children and little bread. (*Spanish*)
Many children, possible, but too many, impossible. (*Russian*)
The last child kills its mother. (*Papiamentu/English/Creole, Caribbean*)

Different twists can be given to one and the same message referring to this issue, as a widespread Arabic proverb illustrates. An Egyptian version emphasizes the affluence and
riches of having many children: 'She is with child, and nurses a child, and has four more
[children] before her'; another version looks at the situation rather from an overburdened
and exhausted woman's perspective:

She is pregnant, she nurses a child, she drives around her other four little ones and she is
  climbing up the mountain to search for a medicine against pregnancy.
  (*Arabic, various countries*)

This variant seem to be referring to a medicine preventing pregnancy (or even provoking
an abortion?). One Russian proverb says fatalistically: 'Do not swear, womb, that you will
not get children', which means so much as: you will get them anyway, even against your
will. It is quite obvious that, as far as proverbs are concerned, nothing much seems to be
done to regulate pregnancies: 'A good-hearted woman is always pregnant', in the words of
a Sinhalese proverb from Sri Lanka. It is also argued that the combination of poverty and
fertility bodes ill for the future:

What's saved if, by going to bed early to spare the candles, your wife then gives birth to
     twins? (*Chinese*)
Two hungry lovers and a single bed means the birth of a beggar. (*Turkish*)
A poor woman is pregnant: good news for the graveyard. (*Arabic, Lebanon*)

PREGNANCY

'Respected!' said the bride on learning she was pregnant. (Oromo)

Pregnancy yields prestige in most cultures: 'A poor girl, until she got pregnant' (*Ladino,
Tunisia*). A pregnant woman must be handled with care, because her child will strengthen
the community, as a Mongo proverb observes, whereas an American English proverb observes that: 'A ship under sail and a big-bellied woman are the handsomest two things that
can be seen.'

Women's irrefutable birth-giving power is acknowledged, for example, in the Minangkabau proverb from Indonesia: 'A cock does not lay eggs.' Some proverbs state explicitly
that living or bearing with a woman is the price a man has to pay for having progeny. As
the Mamprusi say: 'A wife is in the man's compound for the sake of the child.' Or, in Turkish as well as in English: 'He that wants eggs must endure the cackling of hens.'

Pregnancy is the inevitable natural consequence of a woman's having intercourse. This
simple fact is used in proverbs to express that even though the origins of one's doings are
secret, the outcome will be public. As the Swahili in East Africa argue: 'She who is pregnant, is pregnant, even though she wraps herself in a *makaja*', the cloth women wear after
childbirth. Without or with an explicit moral judgment, this is an issue returning again
and again in proverbs all over the world.

A man may get away with it, but women can no more keep their pregnancies secret
than people can hide love; pregnancy is as obvious as cough, a hunchback, or going up a
mountain, according to a class of proverbs popular in various Arabic-speaking areas, for
example: 'Three things cannot be hidden: love, pregnancy and riding a camel.' Here are
some similar examples from other cultures:

The cow receives the bull in secret, but gives birth in public. (*Kurdish*)
A woman hides the penis, she won't hide the belly. (*Mamprusi*)
The tongue shows what it has eaten. (*Lunda*)
A fire and a girl's pregnancy cannot be kept secret. (*Rwanda*)

However, things do not always turn out as expected, as many risks threaten both the future
mother and the unborn child. No wonder, then, that in many languages the delicate status
of a pregnant woman with its uncertain outcome serves as a metaphor, warning against
dangerous anticipation, such as thinking up names, making clothes, making a cradle,
preparing porridge or diapers, and so forth. Such premature behaviour sometimes starts
even before pregnancy, and eloquently reflects how deeply women long for motherhood:

Not even married yet, but prepares the diapers. (*Korean*)
The son in her uterus is only an embryo, and already she is weaving his *burnous* [large
     cloak] for great festivities. (*Arabic, Morocco*)

Before seeing her son she named him. (*Oromo*)
Don't look for the strapping-cloth when the baby is not yet born. (*Hehe*)
One doesn't sew a shawl for an unborn baby. (*Gikuyu*)
As long as the child isn't born don't make a cradle for him. (*Shor*)
Do not boil the pap before the child is born. (*Hebrew*)

Much can go wrong before a child is born, especially in situations where healthcare and medical services are lacking, and multiple dangers surround pregnancy:

Pregnant women have one foot in the grave. (*German*)
A pregnant woman stands facing the gate of a graveyard. (*Vietnamese*)
A pregnant woman is in more serious danger than sailors and horsemen. (*Chinese*)

The more infant mortality constitutes a threat in a particular society, the more numerous seem the warnings against anticipating the child's arrival. I found relatively few such admonitions in Europe, but many in Africa where, moreover, the belief is widespread that if you appear too happy about a pregnancy, an evil spirit could become so jealous as to destroy the unborn baby. This might well be the reason why the Baule from Ivory Coast—among other people (and not only in Africa)—recommend not addressing the pregnant woman as 'mother' yet. This title of honour is not only seen as premature before she has given birth, but it might also prove to conjure up danger for the future mother as well as for her foetus:

Pregnancy is not yet having a child. (*German*)
Pregnancy does not yet mean baby. (*Baule*)
A pregnant woman should not put her unborn child on her list of living children.
(*Papiamentu, Aruba*)

Many proverbs emphasize and repeat that people should first wait and see or, as the Yaka put it wisely and concisely: 'Praise the child, don't praise the pregnancy.' That there is a time for everything also holds for pregnancy: some brides are in trouble because they are already pregnant on the wedding day, as their secret—of having had sex before marriage—will become public soon. In the Western world this used to be a terrible shame: 'June brides, January mothers' (*English, USA*). Other brides, on the contrary, worry whether they will get pregnant soon enough. Their situation is usually much worse. Even though a virgin's untimely and unwished-for pregnancy detracts somewhat from the enormous prestige childbirth otherwise has, it is agreed throughout the world, that 'A pregnant woman earns respect', as it is said in Italian for example. Summarizing, then, in the large majority of proverbs about the topic, the principle holds that 'It is a shame for a girl to be pregnant and for a woman not to be pregnant', as the Oromo in Ethiopia observe tersely, or, in Estonian: 'Having a child is a shame for a girl, an honour for a woman.'

CHILDBIRTH AND CHILDBED

A child is the girdle of marriage. (*Tumbuka*)

Pregnancies and childbirth are killers of women and their babies all over the world. According to a popular Arabic proverb, 'Birth is the messenger of death.' More than four thousand years ago, the Sumerians already carved on a clay tablet their worries about the uncertain fate of a woman in childbirth: 'A sick person is [relatively] well; it is the woman in childbirth who is [really] ill.' Another Sumerian proverb stresses the exhaustion brought about by continuous childbirths: 'A mother who has given birth to eight youths lies down in weakness.' The proverb has been (over-)interpreted in different ways: as a boast on the part of a particularly proud father, but also as an expression of sympathy for the aging, though still fertile, mother who lies down passively in fear of another risky pregnancy, when her husband wants to make love again. Among the Haya, the ninth childbirth is considered risky as such: 'The woman who said: "How well and easily do I give birth," died with the birth of her ninth child', and a Caribbean proverb warns that 'The last child kills its mother', meaning that so often goes the pitcher to the well that it comes home broken at last—in which the pitcher could as well serve as a metaphor for the birth-giving womb, as it actually does in a good many proverbs.

A Papiamentu proverb from the Caribbean observes that for women 'Desire is more powerful than pain.' This does not mean, however, that women's birth-giving and aging does not take its toll: 'Bearing fruits bends the trunk of the banana tree.' This Gikuyu image expresses that maternity inevitably means pain. Some proverbs observe the glaring contrast between the pleasures of sex and the subsequent stressful labour pains for women:

> Making love is a good thing, giving birth is not. (*Creole, Guadeloupe*)
> Even if a thousand women come together, the one who gives birth has to suffer the pain. (*Armenian*)
> Getting pregnant is easy, giving birth is hard. (*Russian*)
> Laughing she got pregnant, crying she delivered. (*Oromo*)
> No rain without thunder, no childbirth without pain, no girl without lover. (*Ladino*)

Whereas others stress that the trouble of giving birth is forgotten as soon as the child has arrived:

> Labour pain, forgotten pain. (*Italian*)
> Women do not remember the labour pains. (*Somali*)
> An egg laid, a hen cackling. (*Spanish, Puerto Rico*)

Some proverbs argue that things are more easily done than dreaded beforehand: 'More suffering in fear than in child's delivery' (*Japanese*). When giving birth women are usually assisted by a midwife, although, as a Ganda proverb stresses: 'A woman in childbirth trembles [only], if somebody is there to help her.' In other words, if nobody were around, she would just help herself without quivering! Several proverbs refer to assistance with delivery. A pregnant woman is warned not to speak contemptuously about a co-wife who has already achieved what she herself still has to do: 'A pregnant wife should not scorn a co-wife's child.' This Mamprusi proverb recommends not to underrate someone else's achievement, but not only that. One co-wife needs the other as a midwife when her own time comes: 'Women give birth with the assistance of their co-wives' is an Acholi proverb from Uganda warning people to be welcoming and polite, because competitors are sometimes forced to help each other. A rival might feel like taking revenge at the very moment you are helpless. In some East African proverbs, the metaphor of the midwife is explicitly used to express people's interdependence in life:

> Insult the midwife, and who will help you next time? (*Sena*)
> Don't insult the midwives while birth is going on. (*Hehe*)
> Do not abuse midwives while childbearing continues. (*Swahili*)

Only a few proverbs reflect a man's reactions to childbirth. Giving birth is clearly considered a women's business, as the word 'midwife' already suggests. A Tswana proverb praises a man's heroism not so much for courageous war or hunting exploits, but for approaching the spot where it all happens—scary ground from a male perspective: 'A hero even steps into the accouchement section.' A man whose wife is giving birth feels the more nervous as he is reduced to passivity: she has to do it and he cannot do anything but express his solidarity. Feeling helpless, a man spontaneously falls ill himself[105]:

> Azzûna [wife of a rabbi] gives birth to a child, and the rabbi feels pain in his bottom.
>   (*Jewish/Arabic, Morocco*)
> The cow calves and the arse of the bull itches. (*Belorussian*)

Very few proverbs pay attention to the fact that women in childbed need extra attention and care. This idea is explicitly referred to in Chinese:

> Patients need activities while new mothers need sleep.
> Building up a woman's health just before childbirth, nourishing her milk just after.
> Stop intercourse until one hundred days after your child is born, if you want to enjoy
>   long happiness with your spouse.

One of the worst things to happen is to give birth to a dead child, or seeing a child you have given birth to die, and, alas, this happens all the time, to the poor in the first place, but also to the rich, as the Sumerians already knew: 'A palace, one day a mother giving birth, the next day a lamenting mother.' The Tamil in India say: 'A child in the grave is a child in the womb,' and indeed, a mother will never get rid of the pain of such a loss, and no other drama can compare to it: 'The grief of the neck lasts six months, the grief of the womb forever' (*Telegu*), in which the 'grief of the neck' signifies the breaking of the marriage cord, i.e. widowhood, while the 'grief of the womb' signifies the loss of a child which immerses one's life in sadness. Some African proverbs mention the loss of several children, so that ultimately one loses hope of keeping any alive:

> She who keeps losing children doesn't invent names anymore. (*Ganda*)
> I give birth, they die, [a woman says], and she gives none of them names.
>   (*Haya, Tanzania*)

Both proverbs refer to the custom that, after the death of one of her children, a mother gives an ugly name or no name at all to the next born, hoping and believing that thus no bad spirit will notice the new pregnancy or be interested in taking the newborn baby away. In addition to this problem, there are numerous other maternal worries, as we have seen.

> She gives birth to them in pain and buries them in pain. (*Ladino, Morocco*)
> A woman who brings forth takes trouble upon herself. (*Ganda, Uganda*)
> She who brings forth a child brings forth a problem. (*Berber, Morocco*)

Nonetheless, childbirth is far from being only sorrow and grief. It is motherhood that grants a wife respect, even among her in-laws, as a Persian proverb stresses: 'A wife is a stranger until she gives birth to a child.' Motherhood and childbirth are praised as the greatest possible asset and benediction:

> A marriage is a joy; the birth of a boy, an honour; the birth of a girl, luck. (*Tajik*)
> A child is the flower of a family garden. (*Turkish*)
> To bear children is wealth; to dress is only colours. (*Tsonga*)

In most cultures proverbs on giving birth once more confirm the importance of having sons instead of daughters. The keen interest in the outcome of a woman's labour mainly represents the hope that she will bring forth a boy:

> Let's pray to the Prophet until the boy comes. (*Arabic*)
> The woman that gives birth to sons has no sorrows. (*Spanish*)
> For her, who has given birth to a son, the sun will rise. (*Nogay*)

A Jewish expression reflects the fact that a girl's birth does not cause the same emotions of joy as a boy's would: 'You are as calm as if you had just given birth to a daughter' (*Hebrew*). Jokingly an Armenian proverb ascribes the following words to a woman badly struggling with her birth pains: 'I would even prefer a girl, if it's quicker.' Giving birth to daughters is thus seen as a mere second-choice solution, after the manner of some result being better than no result at all:

> Whatever they tried, she kept on giving birth to daughters. (*Abazin*)
> It is better to give birth to a girl than to sit idle. [Anything is better than idleness]
>   (*Oromo*)
> Give birth to girls and do not lead a useless life. (*Arabic*)
> Only the house's ghost is happy with the birth of a daughter. (*Chuwash*)

There is also the question of who owns the children. Depending on the rules within a given society, children are attributed to the mother's or the father's family. In the Ovambo society the child belongs to the mother's clan, whereas the father's relatives are not considered relatives of the child; even the father himself is not a relative of the child as one Ovambo proverb explicitly states: 'The family does not spring from the man.' Most other proverbs on the topic mainly stress that the children belong to the husband and his family: 'A woman gives birth to what's yours, but she [herself] is not yours' (*Rwanda*). Several proverbs regretfully observe that, instead of the girl's own family, the in-laws will profit from their daughters' 'production': 'A daughter is like a raindrop: she'll fertilize others' fields' is a Luba example.

What about responsibility for the children a man fathers? Significantly few proverbs deal with this question, as compared to the large numbers interested in men's having sex with women, whether their 'own' or not—and as compared to the many proverbs concerning women's maternal responsibilities. I found only two sayings reminding men of the duties resulting from their sexual activities: 'The thing [penis] responsible for the pregnancy is the same responsible for the child', an Oromo proverb brings men to notice, and an Ashanti proverb from Ghana agrees: 'It is not only the female who gives birth; the male should feel just as responsible.'

Proverbs frequently deal with the tricky question of who actually fathers the children to whom women give birth. A Baule proverb from Ivory Coast conjures the danger by stating that 'Her husband away, a woman can bear, but she cannot conceive.' There is a strong awareness that ultimately the name of the father is the secret of the mother:

Mama's baby, papa's maybe. (*English*, *Jamaica*)
Let the baby be born and he will tell who is his father. (*Spanish*, *Mexico*)
Only the pregnant one will know who is the father of the child. (*Twi*)
The mother knows best whether the child is like the father. (*English*, *USA*)
The mother is known, the father unknown. (*Estonian*)

Conception and death are the two poles between which life is spent, and procreation is considered crucial across the world. Men desire and look for attractive sex partners and for fertile wives who can give them healthy children. Women dream of powerful lovers and well-to-do husbands to have children with, albeit that their wishes and desires are rather neglected in proverbs about love, sex, fertility and childbirth. Usually, both parties seem to have (or have had in the past) a preference for sons. Ultimately, proverbial men derive their prestige from their power physically and economically to dominate in society, whereas proverbial women derive their prestige from their sexual attractiveness, and their birth-giving capacity. Some proverbs present the complementary roles of men and women concisely and cynically thus:

Battlefield for man, childbirth for woman. (*Maori*)
What war is to man, childbirth is to woman. (*Assam*)

Basics of Life Anthology

LOVE

Love is a ring and a ring has no end. (*Russian*): *Mieder 1986: 286; Reinsberg-Düringsfeld 60*

Where love is sown, joy comes up. (*German*): *Geyvandov 43*

A thirsty person dreams of water. (*Persian*): *Shaki 516*

One open lotus, grasp life. (*Japanese*) [To sit intimately together on one lotus flower in
   paradise is a lovers' dream]: *Buchanan 12*

In dreams and love nothing is impossible. (*Hungarian*): *Rauch 180*

The first love is the only true love. (*Arabic*): *Geyvandov 26*

First love and first fruit taste best. (*Portuguese*): *Geyvandov 27*

There is no love like the first. (*Spanish, Mexico*): *Glazer 13*

A young girl never quite gets over her first man. (*English, USA*): *Whiting 1952: 414*

First love is like a snake; if it doesn't destroy you, it will paralyze you. (*Polish*): *Geyvandov 27*

Even if you saw down a willow, she'll grow again. (*Udmurt, RF*): *Geyvandov 27*

When the laurel flowers the girl shivers.
   (*Arabic, Algeria*): *Belamri 30*

Old love does not get rusty. (*Russian; Polish*): *Geyvandov 27*

Old love doesn't rust, and new love is strangled by the Devil. (*Czech*): *Geyvandov 27*

Salt consumed long ago makes you thirsty. (*Karelian, RF*): *Geyvandov 27*

Old ice refreezes easily. (*English, UK; Dutch; French*): *Van Dale 1989: 33*

Old loves and old fires flare up easily. (*Danish*): *Brix 209*

The longer you wash mother-of-pearl, the more beautiful it is. (*Mongolian*): *Geyvandov 57*

The love of young people is like a pair of silver buds, but the love of mature people is like golden flowers. (*Japanese*): *Geyvandov 28*

FALLING IN LOVE

There are a thousand miseries in one love. (*Punjabi, India*): *Champion 424*

The usual occupation of the love-struck is silence. (*Kurdish, Turkey*): *Geyvandov 42*

Who falls in love quickly, will separate quickly. (*Amharic, Ethiopia*): *Geyvandov 60*

Quick loving a woman means quick not loving a woman.
  (*Yoruba, Nigeria*): *Finnegan 402; Ibekwe 86; Champion 607*

To fall in love with a woman quickly is to fall out of love with her quickly.
  (*Papiamentu, Aruba*): *Geyvandov 60*

A tree, blown down by the wind, was more leaves than roots. (*Chinese*): *Geyvandov 56*

A fast river does not run as far as the sea; a fast love does not last a century.
  (*Mongolian*): *Geyvandov 57*

Short love brings a long sigh. (*Russian*): *Mieder 1986: 288*

Love affairs pass and the pain remains. (*Spanish, Colombia*): *Ramírez S. 258*

You can suffer without love, but you can't love without suffering. (*German*): *Geyvandov 46*

Heartache cannot be discarded like a nutshell. (*Udmurt, RF*): *Geyvandov 40*

May Inanna [the goddess of love] pour oil on my heart that aches!
  (*Sumerian, Mesopotamia*): *Alster I 101*

If pangs of love were a disease of the legs, many people would limp.
  (*Wolof, Senegal*): *o.s. P.G. N'Diaye*

Love breeds offences. [Being hurt.] (*Korean*): *Geyvandov 44*

Frost hurts the ears, love the heart. (*Bashkir, RF*): *Geyvandov 46*

No worse disease than love. (*Romanian*): *Geyvandov 47*

No herb will cure love. (*Hebrew, Israel*): *Cohen 1961: 314*

Diseases of the heart are healed with a heart-potion. (*Chinese*): *Geyvandov 47*

Both my pain and my cure proceed from my beloved. (*Persian*): *Roebuck 219*

Break my heart and bring me a plaster. (*Maltese*): *Busuttil 32*

He who wants a rose must respect the thorn. (*Persian*): *Elwell-Sutton 34*

A rose can come from a thorn, a thorn can come from a rose.
  (*Arabic, widespread*): *Lundle & Wintle 60*

Without thorns no love. (*Romanian; Slovenian*): *Gruber 20; Mieder 1986: 286*

The roses fall and the thorns remain. (*Italian*): *Bohn 1857: 108*

The one who wants honey has to endure the stings of the bees. (*Arabic*): *Geyvandov 143*

First she kisses, then she stings. (*Indonesian*): *Geyvandov 226*

If you tease a bee, she will sting. (*Vietnamese*): *Geyvandov 144*

A woman is like a bee, she either gives you honey or a sting.
  (*Portuguese, Brazil*): *Souto Maior 56*

If you do not know the hell of bees, you do not understand the sweetness of honey.
  (*Turkish*): *Geyvandov 44*

The more longings, the more disappointments. (*Bengali, India*): *Geyvandov 192*

I really do love you, but I will not drown myself for you. (*Pashto, Afghanistan*): *Geyvandov 244*

Unlike the singing cicadas, the silent fireflies burn themselves. (*Japanese*): *Buchanan 266*

The mortar seeks the pestle. [reversal of the order of things] (*Malay*): *Champion 453*

If a man runs after a woman, he falls into marriage; if a woman runs after a man, she falls into ruin. (*Khiongbta, Bangladesh*): *Lewin 17*

A hen shall not crow. (*Ovambo, Angola / Namibia*): *Geyvandov 185*

The horse cannot sell itself. (*Tiv, Nigeria*): *Geyvandov 191*

A pond is in search of a field. (*Indonesian*): *o.s. Sylvia Schipper*

If the hay follows the horse, it wants to be eaten. (*Dutch*): *Mesters 58; Ter Laan 250*

Going around with the bit in one hand and the saddle in the other.
  (*Spanish, Uruguay*): *Escobar 56*

The eyes are the gates of love. (*German; Russian*): *Meider-Pfaller 38*

The eye beholds, the heart desires. (*Romanian*): *Gruber 16*

Love starts from the eyes. (*Russian; Romanian*): *Mieder 1986: 287; Gruber 16*

Love is born through the eyes. (*Spanish, Mexico*): *Casasola 31*

Eyes meet, hearts fall in love. (*Uzbek*) *Geyvandov 26*

Love at first sight is a bond between four eyes. (*Assam, India*): *Geyvandov 26*

It is the eyes that wound lovers. (*Hebrew*): *Cohen 1961: 172*

That which the eye has not seen, cannot cause a heartache. (*Creole, Guadeloupe*): *Zagaya 31*

Enamoured eyes don't stay unnoticed. (*Duala, Cameroon*): *Geyvandov 42*

If the heart does not tell, the eyes will show. (*Bulgarian*): *Champion 42*

Eyes give away lovers. (*Norwegian*): *Geyvandov 42*

Love sparkles in eyes. (*Digor, RF*): *Geyvandov 42*

Love is like a mosquito; it cannot stay hidden. (*Pashto, Afghanistan*): *Geyvandov 42*

Love is like a hunchback: it cannot be hidden. (*Ladino, Morocco*): *Dahan 250*

Love, anger, and cough betray their owner. (*Portuguese*): *Champion 251*

Poverty and love are hard to hide. (*Danish*): *Cordry 162*

Three things cannot be hidden: love, pregnancy and riding a camel.
  (*Arabic, several variants, many countries*): *Geyvandov 42*

Love, pregnancy and going up a mountain cannot be hidden. (*Arabic, Egypt*): *Khalil Safadi 6*

Lovers keep their secrets badly. (*Russian*): *Geyvandov 270*

Love cannot be locked away. (*Kirghiz*): *Geyvandov 33*

The extreme form of passionate love is secret love. (*Japanese*): *Buchanan 13*

A secret love is always a true love. (*Slovak*): *Mieder 1986: 284*

What you love passionately is like henna on your hand palm. (*Arabic, Maghreb*): *Cheneb III 143*

Passionate love is the origin of a hundred fruits. (*Japanese*): *Buchanan 13*

Divide your passionately burning love over all the days of your life. (*Ladino, Morocco*): *Stahl 240*

A small fire that warms is better than a large one that burns. (*Danish*): *Bohn 1875: 366*

THE LOGIC OF LOVE

Ardent love and cold reason seldom go together. (*Frisian, Netherlands*): *Beintema 83*

When the heart bends, the mind falls. (*Portuguese*): *Geyvandov 49*

Five senses we have, five senses we lose when we fall in love. (*Spanish, Mexico*): *Glazer 278*

Love is no prison, but it does make people's senses disappear. (*Russian*): *Geyvandov 49*

When love enters through the door, the mind jumps out through the window.
  (*German*): *Geyvandov 49*

Love is a friend of blindness. (*Arabic*): *Geyvandov 48*

Love and blindness are twin sisters. (*Russian*): *Mieder1986: 285*

One, who is in love, is blind with open eyes. (*English, UK*): *Geyvandov 48*

An owl is blind in daytime, a crow is blind at night; but lovers are blind in daytime and at
  night. (*Hindi, India*): *Geyvandov 48*

Blinded by love, a husband does not see his wife's wickedness. (*Sanskrit, India*): *Jha 194*

Love is blind: it descends with as much ease on cow manure as it does on a nice girl.
  (*Switzerland*): *Geyvandov 49*

Love is blind and thinks others don't see either. (*Danish*): *Ley 107*

Love is blind, but the neighbours are not.
  (*Spanish, Mexico/Puerto Rico*): *Ballesteros 45; Díaz Rivera 149*

Keep your eyes wide open before marriage, half-shut afterwards.
  (*Hebrew, Israel; English, USA*): *Cohen 1961: 325; Champion 613*

Love blinds the eyes and only regret will open them. (*Sranan, Surinam*): *Hoen 45*

The beloved one has no pimples. (*Nigeria*): *Akporobaro & Emovon 189*

Love turns pimples [also: pockmarks] into dimples. (*Japanese*): *Lunde & Wintle 63*

Love is blind to blemishes and faults. (*Irish*): *O'Rahilly 22*

The foot of a sweetheart makes a trodden track green. (*Italian*): *Geyvandov 48*

When you are in love, even a monkey is beautiful; but when you are not, even a lotus flower is
  ugly. (*Chinese*): *Geyvandov 75*

A wolf is handsome in the eyes of a lovesick girl. (*English, USA*): *Kin 115*

Love does not notice patches on the trousers. (*Creole, Guadeloupe*): *Ludwig 438*

Love extends even to the crow on the roof. (*Japanese*): *Buchanan 11*

Hot lovers don't feel cold. (*Dutch*): *Mesters 162*

Lovers do not notice the rain. (*Malagasy, Madagascar*): *Geyvandov 34*

Two wet swallows under one umbrella. (*Japanese*): *Buchanan 11*

Love turns the sensible stupid, and the shy wild. (*Russian*): *Geyvandov 49*

Love is following your beloved, even when that means walking through twelve thousand
  mountain passes. (*Korean*): *Geyvandov 34*

For the one who is in love, Baghdad is not far. (*Turkish*): *Haig 34*

The road of love does not know distance. (*Sranan, Surinam*): *Hoen 44*

To a lover going to and fro, a thousand *ri* [± 2.5 miles] is but one. (*Japanese*): *Buchanan 12*

Between lovers, there are no barriers. (*Kurdish, Turkey*): *Geyvandov 33*

Not even God is smart enough to catch a woman in love. (*Yoruba, Nigeria*): *o.s. B. Jeyifo*

Women know how to find their lover even when they are locked up in a chest.
  (*German*): *Wander V 1271*

Women's tricks outwit all. (*Widespread in Europe; e.g. Greek; Russian*): *Haller 464; Graf 252*

When a woman cooks up a trick she can outwit a hundred men.
  (*Abkhaz, Georgia*): *Geyvandov 196*

When the she-hedgehog loves a he-hedgehog, she gives herself to him in spite of the quills.
  (*Arabic, Maghreb*): *Cheneb II 155*

Love does not know barriers between higher and lower [ranks]. (*Japanese*): *Geyvandov 34*

Love lies below the border of reason. (*Japanese*) *Geyvandov 49*

A lover's argument is like a shower in spring. (*Arabic*): *Geyvandov 44*

The saw refuses the corn but ventures to nibble. (*Spanish, Mexico*): *Rubio 53*

To say 'I hate you' is to say 'I love you.' (*Japanese*): *Geyvandov 45*

With the one hand she hits you, with the other she hugs you. (*Tamil, India*): *Geyvandov 44*

Woman is like a shadow, follow her and she flees from you, flee from her and she follows you.
　(*In cultures from Africa to Europe and America*): *Mieder 1986: 193; o.s. I. d'Almeida*

The more a girl runs, the harder a boy chases. (*English, USA*): *Mieder 1992: 251*

Dislike a woman and she will love you, love her and she will dislike you.
　(*Ladino, Morocco*): *Dahan 248*

Where there is love there are many anxieties. (*Mongolian*): *Krueger 71*

Jealousy is the soul of love. (*Japanese*): *Geyvandov 59; Huzii 64*

A woman who is not jealous is a ball that does not bounce. (*Japanese*): *Geyvandov 59; Huzii 64*

Love without jealousy is no love. (*Hebrew, Israel*): *Cohen 1961: 273; Gross 9*

The smile in love is like honey; the smile in jealousy is like a thorn in the heart.
　(*Filipino*): *Chua & Nazareno 88*

Jealousy bites deeper than fleas. (*Icelandic*): *Geyvandov 59*

Jealousy will destroy love. (*Spanish, Mexico*): *Ballesteros 11*

Doubt is the beginning of the disease that kills love. (*Burmese*): *Geyvandov 59*

Better to die by blows than from jealousy fade away. Better to love a dog than a thankless
　woman, for a dog is grateful when he is fed. (*English, USA*): *Coffin & Cohen 145*

LOVE IN MARRIAGE

The gloves you put on, you shall wear. The wife you choose, you shall live with.
　(*Latvian*): *Geyvandov 94*

Let your marriage be like the feathers of a bird: they don't leave her till the end of her days.
　(*Malagasy, Madagascar*): *Geyvandov 115*

Perfect marriage is like blossoming flowers and full moon. (*Chinese*): *Yu Jialou 175*

Husband and wife are like tongue and teeth. (*Burmese*): *Myint Thein 32*

Husband and wife are like chopsticks: always together. (*Vietnamese*): *Geyvandov 113*

Husband and wife are tied together like an axe and the handle of the axe.
　(*Ossetian, RF/Georgia*): *Geyvandov 113*

Husband and wife are each other's spade and pickaxe. [They support each other.]
　(*Kurdish, Turkey*): *Geyvandov 120*

What the yam feels, the knife understands. [The knife is the closest to the yam; the husband,
　the closest to his wife.] (*Yoruba, Nigeria*): *Lindfors & Owomoyela 12*

Loving spouses say a thousand things to each other, without saying a word.
　(*Chinese*): *Geyvandov 42*

Such harmony that not even water can come between them. (*Lithuanian*): *Geyvandov 140*

If the bullock and the cart keep together, what does it matter how many ups and downs
　there are? (*Tamil, India*): *Champion 430*

Love your husband like a friend, fear him like an enemy. (*Catalan, Spain; French*): *Guiter 19*

Do not try to come between the tree and its bark. (*Arabic*): Geyvandov 144

Do not even put a pin between a husband and a wife. (*Spanish, Panama*): Aguilera 119

Do not put a spoon between a husband and a wife. (*Portuguese, Brazil*): Mota 93

Where there is much love, there are few freedoms. (*Spanish*): Champion 304; Geyvandov 40

Obligation suffocates love. (*Uzbek*): Geyvandov 39

Love is a magnificent garden, but the field of marriage is covered with stinging nettles.
  (*Finnish*): Geyvandov 65; Ley 167

Desire of two young lovers, and regret of husband and wife.
  (*Urdu, Pakistan/India*): Geyvandov 115

Happiness is like palm-wine: if you mix it with too much water, it loses its taste.
  (*Akan, Ghana*): Geyvandov 259

Marriage is a battlefield and not a bed of roses. (*Hebrew, Israel*): Cohen 1961: 327

Marriage is the tomb of love. (*Russian*): Mieder 1986: 313

Love leads you to a wonder, money to a marriage. (*French*): Geyvandov 98

You do not long for the one they married you off to, but for the one you love.
  (*Kirghiz*): Geyvandov 39

The bride in her silliness and inexperience calls marriage 'love.' (*Ganda, Uganda*): Walser 439

Wedlock is not 'love me'. [Many see their mistake soon.] (*Kundu, Cameroon*): Ittmann 34

Whoever marries for love, must live in sorrow. (*Spanish, Chile*): o.s. Elba Sáa

Love provides wings, but wings of wax melt with the torch of marriage. (*Russian*): Rauch 141

He that marries for love, dies miserably of anger. (*Italian*): Meier-Pfaller 57

He that marries for love has good nights but sorry days.
  (*English, UK; French; Spanish; Italian*): Reinsberg-Düringsfeld 365

They call you the newly wed one, do not be sad. (*Arabic, Syria/Lebanon*): Fenghali 313

A marriage without love, raining when the sun shines. (*Spanish, Cuba*): Feijóo 17

A marriage without love is like a garden without flowers, a shirt without sleeves or a bull
  without cover. (*Kurdish, Turkey*): Geyvandov 137

Love comes after marriage. (*Icelandic; Inuktitut, Canada*): Geyvandov 65

Who marries without love, lives in distress. (*Portuguese*): Geyvandov 137

Marriage without love is a vexation. (*Estonian*): Geyvandov 137

Sauce makes the couscous, love makes the marriage. (*Berber, Morocco*): Bentolila 79

Love ends at the altar. (*Estonian*): Geyvandov 65

Before the wedding, you say, 'my love', and afterwards you sigh, 'If I had known.'
  (*Creole, Martinique/Dominican Republic*): David 44; ACCT 102

The first night of the marriage is sometimes the last of love. (*Dutch*): Mesters: 34

The woman who marries the man who loves her will do better than the woman who marries
  the man she loves. (*Arabic, widespread*): Lunde & Wintle 85

A wise woman will marry the man who loves her, rather than the one she loves.
  (*Slovenian; Serbian/Croatian*): Mieder 1986: 539; Geyvandov 36

When you love, you are a slave; when you are loved, you are the boss. (*Polish*): Geyvandov 36

Better to be waited-for than to wait. (*Japanese*): Huzii 64

To marry for love is risky, but God smiles at it. (*German*): Meier-Pfaller 52

God brings to all wheat its measurer. (*Arabic, Morocco*): Westermarck 71

The wooden shoe should know the wooden shoe and the boot should know the boot.

(*Russian*): *Geyvandov 61*

If you take a wife, take boot to boot, birch-bark sandal to birch-bark sandal, leather sandal to
leather sandal. (*Estonian*): *Paczolay 179*

Love between unequal people is suspect. (*Spanish, Puerto Rico*): *Fernández Valledor 35*

A bird cannot fly on one wing. (*Kundu, Cameroon*): *Geyvandov 106*

Everyone should marry his equal. (*Arabic/Jewish, Iraq*): *Stahl 417*

He who wants to marry, let him look for a woman who is his equal.

(*Serbian*): *Reinsberg-Düringsfeld 116*

Butter with butter is no sauce. (*Scottish, UK*): *Geyvandov 61*

Bread and cheese is very well, but cheese and cheese is no sense. (*English, UK*): *Williams I 476*

Fine looking and a lesbian, like an itchy bitch in a straw hut.

(*Arabic, Morocco*): *Westermarck 151*

An unmarried man is Satan's brother. (*Arabic, Tunisia*) *Lunde & Wintle* 11

'Oh my troublesome fellow!' said the woman who mourned for a homosexual.

(*Oromo, Ethiopia*): *Cotter 41*

LOVE AND OTHER MEN'S WIVES

Don't place your spoon where your bowl is not. (*Abkhaz, Georgia*): *Geyvandov 213*

A man is allowed to have more than one woman, a good wife has only one man.

(*Vietnamese*): *o.s. Lam Ngo*

Woman is a gazelle skin on which only one man can sit. (*Taka, Congo*): *Beken 1993: 203*

Married women are like elephant tusks: don't touch them.

(*Swahili, East Africa*): *Geyvandov 213; o.s. Anonymous*

Another man's wife is like the mongoose skin: only one person can sit on it.

(*Luba, Congo DR*): *o.s. Clémentine Faïk-Nzuji*

One doesn't taste another man's wife. (*Bassar, Togo*): *Szwark 60*

Do not lure another man's hen. (*Songye, Congo DR*): *o.s. Clémentine Faïk-Nzuji*

One should close one's mouth to someone else's apple. (*Karakalpak, RF*): *Geyvandov 213*

In someone else's millet, don't put your horns. (*Russian*): *Geyvandov 288*

Don't place your foot in someone else's shoe. (*Karachay-Balkar, RF*): *Geyvandov 213*

Do not look at someone else's dish. (*Spanish, El Salvador*): *Sánchez Duarte 178*

Do not hibernate on an open spot; do not love another man's wife. (*Mongolian*): *Geyvandov 213*

Better catch a serpent and suck its poison than to have dealings with another man's wife.

(*Urdu, India*): *Champion 409*

The tastiest dish comes from somebody else's home. (*Spanish, Mexico*): *Casasola 30*

The forbidden fruit always tastes sweeter. (*Spanish, Chile*): *o.s. Frano*

Another man's hen is a goose; another man's wife a beauty. (*Turkish*): *Geyvandov 206*

Another man's wife is always the prettiest. (*Hebrew, Israel*): *Cohen 1961: 374*

To kiss your own wife is like chewing cotton wool. (*Persian*) *Geyvandov* 211

Men love their own compositions and other men's wives. (*Chinese*): *Champion 383*

A horse is fun if it's your own, a wife if she's someone else's.

(*Awar/Chechen, RF*): *Geyvandov 211*

One favours somebody else's wife, but one's own son. (*Russian*): *Rauch 149*

A knife cutting through water will leave no trace. (*Creole, Martinique*): *David 50*

He who makes love to a married woman is killed on her doorstep. (*Egyptian*): *Ibekwe 168*

He who loves somebody else's wife always looks pale, not because of the love he feels but from fear of the husband. (*Spanish, Mexico*): *Casasola 42*

He who loves prickly pears must not fear thorns, and he who loves a married woman must not fear death. (*Maltese*): *Lunde & Wintle 32*

Preheat the oven for somebody else to bake his bread.
   (*Spanish, Bolivia/Costa Rica*): *Barneville Vásquez 20*

Some dress up the altar for others to celebrate mass. (*Spanish, Colombia*): *Acuña 122*

To hang a swing for somebody else to swing on. (*Spanish, Mexico*): *Rubio 101*

I heat up the water and somebody else drinks the *mate* [a hot drink made out of herbs].(*Guaraní, Argentina*): *Moya 196*

Can anyone walk on glowing coals without burning his feet?
   (*Hebrew, Israel*): *Malka 32; Proverbs 6: 28–9*

A woman is like a cluster of palm nuts: if it falls it grows leaves.
   (*Baule, Ivory Coast*): *Arbelbide 86*

True love does not fear infidelity. (*Hungarian*): *Geyvandov 57*

BITTER WORRIES AND SWEET WORDS

The tongue is the translator of the heart. (*Arabic*): *Geyvandov 237*

One who loves intensely, has intense fears. (*Spanish*): *Geyvandov 63*

Fear drives off love. (*Russian*): *Geyvandov 63*

Fear and love are not compatible. (*Lithuanian*): *Geyvandov 63*

Where there is fear there is no love. (*Romanian*): *Geyvandov 63*

Love is a sea: who cannot swim in it, drowns. (*Turkish*): *Geyvandov 34*

Love is bottomless. (*Udmurt, RF*): *Geyvandov 245*

Love is a dark pit. (*Hungarian*): *Mieder 1986: 286*

Love is like a nettle that stings badly. (*Russian*): *Geyvandov 46*

Violent love, violent anger. (*Burmese*): *Myint Thein 67*

Love is like soup, the first mouthful is very hot, and the ones that follow become gradually colder. (*Spanish*): *Champion 304; Geyvandov 26*

Love is like seaweed: pushing it away will not prevent it from coming back.
   (*Fulfulde, Nigeria*): *Akporobaro & Emovon 177*

Love is like seaweed: you go to her, she leaves you, you leave her, she follows you.
   (*Malagasy, Madagascar*): *Geyvandov 34*

Love is like a farm: every day the tasks have to start anew. (*Dutch*): *o.s. A. Idema*

Love is like oatmeal porridge, you have to prepare it every day. (*Irish*): *Geyvandov 34*

Love is like a baby, you have to treat it tenderly. (*Afrikaans, South Africa*): *Geyvandov 54*

Love is like silk: it can be wrapped around the dead and clothe the living.
   (*Malagasy, Madagascar*): *Geyvandov 49*

Love is like the sun to flowers: to the strong she gives strength, the weak she dries up.
   (*Irish*): *Geyvandov 46*

Faithful love will not burn in fire nor drown in water. (*Russian*): *Geyvandov 58*

Love of women is like morning dew, the wind blows, and it's gone. (*Russian*): *Geyvandov 55*

A female heart is as unstable as water rolling on a lotus leaf. (*Thai*): *Champion 472*

A new love will let you forget the old ones. (*Spanish, Mexico*): *Glazer 14*

New loves make us forget old ones. (*Spanish*): *Haller 618*

New saints make us forget the old ones. (*Danish*): *Haller 618*

New dishes give satisfaction; old dishes are given to the fire. (*Latin; German*): *Haller 618*

Love and eggs should be fresh to be enjoyed. (*Russian*): *Mieder 1986: 285*

A change of saddle yields pleasure. (*Arabic, Maghreb*): *Cheneb I 153*

Not a handful but a land full. (*Dutch*): *o.s. A. Broere*

Kiss a mouth and you'll forget the other mouth. (*Ladino / Hebrew, Morocco*): *Dahan 262*

Women are like buses, if one leaves another one will come. (*Spanish, Venezuela*): *Febres Cordero 43*

Women are like shoes, they can always be replaced. (*Rajasthani, India*): *Bhatnagar 67*

Women are like the bullets of a revolver, one comes out the barrel and another one is ready in the cylinder. (*Portuguese, Brazil*): *Souto Maior 71*

Women are like frogs, for every one that dives into the water there are four to come up to the surface. (*Spanish, Peru*): *Arora 165*

Many are the flowers which bloom in the garden, but one flower alone maddens my heart with love. (*Malay*): *MBRAS 29*

To lovers, even water tastes sweet. (*Chinese*): *Geyvandov 43*

When two loving hearts are united, they take a hayloft for a feather bed.
    (*Turkish*): *Geyvandov 51*

With you: bread and onions. (*Spanish, Bolivia*): *Paredes-Candia 59*

With a sweetheart you can have paradise in a hut. (*Russian*): *Krylov 113*

Harmony makes space and love widens the blanket. (*Scandinavian*): *Kuusi 335*

Rather a meal of cabbage when you love each other than a fattened calf when you hate each other. (*Hebrew, Israel*): *Malka 97; OT, Proverbs 16 : 17*

Better a piece of bread in happiness than a gold bar in sorrow. (*Finnish*): *Geyvandov 99*

When poverty enters through the door, love jumps out through the window.
    (*English, UK; German; Danish; Dutch*): *Geyvandov 51*

Of mere love a chimney does not smoke. (*German*): *Meier-Pfaller 41*

Love is a fire: without food it will extinguish. (*Russian*): *Geyvandov 41*

Eating is preferable to amorousness. (*Japanese*): *Buchanan 12*

Love cannot exist without bread and salt. (*Polish*): *Geyvandov 50*

Love can do much, money everything. (*French*): *Champion 148*

If you supply food, fancy presents and love, women remain tame. (*Hindi*): *o.s. Shobha Gupta*

Deposit the money and the wife will arrive. (*Arabic, Maghreb*): *Cheneb I 210*

In both war and love, gold is the winner. (*Spanish, Venezuela*): *Febres Cordero 56*

Poetry softens the relationship between men and women. (*Japanese*): *Buchanan 14*

With sweet words you can break stones. (*Russian*): *Geyvandov 230*

With sweet words you can milk a mountain goat. (*Georgian*): *Geyvandov 230*

All girls lap up sweet words. (*Yiddish*): *Rosten 1970: 217*

Pleasant words are the hunters of men's hearts. (*Persian*): *Roebuck 267*

From the union of heart and tongue love is born. (*Pashto, Afghanistan*): *Geyvandov 61*

Two hearts united will break down a mountain. (*Persian*): *Roebuck 26*

Two hearts can put one mountain on top of another. (*Kurdish*): *Anonymous*

The united couple can make gold out of earth. (*Chinese*): *o.s. Huang Mingfen*

Befriended spouses can pump all the water from the Pacific Ocean. (*Vietnamese*): *Geyvandov 140*

Music is the key to the female heart. (*English, USA*): *Kin 171*

Love teaches music even if you are unaware of it. (*German*): *Haller 201*

A heart without love is a garden without flowers. (*Japanese*): *Geyvandov 43*

The merit of the rose is known to the nightingale. (*Turkish*): *Haig 105*

The gratification of my beloved is dear to me, and the leaf of the rose is very delicate.
  (*Persian*): *Roebuck 196*

Without you, the flowers won't flower, the oaks won't grow so beautifully in the oak garden.
  (*Russian*): *Geyvandov 53*

Love me the way cotton is made: give the thin parts a little extra and connect the broken
  threads. (*Malagasy, Madagascar*): *Geyvandov 57*

Love lifts the coat and the shirt. (*Danish*): *Kjaer Holbek 102*

It's heaven on earth to make love while in love. (*Dutch*): *Mesters 66*

SEX

The pan said: 'My bottom is [made] of gold', and the dipper answered: 'I've just been there.'
  (*Akkadian*): *o.s. Geyvandov 242*

PRIVATE PARTS

The penis does not know what the vagina thinks. (*Igbo, Nigeria*): *Ibekwe 43*

It is the woman's private parts that are shown to the husband. (*Igbo, Nigeria*): *Penfield 113*

Even when the bird's sex is small, he will show it to his wife.
  (*Mossi, Burkina Faso*): *o.s. A. Sawadogo*

Better a short penis than sleeping alone [as a woman]. (*Baule, Ivory Coast*): *Arbelbide 126*

Even if the penis is short, it can cover a woman's sex as well as a Fulfulde hat [can cover a
  man's head]. (*Minyanka, Mali*): *Cauvin 1980: 525*

She who has undressed should not fear a long penis. (*Ganda, Uganda*): *Ibekwe 33*

The wife who hides her private parts will never have children.
  (*Swahili, Tanzania/Zanzibar*): *o.s. Marieke van Twillert*

Sitting on her heel, a woman closes the entrance to numerous offspring.
  (*Rwanda*): *Crépeau 477*

A woman is like a flower: it sprouts only if you water it. (*Guaraní, Argentina*): *Moya 196*

He who is too shy to live in matrimony with his wife will not get children.
  (*Arabic, Syria/Lebanon*): *Feghali 181*

The pregnant woman is not afraid of her husband's penis. (*Ovambo, Namibia*): *Ibekwe 58*

The mother of twins does not fear a huge penis. (*Baule, Ivory Coast*): *Arbelbide 128*

A large penis is like an inheritance for a girl; a large vagina is like beating wheat in a famine.
  (*Tibetan*): *Duncan 218*

A woman with the genitals of a large octopus is stronger than God and even stronger than
the Devil. (*Creole, Guadeloupe*): *Ludwig 426*

What affects the penis affects the vagina. (*Igbo, Nigeria*): *Ibekwe 63*

You only know if something is long or short after you have tried it on.
(*Korean*): *Geyvandov 274*

A man is like pepper: only when you have tasted it, do you know how hot it is.
(*Hausa, Niger/Nigeria*): *Geyvandov 244*

Even a bent sugar spoon will taste sweet. (*Telegu, India*): *Geyvandov 74*

If you cure someone of his impotence, it's your wife that he'll rape.
(*Mossi, Burkina Faso*): *o.s. A. Sawadogo*

You cured his testicles and he used them on your wife. (*Ganda, Uganda*): *Ibekwe 100*

Whenever you cure your enemy's penis, he'll use it to impregnate your wife.
(*Mamprusi, Burkina Faso*): *Plissart 422*

He gets his passage for nothing, and winks at the wife of the captain.
(*Arabic, Egypt*): *Burckhardt 264*

The desiring vagina dies by making a bed for herself on the road. (*Rwanda*): *Crépeau 223*

Has an unfaithful penis ever done damage to an unfaithful vulva?
(*Sumerian, Mesopotamia*): *Gordon 125; Alster I 32*

DESIRE

Desire calls, modesty halts. (*Telegu, India*): *Geyvandov 191*

Who knows the limits of desire? (*Sanskrit, India*): *Geyvandov 191*

Desire has no limit. (*Chinese*): *Geyvandov 192*

Desire is the door that leads to problems. (*Hausa, Niger/Nigeria*): *Geyvandov 192*

Lecherous men are only conquered by lecherous women, and lecherous women are only
conquered by the grave. (*Arabic, widespread*): *Lunde & Wintle 83*

Woman and money tempt even Brahma the creator. (*Telegu, India*): *Murty 228*

In stormy weather, every hole seems like a harbour. (*Spanish, Mexico*): *Casasola 50*

Woman and soup taste the whole year. (*Catalan, Spain; French*): *Guiter 45*

The red fruit of the palm by day and the pleasure of women by night.
(*Maori, New Zealand*): *Geyvandov 256*

A penis does not have shoulders. (*Creole, Guadeloupe*): *Ludwig 435*

The woman too eager to make the bed will not notice that she does not please.
(*Rwanda*): *Crépeau 195*

When the husband has a lover, one stake in the barn burns. When the wife has an affair, all
the buildings burn. (*Komi, RF*): *Geyvandov 136*

If a man is unfaithful to his wife, it is like spitting from a house into the street, but if a
woman is unfaithful to her husband, it is like spitting from the street into the house.
(*Chinese*): *Lunde & Wintle 103*; (*English, USA*): *Kin 265*

If a man sins it is like spitting out of the window, if a woman sins it is like spitting in
through the window. (*Estonian*): *Geyvandov 136*

The husband's sin is left before the threshold; his wife brings everything into the house.
(*Russian*): *Geyvandov 194*

It is better to be content with a bad husband than to wish for the good husband of someone
  else. (*Oromo, Ethiopia*): *Cotter 20*

If the wife is unfaithful, even though she has a child, divorce her, don't love her.
  (*Arabic, Morocco*): *Westermarck 78*

A wife who loves two: may the Devil take her away. (*Spanish, Colombia*): *Acuña 48*

Books, wife, wealth when taken by others are lost. (*Sanskrit, India*): *Jha 182*

When the nanny-goat is in the garden, the billy-goat will look over the fence.
  (*Russian*): *Geyvandov 190*

There where the fence is low, the cow will climb over.
  (*Creole, Marie-Galante*): *Barbotin 39*

She covers herself like eggs in a basket. (*Berber, Morocco*): *Bentolila 35*

The fickle husband mistrusts his wife's faithfulness, the thief fears to have his house robbed.
  (*Arabic, Morocco*): *Messaoudi 112*

If the cow were honest, the bull wouldn't have horns.
  (*Spanish, Argentina/Bolivia*): *Moya 621; Paredes-Candia 212*

When the husband is away, the wife will play. (*English, USA*): *Mieder 1989: 93*

Palm-wine is not kept in a transparent bottle. [A wife is unreliable.]
  (*Krio, Sierra Leone*): *Geyvandov 273*

A horse, a wife and a sword, these three are unfaithful. (*Kashmiri, India*): *Champion 418*

Who ever saw a horse, a woman, or a sword faithful? (*Persian*): *Roebuck 5*

Never trust a horse or a woman. (*Turkish*): *Haig 36*

There is no worse adultery than that of the woman who, while making love to her husband,
  thinks of another man. (*Hebrew, Israel*): *Rosten 1977: 84*

A book and a woman when taken by another man are lost forever.
  (*Sinhalese, Sri Lanka*): *o.s. Alex Gunasekare*

Any piece of rug with an opening for your head, can serve as a poncho.
  (*Spanish, Mexico*): *Casasola 23*

The thief is not to be blamed if he finds the gate open. (*Spanish, Colombia*): *Ramírez S. 207*

The man who sees a saddled horse, will often decide he needs to take a ride.
  (*Spanish, Mexico*): *Ballesteros 65*

No one will ever miss a slice on a loaf that has already been cut.
  (*English, Jamaica*): *Llewellyn Watson 207*

Once the ears have been pierced, any earring can go in. (*Creole, Guadeloupe*): *Ludwig 471*

A girl and sugarcane should not be passed by. (*Oromo, Ethiopia*): *Cotter 6*

Put the light out, all women are alike. (*Arabic, Tunisia*): *Tetiv 131*

Switch the light off, and all women are equal. (*German*): *Meier-Pfaller 60*

All women look the same after the sun goes down. (*English, USA*)

At night all women are equal. (*Italian*): *Raimondi 51*

Under the sheets the black one is as good as the white one. (*Spanish*): *Wander I 350*

After the light has been turned off, we are all the same colour.
  (*Spanish, Dominican Republic*): *Rodríguez D. 288*

In the dark, the queen is worth as much as the black cook.
  (*Portuguese, Brazil*): *Magalhães Júnior 205*

A wife is not like a bedcover. [One cannot simply change her after a while.]
(*Creole, Haiti*): *ACCT 42*

A wife is not a shirt you can change according to your needs. (*Ladino, Morocco*): *Stahl 248*

A woman is not cassava to be valued by roasting and tasting. (*Baule, Ivory Coast*): *Arbelbide 85*

A woman is not a boot, you cannot kick her off. (*Russian*): *o.s. Anna Ravve*

A woman is not a *goesli* [stringed instrument], having played you cannot hang it on the wall.
(*Russian*): *o.s. Anna Ravve*

A woman is not a fiddle you hang on the wall after playing.
(*German; Finnish*): *Kuusi 361; Champion 186*

A wife is not a *kantele* [string instrument] to hang on the wall. (*Finnish*): *Kuusi 70*

Abstinence is the best medicine. (*Tamil, India*): *Champion 429*

A man always desiring women destroys his body; a man always desiring possessions destroys
his life. (*Mongolian*): *Geyvandov 60*

Piety lies between earrings and cheeks, not on top of the mountains.
(*Arabic, Maghreb*): *Cheneb II 81*

Beautiful women are charming like fairies. (*Arabic, Maghreb*): *Cheneb II 81*

Who resisted seduction, does not have to blush. (*Chechen, RF*): *Geyvandov 191*

The great praise of a wise woman is self-control in her manner of life. (*Egyptian*): *Ibekwe 169*

Everything is settled underneath the blankets. (*Spanish, Costa Rica*): *Hernández 59*

I told her: 'I divorce you!' She said: 'Come to bed!' (*Arabic, Iraq*): *Lunde & Wintle 86*

Quarrels between spouses and wind from the west stop when the night falls.
(*Japanese*): *Geyvandov 143*

Unless you want to sleep alone do not curse your wife after sundown.
(*Chinese*): *Lunde & Wintle 338*

During daytime they fight, but at night they sleep together. (*Indonesian*): *Geyvandov 146*

Husband and wife call one another names but they lie under one fur coat.
(*Russian*): *Geyvandov 146*

Two who hate each other in daytime love each other at night. (*Estonian*): *Geyvandov 46*

Better the blows of a sledgehammer than a wife's complaints in bed.
(*Arabic, Lebanon*): *Lunde & Wintle 87*

During the day she is my dustbin, during the night she is my beauty.
(*Arabic, Algeria*): *Belamri 34*

If a husband and his wife go to bed after they have had an argument, the blankets will make
peace between them. (*Kurdish, Turkey*): *Stahl 240*

The promises of the night, made of butter, melt when the first sunrays appear.
(*Arabic*): *Geyvandov 230*

The words of the night are covered with butter; in the morning, they melt away.
(*Arabic, Tunisia*): *Yetiv 60*

PLEASURE

Woman and horse want a worthy rider. (*Greek*): *Politès 8*

A kiss does not come under your shirt. (*Russian*): *Geyvandov 32*

The more they play, the more the dogs get entangled. (*Spanish, Panama*): *Aguilera 280*

Love pushes the branches from each other, joy lifts the clothes. (*Estonian*): *Geyvandov 33*

If a woman is cold, it's her husband's fault. (*Russian*): *Mieder 1986: 8*

Her beauty increases when her neck is caressed. (*Nenets, RF*): *Geyvandov 75*

Stroke a cow before you milk her. (*Hausa, Niger/Nigeria*): *Geyvandov 289*

A woman is like the legs of a hide; if you don't rub them, they won't be yielding.
   (*Ganda, Uganda*): *Walser 372*

A woman is like a bottle of medicine: shake before use.
   (*Portuguese, Brazil*): *Souto Maior 56*

With a hammock as with women: sideways and patiently. (*Spanish, Colombia*): *Ramírez S. 16*

A woman and a guitar are tuned before using them. (*Spanish, Puerto Rico*): *Díaz Rivera 69*

Fire and women burn when you put them into motion. (*Korean*): *Geyvandov 268*

You mustn't rush a lady. (*English, USA*): *Mieder 1992: 359*

The eggplant is eaten slowly. (*Arabic, Morocco*): *Westermarck 76*

Woman must sing and man must accompany her. (*Chinese*): *Geyvandov 61*

If you carve a harp-lute, you must know how to play it.
   (*Ngbaka, Central African Republic*): *Thomas 760*

A woman is like a guitar, as soon as you play her, she sounds. (*Spanish, Mexico*): *Arora 5*

One should know how to tune a woman and a guitar. (*Spanish*): *Meier-Pfaller 61*

The older the violin, the sweeter the music. (*Creole, Belize*): *Ibekwe 119*

At first she acts coyly, later enjoys. (*Turkish*): *Haig 93*

At first shy as a maiden, at last swift as an escaping hare. [First go cautiously, but finally
   boldly.] (*Japanese*): *Buchanan 38; o.s. Keiko Kosunose*

In lovemaking a mature woman is best. (*Japanese*): *Geyvandov 28*

Always marry an older woman; you and you'll benefit from her experience.
   (*Indonesian*): *o.s. Tineke Hellwig*

Old ovens are soon heated. (*English, UK*): *Champion 36*

A new sleeping mat is no pleasure to sleep on. (*Swahili, East Africa*): *Scheven 486*

Fresh young coconut tastes better than the ripe one. (*Filipino*): *Chua & Nazareno 26*

Don't undress, it's still a long way to go to the river. (*Romanian*): *Geyvandov 289*

Do not lift your skirts before you need to wade. (*Adyg, RF*): *Geyvandov 289*

Keep God before you and the trousers closed. (*Dutch*): *o.s. Wibo Westerhof*

If you do not lift the bride's dress, you will not know what is underneath.
   (*Creole, Martinique*): *David 43–4*

More to be feared than a tiger is the scarlet silk-crêpe. [In Japan, scarlet silk-crêpe is used for
   women's undergarments.] (*Japanese*): *Buchanan 269*

Dress to meet your in-laws; undress to meet your husband. (*Chinese*): *Lunde & Wintle 140*

If you feel her thigh, don't fear her sex. (*Mandinka, West Africa*): *Meyer 67*

Do not despise a woman you have not undressed. (*Bemba, Zambia*): *o.s. Marieke van Twillert*

One has to undress the sweetcorn to judge its quality. (*Creole, Guadeloupe*): *Zagaya 233*

A woman is not a corncob to be valued by stripping off its leaves.
   (*Baule, Ivory Coast*): *Arbelbide 85*

Nobody undresses a girl in order to sit beside her and look into her eyes.
   (*Papiamentu, Aruba; Yoruba, Nigeria*): *Geyvandov 263*

The one who dresses a woman is allowed to undress her.

  (*Frisian, Netherlands*): *o.s. Anne van de Zande*

The head thinks of the man, the eyes think of the he-goat. (*Estonian*): *Geyvandov 186*

The one who mounts, commands.

  (*Spanish, Bolivia/Uruguay*): *Barneville Vásquez 31; Escobar 65; Paredes-Candia 93*

A husband is like a rider on his horse. (*Ladino, Morocco*): *Dahan 187*

The horse depends on the rider, the woman depends on the man.

  (*Arabic, Maghreb*): *Cheneb II 130*

Whatever the size of the woman, it's the man who mounts her. (*Ikwere, Nigeria*): *o.s. Sylvester Osu*

A horse rears according to its rider. (*Turkish*): *Haig 35*

THE FIRST TIME AND NEXT

The penis comes erect as if it intends to kill, but the vagina swallows and tames it.

  (*Igbo*): *o.s. Chika N. Unigwe*

A rose untimely opened, will soon fade. (*Turkish*): *Haig 90*

Do not praise the bride after the first night and do not praise the shepherd after his first year.

  (*Hebrew, Iraq*): *Stahl 415*

Do not praise the girl before the morning, do not praise the day before the evening.

  (*Lithuanian*): *Schleicher 171*

With a girl the way you want, with a widow the way she wants. (*Polish*): *Rauch 127*

It is hard to teach unwilling brides how to dance. (*Dutch*): *Mesters 740*

There's no end either to a virgin's resistance or to a wife's resentment. (*Chinese*): *Wintle 86*

A grown-up girl is not afraid of her groom. (*Basque, Spain*): *Geyvandov 109*

Endure, young bride, it's a man. (*Bulgarian*): *Arnaudov 70*

Be quiet and lie down at his side. (*Oromo, Ethiopia*): *Cotter 195*

The mortar is under the bride and still she keeps quiet. (*Berber, Morocco*): *Bentolila 32*

The bride is ashamed to eat, but nonetheless swallows the banana whole.

  (*Bengali, India*): *Geyvandov 254*

He who would eat the kernel, must crack the shell.

  (*English, UK; Polish*): *Bohn 1857: 377; Mieder 1986: 351*

May God have mercy on the husband; as for the wife, she knows what awaits her.

  (*Berber, Morocco*): *Bentolila 81*

Before the time great courage; when at the point, great fear.

  (*English, UK; Spanish*): *Bohn 1855: 200*

The rat will die, and the hole will not be satisfied. (*Arabic, Tunisia*): *Yetiv 75*

Women, land and belly are insatiable. (*Jewish/Arabic, Yemen*): *Alcalay 240*

Water, fire and women will never say 'enough'. (*Polish*): *Rauch 126*

The man as long as he can, the woman as long as she wants to.

  (*Spanish, Bolivia*): *Paredes-Candia 90*

Women's appetite is twice that of a man, their intelligence four times, and their desire eight

  times. (*Burmese*): *Wintle 8*

Women are violent, they even overthrow a man's penis. (*Mapuche, Chile*): *Guevara 54*

Woman is fire bearing fire (*Hebrew, Israel*): *Alcalay 548*

Woman is a fire; if you have to, take a little.

   (*Fulfulde, West Africa*): *Champion 526; Gaden 16; Geyvandov 223*

Woman is like a corncob: if you have no teeth, you hardly eat.

   (*Fang, Cameroon/Gabon*): *o.s. S. Eno-Belinga*

When an old man takes a young wife, he lives in an oasis and she lives in a desert.

   (*Hebrew, Israel*): *Geyvandov 138*

An old man who marries a younger woman will end up finding her with a younger man.

   (*Ladino, Morocco*): *Dahan 312*

An old man is a cold bedfellow. (*English, UK*): *Williams I 467*

Woman is to an old man like a book to an illiterate. (*Russian*): *Geyvandov 138*

To a woman an old man is like a hedgehog to a dog. (*Polish*): *Geyvandov 29*

Lovemaking and baking do not always succeed. (*German*): *Wander I 1149*

The husband mated and surprised his wife. (*Russian*): *Geyvandov 252*

All women kiss their men in their own way. (*Sranan, Surinam*): *o.s. Mavis Noordwijk*

Every man kisses a woman in his own way. (*Papiamentu, Netherlands Antilles*): *Maduro 131*

Everyone caresses his bride in his own way. (*Dutch*): *Harrebomée I 100*

All fingers are different. (*Hebrew, Israel*): *Malka 31*

Do not cook in your neighbour's saucepan. (*Hebrew, Israel*): *Malka 19*

Don't eat a bitten pea, don't take a deflowered woman as a wife. (*Bulgarian*): *Geyvandov 100*

A woman without character flees one penis for another. (*Lega, Congo DR*): *o.s. Malasi*

She left the lyre in the willow and went on to play the lute. (*Arabic*): *Safadi 17*

Lost is the girl who plays with men before her marriage. (*Oromo, Ethiopia*): *Cotter 84*

Why take care of the stalk if the ear has already been lost? (*Spanish, Mexico*): *Rubio 119*

A woman who has not been married several times cannot know what perfect marriage is.

   (*Yoruba, Nigeria*): *o.s. Biodun Jeyifo*

Who has never changed turban has never seen sweetness. (*Arabic, Magrheb*): *Cheneb III 97*

For the chaste woman God suffices.

   (*Spanish, El Salvador/Argentina*): *Sánchez Duarte 4; Moya 305*

For the chaste woman her husband suffices. (*Spanish, Colombia*): *Acuña 46*

He who does not have anything better, sleeps with his wife.

   (*Spanish, Puerto Rico/Cuba/Chile; Portuguese, Brazil*): *Díaz Rivera 39; Sabiduría Guajira 36;*
   Lamenza 220; Cannobio 80

No pilgrimage is complete without a visit to the girls. (*Japanese*): *Lunde & Wintle 41*

The son that runs away retains some value, but a runaway daughter becomes completely

   worthless. (*Chinese*): *Lunde & Wintle 81*

The daughter of shame is bought with a price; the son of shame is cuddled on the lap.

   (*Tibetan*): *Duncan 219*

Saying 'no', a woman shakes her head lengthwise.

   (*Japanese*): *Huzii 90; Buchanan 265; Wintle 120*

When a woman's lips say 'It is enough', she looks at you and her eyes say 'Again'.

   (*Chinese*): *Champion 284*

When a woman says no, she often means yes. (*Swedish*): *Ström 161*

The 'no' of a girl is the 'yes' of a boy. (*Danish*): *Molbech 171*

A woman's nay is a double yea, they say. (*English, UK*): *Williams III 409*

When a lady says no, she means perhaps; when she says perhaps, she means yes; when she says yes, she is no lady. (*English, USA*): *Mieder 1992: 358*

HEAVENLY DELIGHT

Let nothing on earth make you sad as long as you can make love. (*Hungarian*): *Rauch 180*

Nothing is so pleasant to one's physical well-being as having a wife. (*Sanskrit, India*): *Jha 214*

Bed, wine and woman comfort the body. (*German*): *Meier-Pfaller 661*

If a woman loves a man she will give it to him even through a hole in the door.
   (*Arabic, Morocco*): *Lunde & Wintle 84*

The blushes on a woman's cheeks are caused by her husband.
   (*Kurdish, Turkey*): *Geyvandov 123*

Where the heart was in the night the legs wake up in the morning.
   (*Haya, Uganda / Tanzania*): *Geyvandov 205*

The wife who has spent the night with her husband shows it in the way they greet.
   (*Minyanka, Mali*): *Cauvin 1980: 221*

Even your own wife is better in another barn. (*Finnish*): *Kuusi 66*

It's most convenient to make love under one's own roof.
   (*Dutch*): *Harrebomée I 228; Reinsberg-Düringsfeld 251*

When husband and wife give pleasure to each other, the little angels in heaven laugh.
   (*Dutch*): *Mesters 107*

A married girl is like water that has been spat out: no one will drink it again.
   (*Chinese*): *Fabre 28*

The fox was beautiful before it got killed; the bride was beautiful before she got married.
   (*Mongolian*): *Geyvandov 81*

FERTILITY, PREGNANCY, CHILDBIRTH

She who leaves a child behind lives eternally. (*Chagga, East Africa*): *Ibekwe 24*

The gem of the house is the child. (*Sinhalese, Sri Lanka*): *Champion 428*

Take thy luck from the lap of thy sister. (*Arabic, Egypt*): *Burckhardt 73*

The womb that is not carrying, raises another woman's child. (*Oromo, Ethiopia*): *Cotter 4*

STERILITY

Do not accuse the bed of infertility. (*Chinese*): *Geyvandov 196*

The impotent man does not eat seasoned food. (*Lunda, Zambia*): *Milimo 62*

If the pestle were broken, the mortar will be lost. (*Malay*): *Champion 454; MBRAS 15*

The adulterous man peoples the village, the sterile man doesn't.
   (*Taka, Congo DR*): *Beken 1993: 221*

If I had relied on you, o husband, we would never have had children.
   (*Morocco*): *Lunde & Wintle 115*

A barren woman is like a hornless goat: when it slips its halter you no longer have a hold on it.
   (*Ganda, Uganda*): *Walser 373*

An impotent man and a barren woman: where does the child come from?

(*Arabic; Arabic/Moorish, Spain*): *Lunde & Wintle 8*

A marriage without children does not last long for men. (*Arabic, Maghreb*): *Champion 561*

A bride who bears no child after three years of marriage should be divorced.

(*Japanese*): *Buchanan 102*

Rather mud than an infertile wife. (*Andrah, India*): *o.s. Sanjukta Gupta*

A tree that does not bear fruits should be chopped. (*Hebrew, Israel*): *Stahl 238*

A tree that does not bear fruit is cut down and thrown into the fire. (*Romanian*): *Günther 34–5*

Seven years is not too long for a pumpkin vine to start bearing fruit.

(*English, Jamaica*): *Llewellyn Watson 170*

When the sterile one begins to give birth, prepare many cradles!

(*Ladino, Morocco*): *Dahan 167*

Miscarriage is not sterility. (*Minyanka, Mali*): *Cauvin 1980: 61*

The woman whose sons have died is richer than a barren woman. (*Gikuyu, Kenya*): *Ibekwe 25*

The one whose children are buried in her womb will not see their graves.

(*Rundi, Burundi*): *Rodegem 74*

Rather condolences for dead sons than no hope of giving birth to them.

(*Ladino, Morocco*): *Dahan 168*

Better to bear twins than to be sterile. (*Frafra, Ghana*): *Geyvandov 219*

Who does not have children does not know why he lives.

(*Dutch; Danish*): *Mesters 129; Harrebomée I 407; Wander II 317*

Hunger is like sterility, it is never hidden. (*Haya, Tanzania*): *Nestor 33*

A woman without children doesn't know what love is. (*English, UK; Italian*): *Geyvandov 159*

The house without children is a cemetery. (*Sanskrit, India*): *Champion 425*

What can a sterile woman know about the happiness of having children?

(*Telegu, India*): *Geyvandov 276*

A barren sow is never kind to piglets. (*Danish*): *Bohn 1855: 371; Bohn 1857: 18*

A useless person is like a woman who is both lazy and barren. (*Ganda, Uganda*): *Walser 294*

If you do not prepare food, should I hate the [sterile] one who prepares well?

(*Yaka, Congo DR*): *Beken 1993: 207*

A barren woman brings forth visitors. (*Ganda, Uganda*): *Walser 372*

The one who visits the barren one chooses among the dough balls. (*Rwanda*): *Crépeau 428*

A childless donkey will be eaten by the wolves. (*Uzbek*): *Geyvandov 158*

You done no breed, so no laugh after your grannie. (*English, Jamaica*): *Champion 622*

If you have only one child, don't laugh at the childless one. (*Mamprusi, Ghana*): *Geyvandov 257*

A woman without children is a tent without tent pegs. (*Ladino, Morocco*): *Stahl 419*

A pair without children is like an extinguished hearth. (*Finnish*): *Geyvandov 158*

The windows are blind without children. (*Lithuanian*): *Geyvandov 158*

A wife without children is like a day without sun. (*Serbian; Czech*): *Reinsberg-Düringsfeld 174*

Marriage without children, day without sun. (*Czech*): *Geyvandov 158*

A woman without children is a cow without a bell. (*German*): *Wander I 1115*

A married woman without children is like a lonely flower on a mountaintop.

(*Vietnamese*): *Geyvandov 159*

A birdless tree, a barren tree. (*Thai*): o.s. *Terwiel*

Women without brood are like trees without fruit. (*German*): o.s. *Terwiel*

A childless woman, a fruitless tree. (*Tajik; Turkish*): *Geyvandov 159*

Too many leaves, no fruit; a beautiful wife is no child bearer. (*Khionghta, Bangladesh*): *Lewin 15*

Bad luck, our sister: she ate a mule's nail. (*Mapuche, Chile*): *Guevara 58*

She had but just passed the holy tree and already felt signs of pregnancy.

   (*Telegu, India*): *Geyvandov 252*

Happy is he who has children, not unhappy is he who does not. (*French*): *Pineaux 92*

FERTILITY

Two can make ten. (*Mongolian*): *Geyvandov 162*

In the desert there are two kinds of trees: dry ones and green ones. [The desiccated ones are male, the green ones, female: males cannot give birth.] (*Kamba, Kenya*): *Geyvandov 185*

If a bride can be bought, a child cannot. (*Bulgarian*): *Arnaudov 110*

If you are impatient to have a child, you marry a pregnant woman.

   (*Fulfulde, Senegal*): *Gaden 142*

Rooster, horse and wife should be chosen for their breed. (*Spanish, Mexico*): *Casasola 57*

Women and goats: choose them for their breed. (*Spanish, Puerto Rico*): *Fernández Valledor 154*

Women, horses and hunting-dogs: choose them for their breed. (*Portuguese, Brazil*): *Mota 125*

A girl is a peanut seed: she enlarges the clan. (*Woyo, Congo DR*): *Clémentine Faïk-Nzuji 11*

The wealth of a girl is in her frontside. (*Rwanda*): *Crépeau 487*

Girl, bring forth, that we may see [what you're worth]. (*Bembe, Congo PR*): *Jacquot: 76*

The girl grows up in order to raise a family. (*Rundi, Burundi*): *Rodegem 137*

May your daughter fill the house [with boys] and bear fruit, thanks to God. [A marriage wish.] (*Arabic, Maghreb/West Sahara*): *Duvollet 43*

Where the mother sends [her children], the childless goes herself. (*Ganda, Uganda*): *Ibekwe 25*

Who will draw water for the childless old woman? (*Gikuyu, Kenya*): *Barra 71*

Those who have children arrive first at the water; the childless one fetches muddy water.

   (*Taka, Congo DR*): *Beken 1993: 222*

Mothers cuddle and play with children, but women who have no children stay glum.

   (*Sinhalese, Sri Lanka*): o.s. *Alex Gunasekare*

A childless woman has no one to scold. (*Nyanja, Malawi/Mozambique/Zambia*): *Geyvandov 159*

Those who fear children's crying will cry in their old age.

   (*Swahili, East Africa*): o.s. *Aldin Mutembei*

Children are the riches of the poor. (*Japanese*): *Geyvandov 163*

If you have sons what would you need money for? (*Chinese*): *Geyvandov 179*

A house full of sons is like a house full of pearls. (*Kurdish, Turkey*): *Geyvandov 179*

If an elder grows slim, it is his fault. (*Taka, Congo DR*): *Beken 1993: 208*

When the year is a good year, the women of the house have many children.

   (*Oromo, Ethiopia*): *Cotter 152*

And the tree keeps on giving. (*Spanish, Mexico*): *Velasco Valdés 163*

The more children the more luck. (*German*): *Meier-Pfaller 74*

Many children are the riches of Romanians. (*Romanian*): *Günther 36–7*

Just as the fireplace for cooking never has enough firewood, a woman never has enough
   children. (*Punjabi, Pakistan*): *o.s. Nasra Shah*

Some women will conceive if you but shake a pair of breeches at them.
   (*English, UK*): *Williams I 461*

It happens that by leaping over a hedge you become pregnant. (*Estonian*): *Geyvandov 252*

A woman who gives birth to many children will get pregnant from the slightest wind.
   (*Hebrew, Israel*): *Moscona 12*

Every year a child, in nine years twelve. (*Bulgarian*): *Arnaudov 79*

Ill-starred women have two babies a year. (*Pashto, Afghanistan*): *Champion 464*

Where she puts her eye, she gets a baby. (*Spanish, Bolivia*): *Paredes-Candia 82*

A tree with many branches has not a day without wind. [Refers to parents with many
   children.] (*Korean*): *Geyvandov 162*

To bear many children is to shed many tears. (*Shona, Zimbabwe*): *Ibekwe 25*

Many children, many debts; many wives, much malicious gossip.
   (*Vietmanese*): *Geyvandov 163*

May God save us from many children and little bread. (*Spanish*): *Meier-Pfaller 76*

Many children, possible, but too many, impossible. (*Russian*): *Geyvandov 162*

She is with child, and nurses a child, and has four more [children] before her.
   (*Arabic, Egypt*): *Burckhardt 71*

She's pregnant and nurses her child, while four others are on her shoulder, and climbs the
   mountain to obtain a pregnancy remedy. (*Arabic*): *Safadi 16*

She is pregnant, she nurses a child, she drives around her other four little ones and she is
   climbing up the mountain to search for a medicine against pregnancy.
   (*Arabic, Lebanon*): *Frayha I 257*

Do not swear, womb, you will not get children. (*Russian*): *Geyvandov 191*

A good-hearted woman is always pregnant. (*Sinhalese, Sri Lanka*): *o.s. Alex Gunasekare*

What's saved if, by going to bed early to spare the candles, your wife then gives birth to
   twins? (*Chinese*): *Wintle 194*

Two hungry lovers and a single bed signifies the birth of a beggar.
   (*Turkish*): *Lunde & Wintle 82*

A poor woman is pregnant: good news for the graveyard.
   (*Arabic, Lebanon*): *Lunde & Wintle 108; Frayha I 257*

PREGNANCY

'Respected!' said the bride on learning she was pregnant. (*Oromo, Ethiopia*): *Cotter 17*

A poor girl, until she got [or: became] pregnant. (*Ladino, Tunisia*): *Stahl 211*

A pregnant woman is not sent away. [Her child will strengthen the community.]
   (*Mongo, Congo DR*): *Hulstaert 625*

A ship under sail and a big-bellied woman are the handsomest two things that can be seen.
   (*English, USA*): *Franklin 1735*

Do not argue with a pregnant woman. (*Ovambo, Angola/Namibia*): *Geyvandov 269*

A cock does not lay eggs. (*Minangkabau, Indonesia*): *J. van Reenen*

The hen lays the egg, and the cock crows. (*Italian*): *Attanasio 45*

A wife is in the man's compound for the sake of the child. (*Mamprusi, Burkina Faso*): *Plissart 157*

He that wants eggs must endure the cackling of hens. (*Turkish*): *Dagpinar 85*

If you would have a hen lay you must bear with her cackling. (*English, UK*): *Champion 31*

She who is pregnant, is pregnant, even though she wraps herself in a *makaja* [the cloth
  women wear after childbirth]. (*Swahili, East Africa*): *o.s. Marieke van Twillert*

The cow receives the bull in secret, but gives birth in public.
  (*Kurdish, Turkey*): *Geyvandov 272*

A woman hides the penis, she won't hide the belly.
  (*Mamprusi, Burkina Faso*): *Plissart 299; Ibekwe 163*

The tongue shows what it has eaten. (*Lunda, Zambia*): *Milimo 41*

A fire and a girl's pregnancy cannot be kept secret. (*Rwanda*): *Crépeau 82*

She who conceives in secret will give birth in public.
  (*Arabic, widespread*): *Lunde & Wintle 54* (*Also: She who has secretly sinned ... Dargin/Tatar,*
  RF): *Geyvandov 272*

Not even married yet, but prepares the diapers. (*Korean*): *Geyvandov 258*

The son in her uterus is only an embryo, and already she weaves for him a *burnous* [large
  cloak] for great festivities. (*Arabic, Morocco*): *Messaoudi 108*

Before seeing her son she named him. (*Oromo, Ethiopia*): *Cotter 1*

Don't look for the strapping-cloth when the baby is not yet born.
  (*Hehe, Tanzania*): *Madumulla 95*

One doesn't sew a shawl for an unborn baby. (*Gikuyu, Kenya*): *Wanjohi 248*

As long as the child isn't born don't make a cradle for him. (*Shor, RF*): *Geyvandov 258*

Do not boil the pap before the child is born. (*Hebrew, Israel*): *Cohen 1961: 83*

Pregnant women have one foot in the grave. (*German*): *Wander I 1130*

A pregnant woman stands facing the gate of a graveyard. [Literally: stands in front of the
  door of a graveyard.] (*Vietnamese*): *Thái 30*

A pregnant womb that is ill, is ill indeed. An exceedingly pregnant womb is exceedingly ill
  indeed. (*Sumerian, Mesopotamia*): *Alster I 282*

Do not fasten the baby strap while the child is still in its mother's belly.
  (*Ngbaka, Central African Republic*): *Thomas 758*

Do not call the pregnant woman a mother. (*Baule, Ivory Coast*): *Arbelbide 112*

Pregnancy is not yet having a child. (*German*): *Wander IV 418*

Pregnancy does not yet mean baby. (*Baule, Ivory Coast*): *Arbelbide 113*

A pregnant woman should not put her unborn child on her list of living children.
  (*Papiamentu, Aruba*): *Geyvandov 192*

A pregnant woman is in more serious danger than sailors and horsemen.
  (*Chinese*): *o.s. Huang Mingfen*

Praise the child, don't praise pregnancy. (*Yaka, Congo DR*): *Beken 1993: 218*

June brides, January mothers. (*English, USA*): *Mieder 1991: 70*

A pregnant woman earns respect. (*Italian*): *Santoro 63*

It is a shame for a girl to be pregnant and for a woman not to be pregnant.
  (*Oromo, Ethiopia*): *Cotter 78*

Having a child is a shame for a girl, an honour for a woman. (*Estonian*): *Geyvandov 188*

CHILDBIRTH AND CHILDBED

A child is the girdle of marriage. (*Tumbuka, Malawi*): *Milimo 15*

Birth is the messenger of death. (*Arabic, widespread*): *Lunde & Wintle 13*

A sick person is [relatively] well; it is the woman in childbirth who is [really] ill.
   (*Sumerian, Mesopotamia*): *Gordon 146*

A mother who has given birth to eight youths lies down in weakness.
   (*Sumerian, Mesopotamia*): *Alster I 72; Gordon 273*

The woman who said: 'How well and easily do I give birth' died with the birth of her ninth
   child. (*Haya, Tanzania/Uganda*): *Geyvandov 253*

The last child kills its mother.
   (*Papiamentu/English/Creole, Caribbean*): *Llewellyn Watson 142; Zagaya 187; Ludwig 424;
   Barbotin 74*

Desire is more powerful than pain. (*Papiamentu, Netherlands Antilles*): *Hoefnagels 90*

Bearing fruits bends the trunk of the banana tree. (*Gikuyu, Kenya*): *o.s. R. van Lent*

The older, the slower the delivery. (*Dutch*): *Cox 28*

Making love is a good thing, giving birth is not. (*Creole, Guadeloupe*): *Ludwig 435*

Even if a thousand women come together, the one who gives birth has to suffer the pain.
   (*Armenian*): *Geyvandov 222*

Getting pregnant is easy, giving birth is hard. (*Russian*): *Geyvandov 264*

Laughing she got pregnant, crying she delivered. (*Oromo, Ethiopia*): *Cotter 75*

No rain without thunder, no childbirth without pain, no girl without lover.
   (*Ladino/Hebrew, Israel*): *Moscona 156*

Giving birth is bitter, but [the pain] is easily forgotten. (*Russian*): *Geyvandov 220*

Labour pain, forgotten pain. (*Italian*): *Giusti 120*

Women do not remember the labour pains. (*Somali*): *Geyvandov 220*

An egg laid, a hen cackling. (*Spanish, Puerto Rico*): *Díaz Rivera 69*

More suffering in fear than in child's delivery. (*Japanese*): *Huzii 69*

A woman in childbirth trembles [only] if somebody is there to help her.
   (*Ganda, Uganda*): *Walser 287*

A pregnant wife should not scorn a co-wife's child. (*Mamprusi, Burkina Faso*): *Plissart 153*

Women give birth with the assistance of their co-wives. (*Acholi, Uganda*): *p'Bitek 20*

An inhospitable woman is spared until the moment of child delivery.
   (*Hehe, Tanzania*): *Madumulla 166*

Insult the midwife, and who will help you next time? (*Sena, Malawi/Mozambique*): *Milimo 21*

Don't insult the midwives while birth is going on. (*Hehe, Tanzania*): *Madumulla 135*

Do not abuse midwives while childbearing continues.
   (*Swahili, Tanzania/Zanzibar*): *o.s. Marieke van Twillert*

A hero steps even into the accouchement section.
   (*Tswana, Botswana/South Africa*): *Madumulla 47*

Azzûna [wife of a rabbi] gives birth to a child, and the rabbi feels pain in his bottom.
   (*Jewish/Arabic, Morocco*): *Westermarck 66*

The cow calves and the ass of the bull itches. (*Belorussian*): *Geyvandov 217*

A lean little thing of a lady and [moreover] in childbed. (*Arabic, Egypt*): *Burckhardt 103*

They despise the unsightly woman, and she brings forth a splendid little boy.
  (*Ganda, Uganda*): *Walser 71*
Patients need activities while new mothers need sleep. (*Chinese*): *o.s. Huang Mingfen*
Building up a woman's health just before childbirth, nourishing her milk just after.
  (*Chinese*): *o.s. Huang Mingfen*
Stop intercourse until one hundred days after your child is born, if you want to enjoy long
  happiness with your spouse. (*Chinese*): *o.s. Huang Mingfen*
A palace, one day a mother giving birth, the next day a lamenting mother. [Infant mortality
  strikes at high and low alike.] (*Sumerian, Mesopotamia*): *Alster I 219*
A child in the grave is a child in the womb. (*Tamil, India*): *Champion 430*
The grief of the neck [i.e. widowhood] lasts six months, the grief of the womb forever.
  (*Telegu, India*): *Champion 436*
She who keeps losing children doesn't invent names anymore. (*Ganda, Uganda*): *Ibekwe 45*
'I give birth, they die', [a woman says], and she gives none of them names.
  (*Haya, Tanzania*): *Geyvandov 159*
She gives birth to them in pain and buries them in pain. (*Ladino, Morocco*): *Dahan 68*
A woman who brings forth takes trouble upon herself. (*Ganda, Uganda*): *Walser 68*
She who brings forth a child brings forth a problem. (*Berber, Morocco*): *Bentolila 68*
A wife is a stranger until she gives birth to a child. (*Persian*): *Shaki 522*
A marriage is a joy; the birth of a boy—an honour; the birth of a girl—luck.
  (*Tajik*): *Geyvandov 178*
A child is the flower of a family garden. (*Turkish*): *Haig 68*
To bear children is wealth, to dress is only colours.
  (*Tsonga, Mozambique*): *Weidman-Schneider 103, 116*
From the mother's efforts in labour, we expected the birth of a male child.
  (*Arabic, Egypt*): *Burckhardt 18*
Time for labour is destined and, if God wishes, a boy is born after the pains—not a girl—so
  the neighbours' malicious pleasure will fade away. (*Arabic*): *Safadi 4*
Let's pray to the Prophet until the boy comes. (*Arabic*): *Safadi 43*
The woman that gives birth to sons has no sorrows. (*Spanish*): *o.s. Anonymous*
For her, who has given birth to a son, the sun will rise. (*Nogay, RF*): *Geyvandov 179*
You are as calm as if you had just given birth to a daughter. (*Hebrew, Israel*): *Moscona 90*
I would even prefer a girl, if it's quicker. (*Armenian*): *Geyvandov 247*
Whatever they tried, she kept on giving birth to daughters.
  (*Abazin, RF*): *Geyvandov 231*
It is better to give birth to a girl than to sit idle. [Anything is better than idleness.]
  (*Oromo, Ethiopia*): *Cotter 13*
Give birth to girls and do not lead a useless life. (*Arabic*): *Wijnaendts-Francken 107*
Only the house's ghost is happy with the birth of a daughter. (*Chuwash, RF*): *Geyvandov 177*
The family does not spring from the man. (*Ovambo, Angola/Namibia*): *Anonymous*
A woman gives birth to what's yours, but she [herself] is not yours. (*Rwanda*): *Crépeau 473*
A daughter is like a raindrop: she'll fertilize others' fields.
  (*Luba, Congo DR*): *o.s. Clémentine Faik-Nzuji*

The thing [penis] responsible for the pregnancy is the same responsible for the child.

(*Oromo, Ethiopia*): *Cotter 163*

It is not only the female who gives birth; the male should feel just as responsible.

(*Ashanti, Ghana*): *Oduyoye 6*

Her husband away, a woman can bear, but she cannot conceive.

(*Baule, Ivory Coast*): *Arbelbide 158*

The name of the father is the secret of the mother. (*Creole, Martinique/Jamaica*): *David 53*

Mama's baby, papa's maybe. (*English, Jamaica*): *o.s. Anonymous*

The father's identity is the mother's secret. (*Creole, Martinique*): *David 53*

One can always be certain that one's mother is one's mother, but none can tell for sure

whether his father is his father. (*Creole, Guadeloupe*): *ACCT 76*

Let the baby be born and he will tell who is his father. (*Spanish, Mexico*): *Casasola 30*

Only the pregnant one will know who is the father of the child. (*Twi, Ghana*): *Geyvandov 275*

The mother knows best whether the child is like the father. (*English, USA*): *Kin 186*

The mother is known, the father unknown. (*Estonian*): *Geyvandov 166*

Battlefield for man, childbirth for woman.

(*Maori, New Zealand*): *Champion 639; Brougham & Reed 132*

What war is to man, childbirth is to woman. (*Assam, India*): *Champion 415*

4

Female Power

'Each of us a trouser-leg,' said the wife, and she took the whole pair of trousers. (Frisian)

Power is a decisive factor in all times and places, and in proverbs power and profit are central topics. Those who have it want to keep it, those without it dream of having their share. Many proverbs about gender insist on the reasonableness of existing hierarchies and the self-evidence of male superiority. At the same time there is the usual omnipresent fear of losing one's authority and of 'others' conquering the precious domains marked 'males only'. Subordinates are not just submissive recipients of orders. They challenge authority, and women are certainly not the powerless creatures many proverbs declare them to be, nor are they the passive victims some feminist sermons have declared them to be. If they were the incarnation of a submissive silent majority, what purpose would all those disapproving proverbs serve? Publicly denying women's authority or influence is eloquent testimony to the reality of the opposite state of affairs.

Proverbs talk about female power in a variety of ways: from denying its very existence to openly expressing the fear of its destructive effects. The principal rule for women is never to reveal that they do have power, knowledge, and other extraordinary mental or artistic abilities. A wife in particular should not exhibit her talents and qualities (except in the domain of housekeeping and childcare), and she should certainly refrain from openly having the upper hand over her husband, unless she wants to ridicule him in public, thus provoking his anger, and, consequently, risking violence or divorce. Earthly pomp is the prerogative of men, or, as expressed in a Russian proverb: 'A smart woman gives the man glory, a wicked one spreads rumours.' Especially in the West (where ever more women have actually started wearing trousers in the past century), proverbs use them as a metaphor for the male roles and domains. The more smart women feel tempted to put on 'male clothes', the more men are warned against the undesirable consequences of this undesirable inclination:

> Where the wife wears the trousers, the husband changes diapers. (*Letzeburgish*)
> A sensible woman leaves her husband the trousers. (*German/Dutch*)
> Where the wife wears trousers, the Devil is the lord of the house. (*German*)
> Woman is smart in distinguishing her skirt from his trousers. (*Scottish, UK*)
> The cunning wife makes her husband her apron. (*English, UK*)
> When the wife wears the pants, the husband rocks the child. (*Ladino*)
> If your petticoat fits you well, do not try to put on your husband's pants.
> (*Creole, Martinique*)

There are many more examples. In Italian, it is said.: 'Where woman wears the trousers and man the apron things turn out badly.' Badly for whom? Using 'the trousers' as a metaphor, a Fon proverb literally equates anatomy with destiny: 'A woman in trousers, what is dangling inside?' Reluctance *vis-à-vis* the very idea of woman's knowledge and talents is expressed without the slightest reserve, in Chinese, for example: 'A woman should never be outstanding or irregular; her face should not be too pretty, nor her words too clever or her work too good.' The message simply is that men do not like their wives to be cleverer than them. Mediocrity scores as a highly recommendable female quality, especially from a husband's perspective, but even if she is admittedly clever, a woman's destiny is not to follow other than the prescribed female roles:

> If too clever a woman gets married, she does not succeed. (*Twi*)
> A mule that whinnies and a woman that talks Latin never come to any good.
> (*English, USA*)
> Women's wisdom destroys houses. (*Russian*)
> When a woman has no talents, she is already doing very well. (*Chinese*)

In many cultures women economically depend on men (fathers, brothers, husbands, sons) for their very survival, and the domains traditionally ascribed to women tend to prevent them from having access to economic independence. One of the very reasons why proverbs about work have been included in a chapter entitled 'Power' is prompted by the enormous strength and perseverance of women, and especially wives, in their working capacities: 'Even God cannot build what a wife can build', in the words of an Armenian example. In the mean time, female talents are directly connected to the iron rule that a man's talents, such as intelligence, knowledge, and prestige, must always be superior to his wife's, at least in the public domain. Proverbs standing up for this rule try to roar down the echoes of rebellious counter voices whose impact is, ironically, revealed by their very absence.

VERBAL TALENT

Take a smart one, and she does not let you say a word. (Russian)

Being physically the weaker sex, women have strongly developed their verbal talent, and proverbs warn against the dangers of this female quality:

Women! Seven mouths, eight languages to chat in. (*Chinese*)
Listen to your wife once every forty years. (*Turkish*)
Women are nine times more talkative than men. (*Hebrew*)

That women should be excluded from being given the floor, or from speaking at all, is an amazingly widespread idea in proverbs in a large variety of cultures. The difference between the male and the female mouth is expressed in Vietnamese: 'A man with a big mouth is elegant; a woman with a big mouth is bad for the neighbours.' All over the world proverbs stress that women are verbally much too gifted. This aptitude, like other female intellectual talents, is mainly referred to contemptuously. Women's speaking is presented as talkativeness, chattering, twittering, cackling and so forth; what is actually said is simply disparaged, whereas men's talk is praised:

A woman's word is wind in the wind, a man's word is rock in the wall. (*Arabic, Morocco*)
The power of a woman is nothing but a plenitude of talk. (*Hausa, Nigeria/Niger*).
Men talk like books; women lose themselves in details. (*Chinese*)
Man thinks and talks, woman talks and does not think. (*Estonian*)

Not only are women's words being set against men's words, women's words are also set against men's deeds:

Deeds are male, words are female. (*Dutch/Greek/Hebrew/Italian*)
Words are female, deeds are macho. (*Portuguese, Brazil*)
Words wear petticoats, deeds trousers. (*Spanish, Mexico*)

When disparagement does not seem to work, and women's words cannot just be brushed aside as mere vanities, another strategy is developed: women's tongues are presented as dangerous, and even murderous. They are associated with swords, sabres, knives and other cutting objects—alerting men to this serious verbal threat:

Three inches of a woman's tongue can slay a man six feet tall. (*Japanese*)
A wife's long tongue is the flight of steps by which misfortune comes [to the home].
    (*Chinese*)
Even a fifty-tongued man cannot equal a single-tongued woman at abusing.
    (*Sinhalese, Sri Lanka*)
A woman's tongue is sharper than a Turkish sabre. (*Serbian/Croatian*)

AN INBORN QUALITY?

A woman's sword will never rust. (Sumerian)

Long ago the ancient Sumerians already warned against the danger of the female tongue by means of the metaphor of the sword, and the same metaphor has been applied for the same purpose in proverbs in later times and widely different parts of the world:

A woman's sword is her tongue and she does not let it rust. (*Chinese/Hebrew*)
A woman's tongue is a sword. (*Portuguese*)
A woman's tongue is a double-edged sword. (*Romanian*)
A woman's tongue is sharper than a double-edged sword. (*English, USA*)

The tongue is also associated or equated with women's problematic head and brains:

> The intelligence of a woman is in her tongue. (*Arabic*)
> A woman's common sense is in her tongue. (*Portuguese, Brazil*)
> The tongue is babbling, but the head knows nothing about it. (*Russian*)

The use of physical violence is always a sign of verbal weakness. Being physically weaker, women developed their verbal force as a defence mechanism to prevent violence. The dimensions of female tongues are presented as gigantic in European proverbs:

> Women's tongues are longer than their skirts. (*Dutch*)
> Women's tongues are longer than their arms. (*English, UK*)
> Woman's hair is long, but her tongue is even longer. (*Russian; English, USA*)

They are also compared to frightening spears and the devil's broomstick as well as to sharply stinging insects or biting poisonous creatures, such as wasps, scorpions, and serpents, for example in Chinese: 'The language of women: a viper's tongue and a wasp's sting.'

Apparently, Yoruba men in Nigeria are also scared of women's clever talk: 'He who is not smart in speech and argument should not take a talkative wife.' Other proverbs contemptuously qualify women's words as talkativeness, suggesting that this is an inborn female characteristic:

> A fish doesn't need to learn how to swim, a woman doesn't need to learn how to talk.
>   (*Ladino, Morocco*)
> Women are born chatterboxes. (*Japanese*)
> Who will not marry a talkative woman stays a bachelor. (*Mongo*)
> Where women abound, noise abounds. (*Oromo*)

THE JEWEL OF SILENCE
A silent wife is a gift from the Lord. (*Hebrew*)

Logically, then, silence is one of the most appreciated female qualities, as expressed in the Hebrew proverb above. Alas, the Lord does not seem to be very generous on this point, granted the fact that proverbs continue to stress that the last thing women do is keep quiet:

> Silence is a woman's most beautiful ornament. (*Widespread in Europe*)

Or, in a variant with more edge: 'Silence is a fine jewel for a woman, but she seldom wears it' (*Danish; English, USA*). According to a German proverb, ' It is easier for women to give birth than to keep silence.' But a silent woman is found to be a contradiction in terms: 'It is not in the nature of the female tongue to be silent' (*English, USA*). Therefore, it has to be severely controlled, or cut off, if necessary: 'Tell your wife a secret but cut her tongue' (*Hebrew; Yiddish*).

Prevention being better than cure, in many cultures daughters are taught from early childhood that propriety means silence, and that men prefer to marry girls who keep their mouths shut, as (among many others) the following proverbs illustrate:

The clouds that have many dragon-sounds [thunder] are without rain; the maiden who
   talks too much will have no wedding feast. (*Tibetan*)
Daughters should be seen, not heard. (*Dutch*)
A woman and a bitch, one that keeps silence is good. (*Spanish*)
There is no more shining dress for a woman than silence. (*Hebrew / Russian*)
Kind words and few are a woman's ornament. (*Danish*)
The woman and the melon, of both the silent ones are the best. (*Portuguese + Brazil*)
A quiet wife is mighty pretty. (*English, USA*)

Proverbs dream of submissive women quietly performing their duties in the home. The
ideal is a perfect wife who looks up to her husband with admiring eyes: silently, or at most
with a few soft sweet words, she encourages him and makes him feel secure and self-
confident in the tasks he has to perform outside the home. This is, for example, expressed
in Japanese: 'Encouraged by the hen, the cock tells the hour.' Speaking in public is a means
of power and influence, and as a metaphor known worldwide the hen and the cock have
frequently been used to express the assertion that women should leave public space to
men. Communication on an equal footing between men and women is a problem: 'Between
women there is female talk; between men, male talk, but what can a man and a woman talk
of?' a Sinhalese proverb wonders.

   Whenever women's verbal talent is being associated with female intelligence, the message is that for women it is most intelligent not to speak. The Iraqi proverb: 'The intelligence of a woman is in her tongue' means precisely that women's best quality is to be silent.

   In proverbs about women, 'deviant' interests are passionately rejected as undesirable
and 'unnatural'. Women are constantly admonished not to infiltrate domains declared
terra non grata for them.

WORK

The entire world is a hotel for men. (Dutch)

At the beginning of time people never had to work, as they were allowed to cut off a piece
of sky and eat it whenever they were hungry. We have got to work for our daily bread, a Bini
myth from Nigeria tells, because the sky has receded from the earth, and this is due to a
greedy woman. Right from the start, the sky had warned people never to cut off too much,
because then the leftovers would be thrown away, and the sky did not want to end up on
the rubbish heap. People tried to carefully observe the rule never to cut off more than they
were able to eat—until, alas, one day a gluttonous woman transcended the interdiction
and cut a piece of sky so huge that neither she nor anyone else on earth was able to finish
it, and in the end she threw what was left on to the refuse heap. The sky felt terribly in-
sulted and rose up to an inaccessible height. Ever since, humanity has had to toil for its
living.

   This myth teaches people never to waste the means generously put at their disposal;
it also blames the loss of paradise on female misbehaviour, as do so many other stories of
origin. However, it does not speak at all about the differentiation between tasks and labour
assigned to men and women respectively, nor do many other creation myths. Whether or

not their myths of origin refer to such differentiation, most societies have developed ideas about what ought to be considered 'man's' work and what, 'woman's' work. Various reasons have been suggested for this sexual division of labour: differences in physical strength, men's presumed greater skill, or women's childbearing and nursing function. In addition to biological differences, culturally based arguments, such as taboos, have been put forward to justify gender-based task assignments and roles. As a rule it can be stated that there is more emphasis on a gendered division of work in societies where there are more strictly applied policies of sexual segregation.[106] Justifications for a division of tasks have also been inferred from the argument that exposing women and their wombs to danger (hunting, war, travels) would be too risky and therefore not in the best interests of the community. Women were and are indispensable for safeguarding humanity's posterity.

Efficiency has also been put forward as an argument in favour of the gender division of role patterns. Women used to be (and usually still are) the ones nursing their babies. This may have been the main reason why women are usually responsible for tasks that could be performed near the home, the kind of tasks that can be easily interrupted and easily combined with nursing and childcare.[107]

The physical strength argument is questionable in several ways: there is an enormous diversity in male and female bodies, and all men are of course not always physically stronger than all women. In most cases the sexual division of labour cannot be reduced to the actual difference in physical strength, nor can it be justified on the basis of sexual differences as such. It has been created and instituted to their advantage by those who imposed themselves, physically or otherwise, on the top echelons of the society. Through the generations such imposed patterns have been strengthened and structured by the fact that children usually identify with task-related behaviour of adults of the same sex, and younger generations are easily forced by the previous generation into existing patterns or role models.

What do proverbs reveal about work as related to the sexes? What kind of work do they present as more or as less prestigious; what is considered as 'only' women's work and why? And where does the profit go? Are women presented as happily performing and enjoying their tasks? To what extent are male and female tasks in life presented as being opposed to each other, as complementary or as hierarchically ordered?

Answers to such questions may provide some insight in to cross-cultural patterns and possibly contribute to a better understanding of the many ways in which, not only in the past but in many contexts until the present day, people have been excluded, for reasons of not having the right sexual equipment, from working in fields assigned 'male' or 'female'.

'WOMAN'S WORK'

Marry, marry, and who is to keep house? (Spanish)

Food preparation, washing and cleaning are necessary tasks that have to be carried out on a daily basis. The usual solution to this problem has been that upper-class people delegated such tasks to lower-class people—to their slaves or to manual workers they hired for little money. Today, people who can afford it turn to household machines to make their lives more comfortable, and thus save time for occupations considered more interesting and rewarding. Washing and cleaning do not seem to be the kind of tasks many people passionately strive for as a full-time desirable occupation if they are given the freedom of choice. The proof of this can be seen from women's growing call for more equal sharing of household tasks, at least among the privileged educated couples in nuclear family households in today's world.

Generally, domestic work, indispensable as it has always been, has not really enjoyed the high esteem it should be given from those being served. A few proverbs show some awareness of this, such as, for example, a Kundu proverb from Cameroon: 'A bad husband does not see all the work his wife has done.' Or the following Spanish one from Puerto Rico: 'He who enters a clean house and sits down at a table which is set does not know how much it costs.' The sympathy in the perspective is clearly with the person who accomplished the domestic tasks. It is not made clear whether the person who made all those efforts is a man or a woman, but the one who profits is clearly presented as a 'he'. Worldwide the four main tasks associated with women in proverbs could be summarized as the four C's:

- Childcare (from nursing to rocking and all other forms of care)
- Cleaning (including sweeping, washing etc.)
- Cookery (including all the preparations from fetching water, collecting firewood, herbs and other ingredients, to grinding, cooking, baking and so forth)
- Crafts (spinning, weaving, needle work, knitting etc.)

No less than other proverbs, those about work express disapproval of non-conformist behaviour. The question to be dealt with first is to what extent and why tasks are presented as gender-related. The rules and reasons may differ. There is an old Berber story telling why women do not have their own *souk* or market: Long ago women wanted their own souk and decided to boycott the men's souk, but in spite of the men's acceptance—apparently, as the story emphasizes, they needed their permission—nothing ever came of it, because the women wasted their time on beautification and idle talk. The conclusion of the tale is set down in a proverb: 'The women's souk will never take place' (*Morocco*). Market business is thus declared a male domain in the society concerned. Another example comes from the Ashanti culture: 'A woman sells garden-eggs, not gunpowder.' That the woman is not supposed to sell gunpowder is because guns and gunpowder belong to the 'male' sphere of hunting and going to war, whereas taking care of chickens and eggs is a women's business.

Among the Hehe in Tanzania, and also among a number of other peoples, farming tasks are divided along gender lines, as expressed in the following somewhat cryptic proverb: 'Hoe is hen, machete is cock.' It means that since women till the land, their tool is the hoe. It is a men's task to fell trees and clear the land before women can begin their part of the job, the tilling. 'Men plough, women weave' is a Chinese proverb that is further strengthened by a serious warning against role reversal: 'When girls do the ploughing, it will cause drought for three years.' Many other customs regulating the tasks of men and women have been laid down in proverbs:

When the male soul is alive, the female soul does not crack nuts. (*Ashanti*)
A woman does not split the head [of an animal] nor dip the cup into the beer. (*Gikuyu*)

If a man has a cook, why should he burn his fingers? (*Arabic, widespread*)
She may not be the submissive type but she'll wash the napkins. (*Indonesian*)

No further explanation. Proverbs all over the world remind women to do only the work prescribed as appropriate to their kind and not to interfere in the domain of men, and vice-versa. In most cases proverbs simply state that this is the way things are:

When the harvest season is over, women weave, men forge. (*Thai*)
On the sixteenth of the first moon the lamps of the ancestors are extinguished; the boys go to school, the girls behind the spinning-wheel. (*Chinese*)
The daughter at the spinning-wheel and the son at the shield. (*Spanish*)
A father to his desk, a mother to her dishes. (*English, USA*)

In none of the above examples is an explicit difference in valuation being made. However, in most societies forging metal is a highly prestigious and specialized technique, and going to school is usually considered as a more important path to progress—and therefore to power and influence—than staying home and doing handicrafts. Schooling leads to 'the desk', and being in 'the world' is generally considered more important than spending one's life at home. Moreover, proverbs usually reflect serious suspicions regarding women's schooling, or in some cases reject the option outright, because schooling goes against enjoying housewifely duties, or in the words of a Danish proverb: 'Educated women, stupid housewives.' With brains or without, for women there is no escape from destiny, and their ineluctable homely tasks and duties are repeated all over:

Woman has only been created for the house. (*Ladino*)
For a woman, marriage is a profession. (*Portuguese, Brazil*)

In the Persian proverb 'Trust in God is male, worldly cares are female', the message is that male equates the spiritual, and female the material matters, the former being superior, religiously speaking, to the latter. In other proverbs men and women are presented as complementary: 'Woman is a moving wheel; it is the man who brings in the money', says an Arabic proverb from Syria and Lebanon, meaning that men are responsible for bringing in the money and that it is women's role to make sure the tasks around the house are done properly. In other words, both are indispensable for a good household and their tasks make up a whole.

In proverbs, the only female 'profession' leading to economic independence is prostitution. Even though one Minyanka proverb neutrally argues that: 'The prostitute's breadwinner is her bottom', i.e. her livelihood, women who practise the profession are usually severely condemned on moral grounds. Women who earn a living this way are seen as outcasts, but not the male customers:

Like a bucket in the public bath, use a whore but pass her on. (*Arabic*)
A woman who can be hired is as cheap as spittle. (*Hebrew*)

Men are possibly blamed for wasting their money on prostitutes but not for having sex with them: 'Whores affect not you but your money.' (*English, UK*). Although considered a degrading job, proverbs admit that prostitution is a rewarding activity:

'If I get a chance, I will marry; if I fail, I will live by prostitution,' said the spinster.
   (*Oromo*)
A poor whore and a good woman do not exist. (*Spanish*)
Whores' work gives shady money. (*German*)
Women can earn money lying down. (*Portuguese, Brazil*)

Some proverbs compare prostitutes with married women, as Simone de Beauvoir has observed: women give themselves and men take them and remunerate them for their being 'used'. Married women are considered the rivals of prostitutes, and therefore 'A prostitute does not recommend marriage' (*Wolof*). There is a popular proverb all over the Western part of the world that establishes a significant connection (of male wishful thinking?) between wives and prostitutes by including the two roles in marriage: 'A good wife is a perfect lady in the living room, a good cook in the kitchen, and a whore in bed' (*Dutch/English, UK/USA*). In all other examples, prostitution is presented as the opposite of wedlock.

Except for prostitution, all the female tasks and activities mentioned in proverbs are considered to be compatible with decency and virtue in marriage. However, none of those other female tasks is very rewarding in the material sense of the word.

Amongst all the tasks specifically considered female in proverbs, some are only found once or twice whereas others occur everywhere. For example, only one shepherdess is mentioned in a Catalan and French proverb and one female miller in Lithuanian, while two proverbs refer to women shaving sheep. One tailoress (*Arabic*) and some landladies (*Europe*) are mentioned. A Serbian herb woman, an Arabic beautician, five hairdressers, mainly from the Arab world, and one Fulfulde excisor from Senegal are mentioned. There are about fourteen nurses breastfeeding children they have not borne, twenty-one midwives, and plenty of women farmers in proverbs from rural areas all over the world. Among the female farmers' activities are mentioned: raising chickens and pigeons, milking cows, making butter and cheese, and working in the fields, sowing and harvesting. I found also one shopkeeper and several female salespersons:

   The shopkeeper cannot stand the burden and if she does not complain it is because she
      does not have a voice. (*Spanish, Cuba*)
   The woman who sells fans has nothing but her hands to shade her eyes. (*Chinese*)
   When the wife of the confectioner does not sell, she is eating. (*Portuguese*)

It is women who take up the role of mourners in Arabic and Jewish culture. They play this role in their own family, but they can also be hired to wail on the occasion of other people's funerals:

   God save us from the women-mourners. (*Arabic*)
   The afflicted mother, who has lost her children, is not like the woman who weeps for
      hire. (*Arabic, Egypt*)
   A wife who cannot sing a lament, what a pity for her husband's death. (*Ladino*)

Water and firewood are basic supplies. Finding them and bringing them to the house is apparently considered women's work. I found proverbs about those activities only in the Arab world and in Africa south of the Sahara. That fetching water is really hard labour is expressed in a Ladino proverb: 'Who says marriage is easy, should try and fetch water on one's own from a far-away well.' In addition to the gendered task message, respect for water as a precious life-giving liquid is expressed in a beautiful Arabic saying : 'Oh! Joy for the inhabitants of Achqout, when the water bottle gurgles; a woman says "It over-flows"; another one replies "May God hear you".' Water is vital for the household, and a Namibian proverb stresses that concentration is indispensable in carrying out the crucial task of drawing water from the well: 'Don't interrupt a woman fetching water.' In case of drought and water scarcity, a Kundu proverb observes, don't blame the women: 'When the river dries up, one cannot fetch water for the husband's bath.' No one is bound to the impossible is the message, but the proverb no less stresses the division of tasks: one fetches the water and the other takes a bath. Among others, a Yaka proverb further con-firms the idea that fetching water is not a male task, by observing that a man without a wife has a 'water problem': 'The man who has no pitcher is very thirsty', the pitcher serv-ing as a metaphor for a serviceable wife in all senses, and not only as a walking jar. The idea is that in principle he should not lower himself to do such jobs.

Fuel gathering, chopping firewood, and lighting a cooking fire are also presented as female tasks, even though the messages in such proverbs refer to something else:

> The childless one anoints herself before she goes out to chop firewood. (*Rwanda*)
> Fit for wood collecting, unfit for marriage. (*Arabic, Syria/Lebanon*)

The first proverb associates beauty with sterility, and therefore lacking assistance in life. The second one argues that being good at fuel gathering does not as such guarantee that a woman will be a good wife. A Sara proverb from Chad uses the image of a woman's fetching firewood to stress that the world's wages are ingratitude: 'The faggot brought home by the woman becomes the cat-o'nine-tails that beats her.'

Women seem to be no keener on water fetching than men. Proverbs complain about women's reluctance, for example in the earlier-quoted Kru example from Ivory Coast and Liberia: 'He has twenty wives but has not been able to take even one bath.' Apparently, one wife after the other keeps telling the husband that one of the other co-wives has to fetch the water for him... The proverb criticizes a wife for neglect. The same idea is ex-pressed in popular proverbs from the Maghreb:

> A [large] group of women and the waterbag stays empty. (*Ladino*)
> Four women in the tent means an empty water-skin. (*Arabic*)

At an early age, girls are forced to follow the established patterns for female tasks, as appears from an Azeri proverb: 'When discussing marriage, they say I'm small, when dis-cussing fetching water, they say I'm big.' The 'you' in the two following proverbs is men addressing themselves:

> A bad home sends you for water and firewood. (*Rwanda*)
> Don't take a wife who has money, she will treat you with arrogance and say to you:
>   'Fetch water'. (*Arabic, Morocco*)

It is the strong, the wilful, and the wealthy wives—often equated with bad wives—who risk overturning the rules and therewith the wavering status quo of privileges. The message is clear: as long as there are females around, males are not supposed to fulfil such tasks. The reversal of roles is presented as ridiculous in ironical sayings such as: 'Beaten up by his wife, Shyirambe says: "Give me a pitcher, I will go and draw water"' (*Rwanda*). A Bengali proverb from India serving the same purpose ridicules a wife who would take it into her head to refuse to cook meals for her husband: 'My darling wife, please do not cook for me. I shall eat raw rice, please do not cry.'

Time to turn to the C's. Under motherhood we have already talked much about the most important issues involving childcare—the sacrifices, the worries, and the loving care in all its aspects. The other three C's, Cookery, Cleaning and Crafts, will be discussed here.

COOKERY

Already the unborn child said: 'My mother is the best cook.' (Haya)

Everyday and everywhere on earth the first thing people need is food. Even on festive days, there is no rest for those who work in the kitchen. In the words of a Portuguese Brazilian proverb: 'However holy a day may be, the pot still has to boil.' All those dishes are not in the first place for those who actually prepare them, but for those who eat them. A Finnish proverb even observes ironically that: 'The housewife is already satisfied by preparing the meal.' Preparing meals is a strenuous task and proverbs pay extensive attention to it. Without enumerating the incidental dishes and ingredients mentioned in the cooking and baking process, I will examine the main issues and arguments.

First of all, food preparation is considered a women's business. The Dutch motto in my mother's cookery book published in the early twentieth century says (in rhyme in the original): 'The little wife who can cook well, in high esteem is held by man.' Proverbs from cultures in all continents stress, insist, claim, order, and argue that the kitchen is women's domain.

> However smart a woman may be, she'll end up in the kitchen. (*Indonesian*)
> A woman and a sardine will have to face the kitchen. (*Spanish, Argentina*)
> A woman and a frying-pan belong to the kitchen. (*Spanish, Chile*)
> Wife and stove belong in the kitchen. (*Ladino, Morocco*)
> A capable housewife can make a kettle boil, even in snow. (*Tatar*)
> What explodes in the pot won't kill a man. (*Rwanda*)

And so forth. Men tend to idealize their mothers' cooking. Proverbs pay a great deal of attention to the mother's food, stressing that she is an excellent cook, as long as the indispensable ingredients are available: 'Our mother knows how to make a bread, if only she has the flour' (*Greek*). From a child's perspective, the mother herself should be there because her physical proximity sweetens the food:

> If your mother is not there, your bowels ache while eating. (*Ganda*)
> Water is good even if it flows through a canal and a meal served by a mother is good even
>   if it is not fresh. (*Rajasthani*)
> If mother and son agree, just vegetables will be good enough for breakfast. (*Tibetan*)

In times of famine and poverty, it is an art to feed one's children, and mothers exhaust themselves in efforts to overcome the extreme difficulties in such a hopeless situation.

Proverbs referring to motherly despair in poor circumstances originate from cultures and countries where dearth is a dreaded intruder:

> Spring days grow longer and longer and the mother's bread becomes smaller and smaller. (*Tibetan*)
> When the children are numerous, the mother suffers. (*Chinese*)
> Pity comes to a mother when she sees that the food is ending. (*Ganda*)
> If the mother-banana tree is drying up, the young shoots also dry up. (*Yaka*)

Mothers sacrifice their own health and well-being for their children. In the words of a Tonga proverb from Zambia: 'A mother-mouse does not make her own stomach sweet.' Various other animal metaphors express this maternal altruism:

> Since its young have arrived, the crow does not remember what a full stomach feels like. (*Persian*)
> A breeding hen works but does not eat. (*Ngaka Bali-Nyonga*)

Children love to be with their mothers in and around the kitchen, where they are spoiled with delicious tit-bits: 'Who can say "mother", has the mouth full' (*Catalan*). Similar observations come from different parts of the world:

> He whose mother is in the house will eat with oil. (*Arabic, Tunisia*).
> He that has a mother eats cake. (*Catalan*)
> No pap like mother's to nourish. (*English, UK*)
> It is only in your mother's kitchen that you can be choosy. (*Ashanti*)
> He who eats with his mother will not cry for scraps [i.e. favours]. (*Hausa*)
> The child who has a mother has flour [food]. (*Mossi*)
> When one's mother is the cook, one is happy round the year. (*Bengali*)

No matter whether women are young or old, married or unmarried, smart or stupid, zealous or lazy, straight or crooked, gifted cooks or not, whether they like it or not, they have to work in the kitchen, simply because they happen to be born with a female body. Once she is married, proverbs argue, the deal for a woman is to serve a husband—which means, in the first instance, serving him in the kitchen: 'Is it not cooking you have come here for?' says the Ganda husband to his wife who refuses to cook in the morning.

Marriage means for a man not only that he has to support a wife materially but also that he has to swallow the food she serves, whether it is good or bad: 'Every husband is his wife's pig; he eats everything she prepares' (*Estonian*). In an Egyptian Arabic proverb, getting used to bad food comes to mean to reconcile oneself to bad living: 'Whatever the half-blind wife cooks for her husband, he sups on it.'

Most proverbs do not present women's views of the matter. Here is one rare example: 'The wife who prepares food does not enjoy her marriage.' Her task is especially hard in poor circumstances, without gas, water, electricity, and kitchen machines, such as obtain in the Yaka rural areas of Congo where the proverb comes from. Daily food is so important in life, that women are urged to do their utmost to provide good meals. A discontented husband will end up refusing revolting food. Women are reminded that men expect

well-cooked meals, that their own destiny depends on the quality of their services, and
that the preparation of a husband's food really needs to be taken seriously:

> As the man wishes, so the steak is broiled for him. (*Russian*)
> The roots of love are situated in the [man's] belly. (*Berber, Morocco*)
> The one who asks for mashed food has someone to mash it. (*Gikuyu*)
> A wife should not prepare the stew her husband does not like. (*Yoruba*)

As long as she adores him, she may do her utmost in cooking and baking. 'The one you
enjoy feeding is the one you love', says a Digor proverb. The result will be more or less
successful, depending on the wife's talents. Although a good cook is a stroke of luck for
the husband, his food paradise may get lost for other reasons. A wife might become discontented with her husband and lose interest in cooking, therewith denying him his
presumed indefeasible right to good food and well-prepared meals:

> As she is, the wife cooks the cabbage. (*Russian*)
> If a wife is going downhill, she eats what she has put aside for her husband. (*Oromo*)
> A wife does not love her husband, when she lets him starve. (*Taka*)
> Only now and again a wife hates her husband and rice. (*Tamil*)

Beauty and cooking do not seem to go together: 'Prettiness makes no pottage' is an Irish
example of this fundamental wisdom. Another Irish proverb sketches the situation with
mild irony: 'She mightn't be much good to boil a pot of spuds but she'd look lovely carrying them to the table.' Girls are pressed to learn in advance how to please their future
husband's belly with nice meals.

> A young wife is a bad cook. (*Malagasy*)
> A girl who cannot prepare maize-porridge, will not be a good wife for a real man.
>   (*Romanian*)

Apparently a 'real' man does not prepare his own porridge. Many tasks precede the cooking as such. Not only are fuel and water needed, but also the gathering of ingredients,
going to the market, all considered women's work. When the needed elements have been
collected, other tasks lay ahead. The most frequently mentioned tasks—all done by hand,
of course—are:

Grinding:

> The wife grinds and the husband sleeps. (*Russian*)
> The greedy-gut discourages the woman who grinds. (*Rundi*)
> The magical powder of marriage is in the grinding and cooking. (*Taka*)
> A Mulata with an expensive shawl: her sugar mill does not grind burnt cane.
>   (*Spanish, Cuba*)
> Marry the one who knows about *atole* and *metate*.[108] (*Spanish, Mexico*)

Kneading:

> When a woman kneads dough, stay; when she cooks, leave. (*Arabic*)
> If a woman does not like kneading, she sifts the flour all day long. (*German*)

You should judge a maiden at the kneading trough, not at the dance.
  (*Danish/English, USA*)
Even if she is crooked she still kneads the bread. (*Lithuanian*)

And pounding:

> The woman's trills are shouted at the mortar. [Refers to women's songs while crushing
>   sugar cane to be brewed]. (*Gikuyu*)
> The weapon is [in] the mortar. [Mortar is the woman's working tool for making flour: a
>   symbol of food and of hard work]. (*Hehe*)
> The [lazy] daughter-in-law lost her pounder; she found it behind the door. (*Bulgarian*)

Only when the above time-consuming exertions have been finished, can the actual cooking
and baking begin. In proverbs the maternal nourishing is much more explicitly appreciated than the same accomplishments realized by wives whose efforts are rather taken for
granted. Many proverbs even complain that wives are not devoted enough. However, as
exceptionally as generously, a Kurdish proverb acknowledges that: 'In a home where
people have had enough to eat, the housewife is a lioness'—a homage to all those billions
of women of all ages, labouring in kitchens of all kinds, who struggle to feed the hungry
mouths around them, a miraculous daily accomplishment indeed.

CLEANING

When the house is clean and the wife has combed her hair, the world looks good too. (*Portuguese*)

Cleaning here includes straightening up the house, doing the dishes, washing clothes and
so forth. Dirt is part of life and there is an ongoing struggle against it throughout people's
lives. The Filipino proverb is right: 'If your house is dirty, your life is a mess as well.' In
proverbs it goes without saying whose business cleaning ought to be. One of my students
brought me an interesting cartoon in which first the 'evolution of man' is presented in four
stages from ape to homo sapiens; the second drawing shows the 'evolution of woman':
four similar female figures on their knees are scrubbing a floor: no evolution to be noticed.
This is exactly the proverbial ideal: the busy cleaning bees are praised all over the world:

> Look at her at the head of the spring, she washes and wrings [is very zealous].
>   (*Arabic, Algeria*)
> The woman's way—if not by washing, then by ironing. (*Russian*)
> The woman who likes washing can always find water. (*English, USA*)
> The woman who keeps the privy clean will have an easy delivery. (*Japanese*)

What has cleaning the toilet to do with giving birth to a child? It could be just one of those
myths invented to make women do the work that needs to be done. In early twentieth-
century Europe, for example, a psychological theory was made up to justify why women
should willingly wash the dishes: the activity would conduct the surplus of their abundant female emotions via their hands into the lukewarm water so that they would become
more harmonious. Several proverbs equate women metaphorically with cleaning equipment:

Woman is man's soap. (*French*)

A new broom sweeps clean, but an old brush knows the corners. (*Irish/Maltese*)

The first wife is the broom, the second is the lady. (*Spanish; also in Puerto Rico/Mexico*)

A new broom is a good broom. (*Creole, Guadeloupe*)

A woman who gesticulates belongs to the riff-raff washtubs [riff-raffs are disreputable women]. (*Spanish, Cuba*)

The Hebrew proverb 'When the wife wears the pants, the husband washes the floor' expresses an objectionable situation. A French proverb presents the immorality of women who don't wear their cleaning outfit: 'Woman without apron is a woman to everyone.' The best way to prevent a wife from developing bad ideas and unchaste behaviour is to allow her no leisure or idleness: 'An aproned wife has no time to be bad', as it is said in Bulgarian. The ideal housewife keeps cleaning, and in her house there will be no dirt behind the door, as it is said in Digor. Proverbs speak disapprovingly about women who do not particularly like their cleaning job or are not very good at it. In particular, women who seem more interested in their own looks or in what happens outdoors than in doing the dishes, doing the laundry or removing everybody's dirt from the house, are in disgrace:

The woman in finery, the house is filthy but the doorway swept. (*Spanish; also Latin America*)

The more women look in their mirror, the less they look to their house. (*Hebrew*)

Beautiful women and women who like dressing up are considered unsuitable for the work in the house, and proverbs warn men not to be so foolish as to take such a frivolous and unprofitable wife.

CRAFTS

Need teaches naked women how to spin. (Danish)

Need teaches a naked woman weaving. (Czech)

Proverbs remind women constantly to stick to their tasks in life. Spinning is one such task. In all continents it is associated with womanhood, although the material to be spun may be variable, from flax to cotton, from wool to silk. The other crafts are limited to women's manual weaving and needlework, activities also represented in numerous proverbs. Crafts require manual dexterity and in some cases also artistic skills. A Romanian proverb presents spinning as the gendered task *par excellence*, right from the beginning of the world, and sanctioned by God himself: 'When God made the woman, he put beside her the distaff to distinguish her from man.' A Hebrew proverb considers spinning the only female skill, whereas in German women are said to be only good at spinning, crying, and gossiping about their husbands.

Ideally, women should start spinning from young girlhood onwards and continue until their death. Already an early Latin proverb stresses that spinning is exactly what women ought to do. There are proverbs about spinning girls, daughters, brides, wives, widows, and grandmothers. In China girls start working at the spinning wheel as from the age that boys start going to school. Spanish fathers are admonished to oblige their daughters to spin silk: more attractive offers are expected for the hand of daughters who master the art of spinning. In the same sense, an Arabic proverb from Syria and Lebanon promises zealous spinners rewards: 'As long as you will spin in this way, you can count on a silk dress!' The silk dress is the prospect of wealth for those who work hard: suitors will eagerly come and ask for the 'hand' of such suitable wives to be.

To be married or not is not the question, though, as far as spinning is concerned, as the word spinster suggests. The message is that women ought to spin all their lives. An old woman's spinning may be a little slower at a great age, but the activity is only to be abandoned at earthly demise.

A Gikuyu proverb recommendation is: 'Let women spin and not speak' whereas the Chinese as well as the Bulgarians stress that women should follow the rhythm of the hens: up early in the morning, and going to sleep when darkness spreads over the world, because spinning at night would mean the wasteful buying and burning of candles, and 'Spinning by candlelight [is] sleeping by sunlight' would be the world upside down.

Several other proverbs identify women's spinning, weaving and needlework activities not only as a source of profit but also as an excellent means for keeping women from 'loafing', from beautifying themselves, and from 'immoral' thoughts popping up in their heads:

> There is no better woman than she at the distaff. (*German*)
> A good woman thinks only of the distaff. (*Spanish*)
> A woman who knocks about the streets, has no time to spin wool. (*Arabic, Morocco*)
> A woman looking much in the glass spins little. (*French/Catalan/English, USA*)
> The woman who gazes much spins little. (*Spanish, Argentina/El Salvador*)

The harder women work, the less they will be led into temptation—a point which gets an extra dimension in a Maltese proverb: 'The wife who makes lace has no time to fight duels over her husband's infidelities.' Furthermore, women spoiled by their husbands would not do their utmost: 'A petted woman does not spin' is a Bulgarian example. Spinning means patience and much trouble before one spindle is full. In proverbs it is presented as one of women's most profitable tasks, as illustrated in the following Dutch example: 'Two boons: a woman who spins a pound of yarn and a cow that gives a pound of butter': women's spinning is a little goldmine to their husbands and their families all their lives.

The other most frequently mentioned crafts are weaving, knitting, sewing and mending. Proverbs about such tasks present similar observations. Women weave not only for themselves, but also for their men: 'The husband does not weave but is not without shirt, the wife weaves but never wears two shirts at a time' (*Russian*). As wives-to-be, girls are judged by their talents in this domain:

> Thread and linen are the face of a girl. (*Komi*)
> The threaded needle judges the girl. (*Spanish, Argentina*)

Again, the zealous are set off against the lazy ones. Zeal can be a matter of need: 'The dowry of the bride is in her hands,' as it is said in Italian. An Arabic recommendation for a girl is to be able to 'dig a lake with a needle.' In the same spirit the ideal Nenets girl attracts suitors 'by the beautiful clothes made by her hands.' Only a few proverbs give some insight into women's disappointment in their own needlework and other household tasks. Obviously, their marriage dreams are not coming true. Instead, they have to spin, to mend clothes, to darn socks. Even before marriage, men seem to expect women to be at their service: 'Smile a little at one who knows no shame and immediately he will ask you to repair his trousers' (*Karakalpak*). On the whole, such comments from a female perspective or defending women's interests are rather rare. The more needlework done, the more profit: a practical woman enriches her family, she has 'A hand of silver, a hand of gold', as an Arabic proverb from Syria and Lebanon describes her. Or, in Danish: 'A good handicraft has a golden foundation.'

NEVER-ENDING HARD WORK

Work hard, my wife, and I'll dig your grave with a golden shovel. (*Ladino, Tunisia*)

No doubt the Tunisian motto sardonically addresses an overzealous wife who wants to please her husband. Proverbs, mainly from the West, echo that women's work is never finished. Just a few examples among many:

> All things come to an end except woman's work and pain in hell. (*Danish*)
> The hands of a woman and the teeth of a horse are never at a loss.
>   (*Dutch/Flemish/Frisian*)
> Man's work is from sun till moon, woman's work is never done. (*German/English*)
> A woman's work is never at an end. (*Hebrew/English, USA*)

The tasks and roles ascribed to women are tough and women themselves ought to be tough to be able to carry out all that hard labour, and several proverbs about work compare women to pack animals:

> Young wife during the night, beast of burden during the day.
>   (*Arabic, Maghreb/West Sahara*)
> He who has a Galician woman has a mule. (*Spanish, Cuba*)
> Do not become the wife of a donkey; but if you already are one, carry its load. (*Persian*)
> My wife, my buffalo [also: my mule]. (*Russian; Serbian/Croatian*)

One of the oldest known Sumerian proverbs sees women's work as even harder labour than the work done by ox and plough. As to the working capacity of men and women respectively, various proverbs from widely different origins observe that women are (or are to be) most devoted, persevering and efficient, and that it is the men who enjoy being served. Not without irony, a Bulgarian proverb expresses the male love of ease thus: 'When one [of the couple] has to lie down, I lay myself down, and the wife has to serve me; when one has to die, the wife should die, so I can take a new one.' Overall the enormous working capacity of wives and the large extent to which the house depends on her is strongly emphasized:

> A smart woman can do more than ten peasants can. (*Chinese*)
> A single woman's work is better than a hundred men's discourses. (*Tajik*)
> When the wife endures, the house prospers. (*Arabic, Algeria*)

The small pot [the wife] goes to and fro, but the big pot [the husband] does not work.
   (*Hausa*)
Hard work tires a woman but totally wrecks a man. (*Fang*)
The wife grinds, the husband sleeps; the wife weaves, the husband dances. (*Russian*)

A Masai proverb from East Africa contains a warning to those who imagine they are too good to do any work: 'Don't be proud like a father of sons.' The father of sons is very prestigious among the Masai as well as in many other cultures. This glorious achievement can make him so haughty that he refuses to do any work whatsoever. It means that the bulk of the work will be his wife's, while the man lies down the whole day. The proverb reminds those who are not in the same position as the father of sons to do their job as they should. Other proverbs argue, that, sons or no sons, the burden is on the wife anyway.

Significantly, among so many proverbs about hard working and slaving women, I found only one (*Arabic*) proverb stressing that, contrary to men, a woman is a weak creature that has to be protected: 'Fear for the cow; as for the ox, it will labour.' In Islamic as in most other cultures this male ideal only holds for those who belong to the affluent social groups. Everywhere in the world, rural women labour on the land, fetch water, collect wood, and do all the other things considered women's work.

Evidently, a wife of humble origins is likely to be more subservient and to work harder out of pure gratitude for having found a husband from a superior social group. She works like a bride without dowry, as the Bulgarian saying has it. Such a woman is eager to prove by zealous drudgery that she 'deserves' her climb up to a higher position on the social ladder. Among other examples, a Japanese proverb even recommends to choose a woman 'from the rubbish heap' which simply means that such a low-class woman will be a gratefully zealous worker. Such proverbs stress the advantages of hierarchy for the privileged. As soon as it comes to people of the same gender, class, wealth, status, and education, problems as to the division of tasks and labour become unavoidable. This is expressed in proverbs from different cultural backgrounds, but strikingly similar in their interrogative form:

I a queen, you a queen, who is to fetch the water? (*Urdu, India*)
The mother-in-law is great, the daughter-in-law is also great; the pot is burnt, who will
   take it off the fire? (*Kashmiri*)
I'll be the queen and you'll be the queen, but who churns the butter? (*Punjabi*)
I mistress and you miss, who is to sweep the house? (*German/Spanish*)
You a lady and I a lady, but who will put the sewage out? (*Hebrew*)
If she is a princess and he is a prince, who will lead the donkey? (*Arabic-Jewish, Iraq*)

The obvious meaning is that a number of humble tasks need to be done in all homes, that everyone prefers to leave to others. If nobody is willing to do the annoying and necessary jobs, there is a problem. Sharing the tasks equally across the gender lines is not the issue. In the above interrogative proverbs, except for the last one, this familiar struggle is, interestingly, presented as a class issue to be fought between two females who both feel too well bred to undertake the disagreeable and humbling tasks. The implicit disapproval addresses those who are meant to accomplish the 'women's work'. Therefore, as a Dutch proverb observes, it is 'Easier to turn a countrywoman into a lady, than a lady into a countrywoman.'

On the whole, in proverbs at least, wives seem to resign themselves to their household tasks, accepting, with or without complaint, that they have been sentenced for life to perform duties most men look down upon. Nonetheless women's anger and frustration are made visible in proverbs full of revulsion and anger against certain heavy household tasks. Several proverbs, again from a variety of backgrounds, refer to such tasks being a serious cause of irritation and anger for wives, whether they take it out on their husbands or not. In order to prevent undesirable confrontations, husbands are advised to stay out of the way of their wives at moments of great stress and disgust due to imposed female tasks such as cleaning, washing, kneading and baking bread.

> When it's time for a spring-clean, stand aside for the women with a broom. (*Japanese*)
> When women make the bread and do the washing they have the Devil in their body.
> (*Dutch*)
> When the wife returns from washing in the river she feels like flaying her husband alive.
> (*Catalan/French*)
> When rain is falling down on women's wash, the wind is blowing in purgatory. (*German*)
> A woman is worst on the day she is baking. (*Danish*)
> Let her be, she comes from *tannour* [the oven]. (*Arabic, Syria/Lebanon*)

The last proverb is meant to excuse (and perhaps even sympathize with) a woman's bad mood resulting from her having to knead the dough, and baking the daily bread for the whole family standing in front of an unbearably hot oven. All six proverbs in the above section reflect tension, displeasure, and irritation due to the imposed household tasks. Although one Russian proverb belittles a woman's anger—by mockingly observing that: 'The woman was angry with the world, but the world did not notice'—men seem to be rather scared of angry women:

> Beware of an angry woman, more than of an angry man. (*Abkhaz*)
> Fire, water and an angry woman are the three [worst] evils. (*Korean*)

A wife who needs an outlet for her dissatisfaction and frustration is associated with all kinds of negative images—from a wild forest (*Swedish*) to a thorny hedge (*Dutch*), from an ugly piece of furniture (*Frisian*) to a wild sea (*Greek*), from lightning striking a house (*Malagasy*) to a cunning serpent (*Portuguese*). Other proverbs echo signs of more covert protest, resistance or subversive behaviour:

> When the soap comes to an end, the washerwoman rejoices. (*Arabic, Algeria*)
> If the washing woman receives no compliment, the ironing woman can wait.
> (*Papiamentu*)

Whether they like it or not, women are required to accomplish the imposed tasks without going in to the sulks. The ideal is to work in the best of spirits: 'Singing, a wife makes the bed for her husband'—that's what my grandmother taught my mother. Similar ideas have been aired in proverbs from ancient Egypt: 'If a woman does not sing, she doesn't work much either', to contemporary Panama: 'A washing woman who does not sing neither takes the filth away nor removes the stains' (*Spanish*). A Congolese Yaka proverb asks rhetorically: 'Produce your frowns and who will eat your beans?' Two more such views come from Germany and El Salvador, respectively: 'If a girl wants to be honoured, she should do her work with pleasure', and 'To an honest woman, work is pleasure.'

Only five rare proverbs (all stressing an obvious *force majeure* at that) pay attention to the option of reversed roles. If the worst comes to the worst, women are to be involved in men's tasks, a Vietnamese proverb acknowledges: 'When the enemy enters the house, the women must join in the fight.' That necessity knows no laws is also stressed in a Bali-Nyonga proverb from Cameroon: 'In war time even a woman may carry the Ngumba instruments.' The Ngumba are executioner's tools—not to be touched or even to be seen by women in ordinary circumstances. A German proverb observes that: 'A woman will learn to mend nets, when the husband is not at home.' Without specifying circumstances, a Chinese proverb argues that 'A family will flourish if the female can do man's work; it will be on the wane if the male tries to do the female's work.' This proverb distinctly links up with earlier proverbs trying to prevent men from being forced to submit to 'female' tasks considered inferior. Finally, a Ladino proverb from Morocco visibly speaks from a female perspective, stressing that a wife can by all means replace her husband: 'Inside me the "man", inside me the "woman".' It is never suggested that in ordinary circumstances men should be prepared to do women's work. In proverbs, then, a reversal of roles is either unadvisable or not allowed, and, for the sake of the existing order, an endless chorus of proverbial voices relegates women to the domain of the C's.

WHAT TO DO WITHOUT A WIFE?

The best piece of furniture is a wife. (*Dutch*)

Large numbers of proverbs stress that women need a husband and men need a wife. Hundreds of proverbs express wholehearted approval of women's economic dependence on men, and of men's addiction to being served by women. An Azeri proverb explains what being married means for a woman: 'In her house a woman is both mistress and maid', and a Serbian-Croatian proverb from Bosnia-Herzegovina adds that 'A real housewife is as much a slave as she is a lady.' Some proverbs make explicitly clear that, even though they are festively dragged into marriage, women are indeed no better off than slaves: 'Three days she's a queen and three days she's still a princess, and from then on engaged as slave' (*Ladino, Libya*).

Even the husbands' smallest personal chores seem to depend on their wives' services, as reflected in an Arabic proverb from Tunisia: 'Everything comes from his wife, even tying his shoelaces.'

Logically, then, proverbs sing the praises of the 'good mother' and 'good wife' who work like donkeys, whereas women's wealth, power, beauty, and other talents than just housekeeping are presented as a serious threat. Although the mother does much better than the wife, ideally both should do equally well, and their absence is felt as a painful deficit for a man used to being served. This was already expressed in a Sumerian complaint: 'My wife is in the holy place, my mother at the river and I will die of starvation.'

Hundreds of other proverbs confirm their weighty presence, expressing over and again that a man's life is impossible without a woman keeping his house: he will starve, he will die, he will lack food, (washed, ironed and mended) clothes, a bright shining spick-and-span house, and so forth.

> Housewife at home, pancake in honey. (*Russian*)
> The industrious woman's house shines at night. (*Bulgarian*)
> A wife is serviceable in every room. (*Dutch*)

If the female presence is lacking, a scenario of doom and disaster looms up, as can be seen in a whole series of suggestive images. A house without a woman is a meadow without dew (*Czech*); a sauna without smoke. (*Finnish*); a well without a bucket (*Bulgarian*); a place covered with dust (*Adyg*); an empty field (*Uzbek*); a burning-ground (*Tamil*); cattle without a pastor (*Amharic*); a fireplace without a fire (*Turkish*), and so forth. In fact the woman *is* the house, as the Igbo put it. Clearly, women are indispensable from a perspective of male interest. The economic rewards of her zealous presence are emphasized across the world:

> Take wives, they will bring you riches. (*Arabic, Maghreb*)
> With a clever wife, a man will become rich. (*Vietnamese*)
> A wife is a household treasure. (*Japanese*)
> An industrious wife is the best money-box. (*Romanian*)
> A woman with many talents fills the house to the ceiling. (*Portuguese*)
> Poverty is scared to get into the house of an industrious woman. (*Bulgarian*)
> If all women were [real] women, the walls of all houses would be made of coins.
>   (*Armenian*)

There are overwhelmingly more proverbs about the economic and other profits of women to men than vice-versa. In this respect it is significant that in proverbs (but not only there) widows seem to manage their life and household more easily than widowers: 'The widower has three sizes of lice; the widow, three sizes of silver' (*Korean*) or: 'Widows bear flowers, widowers breed maggots' (*Japanese*).

To what extent the respective gender roles have been questioned in the various societies we simply do not know. Why have things not changed more drastically long before the twentieth century? It must have to do with women's economic dependence. There is a meaningful Gikuyu myth about male and female tasks, which explains why men are the rulers. The story tells how, at the dawn of time, women were in charge. They ruled with an iron fist; they were cruel, pitiless and unfair. They made men do everything for them: men tilled the fields, did the cooking, looked after the children, went hunting and protected the home. All the women did was give out orders and mete out punishment if things did not suit them. The men obediently did what they were told. They worked diligently, even though they were treated like slaves. The women were never satisfied and became so demanding that the men decided things could not go on in this way. They resorted to a ruse and decided to impregnate all the women at the same time. This would weaken the women and provide the right moment to overthrow their unjust regime. And so it happened: the men created a new world order and strengthened their grip upon it. Ever since, the Gikuyu community has known justice and peace...

This intriguing story about power relationships significantly relates to male and female tasks in daily life. In the story there is obviously a struggle going on between men and women about who is in charge. Those who rule are exacting and inclined to treat their subordinates as their slaves. The subordinates do the humbler tasks and as soon as the slightest chance appears they will not hesitate to try and change their fate. Finally, the myth explicitly mentions that 'in the beginning' men were fulfilling both male and female tasks. Apparently there was no point in mentioning that as men they could not accomplish the tasks and duties later to be assigned to women as 'women's work'. The men simply did what they had to do because they were forced to, until they established 'a new world order'. The existing order is explained or justified through the invention of a creation myth. Subsequently, the community involved will have to believe and internalize this explanation, which begins to lead a life of its own as a self-evident 'fact'.

In Kenya, in the rural areas, this myth is still referred to today by Gikuyu men who do not wish to do 'women's work'. Even men who would be willing to work in solidarity with their wives or help them may feel reluctant to do so because they are wary of other people who might mock them and think that their women still rule them. This myth in the Gikuyu culture, as well as other myths, beliefs, 'nature', 'tradition', or combinations of those in other cultures, have succeeded in establishing roles as they have been confirmed in proverbs.

After the Russian Revolution, a new proverb was officially launched in the Soviet Union, recommending that: 'Woman should be a comrade to the man, not a maid' but its impact has not been spectacular.[109] It is a matter of gaining or losing privileges. The Romanian complaint: 'Woe the house where man is woman' resonates in other languages as well. Especially in Europe, the 'aproned wife' is a most appreciated category, and the metaphors of exchanging the trousers and the apron have frequently served to conjure up nightmarish scenarios.

Against the continuous danger of blurring roles, all sorts of barricades have been put up, disguised as 'traditions' along gender lines. Having a male or a female body has not much to do with the established patterns. Does being a chief, cracking nuts, cutting a drum, or hunting require more physical strength than gathering wood or fetching water, and carrying those heavy loads home over long distances? Why should a man not rock the child, do the laundry, cook a nice meal or wash the floor? Why should a woman not dip the cup into the beer, mend fishing nets, go to school or work at her desk? Those are not the kind of questions proverbs preoccupy themselves with. It is not change, but keeping things as they are, that they are about.

KNOWLEDGE

The women's side of the house: the side without knowledge. (Burmese)

Knowledge is power, and knowledge is riches; knowledge is no burden, but a lack of knowledge is darker than the night. With knowledge, you are never lost. This is a summary of messages about knowledge to be found in all the corners of the globe. Those who have knowledge are more prestigious, and they usually have more authority and privileges than those who lack knowledge. Everywhere proverbs stress the great importance and impact of knowledge, learning, and wisdom:

> The road to wisdom begins with the alphabet. (*Japanese*)
> Learning is a treasure that follows its owner everywhere. (*Chinese*)
> Learning has no enemy but ignorance. (*English, USA*)
> Learning is better than goods. (*Arabic, Morocco*)
> Learning is wealth that cannot be stolen. (*Philippino*)
> First learn, then form opinions. (*Hebrew*)
> Not to know is bad, not to want to know is worse. (*Wolof*)

FOR MEN ONLY

*Virtuous is a woman without knowledge. (*Chinese, Taiwan*)*

It is the more revealing then to discover that in fact proverbs shout their hardest in denying women this precious gift of knowledge, and preventing them from having access to it. The simple strategies developed are the same as those used to combat women's verbal talents. The first one is to belittle women's intellectual capacities as much as possible. Thus, an abundance of proverbs simply declares that women have no bright mind. Whether referred to as brains, understanding, sense, wisdom, intelligence or knowledge, all such qualities in women are widely scorned or disparaged, if they are not actually declared non-existent right away:

> It is because they are so stupid that women should distrust themselves and obey their husbands. (*Chinese*)
> A woman's sense is wrong sense. (*Telegu*)
> All a woman's intelligence is her home; if she leaves it, she will be worthless. (*Kurdish*)
> Women ask questions, men give the answers. (*Arabic*)
> A woman's intellect is in her heels. [i.e. very limited] (*Lezgi*)
> The wisdom of a woman is wonderful to hear. [Ironic] (*English, UK*)
> The wisest of women still is the greatest of fools. (*Dutch/Yiddish*)
> A wise woman is twice a fool. (*English, USA*)

The second strategy is, again, to present intelligent and knowledgeable women as a frightening destructive force with disastrous effects, and men are told to take heed already in some of the oldest known sources: 'Woman's intelligence can cause a catastrophe' (*Sanskrit*). In the large bulk of proverbs about the issue, men are advised to prefer mediocre wives to smart ones: 'An educated woman and too salty a soup are both unappetizing' is a German observation. A woman without learning or knowledge is more devoted to housekeeping. Moreover, lack of knowledge brings more chances of their being submissive, modest, and more easily controlled. The choice should not be too difficult:

> A morning sun, a wine-bred child, and a Latin-bred woman seldom end well.
> (*English*)

To educate a woman is like putting a knife in the hands of a monkey. (*Hindi/Portuguese*)
Ugly women and stupid girls make an invaluable treasure. (*Chinese*)

Women's striving for knowledge and for success in the world is no positive quality. Instead they are reminded that for them virtue is the priority:

Men should set knowledge before virtue, women virtue before knowledge. (*German*)
History is being made but household duties are neglected. (*Burmese*)

If, in spite of all warnings, a woman does become publicly successful, this will bring her nothing but bad luck. A North American proverb expresses this even more dramatically: 'A woman's fame is the tomb of her happiness.' Schooling and knowledge means growing big feet which means no husband. Especially in European proverbs this is an issue. Fathers are warned that their daughters should not have too much intellectual baggage. Somewhat sadly, a Ladino father worries about his daughter's future thus: 'May you be lucky, my daughter, because knowledge does not help you much.'

Women who are so knowledgeable and self-confident that they dare comment, are sharply disapproved of, especially in proverbs from the West—do they talk back more than women in other continents?

A man doesn't want a woman smarter than he is. (*English, USA*)
A dog is smarter than a woman. It does not bark at its master. (*Russian*)
A hen that crows and a woman who knows Latin never come to a good end.
(*German/Spanish*)

In Europe knowledge and education were in the past referred to as 'Latin', traditionally the language of higher learning. 'A woman who knows Latin will never find a husband nor come to a good end' is a centuries-old proverb found all over Europe, recommending that women be excluded from the academic bulwark. Some variants compare a 'learned' woman to a crowing hen: both deny their due role. Other variants strongly reject intellectual women, associating them with another despicable kind—misbehaving non-submissive girls, as in the following variant: 'A woman who knows Latin and a girl who answers back are good for nothing.'

Until the twentieth century this kind of recommendation against women's higher education was taken very seriously in most European countries, from both sides: parents advised against women studying and universities created rules to exclude them. Academic scholars in Europe used to argue openly that study was totally 'unnatural' for women, leading as it would to increasing sterility and perversity among them, and that women who would be qualified to study had to be considered 'abnormal' and 'monstrous'.[110] Although there was no law preventing women from studying, many male researchers were convinced that women were unable to achieve intellectually and under such conditions legal prohibition was not even necessary: culture itself had the same effect, making women shun studying in order not to spoil their chances of finding a husband. This is exactly what numerous proverbs also unambiguously proclaim.

The European message stressing that a woman who knows Latin turns out badly has crossed the ocean, not only to the United States, but also as part of the cultural baggage of Portuguese and Spanish colonizers. It took root in a number of countries in South America, in literally the same form as well as in other variants such as:

> A learned woman is a lost woman. (*Portuguese/Spanish*)
> The glory of man is knowledge, but the glory of woman is to renounce knowledge.
> (*Portuguese, Brazil*)

The danger of giving a woman the opportunity to gain knowledge is considered risky. All those warnings and recommendations against women's education obviously aim at keeping a balance considered precarious. To maintain that balance, an element of tactful male solidarity is advised, for example in Turkish: 'One does not discuss a man's negative qualities in front of his wife', and in Vietnamese it seems to work: 'In the company of his wife [he is] bright; in the company of his brothers, foolish.'

Only one exception contradicts those popular and significantly numerous messages meant to prevent women from having or even wanting access to knowledge: 'Learned woman is worth two' is a Spanish proverb from Puerto Rico—a women's variant going against the rule?

What about wisdom? 'A wise woman has a great deal to say and remains silent', is a popular proverb all over Asia. Women's wisdom rather consists of not doing certain things: not to intervene in a man's business, for example. In Japan women are told that: 'A wise woman seldom crosses her husband's threshold.'

Many proverbs testify to women's desire for knowledge, often qualified as 'curiosity'. In the Western part of the world this questionable disposition has almost automatically been connected with the story of Eve whose curiosity brought her into contact with the Devil, or was it her wickedness that did so? Both features in the story have been stereotypically projected on to the whole of womankind. In order to control the dangers of women's longing for knowledge, this bad inclination should be suppressed right from the beginning: 'Little girls shouldn't ask questions' (*English, USA*). Women's thirst for knowledge is cause for reproof:

> A curious woman is capable of up-turning the rainbow to find out what's underneath.
> (*Chinese*)
> Woman, thy name is curiosity. (*Widespread in Europe; English, USA*)

Of course, the more knowledge is inaccessible, the more intriguing and desirable it becomes. Clearly, proverbs see a woman's being intelligent, knowledgeable and clever as a serious problem, or, in Russian: 'Good luck for the stupid, bad luck for the smart.'

WOMEN'S ADVICE

Woman's advice brings total chaos. (Sanskrit)

In all continents large numbers of proverbs warn men against women's advice. Apparently female influence is so strong that there is a general clamour against it. In proverbs a woman's (and especially a wife's) advice is presented not only as suspect but as ruinous; it provokes chaos and catastrophe. Therefore: 'He who listens to a woman's advice is a fool', according to a Tamil proverb from India.

The usual arguments justify this view: her supposed ignorance makes her a bad judge, and her wickedness turns the outcome into evil. Women's advice results in evil (*Icelandic*), it will kill a man (*Digor*), or drown him (*Fulfulde*). There is a lack of trust and a lot of fear. An Arabic proverb from Morocco first warns men not to follow up the advice of a wife, and then adds that should a man do so, she would rule over him. There are many, many examples implying such fear of disaster. Here are just a few more, picked randomly from various parts of the world:

> Taking women's advice causes: 'Oh, that I had known!' (*Hausa*)
> If a cow leads the herd, all the cattle will fall into the pool. (*Venda*)
> Woman's intelligence brings destruction. (*Sinhalese*)
> To consult women brings ruin to a man. (*Persian*)
> The advice of a woman is like dust. (*Tibetan*)
> The advice of a clever woman will ruin a walled city. (*Chinese*)

Such messages about female advice—belittled as much as feared—complement the ambiguous views held about female knowledge and intelligence.

A few proverbs admit that in some cases a woman's advice is not always totally worthless. Without specifying anything in particular, a Swedish proverb concedes that: 'Woman's advice can be good sometimes', and this is confirmed in Czech: 'Even women's advice is sometimes good.' In Turkish it is observed that a woman's advice can be useful, but not for men: 'Women's advice is good for women.' A Hebrew proverb advises men to take a woman's advice into account: 'Consult your wife about everything. If she's small, bend down to her.' It is not sure at all, though, what the outcome of this respectful listening is meant to be, as other Jewish proverbs recommend something else:

> Ask your wife's advice and do the opposite. (*Ladino-Jewish, Iraq*)
> Whoever listens to his wife will lose his job. (*Kurdish-Jewish*)

Arabic variants stress the same idea: 'Consult your wife and do the opposite.' And an Italian version of the same message sees the marital consultation as just a matter of the ritual of politeness, a routine must for the sake of making the wife feel that she is taken seriously, but without having further impact on the man's decision: 'Praise the advice of a woman but don't act on it' (*Italian*). Behind all this male advice on female advice lurks the fear of women's hidden power and influence.

Several proverbs refer to the intimate discussions between husband and wife in bed where 'The word of the night annuls the word of the day', as it is said in Berber; or, in Russian: 'I consult with my pillow and then I confer with my wife.' A Hebrew proverb also reveals the impact of women's advice: 'The night-time counsellor wins over the daytime counsellor.' At the complete opposite of the bulk of scornful statements about women's advisory capacities, such proverbs, although they are a small minority, suggest that an intelligent (or even not so intelligent) wife has an impact on her husband's decision-making. Indirectly, then, the strong outcry against women's advice might confirm the exceptional Korean message arguing that 'There is no man who would not listen to his wife.'

'CUNNING' VERSUS 'KNOWLEDGE'

The cunning of woman has beaten man. (Turkish)

'Cunning', 'craftiness', and 'wiliness' are repetitiously connected with women in proverbs: their 'wiles' have become proverbial in the minds of those who invented and transmitted such proverbs. Those destructive sides of cognisance are hardly ever found in the negative sense in proverbs about men. Women's 'cunning' is often associated with donkeys, devils, and the like:

> A cunning woman and a devil always escape. (*Portuguese*)
> A woman's cunning is as great as a donkey's weight. (*Persian*)
> Don't succumb to the wiles of women. (*Sinhalese, Sri Lanka*)
> The cunning of one woman is equivalent to the load of forty donkeys. (*Kazakh*)

Although women are usually denied knowledge and power, in the negative domain of 'cunning' their superiority to man is, paradoxically, acknowledged as so artful that men must be on the alert:

> Women's tricks, fourteen tricks; men's tricks, nothing. (*Arabic, Maghreb W. Sahara*)
> Women's tricks outwit all. (*Greek/German*)
> The cunning of women is strong, and the cunning of the Devil is weak. (*Arabic*)
> What women eat, we are told, is twofold; their cunning is fourfold; their perseverance sixfold and their passions eightfold. (*Sanskrit*)
> A cunning woman always tries to watch her husband. (*Abkhaz*)
> Woman's slyness was put on a cart, but it was too much for the cart. (*Armenian*)
> The female's cunning is equal to her obstinacy. (*English, USA*)

What is referred to as 'cunning' are women's undermining informal forces, experienced as disfiguring cracks in the bulwark of the existing order. As usual, the task of proverbs is to remind society of this imminent danger. As long as the royal road of formal power is inaccessible, other sources of informal power—beauty, love, sex appeal, tears, and pillow talk— are being tapped to attain the desired goals in spite of all the gender barricades put up to keep women submissive. No openly expressed act of rebellion is mentioned, with the exception of the few uncontrolled outbursts of anger we have come across in the context of work.

Women's informal influence is referred to in a Indian Tamil proverb where a woman instructs the youngest of her family by saying that: 'The power of the king depends on the competence of his minister', meaning that the man who makes the money depends on the woman who runs the house. The following examples reflect somewhat apprehensive perspectives on the complex gendered interplay of power:

> A woman's strength is in her tears, a thief's in his lies. (*Bengali*)
> Love conquers even a hero. (*Turkish*)
> Beauty is power. (*Kanuri*)
> No man is a hero to his wife. (*Swahili*)
> No man is a hero to his wife or his butler. (*English, USA*)
> Three kinds of chains you can never shake off: a woman's chains, a king's chains and the soul's chains. (*Wolof, Gambia/Senegal*)

In Africa south of the Sahara, the formidable informal power of women is openly acknow-ledged in proverbs about kings or chiefs from widely different cultures, such as: 'The woman has no king' (*Ndebele*); 'A woman is more crafty than a king' (*Hausa*); 'The wife ignores that her husband is chief' (*Mossi*). Such proverbs express women's disrespect for established authority. Acholi, Chewa and Bari proverbs also stress that women accept no authority in almost literally the same terms: 'Women have no chief' or 'Women have no king.' All at-test to women's considerable power. I have obtained several oral explanations for the Bari statement: women conspire and thus get what they want; women are much more radical than men, and therefore inexorable; and, finally: women are uncontrollable.[111]

Many proverbs—though mostly reluctantly— also admit that it is women who take the final decisions in their men's lives. Here is an Arabic perspective on the final hierarchy of power:

> Who conquers fire? Water. Who conquers water? The slope.
> Who conquers the slope? The horse. Who conquers the horse? The knight.
> Who conquers the knight? The Sultan. Who conquers the Sultan? His wife.
>   (*Maghreb / West Sahara*)

It is not only in Africa that proverbs express directly or indirectly women's enormous im-pact and subversive inclinations. Here are just a few more examples warning men against the dangers of female power, or stating that this is how it is:

> A woman who loves power is her husband's husband. (*Persian*)
> Who wants to live in peace let his wife be in command. (*Dutch*)
> A wife is a giant. (*Ga*)
> Women are a vessel of wood, and he who travels in it is lost. (*Arabic, Morocco*)

In this context a last point to be mentioned is women's persistent willpower, as a serious force presenting a strategy of continuous repetition likely to prove victorious in the end: 'Repeated blows make the drum sound' (*Khiongtha*); 'After saying it many times she [wife] prevails' (*Burmese*), or: 'The man's command is less important than the woman's gong' (*Vietnamese*). A Turkish proverb sees a remarkable difference between men's aging and women's aging: 'An aging man loses his willpower; an aging woman loses her beauty.' This and other proverbs suggest that, ultimately, a wife overrules even a stubborn man. In other words, she gets what she wants. This point is being made in many cultures:

> A woman's willpower will pierce even a rock. (*Japanese*)
> What a girl wants at any price, she'll get. (*Rwanda*)
> What a woman wants, God also wants. [She will make it happen] (*Turkish*)
> When a woman wants to, she can do anything. (*Italian / German*)
> You grow older and forget, and finally agree with the wife's ideas. (*Ladino*)
> Nothing is impossible to a woman of will. (*Gikuyu*)

Is the fear of this strong female will the reason why women without a mind of their own are recommended as the better marriage candidates?

> A woman with her own will, who wants her? (*Irish*)
> If she has a mind of her own, there won't be many with a mind for her. (*English, UK*)
> A girl with a will of her own will not get married. (*Ovambo, Angola*)

Ultimately, then, quite a body of proverbs seem to suggest that women overcome all difficulties in life, and defeat their husbands at all fronts, so that Spanish men are jokingly advised: 'When your wife tells you to jump off a roof, pray God that it be a low one.'

FROM HEALING TO POISONING

Under the veil glistens the poison. (Arabic, widespread)

The female healer with her thorough knowledge of herbs and healing is supposed to also know the negative effects of herbs and medical ingredients, and thus risks the charge of misusing her knowledge, be it by mistake or on purpose. In proverbs she is often suspected or accused of bad intentions. When her own children die, she may be blamed for being the cause of their death: 'The professional woman [poisoner] shows herself by touching her belly' (*Rwanda*). 'Touching one's belly' is a euphemism for killing one's own children. A Rundi proverb observes that the one who has poison in her house takes risks and is likely to endanger her beloved ones: 'The professional poisoner kills her husband if she does not kill her child.' Proverbs connect women and poison in several ways, and women are often compared to animals that produce venom, such as snakes, scorpions, and wasps. In some African proverbs women are explicitly referred to as professional and knowledgeable poisoners.

In a number of proverbs, mostly (but not exclusively) from Africa and the Middle East, in turn, a girl or (co-)wife, a mother-, daughter- or sister-in-law, or an old woman are being put on a par with poison, poisonous animals, poisonous plants, or poisonous inclinations:

> Girls and snakes murder with their mouth. (*Somali*)
> Who has a co-wife will always say: 'My child has been poisoned.' [One first accuses the prime suspect] (*Rwanda*)
> The co-wife is poisonous and the sister-in-law a bitter almond. (*Arabic*)
> A sister-in-law is a poisonous scorpion. (*Arabic, widespread*)
> A stepmother is poison for the whole house. (*Bengali, India*)
> A daughter-in-law is like a snake that enters the house accompanied by music. (*Ladino/Hebrew*)
> When a woman grows old, nothing remains in her but poison and the colour of sulphur. (*Arabic*)

Without further specifying, the poison message sometimes extends to 'womankind' in general, examples of which are to be found in many places in Europe and Asia:

> The most venomous is a woman's heart. (*Thai*)
> There is no such poison in the green snake's mouth, or the hornet's sting, as in a woman's heart. (*Chinese*)
> There are no virtuous serpents. [Meant as a reference to the nature of women.] (*Arabic, Syria/Lebanon*)
> Trust in a woman is like poison to your stomach. (*Arabic-Jewish, Yemen*)
> Between women the venom is the greatest. (*Danish*)
> Venom is the doing of woman. (*English, UK*)
> Woman and wine have their venom. (*Spanish/French*)

Sometimes female 'poison' is associated with other suspect qualities—such as being wicked, beautiful, non-virtuous, or angry—in proverbs from Latin to Russian, from Portuguese to English, from Turkish to Sanskrit[112] or Chinese. The number of proverbs equating women with poison are telling. The fact that women do most of the cooking may have given rise to male fear of food poisoning: how to be sure that your daily food has been prepared without bad intentions? Suspicion of those whose services one cannot do without is a rather common human reaction in unequal relationships such as those between bosses and workers, or colonizers and colonized. Fear of 'the Other's' hidden power provokes suspicion and suspicion provokes fear, and both project evil intentions on to those who are feared.

The subject of gender and power is inexhaustible. It becomes even more complex as soon as women's verbal talents, work, knowledge, cunning, will, and other forms of power are being associated with secrecy and the occult, variously called magic, sorcery, witchcraft, and devilry. Dark forces ascribed to women are another most formidable source of fear reflected in proverbs.

WITCHCRAFT AND OTHER OCCULT FORCES

When the witch is burnt, peace returns to the country. (German)

In many parts of the world, occult powers are part of life, and the stereotypical belief that there is a 'natural' opposition between witchcraft and modernity does not hold.[113] In Europe today the exotic appeal of magical power seems to be finding a growing audience, if we must believe the numerous classified advertisements in Western newspapers with their promises of efficacious remedies against unhappy love relationships, cancer, impotence, loneliness, and other human miseries. Some such advertisements even hold promises for 'punishing' those who cast evil spells upon potential victims. It is all a matter of power, and belief, of course.

Most cultures have terms for what is referred to in European languages as 'magic', 'witchcraft' and 'sorcery'. Thanks to colonization the European terms are not only used by those who study such phenomena but also by those who encounter them in their own cultures. The terms are loaded with connotations, positive as well as negative. There is a certain ambiguity in society's forces, a precarious balance of powers and counter powers, in which those who feel disadvantaged in life are striving for a better balance. Witchcraft plays a role of its own in the complex process of making and remaking social relations and collective identities. The uncertain power balance is always ready to dip either way, serving purposes of accumulating power or of levelling power—inspiring fear among those who have the upper hand—while gossip, rumours, and other elusive forces play a considerable role. What is real and what is imagined cannot easily be distinguished. In proverbs about women the positive side of occult powers is hardly acknowledged, whereas the negative side—in the form of multiple proverbs testifying that witchcraft and evil are hand in glove—is overemphasized, as for example in German: 'Witches always plan evil.' This message of evil is then forcefully connected to presumed mysterious female power.

A person is labelled a witch when members of a community fear that she or he has special powers, which can work either way. In the escalation of social hostilities gossip, as a special form of talkativeness, seems to be the first step. It can be defined as the telling of stories meant to ruin someone's reputation or that of a whole group. Evil words may well have such a destructive effect that they ruin people's lives. The Haya in Tanzania associate the negative force of such words with witchcraft: 'One who speaks evil words is [called] a witch.' As discussed earlier, talkativeness is a quality women are often blamed for in proverbs. The destructive force of women's gossip is warned against, for example in an Arabic proverb: 'The gossip of two women destroys two houses', whereas an English proverb associates gossip with the devil's mailbag. Gossip is the verbal 'forerunner' of what then becomes the next step—witchcraft:

> An aggressive wish to bring misfortune on someone ('May his crops wither!') becomes, through the performative act of magic, the agency of harm. Like gossip and unlike an open verbal declaration of war, magical aggression is secret and can always be disavowed. Witchcraft is in many respects the classical resort of vulnerable subordinate groups who have little or no safe, open opportunity to challenge a form of domination that angers them. In a society that practises magic, those who perceive a lively resentment and envy directed at them from below will easily become convinced that any reverses they suffer are the result of malevolent witchcraft.[114]

According to popular beliefs in early modern Europe, certain people were gifted with uncommon knowledge. Such knowledge consisted of medicinal herbs or incantations, love or fertility potions, and divination, and meant prestige and remuneration for the, mostly poor, healers. This was the positive side of magic, but the negative side was also developed. It has been called 'black magic', a rather problematic term.[115] Witchcraft theory as furthered in influential books such as the *Malleus Maleficarum* (1486), written by two German Dominicans, progressively accentuated women's roles as inclined to evil, as daughters of Eve who had been tempted by the snake in Paradise, and thus believed to be susceptible to the Devil's influence by their very belonging to womankind. In proverbs women have no less often been equated with the Devil because of the Genesis story. The ingrained idea was that, thanks to women and their potions,

> [T]he Devil could inspire love or hate, render people impotent or incapable of sexual intercourse, or even cause them to believe they had been castrated. Witches could also change men into animals, possess them with devils, make them sicken and die, cause floods and hailstorms and fly mysteriously through the air. The two German Dominicans added a self-congratulatory postscript: 'Blessed be the most high who has so far preserved the male sex from such crime.'[116]

From the perspective of Christian orthodoxy at the time, collusion with the Devil meant that a witch would be condemned to death. Many of the accused witches in Europe were not only old and poor, two-thirds of them were widows or spinsters, living on their own, independently from the patriarchal community.

FEMALE WITCHES

A small parcel of sorcery is never small. (Lega)

Although, throughout history, both men and women have been accused of being witches, women have far more often been stereotyped as such. In Europe in the past, aged women especially used to be accused of being witches, and they still seem to make up the bulk of the accused in postcolonial witch-cleansing movements today.

Proverbs are also inclined to associate old women with witchcraft and devilry, but they also repetitiously suggest that all women have the potential of being a witch or a devil. The reason for this stigmatizing message is that in most societies women have been (and often still are) marginalized, for example as the 'strangers' intruding in the households of their in-laws. More importantly, it is the female reproductive functions that have played a major role in setting them apart. The processes related to giving birth have universally been designated as both positive and negative. In proverbs, their life-giving force is appreciated as a positive creative energy, as we have seen, but at the same time male fear has led to women being represented as the ones who radiate awesome and destructive energy. This negative image is strongly stressed in proverbs about occult forces and malevolent practices ascribed to women as a 'deviant' category of people in society. Witches and magicians are usually set apart because of physical particularities—a limp, a hump, blindness, being one-eyed or the 'deviation' of being a woman:

> They are everywhere recognized as being more prone to magic than men, not so much because of their physical characteristics, but because of the social attitudes these characteristics provoke. The critical periods of their life cycle lead to bemusement and apprehension, which place them in a special position. And it is precisely at periods such as puberty, menstruation, pregnancy and childbirth that a woman's attributes reach the highest intensity. It is usually at such times that women are supposed to provide subjects or act as agents for magical action. Old women are witches; virgins are valuable auxiliaries; menstrual blood and other like products are common specifics ... women are the butt of superstitions and jural and religious taboos, which clearly mark them off as a separate class in society. They are made out to be more different from men than they are in fact.[117]

Deviant from whom or what? And why? It has often been suggested that because of their being excluded from or marginalized in religious ceremonies, women would be inclined to enter into subversive initiatives, such as magic or witchcraft, against those who set the dominant norms. Did, or do women attempt to use witchcraft as a means of empowerment, as suggested by various female scholars? It is hard to know.[118]

Proverbs reveal a few clues to how witches are believed to proceed in different cultures. Usually they are supposed to act secretly, so that it is not easy to find out who exactly is a practising witch and who is not. A Baule proverb refers to the risk of unknowingly marrying a witch with all the disastrous resulting consequences: 'To marry a witch is to enter [forever] the forest with the demon [also: with the Devil].'

One becomes a witch either through heredity or by being initiated into the profession by an accomplished professional. The second category is considered worse in a Russian proverb: 'A witch who has learned witching, is more evil than a born witch.' The first category is referred to in a Thai proverb about mother and daughter, as follows: 'If the mother is a witch, when on the point of death she must spit [into the mouth] of her child which thereby receives in heirship the power of witchcraft possessed by her mother.' This way of transmitting witchcraft reveals that in Thai culture a ritual is necessary for such a hereditary transmission.

In a number of African cultures the belief exists that witches kill people by 'eating' their soul, by depriving them of their vitality that is: 'The witch swallows her nearest kin', as the Duala proverb has it, reminding us that witchcraft always takes place among close relatives. This being 'eaten' or 'swallowed' happens without witches ever using their teeth. Nonetheless, people die, according to those who believe and accuse such 'soul eaters' of applying destructive power tricks, reducing people to bones and ashes. This is a widespread African belief, but it also exists elsewhere. The following Russian proverb, for example, refers to the same practice: 'Women's tricks, even without teeth, deal with bones', meaning that women's powers are deadly destructive, and turn their victims into skeletons.

Witches seem to be rather dainty; they do not kill thin people but instead bewitch healthy children and strong people. In the words of a Cameroonian Kundu proverb, 'A witch does not swallow bones.' Here, 'bones' refers to slimness. Actually, thin people are sometimes believed to be witches themselves, because they are thin, and older people, who are often thinner than younger ones, are especially suspect. As a Portuguese proverb argues: 'When a woman is lean without being hungry, you had better leave her alone, otherwise she will eat you.'

Strange behaviour is so suspect that witchcraft is not to be ruled out: 'If a woman shows greater care for a child than its own mother, then surely she is a witch', as it is observed in Bengali culture. People have to balance carefully on the slack-rope in societies where the accusation of witchcraft may strike at any time.

Proverbs acknowledge that people are sometimes wrongly accused of witchcraft. One Arabic proverb from West Sahara refers to an angelic woman envied by others who was falsely accused of witchcraft. A Yaka proverb presenting a happy couple is another example of the effect of envy; again, struck by jealousy, people start gossiping that people's good luck must be suspect. One can thus be happy to the point of being accused of witchcraft. The function of such proverbs is to go against easy gossip and calumny.

Other proverbs associate the work of witches with specific places, for example crossroads, specific hours, preferably after dark, and specific rituals, depending on the cultural context. Demons, devils and witches are believed to use powerful formulas or fetishes. Older women are believed to be especially gifted with occult powers:

> If you see an old woman at a crossroad, do not trouble her. (*English, Jamaica*)
> Do not trust three: a trotting mare, a rushing hare, and an old woman walking with a
>   stick. (*Arabic, Maghreb*)
> The indelicacy of the old woman provokes spells unheard of elsewhere. (*Rundi*)

The night carries secrets and mysteries: 'Night is a witch', as the Hehe in Tanzania say. In the dark things look more mysterious and more frightening, especially in regions where there is no electricity. The night is the time of attack by witches and other nameless terrors:

> A wicked one [a witch] attacks during the night. (*Kundu, Cameroon*)
> Beware of the woman who goes out at night: as a poisonous snare she will destroy your heart. (*Umbundu*)
> If a man has sworn vengeance on you, you may still sleep; but if a woman has sworn vengeance, watch through the night. (*Arabic, Morocco*)
> A black chicken flies at night. (*Indonesian*)
> In the daytime holy but at night she kisses the Devil. (*Romanian*)
> Women who wander about at night are cats or demons. (*Catalan/French*)

Women who wander about at night are associated with evil or with the Devil. Witches are often associated with black cats as reincarnation of witches, or the other way round. The Devil and other demons are also said to wander about at night looking for victims, and so do evil spirits who cannot find a place to rest in the afterlife. Female beauty is no less believed to be a man-bewitching power. In several West African proverbs attractive women are presented as either filching money from men or, worse, casting a bad spell upon the male sex:

> The beautiful woman is either a thief or a witch. (*Bamum*)
> A beautiful woman either steals from you or catches you [i.e. is a witch]. (*Mossi*)
> A very beautiful woman is either a witch or a prostitute. (*Sara*)

Women thus become a mixture of external attractiveness and witchlike forces: 'Woman is a bewitching creature', according to a Japanese proverb. Men are warned that, even in cases of apparent female devoutness and piety, the frightening destructive forces lurk under the surface. In the words of an Arabic proverb: 'If you see an old woman with a rosary, know that she is truly a devil.' The more devout, innocent, and fragile women may look, the more suspect they are, is the suggestion. This is also expressed in Asian proverbs:

> Outwardly a goddess, inwardly a witch. (*Japanese*)
> Started with the dance of the goddesses; ended with the dance of the witches. (*Tamil*)
> There is a day in every man's life when he is a saint, and there is a day in every woman's life when she is a demon. (*Malay*)

Witches are also believed to catch men with words, and thus the seductive female voice may be regarded as a man-bewitching power. This must be one of the reasons why proverbs insist so much on women's silence as a sign of virtue, while stressing the negativity of women's verbal talents. According to a Ladino proverb from Morocco: 'The witch has conquered the beloved and caught him with her beautiful words.' In a number of proverbs love and witchcraft are presented as interconnected, and so are love and the devil:

> If you give your heart to a woman, she will kill you. (*Kanuri*)
> The love of a woman is the Devil's net. (*Portuguese, Brazil*)

Whether concerned with beauty, love, sex, food, or anything else, proverbs continually warn against all aspects of presumed female occult powers. The main point being made is that witches 'catch' men thanks to those special powers. Time and again the warning goes that men should not allow themselves to be enticed into danger or sins by the wiles of female allure. This also holds for witches' illusory wealth, as for example expressed in a German proverb: 'Witches' gold, and musicians' wages vanish at night.'

In most societies family ties are indispensable, and solidarity is basic to the survival of close relatives. Wherever distrust exists, tensions are likely to grow and people suspected of witchcraft may be blamed for every unhappy event that takes place. Witchcraft usually does not concern foreigners. It arises from the close relations one has with one's own kin: 'A stranger is not eaten', as the Kundu in Cameroon put it tersely, but in this case the in-laws do belong to the relatives. The idea is that only those who belong to the clan have an interest in bewitching their own people. Those with whom one lives are those one is supposed to trust, but they are usually also the ones who are envious of each other's success or well-being. Inequalities within the family can lead to jealousy and aggression, for example in the case of co-wives. Such inequalities easily lead to accusations of witchcraft.

In some alarming scenarios sketched in proverbs jealousy is imagined as a force that changes women into witches or devils. Co-wives readily accuse each other of witchcraft when some disaster occurs, and the killing jealousy of witches may cause her envied rivals to lose a child. This explains why in a Congolese Yaka example, a husband worries about his children: 'A polygamous man must be tactful not to lose a child.' He suspects his two co-wives of mutual jealousy and fears their spiteful witchcraft against each other's children. A sterile woman is suspected of being unable to cope with the idea that another woman does have children. Examples of this fearful belief are illustrated in a Sotho proverb simply stressing that 'Childlessness kills,' or a Haya proverb: '"We must become equals", a jealous childless woman says, and she refuses to give you an amulet for your sick child.' A last example, originating from the West African Mossi culture, suggests that the witchcraft-mindedness of a frustrated and vengeful old woman does not shrink from killing younger women's children: 'As the old woman stopped her sorcery, the children lay behind her hut.'

Omnipresent is the deep fear that, as soon as something bad happens to a witch, she will work it off on those who cherish children, prosperity and other elements of happiness in their lives. This suspicion of revenge is also expressed in the following Minyanka proverb from Mali: 'If smallpox has killed the witch's child, let the women with children not laugh.' The quoted examples attach the use of negative powers to specific cases of poignant inequality. The above proverbs are from Africa, but jealousy is also associated with witchcraft, devils and demons in other parts of the world, be it in more general terms:

> A jealous woman is worse than a witch. (*English, USA*)
> A jealous wife is a very witch. (*English, UK*)
> A jealous woman is almost a devil. (*Catalan and French*)
> Jealousy is the Devil's mother. (*Estonian*)
> Horns will grow on the head of a jealous woman. [Based on the belief that a jealous
>   woman would become a demon] (*Japanese*)
> Jealous woman, dangerous woman. (*Spanish, Argentina*)
> Jealousy often calls in the help of witchcraft. (*Creole, Guadeloupe*)

In all the cases so far women's witchcraft is presented as a negative force, resulting in tears and mourning in her surroundings: 'When the witch has finished, there will be red eyes', according to a German proverb.

However, as I have seen in Africa, occult forces are not only feared and considered risky and destructive, but also believed to give access to positive powers. There are indeed two sides to magic and, sometimes, positive counter-powers are believed to be able to undo the harmful effects of the negative, depending on the vital powers of the performer. Occult forces are also being used to beget children or to have a long and happy marriage or, as in a Congolese Yaka proverb, to die as husband and wife at the same moment in old age, instead of having to mourn for your partner and stay behind alone: 'You grind [the ingredients of] the *yindzika-nyanga*, you'll leave [die] together.'[119] Once more, mothers are not to be lumped together with the rest of womankind: they are special, and it is not only the mighty sorcerer, but also the loving mother who is believed to be for her children a protecting positive power, as a Yoruba proverb from Benin stresses: 'No fetish so sacred as the woman-mother.'

The male tendency to embody women with ambivalence easily dips into the projection of evil onto them. In proverbs, this takes various threatening forms; besides witchcraft the most widespread forms are devilry and evil as personified in the Devil or Satan, other demons. The various representations overlap in many proverbs. Female witchcraft and the Devil can be closely connected, as for example in this Russian proverb: 'The Devil has a witch for a wife.' It is significant that women have so frequently been blamed for the wrongs of society, especially in troubled times and places of human history—and not only in proverbs.

DEVIL AND SATAN

When God shut up Satan in Hell, He created woman to replace Satan on earth. (Malay)

Not only are witches believed to be around, threatening peace and order, the world is also believed to be full of supernatural beings personifying evil in the form of devils, demons, and evil spirits. And, of course, there is the Devil presented with a capital letter, as a person in the singular—also called Satan—whose habitat is referred to as Hell. Hell is also the place where devils, demons, and evil are located, where the agents of evil gather and where their victims are tortured. There are incredibly many proverbs about women being associated with devils, evil, and Satan, especially in proverbs originating from the Jewish, Christian and Islamic cultures. The motto at the heading of this section is an Islamic example from Malaysia. Here are a few more from the Arab world and from Islamic Africa:

> Women are the Devil's friends. (*Arabic*)
> Women are the snares of the Devil. (*Arabic, Somalia*)
> If a man tells a woman his secrets, she will lead him onto the Devil's road. (*Kanuri, Nigeria*)

Other examples originate from either the Christian or Islamic tradition, such as the following Yoruba proverb from Benin: 'Take woman for what she is: a sister of the Devil.' North African examples are sometimes of Jewish origin: 'Woman conquers the Devil.' (*Ladino, Morocco*), and Jewish examples can be found in Arab countries, such as Yemen, e.g.

'Women come from the Devil.' Still others combine Christian influences with traditional African religious elements in their warnings against women. In two variants of a proverb I collected in Congo DR, a witch and the Devil appear to be interchangeable:

> To eat with a woman is to eat with the Devil. [Beware of your wife] (*Kongo*)
> To eat with a woman is to eat with a witch. (*Lingala*)

All over Europe, but in other areas too, it is stressed that women know a point more than the Devil. From both Christian Europe and Islamized Africa I found a few rather similar proverbs, arguing that even the Devil has never succeeded in finding out women's secrets, mysteries or ultimate trick:

> The wiles of a woman [which are known to man] are ninety-and-nine, but not even
>   Satan has discovered the hundredth. (*Hausa*)
> Ninety-nine tricks of a woman you can discover, but the hundredth even the Devil did
>   not find out. (*German*)
> The Devil knows everything, except the place where women sharpen their knives.
>   (*Bulgarian*)

In Western proverbs, women's 'knowing' is often associated with the Devil. When women build a house, for example, 'not even the Devil can destroy it', and as it is said in Polish: 'The Devil swallowed a woman, but could not digest her.'

As soon as women's knowledge surpasses the knowledge of men, and hierarchies at risk of being turned upside down, women and the Devil are believed to co-operate, as illustrated in a proverb that can be found in Europe and North America: 'When woman reigns, the Devil rules.' Or, even worse, women's power is presented as so dangerously spectacular that the Devil himself is overruled and has to accept being a woman's subordinate. Here is a Swedish example: 'Where a woman rules the house, there the Devil is the farm-hand.' In numerous proverbs from Europe and both Americas, women, even small ones, are outwitting the Devil without much difficulty:

> The Devil is the Devil, but a woman out-devils him. (*Bulgarian*)
> Woman has deceived the Devil. (*Greek*)
> Women know a lot more than the Devil. (*Italian*)
> It takes a woman to outwit the Devil. (*English, UK*)
> A woman can beat the Devil. (*Irish*)
> Not even the Devil himself has as much malice as a woman. (*Spanish, El Salvador*)
> Woman does what the Devil cannot do. (*Portuguese, Brazil*)
> A woman knows a bit more than Satan. (*English, USA*)

Who says Devil says evil, and both terms are often simply being put on a par with 'woman'. It is said in Spanish as well as in German that: 'He who has a good wife can bear any evil.' However, good wives are an extremely rare species in proverbs. All evil and its agents are heaped on to women's being when it is argued, that 'in her soul roots all the evil of the Devil' (*Italian*) or that 'Women have seven devils in their bodies' (*Dutch/German*). In Europe, in the past, mainly women were suspected and accused of having concluded a pact with the Devil, as witches or even just simply as women, as many proverbs reflect. Similar ideas have also spread and become familiar or even common property in Europe's former colonies. Witchcraft and devilry have thus become narrowly linked through beliefs in which the Devil himself was thought to teach not only 'cunning' but also witchcraft to women. Such beliefs are of course indebted to the Genesis origin story that travelled all over the world with Christianity as well as with Islam.

When reading proverbs such as the following in Hebrew: 'When Satan is likely to fail, he sends a woman', or in Russian: 'Where the Devil is powerless, there he sends a woman as messenger', at first the suggestion seems to be that women would succeed thanks to their female sex appeal, but the same proverb has many popular variants all over Europe (also diffused to Latin America) in which explicitly an old woman is sent:

> Where the Devil cannot succeed, he sends an old woman. (*Polish*)
> Where the Devil fails, he sends an old woman. (*Serbian/Croatian*)
> Where the Devil cannot enter, he sends an old woman. (*Dutch/German*)
> Old women are one point ahead of the Devil. (*Spanish, Argentina*)

In proverbs, then, women in general, and old women in particular, have not only been associated with 'cunning' and witchcraft, but also with 'devilry'. If, in this proverbial reasoning, 'special' powers ascribed to 'woman' enable her to achieve more than the Devil, experience much more than physical attractiveness is likely to play a role. Mysterious female powers are most strongly associated with old age. Not only in European but also in Arabic proverbs, old women are presented as a formidable factor in dealing with the Devil.

In Jewish culture, Satan is originally a demonic figure, a personification of evil. Satan was specifically created for the purpose of causing havoc and evil. Gradually the meaning of Satan has developed more in the sense of 'evil inclination', and this is how he has usually been interpreted later, not only in Jewish sources, but also in Christianity and Islamic sources.[120] Satan, or the Devil, has become an instrument for suppressing forbidden ideas and thoughts: once an idea has been ascribed to Satan or associated with Satan, it is taboo and must be suppressed. In proverbs, the idea of Satan as 'evil inclination' has been projected on to 'woman' as the imagined 'dark' side of 'man'. In the confused minds of those who are struggling to suppress forbidden drives, dreams, and thoughts, women are vehemently blamed for the troubling feelings of guilt men develop in spite of their inexorable religious norms and commandments. Helplessly they opt for the easiest way out by turning women in general, and wives in particular, into the source of their own forbidden 'evil', sometimes literally:

> Sea is the source of salt, woman the source of all evil.
> (*Throughout Mediterranean Europe, and beyond*)
> Women are the root of all evil. (*English, USA*)
> Woman is the source of all evil: only our soul saves us from the harm she does. (*Fon*)
> Daughters and land: root of all evil. (*Bengali*)

Numerous European proverbs seriously argue that all women *are* 'evil', 'the store of all evil', 'at the bottom of all evil', 'inescapable evil', 'indispensable evil', 'essential evil', 'necessary evil', and so forth.

Due to Islamic religious influence, Satan is also referred to in proverbs about women from the Middle East to Europe and South East Asia, with the same familiar messages:

Woman is a man's Satan. (*German*)
Women are the snares of Satan. (*Arabic*)
Women are the whips of Satan. (*Persian*)

It is observed that Satan himself gets 'evil inclinations'—and is in need of prayers!—when he sees attractive girls, as a Punjabi proverb from India playfully argues. Satan is no less resistant to girl power than earthly men.

As we have seen in this chapter, the insecure power balance has resulted in two main strategies: proverbs either belittle women's knowledge and other talents, except for the four C's, of course, or they cry out against female destructive powers and disastrous abilities. The association of women with poison and snakes as producers of poison may be partly derived from the Genesis story of Eve and the snake in paradise. However, there is evidence of similar poison examples in other cultural traditions than the Jewish, Christian and Islamic traditions. Proverbs about witchcraft and devilry are yet another illustration of the fearful obsession of losing control or power over 'deviant' women. The Devil comes in as soon as women start outsmarting their husbands. This obviously most popular belief serves to apologetically argue that if the Devil does not know how to handle women, how could earthly men ever imagine being able to dominate the female sex?

In proverbs, women are easily accused of witchcraft and devilry: spinsters, widows, women after menopause, herbalists, very poor or very rich or very beautiful women, women who know too much, in brief, any female human being breaking the prescribed norms of behaviour in general and of sexual controllability in particular. However, not only some particular female categories but *woman*kind as a whole is frequently presented as 'deviant', and thus suspected of having special powers. It is this obsession, directly or indirectly reflected in proverbs, that leads to women being accused of engaging in destructive practices and wreaking havoc.

In cultural contexts where a growing competition between male and female economic and other activities is taking place, women are easily sought out as agents of destruction. They are accused of bewitching 'out of an innate capacity' and are depicted as a threat to society. This mechanism was applied to 'deviant' women in early Europe, but it applies no less to other contexts: 'Where females gain authority in male-dominated societies in Africa, male suspicion and resentment are focused in the concept of witchcraft, with attitudes, practices and roles that are strikingly similar to those of the European Middle Ages.'[121] Proverbs associating *man*kind with the Devil or Satan seem to be unheard of, at least in proverbs as a genre—even though the Devil, being the director of Evil, is represented as male, but then a Spanish proverb from Puerto Rico happens to know that 'If the Devil were to be born again, he would surely be born female.'

COUNTERMEASURES

Husband is the tie, wife is the parcel: when the tie breaks, the parcel loosens. (*Igbo*)

Whether stature, beauty or love or sex appeal, talents, knowledge or wealth are referred to, the explicit or implicit acknowledgement of female power has led to the invention of

appropriate measures to prevent such misconduct. Ropes, ties, strings and other significant metaphors express the needed control, as in the above Igbo motto, or in an Indian
Marathi example: 'Tie up and carry with you your wife and your money.' The numerous
prescriptions and proscriptions, invented for men's peace of mind, are presented as meant
for women's good and safety. The different measures resemble each other in their obvious
aim to restrict female freedom and ambition. The less freedom a wife has, the better for
the marriage: 'The husband gives freedom to his wife, nothing good is the result' (*Russian*). The proverbs recommending such measures are so numerous that a small selection
has been made, based upon the most frequent issues. Talking about the do's and the don'ts
in marital relationships, they address completely different messages to men than to
women. Men are the craftsmen who 'model' women into wives, thanks to their skills.

MOULDING A WIFE

Model the vase with your own clay, it will result in your own saucepan. (*Arabic, Maghreb/W. Sahara*)

How can problems between spouses be avoided? The common answer is simple. A wife
should never be allowed independence nor superiority. An ideal wife submits on her own
behalf, and that should be that: 'A married girl gives the rein to her husband just like a
newly purchased horse' (*Chinese*). One proverbial tactic is to simply declare that women
are 'naturally' subservient:

> The god of women is a man, therefore all women must obey man. (*Persian*)
> The woman is never in charge. (*Igbo*)
> It is correct to have total authority over one's wife. (*Sanskrit*)

More realistically, other proverbs foresee a large variety of problems. 'The purchased horse
needs training in order to understand that he who drives her is her master', as the Kanuri
say. This is an art, and a Greek proverb warns men: 'Either do not marry at all, or, if you
marry, be the master.' A wife who happens to be superior to her husband in some domain,
is advised to be clever enough to hide her 'male' qualities. That a man must be the master
in wedlock is a rule endorsed and repeated in most cultures. This rule is further specified
in four ways, variants of which we have come across throughout the previous chapters:

- Women should be smaller than their husbands.
- Women should be younger than their husbands.
- Women should be less talented than their husbands.
- Women should be less wealthy than their husbands

The issue of stature has been dealt with in Chapter One, 'The Female Body'. References
to physical size are metaphorically associated with hierarchy promoting objects, as for
example in Oromo: 'A wife and a plough handle are best when shorter than the man.' Sim-
ilarly, a proverb in Danish as well as German advises: 'Give your wife the short knife and
keep the long one for yourself.' And here is an (almost Freudian) Khiongtha ideal from
Bangladesh: 'A big cigar and a small wife.' This proverb also exists in a version where
'young' replaces 'small', thus making it fit in the second above category. As experience

comes with age, more than a few proverbs stress that for a husband, even an experienced one, it is most comfortable to have a young wife without sexual or other life experience, the very reason why the moulding of a widow by a second husband is acknowledged to be highly problematic. The same holds for a woman who is older than her husband: he cannot treat her as his child: 'Only a man who could have been her father, is a good match for his wife' (*Somali*).

Serious modelling must begin right from the wedding day, although, in the best case, the preparatory work has been done long before the wedding day, at the little girl's home: 'Girls and yearling bulls are trained when their stomachs are empty'—in order to become good wives and good oxen respectively, as the Oromo proverb recommends. A young wife is compared to a child that has to grow up under good guidance:

> Start teaching your child right from the beginning [of its life], start teaching your wife on the wedding day. (*Uyghur/Chinese*)
> On the first day of the year make your plans; on the first day of marriage correct your wife. (*Japanese*)
> Wives! Cleanse them and move them in—that's how to handle them. (*Berber*)
> For a house, take a ready one; for a wife, take an unready one. (*Bulgarian*)

The third point, superior talents, has been extensively dealt with in the previous chapter: wives must never exhibit such talents and stay away from all domains proclaimed male. The fourth and last point is wealth. Riches (as well as class) work in favour of the privileged, and proverbs tend to recommend for men to love and marry down, whereas women get the advice to find a husband to look up to: 'Marry above your match and you get a good master' (*Hebrew*). Still, in the inadvisable opposite case, a Turkish proverb subtly reminds women that: 'Even if the woman's candlestick is made of gold, it is the man who puts the candle in.' Unless a woman willingly accepts male superiority in spite of her own wealth and property, such a reversed situation risks creating a dramatic reversal of roles. Directly or indirectly, the frightening message is that a woman who has money 'changes into a man', as a Ghanaian Twi proverb observes, or a man becomes her servant, as a Brazilian proverb warns. Other examples come from Europe:

> Nothing is more unbearable than a rich woman. (*Italian/Latin*)
> A rich woman is conceited and often quarrels with men. (*Russian*)
> I took a wife with money; I swept the house, she was in the field. (*German*)
> In the home of a wealthy woman, she pays, commands and shouts. (*Catalan/French*)

Variants of the last above proverb are also popular in Latin America. Clearly, a woman who is economically independent equals being a 'man', whereas an economically dependent husband equals being a 'woman', and such an economic 'gender change' is considered no good at all.

Women's taking care of the four C's makes them economically depend on men who are seen as the 'natural' economic providers in the family. In proverbs it seems to be 'natural' that wealth, and material property are the domain of men, as concisely expressed in a Vietnamese saying: 'Wealth—man's [property]; work—woman's [property].' An Arabic proverb from Algeria looks into the gendered division of material well being even more pessimistically from a female perspective: 'Men's life is riches, women's life is distress.' In an Indian Telegu proverb the roles are fixed forever by simply presenting women as incapable of managing money and men of taking care of a child: 'Money left in the hands of a woman won't last; a child left in the hands of a man won't live.' In several European proverbs, particularly in German and French, wealthy women and women earning money are associated (as so often) with the Devil. It is strongly believed and defended, then, that earning money for the family is a men's job, and that wives with a job would ridicule their husbands. In many languages the message is that things need to stay as they are: 'The bread earned by the man is the most trustworthy, the laundry washed by the woman is the cleanest' (*Karelian*), or in a Finnish variant: 'The husband's [earned] bread is the tastiest, the wife's clothes the whitest.' Honestly earning money and being wealthy are male qualities, and women's being dependent and 'owned' is taken for granted:

> The man who waits for his wife's wages, will never know abundance. (*Hebrew*)
> Women's earnings: the earnings of mice. (*Korean*)

Her dependence on wedlock leads proverbs to suggesting that a woman has no alternative but to rely on some man: 'A field and a married woman are always someone's property' (*Indonesian*). Therefore, she must have found another 'boss', when she behaves rebelliously, as argued in the following African proverbs.

> A woman does not leap over the enclosure unless she wants to divorce. (*Rundi*)
> A woman who starts to oppose her husband has found a place to go. (*Ganda*)
> If a woman leaves her husband, she goes to [marry] someone else. (*Mamprusi*)

In spite of all the moulding and all the messages stressing and pressing for female dependence, several (mainly European) proverbs observe, jokingly, that marriage tames men.

> The husband is the guest, the wife is the boss of the house. (*Digor*)
> The husband is the head (of the home), the wife is the neck; she turns him whichever
>   way she wants. (*Russian/Frisian/Dutch*)
> Man is the head, and woman the nightcap on top. (*German*)
> He who takes a wife finds a master. (*French/English, USA*)

A struggle is mirrored in which both parties are trying to find a balance that suits them. 'It is easier to rule a country than to rule your wife', a Chinese proverb admits. A practical wisdom is that relationships need some investment. Despising and humiliating one's wife is useless: 'Do not say too many bad things about the wife you cannot divorce' (*Adyg*). If, on the contrary, a husband succeeds in encouraging his wife, and convincing her that her position in wedlock is an attractive and interesting one, she'll more easily commit of her own accord.

> A good husband will make a woman young, a bad one will age the girl. (*Karelian*)
> A good husband makes the wife beautiful, a bad one wears her out. (*Estonian*)
> The husband is the wife's model; when he is upright, she is good. (*Chinese*)

Here, a good wife is the product of her husband's merit. Other examples confirm this idea: 'Good soil gives good grain, a good husband makes a good wife' is a Khionghta proverb from Bangladesh. This profitable policy has already been suggested in an early Egyptian proverb: 'If her chains are pleasant, a wife is tied up twice', and it still holds in later proverbs: 'Who sugars his wife, will find a sweet wife' (*Dutch*); 'The well-fed sheep makes a cloak of its tail' (*Spanish*); 'Only on high water is the water lily at its best' (*Burmese*). Only a husband's full support will bring out the best in a wife, whether or not he thinks of the profits at stake.

Far more frequently, though, proverbs ignore the need for such negotiations or even bluntly advise against such signs of weakness, insisting that the husband moulds at will, and the wife is his 'earthen pot for moulding' in a Kenyan Luo expression. The proverbial directions for such moulding a wife are full of do's and don'ts.

DO NOT PRAISE AND DO NOT TRUST

Do not believe in the roots of yams, muddied water, and woman's words. (Bengali)

In countries as far apart from each other as Iraq, the United States, and Myanmar, proverbs agree that women should not be abundantly praised, although the ideas about the frequency or the amount of praise they possibly deserve varies. An Azeri proverb stresses that praising a wife will lead to nothing good: 'His horse, his sword, his wine, his wife, no man praised them without regret', and an Allagish proverb from Turkey is even more explicit: 'The quite stupid praises his wife; the quite wise praises his dog', whereas in Italian it is good wine, a horse and a wife that should never be praised. Other proverbs reveal a more subtle approach, with instructions to space the praise with prudent intervals:

> Do not praise your wife before seven years. (*Russian*)
> Never praise your wife until you have been married ten years. (*English, USA*)

As a precaution, still others advise against praising a wife until she has passed away. Apparently her getting spoiled or arrogant is too overwhelming a risk to be taken:

> Do not praise a day before sunset, a horse before a year, and a wife before she is dead.
>   (*Czech*)
> If you love your wife, praise her only after her death. (*Burmese*)
> Praise a woman only when she is cremated and her ashes are scattered. (*Bengali*)

The above could be variants on a more general proverb I came across in exactly the same terms in Ethiopia as well as in Scotland: 'If you wish to be blamed, marry. If you wish to be praised, die.' Blaming a wife seems to be more common than praising a wife. I found an exception, though, in an Awar proverb seeing no problem in praising: 'Teach a horse with cuddles and a wife with compliments.'

When it comes to a wife's praising her husband, men are advised to be suspicious: it could just be flattery, and who knows what lies behind a woman exhibiting warm sympathy? It all appears rather worrisome:

> A flattering woman has something bad on her mind. (*Russian*)
> If a woman praises you for climbing a tree, she is praising you to fall. (*Mamprusi*)
> When your wife is affectionate to you, be careful. (*Abkhaz*)

> A woman is seldom more tender to a man than immediately after she has deceived him. (*English, USA*)

The message of distrust is no less widely spread in proverbs referring to other domains. To express that a person that you trusted proves to be unworthy of that trust, a Persian proverb says: 'When I lifted up the tail, I found it was a female.' Literally hundreds of such proverbs refer to women's supposed infidelity, and unreliability. Many proverbs do not even specify: men ought to be suspicious, full stop. Some examples:

> There is no trusting a woman nor a tap. (*English, UK*)
> An elephant, a cobra, an old slave, a loving wife, put not your trust in them. (*Thai*)
> One should trust neither court officers nor women. (*Sanskrit*)
> Trust a woman so long as thy mother's eyes are on her. (*Japanese*)
> Woman is not a chicken cage you hang on your shoulder. [One can never be sure of one's wife.] (*Bassar, Togo*)

Cobra, court officer, yam root, tap, muddy water, wind or weather, are only a few of the items women are associated with in the context of distrust. Men are told not to share with a woman, either their secrets, their love, their trust, or their lives; moreover they should beware of women's attractiveness, promises, feelings, smiles, tears, words etc. Especially tears are a 'fountain of deceit' (*Italian*), in front of which much caution is needed:

> Do not believe a woman's tears. (*Widespread in Latin America*)
> A woman's strongest weapons are her tears. (*English, USA*)
> Women's tears are a sauce to cover vice. (*Latin*)
> A woman's strength is in her tears, a thief's in his lies. (*Bengali*)
> The last resort of a woman is tears. (*Azeri*)

Only a few proverbs take tears seriously. A Hebrew proverb observes that 'A man should take care not to make a woman weep, for God counts their tears', and in Japanese it is acknowledged that women 'treated rudely' have many reasons to cry: 'To have a thousand wettings of the sleeves is a woman's lot.' The wettings are the result of the weeping, as Japanese women used to wipe away their tears with the inside lining of their long kimono sleeves (today they would probably use tissues).

There are also proverbs warning women (and especially girls) not to trust men: 'A woman who trusts a man's oath, will cry both night and day' is a Portuguese example from Brazil. Still, women are represented in proverbs as being most untrustworthy. Especially wives are met with distrust. Earlier, in a Mongo proverb, she was compared to an *inkengi* rat who steals from the house, whereas a more straightforward Korean proverb associates a wife directly with a stranger one cannot trust.

The basic difference between men and women is that men struggle with the question of how to safeguard their paternal certainty, whereas a woman always knows that the child she is carrying is hers. A Chechen proverb may well argue that: 'The ladle knows best what is happening at the bottom of the kettle', but how to be sure that only one ladle was there? That is why the chastity of fiancées is so suspiciously guarded in many cultures. The slightest misbehaviour or even gossip could be explained as dishonour.

NOT TO BE SEEN AND NOT TO BE HEARD

Sit girl, in the corner; if you are virtuous, they will find you. (*Czech*)

Ideal female conduct could actually be summarized in this one commandment: thou shallt not draw attention to thyself, especially not from any man other than thy husband: 'For a woman, display is dishonour', in the words of a Swahili proverb from Tanzania. Even though the definition of display may differ in different cultures, the principle widely applies. The two main commandments: women are not to be seen and not to be heard.

Not to be seen means hiding oneself from the eyes of the world, sticking to the background, silencing oneself, or rather being silenced, covering oneself, and sitting behind three thresholds, as recommended to Russian girls. An Arabic proverb from the Maghreb advises girls 'to stay with their dust until their day arrives', that is to avoid dressing up before the wedding day. However, the rule does not only apply to girls, but more generally to the female species. Here is a Burmese example observing that 'A good dog keeps his tail tucked in; a good woman remains in the background.'

What then happens to those who break the mould and put themselves 'on display'? Here, the Arabic Moroccan proverb applies: 'People wonder at a camel if he climbs a roof.' It refers to a married woman who is seen on the roof terrace by people passing by. Being seen is almost equated with offering oneself as consumption good for passers by, in other words, being a prostitute. Examples from various origins in Europe and the Americas abound in the same sense:

> The woman who sits at the window gossips about everyone and everyone about her.
> (*Portuguese, Brazil*)
> A woman who loves to be at the window is like a bunch of grapes on the wayside.
> (*Italian/English, USA*)
> Woman at the window, mulberry on the wayside. (*Portuguese*)
> Woman at the window wants to sell herself cheaply. (*Spanish*)
> Woman at the window and peas on the pavement are hard to guard. (*Danish*)
> Borderlands of a river, a vineyard along the wayside and a woman passing her time at the
>   window, have no happy ending. (*Catalan/French*)

If not allowed to leave the house, what else can one do than connect with the world through the window? Women inside know everything that happens outside, Arabic proverbs suggest:

> If you have missed some news, ask the cloistered. (*Algeria*)
> If you lose a donkey, ask the women who never go out. (*Maghreb*)

No display also means not to be heard. The beautiful ornament of silence is not women's favourite necklace, as we have seen. Well-behaved girls do not talk, nor do they ask questions, let alone give orders. What utterances other than speaking or arguing are declared taboo? Singing is frowned upon: 'A singing hen and a laughing girl bode no good,' as it is said in Finnish. In fact all female sounds that exceed silence and soft whispering are disapproved of in one proverb or another, as they make girls draw attention to themselves:

A girl should not have too many conversations nor greet too many people.
  (*Arabic-Jewish*, *Yemen*)
A singing bird sells itself. (*Russian*)
Maidens should laugh softly that men hear them not. (*English*, *UK*)

Laughing, especially, is a bad presage, from America to India and Africa:

A maid that laughs is half taken. (*English*, *USA*)
A woman who laughs and accepts your presents, you kiss her whenever you want.
  (*Greek*)
She who laughs often or walks with bold steps is a harlot. (*Bengali*)
A laughing young woman; a whore or a gossip. (*Spanish*)
Laughing she got pregnant, crying she delivered. (*Oromo*)

It goes without saying that shouting and whistling women are sharply disapproved of, as in the following Arabic example from the Maghreb and West Sahara: 'Good woman speaks discreetly, gives with measure, walks and wins [sympathy]; bad woman shouts, gives in extravagance and makes dust fly around.' In Europe and the USA there is even a whole series of proverbs crying out against whistling women; half of the variants equate women who whistle with crowing hens, as quoted earlier, others offer dire consequences of one sort or another:

When girls are whistling, the holy virgin cries. (*Letzeburgish*)
Where a woman whistles, seven churches tremble. (*Czech*)
When a girl whistles the angels cry. (*English*, *USA*)

In fact there is a paradox here: how can girls decently hide themselves, and still fulfil their only sacred duty, before they grow too old? 'The singing woman needs a husband,' as an Albanian proverb says, by way of excuse. Nevertheless, modesty for girls, and for women at large, is consistently stressed, as in this Kru proverb from Liberia: 'Mind your behaviour as long as you are a girl, and the world will be interested in you.'

What happens when the prescriptions are not respected, when the proscriptions are flung to the winds? When wives break out of the moulds husbands have so carefully tried to harden into the desired shape? What can still be done when a woman's power, verbally, sexually, mentally, or otherwise, is experienced as more than a man can handle? As frustration is a bad adviser, proverbs are inclined to recommend bossy solutions.

VIOLENCE

Do not think, husband of mine, that that will startle me. (*Tamil*)

Though violence against women is practised universally, its existence has long been ignored or denied, if not seen as mere customary routine. Today, the issue is more openly debated than in the past, when it was either commonly accepted as a normal part of life or hushed up for the sake of social convenience. At the World Women's Conference of the United Nations in the year 2000, for the first time a resolution was adopted to banish all

forms of violence against women. An important new element inserted in the final docu-
ment of the conference was that emancipation policies should address not only women
but also men.

All over the world proverbs are to be found recommending wife-beating as a 'natural'
tool for forcing women, and especially wives, into submissive behaviour, but they are not
equally numerous in all parts of the world. No less than multiple pregnancies, violence is
apparently seen as a means to control women. A Turkish restaurant owner in London told
me, with some embarrassment, that his father used to say: 'A stick on the back and a child
in the womb'—that was the old way to force your wife into obedience.

Proverbs about violence against women are significantly numerous in countries surrounding the Mediterranean, and in societies those countries have been in contact with.
The similarities in form and content between a number of Iberian and Latin American
proverbs, and the frequency of some popular proverbs about wife-beating all over the
Arab world, are most striking. This certainly does not mean that violence against wives is
not an issue in other areas.

The proverbs concerned offer a broad variation in arguments and attributes in which
the basic starting point is the idea that a wife, being a man's property, can be handled and
disposed of at will. This is reflected in a juridical Mongo proverb arguing that: 'One cannot beat another's wife.' In other words: when a woman other than your own wife inflames
your ire, her husband alone is entitled to punish her physically, because he is the legal
'owner'.

Interestingly, men are advised not to scare away their wives to be prior to the wedding.
A girl might decide to abandon the very idea of marrying such a brute, as stressed in a
Khakass advice from the Russian Federation: 'Do not use the lash before you have
mounted the horse.' Or, as a Haya proverb from Tanzania says: 'With beatings you cannot
find a wife.' Sometimes even indirect signals announce marital violence: 'A man who kicks
his dog will beat his wife' (*English, USA*). Such warnings, though, do not question the le-
gitimacy of beating.

The idea of wife-beating in marriage is usually presented as a matter of fact: this is how
a husband handles his wife, or this is how things go in wedlock, as in the following
Chuwash example: 'After the wedding the kissing-months won't continue uninterrupted,
now and then there is a month of beating as well.'

The wedding is the official date for the 'ownership' to start, and therewith the right
time for establishing male authority: 'What the bride gets used to on the first night, she'll
be used to later' is the way a Ladino proverb puts it, referring to sex, but also to 'moulding'. In order to force the wife into awe and respect, a very popular Arabic proverb suggests, as a first tactic, to teach the cat: 'Beat the she-cat and [that will] teach your bride a
lesson.' This may well be an old practice. In a television interview a young Iranian woman
said that her mother advised her brother to cut the throat of a cat on the wedding night.
As a result, the frightened bride would immediately know who was the boss, and be a good
wife forever. A similar suggestion of substitute threat, though not necessarily related to
the wedding night is to be found in a Russian proverb: 'The husband hit a toad, looking
menacingly at his wife.'

WIFE-BEATING

Beat your wife regularly; if you don't know why, she will know why. (*West Africa*)

Numerous proverbs suggest using violence as an adequate means for showing off one's being a man, especially in societies where men are required to prove that they are 'real' men. An Arabic proverb from the Maghreb compares it to another manly task: 'The man who cannot slaughter his sheep or beat his wife [when she deserves it], it is better for him to die than to live.' Authoritative manly behaviour ought to serve as a preventive measure against female subversion, and violence is no less recommended as an efficient means before or after her actual 'failing': 'To keep your wife on the rails, beat her—and if she goes off the rails, beat her.' (*Spanish, Puerto Rico*).

What kind of men actually practice wife-beating? Research about the topic in cultures and countries in all continents confirms that it takes place in all layers of societies. An Arabic proverb from Syria and Lebanon states that: 'It is not only the villain who beats his wife.' Violence is often the outcome of stress caused by imagined or real lack of control over a wife's social and more specifically sexual behaviour. The way this loss of control is perceived depends partly on the individual man, and to a large extent on the norms prevailing in the community concerned. Violence is not therefore only a domestic problem between husband and wife, it is also related to the real or imagined reputation of the husband concerned in the community and among other men. And of course it is related to the prevailing 'customs' and laws in the countries concerned regarding beating: is it socially accepted or even recommended, or is it disapproved of?[122]

Who are the victims of spousal violence referred to in proverbs? Although there are a very small number of proverbs about husband-beating (to be discussed below), usually it is women who are the victims, just ordinary women, mainly wives who are the objects of domestic violence. Any wife can become a victim, if one takes into account the large numbers of messages, just simply recommending beating as a self-evident practice. Here are a few samples from different corners of the globe:

> Women, like gongs, should be beaten regularly. (*English, USA*)
> A bad woman and a good woman both need the rod. (*Spanish, Argentina*)
> Good horses and bad horses need the spurs, good women and bad women need the whip.
>   (Many variants in both Europe and the America's)
> Do not spare a bullock or a wife. (*Burmese*)
> Caulk a new boat; beat a new wife. (*Khionghta*)

Numerous other proverbs allege arguments of all kinds justifying a husband's brute force whenever he considers the wife's behaviour as subversive or disrespectful. There are hundreds of proverbs furnishing one reason or another in favour of such physical punishment: she is being quarrelsome, naughty, foolish, opinionated, arrogant, impertinent etc.

> A quarrelsome woman is rightly hit. (*Latin/German*)
> If the wife is foolish the lash should be strong. (*Kazakh*)
> Claim-beatings-again tells her husband he is castrated. (*Rwanda*)

Other proverbs stress that the practice of violence is profitable to the man himself: his wife will be sweeter, more chaste, harder working, and thus his own life gets improved. Being beaten will turn her into a good wife; a better wife; a more silent wife; a tamed wife; and it will drive the devils out of her:

> Clubbing produces virtuous wives. (*Chinese*)
> A woman who is beaten is going to be a better wife. (*Korean*)
> The nails of a cart and the head of a woman, they only work when they are hit hard. (*Rajasthani*)
> For who beats up his wife, God improves the food. (*Russian*)
> A nut, a stockfish, and a young wife should be beaten, in order to be good. (*Polish*)
> A woman, a dog and a walnut tree, the harder you beat them, the better they be. (*English, UK/USA*)

Sexuality and violence are quite often linked in proverbs where beating and love are presented as two sides of the same coin. Does this mean that violence is considered or experienced to be a means of sexual pleasure, or does it mean that the argument is used to justify the practice of violence, or to force the wife to stay, or to keep her from being unfaithful? It is difficult to establish the real meaning of proverbs in which beating is (light-heartedly?) recommended over and again as a true sign of a man's affection towards his wife:

> Affection begins at the end of the rod. (*Korean*)
> When two camels love each other, they bite and kick each other. (*Turkish*)
> If you really love your wife you have to beat her. (*Tigrinya, Eritrea*)
> Where there are no punches, there is no affection.
>   (*Spanish, Mexico; Quechua/Spanish, Bolivia/Argentina*)
> Love well; whip well. (*English, USA*)
> Because of love, sticks have broken bones. (*Belorussian*)

Being beaten is even presented as just fun, as making wives happy, because it reminds them that their husbands do not ignore them, as in this Hausa proverb: 'Now the marriage is going to begin, as the neglected wife said, when she was flogged with thorns.' Without being beaten, it is ironically argued, how could a wife be sure that her husband loves her? Without, her marital life would be just boring:

> If your lover hits you, it's only for comfort. (*Romanian*)
> To be beaten by your lover is like eating a raisin. (*Arabic*)
> If you don't thrash your wife, she might think she's already a widow. (*Armenian*)

Some proverbs, especially in Latin America, go so far as to argue that it is being beaten up that makes a wife love her husband: 'Women, like dogs: the more you beat them, the more they love you.' (*Spanish, Argentina*) There is an old Calypso song confirming this pattern of thinking: 'Knock them down, they love you long ... Take a piece of iron and bruise their knees, and they love you eternally.' All this overwhelming love is expressed in proverbs recommending bashing, punching, shaking, thrashing, kicking, trampling, etc. Both fists and feet are to be used, and further helpful instruments specifically mentioned for the purpose are rod, stick, cane, whip, knife, club and hammer.

Violence and fear of one's own emotions often seem to go hand in hand. Being the subject of beating, creates the illusion of being in control, as much as loss of control provokes fear. In the above idea of beating as an expression of love, it is the husband who takes the initiative and is the agent. However, he who falls in love becomes a vulnerable object of uncontrollable emotions. This is aptly expressed in a Spanish proverb from Cuba, which significantly reverses the gendered message of violence as a sign of love: 'If you love your wife, you will be beaten up.' In other words: don't fall in love. In the previous chapters we have come across the enormous fear of being dependent upon women as expressed in proverbs often literally referring to the awesome power of women's bodies, their killing hair, killing eyes, killing tongue, killing skirts, killing hips, their killing beauty, love, sex etc.

There is no explicit reference to sado-masochism in proverbs, and certainly not as it is promoted today in pornographic magazines, films, videos and on internet sites. Nor do women themselves express pleasure in being handled aggressively by men—although some proverbs pretend that women derive pleasure from it. Neither do men in proverbs ever state how much they love being thrashed or whipped by wives, girlfriends or prostitutes, gratefully paying their female partners for the violent experience of being beaten up.

HUSBAND-BEATING

A man knocked down by a woman will not get up again. (Kumyk)

Among hundreds of proverbs about wife-beating, I found no more than about a dozen referring to women's physical violence against men. They all originate from societies where proverbs about wife-beating also occur. Such violence against men seems due to mutual quarrelling or to women's fighting back as a matter of self-defence; in rare cases women are presented as those who take the initiative in such behaviour.[123] In contrast with the numerous proverbs recommending and approving of wife-beating, those addressing violence against husbands express fear, unease, plain indignation or despair, expressed in a Hebrew proverb from Yemen: 'Only God can help when a wife hits her husband.'

In Europe, the idea of husband-beating is condemned, for example by associating a woman who would dare do this with the Devil (who once again takes sides with her here). 'A woman who hits her husband will find her death in the Devil's country' (*Portuguese*).

An American proverb foresees another familiar punishment for such a wife: 'When a woman throws a man over he usually lands on his knees before another woman.' Adequate counter-measures are suggested against such terrible female subversion. As in war, men are advised to strike first, as expressed in the following Bulgarian proverb: 'When you do not thrash your wife's neck once a week, she will snatch at yours.' Some other proverbs express amusement or jest about the very idea: 'If you prostrate yourself before your wife, you keep your teeth intact', it is said in Burmese. At the same time, being a woman's victim is considered a real disgrace for a man, who will feel ashamed in front of the people in his community. Where could he go and lodge a complaint? In the words of a Brazilian proverb: 'He who is hit by a woman doesn't go and complain to the police.'

ANYONE AGAINST?

Hitting a wife is like hitting a sack of flour: the good flies out and the bad remains. (Swedish)

Today more countries legislate against violence within the family, including taking juridical measures to outlaw wife-beating. In addition, ever more women all over the world consider themselves less than before to be their husband's property. In many societies though, even today, men are still publicly being encouraged to keep control over their wives and criticized when they appear to be unable to do so. In such cases wife-beating is condoned; it is often simply viewed as necessary, and culturally expected, for a man to beat his wife. So far, most proverbs we have come across on this subject were fully in favour, strongly stressing that such behaviour should be encouraged. Fortunately, there are also a few fragile voices—even in those cultures that so warmly recommend violence—that also question wife-beating. I found two proverbs, one from Brazil, one from China, categorically against:

> Women should not be beaten, not even with a flower. (*Portuguese, Brazil*)
> A good man does not beat a woman; a good dog does not fight with a chicken. (*Chinese*)

A few others argue that a successful, self-confident man does not need to prove himself by degrading his wife; he has better things to do. The problem is presented as a 'losers'' problem:

> A real man hugs his wife, a weak man hits her. (*Adyg*)
> No-one beats a woman except the wretched man. (*Arabic, Lebanon*)
> A man beats a wife at home only when he has no public status. (*Bengali*)
> Sullen clouds let fall rain, a sullen husband lets fall blows. (*Khiongbta*)

Still others question the envisaged outcome, arguing that brutal behaviour meant to yield a man both a submissive wife and prestige in the community, turn out to having the opposite effect. Instead of the anticipated public 'honour' or 'glory', it produces an embittered wife:

> Whipping a woman gives a man no glory. (*Swedish*)
> You are not honoured for beating your wife. (*Macedonian*)
> A slap does not get a woman. (*Mamprusi*)
> A man should not hit his wife; when one devil is struck out ten new ones go in.
>   (*German/Danish*)
> Women and grapes should not be squeezed because they will be bitter. (*Spanish*)
> You can shut up a hog by beating it but not a woman. (*Spanish, Argentina*)

Several European proverbs compare wife-beating to one part of the body hitting another part. This equates with what we have seen throughout, namely that wives are mostly considered as some man's property:

> Who beats up his wife, beats up his own body. (*Russian*)
> Who beats his wife, beats his head, who beats his oxen, beats his money-bag.
>   (*Bulgarian/Romanian*)

He who hits his wife, hits his own back. (*Swedish*)
He who beats his wife, beats his left hand with his right hand. (*Danish*)

The point being made here is not so much a protest against wife-beating as it is a warning not to damage or incapacitate one's own property, as such behaviour would go against one's own profit and interests, as for example in the Kurdish proverb of Jewish origin stating that 'Whoever hits his wife, hits his fortune.'

Finally, and exceptionally, two proverbs offer alternative positive measures of correction, in the form of loving attention or otherwise pleasant treatment, in Russian: 'Beat your pelt with temper, your wife with tenderness', and in Swahili: 'A wife should not be beaten with a stick but with food and cloth.' Without physical attack, other negative measures—divorce, taking a lover or adding a new co-wife to the family are other quite disastrous moves—are certainly no less humiliating for wives in a situation of dependence:

Punish your wife with a rival rather than using a whip. (*Hebrew*)
Beat wives with wives and not with a stick.(*Arabic, Maghreb*).

A final point to be dealt with is community intervention. Those who see or hear what is going on, what are they supposed to do?

Husband and wife quarrel and the fools take it seriously. (*Persian*)
When husband and wife quarrel, the donkey should not interfere. (*Mongolian*)
When husband and wife quarrel, they get the benefit of neighbours laughing at them.
   (*Danish*)
When husband and wife quarrel, keep your distance. (*Dutch*)
Let the Devil interfere in the quarrels of a married couple. (*Spanish, Puerto Rico*)
One should not interfere in spousal quarrels. (*Spanish, Chile/Cuba*)

No negative sanctions are mentioned. There seems to be no protection for wives. Outsiders should mind their own business. Better to just laugh or give a shrug. It is even likely that the wife concerned would belittle or deny the violent quarrel with her husband: she has to think of her own survival. Where could she go? Significantly, a Twi proverb chooses the husband's side: 'If you find a man fighting with his wife, don't interrupt; only the husband knows what the wife has done to him.'

WOMEN'S REACTIONS

Women will always be blamed for everything. (Sranan)

Where, then, does the experience of wives, the victims of this tragedy, and their own position or interests come in to consideration? Women are advised to keep silent about violence committed against them, because public opinion would not appreciate a battered woman lodging a complaint against her husband. She would embarrass her man through such a daring action, as a Ganda proverb observes: 'Only a shameful wife takes her husband to court.' On the other hand, the Tsonga proverb stressing that 'Women have no court' reflects that little importance is attached to a woman's word anyway. Proverbs do not seem to support and sympathize with such a female counter-initiative, and rarely take into account women's feelings of embarrassment and humiliation when they are the objects of violence.

Indirectly, a few proverbs express some consideration for the uncomfortable situation of the two spouses as they notice both the man's lack of security as the cause of wife-beating and the wife's miserable fate. Tensions due to stress at work or confrontations with other more authoritative people in the outside world easily explode at home where the husband himself tries to work off his frustrations and bad temper on the one he has power over: his wife. Two examples, Ladino and Ganda, respectively: 'Humiliated by the men, he came home to his poor wife'; 'The fool beaten up at a beer party takes it out on his wife.' And yet, such proverbs do not really adopt a victim's perspective.

Another variant on this theme is an Efik proverb from Nigeria; it differs in two ways from the three examples above: it addresses the angry man directly and does so from a female perspective. Its form is a polite but no less reproachful question, and the metaphor usefully serves as a shield to protect the one who quotes the proverb: 'The crab bit you, but you came [home] and bit the water.' In other words: why do you punish me for something somebody else did to you? Still, this proverb only indirectly reflects a woman's thoughts, feelings and reactions as a victim of violence. The proverb is not the right place to look for direct answers to questions such as: How do aggressed women feel? Do they swallow their humiliation? Do they talk or fight back? Do they find ways to escape their fate? If they are able to leave, where do they find shelter? Only incidentally are tiny tips of this dark veil of suffering lifted.

Such widespread terror and violence inevitably fill women not only with a strong sense of fear and with deep feelings of inferiority and inadequacy. However, proverbs pay little attention to such issues. I found only a handful referring to the effect such humiliation has on one's identity. A Tatar proverb draws attention to the loss of women's self-respect in the process: 'If your husband loves you, people respect you; if your husband beats you, people will humiliate you too'; and a Bengali proverb refers to a wife's being ruined by being beaten. An Ovambo proverb accepts the practice as an inescapable 'fate': 'A wife's fate is not easy: you are beaten with a stick and you must be silent, because grown-ups don't cry.'

In a Rwanda proverb from a female perspective, wife-beating is also presented as if it were a fatality that women must bear with: 'A woman beaten for misbehaviour says: "Only she without one can ridicule me"'—one without a vagina, that is. Young wives who are still full of self-confidence are advised not to laugh when older ones are being beaten up, because they will not escape their fate. In other words, don't laugh at someone else's trouble, because 'The same stick will beat both the white and the black hen' (*Sranan*).

That women try to avoid their 'fate' is reflected in a Ganda proverb suggesting a subtle subversive solution: 'If a wife sees the stick that beats her co-wife, she throws it into the wilds.' Women have never stopped looking for means to prevent their husbands from humiliating and beating them, for example by threatening to leave, as in the following Rwanda proverb: 'The stick of a girl is: "Touch me and I'll leave."' The option of quitting marriage and returning home can serve as a preventive means of defence. This is obviously the only hope left in the following Arabic proverb from Syria and Lebanon: 'The house that has raised me, does not forget me'—quoted by a woman mistreated by her mother-in-law and husband to comfort herself with the idea that she can always return home if her life becomes really intolerable.

Women may also succeed in evening up the balance by the various means of power at their disposal discussed earlier, such as their verbal talents, or their indispensability in taking care of the household. If things get really out of hand, suicide is the last resort for a Ganda wife reminding her violent husband that: 'A woman's rope is always ready on the porch.'

Two Arabic proverbs present women talking defiantly back against violence, literally. One blames the husband for having double standards, when, in front of his friends he has to keep up standards of maleness, by showing he has real authority over his wife: 'In public you want to beat me and at home you want to get on well with me?' The wife refuses to play the game. The second proverb, from Syria and Lebanon, represents women's strength as well: 'If I see you in your house I will tear your *izár* [veil]; she replies: first you will have to see me there.' Indeed, a man can only hit his wife when her veil is off, that means: at home. The proverb refers to people who make threats they are unable to perform.

Proverbs reflect a rather uncomfortable state of the art. Numerous proverbs advising violence against women justify such action by first projecting violence on to women themselves, in messages suspecting them and accusing them of using poison or invoking witchcraft, or killing men by their uncontrollable powers. Two earlier-mentioned proverbs, from Chile and Nigeria respectively, directly hint at female sexual violence: 'Women are violent, they even overthrow a man's penis', is Mapuche, and 'The penis comes erect as if it intends to kill, but the vagina swallows and tames it' is Igbo.

Proverbs about violence against women reflect anger as well as helplessness *vis-à-vis* the drives and needs which only women are believed to be able to satisfy.[124] The confused fear of imagined female power, in combination with men's enormous benefit from and dependence on 'women's work' discussed earlier, may well have contributed to the strong aggression so many of the above messages display, notwithstanding much jesting.

The ideal wife, then, is chaste, reserved, faithful, decent, silent, invisible, reliable, zealous, profitable, and willingly lets herself be moulded by her husband into the wished for submissiveness: 'A young wife should be no more than an echo or a shadow in her husband's house', says a Japanese proverb. And her name is 'Yes', as a Wolof proverb has taught us. Finally, if I may, what does the ideal husband look like? In a Hebrew proverb he is described as follows: 'The ideal man has a man's strength and a woman's compassion.' And the ideal man never acts aggressively, I'd like to add.

Female Power Anthology

Each of us a trouser-leg, said the wife, and she took the whole pair of trousers.

    (*Frisian, Netherlands*): *o.s. Beintema 121*

A smart woman gives the man glory, a wicked one spreads rumours. (*Russian*): *Geyvandov 121*

Where the wife wears the trousers, the husband changes diapers.

    (*Letzeburgish*): *o.s. Laure Wolter*

A sensible woman leaves her husband the trousers.

    (*German; Dutch*): *Harrebomée II 420; Mesters 27*

The cunning wife makes her husband her apron. (*English, UK*): *Williams IV 144*

When the wife wears the pants, the husband rocks the child.

    (*Ladino/Hebrew, Israel*): *Rosten 1977: 487; Stahl 244*

If your petticoat fits you well, do not try to put on your husband's pants.

    (*Creole, Martinique*): *Hearn 34*

Where woman wears the trousers and man the apron, there things turn out badly.

    (*Italian*): *Meier-Pfaller 72; Reinsberg-Düringsfeld 216*

A woman in trousers, what is dangling inside? (*Benin*): *Kouavi 83*

A woman should never be outstanding or irregular: her face should not be too pretty, nor her words too clever or her work too good. (*Chinese*): *Geyvandov 218*

If too clever a woman gets married, she does not succeed. (*Twi, Ghana*): *o.s. Peggy Appiah*

A mule that whinnies and a woman that talks Latin never come to any good.

    (*English, USA*): *Brunvand 97*

Women's wisdom destroys houses. (*Russian*): *Geyvandov 268*

Even God cannot build what a wife can build. (*Armenian*): *Sakayan 241*

VERBAL TALENT

Take a smart one, and she does not let you say a word. (*Russian*): *o.s. Anna Ravve*

Women! Seven mouths, eight languages to chat in. (*Chinese*): *Fabre 58*

Listen to your wife once every forty years. (*Turkish*): *Geyvandov 131*

Women are nine times more talkative than men. (*Hebrew, Israel*): *Rosten 1977: 493*

The strength of women is nothing but a plenitude of talk.

  (*Hausa, Niger/Nigeria*): *Champion 535; Geyvandov 200 Whitting 93*

A woman's word is wind in the wind, a man's word is rock in the wall.

  (*Arabic, Morocco*): *Lunde & Wintle 137*

Men talk like books; women lose themselves in details. (*Chinese*): *Fabre 257*

Man thinks and talks, woman talks and does not think. (*Estonian*): *Geyvandov 237*

Deeds are male, words are female.

  (*Greek; Italian; Dutch; Hebrew, Israel*): *Rosten 1977: 160; Cohen 1961: 125, 174; Mesters 107;*
  Bohn 1855: 108; Bohn 1857: 5; o.s. Laure Wolter

Words are female, deeds are macho. (*Portuguese, Brazil*): *Lamenza 181; Rubio 287*

Words wear petticoats, deeds trousers. (*Spanish, Mexico*): *Rubio 287*

Three inches of a woman's tongue can slay a man six feet tall.

  (*Japanese*): *Lunde & Wintle 121; Champion 447*

A wife's long tongue is the flight of steps by which misfortune comes [to the house].

  (*Chinese*): *Champion 382*

Even a fifty-tongued man cannot equal a single-tongued woman at abusing.

  (*Sinhalese, Sri Lanka*): *Champion 428*

A woman's tongue is sharper than a Turkish sabre. (*Serbian/Croatian*): *Mieder 1986: 489*

AN INBORN QUALITY?

A woman's sword [her tongue] will never rust. (*Sumerian, Mesopotamia*): *Geyvandov 200*

A woman's sword is her tongue and she does not let it rust.

  (*Hebrew, Israel; Chinese*): *Cohen 1961: 574; Champion 379*

A woman's tongue is a sword. (*Portuguese, Brazil*): *Souto Maior 36*

A woman's tongue is a double-edged sword. (*Romanian*): *Günther 32–33*

A woman's tongue is sharper than a double-edged sword. (*English, USA*): *Mieder 1986: 51*

A woman has two ears and one tongue, therefore she should listen twice as much as she talks.

  (*Spanish, Chile*): *o.s. Luis Ramírez*

A woman's common sense is in her tongue. (*Portuguese, Brazil*): *Souto Maior 69*

The tongue is babbling, but the head knows nothing about it. (*Russian*): *Günther 53*

The language of women: a viper's tongue and a wasp's sting. (*Chinese*): *Fabre 57*

Woman's vigor is [the] strength of her tongue. [Woman's power is in her nagging.]

  (*Turkish*): *Haig 128*

Women's tongues are longer than their skirts. (*Dutch*): *Harrebomée II 419*

Women's tongues are longer than their arms. (*English, UK*): *Williams I 472*

Woman's hair is long, but her tongue is even longer. (*Russian*): *Geyvandov 235*

A woman's hair is long; her tongue is longer. (*English, USA*): *Mieder 1992: 666*

He who is not smart in speech and argument should not take a talkative wife.

(*Yoruba, Nigeria*): *Areje 45*

A fish doesn't need to learn how to swim, a woman doesn't need to learn how to talk.

(*Ladino, Morocco*): *Dahan 170*

Women are born chatterboxes. (*Japanese*): *Buchanan 267*

Who will not marry a talkative woman stays a bachelor. (*Mongo, Congo DR*): *Hulstaert 600*

Where women abound, noise abounds. (*Oromo, Ethiopia*): *Cotter 58*

THE JEWEL OF SILENCE

A silent wife is a gift from the Lord. (*Hebrew, Israel*): *Alcalay 523*

A wise woman has a great deal to say and remains silent. (*All over Asia*): *Champion 460*

Silence is a woman's most beautiful ornament.

(*English, UK; Greek; Italian*): *Smith & Hesseltine 589; Attanasio 179; Leutsch & Schneidewin 354*

Silence is a fine jewel for a woman, but she seldom wears it.

(*Danish; English, USA*): *Champion 110; Kin 234*

It is easier for women to give birth than to keep silence. (*German*): *Wander I 1366*

It is not in the nature of the female tongue to be silent. (*English, USA*): *Whiting 1977: 494*

Tell your wife a secret, but cut her tongue.

(*Hebrew; Yiddish*): *Cohon 1961: 445; Geyvandov 273*

A marriageable daughter who doesn't chat at all, tells a lot about herself by keeping silence.

(*Greek*): *Leutsch & Schneidewin 354; Van Dijk-Hemmes 13*

The clouds that have many dragon-sounds [thunder] are without rain; the maiden who talks
    too much will have no wedding feast. (*Tibetan*): *Duncan 235*

Daughters should be seen, not heard. (*Dutch*): *Bohn 1857: 311*

A woman and a bitch, one that keeps silence is good. (*Spanish*): *Bergua 343*

There is no more shining dress for a woman than silence.

(*Hebrew*): *Cohen 1961: 456*; (*Russian*): *Graf 144*

Kind words and few are a woman's ornament. (*Danish*): *Cordry 288*

The woman and the melon: of both the silent one is the best.

(*Portuguese, Portugal/Brazil*): *Mota 74; Chaves 894*

A quiet wife is mighty pretty. (*English, USA*): *Kin 279*

Encouraged by the hen, the cock tells the hour. (*Japanese*): *Buchanan 259*

Between women there is female talk; between men, male talk, but what can a man and a
    woman talk? (*Sinhalese, Sri Lanka*): *o.s. Alex Gunasekare*

The intelligence of a woman is in her tongue. (*Arabic, Iraq*): *o.s. Muzan*

WORK

The entire world is a hotel for men. (*Dutch*): *o.s. Anonymous*

'WOMAN'S WORK'

Marry, marry, and who is to keep house? (*Spanish*): *Collins 80*

A bad husband does not see all the work his wife has done. (*Kundu, Cameroon*): *Geyvandov 226*

He who enters a clean house and sits down at a table which is set does not know how much it
  costs. (*Spanish, Puerto Rico*): *Fernández Valledor 60*

The women's *souk* [market] will never take place. (*Berber, Morocco*): *Bentolila 40*

A woman sells garden-eggs, not gunpowder. (*Twi, Ghana*): *o.s. Peggy Appiah*

Hoe is hen, machete is cock. [Women's task is to till the land, their tool is the hoe. It is a
  men's task to fell trees and clear the land before women can begin their part of the job,
  the tilling.] (*Hehe, Tanzania*): *Madumulla 164*

Men plough, women weave. (*Chinese*): *Yu Jialou 31; o.s. Zhang Hongjuan*

When girls do the ploughing, it will cause drought for three years.
  (*Chinese*): *o.s. Huang Mingfen*

When the male soul is alive, the female soul does not crack nuts. (*Ashanti, Ghana*): *Oduyoye 7*

A woman does not split the head [of an animal] nor dip the cup into the beer.
  (*Gikuyu, Kenya*): *Barra 71*

If a man has a cook, why should he burn his fingers? (*Arabic, widespread*): *Lunde & Wintle 133*

She may not be the submissive type but she'll wash the napkins. (*Indonesian*): *o.s. Hellwig*

When the harvest season is over, women weave, men forge. (*Thai*): *Peltier 26*

On the sixteenth of the first moon the lamps of the ancestors are extinguished; the boys go
  to school, the girls behind the spinning-wheel. (*Chinese*): *Fabre 633*

The daughter at the spinning-wheel and the son at the shield. (*Spanish*): *Bergua 265*

A father to his desk, a mother to her dishes. (*English, USA*): *Kin 191*

Educated women, stupid housewives. (*Danish*): *Storm Petersen 23*

Woman has only been created for the house. (*Ladino/Hebrew, Maghreb*): *Dahan 189*

For a woman, marriage is a profession. (*Portuguese, Brazil*): *Vasconcellos 97*

Trust in God is male, worldly cares are female. (*Persian*): *Roebuck 169*

Woman is a moving wheel; it is the man who brings in the money.
  (*Arabic, Syria/Lebanon*): *Feghali 177*

The prostitute's breadwinner is her bottom. (*Minyanka, Mali*): *Cauvin 1980: 78*

Like a bucket in the public bath, use a whore but pass her on.
  (*Arabic, widespread*): *Lunde & Wintle 113*

A woman who can be hired is as cheap as spittle. (*Hebrew, Israel*): *Alcalay 203*

Whores affect not you but your money. (*English, UK*): *Bohn 1855: 22*

'If I get a chance, I will marry; if I fail, I will live by prostitution', said the spinster.
  (*Oromo, Ethiopia*): *Cotter 16*

A poor whore and a good woman do not exist. (*Spanish*): *Bergua 426*

Whores' work gives shady money. (*German*): *Wander II 936*

Women can earn money lying down. (*Portuguese, Brazil*): *Mota 187*

A prostitute does not recommend marriage. (*Wolof, Senegal*): *o.s. Papa Gueye N'Diaye*

A woman has to be: a lady in the street, a maid in the kitchen and a whore in bed.
  (*Many variants, e.g. Dutch; English*): *Champion 45; Williams IV 200; Williams IV 200; Pineaux
  87; Meier-Pfaller 61; o.s. Overmaat*

The first wife is a shepherdess, the second a lady. (*Catalan, Spain; French*): *Guiter 119*

The [female] miller got floury hands. (*Lithuanian*): *Schleicher 162*

The old woman shaved her sheep and dances with her lambs. (*Greek*): *Politès 16*

Women that don't like to spin become good landladies. (*German*): *Wander I 1122*

The wise woman gathers herbs when they are blossoming and have a nice scent.

    (*Sorbian*): *Herrmann 23*

On the heads of orphans hairdressers learn their trade. (*Arabic, Morocco*): *Lunde & Wintle 101*

Better to fool your excisor than your hairdresser. [Excision (female circumcision) only happens once in your life.] (*Fulfulde, Senegal*): *Gaden 22*

The nurse is more friendly than the mother. (*Persian*): *Roebuck 258*

When the midwife is a bad one, she will blame the crescent moon. (*Spanish, Mexico*): *Casasola 25*

The son of a midwife knows everything [lit.: nothing is a secret to him, for the midwife knows all the gossip of the town.] (*Arabic, Lebanon*): *Frayha I 9*

When a woman feeds the cows, even the horns will give milk. (*French*): *Wander I 1132*

Every woman praises her cow [butter]. (*German*): *Wander I 271*

Of her cheesecake are made shoes and blankets. (*Digor, RF*): *Geyvandov 264*

Two smart women do not plant rice on one field. [Rivalry, co-wives.]

    (*Kru, Ivory Coast/Liberia*): *Geyvandov 37*

Do not choose your wife at a dance, but on the field amongst harvesters.

    (*Czech*): *Mieder 1986: 526; Champion 103*

God save us from the women-mourners. (*Arabic, widespread*): *Khalil Safadi 46*

The afflicted mother, who has lost her children, is not like the woman who weeps for hire.

    (*Arabic, Egypt*): *Burckhardt 214*

A wife who cannot sing a lament, what a pity for her husband's death.

    (*Ladino, Morocco*): *Dahan 305*

The shopkeeper cannot stand the burden and if she does not complain it is because she does not have a voice. (*Spanish, Cuba*): *Cabrera n.p.*

The woman who sells fans generally has nothing but her hands to shade her eyes.

    (*Chinese*): *Lunde & Wintle 136*

When the wife of the confectioner does not sell, she is eating. (*Portuguese*): *Chaves 857*

Who says marriage is easy, should try and fetch water on one's own from a faraway well.

    (*Ladino, Morocco*): *Dahan 214*

Oh! Joy for the inhabitants of Achqout, when the water bottle gurgles; a woman says 'It overflows', another one replies 'May God hear you.' (*Arabic, Lebanon*): *Feghali 233–4*

Don't interrupt a woman fetching water. (*Namibian*): *Knappert 197*

When the river dries up, one cannot fetch water for the husband's bath.

    (*Kundu, Cameroon*): *Geyvandov 193*

The man who has no pitcher is very thirsty. (*Taka, Congo DR*): *Beken 1993: 238*

The childless one anoints herself before she goes out to chop firewood. (*Rwanda*): *Crépeau 255*

Fit for wood collecting, unfit for marriage. (*Arabic, Syria/Lebanon*): *Feghali 195*

The faggot brought home by the woman becomes the cat-o'nine-tails that beats her.

    (*Sara, Chad*): *Bon & Colin 95*

Not every woman making a fire knows how to cook. (*Arabic*): *Wijnaendts-Francken 22*

A [large] group of women and the waterbag stays empty. (*Ladino, Morocco*): *Dahan 287*

Four women in the tent means an empty water-skin.

    (*Arabic, Algeria*): *Lunde & Wintle 84*

When discussing marriage, they say I'm small, when discussing fetching water, they say I'm
   big. (*Azeri, Azerbaijan*): Geyvandov 238

A bad home sends you for water and firewood. (*Rwanda*): Crépeau 541

Don't take a wife who has money; she will treat you with arrogance and say to you: 'Fetch
   water'. (*Arabic, Morocco*): Westermarck 71

Beaten up by his wife, Shyirambe says: 'Give me a pitcher, I will go and draw water.'
   (*Rwanda*): Crépeau 392

My darling wife, please do not cook for me. I shall eat raw rice, please do not cry.
   (*Bengali, India*): o.s. Sanjukta Gupta

COOKERY

Already the unborn child said: 'My mother is the best cook.' (*Haya, Tanzania*): Geyvandov 277

However holy a day may be, the pot still has to boil. (*Portuguese, Brazil*): Mota 168

The dish is not for the one who prepares it, but for the one who eats it.
   (*Portuguese, Brazil*): Magalhães Júnior 221

The housewife is already satisfied by preparing the meal. (*Finnish*): Geyvandov 254

The little wife who can cook well, in high esteem is held by man. (*Dutch*): Münch n.p.

However smart a woman may be, she'll end up in the kitchen. (*Indonesian*): o.s. Puntowati

A woman and a sardine will have to face the kitchen. (*Spanish, Argentina*): Moya 489

A woman and a frying-pan belong to the kitchen. (*Spanish, Chile*): o.s. Lyncoyan Silva

Wife and stove belong in the kitchen. (*Ladino, Morocco*): Benazeraf 92

A capable housewife can make a kettle boil, even in snow. (*Tatar, RF*): Geyvandov 128

Let the bride be a blockhead, if she only blows the fire in time. (*Russian*): Geyvandov 265

What explodes in the pot won't kill a man. [Cooking matters are women's concerns.]
   (*Rwanda*): Crépeau 44

Our mother knows how to make a bread, if only she has the flour. (*Greek*): Politès 12

If your mother is not there, your bowels ache while eating. [The presence of the mother
   sweetens the food.] (*Ganda, Uganda*): Walser 64

Water is good even if it flows through a canal and a meal served by a mother is good even if it
   is not fresh. (*Rajasthami, India*): Bhatnagar 75

If mother and son agree, just vegetables will be good enough for breakfast.
   (*Tibetan*): Gergan 122

Spring days grow longer and longer and the mother's bread becomes smaller and smaller.
   [Poverty.] (*Tibetan*): Gergan 58

When the children are numerous, the mother suffers. (*Chinese*): Scarborough 196

Pity comes to a mother when she sees that the food is ending. (*Ganda, Uganda*): Walser 125

If the mother-banana tree is drying up, the young shoots also dry up.
   (*Yaka, Congo DR*): Beken 1993: 91

A mother-mouse does not make her own stomach sweet. [The mother always thinks of the
   child to the extent of forgetting herself: she shares everything with her child: thus her
   own stomach is never satisfied.] (*Tonga, Zambia*): Milimo 12

Since its young have arrived, the crow does not remember what a full stomach feels like.
   (*Persian*): Geyvandov 164

A breeding hen works but does not eat. [A mother works to feed her children in the first
   place.] (*Ngaka Bali-Nyonga, Cameroon*): *Stöckle 233*

Who can say 'mother', has the mouth full. (*Catalan, Spain*): *Guiter 143*

He whose mother is in the house will eat with oil. [He will enjoy rich food.]
   (*Arabic, Tunisia*): *Lunde & Wintle 123*

He that has a mother eats cake. (*Catalan, Spain*): *Guiter 143*

No pap like mother's to nourish. (*English, UK*): *Whiting 1968: 22, 446*

It is only in your mother's kitchen that you can be choosy [and not in someone else's].
   (*Ashanti, Ghana*): *Oduyoye 10*

He who eats with his mother will not cry for scraps [i.e. favours]. (*Hausa, Nigeria*): *Ibekwe 66*

The child who has a mother has flour [food]. (*Mossi, Burkina Faso*): *o.s. Alizata Sawadogo*

When one's mother is the cook one is happy round the year. (*Bengali, India*): *Long I 33*

'Is it not cooking you have come here for?' [says the husband to his wife who refuses to cook
   in the morning]. (*Ganda, Uganda*): *Walser 179*

Every husband is his wife's pig; he eats everything she prepares. (*Estonian*): *Geyvandov 253*

Whatever the half-blind wife cooks for her husband, he sups on it. (*Arabic, Egypt*): *Burckhardt 14*

The wife who prepares food does not enjoy her marriage. (*Taka, Congo DR*): *Beken 1993: 206*

As the man wishes, so the steak is broiled for him. (*Russian*): *Graf 169*

The roots of love are situated in the [man's] belly. (*Berber, Morocco*): *Bentolila 18*

The one who asks for mashed food has someone to mash it. [Unless a man has a wife, he
   cannot expect well-cooked food.] (*Gikuyu, Kenya*): *Ngumbu Ngururu 81*

A wife should not prepare the stew her husband does not like. (*Yoruba, Nigeria*): *Areje 45*

The one you enjoy feeding is the one you love. (*Digor, RF*): *Geyvandov 254*

As she is, the wife cooks the cabbage. (*Russian*): *Graf 146*

If a wife is going downhill, she eats what she has put aside for her husband.
   (*Oromo, Ethiopia*): *Cotter 15*

A wife does not love her husband, when she lets him starve. (*Taka, Congo DR*): *Beken 1993: 219*

Only now and again a wife hates her husband and rice. (*Tamil, India/Sri Lanka*): *Geyvandov 285*

Prettiness makes no pottage. (*Irish*): *O'Rahilly 6*

She mightn't be much good to boil a pot of spuds but she'd look lovely carrying them to the
   table. (*Irish*): *O'Farrell 85*

A young wife is a bad cook. (*Malagasy, Madagascar*): *Geyvandov 112*

A girl who cannot prepare maize-porridge will not be a good wife for a real man.
   (*Romanian*): *Günther 26–7*

The wife grinds and the husband sleeps. (*Russian*): *o.s. Anna Ravve*

The greedy-guts discourages the woman who grinds. (*Rundi, Burundi*): *Rodegem 353*

The magical powder of marriage is in the grinding and cooking.
   (*Taka, Congo DR*): *Beken 1993: 219*

A Mulata with an expensive shawl: her sugar mill does not grind burnt cane.
   (*Spanish, Cuba*): *Cabrera n.p.*

Marry the one who knows about *atole* and *metate*. [*Atole* is a milk drink with cornflour; *metate*
   is a stone for grinding maize.] (*Spanish, Mexico*): *Casasola 119*

When a woman kneads dough, stay; when she cooks, leave. (*Arabic, Syria/Lebanon*): *Feghali 230*

If a woman does not like kneading, she sifts the flour all day long. (*German*): *Wander V 1272*

You should judge a maiden at the kneading trough, not at the dance.

(*Danish; English, USA*): *Hines 197*

The woman's trills are shouted at the mortar. [Refers to women's songs while crushing sugar cane to be brewed.] (*Gikuyu, Kenya*): *Barra 86*

The weapon is [in] the mortar. [Mortar is the woman's working tool for making flour: a symbol of food and of hard work.] (*Hehe, Tanzania*): *Madumulla 97*

The daughter-in-law lost her pounder; she found it behind the door. (*Bulgarian*): *Arnaudov 69*

In a home where people have had enough to eat, the housewife is a lioness.

(*Kurdish, Turkey*): *Geyvandov 128*

CLEANING

When the house is clean and the wife has combed her hair, the world looks good too.

(*Portuguese*): *Chaves 124*

If your house is dirty, your life is a mess as well. (*Filipino*): *Chua & Nazareno 152*

Look at her at the head of the spring, she washes and wrings. [She is very zealous.]

(*Arabic, Algeria*): *Westermarck 186*

The woman's way—if not by washing, then by ironing. (*Russian*): *Krylov 67*

The woman who likes washing can always find water. (*English, USA*): *Kin 275*

The woman who keeps the privy clean will have an easy delivery [also: will have a beautiful child]. (*Japanese*): *Buchanan 232*

Woman is man's soap. (*French*): *Roux de Lincy 226*

A new broom sweeps clean. (*Maltese*): *Busuttil 30*

A new broom sweeps clean, but an old brush knows the corners. (*Irish*): *Champion 47*

The first wife is the broom, the second is the lady.

(*Spanish, Spain/Puerto Rico/Mexico*): *Díaz Rivera 130; Ballesteros 8*

A new broom is a good broom. (*Creole, Guadeloupe*): *Zagaya 29; Ludwig 417*

A woman who gesticulates belongs to the riff-raff washtubs. [Riff-raffs are disreputable women.] (*Spanish, Cuba*): *Sánchez-Boudy 121*

When the wife wears the pants, the husband washes the floor.

(*Hebrew, Israel*): *Rosten 1977: 487*

Woman without apron is a woman to everyone. (*French*): *Ségalen 53*

An aproned wife has no time to be bad. (*Bulgarian*): *Champion 93; Geyvandov 265*

A capable housewife doesn't have dirt behind the door. (*Digor, RF*): *Geyvandov 128*

The good housewife takes care of the house, the wasteful one tears it up with her hands.

(*Russian*): *Reinsberg-Düringsfeld 156*

The woman in finery, the house is filthy but the doorway swept. (*Spanish*): *Bohn 1857: 227*

The more women look in their mirror, the less they look to their house.

(*Hebrew, Israel*): *Cohen 1961: 572*

CRAFTS

Need teaches naked women how to spin. (*Danish*): *Storm Petersen 87*

Need teaches a naked woman weaving. (*Czech*): *Geyvandov 281*

When God made the woman, he put beside her the distaff to distinguish her from man.
   (*Romanian*): *Mieder 1986: 200*

The only skill that women have, is turning the spinning wheel. (*Hebrew, Israel*): *Malka 20*

Spinning, crying and talking about her husband is often all a wife can do.
   (*German*): *Champion 184*

[She was] at home and spun wool. (*Latin*): *Geyvandov 128*

He who has daughters to marry let him give them silk to spin. (*Spanish*): *Collins 326*

As long as you will spin in this way, you can count on a silk dress!
   (*Arabic, Syria/Lebanon*): *Feghali 201*

Let women spin and not speak. (*Gikuyu, Kenya*): *Barra 62*

The women who work behind the spinning wheel stop working; the hens go to sleep.
   (*Chinese*): *Fabre 536*

Spinning by candlelight [is] sleeping by sunlight. (*Bulgarian*): *Arnaudov 73*

During the day we loaf; at night we spin wool. (*Arabic, Lebanon*): *Frayha I 199*

There is no better woman than she at the distaff. (*German*): *Wander I 1121*

A good woman thinks only of the distaff. (*Spanish*): *Wander I 1117*

A woman who knocks about the streets has no time to spin wool.
   (*Arabic, Morocco*): *Messaoudi 122*

A woman who looks much in the glass spins but little.
   (*Catalan, Spain; French; English, USA*): *Guiter 39; Bohn 1957: 18; Mieder 1992: 666*

The woman who gazes much spins little.
   (*Spanish, Argentina/El Salvador*): *Moya 488; Sánchez Duarte 63*

The wife who makes lace has no time to fight duels over her husband's infidelities.
   (*Maltese*): *Lunde & Wintle 98*

A petted woman does not spin. (*Bulgarian*): *Champion 93*

Two boons: a woman who spins a pound of yarn and a cow that gives a pound of butter.
   (*Dutch*): *Joos 141*

The husband does not weave but is not without shirt, the wife weaves but never wears two
   shirts at a time. (*Russian*): *o.s. Anna Ravve*

Thread and linen are the face of a girl. (*Komi, RF*): *Geyvandov*

The threaded needle judges the girl. (*Spanish, Argentina*): *Champion 615*

The dowry of the bride is in her hands. (*Italian*): *Geyvandov 96*

She can dig a lake with a needle. (*Arabic*): *Safadi 18*

I want my suitors to be attracted to the beautiful clothes made by my hands.
   (*Nenets, RF*): *Geyvandov 97*

Smile a little at one who knows no shame and immediately he will ask you to repair his
   trousers. (*Karakalpak, RF*): *Geyvandov 187*

A hand of silver, a hand of gold. (*Arabic, Syria/Lebanon*): *Feghali 230*

A good handicraft has a golden foundation. (*Danish*): *Bohn 1855: 371*

I got married to make up my eyes, and not to darn socks. (*Persian*): *Geyvandov 281*

I got married in order to live comfortably; I found myself carrying the sickle and the baking
   cushion. (*Arabic, Lebanon*): *Frayha I 222*

Gone are the days of face make up, now are the days of childcare. (*Ladino, Morocco*): *Dahan 1303*

The wedding lasts one or two days, but the burden stays. (*Czech; Slovak*): *Ley 94*

Mama, what does being married mean? It means, daughter, kneading dough, weaving, having children and shedding tears. (*Russian*): *Geyvandov 113*

Mother, what is marriage? It is spinning, giving birth and then regret.
(*Dutch; Portuguese; Spanish, Spain/various Latin American countries*): *Bohn 1857: 230, 281, Mesters 149; Moya 356; Mota 115; Souto Maior 54*

The woman who does not stay up at night does not make a long cloth. (*Spanish, Argentina*): *Villafuerte 232; Moya 531*

NEVER-ENDING HARD WORK

Work hard, my wife, and I'll dig your grave with a golden shovel.
(*Ladino, Tunisia*): *Stahl 238*

All things come to an end except woman's work and pain in hell. (*Danish*): *Kjaer Holbek 204*

The hands of a woman and the teeth of a horse are never at a loss.
(*Dutch, Belgium/ Netherlands; Frisian, Netherlands*): *Joos 141; Champion 19; o.s. Pijlman; Callenbach*

Man's work is from sun till moon, a woman's work is never done.
(*Dutch; German; English, UK/USA*): *Mesters 64; Bohn 1855: 45; Storm Petersen 176; o.s. Boogaard*

A woman's work is never at an end. (*English, USA*): *Loomis 1955: 197*

Marriage is easy but housekeeping is hard. (*Hebrew, Israel*): *Cohen 1961: 326*

Young wife during the night, beast of burden during the day.
(*Arabic, Maghreb/West Sahara*): *Duvollet 41*

He who has a Galician woman has a mule. (*Spanish, Cuba*): *Feijóo 24; Sabiduría Guajira 23*

Do not become the wife of a donkey; but if you already are one, carry its load.
(*Persian*): *Geyvandov 289*

My wife, my mule [also: my buffalo]. (*Russian; Serbian/Croatian*): *Geyvandov 265*

The work a woman does is too much even for ox and plough.
(*Sumerian, Mesopotamia*): *Geyvandov 201*

When one [of the couple] has to lie down, I lay myself down, and the wife has to serve me; when one has to die, the wife should die, so I can take a new one. (*Bulgarian*): *Arnaudov 107*

A smart woman can do more than ten peasants can. (*Chinese*): *o.s. Huang Mingfen*

A single woman's work is better than a hundred men's discourses. (*Tajik*): *Geyvandov 265*

When the wife endures, the house prospers. (*Arabic, Algeria*): *Belamri 32*

The small pot [the wife] goes to and fro, but the big pot [the husband] does not work.
(*Hausa, Nigeria*): *Akporobaro & Emovon 163*

Hard work tires a woman but totally wrecks a man.
(*Fang, Cameroon/ Gabon/Equatorial Guinea*): *o.s. Samuel Eno-Belinga*

The wife grinds, the husband sleeps; the wife weaves, the husband dances.
(*Russian*): *o.s. Anna Ravve*

Don't be proud like a father of sons. (*Masai, Kenya/Tanzania*): *Geyvandov 214*

Fear for the cow; as for the ox, it will labour. (*Arabic, Algeria*): *Belamri 32*

She works like a bride without dowry. (*Bulgarian*): *Arnaudov 68*

Choose a woman from the rubbish heap. (*Japanese*): *Buchanan 90*

I a queen, you a queen, who is to fetch the water? (*Urdu, India*): *Champion 408*

The mother-in-law is great, the daughter-in-law is also great; the pot is burnt, who will take
    it off the fire? (*Kashmiri, India*): *Champion 417*

I'll be the queen and you'll be the queen, but who churns the butter?
    (*Punjabi, Pakistan*): *Champion 24*

I mistress and you miss, who is to sweep the house?
    (*Spanish; German*): *Collins 389; Wander I 1138*

You a lady and I a lady, who will put the sewage out? (*Hebrew, Israel*): *Cohen 1961: 287*

If she is a princess and he is a prince, who will lead the donkey?
    (*Arabic/Jewish, Iraq*): *Stahl 414*

It is easier to turn a countrywoman into a lady than a lady into a countrywoman.
    (*Dutch*): *Mesters 114*

When it's time for a spring-clean, stand aside for the women with a broom.
    (*Japanese*): *Wintle 51*

When women make the bread and do the washing they have the Devil in their body.
    (*Dutch*): *Champion 116; Wander I 1133*

When the wife returns from washing in the river she feels like flaying her husband alive.
    (*Catalan, Spain; French*): *Guiter 45*

When rain is falling down on women's wash, the wind is blowing in purgatory.
    (*German*): *Wander I 1134*

A woman is worst on the day she is baking. (*Danish*): *Kjaer Holbek 178*

Let her, she comes from *tannour* [the oven]. (*Arabic, Syria/Lebanon*): *Feghali 234*

The woman was angry with the world, but the world did not notice. (*Russian*): *Geyvandov 222*

Beware of an angry woman, more than of an angry man. (*Abkhaz, Georgia*): *Geyvandov 198*

Fire, water and an angry woman are the three [worst] evils. (*Korean*): *Geyvandov 124*

Better to live in a wild forest than with an angry woman. (*Swedish*): *Ström 162*

An angry wife is a thorny hedge to the house. (*Dutch*): *Joos 114; Mesters 160*

An angry wife is an ugly piece of furniture. (*Frisian, Netherlands*): *Beintema 141*

An angry woman is like a wild sea. (*Greek*): *Politès 6*

An angry wife is like a house [struck by] lightning. (*Malagasy, Madagascar*): *Geyvandov 124*

An angry woman is worse than a serpent. (*Portuguese*): *Chavez 840*

Be on your guard for a wall with cracks, an angry dog, and a nagging woman.
    (*Persian*): *Geyvandov 225*

May God protect us from a woman's anger and a man's blows.
    (*Arabic, Syria/Lebanon*): *Feghali 102–3*

Smoke, smell and angry wives drive a man out of the house.
    (*Papiamentu, Netherlands Antilles; Dutch*): *Maduro 103; Moya 475; Casasola 170; Joos 136*

Four things make a man age prematurely: fear, anger, children and a bad-tempered wife.
    (*Hebrew, Israel*): *Rosten 1977: 87*

Give the angry wife a long rope. (*Spanish, Argentina*): *Moya 305*

Give the wife and the greyhound a long rope, but not so long as to get outside the house.
    (*Spanish, Chile*): *Laval 72*

Give the wife and the goat a long rope, but not so long that you lose both the rope and the
    goat. (*Spanish, Chile*): *Laval 72; Cannobio 79*

Give an unruly wife plenty of rope. (*Spanish*): *Collins 18*

To a wife or a goat one should not give a long rope. (*Spanish, Argentina*): *Moya 305; Villafuerte 22*

When the soap comes to an end, the washerwoman rejoices. (*Arabic, Algeria*): *Westermarck 145*

If the washing woman receives no compliment, the ironing woman can wait.

(*Papiamentu, Netherlands Antilles*): *Brenneker 1993: 51*

Singing, a wife makes the bed for her husband. (*Dutch*): *o.s. Josépha Wesseldijk*

If a woman does not sing, she doesn't work much either. (*Egyptian*): *o.s. Jacco Dieleman*

A washing woman who does not sing neither takes the filth away nor removes the stains.

(*Spanish, Panama*): *Aguilera 136*

Produce your wrinkles and who will eat your beans. (*Taka, Congo DR*): *Beken 1993: 75*

If a girl wants to be honoured, she should do her work with pleasure.

(*German*): *Meier-Pfaller 42*

To an honest woman, work is pleasure. (*Spanish, El Salvador*): *Sánchez Duarte 27*

When the enemy enters the house, the women must join in the fight.

(*Vietnamese*): *Geyvandov 223*

In war time even a woman may carry the Ngumba instruments [which in peacetime she is
   not permitted to even see]. (*Ngaka Bali-Nyonga, Cameroon*): *Stöckle 219*

A woman will learn to mend nets, when the husband is not at home. (*German*): *Wander I 1121*

A family will flourish if the female can do man's work; it will be on the wane if the male tries
   to do the female's work. (*Chinese*): *o.s. Huang Mingfen*

Inside me the 'man', inside me the 'woman'. (*Ladino/Hebrew, Morocco*): *Benazeraf 59*

WHAT TO DO WITHOUT A WIFE?

The best piece of furniture is a wife. (*Dutch*): *o.s. De Beurs*

In her house a woman is both mistress and maid. (*Azeri, Azerbaijan*): *Geyvandov 128*

A real housewife is as much a slave as she is a lady.

(*Serbian/Croatian, Bosnia-Herzegovina*): *Champion 19*

Three days she's a queen and three days she's still a princess, and from then on engaged as
   slave. (*Ladino, Libya*): *Stahl 417*

Everything comes from his wife, even tying his shoelaces. (*Arabic, Tunisia*): *Tetiv 86*

My wife is in the holy place, my mother at the river and I will die of starvation.

(*Sumerian, Mesopotamia*): *Geyvandov 254*

When the housewife is absent, only then does one realize the weight of her presence.

(*Sanskrit, India*): *Long I 20*

Housewife at home, pancake in honey. (*Russian*): *Geyvandov 128*

The industrious woman's house shines at night. (*Bulgarian*): *Arnaudov 74*

A wife is serviceable in every room. (*Dutch*): *o.s. P. de Beurs*

A house without a woman is a meadow without dew. (*Czech*): *Mieder 1986: 539*

House without mistress is like a sauna without smoke. (*Finnish*): *Geyvandov 127*

A house without a woman is like a well without a bucket. (*Bulgarian*): *Geyvandov 127*

A house without a woman is a place covered with dust. (*Adyg, RF*): *Geyvandov 127*

A household with a woman is like a flower bed, a household without one like wasteland.

(*Uzbek*): *Geyvandov 127*

A house without a wife is a burning-ground. (*Tamil, India/Sri Lanka*): *Champion 435*

A house without a woman is like cattle without a pastor. (*Amharic, Ethiopia*): *Geyvandov 127*

A house without a woman is a fireplace without a fire. (*Turkish*): *Geyvandov 121*

A woman is the house. (*Igbo, Nigeria*): *Akporobaro & Emovon 168*

One thousand men can ruin a camp, but to create a home, you need a woman.
   (*Chinese*): *Geyvandov 128*

Take wives, they will bring you riches. (*Arabic, Maghreb*): *Cheneb I 156*

With a clever wife, a man will become rich. (*Vietnamese*): *Geyvandov 121*

A wife is a household treasure. (*Japanese*): *Buchanan 90*

An industrious wife is the best money-box. (*Romanian*): *Geyvandov 133*

A woman with many talents fills the house to the ceiling. (*Portuguese*): *Chaves 860*

Poverty is scared to get into the house of an industrious woman. (*Bulgarian*): *Arnaudov 73*

If all women were [real] women, the walls of all houses would be made of coins.
   (*Armenian*): *Sakayan 222*

The widower has three sizes of lice; the widow, three sizes of silver.
   (*Korean*): *Geyvandov 154; o.s. B. Walraven*

Widows bear flowers, widowers breed maggots. (*Japanese*): *Buchanan 268*

Woman should be a comrade to the man, not a maid. (*Russian*): *o.s. Anna Ivanova*

A wife is the equal of her husband. (*Hebrew, Israel*): *Malka 23*

The wife is equal to the man. (*Arabic, Maghreb*): *Cheneb II 270*

Woe the house where man is woman. (*Romanian*): *Günther 32–33*

KNOWLEDGE

The women's side of the house: the side without knowledge. (*Burmese*): *Geyvandov 269*

The road to wisdom begins with the alphabet. (*Japanese*): *Wintle 6*

Learning is a treasure that follows its owner everywhere. (*Chinese*): *Mieder 1986: 271*

Learning has no enemy but ignorance. (*English, USA*): *Mieder 1986: 271*

Learning is better than goods. (*Arabic, Morocco*): *Mieder 1986: 271*

Learning is wealth that cannot be stolen. (*Filipino*): *Mieder 1986: 272*

First learn, then form opinions. (*Hebrew*): *Mieder 1986: 271*

Not to know is bad, not to want to know is worse. (*Wolof*): *Mieder 1986: 262*

FOR MEN ONLY

Virtuous is a woman without knowledge.
   (*Chinese, Taiwan*): *o.s. H. Vinita Tseng; Zhang Hongjuan*

Feminine wisdom extends to the nose. (*Japanese*): *o.s. Kosunose*

It is because they are so stupid that women should distrust themselves and obey their
   husbands. (*Chinese*): *Lunde & Wintle 28*

A woman's sense is wrong sense. (*Telegu, India*): *Champion 438*

All a woman's intelligence is her home; if she leaves it, she will be worthless.
   (*Kurdish, Turkey*): *Champion 451*

Women ask questions, men give the answers. (*Arabic*): *Lunde & Wintle 90*

A woman's intellect is in her heels [i.e. very limited]. (*Lezgi, RF*): *Geyvandov 71*

The wisdom of a woman is wonderful to hear. [Ironic.] (*English, UK*): *Whiting 1968: 421, 652*

The wisest of women still is the greatest of fools. (*Dutch; Yiddish, Netherlands*): *Stahl 235*

A wise woman is twice a fool. (*Dutch; English, USA*): *Harrebomée II 420; Kin 280*

Woman's intelligence can cause a catastrophe. (*Sanskrit, India*): *Long I 133*

An educated woman and too salty a soup are both unappetizing. (*German*): *Wander I 1116*

A morning sun, a wine-bred child, and a Latin-bred woman seldom end well.
(*English, UK*): *Champion 45*

To educate a woman is like putting a knife in the hands of a monkey.
(*Hindi, India*): *Champion 405*

Ugly women and stupid girls make an invaluable treasure. (*Chinese*): *Geyvandov 81*

Men should set knowledge before virtue, women virtue before knowledge.
(*German*): *Champion 170*

History is being made but household duties are neglected. (*Burmese*): *Myint Thein 14*

A woman's fame is the tomb of her happiness. (*English, USA*): *Hines 290*

May you be lucky, my daughter, because knowledge does not help you much.
(*Ladino, Marocco*): *Benazeraf 48*

Women do not think the silent person is clever. (*Oromo, Ethiopia*): *Cotter 42–43*

A man doesn't want a woman smarter than he is. (*English, USA*): *Mieder 1992: 396*

A dog is smarter than a woman. It does not bark at its master. (*Russian*): *o.s. Anna Ravve*

A hen that crows and a woman who knows Latin never come to a good end.
(*German; Spanish*): *Geyvandov 275; Haller 463; Champion 310; Meier-Pfaller 63*

A woman who knows Latin and a girl who talks back are good for nothing.
(*Europe*): *Wander I 1115; Harrebomée II 420*

A learned woman is a lost woman. (*Portuguese; Spanish*): *Souto Maior 49*

The glory of man is knowledge, the glory of woman is to renounce knowledge.
(*Portuguese, Brazil*): *Souto Maior 67*

Ladies who become doctors do not taste very well. (*Portuguese, Brazil*): *Lamenza 148*

A wise woman is worth nothing. (*Italian*): *Cibotto 1976: 7*

One does not discuss a man's negative qualities in front of his wife. (*Turkish*): *Geyvandov 240*

In the company of his wife [he is] bright; in the company of his brothers, foolish.
(*Vietnamese*): *Geyvandov 270*

When a man is in trouble, a woman laughs. (*English, Jamaica*): *Llewellyn Watson 252*

Learned woman is worth two. (*Spanish, Puerto Rico*): *Díaz Rivera 23*

A wise woman is an invaluable treasure. (*Greek*): *Politès 44*

A wise woman never outsmarts her husband. (*English, USA*): *Mieder 1989: 85*

The intelligence of woman is [in her] ornaments; the ornament of man is [his] intelligence.
(*Hebrew; Yiddish*): *Rosten 321; o.s. Sabine Cohn*

A woman's intelligence is her beauty and a man's beauty is his intelligence.
(*Arabic, Tunisia*): *Lunde & Wintle 83; Yetiv 8*

Intelligence is the ornament of every serious woman. (*Arabic, Lebanon*): *Lunde & Wintle 155*

Choose the sharp girl, even if she is older than yourself. (*Arabic, e.g. Algeria*): *Belamri 26*

A man may teach his daughter Greek, for it is a jewel to her. (*Hebrew, Israel*): *Alcalay 194*

A woman who is either only pretty or only clever is like a person standing on one leg.
   (*Hebrew, Israel*): *Alcalay 551*

When a woman has no talents, she is already doing very well. (*Chinese*): *o.s. Xiaohong Zhang*

A wise woman seldom crosses her husband's threshold. (*Japanese*): *Champion 447*

Little girls shouldn't ask questions. (*English, USA*): *Taylor & Whiting 152*

As soon as she can stand, a girl searches out what is hidden.
   (*Arabic, Algeria*): *Lunde & Wintle 51*

A curious woman is capable of up-turning the rainbow to find out what's underneath it.
   (*Chinese*): *Geyvandov 274*

Woman, thy name is curiosity. (*Widespread in Europe; English, USA*): *Whiting 1977: 494*

Women know a point more than the Devil. (*Italian*): *Reinsberg-Duringsfeld 247*

Good luck for the stupid, bad luck for the smart. (*Russian*): *Geyvandov 271*

WOMEN'S ADVICE

Woman's advice brings total chaos. (*Sanskrit, India*): *Jha 186*

He who listens to a woman's advice is a fool. (*Tamil, India*): *Champion 435*

Don't follow the advice of your wife. [If you do, she will rule over you.]
   (*Arabic, Morocco*): *Westermarck 77*

Often is evil the result of woman's advice. (*Icelandic*): *Geyvandov 268*

A man that listens to his wife's counsel can be considered a dead man.
   (*Digor, RF*): *Geyvandov 131*

Who follows a woman's plan will drown himself. (*Fulfulde, Senegal*): *Gaden 15*

Taking women's advice causes: 'Oh, that I had known!' (*Hausa, Niger/Nigeria*): *Whitting 45*

If a cow leads the herd, all the cattle will fall into the pool. (*Venda, South Africa*): *Champion 591*

To consult women brings ruin to a man. (*Persian*): *Champion 469*

The advice of a woman is like dust. (*Tibetan*): *Gergan 82*

The advice of a clever woman will ruin a walled city. (*Chinese*): *Champion 383*

Women's intelligence brings [contributes to] destruction. (*Sinhalese, Sri Lanka*): *o.s. Gunasekare*

Woman's advice can be good sometimes. (*Swedish*): *Ström 163*

No-one should disregard woman's advice. (*Norwegian*): *Geyvandov 268*

Even women's advice is sometimes good.
   (*Czech, Serbia/Montenegro*): *Reinsberg-Düringsfeld 137*

Women's advice is good for women. (*Turkish*): *Geyvandov 268*

Consult your wife about everything. If she's small, bend down to her.
   (*Yiddish, RF; Hebrew, Israel; English, USA*): *Malka 31; Cohen 1961: 551; Cohen 1912: 35; Geyvandov 131; Mieder 1992: 654; Rosten 1977: 486*

Ask your wife's advice and do the opposite.
   (*Ladino/Hebrew, Iraq*): *Stahl 418; Cohen 1961: 550; Alcalay 547*

Whoever listens to his wife will lose his job.
   (*Kurdish/Hebrew, Turkey*): *Stahl 418; Cohen 1961: 550; Alcalay 547*

Consult your wife and do the opposite.
   (*Arabic, Maghreb/West Sahara*): *Cheneb II 27; Duvollet 41; o.s. Zoelen*

Praise the advice of a woman but don't act on it. (*Italian*): *Geyvandov 268*

The word of the night annuls the word of the day. (*Berber, Maghreb*): *Bentolila 96*

I consult with my pillow and then I confer with my wife. (*Russian*): *Reinsberg-Düringsfeld 137*

The pillow your mother snores on wants for nothing. (*Rundi, Burundi*): *Rodegem 308*

The night-time counsellor wins over the daytime counsellor. (*Hebrew, Israel*): *Stahl 240*

There is no man who would not listen to his wife. (*Korean*): *Geyvandov 132*

'CUNNING' VERSUS 'KNOWLEDGE'

The cunning of woman has beaten man. (*Turkish*): *Haig 128*

A cunning woman and a devil always escape. (*Portuguese*): *Geyvandov 197*

A woman's cunning is as great as a donkey's weight. (*Persian*): *Geyvandov 198*

Don't succumb to the wiles of women. (*Sinhalese, Sri Lanka*): *o.s. Alex Gunasekare*

The cunning of one woman is equivalent to the load of forty donkeys. (*Kazakh*): *Geyvandov 196*

The cunning of women includes always two tricks, and I have just fled from their malicious-
   ness: they wear snakes as belts and scorpions as brooches. (*Arabic, Maghreb*): *Cheneb II 205*

There is no old woman without cunning. (*Spanish, Argentina*): *Villafuerte 251*

Women's tricks, fourteen tricks, men's tricks, nothing.
   (*Arabic, Maghreb/West Sahara*): *Duvollet 40*

Women's tricks outwit all. (*Greek; German*): *Haller 464*

The cunning of women is strong, and the cunning of the Devil is weak.
   (*Arabic, Morocco*): *Westermarck 66*

What women eat, we are told, is twofold; their cunning is fourfold; their perseverance sixfold
   and their passions eightfold. (*Sanskrit, India*): *Champion 427*

A cunning woman always tries to watch her husband. (*Abkhaz, Georgia*): *Geyvandov 277*

Woman's slyness was put on a cart, but it was too much for the cart. (*Armenian*): *Geyvandov 198*

The female's cunning is equal to her obstinacy. (*English, USA*): *Kin 93*

The power of the king depends on the competence of his minister. (*Tamil, India*): *Geyvandov 132*

A woman's strength is in her tears, a thief's in his lies. (*Bengali, India*): *o.s. Shobha Gupta*

Love conquers even a hero. (*Turkish*): *Geyvandov 39*

Beauty is power. (*Kanuri, Nigeria*): *Geyvandov 78*

No man is a hero to his wife. (*Swahili, East Africa*): *Kalugila & Lodhi 32*

No man is a hero to his wife or his butler. (*English, USA*): *Kin 119*

Three kinds of chains you can never shake off: a woman's chains, a king's chains and the
   soul's chains. (*Wolof, Gambia/Senegal*): *Geyvandov 40*

The woman has no king. (*Ndebele, Zimbabwe*): *Pelling 41*

A woman is more crafty than a king. (*Hausa, Nigeria*): *Akporobaro & Emovon 164; Champion 535*

The wife ignores that her husband is chief. (*Mossi, Burkina Faso*): *o.s. A. Sawadogo*

Women have no chiefs. (*Acholi, Uganda*): *p'Bitek 10*

Women have no chief. (*Chewa, Malawi*): *o.s. Mathieu Schoffeleers*

Women have no king. (*Bari, Sudan*): *o.s. Simon Simonse*

Who conquers fire? Water. Who conquers water? The slope. Who conquers the slope? The
   horse. Who conquers the horse? The knight. Who conquers the knight? The Sultan. Who
   conquers the Sultan? His wife. (*Arabic, Maghreb/West Sahara*): *Duvollet 41*

A woman who loves power is her husband's husband. (*Persian*): *Geyvandov 130*

Who wants to live in peace let his wife be in command. (*Dutch*): *Harrebomée II 419*

A wife is a giant. (*Ga, Ghana*): *Geyvandov 200*

Women are a vessel of wood, and he who travels in it is lost. (*Arabic, Morocco*): *Westermarck 69*

Repeated blows make the drum sound; a wife gains her end by asking often.

   (*Khiongtha, Bangladesh*): *Lewin 3*

After saying it many times she [wife] prevails. (*Burmese*): *Hla Pe 50*

The man's command is less important than the woman's gong. (*Vietnamese*): *Thái 35*

An aging man loses his willpower; an aging woman loses her beauty. (*Turkish*): *Geyvandov 81*

A woman's will-power will pierce even a rock. (*Japanese*): *Buchanan 267*

What a girl wants at any price, she'll get. (*Rwanda*): *Crépeau 155*

What a woman wants, God also wants. [Women get everything they wish to get.]

   (*Turkish*): *Haig 128*

When a woman wants to, she can do anything. (*Italian; German*): *Haller 468; Ilg 23*

You grow older and forget, and finally agree with the wife's ideas.

   (*Ladino, Morocco*): *Dahan 203*

Nothing is impossible to a woman of will. [Perseverance.] (*Gikuyu, Kenya*): *Ibekwe 142*

A woman with her own will, who wants her? (*Irish*): *Geyvandov 105*

If she has a mind of her own, there won't be many with a mind for her.

   (*English, UK*): *O'Farrell 57*

A girl with a will of her own will not get married. (*Ovambo, Angola*): *Geyvandov 195*

Woman, being equal or not, wants to be man. (*Spanish*): *Bergua 342*

A woman can't become a man. (*Mamprusi, Burkina Faso*): *Plissart 103*

When your wife tells you to jump off a roof, pray God that it be a low one.

   (*Spanish*): *Champion 310*

FROM HEALING TO POISONING

Under the veil glistens the poison. (*Arabic, widespread*): *Cheneb II 122; Lunde & Wintle 156*

The professional woman [poisoner] shows herself by touching her belly.

   (*Rwanda*): *Crépeau 478*

The professional poisoner kills her husband if she does not kill her child.

   (*Rundi, Burundi*): *Rodegem 292*

Girls and snakes murder with their mouth. (*Somali*): *Geyvandov 234*

Who has a co-wife will always say: 'My child has been poisoned.' [One first accuses the prime

   suspect.] (*Rwanda*): *Crépeau 425*

The co-wife is poisonous and the sister-in-law a bitter almond.

   (*Arabic, Maghreb/West Sahara*): *Duvollet 38*

A sister-in-law is a poisonous scorpion. (*Arabic, widespread*): *Khalil Safadi 122*

A stepmother is poison for the whole house. (*Bengali, India*): *Geyvandov 176*

A daughter-in-law is like a snake that enters the house accompanied by music.

   (*Ladino/Hebrew, Israel*): *Stahl 232*

When a woman grows old, nothing remains in her but poison and the colour of sulphur.

   (*Arabic, Maghreb*): *Westermarck 67; Champion 565*

The most venomous is a woman's heart. (*Thai*): *o.s. Zhang Hongjuan*

There is no such poison in the green snake's mouth, or the hornet's sting, as in a woman's
   heart. (*Chinese*): *Champion 384; o.s. Huang Mingfen*

There are no virtuous serpents. [Meant as a reference to the nature of women.]
   (*Arabic, Syria/Lebanon*): *Feghali 724*

Trust in a woman is like poison to your stomach. (*Arabic-Jewish, Yemen*): *Stahl 241*

Between women the venom is the greatest. (*Danish*): *o.s. Annelies van Hees*

Venom is the doing of woman. (*English, UK*): *Whiting 1968: 619*

Woman and wine have their venom. (*Spanish; French*): *Roux de Lincy 222; Bohn 1957: 18*

A wicked wife is more deadly than a serpent. (*Latin*): *Haller 465*

Better to live with a snake than with an evil wife. (*Russian*): *Geyvandov 125*

Pretty woman and sweet wine are full of secret venom.
   (*Dutch*): *Harrebomée II 42; Roux de Lincy 227*

A beautiful woman, like old wine, is sweet-tasting poison. (*Hebrew, Turkey*): *Stahl 228*

If a woman is without virtue she will be one of three things: selfish, jealous, or poisonous.
   (*Chinese*): *Plopper 260*

No serpent so cruel as an irate woman. (*English, UK*): *Whiting 1968: 508*

WITCHCRAFT AND OTHER OCCULT FORCES

When the witch is burnt, peace returns to the country. (*German*): *Wander II 640*

Witches always plan evil. (*German*): *Wander II 640*

One who speaks evil words is [called] a witch. (*Haya, Tanzania*): *Nestor 61*

The gossip of two women destroys two houses. (*Arabic*): *Geyvandov 243*

A gossip's mouth is the Devil's mail-bag. (*English, UK*): *Champion 81*

FEMALE WITCHES

A small parcel of sorcery is never small. (*Lega, Congo DR*): *o.s. Malasi*

To marry a witch is to enter [forever] the forest with the demon [devil].
   (*Baule, Ivory Coast*): *Arbelbide 141*

A witch who has learned witching is more evil than a born witch.
   (*Russian*): *Geyvandov 275*

If the mother is a witch, when on the point of death she must spit [into the mouth] of her
   child which thereby receives in heirship the power of witchcraft possessed by her mother.
   (*Thai*): *Champion 473*

The witch swallows her nearest kin. (*Duala, Cameroon*): *Geyvandov 124*

Women's tricks, even without teeth, deal with bones. (*Russian*): *Reinsberg-Düringsfeld 29*

A witch does not swallow bones. (*Kundu, Cameroon*): *Ittmann 98*

When a woman is lean without being hungry, you had better leave her alone, otherwise she
   will eat you. (*Portuguese*): *Chaves 916*

If a woman shows greater care for a child than its own mother, then surely she is a witch.
   (*Bengali, India*): *o.s. Sanjukta Gupta*

Jealous of the woman, they have seen her so patient that they accused her of being a witch.
   (*Arabic, Maghreb/West Sahara*): *Duvollet 32*

I agree with my wife [to the point of] being provided with witchcraft.

    (*Yaka, Congo DR*): *Beken 1993: 24*

If you see an old woman at a crossroad, do not trouble her.

    (*English, Jamaica*): *Llewellyn Watson 259*

Do not trust three: a trotting mare, a rushing hare, and an old woman walking with a stick.

    (*Arabic, Maghreb*): *Cheneb II 254*

The indelicacy of the old woman provokes spells unheard of elsewhere.

    (*Rundi, Burundi*): *Rodegem 137*

Night is a witch. (*Hehe, Tanzania*): *Madumulla 130*

A wicked one [a witch] attacks during the night. (*Kundu, Cameroon*): *Ittmann 22*

Beware of the woman who goes out at night: as a poisonous snare she will destroy your heart
    [i.e. by means of devilry]. (*Umbundu, Angola*): *Valente 77*

If a man has sworn vengeance on you, you may still sleep; but if a woman has sworn
    vengeance, watch through the night. (*Arabic, Morocco*): *Lunde & Wintle 129*

A black chicken flies at night. (*Indonesian*): *P. de Haas*

In the daytime holy, but at night she kisses the Devil. (*Romanian*): *Geyvandov 272*

Women who wander about at night are cats or demons. (*Catalan, Spain; French*): *Guiter 39*

The beautiful woman is either a thief or a witch. (*Bamum, Cameroon*): *o.s. Chimoun*

A beautiful woman either steals from you or catches you [i.e. she is a witch].

    (*Mossi, Burkina Faso*): *A. Sawadogo*

A very beautiful woman is either a witch or a prostitute. (*Sara, Chad*): *Bon & Colin 90*

Woman is a bewitching creature. (*Japanese*): *Buchanan 267*

If you see an old woman with a rosary, know that she is truly a devil.

    (*Arabic, Maghreb*): *Champion 565*

Outwardly a goddess, inwardly a witch. (*Japanese*): *Geyvandov 76*

Externally a female Buddha, internally a female devil. (*Japanese*): *Buchanan 264*

Started with the dance of the goddesses; ended with the dance of the witches.

    (*Tamil, India*): *Geyvandov 264*

There is a day in every man's life when he is a saint, and there is a day in every woman's life
    when she is a demon. (*Malay*): *Lunde & Wintle 155*

The witch has conquered the beloved and caught him with her beautiful words.

    (*Ladino, Morocco*): *Dahan 299*

If you give your heart to a woman, she will kill you.

    (*Kanuri, Nigeria*): *Akporobaro & Emovon 180*

The love of a woman is the Devil's net. (*Portuguese, Brazil*): *Souto Maior 67*

Witches' gold, and musicians' wages vanish at night. (*German*): *Wander II 641*

A stranger is not eaten. (*Kundu, Cameroon*): *Ittman 94*

A polygamous man must be tactful not to lose a child. (*Yaka, Congo DR*): *Beken 1993: 207*

Childlessness kills. (*Sotho, Lesotho*): *Geyvandov 158*

'We must become equals', a jealous childless woman says, and refuses to give you an amulet
    for your sick child. (*Haya, Tanzania/Uganda*): *Geyvandov 105*

As the old woman stopped her sorcery, the children lay behind her hut.

    (*Mossi, Burkina Faso*): *o.s. A. Sawadogo*

If smallpox has killed the witch's child, let the women with children not laugh.
  (*Minyanka, Mali*): *Cauvin 1981: 39*

A jealous woman is worse than a witch. (*English, USA*): *Kin 135*

A jealous wife is a very witch. (*English, UK*): *Williams I 467*

A jealous woman is almost a devil. (*Catalan, Spain; French*): *Guiter 39*

Jealousy is the Devil's mother. (*Estonian*): *Geyvandov 206*

Horns will grow on the head of a jealous woman. (*Japanese*): *Buch 232*

Jealous woman, dangerous woman. (*Spanish, Argentina*): *Moya 531*

Jealousy often calls in the help of witchcraft. (*Creole, Guadeloupe*): *Ludwig 432*

When the witch has finished, there will be red eyes. (*German*): *Wander II 640*

You grind [the ingredients of] the *yindzika-nyanga* [strong fetish], you'll leave [die] together.
  (*Yaka, Congo DR*): *Beken 1993: 21*

No fetish so sacred as the woman-mother. (*Yoruba, Benin*): *o.s. Soulé Issiaka Adissa*

The Devil has a witch for a wife. (*Russian*): *Geyvandov 111*

DEVIL AND SATAN

When God shut up Satan in Hell, He created woman to replace Satan on earth.
  (*Malay*): *Champion 456*

Women are the Devil's friends. (*Arabic*): *Geyvandov 197*

Women are the snares of the Devil. (*Arabic, Somalia*): *Andrzjewski 152*

If a man tells a woman his secrets, she will lead him onto the Devil's road.
  (*Kanuri, Nigeria*): *Geyvandov 272*

Take woman for what she is: a sister of the Devil. (*Yoruba, Benin*): *o.s. S. Issiaka*

Woman conquers the Devil. (*Ladino, Morocco*): *Cahan 293*

Women come from the Devil. (*Arabic/Jewish, Yemen*): *Stahl 246*

To eat with a woman is to eat with the Devil. [Beware of your wife's feelings.]
  (*Kongo, Congo DR*): *Roy & Daeleman 17*

To eat with a woman is to eat with a witch. (*Lingala, Congo DR*): *o.s. E. Mboyi*

The wiles of a woman [which are known to man] are ninety-and-nine, but not even Satan has
  discovered the hundredth.
  (*Hausa, Niger/Nigeria*): *Akporobaro & Emovon 164; Geyvandov 275*

Ninety-nine tricks of a woman you can discover, but the hundredth even the Devil did not
  find out. (*German*): *Meier-Pfaller 17*

The Devil knows everything, except the place where women sharpen their knives.
  (*Bulgarian*): *Champion 87*

Man built a house, woman destroyed it; woman built a house and even the Devil himself
  could not destroy it. (*Georgian*): *Geyvandov 128*

The Devil swallowed a woman but could not digest her. (*Polish*): *Champion 249*

When woman reigns, the Devil rules. (*e.g. Italian; English, USA*): *Brunvand: 154; Champion 212*

Where a woman rules the house, there the Devil is the farm-hand. (*Swedish*): *Ström 163*

The Devil is the Devil, but a woman out-devils him. (*Bulgarian*): *Champion 87*

Woman has deceived the Devil. (*Greek*): *Politès 5*

Women know a lot more than the Devil. (*Italian*): *Reinsberg-Düringsfeld 247*

It takes a woman to outwit the Devil. (*English, UK*): *O'Farrell 87*

A woman can beat the Devil. (*Irish*): *Gaffney & Cashman 93*

Not even the Devil himself has as much malice as a woman.

   (*Spanish, El Salvador*): *Sánchez Duarte 168*

Woman does what the Devil cannot do. (*Portuguese, Brazil*): *Lamenza 175*

A woman knows a bit more than Satan. (*English, USA*): *Mieder 1992: 666*

He who has a good wife can bear any evil. (*Spanish; German*): *Bohn 1857: 210; Haller 461*

A wife is either an angel or a she-devil. (*Hungarian*): *Geyvandov 119*

A woman is the cause of death and hell, as in her soul roots all the evil of the Devil.

   (*Italian*): *Loi 89*

Women have seven devils in their bodies. (*Dutch; German*): *Haller 466*

Where a woman rules, the Devil is chief servant.

   (*German; English, USA*): *Champion 186; Mieder 1989: 45*

Where the woman reigns, the Devil is prime minister. (*Spanish, Puerto Rico*): *Díaz Rivera 34*

Woman knows a point more than the Devil.

   (*English, UK; German; French; Italian*): *Bohn 1857: 108; Meier-Pfaller 62; Champion 63;*
   Reinsberg-Düringsfeld 245

In craft women can give points to the Devil. (*English, USA*): *Hines 294*

When Satan is likely to fail, he sends a woman. (*Hebrew, Israel*): *Alcalay 548*

Where the Devil is powerless, there he sends a woman as messenger. (*Russian*): *Rauch 146*

Where the Devil cannot succeed, he sends an old woman.

   (*Polish*): *Mieder 1986: 110* (*with many variants all over Europe, e.g. Serbian/Croatian*): *Champion*
   288; Karadžić 276

Where the Devil cannot enter, he sends an old woman.

   (*Dutch; German*): *Van Dale 1984: 1553; Van Dale 1986: 1549; Cock 279; Wander IV 11*

Old women are one point ahead of the Devil. (*Spanish, Argentina*): *Villafuerte 195; Moya 195*

What the Devil does in one year, an old woman does in one day. (*Arabic*): *Geyvandov 247*

What the Devil does in a year, an old woman does in an hour. (*Arabic, Maghreb*): *Champion 565*

An old woman is worse than the Devil. (*Arabic, Maghreb*): *Champion 565*

Sea is the source of salt, woman the source of all evil.

   (*All over Mediterranean Europe, and beyond; Italian; Spanish; Portuguese, Portugal/Brazil; Greek*):
   Alaimo 68; Chaves 903; Bergua 342; Champion 193; Williams I 470; Raimondi 22; Souto Maior 35

Women are the root of all evil. (*English, USA*): *Mieder 1992: 669*

Woman is the source of all evil: only our soul saves us from the harm she does.

   (*Fon, Benin*): *o.s. Soulé Issiaka Adissa*

Daughters and land: root of all evil. (*Bengali, Bangladesh*): *Jalil 25*

Worst of all evil is the wife. (*Russian*): *Geyvandov 225*

There is a lot of suffering due to women: they are the store of all evil.

   (*Greek; Latin; German*): *Haller 464*

A priest and a woman may be found at the bottom of all evil. (*German*): *Champion 177*

Women are an inescapable evil. (*Latin; English, UK*): *Geyvandov 280*

A woman is an eternal evil. (*Bulgarian*): *Arnaudov 50*

Woman is an indispensable evil. (*Serbian*): *Geyvandov 89*

A woman is a bad creature and we endure her as a necessary evil. (*Greek*): *Haller 464*

Women are necessary evils. (*English, UK*): *Champion 45*

Wives and wind are necessary evils. (*English, UK*): *Williams IV 199; Champion 78*

We should not expect anything good from our rib. (*Russian*): *o.s. Anna Ravve*

A woman' heart betrays the world, because in it evil is found. (*French*): *Roux de Lincy 221*

A woman always attaches herself to the evil. (*Italian*): *Speroni 208*

Woman is man's Satan. (*German*): *Haller 466*

Women are the snares of Satan. (*Arabic*): *Champion 343*

Women are the whips of Satan. (*Persian*): *Champion 469*

Even Satan prays for protection from girls. (*Punjabi, India*): *Champion 424*

If the Devil were to be born again, he would surely be born female.

(*Spanish, Puerto Rico*): *Díaz Rivera 90*

COUNTERMEASURES

Husband is the tie, wife is the parcel: when the tie breaks, the parcel loosens.

(*Igbo*): *Ibekwe 122*

Keep watch on your melon field and your wife is stolen; keep watch on your wife and your melons will be pinched. (*Japanese*): *Wintle 100*

He who loves his wife should guard her [not allowing other men to talk with her].

(*Arabic, Morocco*): *Westermarck 77*

Tie up and carry with you your wife and your money. (*Marathi, India*): *Champion 423*

The husband gives freedom to his wife, nothing good is the result.

(*Russian*): *Geyvandov 282*

A good wife is the workmanship of a good husband. (*English, USA*): *Loomis 1955: 196*

The husband makes the wife and the wife makes the husband. (*Catalan, Spain*): *Guiter 115*

MOULDING A WIFE

Model the vase with your own clay, it will result in your own saucepan.

(*Arabic, Maghreb/West Sahara*): *Duvollet 43*

Woman is the earthen pot for moulding. (*Luo, Kenya*): *o.s. Jolanda Alkemade*

A married girl gives the rein to her husband just like a newly purchased horse.

(*Chinese*): *o.s. Huang Mingfen*

The god of women is man, therefore all women must obey man. (*Persian*): *Champion 469*

The woman is never in charge. (*Ibo, Nigeria*): *Geyvandov 129*

It is correct to have total authority over one's wife. (*Sanskrit, India*): *Jha 47*

The married woman is ruled as [a] purchased horse. (*Chinese*): *o.s. Huang Mingfen*

Either do not marry at all, or, if you marry, be the master. (*Greek*): *Champion 191*

An obedient wife always respects her husband. (*Vietnamese*): *Geyvandov 120*

The cow and the wife know who their boss is. (*Somali*): *Geyvandov 125*

The bow is not stronger than the spear. [A servant is inferior to his master, a woman is inferior to her husband, even when she is rich.]

(*Ovambo, Angola/Namibia*): *Geyvandov 130*

Give your wife the short knife and keep the long one for yourself.

> (*Danish; German*): *Champion 11; Bohn 1857: 348; Kjaer Holbek 97; Reinsburg-Düringsfeld 246*

A big cigar and a small [or: young] wife. (*Khiongtha, Bangladesh*): *Lewin 26*

Only a man who could have been her father is a good match for his wife. (*Somali*): *Geyvandov 30*

Girls and yearling bulls are trained when their stomachs are empty. (*Oromo*): *Cotter 192*

Start teaching your child right from the beginning [of its life], start teaching your wife on
> the wedding day. (*Uyghur, China; Chinese*): *Geyvandov 286; o.s. Huang Mingfen*

On the first day of the year make your plans; on the first day of marriage correct your wife.

> (*Japanese*): *Lunde & Wintle 6*

Wives! Cleanse them and move them in—that's how to handle them. [According to your
> own ideal.] (*Berber, Maghreb*): *Bentolila 109*

For a house, take a ready one; for a wife, take an unready one.

> (*Bulgarian*): *Rauch 25; Arnaudov 62*

Keep the child quiet from the moment it is born, the wife from the first moment [after the
> wedding]. (*Bashkir, RF*): *Geyvandov 116*

If you spoil your wife, she will soon start dancing naked. (*Bengali, India*): *o.s. Shobha Gupta*

Respect your wife but do not lose hold of the reins. (*Kurdish, Turkey*): *Geyvandov 116*

Women, donkeys and nuts demand strong hands. (*Italian*): *Geyvandov 202*

You should ride wicked women and stiff horses with sharp spurs. (*Dutch*): *Mesters 133*

Approach a woman and a horse from the front. (*Polish*): *Geyvandov 202*

Rule a wife and have a wife. (*English, USA*): *Mieder 1992: 654*

A woman is like a goat: she is tethered where the thistles grow. [A wife has to be treated
> harshly.] (*Rwanda*): *Crépeau 476*

A woman is like a horse, he who can drive her is her master.

> (*Kanuri, Nigeria*): *Akporobaro & Emovon 180*

The horse [wife] is worth what the horseman makes of it.

> (*Arabic, Maghreb/West Sahara*): *Duvollet 27*

Marry above your match and you get a good master. (*Hebrew, Israel*): *Cohen 1961: 326*

Even if the woman's candlestick is made of gold, it is the man who puts the candle in.

> (*Turkish*): *Champion 478*

If a woman becomes wealthy, she changes into a man. (*Twi, Ghana*): *o.s. Peggy Appiah*

A poor man married to a rich woman is more of a servant than a husband.

> (*Portuguese, Brazil*): *Mota 167*

Nothing is more unbearable than a rich woman. (*Italian; Latin*): *De Mauri 353*

A rich woman is conceited and often quarrels with men.

> (*Russian*): *Reinsberg-Düringsfeld 114*

I took a wife with money; I swept the house, she was in the field. (*German*): *Wander I 1126*

In the home of a wealthy woman she both commands and shouts.

> (*Spanish, El Salvador*): *Sánchez Duarte 83*

In the home of a wealthy woman, she pays, commands and shouts.

> (*Catalan, Spain; French; also widespread in various countries in Latin America*): *Guiter 45*

Wealth—man's [property]; work—woman's [property]. (*Vietnamese*): *Geyvandov 133*

Men's life is riches, women's life is distress. (*Arabic, Algeria*): *Belamri 30*

Money left in the hands of a woman won't last; a child left in the hands of a man won't live.
(*Telegu, India*): *Champion 437*

Woman who earns, hen that lays, are [worse than] the Devil at home.
(*German; French*): *Wander I 1113*

Where the wife wears trousers, the Devil is lord of the house. (*German*): *Wander I 1139*

The bread earned by the man is the most trustworthy, the laundry washed by the woman is
the cleanest. (*Karelian, RF*): *Geyvandov 113*

The husband's [earned] bread is the tastiest, the wife's clothes the whitest.
(*Finnish*): *Kuusi 74*

The man who waits for his wife's wages will never know abundance.
(*Hebrew, Israel*): *Rosen 419; Gross 81; Malka 24*

Women's earnings: the earnings of mice. (*Korean*): *o.s. B. Walraven*

A field and a married woman are always someone's property. (*Indonesian*): *o.s. Sutedja Liem*

A woman does not leap over the enclosure unless she wants to divorce.
(*Rundi, Burundi*): *Rodegem 291*

A woman who starts to oppose her husband has found a place to go.
(*Ganda, Uganda*): *Cotter 202*

If a woman leaves her husband, she goes to [marry] someone else. [Dependent as she is, she
needs a new 'boss'.] (*Mamprusi, Ghana*): *Geyvandov 281*

Before going to war, say one prayer; before going to sea—two; before getting married—
three. (*Polish; Russian*): *Mieder 1986: 386; Rauch 133*

Land and women are the prey of the strong one. (*Nandi, Kenya*): *o.s. Anonymous*

The husband is the guest, the wife is the boss of the house. (*Digor, RF*): *Geyvandov 217*

The husband is the head (of the home), the wife is the neck; she turns him whichever way
she wants. (*Russian; Frisian, Netherlands; Dutch*): *Mieder 1986: 245; Beintema 93; o.s. De Kruyf*

Man is the head, and woman the nightcap on top. (*German*): *Meier-Pfaller 67*

He who takes a wife finds a master. (*English, USA*): *Hines 286*

Who takes a wife, takes a master. (*French*): *Geyvandov 88*

It is easier to rule a country than to rule your wife. (*Chinese; Georgian*): *Geyvandov 203*

A good husband will make a woman young, a bad one will age the girl.
(*Karelian, RF*): *Geyvandov 123*

A good husband makes the wife beautiful, a bad one wears her out.
(*Estonian*): *Geyvandov 124*

The husband is the wife's model; when he is upright, she is good. (*Chinese*): *Scarborough 210*

Good soil gives good grain, a good husband makes a good wife.
(*Khionghta, Bangladesh*): *Lewin 129*

Do not say too many bad things about the wife you cannot divorce. (*Adyg, RF*): *Geyvandov 199*

If her chains are pleasant, a wife is tied up twice. (*Ancient Egyptian*): *Geyvandov 39*

Who sugars his wife, will find a sweet wife. (*Dutch*): *Mesters 162*

A sweet tongue will be sucked by the lioness. (*Arabic, African*): *Westermarck 77*

The well-fed sheep makes a cloak of its tail. (*Spanish*): *Bohn 1857: 227*

Only on high water is the water lily at its best. (*Burmese*): *Hla Pe 50*

The husband of every newborn girl has already been born. (*Tamil, India*): *Geyvandov 106*

Be careful to honour your wife, for blessing enters a house only because of the wife.

    (*Hebrew, Israel*): *Rosten 1977: 486; Malka 22*

Do not humiliate your wife, she is your home. (*Ovambo, Angola/Namibia*): *Geyvandov 128*

If you don't have a wife, you'll eat with the zebras in the forest and look like them. (*Ovambo, Angola/Namibia*): *Geyvandov 128*

DO NOT PRAISE AND DO NOT TRUST

Do not believe in the roots of yams, muddied water, and woman's words.

    (*Bengali*): *o.s. Shobha Gupta*

His horse, his sword, his wine, his wife—no man praised them without regret.

    (*Azeri, Azerbaijan*): *Geyvandov 237*

The very stupid praises his wife; the very wise praises his dog.

    (*Allagish, Turkey*): *Champion 483*

Everyone knows you should not praise good wine, a horse, nor your wife. (*Italian*): *Alaimo 5*

Praise food when it is digested; the wife when her youth has passed; the hero when he has returned from battle; the grain when it is harvested. (*Sanskrit, India*): *Champion 426*

Do not praise your wife before seven years. (*Russian*): *Mieder 1986: 526*

Never praise your wife until you have been married ten years.

    (*English, USA*): *Mieder 1992: 654*

Do not praise a day before sunset, a horse before a year, and a wife before she is dead.

    (*Czech*): *Champion 102*

If you love your wife, praise her only after her death. (*Burmese*): *Geyvandov 240*

Praise a woman only when she is cremated and her ashes are scattered.

    (*Bengali, India*): *Kagal 200*

If you wish to be blamed, marry. If you wish to be praised—die.

    (*Galla; Scottish, UK*): *Champion 73, 528*

Teach a horse with cuddles and a wife with compliments. (*Awar, RF*): *Geyvandov 240*

With sweet talking and little acts of love, one can drag even an elephant along with one hair.

    (*Tajik*): *Geyvandov 230*

A flattering woman has something bad on her mind. (*Russian*): *Geyvandov 284*

If a woman praises you for climbing a tree, she is praising you to fall.

    (*Mamprusi, Burkina Faso*): *Plissart 102*

When your wife is affectionate to you, be careful. (*Abkhaz, Georgia*): *Geyvandov 284*

A woman is seldom more tender to a man than immediately after she has deceived him.

    (*English, USA*): *Hines 290*

When I lifted up the tail, I found it was a female. (*Persian*): *Roebuck 33*

Trust not bad women, still less good ones. (*Spanish*): *Geyvandov 260*

Do not entrust your life to a woman. (*Greek*): *Haller 464*

Trust neither weather nor women. (*Dutch*): *o.s. Ms Verwijen*

A marriage without trust is like a teapot without a stand. (*Arabic*): *Geyvandov 135*

Woman is not a chicken cage you hang on your shoulder. [One can never be sure of one's wife.] (*Bassar, Togo*): *Szwark 60*

There is no trusting a woman nor a tap. (*English, UK*): *Williams I 477*

An elephant, a cobra, an old slave, a loving wife, put not your trust in them. (*Thai*): *Peltier 13*

One should trust neither court officers nor women. (*Sanskrit, India*): *o.s. Sanjukta Gupta*

Trust a woman so long as thy mother's eyes are on her. (*Japanese*): *Champion 447*

Love your wife but do not trust her. (*Wolof, Senegal*): *o.s. PapaGueye N'Diaye*

Though a woman has given you ten sons, do not trust her. (*Chinese*): *Champion 383*

Woman's tears, a fountain of deceit. (*Italian*): *Raimondi 56*

Do not believe a woman's tears.

> (*Spanish, all over Latin America, e.g. Panama / Bolivia / Chile / Colombia*): *Aguilera 288; Fernández Naranjo 194; Cannobio 70; Acuña 48*

A woman's strongest weapons are her tears. (*English, USA*): *Hines 219*

Women's tears are a sauce to cover vice. (*Latin*): *Geyvandov 202*

The last resort of a woman is tears. (*Azeri, Azerbaijan*): *Geyvandov 2*

A woman's tears are a form of bribery. (*Hebrew, Israel*): *Rosten 1977: 494*

A man should take care not to make a woman weep, for God counts their tears.

> (*Hebrew, Israel*): *Rosten 1977: 320, 493*

To have a thousand wettings of the sleeves is a woman's lot. (*Japanese*): *Buchanan 269*

A woman who trusts a man's oath, will cry both night and day. (*Portuguese, Brazil*): *Mota 126*

The young woman is beautiful, but her heart is an *inkengi* rat. [Inkengi is a rat who steals from the house.] (*Mongo, Congo DR*): *Hulstaert 366*

A woman is like a stranger. [You cannot trust her in everything.] (*Korean*): *Geyvandov 135*

The ladle knows best what is happening at the bottom of the kettle.

> (*Chechen, RF*): *o.s. Anna Ravve*

NOT TO BE SEEN AND NOT TO BE HEARD

Sit, girl, in the corner; if you are virtuous, they will find you. (*Czech*): *Reinsberg-Düringsfeld 80*

For a woman, display is dishonour. (*Swahili, Tanzania*): *Scheven 489*

Sit, girl, behind three thresholds. (*Russian*): *Geyvandov 283*

The girls have to stay with their dust until their day arrives. (*Arabic, Maghreb*): *Cheneb III 117*

A good dog keeps his tail tucked in; a good woman remains in the background.

> (*Burmese*): *o.s. Aris*

People wonder at a camel if he climbs a roof. (*Arabic, Morocco*): *Westermarck 85*

The woman who sits at the window gossips about everyone and everyone about her.

> (*Portuguese, Brazil*): *Mota 125*

A woman who loves to be at the window is like a bunch of grapes on the wayside.

> (*Italian; English, USA*): *Bohn 1857: 93; Loomis: 1956: 176*

Woman at the window, mulberry on the wayside. (*Portuguese*): *Chaves 867*

Woman at the window wants to sell herself cheaply. (*Spanish*): *Bergua 341*

Woman at the window and peas on the pavement are hard to guard. (*Danish*): *Brix 39*

Borderlands of a river, a vineyard along the wayside and a woman passing her time at the window have no happy ending. (*Catalan, Spain; French*): *Guiter 31*

If you have missed some news, ask the cloistered. (*Arabic, Algeria*): *Belamri 34*

If you lose a donkey, ask the women who never go out. (*Arabic, Maghreb*): *Cheneb III 73*

A singing hen and a laughing girl bode no good. (*Finnish*): *Kuusi 52*

A girl should not have many conversations nor greet too many people.

   (*Hebrew, Yemen*): *Stahl 211*

A singing bird sells itself. (*Russian*): *Geyvandov 235*

Maidens should laugh softly that men hear them not. (*English, UK*): *Whiting 1968: 365*

A maid that laughs is half taken.

   (*Yiddish, Europe*): *o.s. Sabine Cohn;* (*English, USA*): *Whiting 1952: 392; Kerschen 64*

A woman who laughs and accepts your presents, you kiss her whenever you want.

   (*Greek*): *Politès 8*

She who laughs often or walks with bold steps is a harlot.

   (*Bengali, India*): *o.s. Shobha Gupta*

A laughing young woman: a whore or a gossip. (*Spanish*): *Bergua 330*

Good woman speaks discreetly, gives with measure, walks and wins [sympathy]; bad woman
   shouts, gives in extravagance and makes dust fly around.

   (*Arabic, Maghreb / West Sahara*): *Duvollet 41*

When girls are whistling, the holy virgin cries. (*Letzeburgish*): *o.s. Laure Wolter*

Where a woman whistles, seven churches tremble. (*Czech*): *Champion 103*

Where a woman whistles, the angels cry. (*English, USA*): *Mieder 1992: 251*

The singing woman needs a husband. (*Albanian*): *Champion 15*

Mind your behaviour as long as you are a girl, and the world will be interested in you.

   (*Kru, Liberia*): *Geyvandov 172*

VIOLENCE

Do not think, husband of mine, that that will startle me. (*Tamil, India*): *Geyvandov 222*

One cannot beat another's wife. (*Mongo, Congo DR*): *Hulstaert 523*

Do not use the lash before you have mounted the horse. (*Khakass, RF*): *Geyvandov 288*

With beatings you cannot find a wife. (*Haya, Tanzania*): *Geyvandov 229*

A man who kicks his dog will beat his wife. (*English, USA*): *Mieder 1989: 85*

After the wedding the kissing-months won't continue uninterrupted, now and then there is
   a month of beating as well. (*Chuwash, RF*): *Geyvandov 112*

What the bride gets used to in the first night, she'll be used to later.

   (*Ladino, Morocco*): *Dahan 226*

Beat the she-cat and [that will] teach your bride a lesson.

   (*Arabic, Maghreb / Tunisia*): *Cheneb I 42; Yetiv 35*

The husband hit a toad, looking menacingly at his wife. (*Russian*): *Geyvandov 231*

WIFE-BEATING

Beat your wife regularly; if you don't know why, she will know why.

   (*West Africa*): *o.s. Irène d'Almeida*

The man who cannot slaughter his sheep or beat his wife [when she deserves it], it is better
   for him to die than to live. (*Arabic, Maghreb*): *Cheneb I 89*

To keep your wife on the rails, beat her—and if she goes off the rails, beat her.

   (*Spanish, Puerto Rico*): *Fernández Valledor 155*

It is not only the villain who beats his wife. (*Arabic, Syria/Lebanon*): *Feghali 175*

Women, like gongs, should be beaten regularly. (*English, USA*): *Kin 22*

A bad woman and a good woman both need the rod. (*Spanish, Argentina*): *Champion 615*

Good horses and bad horses need the spurs, good women and bad women need the whip.
    (*French; many more variants in both Europe and the Americas*): *Roux de Lincy 161*

A bone for my dog, a stick for my wife. (*Hungarian*): *o.s. P. Rauch*

A whip for the horse, a whip for the wife. (*Digor, RF*): *Geyvandov 216*

God why do you punish me? Do I drink no vodka, don't I beat my wife, don't I go to church,
    don't I go to the pub? (*Ukrainian*): *Geyvandov 194*

Do not spare a bullock or a wife. (*Burmese*): *Hla Pe 49*

Caulk a new boat; beat a new wife. (*Khionghta, Bangladesh*): *Lewin 7*

A quarrelsome woman is rightly hit. (*Latin; German*): *Haller 465*

If the wife is foolish the lash should be strong. (*Kazakh*): *Geyvandov 116*

Claim-beatings-again tells her husband he is castrated. [The quarrelsome wife has to be
    punished.] (*Rwanda*): *Crépeau 477*

Clubbing produces virtuous wives. (*Chinese*): *o.s. Xiaohong Zhang*

A woman who is beaten is going to be a better wife. (*Korean*): *o.s. B.Walraven*

The nails of a cart and the head of a woman, they only work when they are hit hard.
    (*Rajasthani, India*): *Bhatnagar 69*

For whom beats up his wife, God improves the food. (*Russian*): *Graf 251*

A nut, a stockfish, and a young wife should be beaten, in order to be good.
    (*Polish*): *Reinsberg-Düringsfeld 172*

A woman, a dog and a walnut tree, the harder you beat them, the better they be.
    (*English, UK/USA*): *Mieder 1992: 665*

Affection begins at the end of the rod. (*Korean*): *Lunde & Wintle 81*

When two camels love each other, they bite and kick each other.
    (*Turkish*): *Geyvandov 44*

If you really love your wife you have to beat her. (*Tigrinya, Eritrea*): *o.s. Ghirmai Negash*

Where there are no punches, there is no affection.
    (*Many variants in Latin America, e.g. Spanish, Mexico; Quechua/Spanish, Bolivia/Argentina:*
    Paredes-Candia 82; Moya 183; Rubio 152; Casasola 34)

Love well; whip well. (*English, USA*): *Champion 613*

Because of love, sticks have broken bones. (*Belorussian*): *Geyvandov 101*

Now the marriage is going to begin, as the neglected wife said when she was flogged with
    thorns. (*Hausa, Niger/Nigeria*): *Whitting 95*

If your lover hits you, it's only for comfort. (*Romanian*): *Geyvandov 44*

To be beaten by your lover is like eating a raisin.
    (*Arabic, e.g. Egypt*): *Geyvandov 44; Champion 510*

If you don't thrash your wife, she might think she's already a widow.
    (*Armenian*): *Geyvandov 202*

Women, like dogs: the more you beat them, the more they love you.
    (*Spanish, Argentina*): *Moya 488*

If you love your wife, you will be beaten up. (*Spanish, Cuba*): *Sánchez-Boudy 45*

HUSBAND-BEATING

A man knocked down by a woman will not get up again. (*Kumyk, RF*): *Geyvandov 122*

Only God can help when a wife hits her husband. (*Hebrew, Yemen*): *Stahl 244*

A woman who hits her husband, in the Devil's country she will find her death.
   (*Portuguese*): *Chaves 931*

When a woman throws a man over he usually lands on his knees to another woman.
   (*English, USA*): *Mieder 1992: 668*

When you do not thrash your wife's neck once a week, she will snatch at yours.
   (*Bulgarian*): *Arnaudov 23*

If you prostrate before your wife, you keep your teeth intact. (*Burmese*): *o.s. Aris*

He who is hit by a woman doesn't go and complain to the police. (*Portuguese, Brazil*): *Mota 316*

Only a shameful wife takes her husband to court. (*Ganda, Uganda*): *Walser 189*

Women have no court. (*Tsonga, Mozambique*): *Champion 596*

ANYONE AGAINST?

Hitting a wife is like hitting a sack of flour: the good flies out and the bad remains.
   (*Swedish*): *Ström 164*

Women should not be beaten, not even with a flower.
   (*Portuguese, Brazil*): *Magalhães Júnior 111*

A good man does not beat a woman; a good dog does not fight with a chicken.
   (*Chinese*): *Fabre 41; Geyvandov 142*

A real man hugs his wife, a weak man hits her. (*Adyg, RF*): *Geyvandov 115*

No-one beats a woman except the wretched man. (*Arabic, Lebanon*): *Frayha II 594*

A man beats a wife at home only when he has no public status.
   (*Bengali, India*): *o.s. Shobha Gupta*

Sullen clouds let fall rain, a sullen husband lets fall blows. (*Khionghta, Bangladesh*): *Lewin 26*

Whipping a woman gives a man no glory. (*Swedish*): *Ström 164*

You are not honoured for beating your wife. (*Macedonian*): *Geyvandov 142*

A slap does not get a woman. (*Mamprusi, Burkina Faso*): *Plissart 286*

A man should not hit his wife; when one devil is struck out ten new ones go in.
   (*German; Danish*): *Meier-Pfaller 60; Kjaer Holbek 184*

Women and grapes should not be squeezed because they will be bitter. (*Spanish*): *Bergua 343*

You can shut up a hog by beating it but not a woman. (*Spanish, Argentina*): *Villafuerte 306*

Who beats up his wife, beats up his own body. (*Russian*): *Graf 206*

Who beats his wife, beats his head, who beats his oxen, beats his money-bag.
   (*Bulgarian; Romanian*): *Mieder 1986: 528*

He who hits his wife, hits his own back. (*Swedish*): *Ström 165*

He who beats his wife, beats his left hand with his right hand. (*Danish*): *Geyvandov 202*

Whoever hits his wife, hits his fortune. (*Kurdish/Hebrew, Turkey*): *Stahl 245*

Beat your pelt with temper, your wife with tenderness.
   (*Russian*): *Reinsberg-Düringsfeld 172*

A wife should not be beaten with a stick but with food and cloths.
   (*Swahili, Kenya*): *o.s. Ahmed S. Nabhani*

Punish your wife with a rival rather than using a whip.

(*Hebrew, Israel*): *Malka 28; Cohen 1912: 36*

Beat wives with wives and not with a stick. (*Arabic, Maghreb*): *Cheneb III 114*

Husband and wife quarrel and the fools take it seriously. (*Persian*): *Shaki 518*

When husband and wife quarrel, the donkey should not interfere. (*Mongolian*): *Geyvandov 144*

When husband and wife quarrel, they get the benefit of neighbours laughing at them.

(*Danish*): *Kjaer Holbek 130*

When husband and wife quarrel, keep your distance. (*Dutch*): *Ter Laan 211*

Let the Devil interfere in the quarrels of a married couple.

(*Spanish, Puerto Rico*): *Díaz Rivera 148*

One should not interfere in quarrels between married couples.

(*Spanish, Chile/Cuba*): *Cannobio 93; Feijóo 17*

If you find a man fighting with his wife, don't interrupt; only the husband knows what the
wife has done to him. (*Twi, Ghana*): *Rattray 139n*

WOMEN'S REACTIONS

Women will always be blamed for everything. (*Sranan, Surinam*): o.s. *Mavis Noordwijk*

Only a shameful wife takes her husband to court. (*Ganda, Uganda*):*Walsov 189*

Humiliated by the men, he came home to his poor wife. (*Ladino/Hebrew, Morocco*): *Dahan 183*

The fool beaten up at a beer party takes it out on his wife. (*Ganda, Uganda*): *Ibekwe 71*

The crab bit you, but you came [home] and bit the water. (*Efik, Nigeria*): *Geyvandov 196*

If your husband loves you, people respect you; if your husband beats you, people will
humiliate you too. (*Tatar, RF*): *Geyvandov 199*

Man's character is spoiled by poverty; a lovely face is spoilt by pimples; the field is ruined by
too much rain; a wife is ruined by too much beating. (*Bengali, India*): *De 7*

A wife's fate is not easy: you are beaten with a stick and you must be silent, because grown-
ups don't cry. (*Ovambo, Namibia/Angola*): *Geyvandov 113*

A woman beaten for misbehaviour says: 'Only she without one can ridicule me.'

(*Rwanda*): *Crépeau 474*

The same stick will beat both the white and the black hen. (*Sranan, Surinam*): *Hoen 19*

If a wife sees the stick that beats her co-wife, she throws it into the wilds.

(*Ganda, Uganda*): *Walser 196*

The stick of a girl is: 'Touch me and I'll leave.' (*Rwanda*): *Crépeau 43*

The house that has raised me, does not forget me. (*Arabic, Syria/Lebanon*): *Feghali 168*

A woman's rope is always ready on the porch. (*Ganda, Uganda*): *Walser 370*

In public you want to beat me and at home you want to get on well with me?

(*Arabic*): *Safadi 45*

If I see you in your house I will tear your *izár* [veil]. She replies: first you will have to see me
there. (*Arabic, Syria/Lebanon*): *Feghali 60*

A young wife should be no more than an echo or a shadow in her husband's house.

(*Japanese*): *Lunde & Wintle 66*

The ideal man has a man's strength and a woman's compassion.

(*Hebrew, Israel*): *Rosten 1977: 321, 493; Gross 75*

5

Messages of Images

Cups and spoons cannot live without tinkling. (*Udmurt*)

Exploring the imagery associated with women in proverbs is a daunting task. When going through my material I found more than a thousand different creative metaphors.[125] At first sight, it looks as if women have been arbitrarily associated with just about anything: objects, plants, animals, natural phenomena such as rain or lightning, places such as kitchens and bedrooms, and spaces such as heaven, earth, hell, water, and so forth. In proverbs, just as in advertisements, surprising comparisons and intriguing images draw people's attention. Thus, a woman may become a sardine (*Portuguese*), a mimosa tree (*Xhosa*), a merino sheep (*Sotho*), a blanket (*Ashanti*), a bee (*German*), a rosehip (*French*), a used potato plot (*Ganda*), a path (*Afrikaans*), a bridge (*Armenian*), a tiger in the house (*Chinese*), a prayer shawl (*Hebrew*), a melon (*Spanish*), a banana tree (*Gikuyu*), moonlight (*Telegu*), a red pepper (*Japanese and Vietnamese*), water (*Bulgarian*), a candlestick (*Turkish*) etc.

How to find some logic in such a mass of mainly unconventional images—or, rather, is there any to be found? Asking this basic question, I started wondering whether there were linkages possible with the various domains of shared human experience that may have imposed some constraints on creators of metaphors. People (probably men in the first place) speak (or used to speak) in proverbial ways about women from their own feelings and experience. It seems logical, then, to see proverbs and their use of figurative language as a mirror, not so much of reality, but of reality as they see it or dream of. If people think in metaphors, their proverbs cannot but convey hidden (perhaps even subconscious) ideas they hold about crucial issues in life. People's images reflect ideals, and across cultures human basic ideals resemble each other in spite of their respective contexts. In ordinary life, ideal relationships are as much striven for as they seem disappointingly difficult to realize, because one person's dreams and ideals get in the way of another person's interests. Those who quote proverbs are inclined to put themselves and their own group in the most attractive and profitable position *vis-à-vis* any group of 'others', and they do so aptly in a rich variety of images.

Images are a most suitable key to decode people's attitudes and strategies regarding desirable as well as undesirable gender relations and hierarchies. They open doors giving access to cherished beliefs and defended interests. Sometimes exactly the same metaphors or comparisons are being used in widely different cultures, and, conversely, different metaphors often convey quite similar messages in the ideas they express due to common human experience. Images here include metaphors, similes and metonyms, even though there is a difference between the three.

In the simile two domains of comparison are linked by means of 'like', as for example in the Luba proverb: 'Woman is like the earth: everyone sits down on her' or in the Hebrew proverb 'A bad woman is like leprosy for her husband.' In different versions of exactly the same proverb, the word 'like' is used on one occasion and omitted on another—not unusual in oral traditions—while the image remains the same. The absence of 'like' shortens and therewith strengthens the link between the two terms of the comparison. Thus the Bulgarian proverb 'Man is fire, woman water' is undeniably a stronger statement than 'Man is like fire, woman like water.' Nevertheless, both variants connect the two different domains. Metonyms could also be considered as a subclass of metaphor, and we do this here for our purpose. As a form of figuration, metonyms do not cross widely dissimilar domains as do metaphors and similes, but they pick out a specific aspect or attitude of something from one and the same domain, and then use this to represent the whole thing. For example, a woman becomes an oven or a stove, because of her being associated with work in the kitchen. She becomes long hair, as in 'Long hair, short ideas', or breast, as in 'The breast that contains milk cannot contain intelligence.' Hair and breast stand then for the person or rather the whole of womankind associated with hair or breast, two parts of the female body apparently considered representative of womankind in many proverbs. All three poetic devices—simile, metaphor, and metonym—are very popular in proverbs.

The two main categories of images are: women as objects, and women as animals. The two overlap in the common metaphor of women as food. A third popular category associates women with specific places and spaces.

WOMEN AS OBJECTS

When a net is worn out, it is thrown away on the shore. (*Maori*)

In proverbs women are often spoken of as being objects to be handled by male subjects. Those objects can be lifeless or living. Among the living objects there are plants and animals, both often turned into food for men, as vegetarian as well as non-vegetarian dishes. Whether considered eatable or non-eatable, the female body has inspired those who invented proverbs in multiple ways. To begin with, the body is referred to as a container, of organs and liquids, of hunger and food, of good and bad feelings. The female body is then a rather special container in its ability to carry unborn humans.

CONTAINERS

A jug breaks only once. (Uzbek)

The container might well be *the* central metaphor for 'woman' all over the world. I found more than a hundred different container metaphors referring to women, from utensils such as bags, baskets, bottles, buckets, calabashes, cups, fishnets, gourds, jars, jugs, kettles, mortars, ovens, pitchers, saucepans, vases, to huge vessels, such as beds, dustbins, rice-bins, vats, washtubs, etc. Other container images referring to women (to protect them or screen them off against seduction) are clothes, coats, kitchens, tents, veils, abodes, fences, hedges, walls, and also caves, pools, holes, stables, houses, ships, and so forth.

The container metaphor is associated with the various ways in which women are seen as serviceable and needed: the children they conceive, carry in their wombs, and give birth to, and the work they do or are expected to do for the family in general and for their husband in particular. The many kitchen container utensils refer to both pregnancies and household profitability:

> A house full of children is a basket full of eggs. (*Dutch*)
> The man who has no pitcher is very thirsty. [It is women's work to fetch water] (*Taka*)
> A woman is a basket full of flour; the hungry come of their own accord. (*Umbundu*)
> A good oven bakes good bread. (*Romanian*)

Most frequently, containers refer to the womb, and its wished-for accessibility or inaccessibility, depending on the situation. Thus, a container is complemented with a 'male' object meant to enter or cover a 'female' object, and thus we find: mortar and pestle; shoe and foot; stocking and leg; candlestick and candle; pot and pot lid; bowl and spoon, pan and dipper, and so forth.

It is repetitiously stressed that access to the female container has to be barred from undesirable intruders until it is officially unlocked. The defloration exercise had (or has, until this very day) to be performed preferably during the wedding night. Loss of virginity or chastity is referred to in the above Uzbek container metaphor of the jug, and also in a Cuban image: 'When a bell breaks, it will never ring again.' The jug or bell ought to be broken by the bridegroom, ideally the one and only man she will ever 'know' in her life. The most familiar fragile 'virginal' containers commonly referred to are glass and crystal. Below are some other container examples referring to virginity, its attractiveness, and its precariousness:

> It will never do to be careless with a little girl and a small bag. (*Japanese*)
> The bottle [is only good] with its seal, the girl with her hymen. (*Arabic*)
> Until the age of twelve the girl is a cup, until the age of sixteen a tub, after the age of
>   sixteen, thank him who takes her out of the house. (*Czech*)
> Precious essences are kept in small vessels. (*Spanish, Chile/El Salvador/Puerto Rico*)

Most container proverbs incessantly insist that a female container needs to be controlled not only before the wedding but for life, or at least until she has reached menopause, because a man wants posterity of his own. This is one of the gravest concerns in container proverbs, whether talking about brides, wives, co-wives, or even widows. In order to close the womb off against external threats, it is advised that vulnerable female containers be safely guarded, and preferably put up in a father's or husband's house.

In addition to serving as an extra protection for the womb, the house also metaphorically coincides with the womb, as in the following Oromo proverb (in which the male pillar image speaks for itself): 'A house without a centre-pole is like a woman without a husband.' The following two proverbs about sex illustrate the same idea:

> Not all nice houses are good to spend the night in. (*Bambara*)
> Coitus interruptus is like dining well within the house and then having to spit it all out on the veranda. (*Thai*)

Earlier we came across the Chinese and English proverb about the unfaithful man whose act was compared to 'spitting from a house into the street', and a woman's unfaithfulness with 'spitting from the street into the house.' Sometimes the woman or her womb becomes a spacious fortress, or a castle. In terms of war, from the owner's perspective, such fortresses and castles are there to be protected and defended, but from an invader's perspective they are to be seized and conquered. The male ownership of the womb has to be negotiated, and ultimately this container will yield, be it of its own accord or being forced by the conqueror. This outcome is less disastrous for a castle that has no real owner yet, but it is a disaster for an owner feeling too weak to properly defend himself or rather his 'property', or for one who has to blame himself for not having taken care well enough. 'Legal' owners tend to speak in worried terms about such threats, as in the following proverb that has travelled all over southern Europe, and also to Latin America. The proverb and its images developed variants under way from one place to another, but the underlying worries subsist:

> He who has a beautiful wife in a castle on the frontier never rests. (*Italian*)
> Who has a handsome wife, or a castle on the frontier, or a vineyard at the main road, is never without war. (*Spanish/Portuguese*)
> He who has a beautiful wife, a castle on the border or windows looking out on the street, will never see the end of the war. (*Portuguese, Brazil*)

From an invader's perspective, however, the castle or fortress looks different, and theirs is a tone of sheer optimism:

> Maidens and castles must yield in the end. (*Yiddish*)
> Women and fortresses that negotiate are half way to being captured. (*Swedish*)
> Neither a fortress nor a maid will hold out long after they begin to parley. (*English, USA*)

Ironically, in the hierarchy defended by proverbs, a woman is not supposed to own such an impressive castle in which she would be able to protect her own precious little container. In proverbs such an idea seems so absurd that it has not been worth considering: women do not own, they are owned. The usual situation is that a woman complies with her father when single; her husband, when married; and her son, after her husband's death, or in a concise Japanese proverb: 'Woman has no house in three generations.'

Some proverbs advise fences, hedges or walls to surround those large containers. More often the small containers are hidden not only under protecting clothes, but also behind thresholds and doors, extra fortified with bolts, bars and keys. Not an easy task, when a girl falls in love, as stated, for example, in Russian: 'Lock and key cannot stop a girl', or in Chinese: 'Keeping a young girl indoors is like having a tiger in the house.'

Being the entrance to the house, the door is a most common metaphor not only for virginity but also for controlling the womb. The closed or locked door represents in turn the protecting or prohibiting father or husband, or the encouraged and praised chastity of daughters and wives who practise restraint of their own accord. Widows' 'doors' are especially problematic, because they lack the indispensable marital control:

> A girl, the door locked and bolted. (*Vietnamese*)
> A stable without a door is a woman without a husband. (*Tibetan*)
> A honourable widow always keeps her door locked. (*Hebrew, Israel*)
> A honest widow, a closed door. (*Spanish, Argentina/Colombia*)

If a woman metaphorically becomes 'a stable' as in the above Tibetan proverb, such an odd term calls for an explanation. It means that a woman as a passive receptacle needs to be protected by a 'door': her father or her brother as long as she is not married, her husband after marriage—otherwise she may seem 'available', as if she invites occupation by any passer by.

The metaphor of a door either refusing or giving access to a female container serves as a yardstick for female morality: a locked or closed door means chastity, whereas an absent or open door means the opposite, even though a closed door cannot be completely trusted either, according to the Argentinean Spanish proverb that 'The Devil comes and goes through a closed door.' Much, for sure, depends on the woman herself. She proves herself to be chaste and faithful, by staying indoors of her own accord. In the words of a North American proverb: 'No padlocks, bolts or bars can secure a maiden as well as her own reserve.' Other proverbs argue that it is a woman's ugliness that protects her virtue best. Virtue can only be tested when 'the door' is left wide open, but most proverbs are not quite eager to take that risk. Open hatches, half-open doors, and closed but unlocked doors, all predict temptation:

> She says: 'I don't love him!' but she doesn't lock her door at night. (*Malagasy*)
> An open door tempts a saint. (*Spanish, El Salvador*)
> Once the hatches are open, the door is open. [Warning to women] (*Spanish, Panama*)
> For a girl there is one door ajar, and it has a wooden bolt, for a man there are forty doors ajar. (*Komi*)

A door ajar means something altogether different for men than for women, and this also holds for the many closed or locked doors or gates which only serve to control women. And then there are proverbs expressing fear of several doors or gates or entrances with access to the same house, an obsession especially strong in Latin American proverbs:

> A house with two doors is difficult to watch. (*Spanish, Colombia*)
> The painted woman leaves her husband through the back door. (*Ladino/Spanish, Puerto Rico*)

A house with two doors, a woman, and a cane plantation: the Devil takes care of them. (*Spanish, Venezuela*)

An adulterous wife needs a home with two entrances. (*Kurdish-Jewish*)

In some rare cases, though, men are advised to concentrate on their wife, their one and only legally owned gate, entrance and house, as in this Chinese example: 'Take care of your own gate, and do not think of other men's wives.' In proverbs, wives are not recommended to lock their husbands up in some container. Instead of using physical strength or economic power, a wife is reminded of other means at her disposal. She incidentally receives the explicit advice, especially in Iberian or Latin American proverbs, to make herself so attractive that her darling husband will be completely bowled over by her, without ever feeling the urge to go and see or even dream of other women. Again the metaphor of the door refers to the entrance the wife's husband might look for in other women's bodies: 'A well-dressed woman draws her husband away from another woman's door' (*Spanish*).

Is this not another effective strategy for keeping somebody in confinement? What is suggested is that not only wives, but women in general, have their own powerful means to dominate men. In the meantime, such proverbs address men: not only do they have closely to watch the access to their wife's container which is likely to interest other men, but they must also resist their own indomitable urge to knock at other intriguing gates or appealing entrances, because such access is as addictive as it is dangerous.

Although the two sides of the gender balance are unequal in most respects, the point being made in the last above proverbs is that, metaphorically (and sometimes literally), not only men imprison women in wedlock, by means of all sorts of restrictive measures. Women are also imagined as forces confining men, by locking them up, so to speak, in their small but nonetheless powerful container, bowl, gourd, jug, jar, vessel—you name it.

FLOWERS, TREES, FRUITS

The beautiful woman is like the giant palm: climb without looking down. (*Bamum*)

Looking down while you climb would make you feel dizzy; so, instead, the Bamum advice is to go ahead and enjoy! Both the pleasure of beauty and the worries about the dangers and disappointments involved with beautiful objects are frequently pondered on in terms of flowers, fruits, plants, and trees. Metaphorically, girls and young women become flowers, attracting bees or birds with their charming colours and forms and fragrances. The main points have been made earlier: men's fascination with female beauty as well as its unreliability and transience. Proverbs also refer to beauty's passing away by means of flower metaphors: roses turning into rosehips (*French*); flowers blooming for just a few days (*Chinese*), and so forth.

Strikingly few proverbs about flowers referring to women come from Africa, hardly any are from south of the Sahara, while relatively many are from Asia, where roses (with their thorns) are apparently the most popular flower in proverbs. In African proverbs beauty seems to be more often associated with food or fruits.

Not only the fascinating freshness of the intact virgin, but also the pain and sadness entailed in enjoyment are emphatically present:

A girl is [like] a rose sought by many. (*Arabic, widespread*)
A girl is like a watermelon that has not been sliced. (*Armenian*)
The laughing of the rose produces tears of rose water as fruit. (*Persian*)
Whoever smells a rose endures the pain of her thorns. (*Turkish*)
Only those who pick the roses feel the thorns. (*Chinese*)
The rose that is smelt by many, loses its fragrance. (*Hebrew*)
The flower is beautiful, but the thorn is sharp. (*Russian*)

The lotus flower appears only in proverbs from south and east Asia. In addition to roses and lotuses, there are peonies and lilies and columbines in Japan, rose laurels in the Arab world, as well as some other flowers and blossoms mentioned here and there in different other languages and cultures: cherry blossom, plum flower, cotton flower, and so forth. In Japanese 'A lotus flower in the mud' refers to a young woman who keeps her chastity 'in spite of immoral surroundings.' A flower in the mud is only one metaphor reflecting the ideals of virginity and chastity. Virginity is expressed here in predictable images such as buds and fresh flowers unfolding their petals. *Au fond*, de-flowering stands for a man taking away a girl's flower of innocence. The other 'extreme' is a woman who has 'known' more than one man which makes her both attractive—believed as she is to be more easily accessible—and dangerous:

Beauty in women is like a flower in the spring; but virtue is like a star in heaven.
     (*English, USA*)
Though the flower of the swamp is white, it is a deadly flower. (*Spanish, Cuba*)

The expression 'Woman of the swamp' is widely used in Cuba. Again and again it is repeated that virtue by far surpasses and outlasts beauty.

   No less than in the container metaphors, then, both female innocence and modesty appear to be cherished ideals in flower metaphors. And so is the fear of women's imagined lack of virtue, unfaithfulness and capriciousness. In Thai it is argued that 'A woman is as capricious as a drop of water on a lotus leaf', and there is a Chinese warning that: 'Woman is as changeable in character as water and poplar flower.' Borrowing from domains other than biology, numerous metaphors stress this message as well, associating women with the weather, the autumn sky, the moon, winter nights, one's luck in life etc.

   The breathtaking beauty of flowers and the radiance of blossoming trees are looked upon with admiration as well as suspicion. Enjoyable flowers soon wither, but this transience makes them no less spoilt and pretentious. Beauty associated with laziness means lack of profit. Metaphorically speaking: fascinating flowers, attractive blossoms, and beautiful foliage are no promise for an abundant harvest, rather are they signs of the opposite, because a beautiful wife is not believed to be a great child-bearer:

Too many leaves, no fruit. (*Khionghta*)
Where there's a lot of blossom there won't be much fruit. (*Japanese*)

Moreover, the most tantalizing fruits of the harvest are believed to be the most disappointing:

The surface beauty of a fig-fruit, inside it are black ants. (*Hehe*)
Red on the outside, rotten inside. [Of fruit and women] (*Spanish, Mexico*)

Tree metaphors confirm such messages. Beautiful women are liable to sickness and die sooner than plain ones, just like beautiful trees: 'A straight tree will be cut down sooner than another one' (*Korean*). Even though beauty is appreciated, it is the profit that counts. Tree metaphors related to profit mostly refer to motherhood and progeny as a wealth of fruits, birds, branches or leaves:

> The beauty of a vine tree lies in its grapes. (*Turkish*)
> A birdless tree, a barren tree. (*Thai*)
> A tree without foliage, even if it is crowned, how can it be beautiful? (*Tibetan*)
> Do not cut down a tree with beautiful flowers. (*Oromo*)

The roots, trunks, branches, leaves, and twigs also stand for the effect a mother has on her children. The most current argument is that good trees bring forth good fruits, and although a bad tree may incidentally succeed in doing that too, the rule is that one knows the fruit from the tree, and the other way round. Thus, a sweet root is believed to guarantee a sweet fruit, a pear tree will not produce apples, there will be no good plant from a bad shrub, and so forth. 'Watch the rose and take the bud' is Turkish advice on marriage in metaphorical terms: look at the tree before eating the fruit, or at the flower before you cut the bud.

A tree without fruits is harshly condemned: cut down and throw on to the fire, is the strong advice. A Mordvin proverb however, defends the poor tree: 'The apple tree can't help not bearing any apples', and a few others advise patience. Flowers, plants, and trees also stand for the extended family of the wife, and a man cannot but accept that he must take care of his in-laws, however grudgingly:

> Plucking the pumpkin you must take the leaves as well. (*Tonga, Zambia*)
> Can you love the berries and hate the shrub that produced them? [Refers to a man who
>   loves a girl but dislikes her mother] (*Sotho*)
> He who loves the *gombo*, loves its leaves. [A *gombo* is a plant] (*Creole, Martinique*)

Flowers, plants, trees, and fruits are also associated with the garden, field, meadow, orchard, or plantation they come from, and people are urged not to pluck and eat them before they are ripe. Fruits and fruit trees growing by the wayside are suspect because of their accessibility to anyone who passes by. Another point is the wisdom that there is a right moment to pluck and enjoy, and one should wait for that moment, day, season, but also to be alert in not letting the right time pass, because those fruits will wither, become overripe, full of worms, or they will rot and be useless. No less than the container, the multiple widespread flower/tree/fruit images in proverbs are very popular.

WOMEN AS ANIMALS

Throughout time the female pigeon made the male pigeon sigh, and the lioness the lion roar. (Arabic)

A third huge field of metaphors about women to be found worldwide are the numerous linkages made with the world of animals. About a hundred different animals are referred to, from disturbing insects or careless birds to beasts of burden such as donkeys and oxen,

from peaceful turtledoves and gazelles to poisonous scorpions or ferocious crocodiles, leo-
pards and wolves. These beasts are associated with women for various presumed qualities
such as beauty or ugliness, strength or vulnerability, working capacity, stubbornness,
stupidity, smartness, fertility or cruelty, or because they are considered to be delicious
food to be eaten—that is to be sexually consummated.

No link can be established between the place of origin of animals and proverbs referring to those animals. Though I did not find frog or fish metaphors among peoples living
in the desert, there are proverbs about lions in European proverbs as well as in North
America; albeit that most tigers figure in proverbs originating from the regions in Asia
where they exist (or used to exist), I also came across them in the Caribbean and South
America. Nonetheless, most frequent are metaphors inspired by animals that people are
familiar with. Having lived with them all their lives, people have carefully observed such
animals in their surroundings. No wonder that birds, dogs, and hens, animals that are
commonplace almost everywhere in the world, are present in people's most common
metaphors in daily language as well as in proverbs about gender roles and behaviour.

Metaphors establish parallels between human and animal behaviour in many ways.
Mothers' love for their children, for example, has been transferred on to animal characters. This exuberant love is projected on to a wide variety of creatures, from insects to
vertebrates, all synonyms in that they express the same worldwide motherly feeling: my
own child is the most fabulous of all. Hearing a mother beetle, cockroach, raven, weasel,
porcupine, or dog express this inborn instinct in emotional words, is the more moving as
it is 'defamiliarizing' this feeling we know from having been a child, or a mother, or both.
Animal metaphors in proverbs confirm the heartfelt love and sympathy we met earlier in
proverbs about mutual mother and child attachment. About women other than mothers,
animal metaphors tell somewhat different stories.

Women's working capacity has been associated with that of hardworking animals—
lucky the man who has a bee for a wife, as it is said in German! Mostly such animals are
beasts of burden: buffalo, camel, cow, donkey, elephant, mare, mule, ox, etc., not forgetting that women have also been associated with poisonous animals such as scorpions or
snakes, as discussed earlier.

The subject of animal metaphors in proverbs would provide an abundance of material
for a full length book essay. Among the large variety of metaphors and themes associating
women with animals, only a few can be discussed here in more detail. I have selected the
hen, and its counterpart the cock, because I found numerous proverbs about them in more
than sixty different languages and in about twenty more countries from all continents.
There must be several reasons for animals being so popular in proverbs, reasons that no
doubt have to do with parallels people see between the animal's behaviour or situation
and their own human experience. In previous chapters we have met the hen together
with her male partner—the hen and her various features being presented as typically
female and contrasted with male characteristics presumed to belong to the cock, whose
name in vulgar language also means 'penis'. Proverbs emphasizing commonalities between women and hens, as well as between men and cocks, cluster around a few basic
points:

- A hen belongs to one cock only, whereas a cock has many hens
- A hen has to be silent, whereas the cock has the right and duty to crow
- A hen lays the eggs and takes care of her chicks as a mother

All three points are surrounded by insights and opinions about how things are in harsh reality and how things ought to be if life were ideal. Only the main arguments will be summarized here. Most of these reflect conflicting gender interests. The cock is presented as the boss and the hens are supposed to submit, but hens often appear not to agree as freely as, ideally, they ought to. This creates conflicts and subversions. Wisely, an Indonesian proverb advises a cock to sometimes cast his pride aside and 'play the hen in the name of peace', but this is quite unusual.

First, ideally, a hen is content with her position as the wife of just one cock, though in practice she is suspected of and blamed for being interested in visiting other cocks as well. She should not even try, goes the threat, because she will always come out of the other cock's henhouse plucked of her feathers. According to the blunt advice of a Chilean Spanish proverb addressed to the cock, if she strays, she needs to be kicked out: 'Do not keep a hen that eats in your house and lays her eggs in somebody else's.' Again, the fear of uncertain fatherhood lies behind the recommendation that a hen who eats in your house and lays her eggs in somebody else's be discarded.

In the meantime, the cocks themselves are met with sympathy for their natural promiscuity. Old or young, it is argued, they are all the same, aren't they? Still, an old rooster whose potency weakens blames his hen for being unreliable. It is stressed that a hen has no existence without her cock, because thanks to him she's got a nest. Better not to quarrel then, she is told. Where else could she go anyway?

Through the force of circumstances, then, a hen decently submits to her position. A sensible hen knows how to behave. Setting an example of decency, she goes to sleep early to avoid gossip; she does not stir at dawn until the cock gives the sign. She stays at home, since a wandering hen does not lay eggs. She does not fly far unless the cock flies with her, aware that a hen flying too high will lose sight of her nest. If, once in a while, she happens to fly away by herself, she'll humbly apologize by saying that it was not her fault: it was the wind that blew her to the other place. The other side of the submissiveness coin is also presented: as soon as the oppressively controlling cock leaves the hen house, or as soon as he happens to die, the hens are suspected of feeling free at last and carelessly enjoying themselves.

Second, it is the cock who does the crowing, in its own henhouse and outside, as he pleases, whereas it is the hen's task to lay the eggs and brood the chicks. It appears that his crowing serves as a badly needed compensation for the hen's unique achievement. All over the world hen and cock have come to serve as a gratefully acknowledged metaphor to spread the wishful wisdom that females ought to be silent whereas males ought to speak. It is forbidden and ought to be forbidden for a hen to crow. Why? First of all, it is forcefully stressed that a hen's speaking would go 'against nature': day itself would refuse to dawn, if the hen would dare crow. Moreover, if she should give it a try, she would completely fail in doing so or at least in doing so aptly. And there is another solid argument: it goes as much against her nature to crow as it is impossible for her to flap her wings in a cock-like way.

Most proverbs, however, do not actually deny the hen's ability to crow, they just find it a very bad idea. Many reasons are advanced against a hen's crowing. God himself in the first place disapproves of such disreputable behaviour. A crowing hen, like a woman who makes herself heard publicly, will end badly, meaning that she will not find a husband. Her crowing will turn the home into a bad house, a sad house, a miserable house, and so forth. From Japan to Russia, from Finland to Namibia, from Argentina to the US, all sorts of variants tirelessly repeat that as soon as a hen starts crowing, she'll bring her influence to bear on the cock or seize power, with all the disastrous consequences this would entail. Her trespassing the rule would not only be a wrong, indecent, saddening thing in itself, but also a foreboding of the most terrible tragedies. A crowing hen means, among other things, the end of peace, one's house falling into ruins, a doomed family, and death catching up with you.

In spite of such disaster scenarios, some proverbs royally acknowledge that the hen need only keep quiet as long as a cock is around or alive. Some proverbs accept her crowing as long as she does not do so in the cock's presence, and if in his presence, then, please, let it not be as loud as he can do it. Rarely it is admitted that the cock's crowing might also be a sign of weakness, for the sake of appearances, a doing as if: 'I am the boss, says father cock, when I am not in, says mother hen.' (*Dutch*)

Why would a hen crow anyway? Is there any profit to be gained from her doing so, or is she only asking for trouble? It can turn out to be advantageous for her to crow, as a few proverbs admit. Crowing hens, who want grain or male company, are sometimes well rewarded for making themselves prominently seen and heard. And so are girls who, God forbid, whistle, and thus succeed in catching attractive boyfriends—though, for sure, they certainly won't bring luck to the house.

Other proverbs reveal a wife's psychological impact and insight in not crowing. The hen is not stupid, they argue, she is keenly aware of what is going on, and would certainly be able to crow and announce the new day, but the cock needs the credit while she doesn't. Isn't she after all the one who is able to give birth to new life? The cock may even need the hen's encouragements before he succeeds in decently crowing, as expressed in the Japanese proverb quoted earlier: 'Encouraged by the hen, the cock tells the hour.' In a rare case, it is the hen who tells the cock to crow, but that is certainly the world upside down, and the large majority of proverbs warmly agree that a good cock is in charge under all circumstances, and crows in all and any henhouses at will, while he severely forbids his hens to talk back, under the threat of violent sanctions in case of non-respect.

Third, the cock lays nothing, as an Igbo proverb dryly observes. Laying eggs and being a mother is a hen's job that leads to another network of metaphors. Once more, familiar issues crop up: beauty is opposed to fertility, and so is noisiness. A hen loses her beauty through pregnancies; the charmingly coloured hen is supposed to be a bad layer of eggs, and a cackling hen is suspected of not laying much. Opinions about clucking and cackling seem to differ. Some proverbs argue that clucking means that the hen wants to lay an egg; others, that she has laid an egg, and still others, that clucking leads to losing one's egg.

The better a hen is being fed, the better she will lay, and laying will make her happy: an egg laid, a hen singing! Several proverbs blame such loudness, one of them comparing a jubilant mother hen to the supposedly more praiseworthy behaviour of the tortoise who lays a thousand eggs in dignified silence. Could this be a little flash of jealousy on the part of one who lays nothing?

Before any eggs can be laid, a nest has to be prepared, a task sometimes considered her own responsibility, and sometimes the cock's. As soon as the nest is ready, she badly wants to lay an egg, and she will do this as soon as she can. However, don't ask her to lay two eggs in a day, and keep in mind that a guinea hen cannot bring forth a ram. As usual, not only the neighbour's hen but also the neighbour's eggs look bigger and more attractive than one's own, and, yes, the neighbour's hen does succeed in laying two eggs at the same time. Incidentally, egg eaters are requested to be aware of the hen's suffering in her accomplishment. The following Caribbean example reminds those who profit, that the enormous exertion and courageous act of giving birth should not be belittled: 'Those who eat an egg do not know whether the hen suffered', thus referring to the ungrateful ones who profit from others' strenuous efforts without taking their suffering and sacrifices into account.

Motherly love is expressed in metaphors about feathers and wings. Her many feathers do not burden the hen, and she succeeds in cherishing all her chicks, by keeping them all under her wings. However, should she not be very interested in her role as a mother, she is strongly reminded that this is not a cock's task but a hen's. Changing roles is strongly disapproved of: woe the unfortunate hen-house where the hen crows and the rooster clucks! He is allowed to ignore the chicks, whereas she is not. This does not mean that her taking care of the young gives her licence to ignore him: he is entitled to enjoy her caressing presence. After giving birth, a hen also may willingly seek opportunities to make love to the cock once again, but she is sternly reminded not to forget about her children. The point being stressed is that, whether she likes it or not, the hen has always more duties at home than the cock. In almost all senses the proverbial scale is being turned in favour of the cock's interests.

WOMEN AS EATABLES

He ate the food and the food ate him. (Zulu)

Food and sex have much in common, both being basic human needs. In proverbs, sex is frequently referred to in terms of desirable dishes. Sexual desire and pleasure are often expressed in food metaphors, from appetite and tasting to dining and dishes, from fruits to chicken, from bread to be sliced (as a metaphor for defloration) to slices of a loaf already cut. And then, there is the sweetness of honey and the hotness of good coffee or soup, no less presented as tantalizing images for sexual 'consumption'. First a few fruit examples:

> You learn the taste of a melon when you bite it. (*Korean*)
> When the figs are ripe, all the birds want them. (*Mandinka, Guinea*)
> Women are like dates, wash and eat. (*Arabic, Algeria*)

The subjects of all this hunger and eating are male only. The only example of a woman eating a fruit 'sexually' is the Bengali metaphor we came across earlier of the banana 'swallowed whole' by the virgin wife: 'The bride is ashamed to eat, but nonetheless swallows the banana whole', but, unlike the men, she is presented as embarrassed and not as one who wholeheartedly enjoys the experience (not in the proverb at least). The meaning is not really clear: does she enter into the experience with shame, or is it that she is ashamed because she does enjoy but is not supposed to show that she likes it? In proverbs the sexual urge of men is frequently presented as 'hunger', and lovemaking as 'eating':

> A hungry crocodile is not choosy. (*Malagasy*)
> When the wife is married to the kitchen, love will soon be hungry. (*German*)
> He who wants to eat another man's hen, has to tie the leg of his own hen. (*Slovene*)

Among the proverbs referring to sexual diseases, there is the food metaphor in the above Zulu motto. It warns against the risks of certain dishes, and recommends selective behaviour: the consequences of one's eating are not to be taken lightly. On the other hand, having sex with a woman can also serve as a medicine to men, as observed in the Irish proverb: 'A woman doesn't have to go out to get the best medicine for her man.'

Metaphorically, women are turned into 'eatable' goods of all kinds that male eaters seem to hunger for, as soon as they see it. In addition to the abovementioned examples, there are all sorts of other fruits: apples, berries, cherries, coconuts, grapes, peaches, pears, and so forth. There are also vegetables (from one's own as well as from other gardens), from carrots (tasting bitter in the case of the mother-in-law) to cabbage, or lettuce. There is cooked food, soup or stew, millet, rice or noodles; there is flour, dough, bread (sliced or unsliced). Women become milk, yoghurt, eggs and cheese; they are appreciated as cakes, cookies, pancakes, sugar, honey, and all sorts of sweets. Men also crack women as nuts, or shells, to savour what they find inside.

As old bulls, donkeys, he-goats, horses, oxen, pigs, or hyenas, they desire to digest preferably young and tender shoots, fresh leaves, soft pears, sweet grapes, etc. A whole series of proverbs metaphorically argues in favour of old men taking very young wives. Thus, all over the world, old animals feast upon young and tasty delicacies. A few examples among remarkably many:

> An old he-goat still likes a green leaf. (*Frisian*)
> The lazy pig eats the soft pears. (*Albanian*)
> The old bull loves fresh grass. (*Thai/Spanish, Argentina*)
> The old hyena gets the best grapes. (*Persian*)
> An old cat likes young mice. (*Spanish, Bolivia/Chile/Cuba/Guatemala/Mexico*)

In proverbs men do not seem to be much choosier than crocodiles, as far as women are concerned. The very hungry, especially, are certainly no vegetarians, but omnivores or fierce carnivorous hunters. In the shape of cats, hawks, sharks, tigers, wolves, and so forth, men metaphorically digest women in the shape of mice, fish, goats, lambs, cows, calves, hens, or chickens. To come back to the hen, she is a favourite dish, both delicious and profitable:

The eagle kissed the hen down to the last feather. (*Russian*)

An old hen gives excellent soup.

(*French, Monaco/Spanish, Chile/Mexico; Papiamentu; Creole, Guadeloupe*)

The old hen gives substance. (*Spanish, Cuba*)

An old hen makes a good stew. (*English, USA*)

Do not turn a hen into broth if its chicks have golden feathers. (*Arabic*)

Fishermen are keen on catching tasty fish. Although fresh fish is not easily caught—the bigger ones, especially, succeed in getting away from the net or the hook—a golden hook is believed to make things easier for the fisherman. Thus, in eating metaphors, women become highly appreciated nourishment for eternally hungry men. The eaters are of course the bigger and stronger animals, and their prospective food logically consists of relatively small and vulnerable fruits, plants, or animals. *En passant*, numerous observations surround this metaphorical consumption, reminding well-intended listeners that there are some rules to be respected, rules that will necessarily put limits to such indiscriminate swallowing of food. The tiger, for example, ought to refrain from tasting married women. Neither should the hyena be allowed to sleep with the goats.

Among the 'weaker' creatures, the lamb, this meek and vulnerable being, should never enter the wild beast's dwelling-place of its own accord. Neither should the cow risk its life by going to a rendezvous with the tiger, nor the goat hazard herself into the forest, and no sheep should be so crazy as to become friendly with the wolf. In proverbs, women are not considered to be able to manage, take care of themselves or defend themselves:

The frivolous partridge hopping around is an easy prey for a hunter's gun.

(*Arabic, Tunisia*)

Don't hurry to the forest, goat, all the wolves will be yours. (*Russian*)

The wild beast cannot live with the lamb. [A girl who runs into somebody's house cannot stay untouched] (*Bari, Sudan*)

Such reminders are addressed to the prospective food rather than to its prospective eaters. One of the main rules of the game for the food is never willingly to offer itself for consumption straightaway, as if being eaten were not bad enough for the experience to be postponed as much as possible:

A woman in search of a husband is like grass looking for a horse. (*Indonesian*)

If the hay follows the horse, it wants to be eaten. (*Dutch*)

It is not only unchaste, but also most dangerous for a dish to volunteer for being eaten, and no mercy is to be expected for such badly behaved grass or hay, or whatever other food inclined to offer itself.

The numerous food metaphors tend to completely overlook women's own appetite. In proverbs, if the very idea of female desire is not too frightening to be dealt with at all, it is referred to in rather negative terms. Female desire is a taboo. Women who dare express interest in 'eating' are referred to in terms of disaster. Or, as the Igbo put it even more forcefully, forwardness in women may be a prelude to Armageddon itself: 'The day a woman tells a man: "come and hug me" is the day the world ends.'

Still, the strongest animals have their weaknesses, and pay a price for their gluttony. Their endless craving is their most vulnerable spot, bowled over as they seem to be by anything appetizing they find on their way. Women use their own strategies to get what they want: their beauty, their cookery, and the prospective motherhood they offer to men:

> The whisper of a pretty girl can be heard further than the roar of a lion. (*English, USA*)
> The lord of the house resembles a bear in the forest, the lady of the house a pancake
>   with honey. (*Russian*)
> The union triumphs over the lion. [Marriage tames the man] (*Arabic, Algeria*)

Some metaphors depict men who come to depend on women as tragic prey to female cruelty, and proverbs worry a lot about the fate of those falling into the hands of female eaters: 'A wife is a panther in your own bed', is a nightmarish Umbundu image. Subversive wives are compared to poisonous animals, such as the snakes or scorpions mentioned before; or they are equated with dangerous carnivores likely to devour their own husbands:

> Who marries a she-wolf often looks at the forest. (*Basque*)
> Better to live with a lion, than to live with a wife. (*Greek*)
> Rather follow a lion or a serpent than a woman. (*Hebrew*)
> Woman to man is either a God or a wolf. (*English, UK*)

Reassuringly, some of those ferocious female creatures are unmasked as fakes, and fall victim to their own incapacity to do any real harm: 'The gazelle who wanted to roar like a lion overworked herself and died', says an Amharic proverb stressing that women cannot but stick to their 'natural' roles. However, unlike food metaphors referring to women, men are evidently not at all presented as appetizing fruits or stew or soup or cookies or juicy animals to be savoured by cheerful female eaters.

GENDERED PLACES AND SPACES

Woman's path takes one ell: from the oven to the threshold. (*Russian*)

Although the metaphors we have come across thus far come from widely different domains, they have in common a tendency first of all to place men and women in opposite categories, and, second, to narrow the relationships between men and women down to terms of male subjects and female objects. In proverbs, those oppositions appear to be quite systematically organized into wished for hierarchies, whether the metaphors belong to the domain of lifeless objects, plants or animals.

HOME AND THE WORLD

There is no blessing in a woman who travels, and there is no blessing in a man who does not travel.
(Arabic, Algeria)

Looking into the domains of location and movement, we find metaphors related to geographical notions, such as earth and sky, water and land, field and forest, or closer by, home and yard. Such spaces have also been translated into oppositions, distance and difference along the lines of male and female.

Women are being associated and equated with home and hearth, and with other metaphors localizing them in, or rather chaining them to, the place where they belong or ought to remain, so that they do not fall a prey to the greedy eyes and hands and penises of men other than their husbands. Thus, proverbs confine them to rooms, homes, houses etc., and have them stay there preferably until the end of their lives. A very popular message in European and Latin American proverbs, compares a virtuous wife with a broken leg: both stay at home, and an English proverb from the UK observes that 'The wife that expects to have a good name, is always at home as if she were lame.' Broken legs and lameness illustrate to what extent the imposed pretext of 'virtue' has been a paralyzing handicap for women in life.

There is an enormous number of proverbs emphasizing that women going out 'walk out of their honour', as it is formulated in a Dutch and Flemish proverb. Some Christian and Islamic proverbs literally insist on this point: a bride enters her husband's house with a veil and leaves it only when she is buried, so that the ideal numbers of times in life women ought to leave the home are limited to two or three:

> A woman is to be from her house three times; when she is christened, married and
>   buried. (*English, UK*)
> A girl must not leave the house more than twice: on the day of her marriage, on the day
>   of her death. (*Arabic, Maghreb / West Sahara*)
> A woman should come to her husband's house in a veil, and leave it in a winding shroud.
>   (*Persian*)
> A woman is well either in the house or in the grave. (*Pashto*)

Separate spaces are to be respected[126] as the appropriate order of things indoors and out of doors, or in the words of an American proverb: 'A woman, a cat and a chimney should never leave the house.' Ovens do not travel either, do they? (*German/Russian*). Many examples equate women with animals that stay at home or stick to one and the same place:

> The men and dogs for the barn, the women and cats for the kitchen. (*English, USA*)
> The woman and the cat have their room in the house, the husband and the dog in the
>   yard. (*Letzeburgish*)
> Women and cats at home; men and dogs in the street. (*Catalan/French*)
> Women and cows do not go abroad. (*Italian*)
> Buffaloes must be kept in stables, gold in purses, and women at home. (*Indonesian*)
> Women and chickens get lost by wandering from house to house. (*Hindi*)

Going to the neighbours, as the chickens do, may look acceptable. But even then, a Spanish proverb from Cuba recommends finding out where the wife really goes, when she says that she is going to visit the neighbours. Ultimately, is she really at home when she is supposed to be there, and what is she up to when she is? 'Don't trust a horse in the field or a woman at home' a Russian proverb warns. In case she should need to leave the home, a decent woman will be (brought) back home early, just like the sheep or the geese, before dark.

Inside the house, the female space *par excellence* is the kitchen; second, the bed or the bedroom, and third, the living room. In the kitchen, metonymically, mothers as well as wives also become the fire, the stove, or the oven; and husbands without a wife are sometimes referred to as a silent kitchen, or a kitchen without a fire, thus stressing that the kitchen can only be brought to life by a woman's presence. Turning women into kitchen utensils, such as a pot or plate or frying pan, or associating them with food prepared in the kitchen, makes it obvious where women are supposed to spend their days.

Indirectly spaces express hierarchies in terms of differences—economic differences, for example—as in the following Vietnamese proverb: 'Without [a] man, the house is an orphan; without [a] woman, only the kitchen [is an orphan]'; or internal female hierarchies in status, for example in a Korean proverb, as expressed in the respective quarters where the lazy mother-in-law and the hard-working daughter-in-law are located, with a man standing in-between, not knowing with whom to take sides: 'Going into the [living] room, the mother-in-law's words sound right; going into the kitchen, the daughter-in-law's words sound right.'

Women are dissuaded from transgressing the borders of their own fixed domain, as their efforts to engage in male roles will only be profitable to those who sojourn in the male domain: 'When a woman makes the giant drum, it is kept in the man's room.' In this Ashanti proverb, the cutting of a large wooden drum as a female achievement is to be annihilated by relegating the result literally to a 'male' space.

Proverbs wholeheartedly agree in that a wife is a profitable interior commodity, useful in all spaces the house possibly contains. Actually, she is praised as the best piece of furniture one can acquire, serving several practical purposes at a time. The tasks assigned to women as female duties inside the home are specified according to the respective spaces where the roles are to be performed, as in a European and North American middle-class proverb with several variants: 'A good wife is a perfect lady in the living room, a good cook in the kitchen, and a harlot in the bedroom.'

Going from the house to the yard or garden is just a small step, but many proverbs see this step as extremely problematic. The metaphor of the rope illustrates the ongoing struggle. The rope connects the husband's dominance as depending on the wife's acceptance: rules cannot be imposed limitlessly, domination and resistance are two sides of the same coin: 'Give the wife and the greyhound a long rope, but not so long as to get outside the house' (*Spanish, Chile*) means that some bargaining is going on. The fear of loss is expressed in another variant from the same country: 'Give the wife and the goat a long rope, but not so long that you lose both the rope and the goat.' The dilemma is clear, the wife wants more space, whereas the husband, whose well-being and posterity depend on her presence, wants to keep her under control. The original Spanish proverb is: 'Give an unruly wife plenty of rope'—arguing that a wife's willingness to being fastened is not endless. The proverb's original form refers to the battle of wills that involves the wife's outburst of anger. The ongoing negotiation led to two other variants in Argentina: 'To a wife or a goat one should not give a long rope' and: 'Give the angry wife a long rope.' Anger and protest may result in her being allowed a little 'more rope' in the complex interweaving of internalized norms and unconsciously adopted values.

In the meantime, a wide variety of proverbs continue to debate whether a woman should be allowed to leave the house at all. This debate depends very much on the extent to which separateness is forced upon men and women in the culture (and the class) concerned. Poor women are usually more 'equal' to their men than rich women who could be set apart because, certainly in the past, their house was being kept by servants or slaves. In developing countries, less well-to-do rural women necessarily still have to go and gather firewood or fetch water at some faraway well or river; usually they also need to work hard on the land for their family's survival. For their relatives, those outside women's activities are badly needed and therefore not really a point of discussion. However, as soon as poorer women marry into another (higher) group or class than their own, such relative freedom of movement may well become problematic, depending on the culture, of course. For example, in the Maghreb a man who wants to marry a rural woman is warned by a friend as follows: 'Hens picking dunghills don't like cages.' (*Arabic*) Such a woman, not used to being confined, might be unwilling to accept such measures of seclusion.

Fences function as protectors and as yardsticks of decency: high fences mean decency, low fences indecency. Metaphorically, both men and women are imagined as fences, especially in Western Europe. A woman becomes her own fence, when she virtuous, or when she is too ugly to inspire any desire in men, and of course the widow is a problematic fence:

> A woman without a mate is like a garden without a fence. (*Slovene*)
> A man without a woman [also: a woman without a man] is like a field without a fence.
>   (*Swedish/Norwegian/Danish/German; Finnish*)
> A widow is a low fence everyone jumps over. (*German*)

A sensible wife enjoys being at home, and only the foolish ones seek fulfilment in going abroad, as a North American proverb stresses. Men, on the contrary, must leave home, to discover other wonderful places on earth than their mother's kitchen. They are encouraged to be on the move: the entire world is theirs to be explored. An Estonian proverb concisely defines the gendered spaces as follows: 'The home is the wife's world, the world is the man's home.' And thus, from Italy to India to Mexico, it has been echoed that the outside world is a man's world, and as far as travelling is concerned: men do and women don't. Travelling is believed to jeopardize a woman's chastity, as dramatically visualized in a Malay proverb: 'A travelled woman is like a garden trespassed by cattle.' Women's travelling, then, has come to be a metaphor for 'unchastity'.

Water is another common metaphor marking out gendered spaces. Women are compared with water in a variety of ways: they are insatiable water; water in opposition to fire (as a metaphor for men); water as more powerful than fire; water not to be trusted; water going wherever it is sent (girls); spilt water (married daughters); unwelcome water (women as a disaster); thirst-quenching water (to a male lover); water you cannot sleep on (beautiful women); muddied water; fresh water and shallow water (both deadly to men); water without badness (a mother); water adapting itself to its surroundings (a wife adapting to her husband), capricious water, and so forth.

Such metaphors confirm the by now familiar qualifications projected on to women in proverbs: dangerous forces, unreliability, required submissiveness and adaptation in

marriage; the loss of daughters to their own parents when they get married; capriciousness—they have all been presented in a variety of ways throughout the previous pages.

Water is not only associated with women, but also with men, depending on whether
it is stagnant or streaming, whether it is 'sedentary' or 'travelling'. Opposed to 'male'
water, 'female' water is referred to as a sea or lake set against a river. As a metaphor for the
irritating mother-in-law who hampers the son-in-law's behaviour: she becomes the duckweed in his river. Metaphors for water containing spaces associate men with flowing water
like rivers, streams or waterfalls, and women with receptacles for streaming water or with
stagnant water containers: springs, wells, pools, ponds, lakes, and seas. Thus they are
contrasting male travellers and immobile females, or in a sexual image: male sperm flowing into the female receptacle. As a mother, a woman is the source of life, even for the
water, and it is acknowledged that the river will always depend on her:

> Every river runs to its mamma. (*English, Jamaica*)
> The source of the river is the source of the family. (*Mongolian*)
> Man is a river, woman is a lake. (*Kurdish*)
> Woman is a lake, man a river. (*Greek; Letzeburgish*)
> A fast, wild stream will not reach the sea. (*Dargin/Russian*)

As the Italian proverb says: 'An angry woman is like a sea without shore.' The hasty, wild
river is a man falling in love, suddenly and passionately. Such a love is believed to end as
abruptly and quickly as it began. It will neither reach the sea nor last a century, in
the words of a Mongolian variant depicting the same image. The streaming river, and the
quiet lakes and ponds waiting for the outside water to come, are a rich source of sex
metaphors, referring in turn to male exertion, female exactingness (rejecting a man's impotence as the sea would a dead bird), fear of women's destructive depths, and a man's
return to his wife in spite of his desire to visit other banks:

> A small, deep pool of water will exhaust the breath. (*Maori*)
> A woman is like the sea which does not admit a dead bird. (*Spanish, Bolivia*)
> Woman is a spring in which all calabashes break. (*Beti*)
> Whatever bank a river has washed, it always returns to its old bed. (*Digor*)

Other sexual metaphors referring to places are bridge, path, road, and street. In many cultures, for a girl going out in the street means losing her good name—which, like water,
will never come back (*Persian*). The opposition of home and street is obvious:

> An egg is never square; a woman of the street is never honest. (*Japanese*)
> A bright woman is a decoration for the house, a foolish woman the amusement of the
>   street. (*Uzbek*)

Whereas girls and women are constantly warned that their honour is easily trampled
upon, men are on the one hand warned not to trust the unreliable paths they would love
to walk upon, and on the other hand advised not to worry about previous passers-by once
they have decided to go for a light-hearted walk:

> A girl is like a bridge; anybody can walk over her. (*Armenian*)
> The woman and the paved road are there to be trampled on. (*Portuguese*)

Woman is like a path, beautiful but sinuous. (*Afrikaans*)
Woman is a path: don't ask who has walked on it or who will walk on it. (*Wolof*)

And, as in the rivers-and-banks metaphor, men are reminded in a road metaphor to return to the 'well-trodden road' after their escapades.

Women's metaphorical and otherwise highly recommended immobility has not prevented proverbs from imagining them as vehicles on the path of life, for example as a bus or a boat—containers again! The maritime means of transport are usually depicted as problematic: the female vessels, boats, or ships are leaky, need mending, and go about without a helm or a sail. And of course they need male guidance:

A woman without a husband, a ship without a helm. (*Portuguese*)
A woman without a husband is a boat without a rudder. (*Vietnamese*)
A woman without husband is a ship without a sail. (*Dutch*)

Other proverbs imagine travelling in female ships as getting lost or shipwrecked. Such frightening metaphors seem to plead against marriage, unless, of course, a good wife can be found, because, in the words of a Turkish proverb: 'A good wife is heaven on earth.'

HERE AND HEREAFTER

Who has a good wife does not need paradise. (*Bulgarian*)

Next to the earth as a man's home, outer spaces are being gendered: sky as well as heaven, paradise, hell, and purgatory. To begin with the last two: women's being associated with the Devil, also associated her with the Devil's dwelling-place: hell. In proverbs women have been associated with the inhabitants of hell, or imagined as the avenue, road, the gate to hell, or the main entrance leading men there straight away. Women, whether or not qualified as 'wicked', are being located in hell, in proverbs of Jewish, Christian or Islamic origin, but also from elsewhere:

There is no hell like an evil wife. (*Hebrew*)
He who has a wicked wife, his hell begins on earth. (*Dutch/German/Italian*)
Hell is lined with grimy housewives. (*Japanese*)
Women are hell, but still no house should be without them. (*Persian*)
Woman is the chief gate to hell. (*Hindi*)
Obedience to women is the entrance to hell. (*Arabic, Maghreb*)
Old maids lead apes in hell. (*English, UK/USA*)
A young wife is a horse on which an old man gallops to hell. (*Polish*)

Purgatory is the place where in the Catholic religion righteous people's souls need to be purified before they get access to eternal felicity. This in-between space figures only in proverbs from Europe or from places outside the Western world that have been in contact with Europe through missionary activities and colonization. No less than hell, purgatory serves as a metaphor for a 'bad' or 'wicked' or 'quarrelsome' wife a man has to live with on earth until the end of his days—divorce being out of the question at the time.

A wicked wife is purgatory on earth. (*German*)
A wicked wife is a daily purgatory. (*Danish*)

The one who has an evil wife is near purgatory. (*Portuguese, Brazil*)
Who has a bad wife has purgatory for a neighbour. (*English, USA*)

Such a tragic life, it is cheerfully suggested, might well redeem a man from the otherwise obligatory sojourn in purgatory in the afterlife. This redemption for husbands even holds for hell, as suggested in Hebrew: 'Whoever has a wicked wife will not see hell', or in Bulgarian: 'He who has a wicked wife does not need hell.'

Moving on to more comforting positive spaces, we enter heaven and paradise. Both are associated with happiness, and happiness is defined as two people being in love with each other, as in the Japanese dream of two lovers sitting together on a lotus flower in paradise. More modest is a Russian dream of paradise in a hut as long as one's sweetheart is there too, or the no less down-to-earth heaven on earth defined in a Dutch proverb as making love while being in love. Evidently, it is not pleasant to be alone, even in such ideal dwelling places as heaven or paradise. In a number of proverbs, heaven is simply defined as having a good mother or a good wife. From a man's perspective, heaven and paradise are metaphors for the reassuring closeness of a 'good' female, whether a man's mother or an idealized paramour/wife:

Heaven is beneath your mother's heel. [You'll find paradise when you respect your mother] (*Indonesian/Turkish*)
A mother's breast, paradise for the child. (*Kabartjaevo-Balkar*)
Paradise on earth is in riding on horseback, gaining information from books, or laying at the breasts of a beautiful woman. (*Arabic*)
Old grain, new butter, a well-bred wife and the back of a horse; these are the four marks of heaven. (*Punjabi*)

A serious issue is the loss of the place called paradise, as explained in the Genesis story of Adam and Eve: 'From a woman came the beginning of sin and because of her we will all perish,' it is said in Hebrew. In Jewish culture, Christian Europe and the Arab world, the impact of this lost-paradise myth has been so powerful that the whole of womankind has been blamed for the behaviour of just one character in just one old narrative:

Only a woman was able to wreck paradise. (*Arabic*)
Adam's rib brings more harm than benefit. (*German*)

Wedlock itself is rarely equated with a stay in paradise. It is seldom seen as a heaven, more often as a hell (if not purgatory), and in the more reasonable cases a combination of both. Features of heaven on earth are a wife's goodness, her friendliness, and her attractiveness, even though female beauty is no less associated with purgatory and hell:

Husbands are in heaven, whose wives chide not. (*Tamil, Sri Lanka/India*)
Woman was placed on earth to show men both paradise and purgatory. (*English, USA*)
Women are paradise for the eyes, a purgatory for the purse, and hell for the soul.
(*All over Europe*)

Comparing purgatory and hell as negative spaces with heaven and paradise as positively connotated spaces, one finds women and men hierarchically and separately positioned *vis-à-vis* each other. In matters of 'badness', several proverbs argue that man is to woman as one devil is to a complete hell. Or, in slightly different terms: if man goes to purgatory, woman goes to hell. In other words, men are less 'bad' than women, according to this logic.

In proverbs, sky and earth have also been associated with men and women respectively. Creation stories about man as the sky and woman as the earth exist in various cultures. A Maori saying refers to a myth about the sky father and the earth mother: 'You and I are both from the sky father and earth mother; this is me, so-and-so, son of such-and-such.' Both sky and earth may serve as metaphors for women and wives. The sky is imagined as a woman in several ways: neither can be understood, both are a mystery, both change unexpectedly, neither can be trusted, and, of course, life without either would be much less complicated:

> Woman and sky cannot be understood. (*Gikuyu*)
> Without wife and wind the sky is always gentle. (*German*)
> A woman's mind and autumn sky [change oft]. (*Japanese*)
> Maids are May when they are maids, but the sky changes when they are wives. (*Yiddish*)

The earth is a more positive metaphor because it is respectfully imagined as the life-giving mother on which we all depend, even though she needs the seed-giving father, as expressed in a harmonious Nogay proverb: 'The rain kisses, the earth smiles.' It is fully stressed that much if not all depends on women in this respect:

> The earth is the mother, the seed the father. (*Amharic*)
> Dear earth, our mother, she feeds us, waters us and clothes us. (*Russian*)
> A house is not built on earth but on woman. (*Turkish*)
> The house is not founded on the earth, but on the wife. (*Serbian/Croatian*)
> The earth is like a mother. [She will never be tired of giving.] (*Mapuche, Chile/Argentina*)

Metaphorically or non-metaphorically, this earth-motherly quality is the most positive side of women to be acknowledged in proverbs: their being able to create new life and to provide men with posterity. The Lingala proverb 'Woman is like the earth: everyone sits down on her' can be interpreted in several ways: people sit on their mother's lap in early childhood, she keeps feeding them until they can take care of themselves. The proverb includes other shades of meaning as well: the one who 'sits down' represents a heavy load for the one who has to bear with the weight. The earth is like a mother: she keeps on giving. The mother's suffering is not so much her ongoing care for her children, but her ongoing worries about all of her children all of her life.

IMAGES IN SEARCH OF HIERARCHIES

Of all animals the female is the better save only in mankind. (Bedouin)

In metaphors, an invented order is confirmed thanks to a simple, effective mechanism. Two sorts of objects, animals, or parts of the human body are selected, which are then associated with men and with women respectively. Those objects have not only been chosen simply for the sake of poetic enjoyment, but also for their underlying purpose. Thus, object and animal metaphors project human situations and behaviour on to objects and animals (and vice versa), either to recommend or to criticize people's conduct.

Such metaphors proclaim required behaviour for both men and women, and justify specific ideas about how things ought to be. They motivate their idea of the nature of things by creating, at will, parallels or contrasts between people's behaviour and the objects, animals or situations that surround them.

If things are the way they are in our surroundings, it is argued—for example in the relationships between hen and cock—then for sure the same situation certainly applies to human females and males as well. On the other hand, if need be, 'nature' is also used to stress the opposite, by arguing: if things are the way they are in the world of the animals, humans are no animals, and their situation is therefore completely different. In both cases, the effect of the argument suits the same interests to be defended. Man and cock are equated, because it suits the argument: the cock does the speaking and he is the master of multiple hens within his henhouse and without.

The purpose of the Bedouin motto at the beginning of this section is not very different: the submissiveness of women is to be justified, and the existing hierarchy has to be kept in place. For the Bedouins, female animals, giving birth and giving milk, are more important because they are more profitable than males; however, by acknowledging that human females are also more profitable than human males the comparison would be going too far. Hence, the parallel between nature and human life has to be turned around in order to suit the argument.

The parallels are adequately chosen: metaphors referring to men and women seem to have been selected in terms of hierarchical oppositions, such as tall versus small, strong versus weak, significant versus insignificant etc. This holds true for the human body, as we have seen. Although most parts of the body are common to men and women alike, in the proverbs differences are created by gendering parts of the body which are neutral as such: parts associated with females are systematically selected among lower or less prestigious parts than those attributed to males, so safeguarding an invented sexual hierarchy. Thus, man is presented as the 'head' of woman's 'body', while she is excluded from being the head by all possible means and arguments. In the same order of ideas, the head is situated higher than the shoulder, and the eye can never rise higher than the brow. As for the hands, if both are compared, she is designated to be the left one and he the right one. However, when he is designated as the 'head', she can become his 'right hand'. The female body or parts of the body are used to belittle women's mental capacity.

The purpose is to 'prove' that 'logically' certain behaviours, professions or skills are not to be displayed by women. This procedure is particularly rigorous when it comes to intelligence. Why would proverbs need to insist so strongly on men's being the 'head' of women and on women's lack of brains? Men need and have talents, knowledge, and eloquence, it is argued, whereas virtuous women neither have nor need such qualities.

The same strategy applies to object metaphors. The big pot rightly dominates the small pot: again, one object, selected from everyday reality on the basis of its 'superiority', is declared male, whereas another, classified lower or weaker in comparison with the other object, is declared female. The Ovambo proverb, 'The bow is not stronger than the spear', stresses that a woman is inferior to her husband, even when she is wealthy. Using very different metaphors, a Burmese proverb aims no less at reassuring those who tend to worry about female power—they shouldn't, because male authority will get the better of it, at sea and ashore, even though it looks quite impressive: 'A big wave! It is under the boat. A big mountain! It is under the foot.' The big waves of the female sea will be controlled by the helmsman who will safely and surely steer his boat across them; likewise, the big mountains of mother earth will be controlled by the male feet walking over them.

Other metaphors spread the same message, by arguing that a 'female' object of apparent power has to be successfully dominated by a 'male' object even though the latter might appear weak on the face of it—as the small string binding the big parcel; the small squirrel lifting the big nut, and so forth.

The idea of hierarchy and control is further confirmed in proverbs referring to location and movement, through metaphors setting male mobility against female immobility, and open male outer spheres of action and influence against closed inner female spheres of action without any public impact. 'Woman' equates both 'womb' and 'home', that which is 'within'. For the sake of female modesty and male security, women are confined to controllable places, such as kitchens, bedrooms, houses etc., whereas men are stimulated to go out into the world without risking their good name. Although women are respected and revered in some cases—and especially as mothers they are—as soon as the idea of female power and superiority pops up, it must be instantly conjured away, as an imminent danger.

Looking into the position of the hen and the cock again (or other female and male animals for that matter), the philosophical question is sometimes brought forward as to whether it is better to be a cock than a hen, to be a female or a male of one's species in life. There is no choice, but all the same, one has to live with the consequences:

> The hen is no bird, the woman is no person. (*Estonian*)
> The hen is no bird, the woman no human. (*Russian*)
> A woman is not a person, a mare is not a horse, a magpie is not a bird, a ruffle is not a
> fish. (*Danish, Norwegian, Swedish; Finnish*)

If a hen is not a real bird, would not this also hold true for the cock? That's not the point. There is no logic: there are interests to be defended. What if one had a choice in life? A few Eastern European proverbs look directly into this question, and are definite about the answer.

> Better be a cock for one day than a hen for a hundred days. (*Digor*)
> It is better to be a bull for a year than a cow for a hundred years. (*Serbian/Croatian*)

On the other hand, as an encouragement to those who complain about the toughness of life, is it not better to be a running hen than to be a dead rooster? This Mexican observation puts an exploited hen on a higher level than a dead cock, but the hierarchy is no less clear. A Kurdish proverb confirms the same idea without making a detour via metaphors: 'It is better to be a male for one day than a female for ten.' In proverbs, women are very, very rarely represented as superior beings *vis-à-vis* men as negligible entities, as it happens in the matrilineal (and matrilocal) Indonesian Minangkabau culture, where, as we have seen, a husband is exceptionally imagined as just 'a little dust on a tree trunk.'

'I won't come back female', is an old Ashanti saying in Ghana, reflecting women's preference for a better position in a next life. No less than direct proverbs about gender relations, proverbial metaphors reproduce a gender hierarchy as an imagined world in which it is self-evident who are the speakers and who the silenced ones; in this world-system there is a clear gender divide between the keepers of knowledge and the ignorant, the travellers and those who stay at home, the eaters and the eatables, and so forth—as if this were the irreversible 'nature of things'.

Messages of Images Anthology

Cups and spoons cannot live without tinkling. (*Udmurt, RF*): *Geyvandov 143*

Woman is like the earth: even a fool sits down on her. (*Luba, Congo DR*): *o.s. Clémentine Faïk-Nzuji*

A woman is like the mimosa tree that yields gum all day long.
   (*Xhosa, South Africa*): *Finnegan 1970: 406*

Which red pepper is not hot; which woman is not jealous? (*Vietnamese*): *Duong 97*

Beware of a beautiful woman as of red pepper. (*Japanese*): *o.s. Keiko Kosunose*

A woman who has borne children is like a used potato plot: from time to time one can dig up
   some potatoes. (*Ganda*): *Walser 373*

Long hair, short ideas. (*Chinese*): *o.s. Huang Mingfen*

WOMEN AS OBJECTS

When a net is worn out, it is thrown away on the shore.
   (*Maori, New Zealand*): *Brougham & Reed 73*

CONTAINERS

A jug breaks only once. (*Uzbek*): *Geyvandov 92*

A house full of children is a basket full of eggs. (*Dutch*): *Joos 138*

A woman is a basket full of flour; the hungry come of their own accord. [She appeals to men
   without having to go and look for them.] (*Umbundu, Angola*): *Valente 43*

When a bell breaks, it will never ring again. (*Spanish, Cuba*): *o.s. Trini Cruz*

It will never do to be careless of a little girl and a small bag. (*Japanese*): *Buchanan 101*

Until the age of twelve the girl is a cup, until the age of sixteen a tub, after the age of sixteen
    thank him who takes her out of the house. (*Czech*): *Reinsberg-Düringsfeld 132*

Precious essences are kept in small vessels.

   (*Spanish, Chile/El Salvador/Puerto Rico*): *Sánchez Duarte 94; Díaz Rivera 26; Champion 616; o.s.*
   Duran

A virginal lap and a warm sun with Christmas are rarities. (*Danish*): *Molbech 158*

An unchaste woman will be unchaste even when confined in a glass vessel. (*Persian*): *Haïm 48*

The house without a centre-pole is like a woman without a husband.

   (*Oromo, Ethiopia*): *Cotter 22*

Not all nice houses are good to spend the night in. (*Bambara, Mali*): *Travélé 46*

Coitus interruptus is like dining well within the house and then having to spit it all out on
    the veranda. (*Thai*): *Lunde & Wintle 122*

Woman is a fortress; man her guard. (*Kurdish, Turkey*): *Geyvandov 40*

Woman is a fortress; man her prisoner. (*Kurdish, Turkey*): *Champion 450*

He who has a beautiful wife in a castle on the frontier never rests. (*Italian*): *Haller 514*

Who has a handsome wife, or a castle on the frontier, or a vineyard at the main road, is never
    without war. (*Spanish; Portuguese*): *Bohn 1855: 197; Haller 515*

He who has a beautiful wife, a castle on the border or windows looking out on the street, will
    never see the end of the war. (*Portuguese, Brazil*): *Souto Maior 52*

Maidens and castles must yield in the end. (*Yiddish*): *Cohen 320*

Women and fortresses that negotiate are half way to being captured. (*Swedish*): *Holm 188*

Neither a fortress nor a maid will hold out long after they begin to parley.

   (*English, USA*): *Brown 1970: 120*

Woman has no house in three generations. (*Japanese*): *o.s. Kosunose*

Lock and key cannot stop a girl. (*Russian*): *Geyvandov 92*

Keeping a young girl indoors is like having a tiger in the house. (*Chinese*): *Wintle 103*

A girl, the door locked and bolted. (*Vietnamese*): *o.s. Lam Ngo*

A stable without a door is a woman without a husband. (*Tibetan*): *Gergan 36*

An honourable widow always keeps her door locked. (*Hebrew, Israel*): *Moscona 117*

An honest widow, a closed door. (*Spanish, Argentina/Colombia*): *Moya 497; Acuña 47*

The Devil comes and goes through a closed door. (*Spanish, Argentina*): *Moya 305*

No padlocks, bolts or bars can secure a maiden as well as her own reserve.

   (*English, USA*): *Kin 215*

She says: 'I don't love him!', but she doesn't lock her door at night.

   (*Malagasy, Madagascar*): *Geyvandov 269*

An open door tempts a saint. (*Spanish, El Salvador*): *Sánchez Duarte 143*

Once the hatches are open, the door is open. [Warning to women.]

   (*Spanish, Panama*): *Aguilera 177*

For a girl there is one door ajar, and it has a wooden bolt, for a man there are forty doors ajar.

   (*Komi, RF*): *Geyvandov 95*

A house with two doors is difficult to watch. (*Spanish, Colombia*): *Acuña 70*

The painted woman leaves her husband through the back door.

   (*Ladino/Hebrew, Morocco*): *Benazeraf 91*

A house with two doors, a woman, and a cane plantation: the Devil takes care of them.

(*Spanish, Venezuela*): *Febres Cordero 43*

The woman who has put on make-up leaves her husband through the other door.

(*Spanish, Puerto Rico*): *Fernández Valledor 155*

An adulterous wife needs a home with two entrances. (*Kurdish / Hebrew, Turkey*): *Alcalay 204*

Take care of your own gate, and do not think of other men's wives. (*Chinese*): *Geyvandov 288*

A well-dressed woman draws her husband away from another woman's door.

(*Spanish*): *Chaves 856; Bohn 1857: 227*

FLOWERS, TREES, FRUITS

The beautiful woman is like the giant palm: you must climb without looking down.

(*Bamum, Cameroon*): *o.s. Chimoun*

Every beautiful rose becomes a rosehip. (*French*): *Gérard 143*

No flower will bloom a hundred days. (*Chinese*): *Geyvandov 82*

Beauty is like a flower that is born and soon withers. (*Spanish, Argentina*): *Moya 186*

A girl is [like] a rose sought by many. (*Arabic, widespread*): *Khalil Safadi 78*

A girl is like a watermelon that has not been sliced. (*Armenian*): *Geyvandov 100*

The laughter of the rose produces tears of rose water as fruit. (*Persian*): *Roebuck 207*

Whoever smells a rose endures the pain of her thorns. (*Turkish*): *Geyvandov 204*

Only those who pick the roses feel the thorns. (*Chinese*): *Lunde & Wintle 64*

The rose that is smelt by many, loses its fragrance. (*Hebrew, Israel*): *Cohen 1961: 438*

The flower is beautiful, but the thorn is sharp. (*Russian*): *Geyvandov 44*

A lotus flower in the mud. (*Japanese*): *Buchanan 264*

Beauty in women is like a flower in the spring; but virtue is like a star in heaven.

(*English, USA*): *Loomis 1955: 197*

Though the flower of the swamp is white, it is a deadly flower.

(*Spanish, Cuba*): *Sánchez-Boudy 34*

Woman is as changeable in character as water and poplar flower.

(*Chinese*): *o.s. Huang Mingfen*

Where there's a lot of blossom there won't be much fruit. (*Japanese*): *Wintle 64*

The surface beauty of a fig-fruit, inside it are black ants. (*Hehe, Tanzania*): *Madumulla 122n*

Red on the outside, rotten inside. [Of fruit and women.] (*Spanish, Mexico*): *Casasola 18*

A straight tree will be cut down sooner than another one. (*Korean*): *Geyvandov 78*

The beauty of a vine lies in its grapes. (*Turkish*): *Geyvandov 74*

A tree with many branches is the beauty of the mountains; a beautiful woman is the house's
ornament. (*Burjat, RF*): *Geyvandov 69*

A tree without foliage: even if it is crowned, how can it be beautiful. (*Tibetan*): *Duncan 214*

Do not cut down a tree with beautiful flowers. (*Oromo, Ethiopia*): *Cotter 113n*

Watch the rose and take the bud. (*Turkish*): *Geyvandov 103*

The apple tree can't help not bearing any apples. (*Mordvin, RF*): *Geyvandov 159*

Plucking the pumpkin, you must take the leaves as well. (*Tonga, Zambia*): *Milimo 51*

Can you love the berries and hate the shrub that produced them? [Refers to a man who loves
a girl but dislikes her mother.] (*Sotho, Lesotho*): *Geyvandov 103*

He who loves the *gombo*, loves its leaves. [A *gombo* is a plant. If you marry a wife, you will have to take her family for granted.] (*Creole, Martinique*): *David 43*

WOMEN AS ANIMALS

Throughout time the female pigeon made the male-pigeon sigh, and the lioness the lion roar.
(*Arabic*): *Wijnaendts-Francken 68*

Lucky the man who has a bee for a wife. (*German*): *Champion 184*

Play the hen in the name of peace. [If you want peace you must cast your pride aside. A cock is proud; a chicken is not.] (*Indonesian*): *o.s. Bekker*

One hen will be as contented with one cock as another with eight.
(*Spanish, Argentina*): *Champion 615*

A hen in someone else's henhouse will always come out plucked.
(*Spanish, El Salvador*): *Sánchez Duarte 112*

Do not keep a hen that eats in your house and lays her eggs in somebody else's.
(*Spanish, Chile*): *o.s. Felipe Ramírez*

An old cock or a young one ... they're all the same! (*Azeri, Azerbaijan*): *Geyvandov 30*

A rooster masters twelve hens, a woman half as many men. (*Spanish*): *Champion 185*

The old rooster blames the hens for being unreliable. (*Creole, Haiti*): *ACCT 50*

A hen without rooster hasn't got a nest. (*Papiamentu, Netherlands Antilles*): *Brenneker 1963: 42*

When a hen is vexed by a rooster, where does it sleep? (*English, Jamaica*): *Llewellyn Watson 232*

The hen says, 'I will sleep early to avoid gossip.'
(*Papiamentu, Netherlands Antilles*): *Brenneker 1963: 43*

The hen knows when it is morning, but she looks at the mouth of the cock.
(*Twi, Ghana*): *Oduyoye 7*

Until the cock crows, the hen does not stir at dawn. (*Tibetan*): *Hla Pe 24*

Woman and hen should be at home, the whole day. (*Spanish*): *Bergua 343*

A hen that wanders much, does not lay eggs. (*Spanish, Colombia*): *Ramírez S. 137*

A woman and a hen: as far as my neighbour's house. (*Spanish*): *Champion 310*

If the hen flies too high, she will lose sight of her nest.
(*Sranan, Surinam*): *Neger-engelse spreekwoorden 36*

If the hen flies not far unless the cock flies with her. (*Danish*): *Bohn 1855: 399*

If the hen wants to go out in the yard, it will tell her keeper, 'The wind blew me here.'
(*Papiamentu, Netherlands Antilles*): *Brenneker 1963: 43*

Make merry hens, the rooster is at the vintage. (*English, UK; Spanish*): *Collins 174*

Run away, chickens, the rooster is dead. (*Portuguese, Brazil*): *Magalhães Júnior 138*

The cock crows, but the hen lays the eggs. (*Hebrew, Israel*): *Cohen 1961: 91*

Every rooster crows in its henhouse. (*Spanish, Cuba*): *Sabiduría Guajira 26*

The rooster, in his henhouse, crows when it pleases. (*Spanish, Venezuela*): *Febres Cordero 30*

The hen should not crow before the cock. (*French*): *Van Dale 1983: 1545*

A hen does not sing in presence of the cock. (*Creole, Martinique*): *David 52*

Where there is a rooster, the hen does not crow.
(*Portuguese, Brazil; Spanish, Argentina*): *Magalhães Júnior 138; Moya 402*

Day does not dawn because the hen crows. (*Burmese*): *Champion 347*

When the hen crows, dawn seldom comes. (*Spanish, Argentina*): *Magalhãs Júnior 373*

Can a hen flap her wings and crow like a cock? (*Tamil, India*): *Champion 432*

A hen that crows in the morning, and a woman who knows Latin, end badly.

(*Spanish*): *Geyvandov 275*

It is a sad house where the cock is silent and the hen crows. (*Czech*): *Mieder 1986: 77*

Woe to the house where the hen crows and the cock keeps silent. (*Romanian*): *Mieder 1986: 228*

There is no peace where the hen crows and the rooster keeps quiet.

(*Portuguese, Brazil*): *Lamenza 145*

When the hen crows, the house goes to ruin. (*Chinese, Japanese, Korean*): *Champion 442*

When a hen crows in the morning, the family is doomed. (*Chinese*): *Shengzi 820*

When the hen crows, death catches up with you.

(*Quecha, Ecuador*): *Santos Ortiz de Villalba 295*

I am the boss, says father cock, when I am not in, says mother hen. (*Dutch*): *o.s. Wessels*

A whistling woman and a crowing hen is neither fit for God nor men.

(*English, UK/Antigua/USA*): *Rhys 54; Smith & Eddins 239*

Where the cock crows, the wife commands. (*Spanish, Costa Rica*): *Hernández 70*

The cock lays nothing. (*Igbo, Nigeria*): *Akporobaro & Emovon 166*

The gaily coloured hen is not always the best layer. (*Serbian/Croatian*): *Mieder 1986: 228*

When a hen clucks, it means she wants to lay eggs.

(*Spanish, Dominican Republic*): *Rodríguez D. 88*

When the hen clucks, it is because she has laid eggs. (*Spanish, Chile*): *Cannobio 55*

A clucking hen lays no eggs. (*Arabic, Lebanon*): *Frayha I 300*

The hen that clucks, loses her eggs. (*Spanish, El Salvador*): *Sánchez Duarte 112*

The better a hen is being fed, the better she lays her eggs.

(*Papiamentu, Netherlands Antilles*): *Maduro 49*

An egg laid, a hen singing. (*Spanish, Puerto Rico*): *Díaz Rivera 82*

A tortoise lays a thousand eggs without anyone knowing it; a hen lays one egg and the whole town knows. (*Malay*): *Lunde & Wintle 70*

Let the hen prepare a nest before laying. (*Welsh, UK*): *Champion 81*

The hen that has settled on her nest, wants to lay an egg. [A woman who stays inside is going to give birth.] (*Portuguese, Brazil*): *Mota 101*

A hen cannot lay two eggs in a day. (*Papiamentu, Netherlands Antilles*): *Brenneker 1963: 42*

The neighbour's hen lays bigger eggs. (*Romanian*): *Günther 128–9*

The neighbour's hen lays two eggs. (*Macedonian*): *Geyvandov 211*

Whoever eats an egg does not realize that a hen must have had a sore behind because of it.

(*Papiamentu, Netherlands Antilles*): *Brenneker 1963: 42*

Those who eat an egg do not know whether the hen suffered. [About those who profit by the misfortunes of others without taking into account their suffering.]

(*Creole, Martinique*): *Hearn 11*

The hen has a lot of chickens, but she keeps them all under her wing. (*Finnish*): *Geyvandov 164*

However many chicks the hen may have, they all go under her wings.

(*Papiamentu, Netherlands Antilles; Sranan, Surinam*): *Brenneker 1963: 43; Neger-engelse spreekwoorden (odo's) 36*

Unfortunate the hen-house where the hen crows and the rooster clucks.

(*Spanish, Mexico*): *Velasco Valdés 53*

A rooster ignores the chickens but the hen is not to ignore him.

(*Papiamentu; Netherlands Antilles*): *Brennker 1963: 41*

When the mother-hen comes to the rooster again, she forgets her children.

(*German*): *Wander I 1775*

WOMEN AS EATABLES

He ate the food and the food ate him. [Refers to nasty diseases caught after an affair with a
   woman of easy virtue.] (*Zulu, South Africa*): *Geyvandov 258*

You learn the taste of a melon when you bite it. (*Korean*): *Geyvandov 274*

A girl is like a watermelon that has not been sliced. (*Armenian*): *Geyvandov 100*

When the figs are ripe, all the birds want them. (*Mandinka, Guinea*): *Sano 49*

Women are like dates, wash and eat. (*Arabic, Algeria*): *Belamri 30*

A hungry crocodile is not choosy. (*Malagasy, Madagascar*): *Geyvandov 38*

When the wife is married to the kitchen, love will soon be hungry. (*German*): *Wander I 1139*

He who wants to eat another man's hen, has to tie the leg of his own hen.

(*Slovenian*): *Geyvandov 213*

A woman doesn't have to go out to get the best medicine for her man. (*Irish*): *O'Farrell 48*

Only a fool would prefer food to a woman. (*Irish*): *Gaffney & Cashman 92*

An unbeaten woman is like unsalted cabbage. (*German*): *Meier-Pfaller 67*

A salad without onions resembles a woman without reason. (*Arabic, Maghreb*): *Cheneb III 188*

A woman without modesty is like a stew without salt. (*Tamashek, West Sahara*): *Champion 590*

Bread, like women, should be eaten hot. (*Spanish, Argentina*): *Moya 423*

Soup, women and coffee should be hot. (*Spanish, Dominican Republic*): *Rodríguez D. 247*

You should not wait till women or soup cool down. (*Letzeburgish*): *o.s. Laure Wolter*

Stew and woman let them simmer until they are readily cooked. (*Spanish*): *Bergua 386*

Five things are nice: long meals, young meat, old fish, pretty women, and wine on the table.

(*Dutch*): *Cock 119*

An old he-goat still likes a green leaf. (*Frisian, Netherlands*): *Beintema 21*

The lazy pig eats the soft pears. (*Albanian*): *Reinsberg-Düringsfeld 117*

The old bull loves fresh grass. (*Thai; Spanish, Argentina*): *Peltier 35; Myint Thein 75; Acuña 59*

The old hyena gets the best grapes. (*Persian*): *Geyvandov 35*

The old hyena gets the good melon. (*Armenian*): *Geyvandov 114*

An old cat likes young mice.

(*Spanish, Bolivia/Chile/Cuba/Guatemala/Mexico*): *Ballesteros 56; Barneville Vásquez 12;
   Sabiduría Guajira 27; Armas 407; o.s. Carlos Iglesias*

For an old donkey, a tender pasture ground.

(*Spanish, Argentina; Portuguese, Brazil*): *Villafuerte 27; Cannobio 32; Mota 162; Lamenza 9*

For an old ox, fresh grass. (*Spanish, Colombia*): *Villafuerte 7*

An old mouse likes fresh cheese. (*Spanish, Argentina*): *Moya 318*

For an old horse, new horseshoes. (*Spanish, El Salvador*): *Sánchez Duarte 20*

The old monkey looks for new shoots. (*Spanish, Bolivia*): *Barneville Vásquez 40*

Old cows like young grass, old men like young wives. (*Khiongtha, Bangladesh*): *Lewin 9*

He that wishes to eat the nut does not mind cracking the shell. (*Polish*): *Mieder 1986: 351*

A thing that does not satiate, creates hunger. [Woman or food.]

   (*Arabic, Egypt*): *Burckhardt 110*

The eagle kissed the hen until the last feather. (*Russian*): *Geyvandov 233*

An old hen gives excellent soup.

   (*French, Monaco; Spanish, Chile / Mexico; Papiamentu, Netherlands Antilles; Creole, Guadeloupe*):
   Suard II 143; Glazer 138; Ballesteros 62; Brenneker 1963: 42; Ludwig 468; o.s. Prieto

The old hen gives substance. (*Spanish, Cuba*): *Sabiduría Guajira 44*

An old hen makes a good stew. (*English, USA*): *West 43*

Do not turn a hen into broth if its chicks have golden feathers. (*Arabic*): *Lunde & Wintle 15*

A young girl and fresh fish are tasty. (*Estonian*): *Geyvandov 81*

Where the sea is deep blue, there the shark swims; when the woman is attractive, men have
   desire, and get her. (*English, Hawaii*): *Judd 15*

The fish that got away was bigger. (*Burmese*): *Myint Thein 83*

Woman and sea fish are difficult to catch. (*Portuguese*): *Chaves 896*

It's easy to catch a fish with a golden hook. (*German*): *Geyvandov 51*

Even the tiger will not bite a married woman. (*Korean*): *Geyvandov 126*

One does not allow the hyenas to sleep with the goats. [One does not allow young men to
   sleep in the same place with young women.] (*Ovambo, Namibia / Angola*): *Geyvandov 251*

The wild beast cannot live with the lamb. [A girl who runs into somebody's house cannot
   stay untouched.] (*Bari, Sudan*): *Spagnolo 352*

The cow is safe only at the tiger's mercy. (*Burmese*): *o.s. Anonymous*

Crazy is the sheep that confesses to the wolf. (*Spanish, Colombia*): *Acuña 47*

Woe the sheep that unburdens its heart to a wolf. (*Moldovan*): *Geyvandov 283*

The frivolous partridge hopping around is an easy prey for a hunter's gun.

   (*Arabic,Tunisia*): *Yetiv 44*

Don't hurry to the forest, goat, all the wolves will be yours. (*Russian*): *Geyvandov 91*

The day a woman tells a man: 'come and hug me' is the day the world ends.

   (*Igbo*): *o.s. Chika N. Unigwe*

A woman in search of a husband is like grass looking for a horse.

   (*Indonesian*): *o.s. Maya Maya Sutedja-Liem*

If the hay follows the horse, it wants to be eaten. (*Dutch*): *Mesters 58; Ter Laan 250*

The hay doesn't follow the stallion. (*Dutch*): *Mesters 58*

The whisper of a pretty girl can be heard further than the roar of a lion.

   (*English, USA*): *Mieder 1992: 251*

The lord of the house resembles a bear in the forest, the lady of the house a pancake with
   honey. (*Russian*): *Graf 1960: 233*

The union triumphs over the lion. [Marriage tames the man.] (*Arabic, Algeria*): *Belamri 42*

Who marries a she-wolf often looks at the forest. (*Basque*): *Geyvandov 91*

Better to live with a lion, than to live with a wife. (*Greek*): *Haller 464*

Rather follow a lion or a serpent than a woman. (*Hebrew, Israel*): *Rosen 423; Alcalay 547*

Woman to man is either a God or a wolf. (*English, UK*): *Champion 45*

The gazelle who wanted to roar like a lion overworked herself and died.
   (*Amharic, Ethiopia*): *Geyvandov 249*
A wife is a panther in your own bed. (*Umbundu, Angola*): *Valente 44*

GENDERED PLACES AND SPACES

Woman's path takes one ell: from the oven to the threshold. (*Russian*): *Graf 1963: 72*
The rain kisses, the earth smiles. (*Nogay, RF*): *Geyvandov 184*

HOME AND THE WORLD

There is no blessing in a woman who travels, and there is no blessing in a man who does not
   travel. (*Arabic, Algeria*): *Westermarck 136*
Broken legs and chaste women should keep chair and room. (*Dutch*): *Mesters 15*
A married woman, a broken leg, and at home.
   (*Spanish, Argentina / Chile / Panama*): *Moya 488; Cannobio 79; Aguilera 119*
An honourable woman and a broken leg should stay inside. (*Spanish, Panama*): *o.s. Anonymous*
The wife that expects to have a good name, is always at home as if she were lame.
   (*English, UK*): *Bohn 1855: 43*
When a woman leaves the house one foot, she walks a hundred feet out of her honour.
   (*Dutch; Flemish, Belgium*): *Cock 320*
A woman is to be from her house three times; when she is christened, married and buried.
   (*English, UK*): *Bohn 1855: 304*
A girl must not leave the house more than twice: on the day of her marriage, on the day of
   her death. (*Arabic, Maghreb / West Sahara*): *Duvollet 41*
A woman should come to her husband's house in a veil, and leave it in a winding shroud.
   (*Persian*): *Haig 248*
A woman is well either in the house or in the grave. [The 'purdah' concealment is good for
   women.] (*Pashto, Afghanistan*): *Champion 463*
A woman, a cat and a chimney should never leave the house. (*English, USA*): *Mieder 1992: 665*
Women and ovens stay at home. (*German; Russian*): *Wander I 1124; Graf 252*
The men and dogs for the barn, the women and cats for the kitchen. (*English, USA*): *Adams 62*
The woman and the cat have their room in the house, the husband and the dog in the yard.
   (*Letzeburgish*): *o.s. Laure Wolter*
Women and cats at home; men and dogs in the street. (*Catalan, Spain; French*): *Guiter 37*
Women and cows do not go abroad. (*Italian*): *Cibotto 1976: 4*
Buffaloes must be kept in stables, gold in purses, and women at home.
   (*Indonesian*): *o.s. Sylvia Schipper*
Better for a man to go abroad and for a woman to stay at home. (*Tibetan*): *Gergan 63*
Women and chickens get lost by wandering from house to house. (*Hindi, India*): *Champion 405*
A woman and a chicken, let them go only as far as the neighbour's house.
   (*Portuguese, Brazil*): *Magalhães Júnior 137*
When your wife tells you she will visit her neighbour, find out where she goes in.
   (*Spanish, Cuba*): *Cabrera n.p.*

Don't trust a horse in the field or a woman at home. (*Russian*): *o.s. Anna Ravve*

Wives and sheep should be brought home early. (*Portuguese*): *Champion 253*

It's getting dark, the women go home. (*Arabic*): *Safadi 44*

Decent women and geese go home early. (*Dutch*): *o.s. Martha Beker*

A woman's place is at home. (*Spanish, Mexico*): *Glazer 177*

A woman's sphere is in the home. (*Hebrew, Israel*): *Cohen 1961: 572*

No child, silent house; no wife, silent kitchen. (*Vietnamese*): *Dình Khuê Duong 27*

A man without a wife is a kitchen without a fire. (*Dutch*): *Harrebomée II 29*

A man without a wife is like a kitchen without a knife. (*English, Jamaica*): *Llewellyn Watson 254*

Without [a] man the house is an orphan; without [a] woman only the kitchen [is an orphan].
   (*Vietnamese*): *Geyvandov 126*

Going into the [living-]room, the mother-in-law's words sound right; going into the kitchen,
   the daughter-in-law's words sound right. (*Korean*): *o.s. B. Walraven*

When a husband dies, his bed remains his wife's; when a wife dies, her bed is thrown into the
   lake. (*Chinese*): *Fabre 61*

When a woman makes the giant drum, it is kept in the man's room. (*Ashanti, Ghana*): *Oduyoye 7*

A wife is useful in every room. (*Dutch*): *o.s. P. de Beurs*

A good wife is a perfect lady in the living room, a good cook in the kitchen, and a harlot in
   the bedroom.
   (*Dutch; English, UK/USA; French; Spanish*): *Mieder 1992 : 635; Champion 45; Williams IV 200;
   Pineaux 87; Meier-Pfaller 61; o.s. Overmaat*

Hens picking dunghills don't like cages. (*Arabic, Maghreb*): *Cheneb III 156*

An egg is never square; a woman of the street is never honest. (*Japanese*): *Geyvandov 189*

A bright woman is an ornament for the house, a foolish woman the amusement of the street.
   (*Uzbek*): *Geyvandov 121*

A woman without a mate is like a garden without a fence. (*Slovenian*): *Mieder 1986: 540*

A man without a woman [also: a woman without a man] is like a field without a fence.
   (*Swedish; Norwegian; Danish; German; Finnish*): *Kuusi 52, 197*

A widow is a low fence everyone jumps over. (*German*): *Meier-Pfaller 52*

A sensible wife looks for her enjoyment at home; a silly one—abroad.
   (*English, USA*): *Hines 286*

Where can one better be than in mother's kitchen. (*Flemish, Belgium*): *Champion 17*

The home is the wife's world, the world is the man's home. (*Estonian*): *Mieder 1986: 231*

Women do not travel to far countries. (*Hebrew, Israel*): *Rosen 419*

A travelled woman is like a garden trespassed by cattle. (*Malay*): *Champion 456*

Man is fire, woman water. (*Bulgarian*): *Geyvandov 224*

Water is more powerful than fire. (*Shor, RF*): *o.s. Dobrinka Parusheva*

Put not your trust in a sword, woman, mare or water. (*Pashto, Afghanistan*): *Champion 463*

Women are like unwelcome water. [They are disastrous.] (*Chinese, Taiwan*): *o.s. H.V. Tseng*

Woman is fresh water that kills, shallow water that drowns. [She is a dangerous creature with
   deceitful looks.] (*Fulfulde, Senegal*): *Gaden 16*

Water and one's mother do not have badness. [In one way or another they can always be helpful.] (*Oromo, Ethiopia*): *Cotter 170*

A woman is as capricious as a drop of water on a lotus leaf. (*Thai*): *Lunde & Wintle 121*

Man is like the Nile, woman like the Mediterranean Sea. (*Arabic*): *o.s. Anonymous*

A man's mother-in-law is as duckweed on a river. (*Vietnamese*): *Nguyen 196*

Every river runs to its mamma. (*English, Jamaica*): *Champion 632*

The source of the river is the source of the family. [The mother.] (*Mongolian*): *Geyvandov 163*

Man is a river, woman is a lake. (*Kurdish, Turkey*): *Lunde & Wintle 83*

A fast, wild stream will not reach the sea. (*Dargin, RF*): *Geyvandov 57*

An angry woman is like a sea without shore. (*Italian*): *Geyvandov 271*

Beware of still waters and quiet women. (*Spanish, El Salvador*): *Sánchez Duarte 113*

May God save me from quiet waters, wild ones I can handle myself. (*Spanish*): *Geyvandov 224*

Woman is a lake, man a river. (*Greek; Letzeburgish*): *Politès 9; o.s. Wolter*

A small, deep pool of water will exhaust the breath.

   (*Maori, New Zealand*): *Brougham & Reed 70*

A woman is like the sea which does not admit a dead bird. (*Spanish, Bolivia*): *Paredes-Candia 136*

Woman is a spring in which all calabashes break. (*Beti, Cameroon*): *o.s. Peter Geschiere*

Whatever bank a river has washed, it always returns to its old bed. (*Digor, RF*): *Geyvandov 56*

A good name is like water; once gone, it will never come back. (*Persian*): *Geyvandov 243*

A girl is like a bridge; anybody can walk over her. (*Armenian*): *Sakayan 245*

The woman and the paved road are there to be trampled on. (*Portuguese*): *Chaves 895*

Woman is like a path, beautiful but sinuous. (*Afrikaans, South Africa*): *Geyvandov 76*

Woman is a path: don't ask who has walked on it or who will walk on it.

   (*Wolof, Senegal*): *o.s. P.G. N'Diaye*

Never run after a woman. They are like streetcars. Stand still, for another one will come

    along soon. (*English, USA*): *Mieder 1986: 50*

A woman without a husband, a ship without a helm. (*Portuguese*): *Chavez 954*

A woman without a husband is a boat without a rudder. (*Vietnamese*): *Nguyen 127*

A woman without husband is a ship without a sail. (*Dutch*): *o.s. Verbeek*

A house without woman is a lantern without light, a ship without a helm.

   (*Danish*): *Kjaer Holbek 135*

Women are vessels of wood and he who travels in them is lost. (*Arabic, Maghreb*): *Champion 565*

Vicious woman is a man's shipwreck. (*Swedish*): *Ström 162*

A faithless wife is the shipwreck of a home. (*English, USA*): *Kin 6*

A good wife is heaven on earth. (*Turkish*): *Geyvandov 184*

HERE AND HEREAFTER

Woman is like the earth: everyone sits down on her.

   (*Lingala, Congo DR*): *o.s. Clémentine Faik-Nzuji*

Who has a good wife does not need paradise. (*Bulgarian*): *Arnaudov 49*

Woman is the chief gate to hell. (*Hindi, India*): *Champion 405*

Obedience to women is the entrance to hell. (*Arabic, Maghreb*): *Cheneb II 66*

Obedience to women makes one enter hell. (*Arabic, Morocco*): *Westermarck 77*

Old maids lead apes in hell.

   (*English, UK/USA*): *Whiting 1977: 274; Smith & Hesseltine 471; Browning 404*

A young wife is a horse on which an old man gallops to hell. (*Polish*): *Geyvandov 138*

A wicked wife is purgatory on earth. (*German*): *Haller 466*

A wicked wife is a daily purgatory. (*Danish*): *Haller 466*

The one who has an evil wife is near purgatory. (*Portuguese, Brazil*): *Lamenza 235*

Who has a bad wife has purgatory for a neighbour. (*English, USA*): *Loomis 1955: 198*

Whoever has a wicked wife will not see hell. (*Hebrew, Israel*): *Rosen 413*

He who has a wicked wife does not need hell. (*Bulgarian*): *Geyvandov 124*

There is no hell like an evil wife. (*Hebrew, Israel*): *Rosten 1977: 248, 494*

He who has a wicked wife, his hell begins on earth.

   (*Dutch; German; Italian*): *Mesters 67; Haller 465; Giusti 87*

Hell is lined with grimy housewives. (*Japanese*): *Lunde & Wintle 15*

Women are hell, but still no house should be without them. (*Persian*): *Lunde & Wintle 155*

Paradise is open at the command of mothers. (*Arabic, Egypt*): *Champion 521*

Heaven is beneath your mother's heel. [You will find paradise when you respect your
   mother.] (*Indonesian; Turkish*): *o.s. Sylvia Schipper; A.P. Kwak*

Paradise on earth is in riding on horseback, gaining information from books, or laying at the
   breasts of a beautiful woman. (*Arabic, Maghreb*): *Wijnaendts-Francken 66*

Old grain, new butter, a well-bred wife and the back of a horse; these are the four marks of
   heaven. (*Punjabi, India*): *Champion 424*

Women hold up half the sky. (*Chinese*): *Wintle 139*

Women are the pillars of half of Heaven. (*Chinese*): *o.s. Huang Mingfen*

From a woman came the beginning of sin and because of her we will all perish.

   (*Hebrew, Israel*): *Alcalay 544; Ben Sira 25: 24*

A single woman destroyed paradise. (*Arabic, widespread*): *Lunde & Wintle 155*

Only a woman was able to wreck paradise. (*Arabic, Lebanon*): *Cattan 149*

Adam's rib brings more harm than benefit. (*German*): *Meier-Pfaller 63*

Husbands are in heaven, whose wives chide not. (*Tamil, Sri Lanka/India*): *Champion 432*

Woman was placed on earth to show men both paradise and purgatory.

   (*English, USA*): *Brown 1970: 113*

Women are paradise for the eyes, a purgatory for the purse, and hell for the soul.

   (*Estonian; German; French, Luxemburg; Spanish*): *Champion 132; Geyvandov 79; Wander II 527;
   Meier-Pfaller 63*

If a bad man is like a devil, a bad woman is like an entire hell.

   (*Danish*): *Champion 110; Geyvandov 197*

An angry man is a devil, an angry woman a hell. (*English, UK*): *Meier-Pfaller 661*

Man goes to purgatory, woman goes to hell.(*Creole, Martinique*): *David 52*

Rather hell with a quarrelsome husband than paradise in my father's house.

   (*Hebrew, Israel*): *Stahl 217*

She that hath a bad husband hath a hell within her own house.

   (*English, USA*): *Loomis 1955: 198*

You and I are both from the sky father and earth mother; this is me, so-and-so, son of such-
   and-such. (*Maori, New Zealand*): *Brougham & Reed 70*

Woman and sky cannot be understood. (*Gikuyu, Kenya*): *Barra 62*

Without wife and wind the sky is always gentle. (*German*): *Meier-Pfaller 60*

A woman's mind and autumn sky [change oft]. (*Japanese*): *o.s. Keiko Kosunose*

Maids are May when they are maids, but the sky changes when they are wives.
    (*Yiddish*): *Cohen 320*

Don't trust the sky in March; don't trust a woman, even when she prays.
    (*Berber, Algeria*): *Taos Amrouche 127*

A clear sky and a smiling woman are not to be trusted. (*Swedish*): *Holm 187*

The earth is the mother, the seed the father. (*Amharic, Ethiopia*): *Geyvandov 104*

Dear earth, our mother, she feeds us, waters us and clothes us. (*Russian*): *Graf 1960: 75*

A house is not built on earth but on woman. (*Turkish*): *o.s. A.P. Kwak*

The house is not founded on the earth, but on the wife. (*Serbian/Croatian*): *Rauch 112*

The earth is like a mother. [She will never be tired of giving.]
    (*Mapuche, Chile/Argentina*): *Koessler-Ilg 123*

IMAGES IN SEARCH OF HIERARCHIES

Of all animals the female is the better save only in mankind. (*Bedouin*): *Champion 333*

The shoulder is lower than the head. (*Kweli, Cameroon*): *Geyvandov 129*

No matter how high an eye rises, it will never rise beyond the brow.
    (*Armenian*): *Geyvandov 244*

The bow is not stronger than the spear. (*Ovambo, Angola/Namibia*): *Geyvandov 130*

A big wave! It is under the boat. A big mountain! It is under the foot. (*Burmese*): *Hla Pe 67*

The hen is no bird, the woman is no person. (*Estonian*): *Paczolay 27*

The hen is no bird, the woman no human. (*Russian*): *o.s. Anna Ravve*

A woman is not a person, a mare is not a horse, a magpie is not a bird, a ruffle is not a fish.
    (*Danish; Norwegian; Swedish; Finnish*): *Kuusi 44, 113*

Better be a cock for one day than a hen for a hundred days. (*Digor, RF*): *Geyvandov 232*

It is better to be a bull for a year than a cow for a hundred years.
    (*Serbian/Croatian*): *Mieder 1986: 50*

It is better to be a running hen than to be a dead rooster. (*Spanish, Mexico*): *Ballesteros 366*

It is better to be a male for one day than a female for ten. (*Kurdish, Turkey*): *Champion 450*

The husband is like a little dust on a tree trunk. (*Minangkabau, Indonesia*): *o.s. Joke van Reenen*

Epilogue

Proverbial Imagination in an Age of Globalization

A hundred male and a hundred female qualities make a perfect human being. (*Tibetan*)

'**M**en and women have been moulded from the same clay.' This was the old Sumerian proverb with which we began. In the previous chapters we have addressed the most frequently encountered topics, and the main ideas mirrored in proverbs, relating and opposing women to men, and men to women in hierarchical patterns. From the thousands of proverbs at my disposal, general similarities were apparent in widely different parts of the world. Cross-culturally, different metaphors frequently convey the same message, about daughters, wives or widows, in-laws, old age, beauty, love, pregnancy, and so forth. Even exactly the same images occur across cultures, for example, of the womb as a fragile pot (needing protection), of women as horses (needing fierce male riders), or as hens (needing cocks to speak on their behalf), or as food (with men as avid eaters).

Next to conspicuous similarities, proverbs also express cultural differences, of course. Having many daughters, for example, is considered disastrous in dowry cultures, and causes mixed feelings in bride-wealth cultures, where daughters and sons are both needed. Local situations may result in different observations: there is, for example, the precious value of water praised in regions where drought is a regular occurrence; the attractive luxury of plumpness and fatness stressed in places where hunger is a threat; the importance of a warm fire or warm hands and blankets in places where people suffer from cold freezing winters. I found many more poetic proverbs referring to flowers in Asia than in Europe, and many more about food and its scarcity in Africa. Proverbs about veils are common in Islamic countries in the Arab world and Asia, and are rare in Europe and the Americas—to give just a few examples.

Even though local geographic and cultural differences play a role generally speaking, some similarities are quite overwhelming. This holds especially true for the large variety of prescriptions and proscriptions circulated worldwide to keep women under control within a marked-out gendered space. This control has to do with male insecurity about their actual fatherhood as far as their wives' pregnancies are concerned. In proverbs, women's physical strength, their working capacity, their endurance, their profitability for men, and their power, have led to all kinds of measures, even the use of brutal strength, meant to prevent women from branching out in life, as this branching out would neither serve female submissiveness nor be in the interest of their willingly fulfilling their cooking and cleaning duties at home. Those recommended restrictions for women are quite the opposite of the messages addressed to men, which brim with stimulating activities and freedom of movement in the public domain and the world at large. In proverbs, female behaviour qualified as 'deviant' is usually stigmatized as 'badness'.

Book collections of proverbs contain strikingly many proverbs about 'woman' as a separate category. Among those proverbs, those underlining negative qualities and rigidly fixed role patterns form a considerable majority; even the proverbs about mothers set them inflexibly on a pedestal. Most proverbs comment upon women from a male perspective or defend male privileges and interests, whereas proverbs judging men from a female perspective are quite rare.[127]

Why would there be so many proverbs judging women negatively—especially those about wives? According to psychologists, the biological fact of women's carrying their children in the womb, giving birth to them and nursing them has a serious impact. In their early period of life, boys strongly identify with their mothers as caregivers, because women play much more of a role in childcare than male adults. In order to learn 'to be a man' boys must first learn 'not to be a woman', and not to depend on women. The male need for dominance has been attributed to the intense early dependence of the son on the powerful mother: if subsequent socialization strongly pressures young boys toward sturdy 'masculinity', this could lead to developing their need to devalue feminine activities and to stress the superiority of male roles, most explicitly in societies where male dominance is strong. The exaggerated need to 'destroy' women, as many proverbs confirm, has even led to the creation of a Spanish proverb warning men against belching forth all those terrible insults: 'When you speak [contemptuously] about women, think of your mother', and indeed, as we have seen, the general contrast between messages about women as such (and especially wives) and about mothers is quite amazing. Obviously, much depends on a mother's behaviour vis-à-vis her sons in early childhood.[128]

I have often been asked whether there are no women's countervailing proverbial views of men. There are indeed a few in this book, as we have seen, but they represent what is, in truth, a small, small minority. Women's voices have usually been silenced, and wherever they did come across, their ideas have often been belittled. Relatively recent Western feminist slogans (or should I say modern proverbs?) such as 'A woman without a man is a fish without a bicycle' or 'Boss in one's own belly' date from the sixties of the last century only.

Public language inevitably influences sex role socialization, and, no doubt, the public genre of the proverb has reinforced stereotype images of women, 'women's work' and women's roles as girls, wives, mothers, widows, etc.:

> Those women who do not fit the composite picture are marginalized by their own social group, other women, as well as men. Thus one encounters such generalized statements as: women cannot keep a secret, they demand impossible feats from men, they prove to be unfaithful. ... Yet the fact remains that it is a composite picture which mediates against the individual woman to be a person.[129]

The traditional division between male creation and female procreation, and the negative comments poured out (for example, by means of proverbs) on women who dare(d) venture beyond the female domain must have efficiently contributed to most women's lack of (self-) confidence in challenging the division of roles, and no less to men's being uncomfortable with questioning and changing the old reassuring patterns. Although proverbs mainly present a male dominant perspective, women have no doubt agreed willingly, as the vested interests and loyalties in a woman's life have usually been (and often still are) dependent upon the men in her life, her father, her husband, and her son, as expressed in a Korean proverb: 'Three men determine the fate of every woman.'

That there is less evidence of uncharitable proverbs about men does not mean that women are more angelic than men, nor does it mean that women do not have negative ideas or make negative statements about men. If there has existed a repertoire of women's proverbs or other genres, they have usually been hidden from the public story and the public culture, and thus far they have hardly been transcribed.[130] This obvious imbalance may have to do with the fact that in societies where women's roles were (or still are) confined to the female domain, women did not dare (or were not allowed to) speak out in public as freely as men do. They used to keep their views to themselves or expressed them, if not in proverbs, then certainly in songs and stories performed only within their own social group. Given such concealment 'strategies', no surprise that such views have had far less impact than the public genre of the proverb.[131]

Many proverbs present women as neatly arranged objects, judged by their appearance and their usefulness. A wife should no more be shared by her owner than other cherished objects, such as horses, knives, guns etc., because lent to others such property would be returned 'spoiled' (meaning pregnant?). Their precarious economic situation has made women inevitably see themselves through the eyes of those who ought to desire, protect and take care of them. This tactics has led many women to spend incredible energy on their appearance, by means of clothes, cosmetics and jewellery, and other beautifying practices, as indispensable investments to seduce and finally induce a man into marriage in order to get their only piece of cake in life.

Women are mainly seen as dependent on men economically, and men on women, sexually. Proverbs about love and sex reflect hierarchical relations, sexual stereotypes and double gender standards in which, at first sight, women are mainly presented as objects and victims of male power. According to a number of proverbs, masculinity, and being a 'real' man, can only mean to 'possess' a woman, or preferably women, and not the reverse. That is why love is so often presented as a frightening emotion, a dark pit, a sea you drown in, and so forth.

There is, however, another side to this story. Not only women are 'objects'; in certain respects men are objects too, not only because they allow themselves to be manipulated by their own desire and therefore by women, but also by their being in want of a mother. Without being aware of it, a man often sees his wife as an extension of his mother and she may intuitively respond to this need by treating him as her child.[132] Such a wife mothers and protects (and even risks suffocating) her husband no less than did his own mother. She thus continues the spoiling praise and comforting adoration his mother had surrounded him with right from his birth as a male child. Possibly such spoilt boys remain immature for their whole lives, and their wives may see such husbands as mere children within their power, even though these 'children' hold important positions in society as soon as they leave the house. Many proverbs spread the message how much men are, or expect to be, spoilt, and how extremely dependent they are on their wives' care, in spite of or thanks to all their efforts of belittling those same wives.

'Being born a woman means a wasted life', an anonymous Bhutanese rural woman observed resignedly in a TV report about development issues. Internalized gender messages had apparently convinced her that there was no way out of the hierarchy—exactly the message found in proverbs. She had given up the idea of change during her lifetime. Numerous women all over the world, however, are enjoying today more freedoms than their grandmothers, and even their mothers could have dreamt of. Successful women have more education, and more prestigious jobs than women ever had in previous generations. They set an inspiring example to their sisters, friends, and daughters. In Bengali, there is a recent popular slogan encouraging education for women: 'Give me an educated mother, and I'll give you a prosperous nation.'[133]

Nonetheless, there are also societies and cultures in which the changing roles of women are being regarded as a betrayal of 'tradition' or religion.[134] In such societies, the boundaries between the local and the outside worlds are strictly guarded, for example, in fundamentalist circles in Islam which categorically reject globalization, and more specifically Westernization, contesting its customs, artistic creations, ideas about love, life and death, philosophy, and especially women's rights. The resistance against globalization seems to be notably structured around female identity: 'so constant has been the typology of women's roles and status for fifteen centuries, that female identity remains at the centre of Muslim society', in the words of El-Khayat, a psychiatrist and anthropologist from Morocco.[135] However, there are other Islamic views where signs of hybridization can be found: Mullah Mohammed Khatami was quoted in the *Herald Tribune* (10 Dec. 1997) thus: 'Our era is an era of preponderance of Western Culture and Civilization, whose understanding is imperative. Islamic nations would succeed in moving forward only if they utilize the positive scientific, technological and social accomplishments of Western Civilization, a stage we must inevitably go through to reach the future.'

Violations of the boundaries of deeply held systems of norms (and interests) are still often considered taboo. This may explain the, sometimes violent, opposition to changing traditions. Globalization provokes not only new debates but also a hardening of local perspectives on gender differences.

A cross-cultural analysis of gender traditions contributes to a greater awareness of legacies we either still accept as 'natural' or, on the contrary, believe we have left far behind us. Such legacies are gradually disappearing, and partly they have indeed disappeared, but there is quite some baggage we still carry along, often even without questioning whether we agree or not, brainwashed as we are by a varied 'traditional' gender chorus that seems at times alien but at times also strangely familiar.

Today, from certain perspectives, many of the proverbs discussed in this book may look disturbing, and their messages quite 'politically incorrect'. But it would be a regrettably shortsighted reaction to reject or suppress, or even censor those cross-cultural ideas from the past, without further reflection.[136] It is absolutely important to be aware of the sexist sentiments expressed in proverbs, because they have formed, and still form, part of the daily conversation in society after society, thus modelling people's gendered legacies, and their identities. Negative messages about women easily reverberate in the minds of male policy makers, and risk undercutting progressive legislation.[137] In order to change formerly accepted mentalities we first need to get back to the underlying thoughts and beliefs, as the southern African women's example below aptly illustrates.

Language and culture are not static, in spite of what the proverbs would want us to believe. Ideas about femininity and masculinity, located in both men and women, are changing along with people's positions, experience, and awareness of their own situation. In this respect, the re-quotation of proverbs about women definitely has a consciousness-raising function—as women's groups in southern Africa confirmed in enthusiastic letters to the publisher, after they had worked with one of my early collections of proverbs from all over Africa south of the Sahara.[138] The women reported that, in their meetings, they had discussed the proverbs about women's phases of life, basics of life, power, etc. They found the proverbs intriguing, both in the way they mirrored their own internalized ideas about 'being a woman', and in the ways straightforward male dominance was revealed. After intense discussions, they had started turning the messages in the proverbs upside down, by replacing in each statement the word 'man' by the word 'woman', and vice versa. This appeared to be a hilarious exercise that provoked roars of laughter, but also served as a great eye-opener *vis-à-vis* their own situation. Their practical strategy was not one of avoiding or boycotting the legacies of oral tradition, but to re-appropriate those legacies. They succeeded not only in exposing the implicit meanings, but also to subvert those very meanings. Thus, for them, looking into proverbs became a way of looking back to 'the tradition', and a way to look forward to gender relations in a changing world. This is a refreshingly relevant way of reflecting on cultural legacies.

Proverbs are part of humanity's eventful cultural history, and we have to understand its lessons, before deciding which part of our various 'traditions' we want to pass on to our children and grandchildren. Thanks to globalization, cultures have become more intertwined than ever before, and we have more access to and more information about each other's traditions than ever before. We know much more about our respective cultural differences than we do about what we have in common. Now that globalization and migration interact with local realities in many ways, positively and negatively, it becomes highly rewarding to re-examine our various traditions together—in mixed (gender and culture) company.[139]

Our first question was: How do we learn to think and speak and write and meet inclusively instead of exclusively? We are those family members, referred to in Chapter One, originating from widely different cultures across the world, still quite unfamiliar with each other, who have now come to meet for conversation in unexpected ways and unthought-of places—quite *étonnés de se trouver ensemble*. No less astonished than the proverbs themselves, like us originating from all continents, and meeting for conversation, in one and the same book. A cosmopolitan conversation has begun thanks to globalization, but this conversation is no less rooted in what people already had in common: their male or female bodies, and their basic human needs shared within living memory.

In proverbs, we have seen, two main views of men as well as women are constantly echoed. Men are inexorable tyrants and shameless profiteers, and men are insecure, fearful beings. Women are not only lamentable victims, but also extremely powerful. Powerful in their appealing beauty, awesome (pro-)creativity, vigorous working capacity, and strong will. Both contradictory gender views are made visible in proverbs, one openly and directly, and the other mostly hidden between the lines. Another conclusion is that the world imagined in proverbs is changing rapidly in some respects, and slowly but surely in other respects, thanks to the ongoing integration of male and female roles and domains.

How far have we progressed along the road towards cosmopolitan citizenship? The outcome of our comparative efforts in this book might serve as an enlightening beacon for future gender orientation. In order to define where we want to go, and where we do not want to go, as men and women today, we first of all need to know where we come from. May experience, this aged 'Mother of all Sciences', and the proverbs she gave birth to, give us a good sense of direction.

Endnotes

Prologue

1. Cf. Theodore Zeldin, *Conversation. How Talk Can Change Our Lives*, London 1998/New Jersey 2000: 44.
2. 'Alphabet of Ben Sira'. *Rabbinic Fantasies: Imaginative Narratives from Classical Hebrew Literature*, Philadelphia 1990; Louis Ginzburg, *The Legends of the Jews*, vol. I: 65.
3. This is what Alan Dundes (ed., *Sacred Narrative: Readings in the Theorie of Myth*, Berkeley/Los Angeles/ London 1984: 278–9) suggests, correlating such stories with highly patriarchal social organization. He sees a common denominator in myths of creation in which self-sufficient non-female creators create and procreate; an interesting idea, even though it is speculation, as he himself admits.
4. Fokke Sierksma, *Religie, sexualiteit en agressie: Een cultuurpsychologische bijdrage tot de verklaring van de spanning tussen de sexen*. Groningen 1979; for male dominance as a reaction to a perception of female power, see also Peggy Reeves Sanday, *Female Power and Male Dominance: On the Origins of Sexual Inequality*, Cambridge 1981: 182.
5. E.g. Fatima Mernissi, *Le harem politique: Le prophète et les femmes*, Paris 1987; Ghassan Ascha, *Du statut inférieur de la femme en islam*, Paris 1987; Leila Ahmed, *Women and Gender in Islam: Historical Roots of a Modern Debate*, New Haven 1992; oral information Henk Bodewitz.
6. *Guide to the Religious Status and Sacred Duties of Women* referred to in: I. Julia Leslie, 'Recycling Ancient Material: An Orthodox View of Hindu Women', Léonie J. Archer, Susan Fischler, Maria Wyke, eds. *Women in Ancient Societies: An Illusion of the Night*, London 1994: 233–251; and I. Julia Leslie, *The Perfect Wife: The Orthodox Hindu Woman According to the Stridharmapaddhati of Tryambakayajvan*, Delhi 1989.
7. As described by Martin Brauen, 'Die Frau im Buddhismus', Gisela Völger, and Karin von Welck, *Die Braut: geliebt, getauscht, geraubt: Zur Rolle der Frau im Kulturvergleich*, Köln 1985, vol. I: 194–201.
8. In 2002 Bulgarian specialists of Eastern European oral traditions told me that this same story continues to circulate in Eastern Europe nowadays.
9. James Obelkevich, 'Proverbs and Social History', Wolfgang Mieder, ed., *Wise Words: Essays on the Proverb*. New York/London 1994: 213.
10. The term 'oral cultures' is used here to indicate that, even though in all contemporary cultures literacy is quite widespread today, oral traditions play a relatively more important role in cultures with limited literacy.
11. David Levinson, and Martin J. Malone, *Toward Explaining Human Culture*, New Haven 1980: 267; 'The concept of female pollution and the ritual associated with it are often used by men to control women.' (Ibid. 279) See also: Walter J. Lonner, 'The Search for Psychological Individuals'. Harry C. Triandis, and William W. Lambert, eds., *Handbook of Cross-Cultural Psychology*. Boston 1980, vol. I: 147; John E. Williams, and Deborah L. Best, Measuring Sex Stereotypes: A Multinational Study, Rev. ed., Newbury Park 1990.
12. As Franco Moretti has observed, 'close reading' and 'distant reading' have both advantages in comparative literature, both need each other, and there is no need anymore to settle the controversy between the two. Close reading has the advantage of looking closely at an oral or written text in the context of a particular culture. Distant reading 'allows you to focus on units that are much smaller or much larger than the text: devices, themes, tropes—or genres and systems. And if, between the very small and the very large, the text itself disappears, well, it is one of those cases when one can justifiably say, Less is more. If we want to understand the system in its entirety, we must accept losing something.' ('Conjectures on World Literature', *New Left Review* Jan.–Febr. 2000: 57, 61)

13. *The Penguin Dictionary of Proverbs*, 197; no language or cultural source mentioned.
14. Ibid.
15. Whether this acceptance is as general as it is supposed to be in the common oral context, is not usually a subject for discussion—neither in the community where the proverbs are used nor by proverb researchers—but it is of course a relevant question, particularly in the context of this book. The power of the proverbial word is obviously so impressive that its eternal truth and invaluable wisdom have been passively swallowed or even romanticized as 'one man's wit and all men's wisdom', in the words of Lord John Russell, quoted without critical comment by Archer Taylor ('The Wisdom of Many and the Wit of One'. Wolfgang Mieder, and Alan Dundes, eds., *The Wisdom of Many: Essays on the Proverb*, Madison 1994: 3). No less than uncritical readers or listeners, scholars have often been taken in by the proverbs' so-called unshakable value, instead of looking into their underlying assumptions. Here are three examples, respectively from Europe, Asia, and Africa. In his introduction to a large collection of European proverbs, Karl Friedrich Wilhelm Wander (*Deutsches Sprichwörterlexikon*, Augsburg 1987: v), for example, approvingly quotes the nineteenth-century scholar Venedey (1842) who called language 'the heart of a people' and proverbs 'the veins carrying blood to all parts of the body', thus underlining their crucial importance. Proverbs, in his words, carry 'the colour and character of a people along with the knowledge of its morals and customs' and thus they reveal peoples' ideas and mentality. Proverbs, he argues, are 'the people's spirit'; circulating among the people like coins going from hand to hand, they have become the people's common property through frequent use. Who represents *the* people's spirit here? In his Asian collection, Justin Wintle (*The Dragon's Almanac: Chinese, Japanese and Other Far Eastern Proverbs*, Singapore 1983: ix) takes a little more distance, observing that 'in the Far East … proverbs are as common as chopsticks' so that 'it is difficult to think for oneself against the ritual clatter of ancestral wisdom' in a context where the 'art of conversation, particularly among older people, still depends on the individual's dexterity at trading one pertinent adage for another … in the revered thought-forms of the past.' In the preface to his African Gikuyu collection, the Kenyan G. Barra (*1000 Gikuyu Proverbs*, Nairobi 1984: iii) calls proverbs 'the essence of eloquence, [and] the true wisdom written by God into the hearts of people, and a precious heritage which should not be lost in the present times of change.'
16. Looking critically into Kenyan oral art forms, Masheti Masinjila criticises the unconditional acceptance of the cultural legacies from oral societies, especially as far as women's 'institutionalized marginality' is concerned. In his introduction to a highly interesting volume entitled *Contesting Social Death: Essays on Gender and Culture* (ed. by Wanjiku M. Kabira, Masheti Masinjila, and Milton Obote, *Nairobi* 1997), he argues that the question 'why the process of consigning women to the private (domestic) sphere, that was/is part of a general culturally legitimized oppression of women on the basis of their sex, has ceased being unimportant.'
17. Information provided by Dr Megna Guhathakurta (*Dakha, Bangladesh*).
18. Kwesi Yankah, 'Proverbs: The Aesthetics of Traditional Communication', *Research in African Literatures*, vol. 20, 1989a (3): 330.
19. Ibid. 333.
20. Kwesi Yankah, ibid. 333. See also Lêjdji Bellow, '"Je cours plus vite que ma rivale"' [I run faster than my rival] : 'Paroles de Pagne chez les Gens-Mina au Sud Togo'. *Cahiers de Littérature Orale* 19 (1986): 29–67. The title of her article refers to a popular textile print with the same message. All kinds of codes unknown to outsiders play a role in textile forms of communication in West Africa as well as East Africa (Rose-Marie Beck, *Texte auf Textilien in Ostafrika : Sprichwörtlichkeit als Eigenschaft ambiger Kommunikation*, Köln 2001).
21. Yankah 1989b: 99: 'The most important visual art forms that embody proverbs are gold weights, spokesman staffs and umbrella tops. While simple designs of objects like crab, elephant, snake, often call for different informants, composite designs often elicit a single proverb, for example a gold weight depicting a man with a pot in his hand while he smokes a pipe, refers to the proverb… "We may smoke the pipe even when we carry gunpowder," often used to mean one cannot entirely sacrifice pleasure in times of crisis.'
    Some peoples in Central Africa use a proverb cord to visualize and teach proverbs to children. This cord is a liana to which all kinds of objects are attached—a chicken leg, herbs, a piece of cloth, and so on (Ngandu-Myango Malasi, *Mutánga : La corde à proverbes des Lega du Kivu Maniema (Congo)*, Gent 2000). Each object represents a proverb and the cord is used as an educational tool. Other non-verbal proverbs channels are musical instruments, for example talking drums (John F. Carrington, *Talking Drums of Africa*, London 1949), horns or trumpets (J.H. Kwabena Nketia, *The Music of Africa*, London 1979).
22. Jan Vissers, *Spreekwoordenboek in beeld: Een aparte kunst uit Cabinda*. 4th. ed., Berg en Dal 1989.
23. As earlier observed by L. Rörich, and W. Mieder, *Sprichwort*. Stuttgart 1977: 60.

24. Said-sayings consist of three parts: an observation, a central part in which the speaker is presented, and a third part referring to the situation in which the observation is being made. So far I found them only in Europe and Africa. Said-sayings are also called wellerisms, after the character Samuel Weller in Charles Dickens' novel *The Pickwick Papers*, who used them frequently.

25. E.g. Kwesi Wiredu, Are There Cultural Universals? In: *The Monist* , vol. 78, 1, January 1995: 56–57.

26. Comparative research such as ours would not be possible without careful translations. Fortunately the University of Leiden is famous for its study of languages and cultures from all over the world, and I was privileged in always finding colleagues and visiting scholars willing to help solve problems I was struggling with regarding cultural idioms or context references.

27. 'In the absence of the situation there is no proverb', as, for example, J. Brookman-Amissah put it in his article: Some observations on the proverbs of the Akan-speaking peoples of Ghana, *Afrika und Übersee*, Band LV, 1971–72, 264. A great deal of information is indeed needed to analyse each and every full contextual meaning, function and effect of a proverb, its original or acquired figurative sense; the speakers and listeners involved (gender, age group, position in society); proverbial currency, acceptance and impact. An intercultural comparative approach does not allow for the proverbs' 'interactional elegance, the multiple meaning relations it contracts with the surrounding discourse, and the skills embodied in its spontaneous deployment' in the words of Kwesi Yankah, in: Proverbs: The Aesthetics of Traditional Communication, *Research in African Literatures*, vol. 20, 1989 (3) 328.

28. As observed earlier, there are losses and gains both ways. A local in-depth study misses the comparative dimension, whereas a comparative study misses the local in-depth information. Extensive studies and anthologies of proverbs originating from many local cultures have been published in all continents. Much work has been done on the proverb in the local or regional cultural context, and relatively little from a cross-cultural comparative perspective. Ideally, both approaches need to complement each other. In spite of the local 'losses', and in spite of the limitations of which I am fully aware, the current enterprise has proved to be a great challenge.

29. Yankah 1989b: 136.

The Female Body

30. This proverb may have travelled over with Africans who were transported as slaves to the Caribbean. There are certainly oral traditions that can be proved to have been transferred from Africa to the other side of the ocean, but in this case I hesitate, because the same proverb also exists in Dutch—did it come to the Netherlands from Surinam which was a Dutch colony until 1975, or was it simply thought up independently in such widely different parts of the world? Impossible to answer such questions.

31. Best and Williams 179; Desmond Morris, *The Human Sexes*. London 1997: 13.

32. Rainer Knussmann, *De man: een vergissing der natuur*, Utrecht 1983; Julian V. Roberts, and C. Peter Herman, 'The Psychology of the Height: An Empirical Review', C. Peter Herman, Mark P. Zanna, E. Tory Higgins, eds., *Physical Appearance, Stigma, and Social Behavior: The Ontario Symposium*, New Jersey/London. Vol. 3: 113–40.

33. Personal information: Kwame Oppong (*Accra*).

34. E.g. Knussmann 101

35. As Elias and others have suggested, 'female chastity and modesty appear to be a displacement of men's fear and their own uncontrolled desire by inversion': Efrat Tseëlon, *The Masque of Femininity: The Presentation of Woman in Everyday Life*, New Delhi 1995: 27–28; N. Elias, *The Civilizing Process*, Oxford 1939.

36. Knussmann 92–99.

37. In the Hebrew Bible, the verb meaning 'to own' or 'to be lord over' is *ba'al*. It also means: 1) to marry a woman (i.e. to own her); 2) to have sex with a woman (i.e. to possess her physically). As a substantive it means: 1) lord, owner; 2) husband; 3) male sex partner; 4) and probably also rapist. The same word refers to the Canaanite god *Ba'al*. Personal information Mark Geller.

38. Majnun and Leila are the Persian equivalents of Romeo and Juliet.

39. Robert Hertz 89. This classical essay was published in English as *Death and the Right Hand* (Aberdeen 1960).

40. According to evolution theorists, the sexually distinctive parts of the human body have been shaped by the power of human evolution, and sexual selection seems to have shaped penises, vaginas, breasts, buttocks, beards, hair and so forth into sexual attractiveness across human cultures today. See, for example, Knussmann, Morris.

41. An anthology of songs, hymns and poems assembled between c.1000–c.400 BCE, regarded as the foundation of Chinese literature.

42. Personal information: Xiaohong Zhang and Kristofer Schipper.
43. Cf. Dundes 1984: 281: 'The combination of puritanical publishing standards in the United States with similar collecting standards may well explain in part the lack of data.'
44. Personal information: Irwan Abdallah.
45. See earlier comments on this proverb in the Prologue, p. 16.
46. This is still the case, as appears from *The Vagina Monologues* by Eve Ensler (New York 1998).
47. There are other female parts of the body considered cold in proverbs; among them, knees and breasts are mentioned most often.
48. In J.T. Milimo, *Bantu Wisdom*, Lusaka 1972: 16.
49. Personal information: Sanjukta Gupta.
50. In many cultures women are compared to shoes and slippers.
51. This has been demonstrated by research: e.g. Arthur Marwick, *Beauty in History: Society, Politics and Personal Appearance c.1500 to the Present*, London 1988: 385.
52. Alison Dakota Gee, 'In the Eye of the Beholder', *Sunday Morning Post (Hong Kong)*, 8 Aug. 1999: 10.
53. Ibid. 9.
54. Morris 47–48; see also John Carl Flügel, *Studies in Feeling and Desire*, London 1955: 43.
55. This issue will be further discussed in Chapter Four, 'Female Power'.
56. Efrat Tseëlon 6.
57. Russian Federation.

Phases of Life

58. Carol R. Ember, 'A Cross-cultural Perspective on Sex Differences', Ruth H. Munroe, Robert L. Munroe and Beatrice B. Whiting, eds. *Handbook of Cross-Cultural Human Development*, New York/London 1981: 543: 'Where one sex is chosen as the core of the residential group, as the core of the unilineal descent group, or as the inheritor of property, it could be either males or females, but by far most societies favour males ... [The Ethnographic Atlas] shows that eighty-nine percent of the societies in which married couples live with or near kin have a unilocal rule of residence (a rule stipulating that the couple lives with or near the kin of one sex); eighty-five percent of the societies with inheritance of real property have unilineal inheritance rules (only one sex inherits); eighty-two percent of societies with movable property have only one sex inheriting such property; and eighty-nine percent of societies with lineal descent groups have unilineal groups (membership in such groups is passed through only one sex).' It is not clear why this is so. Several suggestions have been made (George Peter Murdock, *Outline of World Cultures*, New Haven 1949; Carol R. Ember, and Melvin Ember, 'The conditions favoring matrilocal versus patrilocal residence', *American Anthropologist* 73 (1971): 571–594 etc.). No doubt it has to do with the fact that most unilocal societies have patrilocal residence. This inevitably means residence change for brides who have to follow the rule. Thus a girl has to go and live 'elsewhere', i.e. with the family of her husband who stays comfortably at home, in his familiar surroundings. In urban situations those percentages are rapidly changing.
59. This traumatic separation is hardly ever referred to in proverbs from a girls' perspective, but there are women's songs and stories about it all over the world.
60. All sorts of beliefs and presages regarding the sex of the future child have been developed in cultures worldwide ever since the beginning of human history. Two ancient examples of omens considered 'favourite' (i.e. for the preferred male posterity) come from Mesopotamia: 'If a man's penis is long and thick: that man will beget sons'; 'If the nose of a woman is symmetrical: [she will give birth to] sons. If a man has intercourse with a woman on waste land, it is believed that she will give birth to a girl; if he sleeps with her in a field or a garden [fertile, "civilized" underground], she will bear a boy. ' (Marten Stol, *Women's History*, Leiden 1995: 206).
61. The importance of fertility will be discussed in Chapter Three.
62. That is the very reason why usually only the men in the family are entitled to inherit land and to possess 'immovable' property.
63. Jack Goody, 'Bridewealth and Dowry in Africa and Eurasia', Jack Goody, and S.J. Tambiah, *Bridewealth and Dowry*, Cambridge 1973: 6: 'it is wealth for, not to, the bride.'
64. Ibid. 6, 7: It is 'the result of a bargain and has a specific intention: that of linking the daughter to a particularly desirable son-in-law.' Matrilineal societies tend to have lower bride-wealth payments than patrilineal societies, because the family of the bride retains more rights and influence in the former than in the latter. The transfer of property corresponds to the transfer of rights over spouses. So bride-wealth goods flow in an opposite direction to the transfer of the bride.

65. Cf a similar construction used to present the opposite message—the more the better—in an Estonian proverb regarding the birth of sons: 'One son, no son; second son, half son; third [one is] a son.'

66. Goody, ibid, 46. 'The dowry is virtually confined to Europe and Asia. It is absent from Africa, except where that continent has been penetrated by Islam or other universalistic world religions, though the words *dot* and *dowry* are often used for bride-wealth in Francophone and Anglophone areas' (ibid. 22). Here, we have only discussed the main rules. Wide variations exist, even within one cultural system. The prevailing principle usually was (and in many cases still is) that if a man wants to marry a girl she is to be relinquished by another man, usually her father or her brother (Claude Lévi-Strauss, *Anthropologie structurale*, Paris 1973), and that young women are exchanged in the interest of enhancing the glory of male status (Georges Balandier, *Anthropo-logiques*, Paris 1974).

67. See Edmund I. Gordon, *Sumerian Proverbs: Glimpses of Everyday Life in Ancient Mesopotamia*, Philadelphia 1959: 452. There are other old references to very young child brides from the same culture (on clay tablets of at least 2500 years BCE but the proverbs must have been transcribed from earlier oral traditions), mentioning the taboo of marital relations with little girls: before puberty a married girl child should not sit in her husband's lap (ibid: 47). Another variant speaks about childishly 'farting in her husband's lap' (see Bendt Alster, *Proverbs of Ancient Sumer: The World's Earliest Proverb Collections*, Bethesda 1997, vol. I: 9). Ancient Sumerians made a lot of fuss about such an incident, as mentioned in a proverb: 'A thing which has not occurred since time immemorial: a young girl broke wind in her husband's lap', suggesting that she was too young to be married. I thank Marten Stol for his comments on this issue.

68. See for more detailed information on the subject of bride kidnapping: Gisela Völger, and Karin von Welck, *Die Braut: geliebt, getauscht, geraubt: Zur Rolle der Frau im Kulturvergleich*, Köln 1985: Vol. I 102–7.

69. A girl adapts to her groom, just as something in a kosher kitchen that is neither meat nor dairy can adapt to both.

70. For this information I am indebted to the *Encyclopedia Britannica* where many more details on polygamy can be found. It is not possible here to go into the various theories trying to explain the occurrence of polygyny throughout the world (201–2). For a comparative study see Peter Brettschneider, *Polygyny: A Cross-Cultural Study*, Uppsala 1995.

71. 'Unofficial' relations and love affairs will be discussed later: see under 'Love' in Chapter Three.

72. The American variant might well be of Chinese origin. Another Chinese variant is: 'A girl can't drink tea from two families.' In China it mainly refers to a widow who might wish to remarry. This is advised against by means of proverbs in other cultures as well. If in a number of cultures the wife of a dead husband cannot just freely remarry, as we shall see below in the section on Widows, the idea of a wife having two living husbands at the same time seems totally unthinkable to men in most societies.

73. Amidst the large numbers of proverbs about co-wives, I found only one referring to the possibility of a wife with two husbands: 'If it is to their advantage, two men will share one wife' (*Arabic*), or in a Tunisian variant: 'If there is any profit in partnership, two will share a woman.' This is indeed unheard of in Muslim proverbs. Is it a joke or meant to be ironic? Not likely, since it is stressed that such a liaison is only desirable if it is to *their* [i.e. the men's] advantage. What the wife concerned thinks is of no matter.

74. According to the *Encyclopedia Britannica*, it even seems debatable as to what extent the existing varieties of the phenomenon of a woman sharing various men 'may properly be described as polyandrous marriage'.

75. Perhaps both are of Jewish origin.

76. In Polynesia and Melanesia polygamy hardly exists, mainly because of Christian influence. More governments have successfully tried, or are trying, to abolish the system, and groups such as *Sisters in Islam* are openly taking action against it. In Turkey it is forbidden, while in Malaysia, Syria and Egypt a man needs special permission from the court. In Morocco a man needs permission from his first wife. In a number of African countries polygamy has been abolished, e.g. in Tunisia, Ivory Coast, Zimbabwe, Botswana, and Namibia. However, as long as polygamy is justified by a Koran interpretation allowing a man to have four wives, it will not be easy to abolish the practice in Islamic societies. On the other hand, girls become more educated, they have better jobs, and are economically more independent, and have therefore a greater say in matters concerning their own lives.

77. The Japanese word for widow means literally 'the one who has not yet died'.

78. The custom of the dowry existed until the end of the nineteenth century in western Europe and continues to do so in many parts of southern Europe and the Mediterranean. Olwen H. Hufton, *The Prospect before her: A History of Women in Western Europe*. Vol. I *1500–1800*, London 1995; Jack Goody, *The European Family: An Historico-Anthropological Essay*, Oxford 2000.

79. See Hufton; Goody 2000.

80. Until this very day 'in societies in which it is often felt that it is the woman's fault if her husband gets ill, the growing debilitation of a man dying of Aids is blamed on his wife's lack of care. When he dies she may be driven from the village' (Caroline Moorehead, 'A Word of Silence', *Widows: Life after Death* (special issue of *Index on Censorship*) March/April 1998: 43.

81. It reminds of the earlier quoted proverb about the woman with attractive breasts, also Spanish: 'A woman with big breasts you should marry, bury, or put in a nunnery', see Chapter One, The Female Body.

82. A capon is a castrated rooster.

83. Jack Goody, *Food and Love: A Cultural History of East and West*, London 1998: 163.

84. The levirate may have been meant as an essential form of economic support for the widow and her children but it is also a system in which the widow herself has no choice: 'Stories abound of women who have refused the marriage imposed on them only to find themselves evicted from their homes, their children taken away by the husband's family, their possessions and land seized ... Where the tradition of the levirate once brought with it a certain security, an obligation on the husband's family to care for his widow, the breakdown in social structures and increasing urbanization have removed even those safeguards' (Moorehead 38–9).

85. Only one, Japanese, proverb goes against a woman's marrying a widower, arguing that he will always hold dearly the memory of his dead wife.

86. See also Chapter Three, on sexual experiece vs virginity.

87. In a special issue of *Index on Censorship*, Caroline Moorehead looks at the world of the widows from a global perspective: 'What all widows share ... is the fact that there are far more of them than widowers' (37). Almost all married women will find themselves widowed at some moment. However, there are huge differences in human rights among widows. In the West a widow may suffer from loss of income and loss in status, but she is not legally discriminated against. In many other parts of the world, 'cultural norms and taboos, customary and state laws governing inheritance, and most devastatingly, Aids, all combine to make widowhood a time of nightmare' (ibid). In many places the human rights of widows continue to be violated, as Margaret Owen has demonstrated in her book *A World of Widows* (London 1996).

88. A rope tie used to hobble cattle during milking.

89. For more details, see pp. 140–46.

90. In this book, stepmothers are not discussed as a category, because being a stepmother is not a phase of life for women in general; their imagined stereotypical wickedness, notoriously presented in stories as well as in proverbs all over the world is comparable to the qualities associated with mothers-in-law, to be discussed in the next part of this chapter. The word stepmother figures sometimes interchangeably with mother-in-law in proverbs carrying the same negative message.

91. This idea is also put forward by psychoanalysis. Psychoanalysts argue that a young child recognizes itself in the mother's eyes. A daughter reads in the mother's gaze all her anxieties, conflicts, tensions and frustrations related to being a woman, and, as a result, a daughter experiences her mother's approval or disapproval at all levels. A son may experience his mother's look as a confirmation of how special he is simply by being physically different from her: her gaze may well express that he is the one destined to realize all her unfulfilled hopes and forbidden dreams for what she has not been able or not been allowed to do as a woman. This is well illustrated in an Arabic saying about mothers' idealizing their sons: 'As many times as a woman gives birth, so many clever men there are on earth.'

92. A sister-in-law also gets a very negative image: 'The sister-in-law is a stinging nettle, or a birchen splinter' (*Russian*); 'The mother-in-law is a fever and the sister-in-law is a poisonous scorpion' (*Arabic, Lebanon*); 'The elder sister of one's husband is as authoritative as one's mother-in-law, and the younger sister is as terrible as the King of Hell' (*Chinese*); 'Two sisters-in-law hit each other, the mother-in-law paid the penalty for it' (*Bulgarian*), etc.

93. Harriet G. Rosenberg, 'Complaint Discourse, Aging, and Caregiving among the !Kung San of Botswana', Jay Sokolovsky, ed., *The Cultural Context of Aging: Wordwide Perspectives*, New York/Westport/London 1990: 19–41: 'In the less developed nations, the gender ratio above age sixty is relatively close, about ninety men for every hundred women, while in the more developed world there are twenty percent fewer males than females still alive' (17).

94. There are many other fascinating metaphors on sex. On sex, see Chapter Three; on metaphors, Chapter Five.

95. Large numbers of proverbs insist that not only old women, but women of all ages should behave modestly and timidly.

96. Proverbs in many languages warn against any woman's whistling, because it is supposed to bring bad luck. In the Rundi culture it is believed that old women can chase red ants by whistling.

97. It exists in about twenty percent of human societies (Steven M. Albert, and Maria G. Cattell, *Old Age in Global Perspective: Cross-Cultural and Cross-National Views*, New York 1994).

98. David Gutmann (*The Cross-Cultural Perspective: Notes Toward a Comparative Psychology of Aging*, Michigan 1977) has argued that this greater access to influence has to do with the supposed masculinization of older women, based on the idea that women become more like men after menopause. This would mean that they become more assertive and less submissive to the many constraints that societies have so often placed on younger women and wives. There are indeed anthropological testimonies confirming this 'late-life women's liberation' in Gutmann's terms, although proverbs give very little evidence to justify the use of this optimistic expression. It seems more realistic to speak in terms of an ongoing asymmetry between men and women, which is somewhat soothed with age in some respects (see also Albert and Cattell 1994).

Basics of Life

99. A *ri* is about 2.5 miles.

100. The Arabic comment provided with the proverb stresses that sexual relations between women are held in contempt both by men and women. One other Arabic proverb refers negatively to unmarried men: 'An unmarried man is Satan's brother.' The negative connotations of sex, whether homosexual or heterosexual, is expressed in another Arabic proverb: 'Dearth is a chastisement from God, and the people increase [it] through [intercourse with] lads and women.' (*Arabic, Morocco*)

101. *Mate* is a hot drink made out of herbs.

102. In past anthropological and folklore research from the nineteenth and early twentieth centuries, sex has often been censored or only referred to in rather indirect ways due to Victorian and conservative moral and middle-class norms, often operating together. In Europe, information about sexual matters was considered embarrassing and has therefore been screened and bowdlerized in many ways.

103. Guy Bechtel, *De vier vrouwen van God*, Kampen/Averbode 2001.

104. Constantina Safilios-Rothschild, *Love, Sex and Sex Roles*. New Jersey 1977: 56.

105. A few proverbs refer to this psychic reaction, somewhat like the couvade, a custom practised among some peoples—at least in the past—according to which a man takes to his bed while his wife is in childbirth.

Female Power

106. Details of such assignments can only be explained in the particular cultural contexts concerned, and cannot be discussed here. See Ember 1981; Reeves Sanday 76.

107. One of the far-reaching consequences of such a rather generalized ongoing division of role patterns has been that those who looked for gendered technological activities in human history found no technological activities strictly assigned to females in small-scale societies—researchers apparently did not consider food preparation and spinning as high tech. All over the world, however, a number of such professional activities strictly reserved for men have been found to exist: hunters and butchers are one such main category; blacksmiths or, more generally, processors of unmanageable raw materials such as iron, stone, bone and wood are another. See, for example, Levinson and Malone, ch. 26.

108. *Atole* is a milk drink with cornflour; *metate*, a stone for grinding maize.

109. *o.s.*: Anna Ivanova.

110. Margo Brouns, 'Het verlies van de wetenschappen' ('Loss of the Sciences'), *De Gids* Sept. 2000: 677–87.

111. *o.s.* Simon Simonse.

112. Cf. P.V. Kane, *History of Dharmaśāstra: Ancient and Mediaeval Religious and Civil Law*, Poona 1941, vol. 2: In texts such as the Mahabharatha and other texts 'women are charged with serious moral lapses (...) there is nothing more wicked than women, who are the edge of a razor, poison, snake and fire in one' (577–8) I thank my Leiden colleague Henk Bodewitz for referring me to this book from India.

113. See witchcraft and modernity: John Lionel Comaroff, and Jean Comaroff, *Modernity and its Malcontents: Ritual and Power in Postcolonial Africa*, Chicago 1993. In Africa as well as elsewhere, as Peter Geschiere has argued, witchcraft 'continues to be a key concept in discourses on power, despite modern processes of change (or perhaps because of them)' (*The Modernity of Witchcraft: Politics and the Occult in Postcolonial Africa*, Charlottesville 1997: 7–8).

114. James C. Scott, *Domination and the Arts of Resistance: Hidden Transcripts*, New Haven 1990: 143–4.

115. Hufton 1995: ' "Black" magic implied the recognition that someone had a key to unlock this force with malice ... The person in possession of this key was the witch (either male or female)', 343.

116. Ibid. 345. The two Dominican authors of the *Malleus Maleficarum* emphasized women's 'inability to keep silent and hence their habit of dragging others into their conspiracies, their insatiable lust, which could

prompt them even to accept the Devil as a lover, and their susceptibility to passion (hysteria), which made them vengeful, [those] were all attributes which converted them into helpmates of the Devil.'

117. Marcel Mauss, *A General Theory of Magic*, London 1972: 28.

118. See for example Marianna Hester, *Lewd Women and Wicked Witches: A Study of the Dynamics of Male Domination*, London 1992, Mary F. Daly, *Gyn/ecology: The Metaethics of Radical Feminism*, London 1979, Amba Oduyoye, 'The Asante Woman: Socialization through Proverbs', *African Notes* Vol. 8., No. 1 (1979): 5–11. One could speculate that, because of the subdominant position women had been manoeuvred into, men may have subconsciously feared their revenge, thus projecting their own fear onto 'woman' as the incarnation of an ongoing threat to the status quo. Such presumed magical powers are 'real' in a particular society as long as public opinion continues to believe that females practise magic.

119. Among the Yaka the *yindzika-nyanga* is considered to be a strong fetish.

120. In Hebrew *'yetzer ra'* means 'evil inclination', it is an instrument for suppressing taboo ideas and thoughts. Satan, 'one who leads astray', could function in the same way. I thank Mark Geller for this information.

121. Judith Hoch-Smith, and Anita Spring, eds., *Women in Ritual and Symbolic Roles*, New York 1978: 248. See also Hufton 1995.

122. See, for example, Dorothy Ayers Counts, Judith K. Brown, and Jacquelyn C. Campbell, *Sanctions and Sanctuary: Cultural Perspectives on the Beating of Wives*, Boulder/San Francisco/ Oxford 1992; Miranda Davies, comp., *Women and Violence*, London/New Jersey 1994.

123. Ibid. See also Henrietta Moore, *A Passion for Difference: Essays in Anthropology and Gender*. Cambridge 1997: 66–70

124. I thank therapist Marga van Gelderen for enlightening discussions about the connection between anger and helplessness.

Messages of Images

125. All are referring to the various categories of women discussed in this book. This huge figure doesn't even take into account the innumerable other metaphors referring to more specific details, such as beauty, love, eyes, dress, or some specific quality of mind or body, such as quarrels, anger, happiness, sadness, weakness, illness, and other aspects conceived in a rich variety of metaphors.

126. One may wonder what kind of women the proverbs have in mind, because being cloistered in a house does not hold of course for women who do have to work on the land for their daily bread, clean other people's houses, sell produce at market, etc.

Epilogue: Proverbial Imagination in an Age of Globalization

127. Amba Odudoye examined the crucial impact of negative proverbial imagery about women for the Ashanti culture in Ghana. She studied proverbs about women in a large collection of Twi proverbs from Ghana, and found that most of them had negative connotations. Her insightful observations about the impact of proverbs in the Ashanti society might well hold true for other cultures as well. See for Europe e.g. K. Daniels, 'Geschlechtsspezifische Stereotypen im Sprichwort: Ein interdisziplinärer Problemaufriss', *Literatur in Wissenschaft und Unterricht* 16: 18–25, and Cox. On the basis of his European collection Cox agreed to the 'generally sexist features' of proverbs, adding that the main dictionaries in Europe consist of 'male-made collections', 334. Yisa Kehinde Yusuf ('The Sexist Correlation of Women with the Non-Human in English and Yoruba Proverbs', *De Proverbio: An Electronic Journal of International Proverb Studies* 3.1 [1997]), compared Yoruba and English proverbs, and observed that they are 'remarkably comparable in the intensity of their cumulative misogyny', 1. Commenting upon Japanese proverbs about women Hiroko Storm ('Women in Japanese Proverbs', Peter Knecht, ed., *Asian Folklore Studies* 51 (1992): 167–82) also found few proverbs describing women positively, and many with negative connotations.

128. See for example Nancy Chodorow, *The Reproduction of Mothering: Psychoanalysis and the Sociology of Gender*, Berkeley 1978. J. and B. Whiting, *Children of Six Cultures: A Psycho-Cultural Analysis*. 4th ed., Cambridge 1979: 193 see male aggression and domination as a psychodynamic reaction to a perception of female power. Does it all start from the female faculty of birth-giving? See the earlier discussed procreation by male creators in creation stories; see also Peggy Reeves Sanday whose book has the significant title *Female Power and Male Dominance*, or Jean Stockard, and Miriam M. Johnson, 'The Origins of Male Dominance', *Sex Roles* Vol. 5, No. 2 (1979): 210: Men 'continue throughout their lives to be threatened in different ways and on different levels with an identity problem and a fear of dependency linked to this identity problem. The institutional arrangements embodying male dominance and the cultural justification of male dominance ordinarily serve to help males cope with these traits.' The problem would then disappear when men

also participate actively in early childcare. This idea might well find support in the underlying fear and insecurity expressed in so many proverbs regarding women's power. Dutch psychoanalyst Tonja Kivits ('Moeders zullen altijd prinsjes blijven kweken', *Opzij* mei 1999: 15–18) explains macho behaviour as follows: 'The mother of a macho has projected on to her young son all her unrealisable desire for male power: her son has to become a "real man", whereas for the "female" side of his personality there is no space or attention. In the [mother-son] relationship the father has hardly any place or he is even completely absent. This close relationship is precisely found in social groups or societies where the woman herself is oppressed. ... Women thus continue their own oppression via their sons ... because of the fact that mothers are mothering always and everywhere and establish the first early bond with their children.'

129. Oduyoye 5.
130. 'When one scholar collected some women's proverbs in Twi, some Twi-speaking males to whom she reported them expressed shock at their contents.' Personal information: Kwame Anthony Appiah. That those proverbs were experienced as 'shocking' is quite ironical, given the bulk of 'male' messages *sans gêne* uttered in public. Those female Twi proverbs apparently belonged to the 'hidden transcript' in James C. Scott's terms. Thus, gradually, the proverb may have come to be seen as a 'male' genre.
131. This is nothing new: in all unequal human relationships, dominant groups allow themselves to speak freely and openly about their subordinates. Being in power, they can afford to do so without risk. Slaves, serfs, servants, colonized and other subdominant subjects keep their thoughts and comments on their superiors to themselves, since they are afraid of the repercussions such boldness might provoke. But among their equals they do, of course, discuss in detail the 'master's' peculiarities, often without the superior's awareness of the very existence of any such comments. Colonial Europeans, for example, generally had no idea what Africans thought of them. Communication on an equal footing was impossible in colonial relations. Cf. my book *Imagining Insiders. Africa and the Question of Belonging* (London 1999).
132. Safilios-Rothschild 1977.
133. *o.s.* Manzoor Elahee (*India*).
134. Today in many communities around the globe (groups of) women are still associated with 'tradition' whereas men usually allow themselves to profit from 'modernity'.
135. 1997, Quoted in *Rawoo Report on Globalization* 2000.
136. Recently, specialists of Chinese proverbs in Beijing told me that the Government intends to censor Chinese proverb collections and dictionaries, so that traditional proverbs with negative messages about gender will no longer be available for study.
137. In a review of my African proverbs collection in *Revue de Littérature Comparée*, 1993 (1), Liz Gunner, for example, mentioned a Ugandan speaker at a recent conference in Germany who 'complained bitterly about the negative pull of proverbs embedded in the minds of male Ugandan policy makers. He claimed, both in sorrow and in anger, that proverbs maligning women whispered stubbornly in the subconscious of the most progressive of men working under the new order.' p193.
138. *'Source of All Evil'. African Proverbs and Sayings About Women*, published in Nairobi in 1991 and in Johannesburg in 1992.
139. Such dialogues reveal no less effectively what we share, globally, than what divides us. There is a worldwide growing awareness of the irrationality on which most existing gender dichotomies have been based, an awareness that has become more confident than ever before. Still, the Mecca of equal opportunities looks far away for those who look into the global human rights situation. In the late 1990s the Japanese Soka Gakkai Peace Committee organized a Travelling Gender and Human Rights Exhibition, which also came to Europe. This exhibition presented and provided statistics and photographs to underscore its argument that in virtually all societies women continue to confront discrimination as women: their labour is rewarded at an average of forty percent less than for the same job performed by a man. Women do about two-thirds of the world's work and produce, process and market three-fifth of the world's food; they receive one-tenth of the world's income, and own less than one-hundredth of the world's property. Nevertheless, it must be stressed that everywhere in the world human rights discussions have made a difference. In the majority of countries laws have been or are being created to protect women's rights and to prevent violence against women, and equal opportunities become ever more self-evident globally.

Languages, Cultures and Countries

Geographical borders, linguistic borders and cultural borders do not always coincide. For practical reasons I have classified the proverbs only according to the languages and the countries they originate from, as far as I was able to find out about both. I had to take decisions that may sometimes stroke against the hair of cultural coherence: I have not, for example, dealt with Jewish or Christian or Islamic or Buddhist proverbs as separate categories. Although religion is an important cultural factor, it is not the only one, and it is not necessarily bound up with language. Definite linguistic and cultural boundaries of proverbs are often difficult to establish, because proverbs are fond of travelling. They are generously shared, first within the community of origin, but then easily move with their owners, from their place of birth to wherever else in the world they find their way, thanks to human conversation.

It is no surprise, then, that the same (or very similar) proverbs are frequently found in neighbouring countries all over Europe; or that some proverbs have spread all over the Commonwealth, or all over the Spanish-speaking world. With wars, crusades, the slave trade, colonization, and migration, proverbs spread to new cultural contexts, where they settled in their original form or underwent changes in form or content due to local cultural influences.

The same popular proverbs re-occur in almost all Arabic-speaking countries. Arabic spread with Islam to Africa, and to south-east Asia. Some Arabic and Hebrew proverbs are quite similar. Moreover, locally, a Jewish proverb from Morocco or Yemen or Libya has been coloured by Arabic culture, and Jewish proverbs are sometimes quoted in the Arabic language, and also the other way round. To some extent Hebrew is spoken by Jews all over the world, but Jewish proverbs also exist in many other languages.

West African proverbs found their way, via the slave trade, to the Caribbean and the Americas. In the process, an Afro-Cuban proverb may have acquired a Spanish and/or Christian flavour. In the Caribbean many proverbs exist in local Creole language-forms alongside official languages. Many other proverbs in Latin America can be traced back to Iberian origins, and so forth.

In this book there are proverbs originating from one language spoken in more than one country, and there are proverbs originating from different languages spoken in one and the same country. Sometimes a language is spoken on both sides of the border of two neighbouring countries, or even in a number of countries. Ultimately, a classification along the lines of languages and nation-states, as far as possible, appeared to be the least problematic solution. 'As far as possible' has to be added indeed: sometimes sources mentioned only the country (e.g. Nigeria), or the region (e.g. West Africa), or only the language: e.g. English, a language spoken in many countries, or Uyghur (spoken partly in China and partly in the Russian Federation), or Bengali, spoken in India and in Bangladesh. Some ancient civilizations, such as Mesopotamia, or the Roman Empire, have disappeared altogether, and their languages are dead, but their proverbs survive. When proverbs are quoted in the main text, the language of origin is given, whereas in the anthologies at the end of each chapter, in addition to the languages, the countries or regions of origin have been included as well.

Below, the alphabetical list of languages mentions all the countries where the languages are spoken (or were spoken, in the case of languages that are no longer alive today, such as Sumerian or Latin), so that readers can easily relate even the lesser-known languages to their respective contexts of origin.

The proverbs have been translated as literally as possible. I have often consulted and checked unclear translations and meanings with knowledgeable native speakers or specialists in the cultural field concerned. Sometimes a word has been added for reasons of clarity. Such a word has been put in [-] brackets. Wherever necessary, a brief explanation has been added, also in [-] brackets. It regularly occurs that proverbs exist in more than one language. In the anthology, for each proverb, the countries as well as the languages of origin have been mentioned in cases where the country of origin is not self-evident.

All the oral and written sources of the proverbs mentioned are to be found in the anthologies at the end of each section. About 4000 proverbs about women have been included in the anthologies. The proverbs in this book originate from more than 240 languages and from at least 150 countries. This is, of course, only a modest inventory of all there is. Millions more could be collected and studied, but the selection in this volume is a reasonable sample which mirrors a fair profile of women's representations in proverbs worldwide.

LIST OF LANGUAGES, CULTURES AND COUNTRIES[1]

Abazin – Russian Federation

Abkhaz – Georgia, Russian Federation, Turkey

Acholi – Uganda, Sudan

Adangme – Ghana

Adyg – Russian Federation

Afar – Djibouti, Eritrea, Ethiopia

Afrikaans – South Africa

Agmari – India

Akan – *see* Ashanti

Akkadian – Mesopotamia

Albanian – Albania, Italy, Macedonia, Turkey

Allagish – Turkey

Amharic – Ethiopia

Andrah – India

Arabic – Middle East (e.g. Iraq, Lebanon, Libya, Oman, Saudi Arabia, Syria, Yemen), Maghreb (Algeria, Egypt, Morocco, Somalia, Sudan, Tunisia), other Muslim countries, Spain

Armenian – Armenia, Azerbaijan, Georgia, Turkey, other parts of former USSR

Ashanti/Asante (Twi, Akan language group) —Ghana, Ivory Coast

Assam – Bangladesh, Bhutan, India

Awar – Russian Federation, Azerbaijan

Azeri – Azerbaijan, Iran

Baatomun – Benin, Nigeria

Bambara – Mali, Nigeria, Burkina Faso, and several other West African areas

Bamum – West Africa (e.g. Cameroon)

Bari – Sudan

Bashkir – Russian Federation

Bassar – Togo

Basque – France, Spain

Baule – Ivory Coast

Bedouin – Bahrain, Iraq, Jordan, Kuwait, Oman, Qatar, Saudi Arabia, Syria, United Arab Emirates, Yemen

Belorussian – Belorus, Lithuania

Bemba – Zambia, Congo DR, Tanzania

Bembe – Congo PR

Bengali – Bangladesh, India

Berber – several areas in Northern Africa (e.g. Algeria, Libya, Morocco, Tunisia)

Beti – Cameroon

Bhojpuri – India

Bihari – India, Nepal

Bisa – Burkina Faso, Ghana, Togo

Bulgarian – Bulgaria, parts of Greece, Moldova, Romania, Ukraine

Bulu – Cameroon, Equatorial Guinea, Gabon

Burjat – Russian Federation, Mongolia

Burmese – Myanmar

Catalan – Andorra, France, Spain

Chagga – Tanzania, East Africa

Chechen – Russian Federation

Cherkess – Russian Federation

Chewa – Malawi, Zambia, Zimbabwe

Chinese – China, Taiwan

Chuwash – Russian Federation, Estonia, Kazakhstan, Kyrgyzstan, Uzbekistan

Creole – Bahamas, Belize, Dominican Republic, French Antilles, Guadeloupe, Haiti, Jamaica, Marie-Galante, Martinique, Saint Lucia, Trinidad and Tobago (NB all various countries and areas have their own Creole languages. Thus Haitian Creole differs from Trinidadian Creole, etc.)

Croatian – *see* Serbian/Croatian

Czech – Czech Republic, Serbia and Montenegro

Danish – Denmark

Dargin – Russian Federation

Digor (dialect of Ossetian) – Russian Federation

Duala – Cameroon

Dutch – Belgium, France, Germany, Netherlands, Netherlands Antilles, Surinam

Efik – Nigeria

Egyptian, Ancient – Ancient Egypt

English – Australia, Canada, Caribbean, Antigua and Barbuda, Hawaii, Jamaica, Ireland, New Zealand, Philippines, UK, USA, many countries in Sub-Saharan Africa

Estonian – Estonia and surrounding regions

Fang – Cameroon, Equatorial Guinea, Gabon

Filipino/Tagalog – Philippines

Finnish – Finland

Fiote – Angola and Cabinda, Congo DR, Gabon

---

[1] I thank my Leiden colleagues Uwe Blaesing (Comparative Linguistics) and Felix Ameka (African languages) for their linguistic comments on this list. In a few cases the name of the language may differ from the name of the culture. In such instances I have opted for the name of the people/culture, because proverbs are part of the culture. Thus in Africa we find Mampruli for the language and Mamprusi for the people and their culture. The same holds for Moore and Mossi.

Flemish – Belgium

Fon – Benin, Togo

Frafra – Ghana, Burkina Faso

French – Belgium, Canada, France, Luxembourg, Monaco, Switzerland, USA, many countries (formerly) governed by France

Frisian – Netherlands, Germany

Fulfulde – West Africa (e.g. Nigeria, Senegal; also spread as far as Sudan)

Ga – Ghana

Gagauz – Moldova, Russian Federation

Galla – *see* Oromo

Ganda – Uganda

Georgian – Georgia, Israel

German – Austria, Germany, Switzerland, USA (Pennsylvania)

Gikuyu/Kikuyu – Kenya

Giryama – Kenya

Greek – Greece

Guaraní – Argentina, Brazil, Paraguay

Hausa – West Africa (e.g. Niger, Ghana, Togo, Burkina Faso, Mali, and as far as Sudan)

Haya – Tanzania, Uganda

Hebrew – Israel (and spoken by Jews elsewhere in the Middle East, e.g. in Iraq, Morocco, Turkey, Yemen etc., and elsewhere in the world at large)

Hehe – Tanzania

Hindi – India

Hungarian – Hungary, Romania, Slovakia, Yugoslavia and Montenegro

Icelandic – Iceland

Igbo – Nigeria

Ikwere – Nigeria

Ila – Zambia

Indonesian – Bahasa Indonesia — Indonesia

Inuit, Inuktitut – Canada

Irish – Ireland

Italian – France (including Corsica), Italy, Switzerland

Jaba – Liberia, Nigeria

Japanese – Japan

Kabardino-Cherkess – Russian Federation, Turkey

Karachay-Balkar – Russian Federation, Armenia, Azerbaijan, Kazakhstan, Kyrgysztan, Uzbekistan

Kalmuk – Russian Federation

Kamba – Kenya

Kanuri – Niger, Nigeria

Karakalpak – Russian Federation, Afghanistan, Kazakhstan, Kyrgyzstan, Turkmenistan, Uzbekistan

Karelian – Russian Federation

Kashmiri – India, Pakistan

Kazakh – Afghanistan, China, Iran, Kazakhstan, Kyrgyzstan, Mongolia, Russian Federation, Tajik-istan, Turkey, Turkmenistan, Ukraine, Uzbekistan

Khakass/Chakas – Russian Federation

Khmer – Cambodia, Thailand, Vietnam

Khiongtha – Bangladesh

Kirghiz – Afghanistan, China, Kyrgyzstan, Tajikistan

Komi – Russian Federation

Kongo/Kikongo – Congo DR

Korean – China, North and South-Korea, Japan

Krio – Sierra Leone

Kru – Ivory Coast, Liberia

Kumyk – Russian Federation, Turkey, Kazakhstan

Kundu – Benin, Cameroon, Chad, Central African Republic, Ghana, Niger, Nigeria, Togo

Kurdish – Armenia, Iran, Iraq, Syria, Turkey

Kweli – Cameroon

Ladino – spoken by Sephardic Jews in the Balkans, Middle East (e.g. Libya, Iraq, Israel), Maghreb (e.g. Morocco, Tunisia), Greece, Turkey

Lak – Russian Federation

Lao – Laos

Latin – former Roman Empire

Latvian – Latvia

Lega – Congo DR

Letzeburgish – Luxembourg

Lezgian – Azerbaijan, Russian Federation

Lingala – Congo DR

Lithuanian – Lithuania

Lokaniti – Myanmar

Luba – Congo DR

Lunda – Angola, Congo DR, Zambia

Luo – Kenya, Uganda

Macedonian – Albania, Austria, Bulgaria, Greece, Macedonia

Makua – Mozambique

Malagasy – Madagascar and adjacent islands

Malay – Malaysia

Malayalam – India

Maltese – Malta

Mamprusi-Mampruli – Burkina Faso, Ghana, Togo

Mandinka – West Africa (e.g. Gambia, Guinea, Guinea-Bissau, Ivory Coast, Mali, Senegal)

Maori – Cook Islands, New Zealand

Mapuche – Argentina, Chile

Marathi – India

Masai, Maasai – East Africa (e.g. Kenya, Tanzania)

Mboshi – Congo PR

Mende – Liberia, Sierra Leone

Minangkabau – Indonesia, Malaysia

Minyanka – Mali

Moldovan/Moldavian – Moldova

Mongo – Congo DR

Mongolian – China, Mongolia

Moore – *see* Mossi

Moorish – Algeria, Mali, Mauritania, Morocco, Niger, Senegal, Spain

Mordvin – Russian Federation

Mossi/Moore – West Africa (e.g. Burkina Faso)

Multani – India, Pakistan

Nama – Namibia

Nandi – Kenya

Ndebele – South Africa, Zimbabwe

Nenets – Russian Federation

Neo-Aramaic – Iraq

Nepalese/Nepali – Bhutan, Nepal

Ngaka Bali-Nyonga (dialect of Mungaka) – Cameroon

Ngbaka – Central African Republic

Ngwana – Congo DR

Nubian/Nobiin – Sudan, Egypt

Nogay – Russian Federation

Norwegian – Norway

Nubian/Nobiin – Egypt, Sudan

Nyanja – Malawi, Mozambique, Zambia

Oromo – Ethiopia, Kenya

Ossetian – Georgia, Russian Federation

Ovambo – Angola, Namibia

Palaung – China, Myanmar

Papiamentu – Aruba, Caribbean, Netherlands Antilles, Surinam

Pashto/Pashtu – Afghanistan, Pakistan

Persian – Iran

Pidgin (i.e. Jamaican Pidgin) – Jamaica (NB Various countries have their own Pidgin languages)

Polish – Poland

Portuguese – Brazil, Portugal including (former) Portuguese colonial territories, Spain

Punjabi – India, Pakistan

Quecha – Bolivia, Ecuador, Peru

Rajasthani – India

Romanian – Moldova, Romania

Ronga – Mozambique, South Africa, Zimbabwe

Rundi – Burundi

Russian – Russian Federation and other former republics of USSR/Soviet sphere of influence

Rwanda/Kinyarwanda – Burundi, Congo DR, Rwanda, Uganda, Tanzania

Sanskrit – India

Sara – Central African Republic, Chad, Sudan

Scottish – UK

Sena – Malawi, Mozambique

Senufo – Ivory Coast, Mali, Burkina Faso

Serbian – *see* Serbian/Croatian

Serbian/Croatian (now known as Serbian, Croatian or Bosnian, depending on the ethnicity of the speaker) – Bosnia and Herzegovina, Croatia, Macedonia, Yugoslavia and Montenegro

Shona – Zimbabwe

Shor – Russian Federation

Sinhalese – India, Maldives, Sri Lanka

Slovak – Slovakia

Slovenian – Austria, Italy, Slovene

Somali – Djibouti, Ethiopia, Kenya, Somalia

Songye – Congo DR

Sorbian – Germany

Sotho – Botswana, Lesotho, South Africa

Spanish – both Americas (e.g. Antigua and Barbuda, Argentina, Bolivia, Chile, Colombia, Costa Rica, Cuba, Dominican Republic, El Salvador, Guatemala, Mexico, Panama, Peru, Puerto Rico, Uruguay, Venezuela), Morocco, Philippines, Spain including Canary Islands

Sranan/Sranantongo – Aruba, Netherlands, Netherlands Antilles, Surinam

Sukuma – Tanzania

Sumerian – Mesopotamia

Swahili – East Africa (e.g. Congo DR, Kenya, Tanzania, Zanzibar)

Swedish – Finland, Sweden

Swiss – Austria, France, Germany, Italy, Liechtenstein, Switzerland

Tagalog – *see* Filipino

Tajik – Afghanistan, China, Tajikistan, Uzbekistan

Tamashek – West Sahara

Tamil – India, Sri Lanka

Tangut – China

Tatar – Bulgaria, China, Romania, Russian Federation, Turkey

Tati – Azerbaijan, Iran, Russian Federation

Telegu – Bahrain, Fiji, India, Malaysia, Mauritius, Singapore

Thai – Thailand

Tibetan – Buthan, India, Nepal, Tibet

Tigrinya – Ethiopia, Eritrea

Tiv – Nigeria

Tonga – Zambia, Zimbabwe

Tsonga – South Africa, Mozambique, Swaziland, Zimbabwe

Tswana – Botswana, South Africa

Tumbuka – Malawi, Zambia

Turkish – Cyprus, Turkey, also elsewhere in Europe and the Middle East

Twi – *see* Ashanti

Udmurt – Russian Federation

Ukrainian – Ukraine

Umbundu – Angola

Urdu – India, Pakistan

Uyghur – China, Kazakhstan, Kyrgyzstan, Russian Federation, Uzbekistan

Uzbek – Afghanistan, China, Kazakhstan, Kyrgyzstan, Tajikistan, Turkmenistan, Uzbekistan

Vai – Liberia, Sierra Leone

Venda – South Africa

Vietnamese – Vietnam

Welsh – UK (Wales)

Wolof – Gambia, Senegal

Woyo – Congo DR

Yaka – Congo DR

Yakut – Russian Federation

Yiddish – most countries with a Jewish population in Europe (e.g. Netherlands, Russian Federation), Israel

Yoruba – Benin, Nigeria, Togo

Zulu – South Africa, Swaziland

Bibliography

'Alphabet of Ben Sira'. *Rabbinic Fantasies: Imaginative Narratives from Classical Hebrew Literature*. Trans. D. Stern, and M.J. Mirsky. Philadelphia 1990.

Abela, Ferdinand Joseph. *Proverbes populaires du Liban-Sud: Saïda et ses environs*. Paris 1981.

ACCT (Agence de coopération culturelle et technique). *1000 proverbes créoles de la Caraïbe francophone*. Paris 1987.

Acuña, Luis Alberto. *Refranero colombiano: Mil y un refranes*. Bogotá/Colombia 1989.

Adams, Owen S. 'Traditional Proverbs and Sayings from California'. *Western Folklore* 6 (1947): 59–64.

Aguilera, Luisita. *Refranero panameño: Contribución a la paremiologia ispano-americana*. Santiago 1955.

Ahmed, Leila. *Women and Gender in Islam: Historical Roots of a modern Debate*. New Haven 1992.

Akporobaro, F.B.O., and J.A. Emovon. *Nigerian Proverbs: Meanings and Relevance Today*. Lagos 1994.

Alaimo, M.Emma. *Proverbi Siciliani*. Florence 1974.

Albert, Steven M., and Maria G. Cattell. *Old Age in Global Perspective: Cross-Cultural and Cross-National Views*. New York 1994.

Alcalay, Reuven. *Words of the Wise: An Anthology of Proverbs and Practical Axioms*. Jerusalem/Ramat-Gan 1970.

Alster, Bendt. *Proverbs of Ancient Sumer: The World's Earliest Proverb Collections*. 2 vols. Bethesda 1997.

Amrouche, Marguerite Taos. *Le grain magique: Contes, poèmes et proverbes berbères de Kabylie*. Paris 1966.

Anderson, Inzett, and Frank Cundall. *Jamaica Proverbs and Sayings*. Shannon (Ireland) 1972.

Andrzejewski, Bogumil Witalis, and Ioan Myrddin Lewis. *Somali Poetry: An Introduction*. Oxford 1964.

Arbelbide, Cyprien. *Les Baoulés d'après leurs dictons et proverbes*. Abidjan 1975.

Archer, John, and Barbara Lloyd. *Sex and Gender*. 1982. Cambridge 1985.

Areje, Raphael Adekunle. *Yoruba Proverbs*. Ibadan 1985.

Armas, Daniel. *Diccionario de la expresión popular guatemalteca*. Guatemala-City 1971.

Armbrister, Hilda. 'Proverbs from Abaco, Bahamas'. *Journal of American Folklore* 30 (1917): 274.

Arnaudov, Michail. *Bŭlgarski Poslovici: Bŭlgarski pritči ili poslovici i charakterni dumi, sŭbrani ot P.R. Slavejkov*. Sophia 1972.

Arora, Shirley L. *Proverbial Comparisons in Ricardo Palma's 'Tradiciones Peruanas'*. Berkeley/Los Angeles 1966.

Ascha, Ghassan. *Du statut inférieur de la femme en islam*. Paris 1987.

Atkinson, Mary J. 'Familiar Sayings of Old Time Texans'. *Publications of the Texas Folk Lore Society* 5 (1926): 78–92.

Attanasio, Sandro. *Parole di Sicilia: Frasi, espressioni, detti, paragoni, proverbi e 'vastasate'*. Milan 1977.

Ayers Counts, Dorothy, Judith K. Brown, and Jacquelyn C. Campbell. *Sanctions and Sanctuary: Cultural Perspectives on the Beating of Wives*. Boulder/San Francisco/Oxford 1992.

Balandier, Georges. *Anthropo-logiques*. Paris 1974.

Ballesteros, Octavio A. *Mexican Proverbs: The Philosophy, Wisdom and Humor of a People*. Austin/Texas 1979.

Bamgbose, Ayo. 'The Form of Yoruba Proverbs'. *Odu: University of Ife Journal of African Studies* 4 (1968), No.2: 74–86.

Barbotin, Maurice. *Dictionnaire du créole de Marie-Galante*. Hamburg 1995.

Barneville Vásquez, Roger de. *Modismos, refranes, frases hechas y otras expresiones empleadas en el oriente de Bolivia*. Santa Cruz de la Sierra 1988.

Barra, G. *1000 Kikuyu Proverbs*. 1939. Nairobi 1984.

Bechtel, Guy. *De vier vrouwen van God*. Trans. Michel Perquy. Kampen/Averbode 2001.

Beck, Rose-Marie. *Texte auf Textilien in Ostafrika : Sprichwörtlichkeit als Eigenschaft ambiger Kommunikation*. Köln 2001.

Bedi, Sohindar Singh. 'Women in the Folksayings of Punjab'. Sen Gupta 167–76.

Beem, H. *Jerosche: Jiddische spreekwoorden en zegswijzen uit het Nederlandse taalgebied*. 1959. Assen 1970.

Beintema, Tabe. *Moai sa, Sikke: Frysk sprekwurdeboek mei Nederlânske oersetting, ferklearring of taljochting—Goed zo Sicco: Fries spreekwoordenboek met Nederlandse vertaling, verklaring of toelichting*. Drachten 1990.

Beken, Alain van der. *Proverbes et vie yaka*. St Augustin 1978.

Beken, Alain van der. *Proverbes yaka du Zaïre*. Paris 1993.

Belamri, Rabah. *Proverbes et dictons algériens*. Paris 1986.

Bellow, Lêdji. ' "Je cours plus vite que ma rivale": Paroles de Pagne chez les Gens-Mina au Sud Togo'. *Cahiers de Littérature Orale* 19 (1986): 29–67.

Benazeraf, Raphaël. *Refranero: Recueil de proverbes judéo-espagnols du Maroc*. Paris 1978.

Bentolila, F. *Proverbes berbères: Bilingue français-berbère*. Paris 1993.

Bergua, José. *Refranero Español precedidos del Libro de los proverbios morales de Alonso de Barros*. Madrid 1988.

Bhatnagar, Manju. 'Women in Rajasthani Folklore'. Sen Gupta 59–78.

Bläsing, Uwe. *Tsuwaschische Sprichwörter und sprichwörtliche Redensarten*. Wiesbaden 1994.

Boatwright, Mody C., ed. *Texas Folk and Folklore*. Dallas 1954.

Boecklen, Adolf. *Sprichwörter in 6 Sprachen*. Stuttgart 1945.

Bohn, Henry George. *A Polyglot of Foreign Proverbs*. London 1857.

Bohn, Henry George. *Handbook of Proverbs*. London 1855.

Bon, Michel, and Roland Colin. 'Les proverbes facteurs de développement'. *Développements et Civilisations*. Sept.–Dec. 1970: 83–123.

Bradley, F.W. 'South Carolina Proverbs'. *Southern Folklore Quarterly* 1 (1937): 57–101.

Brauen, Martin. 'Die Frau im Buddhismus'. Völger & Von Welck I: 194–201.

Brenneker, Paul Hubert Frans. *Proverbio*. Curaçao 1963.

Brettschneider, Peter. *Polygyny: A Cross-Cultural Study*. Uppsala 1995.

Brix, Hans. *Danske ordsprog, udvalgt og indledt af*. Kopenhagen 1944.

Brookman-Amissah J. 'Some observations on the proverbs of the Akan-speaking peoples of Ghana'. *Afrika und Übersee*. Vol. IV (1971–72): 262–67.

Brougham, Aileen E., and A.W. Reed. *Maori Proverbs*. Auckland 1963.

Brouns, Margo. 'Het verlies van de wetenschappen'. *De Gids* Sept. 2000: 677–87.

Brown, Donald E. *Human Universals*. New York 1991.

Brown, Raymond Lamont. *A Book of Proverbs*. New York 1970.

Browning, David Clayton, comp. *Dictionary of Quotations and Proverbs: The Everyman Edition*. 1951. London 1989.

Brunvand, Jan Harold. *A Dictionary of Proverbs and Proverbial Phrases from Books Published by Indiana Authors before 1890*. Indiana 1961.

Buchanan, Daniel Crump. *Japanese Proverbs and Sayings*. Oklahoma 1965.

Burckhardt, John Lewis. *Arabic Proverbs: Or the Manners and Customs of the Modern Egyptians*. 1875. London 1980.

Busuttil, E.D. *Gabra ta Qwiel maltin u qwiel inglizi li jaqblu maghhomi*. n.p. 1971.

Cabrera, Lydia, comp. *Refranes de negros viejos*. La Habana 1955.

Cannobio, Agustín G. *Refranes Chilenos*. Santiago 1901.

Carmody, Denis Lardner, John Carmody, and Robert L. Cohen. *Exploring the Hebrew Bible*. Englewood Cliffs 1988.

Carrington, John F. *Talking Drums of Africa*. London 1949.

Casasola C., José. *Dichos mexicanos: Explicaciones y comentarios*. México n.d.

Cattan, Henry. *The Garden of Joys: An Anthology of Oriental Anecdotes, Fables and Proverbs*. London 1979.

Cauvin, Jean. *Comprendre les proverbes*. Saint-Paul 1981.

Cauvin, Jean. *L'image, la langue et la pensée. I: L'Exemple des proverbes (Mali) II: Recueil de proverbes karangasso*. 2 vols. St Augustin 1980. Vol. I.

Champion, Selwyn Gurney. *Racial Proverbs. A Selection of the World's Proverbs Arranged Linguistically*. London 1938.

Chaves, Pedro. *Rifoneiro Português*. Pôrto 1945.

Chen, John T.S. *1001 Chinese Sayings*. Hongkong 1973.

Cheneb, M. ben. *Proverbes arabes de l'Algérie et du Maghreb*. 3 vols. Paris 1905–1907.

Chodorow, Nancy. *The Reproduction of Mothering: Psychoanalysis and the Sociology of Gender*. Berkeley 1978.

Chua, Romulo L., and Rodolfo L. Nazareno. *Ang Mahalaga Sa Buhay: A Handbook of Filipino Values*. Eds. E. Albert, and S.J. Alejo. Quezon City 1992.

Cibotto, Gian Antonio. *Proverbi del Veneto*. Florence 1976.

Cock, A. de. *Spreekwoorden en zegswijzen*. Gent 1908.

Coffin, Tristam Potter, and Henning Cohen, eds. *Folklore in America*. Garden City 1966.

Cohen, Arthur. *Oude Joodsche spreekwoorden*. Trans. J. Herderscheê. Deventer 1912.

Cohen, Israel. *Dictionary of Parallel Proverbs in English, German and Hebrew*. Jerusalem 1961.

Collins, J. *A Dictionary of Spanish Proverbs*. London 1823.

Comaroff, John Lionel, and Jean Comaroff. *Modernity and its Malcontents: Ritual and Power in Postcolonial Africa*. Chicago 1993.

Coping with Globalization: The Need for Research Concerning the Local Response to Globalization in Developing Countries 20, RAWOO, The Hague, 2000.

Cordry, Harold V. *The Multicultural Dictionary of Proverbs: Over 20000 Adages from More Than 120 Languages, Nationalities and Ethnic Groups*. McFarland 1997.

Cotter, George. *Ethiopian Wisdom: Proverbs and Sayings of the Oromo People*. Ibadan 1996.

Courville, Cindy. 'Reexamining Patriarchy as a Mode of Production: The Case of Zimbabwe'. Stanlie M. James, and Abena P.A. Busia, eds. *Theorizing Black Feminisms: The Visionary Pragmatism of Black Women*. London/New York 1993: 32–43.

Cox, Heinrich Leonard, and A.M.A. Cox-Leick. *Spreekwoordenboek in vier talen: Nederlands, Frans, Duits, Engels*. Utrecht 1988.

Crépeau, Pierre, and Simon Bizimana. *Proverbes du Rwanda*. Tervuren 1979.

Cruz Brache, José Antonio. *5600 refranes y frases de uso común entre los dominicanos*. Santo Domingo 1978.

Dagpinar, Aydin. *A Dictionary of Turkish-English/English-Turkish Proverbs and Idioms*. Istanbul 1982.

Dahan, Hanania. *Otsar ha-pitgamin shel Yehude Maroko: Be-tseruf hashva'ot u-makbilot mi-mekorot Yehudiyim va-aherim*. 2 vols. Tel-Aviv 1983. Vol. 1.

Dale, van. *Spreekwoordenboek in vier talen. Nederlands/Frans/Duits/Engels*. Utrecht 1989.

Daly, Mary F. *Gyn/ecology: The Metaethics of Radical Feminism*. London 1979.

Daniels, K. 'Geschlechtsspezifische Stereotypen im Sprichwort: Ein interdisziplinärer Problemaufriss'. *Literatur in Wissenschaft und Unterricht* 16 (1985): 18–25.

David, B., and J.P. Jardel. *Les proverbes créoles de la Martinique*. Paris 1969.

Davies, Miranda, comp. *Women and Violence*. London/New Jersey 1994.

Davison, Jean. *Gender, Lineage, and Ethnicity in Southern Africa*. Boulder 1997.

De, Sushilkumar, ed. *Bangla Prabad*. Calcutta 1946.

Díaz Rivera, María Elisa. *Refranes usados en Puerto Rico*. Río Piedras 1984.

Dijk-Hemmes, Fokkelien van. 'Want eerst is Adam geformeerd en daarna Eva. . .' *Ro* 1982: 25–41.

Dình Khuê Duong. *La littérature populaire vietnamienne*. Saigon 1968.

Duncan, Marion H. *Love Songs and Proverbs of Tibet*. London 1961.

Dundes, Alan, ed. *Sacred Narrative: Readings in the Theory of Myth*. Berkeley/Los Angeles/London 1984.

Duvollet, Roger. *Proverbes et dictons arabes. Algérie/Tunisie/Maroc/Sahara*. n. p. 1980.

Elias, N. *The Civilizing Process*. 2 vols. Oxford 1939.

Elwell-Sutton, Laurence Paul. *Persian proverbs*. John Murray. London 1954.

Ember, Carol R. 'A Cross-cultural Perspective on Sex Differences'. Ruth H. Munroe, Robert L. Munroe and Beatrice B. Whiting, eds. *Handbook of Cross-Cultural Human Development*. New York/London 1981: 531–80.

Ember, Carol R., and Melvin Ember. 'The conditions favoring matrilocal versus patrilocal residence'. *American Anthropologist* 73 (1971): 571–594.

Emrich, Duncan. *Folklore on the American Land*. Boston 1972.

Ensler, Eve. *The Vagina Monologues*. New York 1998.

Ernest W. *The Folklore of Orkney and Shetland*. London 1975.

Escobar, Washington. *Refranero uruguayo: Pequeña biblia gaucha. Dichos, máximas y sentencias del habla popular colectadas oralmente en Tacuarembó*. Montevideo 1963.

Fabre, Alfred. *Film de la vie chinoise: Proverbes et locutions*. Hongkong 1937.

Faïk-Nzuji Madiya, Clémentine. *Les droits de la personne dans les proverbes africains*. Louvain-la-Neuve 1986.

Febres Cordero, Julio. *Porsiacaso de Refranes*. Caracas 1987.

Feghali, Michel. *Proverbes et dictons syro-libanais*. Paris 1938.

Feijóo, Samuel. *Refranes, adivinanzas, dicharachos, trabalenguas, cuartetas y décimas antiguas de los campesinos cubanos*. La Habana 1961.

Fergusson, Rosalind. *The Penguin Dictionary of Proverbs*. 1983. Harmondsworth 1986.

Fernández Naranjo, Nicolas, and Dora Gómez de Fernández. *Diccionario de bolivianismos*, La Paz/Cochabamba 1967.

Fernández Valledor, Roberto. *Del refranero puertorriqueño en el contexo hispánico y antillano.* Madrid 1991.

Finnegan, Ruth. *Oral Literature in Africa.* Oxford 1970.

Flügel, John Carl. *Studies in Feeling and Desire.* London 1955.

Foucault, Michel. *The History of Sexuality.* 2 vols. New York 1980.

Franklin, Benjamin. *Poor Richard's: The Almanacks for the Years 1733–1758.* New York 1964.

Frayha, Anis. *Modern Lebanese Proverbs.* 2 vols. Beirut 1953.

Gaden, Henri. *Proverbes et maximes peuls et toucouleurs (traduits, expliqués et annotés).* Paris 1931.

Gaffney, Sean, and Seamus Cashman. *Proverbs and Sayings of Ireland.* 1974. Dublin 1992.

Gee, Alison Dakota. 'In the Eye of the Beholder.' *Sunday Morning Post* (Hong Kong). 8 Aug. 1999 : 6–10.

Gee, Ellen M., and Meredith M. Kimball. *Women and Aging.* Toronto 1987.

Gérard, Alain. *Paraulo de Provenço—Paroles de Provence.* Nonette 1984.

Gergan, Rev. J., and Waltern Asboe. 'A Thousand Tibetan Proverbs and Wise Sayings with Short Explanations of Obscure Phrases from Ladakh, Spiti, Lahaul and Naris Skor-gSum'. *Journal of the (Royal) Asiatic Society, Calcutta Branch.* VIII Letters. Repr. with an Introduction by S.S. Gergan. Delhi/Sterling 1976.

Geschiere, Peter. *The Modernity of Witchcraft: Politics and the Occult in Postcolonial Africa.* Charlottesville 1997.

Geyvandov, Eduard Aratyunovich. *Zhenshchina v poslovitsakh i pogovorkakh narodov mira.* Moscow 1995.

Gilmore, David D. 'The Manhood Puzzle'. Brettell, Caroline B. and Carolyn F. Sagent, eds. *Gender in Cross-Cultural Perspective.* 2nd ed. New Jersey 1993: 185–97.

Ginzburg, Louis. *The Legends of the Jews.* Trans. Henrietta Szold. 7 vols. Philadelphia 1967–1969.

Giusti, Giuseppe. *Raccolta di proverbi Toscani.* Livorno 1971.

Glazer, Mark. *A Dictionary of Mexican American Proverbs.* New York/Connecticut/London 1987.

Gluski, Jerzy. *Proverbs—Proverbes—Sprichwörter—Proverbi—Proverbios—Poslovicy: A Comparative Book of English, French, German, Italian, Spanish and Russian Proverbs.* Amsterdam/New York 1971.

Goody, Jack, and S.J. Tambiah. *Bridewealth and Dowry.* Cambridge 1973.

Goody, Jack. 'Bridewealth and Dowry in Africa and Eurasia'. Goody & Tambiah 1–58.

Goody, Jack. *Food and Love: A Cultural History of East and West.* London 1998.

Goody, Jack. *The European Family: An Historico-Anthropological Essay.* Oxford 2000.

Gordon, Edmund I. *Sumerian Proverbs: Glimpses of Everyday Life in Ancient Mesopotamia.* Philadelphia 1959.

Graf, Adolf Eduard. *6000 deutsche und russische Sprichwörter.* 3 Auflage. Halle 1960.

Gray, James. *Ancient Proverbs and Maxims From Burmese Sources: Or the Niti Literature of Burma.* London 1886.

Gross, David C., and Esther R. Gross, ed. *De wereld is in handen van dwazen en andere spreekwoorden, spreuken, aforismen, wijsheden en onvergetelijke citaten uit de schatkamer van de Joodse cultuur.* Trans. Henk Buma. Delft 1995.

Gruber, Jona. *750 rumänischen Sprichwörter – 750 proverbe romanesi.* Bukarest 1973.

Guarnieri, Juan Carlos. *Sabiduría y folklore en el lenguaje campesino rioplatense.* Montevideo 1971.

Guevara, Tomás. *Folklore Araucano.* Santiago 1911.

Guiter, Henri. *Proverbes et dictons catalans.* Forcalquier 1969.

Gunner, Liz. 'New African Oral Literatures'. *Revue de Littérature comparée* 1 (1993): 91–99.

Günther, Johannes. *Russkie poslovicy—Russische Sprichwörter.* München 1958.

Gutmann, David. *The Cross-Cultural Perspective: Notes Toward a Comparative Psychology of Aging.* Michigan 1977.

Ha, Tae Hung. *Maxims and Proverbs of Old Korea.* Seoul 1970.

Haig, Kerest. *Dictionary of Turkish-English Proverbial Idioms.* Istanbul 1951. Amsterdam 1969.

Haïm, Sulaimān. *Persian-English Proverbs.* Tehran 1956.

Hall, Robert A. jr. 'Haitian Creole: Grammar—Texts—Vocabulary'. *The American Anthropological Association* 55, Part 2, Memoir 74, April–June 1953.

Haller, Joseph. *Altspanischen Sprichwörter.* Regensburg 1883. Vol. 1.

Hamutyinei, M.A., and A.B. Plangger. *Tsumo-Shumo: Shona Proverbial Lore and Wisdom.* Harare 1974.

Harrebomée, Pieter Jacob. *Spreekwoorden der Nederlandschen taal.* 3 vols. 1858–1870. Utrecht 1991.

Hazan-Rokem, Galit. *Proverbs of the Jews from Georgia and Israel.* Hebrew text. Jerusalem 1993.

Hearn, Lafcadio. '*Gombo Zhèbes*'. *Little Dictionary of Creole Proverbs Selected from Six Creole Dialects.* New York 1885.

Hendricks, George D. 'Texas Folk Proverbs'. *Western Folklore* 21 (1962): 92.

Henríquez Ureña, Pedro. *El Español en Santo Domingo.* 1940. Santo Domingo 1975.

Herg, E. *Deutsche Sprichwörter im Spiegel fremder Sprachen.* Berlin/Leipzig 1933.

Hernández H., Hermógenes. *Refranes y dichos populares.* San José de Costa Rica 1987.

Herrmann, Gerhard, comp. *Hojaca Knižka. Serbske přislowa (Das Heilebuchlein. Sorbische Sprichwörter).* Trans. Elke Nagel. Bautzen 1992.

Hertz, Robert. *Death and the Right Hand.* Trans. Rodney Needham, and Claudia Needham. Aberdeen 1960.

Hester, Marianna. *Lewd Women and Wicked Witches: A Study of the Dynamics of Male Domination.* London 1992.

Hines, Donald M. *Frontier Folksay: Proverbial Lore of the Inland Pacific North-west Frontier.* n.p. 1977.

Hinton, Perry R. *Stereotypes, Cognition and Culture.* Hove 2000.

Hla Pe, U. *Burmese Proverbs.* London 1962.

Hoch-Smith, Judith, and Anita Spring, eds. *Women in Ritual and Symbolic Roles.* New York 1978.

Hoefnagels, Peter, and Shon We Hoogenbergen. *Antilliaans spreekwoordenboek: Spreekwoorden en zegswijzen.* Curaçao 1980. Amsterdam 1991.

Hoen, Guno. *Sranan odo buku.* 1988. Paramaribo 1989.

Hoffman, W.J. 'Folklore of the Pennsylvania Germans'. *Journal of American Folklore* 2 (1889): 191–202.

Honeck, Richard P. *A Proverb in Mind. The Cognitive Science of Proverbial Wit and Wisdom.* Mahwah 1997.

Hufton, Olwen H. *The Prospect before Her: A History of Women in Western Europe.* Vol. 1 *1500–1800.* London 1995–.

Hulstaert, G. *Proverbes mongo.* Tervuren 1958.

Huzii, Otoo. *Japanese Proverbs.* Tokyo 1940.

Ibekwe, P. *Wit and Wisdom of Africa: Proverbs from Africa and the Carribean.* Trenton 1998.

Issa, Amadou, and Roger Labatut. *Sagesse des Peuls nomades.* Yaoundé 1973.

Ittmann, Johannes. *Sprichwörter der Kundu (Kamerun).* Berlin 1971.

Jablow, Alta. *Yes and No: The Intimate Folklore of Africa.* Westport 1961.

Jacquot, A. *Etudes béembe (Congo), esquisse linguistique: Devinettes et proverbes.* Paris 1981.

Jalil, Alamgir. 'Women in Folklore of East Pakistan'. Sen Gupta 20–32.

Jha, Tarinish, et al., eds. *A Dictionary of Sanskrit Idioms and Proverbs.* 2nd ed. Allahabad 1975.

Joos, Amatus Honoratus. *Schatten uit de volkstaal.* Gent 1887.

Judd, Henry P. *Hawaiian Proverbs and Riddles.* New York 1988.

Kalugila, L., and A.Y. Lodhi. *More Swahili Proverbs from East Africa.* Uppsala 1980.

Kane, P.V. *History of Dharmaśātra: Ancient and Mediaeval Religious and Civil Law.* 5 vols. Poona 1941. Vol. 2.

Karadžić, Vuc Stepanović. *Volksmärchen der Serben. Nebst einem Anhange von mehr als 1000 serbischen Sprichwörtern.* Trans. Wilhelmine Karadžić. Berlin 1854.

Kayal, Akshaykumar. 'Women in Folklore of West Bengal'. Sen Gupta 177–200.

Kerschen, Lois. *American Proverbs About Women. A Reference Guide.* Westport, Connecticut 1998.

Kin, David, ed. *Dictionary of American Proverbs.* New York 1955.

Kivits, Tonja. 'Moeders zullen altijd prinsjes blijven kweken'. *Opzij* mei 1999: 15–18.

Kjaer, Iver, and Bengt Holbek. *Ordsprog i Danmark: 4000 Ordsprog fra skrift og tale gennem 600 år.* Kopenhagen 1969.

Kloeke, Gesinus Gerhardus. *Kamper spreekwoorden (uit 1550).* Assen 1967.

Knappert, Jan. *Namibia, Land and Peoples, Myths and Fables.* Leiden 1981.

Knussmann, Rainer. *De man: een vergissing der natuur.* Trans. T.W. Rutten-Kooistra. Utrecht 1983.

Koessler-Ilg, Bertha. *Tradiciones Araucanas.* La Plata 1962.

Kouaovi, Ahlin Bernard Mathias. *Proverbes et dictons du Bénin.* Porto-Novo 1981.

Krueger, John R. 'Mongolian Folktales, Stories, and Proverbs'. *The Mongolian Society Occasional Papers* 4 (1967).

Krylov, Konstantin Arkadyevich. *Russian-English Dictionary of Sayings and Proverbs in Russian and English.* New York 1973.

Kuusi, M. *Proverbia Septentrionalia: 900 Balto-Finnic Proverb Types with Russian, Baltic, German and Scandinavian Parallels.* Helsinki 1985.

Kuzwayo, Ellen. *Call Me Woman.* 1985. London 1998.

Laan, K. ter. *Nederlandse spreekwoorden, spreuken en zegswijzen.* Amsterdam 1988.

Lakoff, George, and Mark Turner. *More than Cool Reason: A Field Guide to Poetic Metaphor.* Chicago/London 1989.

Lakoff, George. *Women, Fire, and Dangerous Things: What Categories Reveal About the Mind.* Chicago 1990.

Lambert, W.G. *Babylonian Wisdom Literature.* Oxford 1960.

Lamenza, Mario. *Proverbios.* Rio de Janeiro 1950.

Landmann, Salcia. *Jiddische anecdoten en spreekwoorden.* Trans. C.W. Meyer-Bossema. Baarn n.d.

Laval, Ramón A. *Paramiología Chilena.* Santiago 1928.

Le Roux de Lincy, M. *Le livre des proverbes français.* 2 vols. Paris 1859.

Lehman-Nitche, Robert. *Textos Eróticos del Río de la Plata.* Buenos Aires 1981.

Leslie, I. Julia. 'Recycling Ancient Material: An Orthodox View of Hindu Women'. Léonie J. Archer, Susan Fischler, Maria Wyke, eds. *Women in Ancient Societies: An Illusion of the Night.* London 1994: 233–51.

Leslie, I. Julia. *The Perfect Wife: The Orthodox Hindu Woman According to the Stridharmapaddhati of Tryambakayajvan.* Delhi 1989.

Leutsch, Ernst Ludwig von, and Friedrich Wilhelm Schneidewin. *Corpus Paroemiographorum Graecorum*. 2 vols. 1839–1851. Göttingen 1965.

Levinson, David, and Martin J. Malone. *Toward Explaining Human Culture*. New Haven 1980.

Lévi-Strauss, Claude. *Antropologie structurale*. 8 vols. Paris 1958–1973.

Lewin, Capt. Thomas Herbert. *Hill Proverbs of the Inhabitants of the Chittagong Hill Tracks*. Calcutta 1873.

Ley, Gerd de. *1001 buitenlandse spreekwoorden*. Antwerpen/Amsterdam 1993.

Lindfors, Bernth O., and Oyekan Owomoyela. *Yoruba Proverbs: Translation and Annotation*. Athens/Ohio 1973.

Littmann. See Safadi.

Loi, S. *Proverbi Sardi*. Milano 1972.

Long, J. *Prabadamala*. 2 vols. Calcutta 1869.

Lonner, Walter J. 'The Search for Psychological Individuals'. *Handbook of Cross-Cultural Psychology*. Harry C. Triandis, and William W. Lambert., eds. 6 vols. Boston 1980. 1: 143–204.

Loomis, C. Grant. 'Proverbs in the Farmer's Almanac(k)'. *Western Folklore* 15 (1956): 172–78.

Loomis, C. Grant. 'Proverbs in the Golden Era'. *Western Folklore* 14 (1955): 196–99.

Ludwig, Ralph, et al. *Dictionnaire créole français (Guadeloupe)*. n.p. 1991.

Lunde, Paul, and Justin Wintle. *A Dictionary of Arabic and Islamic Proverbs*. London 1984.

Madumulla, J.S. *Proverbs and Sayings: Theory and Practice*. Dar es Salaam 1995.

Maduro, Antoine Johannes. *Spreekwoorden en zegswijzen: Nederlands, Spaans, Portugees, Papiaments*. Willemstad 1990.

Magalhães Júnior, R. *Dicionário de provérbios, locuções e ditos curiosos bem como de curiosidades verbais, frases feitas, ditos históricos e citações literárias, de curso corrente na língua falada e escrita*. Rio de Janeiro 1974.

Maity, Pradyot Kumar. 'Co-Wives in Bengali Folklore'. Sen Gupta 295–305.

Malasi, Ngandu-Myango. *Mutánga : La corde à proverbes des Lega du Kivu Maniema (Congo)*. Gent 2000.

Malka, Victor. *Proverbes de la sagesse juive*. Paris 1994.

Marwick, Arthur. *Beauty in History: Society, Politics and Personal Appearance c. 1500 to the Present*. London 1988.

Marwick, Max G., ed. *Witchcraft and Sorcery: Selected Readings*. 2nd ed. London 1990.

Masinjila, Masheti. Introduction. *Contesting Social Death: Essays on Gender and Culture*. Ed. by Wanjiku M. Kabira, Masheti Masinjila, and Milton Obote. Nairobi 1997: ix–xviii.

Mauri, L. de. *5000 Proverbi e motti Latini*. Milan 1990.

Mauss, Marcel. *A General Theory of Magic*. London 1972.

MBRAS (Malay Branch of the Royal Asiatic Society). *The Book of over 1,600 Malay Proverbs, with Explanations in English*. Monograph 22, Kuala Lumpur 1992.

Meier-Pfaller, Hans-Josef, ed. *Das grosse Buch der Sprichwörter*. Esslingen am Neckar 1980.

Menarini, Alberto. *Proverbi Bolognesi*. Milan 1971.

Mernissi, Fatima. *Le harem politique: Le prophète et les femmes*. Paris 1987.

Messaoudi, Leïla. *Proverbes et dictions du Maroc*. Paris 1987.

Mesters, G.A. *Prisma spreekwoordenboek*. Utrecht 1986.

Meyer, Gérard, Jean-Raphaël Camara, and Fonsa Camara. *Proverbes malinké: A l'ombre des grands fromagers*. Paris 1985.

Mieder, Wolfgang, ed. *A Dictionary of American Proverbs*. Oxford 1992.

Mieder, Wolfgang. *American Proverbs: A Study of Texts and Contexts*. Bern 1989.

Mieder, Wolfgang. *The Prentice Hall Encyclopedia of World Proverbs*. Prentice Hall 1986.

Milimo, J.T. *Bantu Wisdom*. Lusaka 1972.

Molbech, Christian. *Danske ordsprog, tankesprog og rijmsprog af trykte og utrykte Kilder*. Kopenhagen 1850.

Moore, Henrietta. *A Passion for Difference: Essays in Anthropology and Gender*. 1994. Cambridge 1997.

Moorehead, Caroline. 'A Word of Silence'. *Widows: Life after Death* (special issue of *Index on Censorship*) March/April 1998: 36–46.

Moretti, Franco. 'Conjectures on World Literature'. *New Left Review* Jan.–Feb. 2000: 54–68.

Morris, Desmond. *The Human Sexes*. London 1997.

Moscona, Isaac (Isak). *Pearls of Sefarad*. Hebrew text. Tel-Aviv 1981.

Mota, Leonardo. *Adagiário brasileiro*. Belo Horizonte 1987.

Moya, Ismael. *Refranero: Refranes, proverbios, adagios, frases proverbiales, modismos refranescos, giros y otras formas paremiológicas tradicionales de la República Argentina*. Buenos Aires 1944.

Münch, Wilma. *Kook- en Huishoudboek voor het Platteland*. Utrecht 1932.

Murdock, George Peter. *Outline of World Cultures*. New Haven 1949.

Murty, Radhakrishna. 'Women in the Folklore of Andhra'. Sen Gupta 223–30.

Myint Thein, Maung. *Burmese Proverbs Explained in Verse*. Singapore 1984.

Neger-engelse spreekwoorden (odo's): Opnieuw verzameld. 5 vols. Paramaribo 1924–1925.

Nestor, Hellen Byera. *500 Proverbs (Haya)—Methali—Emigani*. Nairobi 1977.

Ngumbu Njururu. *Gikuyu Proverbs*. Nairobi 1983.

Nguyen, Lan. *Dictionnaire des locutions et proverbes français-vietnamiens*. Hanoi 1992.

Njoku, John E. Eberegbulam. *A Dictionary of Igbo Names, Culture and Proverbs*. Washington D.C. 1978.

Nketia, J.H. Kwabena. *The Music of Africa*. London 1979.

Nyembezi, Cyril Lincoln Sibusio. *Zulu Proverbs*. 1954. Johannesburg 1963.

O'Farrell, Padraic. *Irish Proverbs and Sayings: Gems of Irish Wisdom*. 1980. Dublin 1990.

O'Rahilly, Thomas F. *A Miscellany of Irish Proverbs*. Dublin 1922.

Obelkevich, James. 'Proverbs and Social History'. Wolfgang Mieder, ed. *Wise Words: Essays on the Proverb*. New York/London 1994: 211–52.

Obenga, Théophile. *Littérature traditionelle des Mbochi (Congo-Afrique Centrale)*. Paris 1984.

Oduyoye, Amba. 'The Asante Woman: Socialization through Proverbs'. *African Notes* 8 (1979), No.1: 5–11.

Ottley, C.R. 'Sayings of Trinidad and Tobago'. *Creole Talk (Trinibagianese) of Trinidad and Tobago: Words, Phrases and Sayings Peculiar to the Country*. Trinidad 1971.

Otto, August. *Die Sprichwörter und sprichwörtlichen Redensarten der Römer*. Leipzig 1890.

Owen, Margaret. *A World of Widows*. London 1996.

p'Bitek, Okot. *Acholi Proverbs*. Nairobi 1985.

Paczolay, Gyula. *Magyar-eszt-német-angol-finn-latin közmondások és szólások*. Veszprem 1987.

Paredes-Candia, Antonio. *Refranes, frases y expresiones populares de Bolivia: 1495 paremias*. La Paz 1976.

Parker, Enid. 'Afar Stories, Riddles and Proverbs'. *Journal of Ethiopian Studies* 9 (1971), No.2: 219–87.

Pelling, J.N. *Ndebele Proverbs and Other Sayings*. Harare 1977.

Peltier, Anatole-Roger. *Dictons et proverbes thaï*. Bangkok 1980.

Penfield, Joyce. *Communicating with Quotes: The Igbo Case*. Westport/London 1983.

Person, Henry A. 'Proverbs and Proverbial Lore from the State of Washington'. *Western Folklore* 17 (1958): 176–85.

Pineaux, Jacques. *Proverbes et dictons français*. Paris 1960.

Pinker, Steven. *The Language Instinct: The New Science of Language and Mind*. London 1995.

Plissart, Xavier. *Mamprusi Proverbs*. Tervuren 1983.

Plopper, Clifford H. *Chinese Religion Seen Through the Proverb*. Shanghai 1926.

Pokhrel, Shanta. *Nepalese Women*. Kathmandu 1982.

Politès, Nikolaos. *Meletai peri tou biou kai tès gloossès tou Hellènikou laou*. 1902. Athens 1965.

Préval, Guerdy. *Proverbes haïtiens illustrés*. Ottawa 1985.

Pukui, Mary Kawena. *'Ōlelo No'eau: Hawaiian Proverbs and Poetical Sayings*. Honolulu 1983.

Raimondi, Piero. *Proverbi Genovesi*. Florence 1975.

Ramírez Sendoya, J. Pedro. *Refranero del Gran Tolima*. Bogotá 1952.

Rattray, Robert Sutherland. *Ashanti Proverbs*. Oxford 1916.

Raub, Julius. *Plattdeutsche Sprichwörter und Redensarten zwischen Ruhr und Lippe*. Münster 1976.

Rauch, Karl. *Sprichwörter der Völker*. Düsseldorf/Köln 1963.

Rayner, John L. *Proverbs and Maxims*. London/New York/Toronto/Melbourne 1910.

Reeves Sanday, Peggy. *Female Power and Male Dominance: On the Origins of Sexual Inequality*. Cambridge 1981.

Reinsberg-Düringsfeld, Otto von. *Die Frau im Sprichwort*. Leipzig 1862.

Reyes, Elma. 'Women in Calypso'. Ellis, Pat., ed. *Women of the Caribbean*. Londen/New Jersey 1986: 119–21.

Rhys, Jean. *Smile Please: An Unfinished Autobiography*. 1977. Harmondsworth 1982.

Roberts, Julian V., and C. Peter Herman. 'The Psychology of the Height: An Empirical Review'. C. Peter Herman, Mark P. Zanna, E. Tory Higgins, eds. *Physical Appearance, Stigma, and Social Behavior: The Ontario Symposium*. New Jersey/London. Vol. 3: 113–40.

Rodegem, Firmin M., ed. *Sagesse kirundi: Proverbes, dictions, locutions usités au Burundi*. Tervuren 1961.

Rodríguez D., Emilio. *Refranero Dominicano*. Santo Domingo 1950.

Roebuck, Thomas. *A Collection of Proverbs in Persian and Hindustanee Languages*. Part I: *Persian*. Calcutta 1824.

Rörich, L., and W. Mieder. *Sprichwort*. Stuttgart 1977.

Rosen, Jechezkel. *Selected Proverbs and Sayings*. Hebrew text. Tel-Aviv 1992.

Rosenberg, Harriet G. 'Complaint Discourse, Aging, and Caregiving among the !Kung San of Botswana'. Jay Sokolovsky, ed. *The Cultural Context of Aging: Worldwide Perspectives*. New York/Westport/London 1990: 19–41.

Rosten, Leo. *Leo Rosten's Treasury of Jewish Quotations*. 2nd edition. Toronto/New York/ London 1977.

Rosten, Leo. *The Joys of Yiddish*. London 1970.

Roy, H. van, and J. Daeleman. *Proverbes Kongo*. Tervuren 1963.

Rubio, Darmo. *Refranes, proverbios y dichos y dicharachos mexicanos*. México 1940.

Sabiduría Guajira. *Selección de Samuel Feijóo*. La Habana 1965.

Safadi, Dalal Khalil, and Victoria Safadi Basha. *A Thousand and One Arabic Proverbs*. Ed. Enno Littmann. Beirut 1954.

Safilios-Rothschild, Constantina. *Love, Sex and Sex Roles*. New Jersey 1977.

Sakayan, Dora. *Armenian Proverbs: A Paremiological Study with an Antology of 2500 Armenian Folk Sayings*. New York 1994.

Sánchez Duarte, Eloisa. *Refranes de mi tierra: Poesía de América y de otros Países*. San Salvador 1978.

Sánchez-Boudy, José. *Guante sin grasa, no coge bola: El refranero popular cubano: los refranes del chuchero, de los estibadores, de la bodega, del amor, del guaguero—y otros estudios*. Miami 1993.

Sano, Mohammed Lamine. 'Proverbes'. *Littérature guinéenne*, Special issue of *Notre Librairie* Jul.–Sept. (1987): 44–49.

Santoro, Caterina. *Proverbi Milanesi*. Florence 1975.

Santos Ortiz de Villalba, Juan, comp. *Sacha Pacha: Mitos, poemas, sueños y refranes de los quichua amazónicos*. Quito 1989.

Scarborough, W. *A Collection of Chinese Proverbs*. Shanghai 1926.

Scheven, Albert. *Swahili Proverbs: Nia zikiwa moja, kilicho mbali huja*. Washington D.C. 1981.

Schipper, Mineke. *Imagining Insiders: Africa and the Question of Belonging*. London and New York 1999.

Schipper, Mineke. *Source of all Evil: African Proverbs and Sayings on Women*. London and Chicago 1991.

Schipper, Mineke, ed. *Unheard Words: Women and Literature in Africa, the Arab World, Asia, the Caribbean and Latin America*. London and New York 1985.

Schleicher, August. *Litauische Märchen, Sprichworte, Rätsel und Lieder*. Weimar 1857.

Scott, James C. *Domination and the Arts of Resistance: Hidden Transcripts*. New Haven 1990.

Ségalen, Martine. 'Le mariage, l'amour et les femmes dans les proverbes populaires français (suite)'. *Ethnologie française* (suite) 6 (1976): 33–88.

Sen Gupta, Sankar. *Women in Indian Folklore: Linguistic and Religious Studies*. Indian Publication Folklore Series 15. New Delhi 1969.

Shaki, Mansour. *A Modern Persian Phrase-Book*. Prague 1963.

Shengzi, Han, ed. *Zhongguo chengyu fenlei da cidian*. Beijing 1990.

Sierksma, Fokke. *Religie, sexualiteit en agressie: Een cultuurpsychologische bijdrage tot de verklaring van de spanning tussen de sexen*. Groningen 1979.

Sierra García, Jaime. *El Refrán Antioqueño en los Clásicos*. Medellín 1990.

Singer, A.P. *Arabic Proverbs*. Cairo 1913.

Smith, Morgan, and A.W. Eddins. 'Wise Saws from Texas'. *Straight Texas, a Publication of the Texas Folklore Society* 13 (1996).

Smith, William George, and Janet E. Heseltine. *The Oxford Dictionary of English Proverbs*. Oxford 1982.

Souto Maior, Mario. *A mulher e o homem na sabedoria popular*. Recife 1994.

Spagnolo, Emilio, ed. *I predoni del Sahara*. Verona 1973.

Speroni, Charles. 'Proverbs and Proverbial Phrases in Basile's "Pentameron"'. *Modern Philology* 24 (1976): 180–276.

Spezzano, Francesco. *Proverbi Calabresi*. Milan 1970.

Stahl, Avraham. *Proverbs of Israel*. Hebrew text. Tel Aviv 1978.

Stampoy, Pappity. *A Collection of Scotch Proverbs*. Los Angeles 1955.

Stockard, Jean, and Miriam M. Johnson. 'The Origins of Male Dominance'. *Sex Roles* 5 (1979), No.2: 199–218.

Stöckle, Johannes. *Traditions, Tales and Proverbs of the Bali-Nyonga*. 2 vols. 1994.

Stol, Marten. 'Women in Mesopotamia'. *Journal of the Economic and Social History of the Orient* 38 (1995): 123–44.

Stol, Marten. *Women's History*. Leiden 1995.

Storm Petersen, Robert. *Danske ordsprog*. Kopenhagen 1948.

Storm, Hiroko. 'Women in Japanese Proverbs'. Peter Knecht, ed. *Asian Folklore Studies* 51 (1992): 167–82.

Ström, Frederik. *Svenskarna i sina ordspråk, jämte sjutusen svenska ordspråk*. Stockholm 1926.

Suard, François, and Claude Buridand. *Typologie et fonctions*. Vol. 2 of *Richesse du proverbe*. 2 vols. Lille 1984.

Subramanian, K. 'Women in Folksayings in Tamil Land'. Sen Gupta 109–14.

Szwark, Marian. *Proverbes et traditions des Bassars du Nord Togo*. St Augustin 1981.

Taylor, Archer. 'The Wisdom of Many and the Wit of One'. Wolfgang Mieder, and Alan Dundes, eds. *The Wisdom of Many: Essays on the Proverb*. 1981. Madison 1994: 3–9.

Taylor, Archer, and Barlett Jere Whiting. *A Dictionary of American Proverbs and Proverbial Phrases, 1820–1880*. Cambridge 1958.

Thái, Kiém Van. 'Introduction à l'étude des proverbes vietnamiens'. *The Vietnam Forum* 1 (1983), No.2: 27–40.

Thomas, Jaqueline M. *Ngbaka-Ma'bo (République Centrafricaine) Contes, Proverbes, Devinettes ou Enigmes, Chants et Prières*. Paris 1970.

Thompson, Harold W. *Body, Boots and Britches: Folktales, Ballads and Speech from Country New York*. Syracuse 1979.

Titelman, Gregory Y. *Popular Proverbs and Sayings*. New York 1997.

Travélé, Moussa. *Proverbes et Contes Bambara (Bambara et Malinké)*. 1923. Paris 1977.

Tseëlon, Efrat. *The Masque of Femininity: The Presentation of Woman in Everyday Life*. London and New Delhi 1995.

Valente, P. José Francisco. *Selecção de provérbios e adivinhas em Umbundu*. Lisboa 1964.

Vasconcellos, Eliane. *La femme dans la langue du peuple du Brésil*. Paris 1994.

Velasco Valdés, Miguel. *Refranero popular Mexicano*. México 1967.

Villafuerte, Carlos. *Refranero de Catamarca*. Buenos Aires 1972.

Vincent, Jeanne-Françoise. *Traditions et transitions: Entretiens avec des femmes beti du Sud-Cameroun*. Paris 1976.

Vissers, Jan. *Spreekwoordenboek in beeld: Een aparte kunst uit Cabinda*. 4th ed. Berg en Dal 1989.

Völger, Gisela, and Karin von Welck. *Die Braut: geliebt, getauscht, geraubt: Zur Rolle der Frau im Kulturvergleich*. 2 vols. Köln 1985.

Walser, Ferdinand. *Luganda Proverbs*. Berlin 1982.

Wander, Karl Friedrich Wilhelm. *Deutsches Sprichwörterlexikon*. 5 vols. Leipzig 1867–1880. Augsburg 1987.

Wanjohi, Gerald Joseph. *The Wisdom and Philosophy of the Gikuyu Proverbs: The Kihooto World-View*. Nairobi 1997.

Watson, G. Llewellyn. *Jamaican Sayings: A Study of Folklore, Aesthetics and Social Control*. Tallahasse 1991.

Weidman-Schneider, Susan. *Jewish and Female: Choices and Changes in Our Lives Today*. New York 1984.

Werner, Roland. *Grammatik des Nobiin (Nilnubisch): Phonologie, Tonologie und Morphologie*. Hamburg 1987.

West, John O. *Mexican-American Folklore*. Little Rock 1988.

Westermarck, Edward. *Wit and Wisdom in Morocco: A study of Native Proverbs*. New York 1930.

Whiting, Bartlett Jere. *Early American Proverbs and Proverbial Phrases*. Cambridge 1977.

Whiting, Bartlett Jere. *Proverbes, Sentences and Proverbial Phrases: From English Writings Mainly Before 1500*. Cambridge Mass/Oxford 1968.

Whiting, Bartlett Jere. 'Proverbs and Proverbial Sayings'. *The Frank C. Brown Collection of North Carolina Folklore*. 7 vols. Durham 1952. Vol. 1.

Whiting, Beatrice B., and John W.M. Whiting. *Children of Six Cultures: A Psycho-Cultural Analysis*. 4th ed. Cambridge 1979.

Whitting, C.E.J. *Hausa and Fulani Proverbs*. Lagos 1940.

Wijnaendts-Francken, C.J. *Arabische spreekwoorden en zegswijzen*. Haarlem 1936.

Williams, John E., and Deborah L. Best. *Measuring Sex Stereotypes: A Multinational Study*. Rev. ed. Newbury Park 1990.

Williams, John E., and Deborah L. Best. *Measuring Sex Stereotypes: A Thirty-Nation Study*. Beverley Hills 1982.

Williams, T.W., ed. *Lean's Collectanea*. 4 vols. London 1903.

Wintle, Justin. *The Dragon's Almanac: Chinese, Japanese and Other Far Eastern Proverbs*. Singapore 1983.

Wolter, L. *2500 Spréch a Spréchwierder, Ein Sammlung vum –*. Lëtzebuerg 1986.

Wortabet, John. *Arabische wijsheid: Spreuken en spreekwoorden*. Deventer 1913.

Yankah, Kwesi 1989a. Proverbs: 'The Aesthetics of Traditional Communication'. *Research in African Literatures*. Vol. 20 (1989), 3: 325–46.

Yankah, Kwesi 1989b. *The Proverb in Context of Akan Rhetoric: A Theory of Proverb Praxis*. Bern 1989.

Yetiv, Isaac. *1001 proverbs from Tunisia*. Washington D.C. 1987.

Yoffie, Leah Rachel. *Yiddish Proverbs, Sayings, etc., in St. Louis, Missouri*. Lancaster/New York 1920.

Yu Jialou. *Hanyu chengyu yingyi cidian* (A Dictionary of Chinese Idioms with English Translations). Hefei 1991.

Yusuf, Yisa Kehinde. 'The Sexist Correlation of Women with the Non-Human in English and Yoruba Proverbs'. *De Proverbio: An Electronic Journal of International Proverb Studies* 3 (1997), No.1.

Zagaya. *Proverbes créoles en Guadeloupe*. Madrid 1965. zaza.com/awomansplace/description.html

Zeldin, Theodore. *Conversation: How Talk Can Change Our Lives*. London 1998. New Jersey 2000.

Index

For chapter and section topics, which have not been included here, please, consult the table of contents. All languages referred to in this book have been included. For corresponding cultures or countries, please consult the section Languages, Cultures and Countries pp. 402–405